Comparative Politics

Political Economy, Political Culture, and Political Interdependence

Third Edition

Monte Palmer

THOMSON
WADSWORTH

Australia • Canada • Mexico • Singapore • Spain
United Kingdom • United States

THOMSON
™
WADSWORTH

Publisher: *Clark Baxter*
Executive Editor: *David Tatom*
Assistant Editor: *Rebecca Green*
Editorial Assistant: *Cheryl Lee*
Technology Project Manager: *Michelle Vardeman*
Senior Marketing Manager: *Janise Fry*
Marketing Assistant: *Teresa Jessen*
Marketing Communications Manager: *Kelley McAllister*
Senior Project Manager, Editorial Production: *Kimberly Adams*

Executive Art Director: *Maria Epes*
Print Buyer: *Barbara Britton*
Permissions Editor: *Stephanie Lee*
Production Service: *Pre-Press Company, Inc.*
Copy Editor: *Mark Mayell*
Cover Designer: *Sue Hart*
Cover Image: *Zap Art/Getty Images*
Cover Printer: *Transcontinental Printing/Louiseville*
Compositor: *Pre-Press Company, Inc.*
Printer: *Transcontinental Printing/Louiseville*

For more information about our products, contact us at:
Thomson Learning Academic Resource Center
1-800-423-0563

For permission to use material from this text or product, submit a request online at **http://www.thomsonrights.com.**
Any additional questions about permissions can be submitted by email to **thomsonrights@thomson.com.**

ExamView® and ExamView Pro® are registered trademarks of FSCreations, Inc. Windows is a registered trademark of the Microsoft Corporation used herein under license. Macintosh and Power Macintosh are registered trademarks of Apple Computer, Inc. Used herein under license.

Library of Congress Control Number:
2005927019

ISBN 0-534-60267-3

Thomson Higher Education
10 Davis Drive
Belmont, CA 94002-3098
USA

Asia (including India)
Thomson Learning
5 Shenton Way
#01-01 UIC Building
Singapore 068808

Australia/New Zealand
Thomson Learning Australia
102 Dodds Street
Southbank, Victoria 3006
Australia

Canada
Thomson Nelson
1120 Birchmount Road
Toronto, Ontario M1K 5G4
Canada

UK/Europe/Middle East/Africa
Thomson Learning
High Holborn House
50–51 Bedford Row
London WC1R 4LR
United Kingdom

Latin America
Thomson Learning
Seneca, 53
Colonia Polanco
11560 Mexico
D.F. Mexico

Spain (including Portugal)
Thomson Paraninfo
Calle Magallanes, 25
28015 Madrid, Spain

Brief Contents

Contents

PREFACE

The field of comparative politics is witnessing an ongoing debate over the relative importance of economic, cultural, and international factors in the shaping of political events. Some of the current comparative government texts embrace one perspective to the detriment of the others, while other texts ignore the debate altogether. The present text starts from the premise that each of the above approaches offers important insights into comparative political analysis but that none, of itself, adequately conveys the richness of the political process. The text also integrates the insights provided by culture, economics, and international interdependence with the traditional comparative emphasis on institutions, elites, parties, groups, and mass behavior.

The vision of comparative politics presented in this text also integrates the "political development" and "advanced industrial society" perspective of comparative politics and stresses the defining issues of the coming decade: democracy, human rights, economic reform, social equality, and environmental degradation.

The third edition of *Comparative Politics* also reflects the changes that have occurred in the world community since the publication of the second edition. The third edition of *Comparative Politics* has been extensively revised and contains a much-needed chapter on the European Union. It also addresses the influence of the war on terror on the politics of the diverse countries covered in this text. That influence has been profound.

The third edition has been written with the student in mind. Every effort has been made to make this edition both readable and informative. Jargon has been kept to a minimum. Terms that are defined in the glossary are printed in boldface type the first time they appear in each chapter. Thus, the same term may appear in boldface in more than one chapter.

Also, you can find the book's companion Website at http://political science.wadsworth.com/palmer03/, where additional materials and updates will be posted. A Multimedia Manager with Instructor Resources CD is available to all adopting instructors. It includes a Test Bank in Microsoft® Word and ExamView® computerized testing, an Instructor's Manual, PowerPoint® Lecture Outlines, and video clips. Please contact your Wadsworth representative for details.

ACKNOWLEDGMENTS

Ted Peacock and Dick Welna inspired this book. Ted's retirement from the publishing business is a matter of great sorrow for all who knew him. I shall miss working with both him and Dick. Ted was very pleased by Wadsworth's acquisition of F. E. Peacock, Publishers, as am I. It has been a pleasure working with David Tatom and Rebecca Green on the third edition of *Comparative Politics*.

I would like to thank the instructors who reviewed *Comparative Politics* for its third edition: David Coates, Wake Forest University; Edward Fox, Western Connecticut State University; Ronald A. Francisco, University of Kansas; Chris Hamilton, Washburn University; Xiaobo Hu, Clemson University; Paul J. Kubicek, Oakland University; Patricia H. Kushlis, University of New Mexico; and Jane G. Rainey, Eastern Kentucky University.

I wish to express my deepest appreciation to all of the people that have assisted with this book over the course of its three editions. Of these, my greatest thanks goes to my wife, Princess Palmer.

Monte Palmer
Tallahassee, May 1, 2005

An Introduction to Comparative Politics

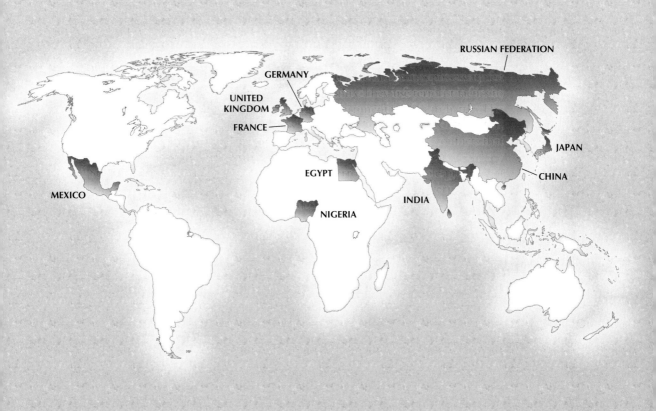

1

❖

An Introduction to
Comparative Politics

The twenty-first century confronts the world community with an era of un-precedented change. The countries of Western Europe are evolving into a European supra-state that may soon rival the economic and military power of the United States. China and India, two countries that collectively possess more than 30 percent of the world's population, are primed to become major ac-tors on the world stage. Both are nuclear powers and possess unlimited economic potential. Fears of a nuclear confrontation between the United States and Russia have faded only to be replaced by an upsurge in global terror that has struck at the very heart of the United States.

Countries also are becoming global. Communications between countries have become instantaneous as has the growing homogenization of global culture. Economist, now speak of a global economy, and rare is the major corporation that is not global in its operation. Individual countries cling jealously to their sovereignty, but the challenges they face are global in scope. Not the least of these challenges are terror, nuclear proliferation, crime, drugs, immigration, environ-mental decay, and AIDS. All require international cooperation for their solution. Rare is the decision made by an independent country that is not influenced by its global environment.

The world community is changing in other ways as well. Transitions to democracy and capitalism promise a world that is both free and prosperous. The combination of democracy and capitalism has brought an unparalleled quality of life to the United States, Canada, Japan, Australia, New Zealand and the countries of Western Europe–a cluster of countries often referred to as the first world. The countries of the first world are the elite of the world community. They monopolize most of its wealth, consume most of its energy, and dominate the activities of United Nations (UN) and other international bodies.

Many of the less fortunate countries of the world, often referred to as the third world, are now embracing democracy and capitalism in the hope that they, too, will attain the quality of life enjoyed by the citizens of the first world. We use the term *third world* simply because the scholars and media of the third world have adopted the term to describe their plight. They believe that it is important to publicize the fact that the world does have a class system that works to the advantage of its wealthy and powerful members.

While it is convenient to use terms such as *first* and *third worlds* to describe large clusters of countries, it would be a profound mistake to believe that the countries of the first world have arrived at some mystical level of development. All fall short of meeting the six standards of good government contained in the Charter of the United Nations and related documents. Good governments, according to the United Nations are stable, democratic, concerned about the rights of their citizens, capable of sustained economic growth, provide all citizens with equal access to life's opportunities, and are protective of the environment (World Bank, 1992a, 1992b).

Recent transitions to democracy and capitalism have seen many countries of the third world make dramatic progress in meeting the UN's standards of good government. The picture, however, remains uneven. China's transition to capitalism has produced exceptional economic growth, but it has made few gains in the area of democracy and human rights. Nigeria has become more democratic, but remains mired in poverty despite abundant oil wealth. Few have manifested much concern for the environment.

Unfortunately, many countries of the world have made little progress towards providing a more democratic, humane and prosperous life for their citizens. Often referred to as the fourth world, they remain enmeshed in poverty, dictatorship, and despair (Palmer 1997). Many, such as Angola, Rwanda, and Afghanistan, are racked with tribal conflict if not civil war.

In the this and the chapters which follow, we explore a variety of question that will have much to say about the way countries of the world will do politics during the coming decade. What forces are driving globalization? Can the transitions to democracy and capitalism be sustained? Why do staggering inequalities remain in a world of plenty? Why has terror replaced communism as the major threat to global security? In the process of answering these and related questions, we examine the political process in 10 of the world's global and regional powers: Great Britain, France, Germany, Japan, Russia, China, India, Mexico, Egypt, and Nigeria. We also examine the politics of the European Union.

Before we begin this venture a few words are in order about politics and the comparative analysis of politics.

CONFLICT AND COOPERATION:
THE TWO FACES OF POLITICS

Two definitions of **politics** have found wide acceptance among political scientists. The first suggests that *politics is the process of deciding "who gets what, when, and how"* (Lasswell 1958). The second definition is similar, suggesting that *politics is the authoritative allocation of scarce values* (Easton 1953). Both definitions address the main source of conflict in human societies: a shortage of the things that people value most. While different people value different things, most place a heavy emphasis on money, power, prestige, and security—values that are always in short supply (Maslow 1954; Glazer and Konrad 2003). This is as true of tribal societies as it is of modern states and the international community. All societies must cope with conflict over scarce values.

Politics involves conflict over scarce values, but it also involves cooperation. Human beings are social animals. Their survival and development depend on their ability to maintain effective social organizations (Parsons 1977). The more a society succeeds in generating cooperation among its members, the more developed and prosperous it is likely to become. Tribal and village societies evolved into countries in order to achieve greater security, wealth, prestige, and power (Herz 1959). The same process is evident in the unification of Western Europe. Most Western European leaders believe that a unified Western Europe will enjoy greater wealth, power, prestige, and security than a Western Europe divided against itself.

Conflict is the enemy of social organization. If unchecked, it fragments societies into warring factions and squanders valuable resources. This, unfortunately, is the scenario currently being played out in many areas of the third world.

Politics, then, has two faces: conflict and cooperation. Wars, revolutions, terrorism, intimidation, assassinations, and ethnic conflict are all part of the political process. Politics, however, also involves **conflict management** and the establishment of stable societies in which individuals are able to cooperate for their common good. If conflict is to be managed, some mechanism must exist for allocating scarce resources in an authoritative and orderly manner. **Governments** are that mechanism. They are the authoritative element in the political process. It is they who make and enforce the laws concerning "who gets what, when, and how."

Governments are created to manage conflict, but they also are the focal point of that conflict. The act of establishing governments invariably creates winners and losers; the winners seek to consolidate their position, and the losers press for change. By controlling the government, the winners in a political conflict acquire three means of conflict management: coercion, persuasion, and economic rewards. In a few societies, the winners rule mainly by coercion, using their control over the police and the army to impose their authority on a reluctant population. Regimes that rule by force alone, however, often are short-lived and unstable. Violence begets violence.

All governments use coercion, persuasion, and economic rewards as techniques for managing conflict, but the extent to which they use each of these techniques varies from country to country. The most effective governments in achieving democracy, stability, and other goals of good government (a topic to be discussed shortly), place persuasion and economic rewards above coercion. A mark of their success is the fact that they use coercion sparingly.

Conflict can be managed, but cannot be eliminated. Continuing tension between the winners and losers is the essence of politics. Some governments manage conflict better than others, but all political systems are in a state of flux as diverse groups in the society attempt to protect or extend their share of society's resources.

American history, for example, is a pageant of change produced by constant tension between the rulers and the ruled. In the early years of independence, American politics was dominated by a quasi-aristocracy of wealthy landowners (Beard 1913). Over time, the winner's circle was expanded to include all white males and eventually white females, black Americans, and other groups. Nevertheless, the process of assuring equal opportunities for all citizens remains incomplete.

Controlled conflict can be a positive force in the development of societies. Without conflict, there would be little incentive for change and societies would remain stagnant (Olson 1982). Thomas Jefferson even suggested that revolutions "from time to time" were not necessarily a bad thing. The challenge of government is to manage conflict in a manner that promotes the development of society rather than its destruction.

Governments that have endured over long periods of time usually are those in which the winners have been able to persuade their fellow citizens that the rules are **legitimate**—that *they are in the best interests of all citizens and should be voluntarily followed.* Some governments attempt to persuade people of their legitimacy on religious grounds, claiming that the established order has been decreed by God. This is certainly the case in Iran, a country governed by religious leaders. Communist leaders in the former U.S.S.R. and the People's Republic of China attempted to gain legitimacy by socializing (indoctrinating) their citizens to view Marxism as the path to a just society. Western democracies base their legitimacy on an electoral process that allows citizens a more or less equal voice in the selection of leaders.

Establishing legitimacy, however, involves far more than socialization or indoctrination. It also is a matter of economic self-interest. Western democracies receive the support of their citizens because the majority of those citizens have an acceptable standard of living. Economics is only one of several factors influencing political behavior, but it is an important one (Lewis-Beck 1990).

COMPARATIVE ANALYSIS

Political scientists attempt to understand why political events unfold as they do and, on this basis, to predict how they are likely to unfold in the future. Political scientists who specialize in comparative politics believe that the objectives of explanation and prediction are most fruitfully achieved by examining and comparing the political process in a broad range of political, economic, and socio-cultural environments (Dogan and Pelassy 1990). *By placing the study of democracy in comparative perspective, for example, we are better able to understand what makes democracy work and why democracy succeeds in some countries and fails in others.* By the same token, comparing the experience of different countries may help us to understand the dynamics of such critical issues as poverty, violence, and environmental decay.

The study of democracy, for example, can be approached by conducting case studies that examine how democracy has succeeded or failed in specific countries. Democracy also can be studied globally by attempting to identify those factors that distinguish democracies from other political systems The same principle applies to all other issues of interest to political scientists.

A second practical benefit of comparative political studies is that they provide a vast laboratory of political experience that may be transferable from one country to another. Many of the proposals for national health legislation in the United States, for example, have drawn heavily upon the experience of long-established health programs in Europe and Canada. While the European and Canadian programs are not without their drawbacks, they do provide important insights into the challenges involved in providing affordable health care. The experience of other countries also is relevant in areas such as crime and social welfare. The murder rate for the United States, for example, is more than 20 times greater than the murder rate in the states of Western Europe. Perhaps the United States has something to learn from the criminal justice programs of its peers.

STATES, GOVERNMENTS, AND POLITICAL SYSTEMS

All societies create rules, laws, and other organizational mechanisms for determining how the scarce resources of society will be allocated. Such institutions, commonly referred to as governments, are the grand prize of politics. The winners in the political contest use their control of governmental institutions to give expression to their values and to achieve their goals. They also use those institutions to manage conflict within society.

In primitive societies, the mechanism for enforcing the rules—the government—consisted of little more than a tribal chief and a council of elders. As societies became more complex, informal rules were codified into law and casual meetings of tribal leaders evolved into the complex governmental institutions that we know today. A few tribal societies remain, but most eventually gave way to a more common comprehensive entity we know as the state.

According to international law, a **state** is *a well-defined geographic area in which the population and resources are controlled by a government* (Brierly 1963). States are also said to have sovereignty, a tricky term that implies that a state, or more precisely its leaders, can do as they wish within the state's territory (Nordlinger 1981; Evans, Rueschemeyer, and Skoupol 1985; Brown 2002; Steinberger 2004). As described in the report of an international commission convened after World War II,

A sovereign state at the present time claims the power to judge its own controversies, to enforce its own conception of its rights, to increase its armaments without limits, to treat its own nationals as it sees fit, and to regulate its economic life without regard to the effect of such regulations upon its neighbours. These attributes of sovereignty must be limited.[1]

Knowing the type of political system that a country possesses provides important clues about how it does politics. In this regard, political scientists have found it useful to classify the countries of the world into three basic categories based on their political systems: democratic, authoritarian, and quasi-democratic or mixed. Each of these main categories, in turn, possesses numerous variants, many of which are discussed in later sections of the book.

Each type of political system is presumed to have both strengths and weaknesses (Caporaso 1989). Understanding these strengths and weaknesses helps comparative political analysts to predict and explain the goals that each type of political system can best achieve.

Democratic Political Systems

The precise nature of democracy has long been a topic of debate among political scientists (Gillespie 1987). Many scholars see its essence as the ability of the masses to hold their leaders accountable (Bollen 1979; Sartori 1965). As Joseph Schumpeter warned more than 50 years ago, "Democracy does not and cannot mean that people actually rule. . . . Democracy means that people have the opportunity of accepting or refusing the men who rule them" (Schumpeter 1950, 284–85). The end result is what counts, not how people get there.

Other scholars, by contrast, suggest that leaders only can be held accountable if a clear set of procedures are followed. (Lipset 1960). Of these, five are of particular importance (Dahl 1971, 1985).

1. Leaders must be elected in free and fair elections open to all citizens, regardless of race, creed, color, gender, educational level, or economic status.

2. Elections must be held at regularly scheduled intervals. One-time elections are not enough.

3. The electorate must have the opportunity to choose from among a meaningful slate of candidates.

4. The electorate must possess sufficient information to evaluate the choices before it. Forcing people to vote in an informational vacuum makes a mockery of the very concept of democracy.

5. Those elected must be allowed to rule. Many countries in the world, including some examined in the present text, maintain the fiction of democracy while the military rules from behind the scenes. Democratically elected leaders take office, but they do not rule.

---

[1]Stubbs (1941) cited in Brierly (1963, 47) from the *International Conciliation Pamphlet,* 1941.

This said, there is little agreement on how the requirements of democracy are best achieved. The framers of the United States Constitution believed that democracy was best served by balancing power between the executive and the legislative branches. This, in their view, would keep either branch of government from oppressing the people. To be on the safe side, they added the Supreme Court with the power to declare acts of the congress and the president unconstitutional. The American pattern of democracy is referred to as the **presidential model of democracy.** The British, by contrast, only vote for the members of the House of Commons. The members of the House of Commons then elect the leader of the majority party in the House of Commons to be the prime minister. There is no separation of powers and the prime minister and cabinet can do as they wish as long as they have the support of the House of Commons. The British model is an example of the **parliamentary model of democracy** because all power, at least in theory, resides with parliament. France has attempted to combine the presidential and parliamentary models of democracy in the hopes of achieving the best of both systems. It is not clear that this has happened, but it has made for interesting politics. Most democracies in the world are a variation of the presidential and parliamentary models.

However constituted, democracy seems to work best when certain conditions are present. Particularly important is the presence of political parties, pressure groups and a free and active mass media. All stimulate citizen participation in the political process and keep a watchful eye on the policies of elected leaders. Countries with an active array of political parties, citizen action groups, the mass media and all other non-governmental groups often are referred to as a **civil society** (Keane 2003; Baker 2002, DeLue 2002).

Democracy also works better when political leaders believe in the democratic process. Barring this, they use the power of the state to subvert democracy rather than strengthen it. As we shall see in the discussion of Russian politics (Chapter 7), some observers fear that Russia's democratically elected leaders are less committed to democratic procedures than they might be.

Citizens, too, must support the democratic process. Democracy works best when individuals believe in the **legitimacy** of the political institutions. That is to say, they believe that their political institutions are fair and well suited to their needs. They play by the rules of democracy because they believe in and benefit from democracy.

In much the same manner, democracy seems to work better in a cultural climate of tolerance, equality, openness, and mutual trust (Maiz and Requejo 2005). Citizens must be convinced that other individuals and other parties will not take advantage of an election victory to irreparably harm their interests and subvert the democratic process.

Finally, political scientists have long noted that democracies seem to prosper in countries that enjoy a high standard of living and education. Prosperity provides the citizens of a country with a strong economic motive for making their institutions work. Political legitimacy is reinforced by economic performance. Education, in turn, builds an informed electorate, helps people understand their responsibilities as citizens an tends to foster a climate of tolerance, openness and, mutual trust.

Authoritarian and Quasi-Democratic Political Systems

Authoritarian regimes are *characterized by the concentration of power in the hands of a single dictator or a small group of powerful individuals.* The advantage of dictatorial regimes lies in the ability of their leaders to pursue a narrow set of goals with ruthless efficiency. Mass emotions and the reconciliation of group interests are of less concern to dictators than they are to democratic politicians who must face the electorate on a regular basis. If the goal of the ruling elite is rapid economic development, all of the country's resources can be focused on that goal (O'Kane 2004). The economic development of South Korea, Brazil, Singapore, Taiwan, and other countries of the third world that now are approaching economic parity with the first world was led by dictatorial regimes. Without strong governments, moreover, many countries of the third world would either fragment into mini-states of questionable viability or dissolve into civil war. This tragic situation is discussed in Chapter 12, "Nigeria: The Politics of Hope and Despair." Economic growth, however, does not guarantee equality.

The disadvantage of authoritarian regimes is that the public has little to say about either the goals pursued by the regime or the manner in which those goals are implemented. The assumption that authoritarian regimes can promote economic development more efficiently than democratic regimes is also open to challenge (Weede 1983, 1984). While authoritarian regimes have facilitated economic development in a handful of states, they have failed miserably in others. The collapse of the U.S.S.R. revealed how profoundly inefficient authoritarian regimes could be. The goals of many authoritarian regimes, moreover, have little to do with either economic development or the advancement of the population. Many dictators seize power with the best of intentions only to lose sight of their developmental goals once they have become entrenched in office. Unlike democracies, authoritarian regimes have no built-in corrective mechanisms to put them back on track.

Authoritarian states come in numerous varieties. Traditional monarchies were generally content to dominate the political system, leaving economic activity to the business community and culture to the church. The same is true of most military dictatorships. **Totalitarian societies** such as Nazi Germany and the Soviet Union, by contrast, *placed all political, economic, and cultural activity under the direct control of the state* (Friedrich and Brzezinski 1956). The topic of totalitarianism is a controversial one, and it is examined at greater length in the discussion of Russian politics (Chapter 7).

Theocracies, are countries that are *ruled by religious leaders.* Their goal is to use the full power of the state to assure mass compliance with a particular set of religious doctrines. Iran is currently the world's only pure theocracy, but an increasing number of countries are strengthening the links between their political and religious institutions.

Many states of the third world have *political systems that blend democratic and authoritarian tendencies* into **quasi-democratic** political systems. Most possess democratic legislatures, but real power lies with a dictator of one form or another. This topic will be explored in our discussion of Egyptian politics (Chapter 11).

Transitions from Authoritarian Rule to Democracy

Transitions from authoritarianism to democracy surged with the collapse of the Soviet Union and the end of the cold war. Indeed, the 20 years since the end of the cold war has seen the emergence of more than 50 new democracies, and the beat continues. Today, the world possesses some 192 independent countries of which 64 percent are democracies. (Karnatnycky 2002)

Unfortunately, not all of the world's new democracies live up to western standards of democracy as previously outlined. As the president of Freedom House, an organization that charts the world's transition to democracy, would note:

> Many of the world's 52 newest electoral democracies are weak and fragile, have a poorly evolved rule of law, and are plagued by endemic corruption and influential oligarches. Some confront debilitating ethnic and sectarian strife or its legacies. In short, most new democracies need the engagement and support of established democracies (Karnatnycky 2002, p. 50).

The rush to democracy is easy to understand. Most people do want a voice in controlling their own destinies. They have also tired of secret police and death squads and have been disillusioned by the failure of authoritarian governments to provide rapid development and an abundant quality of life. Dissatisfaction with authoritarian rule has also been accelerated by a global explosion in education and information. Satellites and the Internet have increased mass demands for greater freedom and a better quality of life as has an explosion of civic actions groups (NGOs) in many countries of the third world. All have also made it more difficult for authoritarian regimes to disguise their failures. Internal pressures for democracy have been matched by western pressure to promote democracy on a global scale. Democracy, in the Western view, is the best way to end global conflicts and the annihilation threatened by the cold war. Democracies may dispute, but they seldom take up arms against each other (Ray 1995). As a result of these pressures, even the world's most authoritarian governments are allowing greater democracy at the grass-roots level, a topic discussed at length in our examination of Chinese politics in Chapter 8.

This does not mean that the transition to democracy will be smooth and without its failures (Diamond, Linz, and Lipset 1990). The problems are many. Emerging democratic regimes often flirt with the authoritarian practices of their predecessors (Skene 2003). The authoritarian regimes in many countries are deeply intrenched and have largely resisted western pressure for reform. That pressure, itself, has been less than it might be. The United States promised democracy in Iraq and Afghanistan but is unlikely to succeed in either. Nor has it made a serious effort to promote democracy in other areas of the oil rich Middle East (Palmer 2002). A grand democratic initiative for democracy was announced with great fanfare in 2003, but was soon abandoned when Saudi Arabia and Egypt complained that Arab culture wasn't compatible with American notions of democracy. Democracy is important, but so is oil.

The countries of the third world have also found it difficult to overcome feelings of distrust among different religious and ethnic groups. Democracy is difficult to achieve when people fear that the victors will use their power to punish their enemies or impose a religious government. The danger also exists that religious and ethnic groups will merely use democracy as a means of breaking away and establishing their own country. Other problems also exist. Most countries of the third world are also hopelessly corrupt and lack effective political institutions capable of meeting the need of their populations. Democracy takes the blame, and extremists promise that authoritarianism will bring a quick end to their misery. Some of these problems can be overcome with education and experience, but that will take time.

Components of Comparative Political Analysis

Three basic components of comparative political analysis are studied throughout this text:

1. The political institutions through which the government of a country allocates resources.
2. The actors who give life to these institutions and carry out the work of governments.
3. The broader economic, cultural and international contexts in which the political process takes place.

The study of formal **political institutions** is an important aspect of comparative analysis because these governmental structures represent the arena of political conflict. It is the executives offices, legislatures, courts, bureaucracies, and other agencies of government that authoritatively allocate the scarce resources of the state.

Politics, however, encompasses much more than the formal institutions of government. It also includes the **actors** who give life to those institutions. Many political scientists find elites to be the critical element in the political process because elites run the political institutions and decide who gets what, when, and how. Other political scientists find the essence of the political process to be the interplay of political parties and pressure groups. Elites, they point out, do not exist in a vacuum. It is the support of political parties and pressure groups that makes them effective. Still other experts focus on the masses or public, recognizing that governments and elites must gain public support if they are to endure.

In addition to institutions and actors, many comparative political analysts have also found it useful to study the broader cultural, economic, and international contexts in which politics occurs. Advocates of a cultural approach to politics believe the way people behave politically is profoundly influenced by the culture in which they have been raised. The more one understands the culture of a society, they argue, the easier it will be to predict the pattern of its politics. Political economists, in turn, find politics to be indivisible from economics. In their view, it is difficult to find any form of political activity that is not influenced in one way or another by economics. Finally, a growing number of comparative political scientists find domestic politics to be profoundly influenced by broader international pressures. The countries of the world are becoming increasingly interdependent, and all must adjust to the demands of the international community.

THE STRUCTURES OF GOVERNMENT

Governments consist of three basic elements: legal and organizational structures, decision makers (elites), and administrative officials (bureaucrats). All are critical to the political process. Laws, procedures, and organizational arrangements are inanimate structures. Much like an automobile, political structures such as laws, constitutions, and organizational charts are devices that help people get from one point to another. They have no life of their own. The analysis of political structures helps us to predict and explain political events in a variety of ways (Fried 1966).

First, political structures such as laws, regulations, voting procedures, and organizations, favor some groups over others (Lijphart 1990). Some political arrangements concentrate wealth and power in the hands of a narrow elite, while others fragment power and wealth among a broad range of groups. The more political structures distribute the resources of a society equitably, the more likely they are to be supported by a broad cross section of the population.

Second, the organizational complexity of political structures influences the type of activities a government can pursue successfully (Alexander and Colmy 1990). Simple machines are designed to perform simple tasks; complex machines perform complex tasks. The same is true of political structures. In the few primitive and tribal governments that remain, for example, the tribal chiefs perform the full range of governmental functions. One individual or a small group of individuals makes and implements decisions and resolves disputes among members of the tribe. The chief also assesses the concerns of the population and assures that support for the clan or tribe is not lagging. The division of political labor is minimal.

Modern political structures, by contrast, are very complex. One institution is assigned responsibility for making decisions, while other institutions are charged with implementation of those decisions and adjudication of disputes. Still other specialized institutions exist to assess the demands of the population and to build support for the system. The greater division of labor of modern political structures enables their leaders to better mobilize the state's human and material resources in support of their objectives. Nowhere is this difference between primitive and modern governments clearer than in the area of warfare. Modern wars employ weapons of mass destruction and are fought by armies numbering in the millions. Primitive wars are fought with arrows and spears by tribal warriors.

Third, the flexibility of structural arrangements influences the capacity of a political system to adapt to changing circumstances. Democratic political arrangements tend to be flexible and adaptive. As circumstances change, disadvantaged groups can alter the rules of the game by participating in elections and open debate. For the most part, violence is avoided. Dictatorial regimes, in contrast, tend to be rigid. When circumstances change, few provisions exist for redressing the balance between the winners and the losers. Virtually all the countries experiencing extreme political violence in the world today possess nondemocratic political systems. Flexible political structures, then, are more likely to change by evolution, while rigid political structures are likely to change only by violence or revolution.

Fourth, many people believe that political structures can be used to change or control undesirable aspects of human nature. The framers of the U.S. Constitution, for example, believed that people naturally craved power. Elected leaders, in their view, would be tempted to transform themselves into kings. To combat this presumed defect in human nature, power was divided between the executive and the legislative. The ambition of one branch would check that of the other (Mendelson 1980). The Mexican and Brazilian constitutions attempt to control their leaders by limiting presidents to a single term.

In one way or another, most modern political structures attempt to control power and corruption by forcing politicians to work within a maze of laws and procedures. Decisions require ratification by a variety of groups, and all are open to legal challenge. Each year the number of hoops through which politicians must jump seems to increase. Legal and organizational constraints may limit abuses of power but, as we are constantly reminded, do not eliminate them. Excessive rules and regulations, moreover, often choke the political process by fragmenting power among too many institutions or actors. The logical outcome of too many checks and balances is no movement at all.

THE HUMAN DIMENSION OF POLITICAL INSTITUTIONS

While structural arrangements influence the performance of governmental institutions such as parliaments and administrative agencies, those institutions are far more than lifeless structures. Institutional performance is also a function of the decision makers and bureaucrats who control and manage the political structures. Much as the driver of an automobile determines its destination and chooses the route to be followed, the drivers of governmental institutions determine the goals that those institutions will pursue and the speed and ruthlessness with which they will be pursued. Much also depends on the skills of political leaders and bureaucrats. Some individuals get more out of their machinery than others.

It is the human element in governmental institutions that seemingly provides them with a life of their own. Institutions outlive the individuals who created them because they develop an organizational or institutional culture that is passed on from one generation to another. A new member of the British Parliament, for example, is immediately confronted with traditions and practices that have evolved over the centuries. To violate these traditions is to be ostracized by other members of Parliament and to lose the support of constituents who believe in the parliamentary system and who expect their representatives to play by the rules. Things change in Britain, but they change very slowly.

Political institutions that evolve slowly over time, earning a respected place in the society, are said to be **institutionalized** (Huntington 1991; Bollen and Jackman 1985). Samuel Huntington defines **institutionalization** as *"the process by which organizations and procedures acquire value and stability."* (Huntington 1968, 12).

Most political institutions in the first world are well institutionalized, and one can predict with reasonable confidence that established patterns of operation will persist over time. By contrast, most institutions in the Third World are poorly institutionalized and change frequently. Together, the countries of Latin America have had more than 200 constitutions in the same time period in which the United States has had one. Because constitutions in Latin America and other countries of the third world change so frequently, they are often viewed with cynicism by the populations affected.

ACTORS IN THE POLITICAL ARENA

The individuals and groups that give direction to the political process are often referred to as **political actors.** Elites and bureaucrats are political actors, as are individual citizens attempting, by one means or another, to influence their governments. Political parties and pressure groups are also considered actors, for both represent individual citizens who are taking collective action to achieve their political objectives.

Elites: The Movers and the Shakers of the Political Arena

Inequality is a fact of political and economic life. Some individuals simply have more influence over the political process than others. *Those individuals who dominate the policy-making process* are referred to as **political elites** (Putnam 1976). As expressed by Bill and Hardgrave, elites are *"the people who create institutions and write constitutions; personalities who plan, plot, dictate, and decide"* (Bill and Hardgrave 1981, 161).

Most of these decision makers occupy senior government positions. Others may exert political influence by virtue of their extraordinary financial resources, status in society, or ability to speak for the members of a large group such as a labor union or religious community. In many states of the third world, the military dominates the elite structure. Even when the generals are not in office, they cast a long shadow over the political process. Elites play a predominant role in setting the policy agenda, and usually have the final voice in determining who gets what, when, and how. In most instances, *they* "get most of what there is to get" (Lasswell 1958).

Types of Elites: Unitary and Pluralistic. Many societies possess a single **unitary elite** in which decision-making authority is concentrated in the hands of a small group of individuals. A government with a unitary elite is often referred to as an **oligarchy.** Unitary elites are common in dictatorships but can also occur in democracies when a single group of elected officials enjoys extraordinary power. In the British political system, for example, enormous power is concentrated in the hands of the prime minister and the Cabinet. Various groups may offer their opinions, but it is Britain's unitary elite that usually makes the final decision.

In other societies, *political power is distributed among a broad range of decision makers.* Some may dominate the shaping of economic policy, while others dominate policy making in the areas of education or health. Such elites are often referred to as **pluralistic elites** (Dahl 1961). The United States is a prime example of a country with a pluralistic elite structure. Even a subcommittee of the U.S. Congress can block national policy until its demands have been met.

Which is better, governments dominated by unitary elites or governments dominated by pluralistic elites? This question does not have a simple answer. A major advantage of pluralistic elites is their responsiveness to diverse groups and interests. Most segments of society can make their voices heard, and governmental decisions tend to emphasize compromise and reconciliation. The more elites fight among themselves, moreover, the more inclined they are to seek support among the masses. Advocates of law and order, by contrast, are often distressed by political institutions that find it difficult to make firm decisions. Coherent and farsighted programs are often watered down by the need for compromise because too many groups are involved in the decision-making process. A major advantage of unitary elites is their ability to take decisive action without endless delay and compromise. The difficulty is they often take extreme positions without concern for the opinions of their citizens.

In one of the classic works of comparative politics, *The Iron Law of Oligarchy* (1915/1959), Robert Michels argues that all political organizations tend to become oligarchies. Once individuals are in positions of authority, Michels explains, they consolidate their power by manipulating organizational procedures, placing supporters in high positions, and managing the information they make available to the general public. If Michels's view is correct (and many political theorists believe it is), rule by oligarchies, or small groups of individuals, is inevitable, regardless of how democratic the governmental structure may be (Dye 1976).

Elites and Political Analysis. Understanding the values and predispositions of a country's leaders often provides important insights into the policies they are likely to pursue. If the values of Hitler and Stalin had been better understood by western democracies, the world might have been spared infinite suffering. In much the same manner, elite values have much to say about the practice of democratic principles. The commitment of India's leaders to these principles has helped to sustain that country's democracy through more than four decades of economic and social adversity. The commitment of Russia's leaders to democracy, by contrast, is less certain. Can former communists become converted democrats, or is the West deluding itself in thinking that this is the case?

The politics of a state is also influenced by the openness or flexibility of its elites. Absolute monarchies represent a closed elite in which the recruitment of new members is restricted to the royal family or a narrow group of aristocrats. Unless the elite group is willing to relinquish its authority, violence is the only path to political change. The British monarchy gradually gave up its political authority and has survived as an institution; the French monarchy did not give way to popular demands for change and was crushed. The more open the process of elite recruitment, the more peaceful the process of political change is likely to be.

In sum, the role of political elites in the political process is extremely important. Political elites have more to say about the allocation of a society's scarce resources than any other individuals in a society. Many people also believe that they receive a disproportionate share of those resources. Whatever the case, the values, perceptions, and skills of the ruling elite greatly influence the course of politics in a society.

Bureaucrats: The Functionaries of Government

Elites play a dominant role in deciding who gets what in a society, but their decisions are not self-enforcing. The **bureaucrats** (administrators) are responsible for *seeing that decisions are implemented*. This is especially the case in today's world, a world in which governments are faced with the need to make informed decisions on topics as complex and diverse as nuclear waste, crime prevention, the ozone layer, international trade, health care, drugs, and a crumbling natural environment, to mention but a few. Decisions in such complex areas cannot be implemented by a handful of cronies or a council of tribal elders. Rather, each area of decision making requires its own specialized agency.

As decision making grows more complex, the influence of bureaucrats increases proportionally (Blau and Meyer 1987). In many instances, it is they, not the elites, who determine which policies the government will pursue and how those policies will be implemented (Aberbach 1981). The behavior of bureaucrats influences policy decisions in a variety of ways, the following of which are among the most important.

1. *Political leaders are generalists, while bureaucrats possess the specialized technical information that political elites need to make informed policies.* The more complex the issue, the more heavily a political elite must rely on the expertise of bureaucrats.

2. Bureaucrats decide how quickly and efficiently elite decisions will be executed. Elites, by definition, are few in number. They simply lack the time and energy to keep tabs on everything. Two or three programs can be highlighted for special attention, but seldom more. Bureaucrats, by contrast, number in the tens if not hundreds of thousands. They know how to manipulate the complexities of the administrative apparatus. Programs that have the approval of functionaries are executed with dispatch, while others tend to lag—waiting, perhaps, for a change of regime.

3. *Bureaucrats constitute an important pressure group.* Bureaucrats occupy a privileged position in most societies, receiving generous salaries and, barring extraordinarily poor behavior, a guaranteed job for life. In the view of many, it is the bureaucrats who receive most of what there is to be gotten. While efforts to curb the costs of bureaucracy are frequent, successes are few.

4. *The capacity of a bureaucracy to execute elite decisions depends on the skills of its members.* Japanese bureaucrats are generally credited with orchestrating Japan's phenomenal economic growth, and the cold efficiency of German bureaucrats is legendary. The bureaucrats of many newly independent countries, by contrast, lack the skill and experience to implement programs in a timely and efficient manner. However farsighted the decisions of the elites may be, their decisions are not being implemented effectively.

5. *Public attitudes toward the government are directly influenced by the behavior of bureaucrats.* Few people come in contact with their leaders, but virtually

everyone comes in contact with bureaucrats. When public officials are honest, service-oriented, and impartial, they help to build a strong bond of legitimacy between government and citizens. Bureaucratic behavior characterized by indifference, favoritism, and corruption, by contrast, breeds mass hostility. Changing dysfunctional bureaucratic behavior, unfortunately, is a slow process at best. Once in place, a bureaucratic culture tends to perpetuate itself as new officials acquire the attitudes of the old.

In an ideal world, bureaucrats would be responsive to the policy directives of elected leaders, efficient in the performance of services, creative in finding solutions for society's problems, courteous and helpful in their dealings with the public, objective in offering advice to political leaders, sparing in the expenditure of public funds, and unobtrusive and restrained as a pressure group. The more the bureaucracy of a country approaches this model, the better positioned the country will be to achieve the goals of good government. As the country chapters in this book will illustrate, this scenario is rare indeed.

Masses, Classes, and Politics

While elites and bureaucrats are key actors in the making and implementation of political decisions, the politics of a country also depends on the opinions and support of its population—the **masses,** as *the public* may be referred to by political theorists.

The analysis of mass political behavior offers two powerful tools for comparative political analysis. The first focuses on the intensity of mass **demands** for a reallocation of society's scarce resources. Mass discontent is a major source of the tension and conflict that permeate all political processes. While the masses may display remarkable patience with their political leaders, the tolerance of even the most docile population has its limits. In the present era of instant communications, moreover, the masses have been made acutely aware of the gap between their lives and those of the ruling classes. If mass demands are moderate, the pace of political change is likely to be moderate and evolutionary. As the intensity of mass demands increases, the probability of political violence also increases (Feierabend, Feierabend, and Nesvold 1967).

The second tool focuses on the extent of mass **support** for political institutions. The more individuals support their political institutions, the stronger those institutions will be. Support for the political system is expressed in a variety of ways. It is shown by obeying the laws of the land, paying taxes, serving in the military, cooperating with government agencies, and participating in elections. Political support also encompasses loyalty, discipline, and hard work. Anything that strengthens the ability of the political system to function effectively is supportive. One should not lose sight of the fact that it is the common people who do most of what gets done in a country. In times of war, for example, the elites give the orders, the bureaucrats mobilize the masses, and the masses do the fighting. The same arrangement also is found in peacetime; that is, the elites set the goals for the nation, the bureaucrats work out the details, and the masses do the work. The masses staff the factories, farms, offices, and mines that generate a society's wealth; and the masses pay most of the taxes. Political institutions can endure without the support of the masses, but they cannot prosper.

The masses, then, have a major impact on the political process. Many decisions made by elites are, in reality, forced by mass pressures. It is often the level of mass support that determines what the government can and cannot accomplish. It is hard to fight wars if the soldiers are demoralized, just as it is difficult to feed the people of a country if its workers are sluggish.

For all of their impact on the political process, the influence of the masses is seldom direct. As a unit, the masses are simply too big, too diverse, too unstructured, and too beset by internal contradictions to focus on more than a handful of issues. Even then, mass opinion is often the product of information provided by the elites or by the diverse political parties and groups to which most people belong.

Collective Action: Groups and Interests

While individual citizens play an important role in the political process, their influence is far stronger when they come together as a group. Indeed, most political activity is group activity. *Groups that form for the express purpose of influencing governmental policies* are often referred to as pressure groups or interest groups.

Pressure groups evolved *to protect their members from capricious acts of the government by means of collective action*. During the early years of the Industrial Revolution, the exploitation of workers was openly condoned by the governments of the day. Individual workers, by themselves, had little recourse against the system. It was only after the establishment of labor unions that rampant exploitation subsided. Groups also evolved to *promote the special interests of their members*. Often, this has meant securing a larger share of society's resources for members of the group. Workers wanted higher wages and better working conditions. Employers wanted fewer taxes and protection from foreign competition. Finally, pressure groups evolved to *impose a particular view of social morality on society as a whole*. Pressure groups have been responsible for the enactment of a broad range of social legislation, including child labor laws, Prohibition, and environmental legislation.

As governments grew larger and more complex, the need for collective action became imperative and pressure groups began to play an integral part in the political process. It is now impossible to envision politics in the United States or any other modern society without pressure groups. The strategies of pressure groups differ markedly from country to country, but the fundamental principle remains the same: collective action is more effective in bringing about changes in governmental policy than action by individuals working alone.

In addition to being one of the basic units of political action, pressure groups also play an important role in the **linkage** of the elites and masses. Pressure groups, for example, *provide an important channel of communication between political leaders and key segments of the population*. Group members are provided with the opportunity to articulate interests, while political leaders are given the opportunity to build support among group members.

Pressure groups also simplify mass–elite relationships by aggregating the demands of their members. Rather than having to cope with the random demands of millions of disorganized workers, political leaders can focus on the precise demands of labor union leaders. If union leaders agree on a contract, the rank and file usually go along and sustained conflict is avoided. By satisfying a limited number of group demands, then, political leaders are often able to control and mobilize many of the best-organized groups in society (Kornhauser 1959).

Other functions of pressure groups are to advise their members on issues and shape their attitudes toward the government and its leaders. If the major groups in society support the existing order, its stability is largely assured. The opposite is equally true. Rare, indeed, is a government that can survive the sustained opposition of the dominant groups in society.

Groups and Political Analysis. Group analysis can be a very powerful tool in comparative politics. Indeed, some scholars believe that group analysis is more effective in predicting and explaining political events than either elite analysis or mass analysis (Truman 1951). Most elites, after all, do not get to be elites without the support of a strong group. They must be careful not to alienate group members. In much the same manner, it is the group that gives structure and direction to the masses. Without structure, these scholars say, the masses are a herd, a mob. It is the act of organization that transforms the masses into a political force.

Several dimensions of group analysis are particularly useful in predicting and explaining political events. Government policies generally reflect the views of the most powerful groups in society. The greater one's ability to chart the group map of a society, the easier it will be to chart the direction of its leaders. In this regard, the influence of groups often results from several factors including organizational structure, the dedication of group members, cohesion, adequate finances, access to the centers of power, the ability to threaten the dominant elites, and the extent to which group goals are embraced by the general population (Truman 1951).

Some of these factors are more important than others in determining a group's strength. Leaders rarely disregard the views of groups that keep them in power. They also attempt to accommodate those groups that are in the strongest position to challenge their authority. Many governments in the Middle East, for example, now find themselves challenged by religious fundamentalists demanding an Islamic (Muslim) government. While attempting to crush the militants, these governments have also brought their policies more in line with Islamic principles, a topic discussed at length in our examination of Egyptian politics (Chapter 11). A small but cohesive group of dedicated members will often have more influence on policy than a larger group whose members are apathetic or divided among themselves. Groups that vote as a solid bloc get the attention of politicians.

In many instances the solidarity of groups is undermined by the diverse interests of their members. A successful businessperson from working-class origins, for example, may be torn between the demands of the business community and sympathy for the rights of workers. He or she may resolve this internal conflict simply by not taking sides. *Groups whose members are divided by conflicting religious, ethnic, economic political, or other loyalties* are said to have **cross cutting cleavages.**

Because the interests of their members are contradictory or cross-cut, these groups find it more difficult to take concerted political action than those whose members share common political values (Lipset and Rokkan 1967).

Political Parties and Party Systems

Pressure groups attempt to achieve their objectives by exerting pressure on the government. Political parties, by contrast, attempt to achieve their objectives by controlling the government. A **political party** is generally defined as *a group of individuals working together to achieve common goals by controlling all or part of the government* (Epstein 1967; Lawson 1976; Robertson 1976; Sartori 1976). Often the ruling party determines who will run the institutions of government and how the resources of society will be allocated.

Major Types of Political Parties. Political parties take a variety of forms depending on their primary objectives. The primary objective of the Republican and Democratic parties in the United States is to win elections. Each has a basic program that it would like to pursue, but it will readily sacrifice that program to achieve its goal of winning elections. Much the same is true of the major political parties in the United Kingdom and Germany. Such parties are often referred to as **catch-all parties** because *they are willing to relax ideological concerns in order to appeal to a broad spectrum of the voting public* (Kirchheimer 1966).

Catch-all parties thrive by capturing the center of the political spectrum and generally avoiding extremist positions that would alienate a large group of voters. They ask little of their supporters and tend to have loose organizational structures. While some people formally join catch-all parties, most of their adherents do not. Meetings and conventions are attended only by the party faithful, and most party affairs are managed by a small cadre of leaders who speak in the name of the party.

At the opposite end of the party hierarchy from catch-all parties one finds mass-membership or devotee parties. **Devotee parties** *have well-defined ideological goals and expect members to devote their lives to the achievement of those goals* (Duverger 1954). While strategic alliances might be made for the sake of achieving power, ideology is more important than votes. Devotee parties have tight organizational structures, with party leaders serving in the role of high priests. Party members are expected to belong to a variety of party study groups and social organizations and to spend most of their free time in organizational work. The integration of members' lives within the party framework provides them with a sense of belonging and reinforces their ideological commitment by enabling them to feed on the zeal of the group. The early communist parties of Russia and China are perhaps the best examples of devotee parties. Party members were dedicated to Marx's vision of a communist utopia in which individuals would give according to their abilities and take according to their needs. The orders of party leaders were absolute and executed with discipline. Indeed, it was the dedication and discipline of party members that enabled relatively small parties to seize control of two of the largest countries in the world. Once in office, both communist parties lost much of their revolutionary zeal, a phenomenon that is examined in Chapters 7 and 8.

Social Democrats: From Mass Membership to Catch-All Parties. Between the extremes represented by the catch-all and devotee parties lies a bewildering array of party arrangements (Janda 1980). Many of the early Social Democratic parties of Europe, for example, attempted to create mass-membership parties dedicated to both socialism and democracy (Neumann 1956, 395-42). The government was to manage economic activity for the mutual benefit of all citizens, but the country itself would remain a democracy. Much like the devotee parties, the early Social Democratic parties attempted to integrate all aspects of their members' lives within the party community. In addition to attending regularly scheduled branch meetings, party members were encouraged to join socialist labor unions, to participate in socialist study groups, and to spend their free time in party recreational activities. The party also furnished members with health care and other social services that were seldom provided by employers. In recent years, many Social Democratic parties have taken on the characteristics of large catch-all parties. While reference to socialism has been retained in the party name, they no longer advocate the nationalization of industry. Rather, they now argue the state's responsibility is to provide its citizens with health care, education, and related social services. This more moderate position has increased the voting base of Social Democratic parties by broadening their appeal beyond the working class. It has also weakened their organizational structure by diluting the ideological fervor of their members.

Still other political parties *focus on a narrow range of issues.* The Green parties of Europe, for example, are concerned primarily with environmental and related social issues. As such, they are often referred to as **single- or limited-issue parties.** While Green parties have been too narrowly focused to gain power, they have been extremely effective in publicizing the serious environmental and social problems facing Europe. Many countries in the third world, by contrast, created large single political parties that were designed to prevent political conflict by forcing all the major groups within the confines of a single party. Competitive political parties, in their view, created conflict by accentuating ethnic, religious and political differences in their societies. In reality, most lacked a clear ideology other than keeping the regime in power. Examples of large single parties are to be found in the discussion of Mexican and Egyptian politics.

Political Parties and Political Analysis. The bewildering array of political parties found throughout the world makes them difficult to classify (Gross and Sigelman 1984; Sartori 1976). Classification is made more complicated by the constant evolution of political parties. Mass-membership parties are evolving into catch-all parties, and the large single parties are splintering into a multitude of minor parties. Even the former communist parties are taking on democratic trappings.

Ideological Classifications: Left, Right, and Center. For practical purposes, most comparative political analysts find it useful to classify political parties on the basis of their ideology, a practice that evolved in revolutionary France. The French parliament of the era took the shape of a large semicircle in which supporters of the church and monarchy sat on the far right, while advocates of direct popular democracy sat on the far left. Over time, it became customary to refer to *monarchists, supporters of the church, and extreme nationalists* as the **far right.** The **moderate or democratic right** consisted of a broad range of *parties favoring private property, free enterprise, low taxation, and law and order.* The **far left** consisted of the *communists, anarchists, and other parties advocating a mass revolution by violent means.* The **moderate left** was the preserve of the Social Democrats, while the political **center** was dominated by *largely middle-class parties that advocated a reasonable balance between capitalism and social welfare.*

As the middle class has grown, so have the parties of the center. Definitions of right and left have also shifted with time. With rare exception, monarchist parties have become a footnote in history, as have the anarchists. Christian Democratic parties now dominate the center right of many European countries, advocating programs that support private enterprise and champion moral responsibility. Social Democratic parties are inching ever closer to the political center, downplaying their socialist origins. Communist parties continue to dominate the far left but have fallen out of favor. The center is where the voters are.

Political systems in which the dominant parties cluster near the political center generally are more stable, more moderate, and more democratic than those in which the parties are polarized at the extreme left and right. It is relatively easy for moderate parties to compromise their differences, but extremist parties find it far more difficult to do so. (Budge, Robertson, and Hearl 1987; Kim and Fording 1994). How, for instance, can the views of an anti-religious communist party calling for total state ownership of the means of production be reconciled with those of an ultra-nationalist party advocating the fusion of church and state and a revival of laissez-faire capitalism? This is one of the many challenges facing Russia and the other newly independent states created by the collapse of the Soviet Union. Similar patterns of extreme polarization exist throughout the third world.

THE CONTEXT OF POLITICS: ECONOMICS, CULTURE, AND INTERNATIONAL INTERDEPENDENCE

Although political institutions and political actors occupy center stage in the political process, that process is profoundly influenced by the broader economic, cultural, and international context in which it occurs. Indeed, some comparative analysts believe that the behavior of any country is largely a reflection of its cultural and economic systems, together with its position in the global community. Whether or not one accepts this point of view, efforts to predict or explain the politics of any country in the modern world would be incomplete without a close look at these three factors.

Economic Systems and Comparative Politics

Advocates of a **political economy** approach to comparative political analysis find *most areas of political life to be shaped by economic relationships* (Clark 1991; Calabrese and Sparks 2004; Clemens 2004). The more one understands the link between economics and politics, in their view, the easier it will be to explain and predict political events.

Although political economists are unified in their belief that economic factors underlie most forms of political activity, they disagree violently over the best strategy for achieving a prosperous and equitable society (Staniland 1985; Gilpin 1987). The dominant schools of political economy are Marxism, free-market (neoclassical) capitalism, and state capitalism. Marxists argue that prosperity and equality are best assured by a socialist economic system in which the government owns the factories, farms, and other means of production. Neoclassical or free-market economists, by contrast, argue that only the free market can assure prosperity and equality. It is the free flow of economic activity unencumbered by the government, in their view, that leads to a society of plenty. While socialists argue that growth and prosperity require government control, free-market capitalists see the government as the enemy of equality and prosperity. State capitalists, in turn, argue that prosperity and equality require both capitalism and a strong dose of government planning.

The United States and many of its allies favor free-market capitalism. Japan and many of the newly industrialized countries of Asia are advocates of state capitalism. Until the 1990s, Russia and China adhered to socialist economic principles. The countries of the third world have experimented with various combinations of socialism (Marxism), free-market capitalism, and state capitalism. As we will see in subsequent chapters, adherence to differing economic philosophies has led to dramatic differences in how countries do politics. Indeed, it is difficult to understand the political process in the world today without some awareness of the basic components of Marxism, free-market (neoclassical) capitalism, and state capitalism. Accordingly, we will explore these topics next.

Marxism.   The world's most famous political economist was Karl Marx (Coker 1934). A philosopher of the mid-nineteenth century, Karl Marx witnessed both the rewards and the abuses of industrialization in Europe. For the first time in human history, industrialization had made it possible for society to provide an advanced quality of life for all of its citizens. The problem, from Marx's perspective, was that the fruits of industrialization were monopolized by *a narrow class of industrialists and merchants* he referred to as the **bourgeoisie.** While the bourgeoisie reaped huge profits, the majority of *the working class*—the **proletariat**—lived in poverty and squalor. Industrialization had made it possible for human society to attain new heights of prosperity and intellectual development, but that goal had been subverted by the greed of the capitalist bourgeoisie.

How, then, Marx asked, could the fruits of industrialization be used for the development of mankind? The task would not be easy, for the political process was controlled by the rich and powerful. Governments, in Marx's words, were

Marx's theory of class conflict may have stemmed in part from his knowledge of London's slums. Dudley Street, shown here in a woodcut by Doré, was close to Dean Street, where Marx once lived with his family. Both of Marx's sons and his daughter died from illnesses related to undernourishment and poor living conditions.

merely a "committee of the rich" charged with keeping the masses in servitude. The masses, moreover, were distracted from their true economic interests by myths of religion and nationalism. Indeed, Marx went so far as to refer to religion as the "opiate" of the masses. The solution, Marx reasoned, was for the masses to come together as a class and seize power from the rich. This accomplished, the masses would use their control of the means of production to assure that everyone received an equitable share of society's wealth.

Fundamental to this argument was Marx's belief that human nature was basically good. With ample resources at their disposal, the working class would be more than willing to "give according to their abilities and take according to their needs." *Everything would be owned in common,* hence the reference to a Marxist society as a **communist** or communal society.

Friedrich Engels, an early colleague of Marx, believed that the state would simply "wither away" once communism had been achieved. The Marxist utopia would be a worker's paradise. It would also be free of religious and national conflict, for religions and nations would cease to exist.

Marx believed that his theory of class conflict underscored the scientific and inevitable unfolding of history. The historical role of capitalism was to industrialize society, and the role of the proletariat was to seize power from the bourgeoisie and use the fruits of industrialization to establish a truly humanistic state. This process was inevitable and could not be reversed. While Marx believed that he had discovered a scientific principle of social evolution, his philosophy was also highly moralistic. In his view, it was the moral obligation of the proletariat to seize the means of production and to use its profits to create a just society.

Communism, as practiced in the states of the former Soviet Union and in the People's Republic of China, proved to be profoundly inefficient. Although important gains were made in the areas of education, health care, and social services, productivity was sluggish and the quality of workmanship was poor. The failure of **Marxism** in the Soviet Union and China will be discussed at length in Chapters 7 and 8, respectively.

Free-Market Capitalism.   The capitalist version of political economy is as simple and as beguiling as that of the Marxists. Capitalist political economy finds its origins in the works of Adam Smith (1776) and other "classical" economists of the eighteenth and nineteenth centuries. Individuals, in the view of Adam Smith, were rational economic actors. Each was primarily concerned with maximizing his or her economic self-interest. Industrialists and merchants wanted to sell their goods at the highest possible price, just as workers wanted to receive the highest possible wages for their labor. Ultimately, the price of goods and labor was determined by the law of supply and demand. Adam Smith described this principle as an "unseen hand" regulating the marketplace.

Adam Smith believed the free market provided the key to social and economic development. Technological development was assured because individuals would always seek to increase their wealth by inventing new goods and services. The production of new goods and services, in turn, would provide jobs for the masses. Indeed, as the number of factories increased, there would not be enough workers to go around, and wages would be driven up by the law of supply and demand. Increased wages would enable workers to buy more goods, thereby stimulating ever-faster economic development. Finally, competition among producers would assure that goods were reasonably priced. By the very nature of the free market, successful products would be overwhelmed by lower-priced imitators. Adam Smith's world, then, would be an abundant world. By attempting to increase his or her personal wealth, each individual would assure that there was enough for all. Some people would be richer than others, but that determination would be made by the market.

Adam Smith's idyllic version of an abundant society required an undistorted free market. In the real world, unfortunately, distortions in the free market lurk around every corner (Edwards 1985). The most influential of these are monopolies and governments. In Adam Smith's ideal world, the pursuit of wealth would lead to greater innovation and productivity. In the real world, it often leads to monopolies and price fixing. How can the law of supply and demand work effectively if manufacturers agree among themselves to charge a common price for their goods and to pay a common wage to their workers? It cannot. In much the same manner, it is difficult for the free market to work effectively in an environment of excessive regulation and taxation. Taxes reduce innovation and productivity by reducing rewards. Why should people work hard and innovate if the fruits of their labor are merely absorbed by the government? Regulations also cripple productivity by distorting the law of supply and demand. It is not the market that determines the type, cost, and quality of goods, but the government.

The modern advocates of free-market economics are referred to as **neoclassical economists** (Friedman and Friedman 1980). They have taken the classical economic theories of Adam Smith and other capitalist philosophers and adapted them to fit the needs of the present era. *Neoclassical economists, accordingly, argue for a world in which monopolistic practices are prohibited and in which the economic role of governments is reduced to facilitating free-market competition.* Currencies are to be strong, taxes low, and regulations few. International trade, also, is to be free of tariffs and monopolistic practices, allowing each state to seek the highest price for its goods and labor. If Mexican labor is willing to work for less than U.S. labor, so be it.

The neoclassical vision of a capitalist world is of far more than theoretical interest, for it has become the guiding vision of the International Monetary Fund, the World Bank, and other international economic agencies. It is that vision that the states of the first world are attempting to establish throughout the third world, including Russia (Walters and Blake 1992).

In reality, of course, Adam Smith's abundant society is as much a utopian vision as Karl Marx's ideal society whose inhabitants give according to their abilities and take according to their needs. Most states of the first world maintain enough of a **free-market economy** to benefit from the energy of human initiative. Most forms of economic activity, however, are regulated by the state in one way or another. In reality, the political process in most countries of the West represents a continuing effort to strike a balance between the raw energy of free-market competition and the need to regulate the excesses of that competition. Canada, Britain, and most other "free-market states" also provide a broad array of welfare services, most of which are managed by the state.

State Capitalism.   A third version of political economy is referred to as state capitalism (Edwards 1985). **State capitalism** accepts the proposition that capitalist competition is the most effective way to generate economic growth, but it rejects the principle that the free market is the most efficient way to regulate the economy. From the point of view of the state capitalists, the economy is simply too important to be left to the "unseen hand" of the marketplace. Individual capitalists, in their view, are too concerned with immediate profits to recognize either their own long-term interests or those of the country as a whole.

The basic formula of state capitalism, accordingly, calls for most economic activity to be in the hands of individual capitalists. The desire for wealth is a powerful motivator that must not be destroyed. Political leaders, however, determine those industries that are best suited to the needs of the country. The government then uses its power and resources to support private-sector firms that invest in these areas. Priority firms receive special financing, pay lower taxes, and are protected from foreign competitors during their formative years. The principle of competition, however, is retained. Several national firms compete in each area, thereby assuring that market forces will produce quality products at a reasonable price. Japan and the **tigers of Asia**—*Taiwan, South Korea, and Singapore—are the world's foremost advocates of state capitalism* (Wang 1994). Germany also inclines toward state capitalism.

State capitalism has produced many variations, depending upon the circumstances of the country. The *ideal version of state capitalism* is often referred to as **growth with equity** (Todaro 1997). *Under the doctrine of growth with equity, the government uses the power of the state both to develop the economy and to assure that all members of society share in the benefits of that development.* Japan and Germany have an enviable record of achieving both growth and equity. Many of the newly industrialized states of Asia and Latin America, by contrast, have stressed growth at the expense of equity. The power of the state has been used to assure that mass protests do not stand in the way of economic development.

The world's most recent convert to state capitalism has been the People's Republic of China. While the communist regime remains firmly in control, communism, as an economic system, is becoming a thing of the past. This topic is discussed in Chapter 8.

Political Economy and Comparative Political Analysis. Despite their philosophical differences, most political economists share the following propositions that illustrate the major focus of political economy research in the study of comparative politics.

1. *Political conflict is largely economic conflict.* As a general principle, political conflict will usually be more intense in societies with declining economic resources than it is in societies with increasing economic resources (Davies 1963). By the same token, one can usually predict that political violence will reflect the distribution of wealth within a society. The greater the disparities of wealth, the greater the potential for political violence. One sees this today in the growing political turmoil in the third world.

2. *Economic prosperity reduces conflict.* Support for political institutions and political leaders is based on their ability to meet the needs of their citizens. The most legitimate political systems in the world are also among the most prosperous. The abundant distribution of wealth increases tolerance among competing groups, as all share a common interest in assuring that the system survives.

3. *The goals that a regime can pursue are limited by its financial resources.* Rich states have a broader range of options than poorer states, but all states have finite resources. The better a state's economic situation is understood, the easier it is to predict what policies political leaders can or cannot pursue, as well as the consequences of those choices.

4. *All things being equal, wealthier individuals and groups will have more political influence than poorer individuals and groups.* Political leaders generally pursue policies

that are favored by their financial supporters. This proposition has withstood the test of time so consistently that it requires little elaboration.

5. *Most political parties and pressure groups evolve to promote the economic interests of their members.* While the fit is far from perfect, the parties to the right of center are favored by the prosperous segments of society, while the parties to the left are favored by the working class.

6. *As general principle, the political activities of individuals will mirror their economic interests.* This approach to political economy is often referred to as public choice analysis. The basic premise of public choice analysis is that individuals are "egotistic, rational, utility maximizers" (Mueller 1979, 1; Austen-Smith 2005). Greed is the great political motivator. In some instances, the link between economic logic and political behavior is direct, with individuals supporting the candidate or position that is most likely to provide an immediate economic payoff such as lower taxes or increased welfare payments. More often than not, however, individuals vote according to their general assessments of how well the country is doing. If the country is viewed as prospering, the incumbents are supported. If the country is perceived to be in an economic decline, the ruling party or coalition is frequently turned out of office (Lewis-Beck 1988). This is not always the case, but such patterns occur with sufficient frequency to establish economics as one of the primary predictors of mass voting behavior.

Most of the principles of political economy also apply to politics at the international level. As with domestic politics, international politics is underscored by conflict over scarce resources. Conflict management at the international level often involves economic payoffs. Rich states usually enjoy greater influence in the inter-national arena than poor states. Much like individuals, states may be predicted to act as rational utility maximizers in pursuing their economic interests. The more one examines the economic dimensions of international politics, political economists argue, the greater will be one's ability to explain and predict international political events (Frieden and Lake 1987).

Culture and Comparative Politics

Economics is an important aspect of comparative political analysis, yet it is but one part of a very complex puzzle. As Karl Marx himself would note, people often have a difficult time understanding their own economic self-interest. Rather than behaving as rational economic actors, observed Marx, people often allow themselves to be swayed by the emotions that accompany religion and nationalism. Economics is important, but so are security, freedom, power, pride, religiosity, love, belonging, nationalism, and a list of other values too long to mention (Maslow 1970; Kroeber and Kluckhohn 1963).

What Karl Marx was referring to, of course, was the influence of culture on politics. The way people respond to their political leaders and political institutions depends on what they consider to be important. It is culture that tells people what they should consider important, that defines standards of good and bad and right and wrong, and that provides individuals with an identity (Jung 2002).

It tells individuals who they are and what they are. Culture also defines the roles that an individual is to play in life and explains how those roles are to be played (Douglas and Wildaysky 1982). It tells individuals what is expected of them and how to get along with other people (Gross and Rayner 1985). Beyond that, culture provides individuals with religions and ideologies that explain how their society came to exist, why it is the best of all possible worlds, and why some individuals should have more of the good things of life than others.

The Two Faces of Culture. Because culture is such a broad and complex phenomenon, it may be helpful to view culture as having two faces: an external face and an internal face. The **external face of culture** consists of *national myths, ideologies, religions, and other belief systems that a society uses to socialize or "program" its citizens.* **Socialization** is *the process of indoctrinating people into their culture.* The socialization process begins with the parents and continues through a wide variety of religious, social, and political institutions. The schools play a major role in the socialization process, as does the mass media. The more effective a society is at socializing its citizens, the more likely it is that those citizens will absorb a common set of political, economic, and social values.

The second face is the **internal face of culture.** It is based on the psychology of the individual and consists of the cultural beliefs that have actually been absorbed by the citizens of a society. It is important to recognize the differences between the two faces of culture. External culture is the content of socialization; it is what a society would like its people to believe. Internal culture, by contrast, is what people actually believe. It consists of the predispositions, values, and attitudes that shape the way in which they view their world. This does not mean that values and attitudes do not always determine behavior. For example, people often have a strong emotional feeling for one party but vote for another one for economic reasons. The converse is equally true. Nevertheless, the more individuals buy into their culture, the more cohesive society is likely to be.

Political socialization in most first world societies is very effective. Parents, peers, schools, churches, and the media all convey more or less the same message: "The political system is fair, and it must be supported. It may not be perfect, but all things considered, it is the best one for us."

Many less-developed countries are experiencing a great deal of cultural turmoil. The government has one vision of what society should look like, while religious, ethnic, regional, and political groups have other ideas. Individuals in such societies tend to be poorly socialized. The message presented by the government in the media and in the schools conflicts with that being presented by parents and by religious or ethnic associations. Who is to be believed: the state, the church, or the family? Should ethnic and religious loyalties be set aside for the sake of the unity of the country, or should each ethnic group fight to create its own independent country?

Diversity in Culture. The cultural values and predispositions that individuals absorb from the socialization process provide them with a **cultural map** for making choices about politics, economics, and almost everything else of impor-

Bob Krist / CORBIS

Cultures often change gradually, as a result of outside influences. Here, a Chinese woman and her son are shown outside a McDonald's restaurant in northeastern Beijing.

tance in their lives. Individuals are bombarded with so many pieces of information on a daily basis that they cannot possibly worry about them all. Their cultural map helps them sort things out. If communism is bad, everything related to communism is bad. If democracy is good, everything related to democracy must also be good. As a practical matter, most attitudes and opinions come prepackaged in the cultural map. The more an individual's cultural map is understood, accordingly, the easier it will be to predict and explain his or her political behavior.

As most individuals are socialized to accept the culture of their society, it is reasonable to assume some degree of cultural uniformity among the citizens of that society. Not all Americans share the same cultural map, but the cultural map internalized by most Americans tends to be distinct from the cultural map internalized by most Russians or most Chinese.

While it is reasonable to say that certain values or attitudes are very prevalent in German or Russian society, it would be profoundly inaccurate to suggest that all Germans or all Russians possess the same cultural map. If they did, predicting German or Russian politics would be remarkably simple. Quite obviously, this is not the case. While most Germans share some values in common, the variations within German society remain infinite. Most Germans, as will be elaborated in

Chapter 5, possess a strong commitment to democratic principles. A minority, however, continue to manifest the fascist views of an earlier era. Culture, moreover, is forever changing. The authoritarian virtues of an earlier era are being replaced by more liberal and egalitarian values of the present era. The ebb and flow of change occurs within all cultures.

Political Culture. Culture not only possess an external face and an internal face, but it also comes in several varieties. It is now common to speak of political culture, economic culture, and artistic culture, among others. **Political culture** is that aspect of culture that seems to have the greatest influence in shaping the way people behave politically (Almond 1956). From the **external** perspective, political culture consists of ideologies, myths, and religions that individuals are socialized to believe. It is the content of political socialization. From the **internal** or individual perspective, political culture focuses on people's orientations to politics: their attitudes and opinions about political leaders, political movements, political events, and political institutions. It encompasses their feelings of legitimacy and alienation, their sense of national identity, and the political groups with which they identify.

Unfortunately, it is not always easy to draw a clear line between what is political and what is not (Inglehart and Abramson 1994). The **economic culture** of a society, *or the value that it places on hard work and innovation,* plays a critical role in determining both the quality of life that its citizens will enjoy and the resource base that will be available to its politicians. **Artistic culture** is also intensely political. *Politics lives on symbols, and it is the arts that give expression to those symbols.* As such, they are part and parcel of the processes of political control and political mobilization. While it is useful to speak of a political culture, it is important that the line between political culture and other specialized cultures not be drawn too precisely. It is difficult to find any dimension of culture without political relevance.

Culture and Comparative Political Analysis. Culture has become such an important dimension of comparative politics that its uses as an analytical tool are not easily summarized. The following points, however, are among the most important.

First, the type of culture that a society possesses often influences the type of political system that it can sustain (Mueller and Seligson 1994). Democratic political systems seem to work best in cultures that emphasize tolerance, individual freedom, trust, civic responsibility, and the belief that individuals can play a major role in shaping their own destinies (Almond and Verba 1963). Cultures that preach racial or religious purity provide a difficult environment for democracy, as do cultures that stress the values of obedience, conformity, and power. Following the end of World War II, many people openly questioned whether the cultures of Germany and Japan could sustain democratic regimes. They survived, but they also underwent changes. The same questions are now being asked in regard to the countries of the former Soviet Union, a region profoundly lacking in democratic traditions.

Second, cultural problems also challenge the internal cohesion of many countries in the third world, some of which remain mosaics of diverse ethnic, tribal, and religious groups united by little more than a common colonial history (Diamond 1994). Cultural attachments to ethnic or religious groups remain stronger than cultural attachments to the state, and interactions among members of different ethnic and religious groups are marked by suspicion and distrust. The tragic results of this state of affairs in Nigeria are examined at length in Chapter 12.

Third, culture influences the ability of political leaders to control their populations and to mobilize those populations in support of their policy objectives. During the Second World War, the fascist regimes in Germany and Japan used nationalistic symbols to wring extraordinary sacrifices from their populations, as did the British and the Americans. Such sacrifices were made possible by the intense sense of national identity among the populations involved. The collapse of the U.S.S.R. in 1991, by contrast, was underscored by a lack of cultural support among its citizens. Slogans and other symbols calling for increased sacrifice and productivity fell on deaf ears. The Soviet state was strong enough to control its citizens by force, but it lacked the cultural symbols necessary to mobilize the Soviet population in support of its goals.

Finally, cultural analysis helps us to predict the future course that the politics of a country is likely to take. Cultures are always changing and evolving. German and Japanese cultures, for example, have become increasingly democratic over the course of the past five decades. Most students of Germany and Japan feel confident that the democracies of both countries now rest on a firm bedrock of democratic culture. Authoritarianism, in their view, has become a thing of the past.

Some cultural analysts find the countries of the First World to be developing a post-material culture (Inglehart 1990). The culture of hard work and productivity that created their prosperity and world dominance now shows signs of eroding as concern for leisure time and the environment outpace the drive for wealth. Not all cultural analysts, however, are convinced that this situation is permanent, arguing that economic values will reassert their influence during periods of scarcity (Flanagan 1987).

International Interdependence and the Evolution of Globalization

The evolution of nation states in the seventeenth century gave birth to a pattern of international relations in which each country was a law unto itself. No international organizations existed and relationships between countries were dictated largely by security interests. If one country became too powerful, others would coalesce in an effort to keep it in check. International relations specialists refer to this as the balance of power system. Sometimes the balancing was informal; other times it found expression in formal alliances. Nothing, however, was written in stone and each country honored its commitments based on its own interests.

In the meantime, countries attempted to increase their economic and military power via industrialization. They traded with each other, but most sought colonies to provide closed markets and a reliable supply of raw materials. Colonies were an extension of the nation's power and were prized as a source of national pride.

The two big winners in the rush to industrialization and global power were Britain and France. Both established global empires and they were the super powers of the balance of power era. The latter quarter of the nineteenth century would see them joined by Germany, Japan, Russia and the United States, each of whom sought their own colonial empire. American colonies were few, but the Monroe Doctrine left little doubt that the U.S. considered Latin America to be its private preserve.

Then as now, economic ties between countries were developing faster than political ties. Norman Angel, a leading economist of the era ,went so far as to argue that the complexity of the economic ties between major powers made war impossible. Economics was a rational science and no rational leader would sacrifice the economic interests of his country by rushing head long into a global conflict (Angel 1914). Angel, unfortunately, misjudged the intensity of nationalistic emotions (culture) and the lust for power among ruling elites. Perhaps he also misjudged the persuasive power of greed.

Whatever the case, 1914 would see the world erupt in flames as Germany invaded France and Britain and the U.S. belatedly joined with the French to stem the German threat. Germany was ultimately defeated, but only after the world had suffered horrendous losses. The balance of power system for managing international conflict was no longer viable.

That, at least, was the message of President Wilson as he forced the world powers to accept the creation of the League of Nations. In his view the League of Nations would be an international government capable of managing conflict before it erupted into another global confrontation. Global conflicts, he argued, required global solutions. The major powers could not prevent the creation of the League of Nations and so they merely forced a provision stipulating that all decisions had to be unanimous. No major power could be forced to do anything against its will. Even the U.S. Congress refused to give the League of Nations any effective power.

President Wilson's logic was impeccable. The dust hardly had settled on the peace treaty ending World War I before the world embarked upon a vicious arms race that would lead to a level of carnage and brutality unimaginable only a few years earlier. Germany emerged as the dominant power in the West; Japan as the dominant power in the East. Each was driven by a virulent fascist ideology that glorified the state as the expression of racial supremacy. The power of both could have been balanced long before they menace the security of the free world, but the balance of power system collapsed. Britain and the Soviet Union chose to manage conflict by appeasing the aggressor. The U.S. for its part, sank into an isolationist stupor pretending that what happened in the rest of the world wasn't its concern.

The devastation of World War II forced the creation of the United Nations, but once again the major powers were unwilling to relinquish their sovereignty. All the world's nations could join the UN, but the victorious powers retained a veto power. Each—the U.S., Britain, France, the Soviet Union and China—could block the power of the UN. This didn't seem to be an insurmountable problem at the time. Surely the winners of the heroic war against the fascist powers could cooperate to maintain the peace.

Alas, the world had changed. When the ashes of World War II had cleared there were only two super powers: the United States and the Soviet Union. The United States espoused democracy and capitalism; the Soviet Union championed Marx's slogan of "from each according to his abilities; to each according to his needs." The state would use its ownership of the economy to promote rapid industrial development and to assure that all people received adequate food, housing, education, and health care. Democracy would emerge once economic development and social equality had been achieved. Communist slogans were extremely popular, and communist parties became powerful forces in all but the Anglo countries. Democracy and capitalism were pitted against authoritarianism and socialism. The Communist Party seized power in China in 1949 raising fears that communism would soon become the dominant political force in the world. The cold war had begun and the United Nations was hopelessly divided. Neither the United States nor the Soviet Union could force their will on the world community. Each balanced the other in what international relations specialists began to call a **bi-polar** system. Popular commentators began to refer to the balance of terror. Nuclear missiles had become the weapon of choice.

Curiously, the balance of terror produced a remarkably stable world for some 40 years. Fearing the devastation of a nuclear conflagration, the U.S. and the Soviet Union fought proxy wars in Korea, Vietnam and Afghanistan in a perpetual game of checkmate. In the final analysis, the seductive lure of capitalism and democracy proved more powerful than socialism and authoritarianism. The Soviet Union collapsed in 1991, splintering into some 15 independent countries. There was neither war nor revolution. The Soviet Empire, one of the twin superpowers of the cold war era, simply dissolved. Of these, the dominant country was Russia, the core of the old Soviet Union. Russia's new leaders, all former communists, began a painful transition to capitalism and democracy. China, while retaining a communist political system, began a transition to capitalism that would transform it into one of the world leading economic powers. The transitions of both Russia and China remain incomplete, a topic discussed at length in Part 3 of this book.

The collapse of the Soviet Union in 1991 marked a dramatic turning point in world affairs. The cold war that had maintained the world on the brink of a nuclear holocaust for more than four decades had come to an end. The United States, now the world's remaining superpower, proclaimed the existence of a new world order based on international cooperation and international inter-dependance. The goals of the new world order were to build an international community that was democratic, stable, prosperous, humane, equitable in the distribution of life's opportunities, and protective of the environment. Capitalism would lead to economic prosperity. International relations specialists began to speak of a **uni-polar** system. There was one superpower and no balancers. Pundits began to refer to the pax Americana. Henceforth, the countries of the world would find their domestic politics shaped by the demands of the United States and its major allies.

Hardly had the cold war come to an end and the pax Americana established than the world was faced with a new war, a war on terror. Attacks on the U.S.

began in 1993 and reached a crescendo on September 11, 2001. The threat of Jihadist terror has been unrelenting since that date. The September 11th attacks were blamed on Osama bin–Laden and his al–Qaeda network., but his is but one of a multitude of Jihadist groups that have vowed revenge on the U.S. and its allies for their domination of the Islamic world and support for Israel .

Terror, of course, was not new. Nor, was it primarily Muslim. The IRA, Eta, Tamil Tigers, Drug gangs, Skin Heads, Red Guards, Weathermen, Contras to mention but a few of the more prominent terrorist groups, had all been part of the political scene during the 40 years of the cold war.

The new terror, however, was different. It was not limited to localized targets but challenged the very existence of the new world order proclaimed with the fall of the Soviet Union. The leader of every major industrialized country now warns that a major terrorist attack is imminent and will eventually succeed. The peace dividend heralded at the end of the cold war has given way to soaring defense budgets and draconian security measures. Unlike the cold war, the war on terror has become a hot war.

Globalization: Economic, Cultural, Political

Whatever the fanfare accompanying the proclamation of a new world order or the despair that followed the September 11th attacks on the United States, the globalization of the world community had become a reality. Rare is the large corporation that is not global in its operations. Cultural boundaries that had endured for centuries have now been blurred by satellite television and the Internet. Drugs, disease and terror and other scourges to humanity have also become global in their reach and demand ever higher levels of international cooperation. One way or another, international pressures are becoming a major determinant of how individual countries do politics (Lagon 2003).

Economic Globalization. World economic affairs are managed by international institutions such as the World Bank, the International Monetary Fund, the World Trade Organization, and the G-8 group of world economic powers (see box p. 37). Multinational corporations are so vast and powerful that they evade regulation by any single country, the United States included. Some have budgets larger than most countries. Indeed, the annual revenues of Exxon-Mobil Corporation are only slightly less that the annual revenues of the entire continent of Africa. (*Guardian,* June 16, 2003, www). If taxes, wages or environmental regulations became to stringent in one country, the multinationals merely shift the bulk of their operations to countries where laws are more forgiving. Indeed, many American multi-nationals have their corporate headquarters in small countries that impose few taxes, yet do most of their business in the U.S. The *Wall Street Journal* reported that some 60 percent of U.S. corporations paid no tax duing the boom years between 1996 and 2000. Foreign corporations, many owned by Americans, paid even less (*Wall Street Journal,* April 6, 2004, p1). So great has been the pace of economic globalization that economists have begun to speak of a **world economic system** with a logic of its own (Cohen 2005).

International Monetary Fund (IMF) and the World Bank

These two organizations were established at the end of World War II to facilitate the reconstruction of a war-torn Europe and to reestablish order within the world economy. Once the reconstruction of Europe was complete, the IMF and the World Bank became the major economic agencies charged with stimulating economic development in the poorer states of the third world. The World Bank and IMF loans are designed to facilitate the economic development of the states of the third world and to assist them in paying their debts to their creditors, most of whom reside in the first world. The World Bank makes long-term loans, and the IMF specializes in short-term loans. The World Bank has also placed increased emphasis on stimulating democracy in the states that it assists. Both organizations are controlled by member countries with voting power reflecting the size of a state's financial contribution. Countries that follow the "rules" of the international system receive loans, and those who break them do not. As most third world states are hopelessly in debt, the IMF and the World Bank exert enormous influence over their domestic politics.

The World Trade Organization (WTO)

The WTO is designed to regulate the level of tariffs that countries can place on the exports of their competitors. As in the case of the international political system, the international economic system works best when the major powers are in agreement. Nothing can be imposed on a major power against its will (Ranis 2005).

Some political observers believe that the powerful countries of the first world use their dominant economic power to keep third world countries in a permanent state of dependence or poverty. This view is referred to as **dependency theory** (Cardoso 1972; Frank 1984; Chilcote 1981; Wallerstein 1984). The central theme of dependency theory is strikingly simple. The international society, like all societies, suffers from a shortage of scarce resources. If some states are to be rich, others must be poor. Much as in colonial days, the large industrial countries of the West increase their wealth by using the third world as a cheap source of raw materials. They also use the poor countries of the third world as a dumping ground for industrial products they can't sell elsewhere. In the eyes of the dependency theorists, nothing has really changed. Old-fashioned military colonialism has merely been replaced by more insidious forms of economic and cultural colonialism. While the countries of the third world are nominally independent, the first world continues to dictate the pace of their economic, political, and social development.

Not so, say free market economists. Economic globalization is merely forcing the world to become more rational. Rather that every country attempting to produce everything, each country will specialize in what it can do best and most profitably. In formal terms, each country will pursue its **comparative advantage** (Chenery and Syraquin 1975). The result will be more jobs, greater innovation, higher quality and cheaper prices. Everyone benefits. At present, the comparative advantage of the countries of the third world is cheap labor, unenforced environmental regulations, dismal safety standards and low taxes.

Which view is correct? This is a matter of great debate (Eschle and Maiguaschca 2005). The advocates of economic globalization provide an avalanche of statistics suggesting that the world transition to capitalism has resulted in dramatic reductions in poverty. World Bank statistics, by contrast, suggest that approximately 24 percent of the world's population continue to exist on $1 per day. Other estimates suggest that the figure may be as low as 18 percent or even 7 percent depending on the calculations used (*Economist,* March 13, 2004, pp. 69–71). While economists debate the proper techniques for measuring abject poverty, the United Nations predicts that every third person will be a slum dweller within 30 years. As things currently stand, some 940 million people, about one-sixth of the world's population "already live in squalid, unhealthy areas, mostly without water, sanitation, public services or legal security"(Vidal 2003).

Has the transition to capitalism made things worse, or has it made things better? Probably both. World productivity has increased, but much of the wealth has gone to the countries of the first world (Bishop 2001). All in all, the transition to capitalism has expanded wealth for a broader segment of society in most countries, but done little to eliminate the misery of the lower classes.

Who's to blame? More debate! Dependency theorists, as previously noted, place all of the blame on a global economic system that exploits the poor countries for the benefit of the rich. Amartya Sen, Nobel prize-winning economist, places the blame on the weakness of democracy in much of the third world (Sen 2002). Democracies, in his view, have less abject poverty because the voters will not tolerate the corruption and inefficiencies that fuel poverty. A middle view suggests that the problem is not economic globalization, but the unwillingness of the rich countries to play by their own rules. The United States, for example, demands that the poor countries remove price supports and open their markets to free trade at the same time that it spends billions of dollars to support American farmers (Pickel 2005). As a result, the U.S. dumps agricultural products abroad at a price far lower than their actual cost. Farmers in the third world can't keep pace and are forced into poverty.

Cultural Globalization. Cultural globalization began during the colonial era as all but the remotest areas of the globe were colonized by the European powers. English and French became the second language in large parts of Asia and Africa with smaller outposts embracing Dutch, Portugese, Italian and German. Christian missionaries followed in the wake of the colonialists making Christianity the dominant faith in the world today, only slightly ahead of Islam. When people speak of cultural globalization today, however, it is more likely the influence of the American pop-culture to which they are referring. Hollywood, the Coca-Cola Company, and McDonald's Corporation have been the conquering hero's of American culture, as have country, rock, and MTV. American films, TV, and videos dominate some 70 percent of the European market and 50 percent of the Japanese market. The opening of a new McDonald's in the countries of the third world has become a major cultural event.

Most scholars decry the erosion of the world's cultural diversity (Beck 2003). Some, however, find it a sign of progress and have coined the term "creative destruction." (Cowen 2002). Cultural globalization, in this view, promotes economic and political globalization. It also does away with traditional cultural practices that the West finds abhorrent, not the least of which is the seclusion of women in many areas of the Islamic world. Whichever view one adopts, the pace of cultural globalization appears unstoppable and many scholars now speak of evolving cultures and hybrid cultures (Tomlisom 1999). Others note that both cultural and political globalization are being driven by economic globalization.

Whatever the theoretical debate, a recent global survey found American culture rejected by all but the Japanese. And yet it continues to ride the wings of the Internet and satellite television to greater heights, its appeal seemingly irresistible among the world's youth (Pew Global Attitudes Project 2001). The French spend some $3 billion a year to stem the American onslaught in the French speaking world and a growing range of countries have limited the access of American films to domestic markets (Baughn and Buchanan 2001).

Americans would like to think that there was more to their culture than Coca-Cola and MTV (Hurrison and Huntington 2002). Democracy, human rights, social equality and the separation of church and state (secularism) are the pillars of American culture just as they are pillars of the Western European culture. They are equally the values that are aspired to by millions of people who continue to live under authoritarian rule. The World Bank and the various aid granting agencies of the first world are using their tremendous influence to further the causes of democracy and human rights in the less democratic areas of the world, but with far less enthusiasm than they are pushing the cause of economic globalization. Organizations that rank democracy and human rights now find the world somewhat more human than it was a few decades ago, but the road remains long and difficult.

Political Globalization.   The United Nations provides a loose framework for political globalization, but possesses no independent powers of its own (Letner 2004; Nowotny 2004). Much the same is true of an expanding body of international law presided over by the International Court of Justice (World Court). At a lower level, hundreds if not thousands of international organizations exist to regulate everything from measurement standards to trademarks (Roden 2005; Vogel and Kagen 2004). A massive network of international non-governmental organizations (NGO's), well over 50,000 by some counts, work to promote democracy, alleviate hunger, save endangered species, and a thousand other causes important to their sponsors. They, in turn, are linked to an incalculable number of local NGO's, some of which may be little more than a local farm cooperative designed to increase the productivity of its members. All are referred to as non-governmental organizations because they are not officially sponsored by a government. Some of the international NGO's are religious groups. Others are private organizations devoted to a particular cause. CARE, Catholic Charities, Save the Whales, Save the Children, Doctors without Frontiers, the International Red Cross, and Amnesty International are all examples of international NGO's that do have an impact on the politics of individual countries. Many provide essential services to the poor of the world and help to compensate for the retched services provided by most governments in the third world. Some scholars now argue that an international civil society of non-governmental groups is emerging that will force the governments of the world to pay greater attention to the critical issues of poverty, refugees, human rights, and the environment (Fisher 2003).

While a vast framework for political globalization exists, it lacks either the promise of vast wealth or the seductiveness of pop-culture. For better or worse, the world community continues to be a community of nations. It is they who decide the fate of the world and they do so on the basis of their own national interest. (Hoffman 2002) The greater the military and economic power of a country, the greater its role in shaping the affairs of the international community.

As the world's most powerful military and economic power, the United States has the major voice in determining how much pressure will be placed on the countries of the world to conform to international rules. The U.S. has been the driving force in the economic and cultural globalization of the world as well as its fight against terrorism. The U.S. has dragged its feet in areas of the environment, human rights, hunger, and democracy, pious statements from Washington not withstanding.

The power of the United States makes the rest of the world nervous. This is because the United States finds itself at odds with the United Nations, rejects the existence of an International War Crimes Tribunal and consistently blocks international agreements calling for stringent environmental regulations and birth control. A senior advisor to Tony Blair, the British prime minister and staunch ally of the United States, claims that American policy has set the world back by 10 years (Jonathon Porritt quoted Brown 2004).

The U.S. has also been forced to recognize the limits of its power. America's wars on terror, drugs, illegal immigration, and nuclear proliferation have all suffered from a lack of international coordination and cooperation. Least there be any doubt in the matter, the American and British effort to "go it alone" in Iraq soon found the U.S. begging its allies to contribute troops to the occupation of Iraq.

For all of the weakness of the era of American dominance, it is likely to remain for some time. While most countries are spending less on defense, the United States is spending more. Recent years have seen annual increases in the U.S. defense budget match the total defense budget of China, a projected superpower of the future (Daalder and Lindsay 2003). The European Union has the size and wealth to challenge the United States but, as we shall see in the next chapter, it is unlikely to reach its full potential for some time. Pressures of globalization will increase apace.

Terror and its Causes

The world has learned to live with crime, drugs, sprawling slums, AIDS, and the degradation of the environment as unfortunate as they may be. Whether this co-existence can be sustained over time remains to be seen. The world, however, cannot live with a terror that strikes at the heart of the most powerful nations on earth (White 2003). No one is immune—no country and no individual. Unfortunately, neither scholars nor politicians have been able to forge a common definition of terror. Each country has its own definition of terror and the United States uses several simultaneously. Needless to say, this is a source of some confusion.

Many scholars define **terrorism** as politically motivated acts of violence committed by an individual or small groups of individuals. This is the definition employed in this book. Terrorist acts include: assassination, kidnaping, hijacking, bombs planted in cars, trains, ships and air craft; suicide bombers and chemical attacks, to mention but the most obvious. Small nuclear devices may soon come on line. All are readily employed by small groups of individuals who strike with deadly precision and then fade undetected into the broad mass of society. The U.S. Army refers to such attacks as low intensity conflict.

The objective of the terrorists is not to occupy all or part of a country, but to terrorize political leaders into compliance with their objectives. Osama bin Laden's attacks on the United States were not designed to occupy the United States but to force an American withdrawal from the Islamic world. It is also possible that bin Laden believed that the shock of his attacks would throw the U.S. into chaos and precipitate a civil war. The September 11th strikes did not succeed in these objectives, but the war goes on. Particularly vulnerable are the Middle Eastern oil supplies upon which the economies of the world depend. Saudi Arabia, alone, possesses some 25 percent of the world's oil supplies and is the target of sustained attack by Jihadist terrorists.

Other popular definitions of terrorism blend acts of terror committed by individuals and small groups with **guerilla warfare.** Guerilla groups possess armed militias and are intent on seizing all or part of a country. They use terrorist tactics to achieve their objectives but they also engage government troops in battle. The FARC in Columbian, for example, possess some 10,000 armed troops. Some estimates suggest the number may be as high as 20,000. In many cases, conflicts that begin with terrorism by small groups escalate into full scale guerilla wars.

Still other definitions of terrorism stress that terror is not the sole preserve of fanatics and independence movements. Terror is also used by governments to achieve their policy objectives. The United States, for example, actively encouraged Muslim terrorists and guerrilla groups to attack Soviet targets in Afghanistan during the 1980's. The Soviet Union was the sworn enemy of the United States and Soviet control of Afghanistan threatened U.S. interests in the Middle East. The Soviets were driven from Afghanistan and bin Laden and other terrorists groups nurtured by the U.S. turned upon their former patron. Russia uses terror to combat separatist groups in the breakaway province of Chechnya and Israel uses terror to counter terrorist attacks by Palestinians demanding an end to Israeli occupation of the West Bank and Gaza Strip. Authoritarian governments in Latin America are renown for their use of death squads to eliminate domestic opponents. Terrorist tactics employed by governments are referred to as **state terrorism.** Most governments of the world, although reluctant to admit it, resort to state terrorism in one guise or another.

Terror: Islam versus Globalization. Why, then, has terror chosen the present era to explode as a global force capable of challenging the power of the new world order established by the United States and its allies? The opponents of globalization argue that the answer to this question lies in the astronomical pace of globalization that has occurred since the end of the cold war (Tetreault and

Denmark 2004). Western pop-culture assaults traditional religious beliefs and erodes social values that have endured for centuries. The global transition to capitalism being imposed on the world community by the world's economic powers is accentuating unemployment and shattering the social safety nets upon which the world's disadvantaged depend. The wealth and glitzy lifestyles promised by the transition to capitalism have benefitted the prosperous, but not the poor. It may do so in time, but for the moment, hopes for a better life are fading. Fading also, are much ballyhooed promises for democracy. The transition to democracy remains largely verbal, and repressive regimes continue to rule most countries of the third world. Advocates of democracy are thrown into prison as are moderate religious leaders seeking greater morality in government. With the moderates in prison, the way is paved for extremism and violence. A global world holds tremendous promise for the future. For the present, however, the transition to globalization has the world in turmoil.

Islam and the War on Terror. While the world's leaders acknowledge that the pace of globalization has caused "social dislocations," their struggle against terror has been overwhelmingly focused on a single religion: Islam. This was probably inevitable. The perpetrators of the Sept.11th attacks were Muslim extremists as were their supporters. The United States and its allies added to the impression that Islam was the culprit by accusing Islamic schools, charities, and religious centers of supporting terror and inflaming hostility toward the West. Many governments of the Islamic world were also accused of supporting Jihadist terror, not the least of which was Saudi Arabia, a long time ally of the United States. There was some truth in the U.S. accusations, but little care was taken to distinguish between fact and fiction (Palmer and Palmer 2004). Preachers and politicians added to the fray by proclaiming a new crusade. All of this has given Muslims, the adherents of the Islamic faith, the impression that the United States and its allies have declared war on Islam. This impression has been reinforced by the U.S. occupation of Iraq, the bombing of Afghanistan and an endless stream of threats against Iran and Syria.

This is unfortunate, for Muslims have not declared war on the West. The terrorist attacks have been perpetrated by a small group of religious extremists who have declared a holy war, a Jihad, against the West. They have also terrorized Israel and everyone else who has stood in the way of their vision of an idealized theocracy based on life in seventh century Arabia. Their primary victims, moreover, have been Muslims. Extremist violence had erupted in the Islamic world three decades before it reached the west with more than 100,000 people perishing in Algeria alone. The overwhelming majority of Muslims abhor violence and want nothing more than to live in a peaceful, secure, and democratic environment. They are the natural allies of the West in the war on terror and their support is essential if the Jihadists are to be defeated. This is not a minor point, for Islam is a global faith with well over a billion adherents. It may soon have a billion and one-half adherents. Islam is the second religion of Europe and North America and the dominant faith of the Middle East, Central Asia, and much of South Asia.

How, then, does one reconcile the fact that the Jihadists have found significant support in the Islamic world with the equally compelling fact that the vast majority of Muslims abhor violence and want nothing more than to live their lives in a peaceful, secure, and democratic environment?

Islam, Christianity, and Judaism.   The first step in understanding this apparent contradiction is to provide a basic understanding of the Islamic faith. A basic understanding of Islam is also essential to understanding the growing influence of the Islamic faith in the countries examined in this text. This should not be a difficult task, for Christian and Jewish students know far more about Islam than they realize.

Muslims, Christians, and Jews worship the same God. They also honor the same prophets. Abraham and Moses are key figures in the Islamic faith and Christ is honored as a major prophet. He is not recognized as the son of God, but the Koran, the word of God as revealed to the Prophet Mohammed, devotes a separate chapter to Mary and does recognize the virgin birth. Indeed, Muslims view the Islamic faith as the successor to Judaism and Christianity. God, in the Islamic view, selected the Jews as his chosen people, but despaired when they strayed from the path of righteousness. Christ was sent by God to return humanity to the path of righteousness, but Christians also strayed. God selected Mohammed to be his third, and final, prophet.

God's message as revealed to the Prophet Mohammed, stressed peace, equality, compassion, and development. It sought to reduce social conflict by eliminating money gouging (interest) and by requesting the rich to give generously of their wealth. Women were requested to dress prudently as a means of curbing the excesses of overly aggressive males. The Koran says nothing of veiling or the forced seclusion of women. It does allow men to marry four wives, but that was a major advance over the unbridled polygamy of the pre-Islamic era. It was also a means of providing for the welfare of women in a society in which large numbers of men perished in tribal wars. Few Muslims today take second wives.

The Koran calls upon Muslims to convert non-believers to the Islamic faith, the exception being Jews and Christians. They, as believers in the one God, are referred to as "people of the book." Christians and Jews are allowed to live in peace among Muslims in exchange for payment of a special tax. Both prospered under Islamic rule and Jewish groups fared much better in the Islamic world than they did in a Christian Europe.

Islam, as all religions, calls upon its adherents to protect their faith. Barring this, it would be difficult for any faith to survive. Wars to expand and protect the Islamic faith are referred to as **Jihads** or holy wars. A Jihad, however, is much more than a holy war against the enemies of Islam. Muslims are also instructed to declare a Jihad against the enemy that lies within. The temptations of the Devil are unrelenting, and the struggle for individual purity must be just as unrelenting.

The relationship between Islam and the West, then, possess two basic dimensions. The first dimension is a long tradition of tolerance among peoples who share a similar religious and cultural heritage. The second dimension is a tradition of conflict that erupted whenever one faith expanded into the territory of the other. Muslim armies pushed the crusaders from the holy lands just as Muslim advances into Spain and Eastern Europe were repulsed by Christian forces. Not unexpectedly, rise of Muslim extremism in the modern era corresponds closely with the colonization of the Middle East. Indeed, the vast majority of the world's hot spots are to be found in the Islamic world. These would certainly include the Palestinian-Israeli conflict, the war in Chechnya, the enduring struggle between India and Pakistan in Kashmir, the simmering conflict in Kosovo, and the American occupation of Iraq. All have pitted occupied Muslims against a non-Islamic power.

Terror and Comparative Politics

Most, if not all, of the countries of the world have been threatened by the surge of terror emanating from the Islamic world. Many have been the targets of that terror. Others have been accused of aiding and abetting that terror and find themselves under enormous pressure from the United States an its allies. Most of the latter now experience economic sanctions as well as veiled or not so veiled attacks. Few welcome the prospect of being transformed into another Iraq or Afghanistan and rare is a policy decision that is not weighted in terms of the American reaction.

All of the countries in this book have increased their defense budgets, negating the much anticipated peace benefit promised by the end of the cold war. Spending on social services and welfare have suffered apace. Human rights have also suffered as security measures have reached an intensity not approached during the long struggle with the Soviet Union. Muslims, a very large minority in Europe, North America, and the non-Muslim countries of Asia and Africa have come under extraordinary surveillance. In some cases, the war on terror has served as a pretext for the persecution of Muslims. Security measures have also targeted Islamic charities and educational institutions. Such measures, even if justified, pose a direct threat to all religious charities and institutions. How does one curtail Islamic institutions without threatening the rights of Christian and Jewish institutions based on a similar theological foundation?

The war on terror has also found the United States retreating from its much vaunted plans to promote democracy and freedom in the Islamic world, the hastily cobbled together political system of Iraq notwithstanding. The U.S. favors democracy, but not if that democracy might lead to Islamic rule. The U.S. has not diminished the pace of economic and cultural globalization. One way or the other, the frustrations and psychological tensions that fuel terror are likely to increase. The war on terror will be a long one.

PUTTING THE PARTS TOGETHER:
ANALYZING TOTAL SYSTEMS

Each of the diverse components of comparative political analysis reviewed in this chapter offers important insights into the ways in which societies decide who gets what, when, and how. Politics, however, is more than the sum of its parts. It is a total process that involves the continuous interaction or meshing of those parts. All components of the political process are influenced to some extent by the others.

Efforts to predict or explain politics that focus on a single factor, such as economics, elites, or culture, often produce results that, while persuasive, are one-sided and incomplete. In this regard, one is reminded of the parable of the three blind men and the elephant.

The first blind man seized the elephant's trunk and pronounced him to be long and tubular, much like a giant snake. The second encountered the elephant's ear and found him to be thin, flat, and supple. The third came to his tail, declaring him to be much like a whip.

The more political analysis can integrate all the various dimensions of the political process, the more accurate it is likely to be.

USING THIS TEXT

In the chapters that follow, we use the perspectives of comparative political analysis outlined in Chapter 1 to examine the politics of the European Union, United Kingdom, France, Germany, Japan, Russia, the People's Republic of China, India, Mexico, Egypt, and Nigeria. Each chapter begins with an examination of the *history* of the country in question. This historical survey is followed by review of the country's *political institutions* and a discussion of the *elites, political parties, pressure groups, and masses* that give life to those institutions. This accomplished, we turn next to the broader *cultural, economic, and international context* underlying the political process in each country. Finally, we conclude each country study by examining the challenges that the country faces in the areas of *democracy, stability, human rights, economic growth, quality of life, and concern for the environment*, which are the criteria established by the United Nations and its related agencies as the standards of good government.

Updates of elections and other major events shaping the politics of the countries examined in this book can be found at http://politicalscience.wadsworth.com/palmer03.

REFERENCES

Aberbach, J. 1981. *Bureaucrats and Politicians.* Cambridge, MA: Harvard University Press.

Alexander, Jeffrey C., and Paul Colmy, eds. 1990. *Differentiation Theory and Social Change.* New York: Columbia University Press.

Almond, Gabriel A. 1956. "Comparative Political Systems." *Journal of Politics* 18: 391–409.

Almond, Gabriel, and Sidney Verba. 1963. *The Civic Culture.* Princeton, NJ: Princeton University Press.

Angell, Norman. 1914. *The Great Illusion.* London: Heinemann.

Austen-Smith, David. 2005. *Positive Political Theory II Strategy and Structure.* Ann Arbor, MI: University of Michigan Press.

Baker, Gideon. 2002. *Civil Society and Democratic Theory: Alternative Voices.* NY: Routledge.

Baughn, Christopher and Mark A. Buchanan. 2001. (Nov.–Dec.) "Cultural Protectionism." *Business Horizons Now* 44(6): 5–16.

Beard, Charles A. 1913. *An Economic Interpretation of the Constitution of the United States.* New York: Macmillan.

Beck, Ulrich, Nathan Snaider and Rainer Winter, eds. 2003. *Global America: The Cultural Consequences of Globalization.* Liverpool: Liverpool University Press.

Berger, Peter L. and Samuel P. Huntington, eds. 2002. *Many Globalizations: Cultural Diversity in the Contemporary World.* NY: Oxford University Press.

Bill, James A., and Robert L. Hardgrave, Jr. 1981. *Comparative Politics: The Quest for Theory.* Lanham, MD: University Press of America. (Originally published in 1973.)

Bird, Graham. 1995. IMF *Lending to Developing Countries: Issues and Evidence.* London: Routledge.

Bishop, Matthew. 2001 (June 16). "The New Wealth of Nations: A Survey of the New Rich." *The Economist,* 3–22.

Blau, Peter, and M. Meyer, eds. 1987. *Bureaucracy in Modern Society.* 3rd ed. New York: Random House.

Bollen, Kenneth. 1979. "Issues in the Comparative Measurement of Political Democracy." *American Sociological Review* 44: 572–87.

Bollen, Kenneth, and Robert Jackman. 1985. "Political Democracy and the Size Distribution of Income." *American Sociological Review* 50: 438-57.

Brierly, J. L. 1963. The *Law of Nations: An Introduction to the International Law of Peace.* New York: Oxford University Press.

Brown, Paul. 2004 (April 14). "World Set Back 10 Years by Bush's New World Order, Says Blair Aide." *The Guardian Unlimited,* online.

Brown, Chris. 2002. *Sovereignty, Rights, and Justice: Internatioanl Political Theory Today.* Malden, MA: Blackwell Pub.

Budge, Ian, David Robertson, and Derek Hear, eds. 1987. *Ideology, Strategy and Party Change.* MA: Cambridge University Press.

Calabrese, Andrew and Colin Sparks. 2004. *Toward a Political Economy of Culture: Capitalism and Communication in the Twenty-First Century.* Lanham, MD: Rowman & Littlefield Pub., Inc.

Caporaso, James A., ed. 1989. *The Elusive State: International and Comparative Perspectives.* Newbury Park, CA: Sage.

Cardoso, Fernando H. 1972 (July–Aug.). "Dependency and Development in Latin America." *New Left Review* 74: 83–95.

Chenery, Hollis, and Syraquin Moshe. 1975. *Patterns of Development, 1950–1970.* New York: Oxford University Press for World Book.

Chilcote, Ronald H. 1981. *Theories of Comparative Politics: The Search for a Paradigm.* Boulder, CO: Westview.

Clark, Barry S. 1991. *Political Economy: A Comparative Approach.* New York: Praeger.

Clemens, Walter C. 2004. *Dynamics of International Relations: Conflict and Mutual Gain in an Era of Global Interdependence.* Lanham, MD: Rowman & Littlefield Pub.

Coker, Francis. 1934. *Recent Political Thought.* New York: Appleton Century Crofts.

Cohen, Theodore, 2005. *Global Political Economy Theory and Practice,* NY: Pearson/Longman

Cowen, Tyler. 2002. Creative Destruction: How Globalization is Changing the World's Cultures. Princeton, NJ: Princeton University Press.

Daalder, Ivo H. and James M. Lindsay. 2003 (Winter). "The Globalization of Politics: American Foreign Policy for a New Century." *Brookings Review* 21: 12–18.

Dahl, Robert A. 1961. *Who Governs.* New Haven, CT: Yale University Press.

Dahl, Robert. 1971. *Polyarchy: Participation and Opposition.* New Haven, CT: Yale University Press.

Dahl, Robert. 1985. *A Preface to Economic Democracy.* Berkeley, CA: University of California Press.

Davies, James. 1963. *Human Nature and Politics.* New York: Wiley.

DeLue, Steven M. 2002. *Political Thinking, Political Theory, and Civil Society.* NY: Longman.

Diamond, Larry, ed. 1994. *Political Culture and Democracy in Developing Countries.* Boulder, CO: Lynne Rienner.

Diamond, Larry, Juan L. Linz, and Seymour Lipset. 1990. *Politics in Developing Countries: Comparing Experiences with Democracies.* Boulder, CO: Lynne Rienner.

Dogan, Mattei, and Dominique Pelassy. 1990. *How to Compare Nations: Strategies in Comparative Politics.* Chatham, NJ: Chatham House.

Douglas, Mary, and Aaron Wildaysky. 1982. *Risk and Culture.* Berkeley: University of California Press.

Duverger, Maurice. 1954. *Political Parties: Their Organization and Activity in the Modern State.* New York: Wiley.

Dye, Thomas R. 1976. *Who's Running America?* Englewood Cliffs. NJ: Prentice Hall.

Easton. David. 1953. *The Political System: An Inquiry into the State of Political Science.* New York: Knopf.

The Economist. 2004 (March 13). "Special Report: Global Economic Inequality." 60–71.

Edwards, Chris. 1985. *The Fragmented World: Competing Perspectives on Trade, Money; and Crisis.* New York: Methuen.

Epstein, Leon D. 1967. *Political Parties in Western Democracies.* NY: Praeger.

Eschle, Catherine and Bice Maiguaschca, eds. 2005. *Critical Theories, International Relations and "The Anti-Globalization Movement": The Politics of Global Resistance.* NY: Routledge.

Evans, Peter, Dietrich Rueschemeyer, and Thelda Skoupol. 1985. *Bringing the State Back In.* MA: Cambridge University Press.

Feierabend, I. K., R. L. Feierabend, and B. A. Nesvold. 1967. "Social Change and Political Violence: Cross National Patterns." In *Violence in America: Historical and Comparative Perspectives,* G. D. Graham and T. R. Gurr, eds. NY: Bantam Books.

Fisher, Julie. 2003. "Local and Global: International Governance and Civil Society." *Journal of International Affairs* 57: 12–31.

Flanagan, Scott. 1987. "Value Change in Industrial Societies." *American Political Science Review* 81(4): 1303–19.

Frank, Andre. 1984. *Critique and Anti Critique: Essays on Dependence and Reformism.* New York: Praeger.

Fried, Robert C. 1966. *Comparative Political Institutions.* New York: Macmillan.

Frieden, Jeffry A., and David A. Lake. 1987. *International Political Economy: Perspectives on Global Power and Wealth.* New York: St. Martin's.

Friedman, Milton, and Rose Friedman. 1980. *Freedom to Choose.* New York: Harcourt Brace Jovanovich.

Friedrich, Carl, and Zbigniew K. Brzezinski. 1956. *Totalitarian Dictatorship and Autocracy.* New York: Praeger.

Gillespie, Charles G. 1987. "From Authoritarian Crisis to Democratic Transition." *Latin American Research Review* 22: 165–85.

Gilpin, Robert. 1987. *The Political Economy of International Relations.* Princeton, NJ: Princeton University Press.

Glazer, Amihai and Kai A. Konrad, eds. 2003. *Conflict and Governance.* NY: Springer.

Gross, Donald A., and Lee Sigelman. 1984. "Comparing Party Systems: A Multi Dimensional Approach." *Comparative Politics* 2: 463–79.

Gross, Jonathan, and Steve Rayner. 1985. *Measuring Culture.* New York: Columbia University Press.

Helliner, Eric and Andreas Pickel, eds. 2005. *Economic Nationalism in a Globalizing World.* Ithaca, NY: Cornell University Press.

Herz, John H. 1959. *International Politics in the Atomic Age.* New York: Columbia University Press.

Hoffman, Stanley. 2002 (July–Aug.). "Clash of Globalizations." *Foreign Affairs* 81(4): 104.

Huntington, Samuel P. 1968. *Political Order in Changing Societies.* New Haven, CT: Yale University Press.

Huntington, Samuel P. 1991. *The Third Wave.* Norman, OK: University of Oklahoma Press.

Inglehart, Ronald. 1990. *Culture Shift in Advanced Industrial Society.* Princeton, NJ: Princeton University Press.

Inglehart, Ronald, and Paul R. Abramson. 1994 (June). "Economic Security and Value Change." *American Political Science Review* 88(2): 336–54.

Janda, Kenneth. 1980. *Political Parties. A Cross National Survey.* New York: Free Press.

Jung, Hwa Yol, ed. 2002. *Comparative Political Culture in the Age of Globalization: An Introductory Anthology.* Lanham, MD: Lexington Books.

Karnatnycky, Adrian. 2002 (Summer). "Making Democratization Work: Overcoming the Challenges of Political Transitions. *Harvard International Review* 24(2): 50–55.

Keane, John. 2003. *Global Civil Society?* MA: Cambridge University Press.

Keohane, Robert O., and Joseph S. Nye. 1989. *Power and Interdependence.* 2nd ed. Glenview, IL: Scott, Foresman.

Kim, HeeMin, and Richard Fording. 1994. "Measuring Voter Ideology: A Cross National Analysis of Western Democracies, 1949–1982." Paper presented at the APSA Convention, New York.

Kirchheimer, Otto. 1966. "The Transformation of the Western European Party Systems." In *Political Parties and Political Development,* ed. Joseph La Palombara and Myron Weiner. Princeton, NJ: Princeton University Press.

Kornhauser, William. 1959. *The Politics of Mass Society.* Glencoe, IL: Free Press.

Kroeber, A. L. and Clyde Kluckhohn. 1963. *Culture: A Critical Review of Concepts and Definitions.* New York: Vintage.

Lagon, Mark P. 2003 (Winter). "Visions of Globalization: Pretexts for Prefabricated Prescriptions—and some Antidotes." *World Affairs* 165(3): 142–49.

Lasswell, Harold D. 1958. *Politics: Who Gets What, When, How.* New York: World Publishing Co.

Lawson, Kay. 1976. *The Comparative Study of Political Parties.* New York: St. Martin's.

Lenter, Howard. 2004. *Power and Politics in Globalization: The Indispensable State.* NY: Routledge.

Lewis Beck, Michael S. 1988. *Economics and Elections.* Ann Arbor, MI: University of Michigan Press.

Lewis Beck, Michael S. 1990. *Economics and Elections: The Major Western Democracies.* Ann Arbor, MI: University of Michigan Press.

Lijphart, Arend. 1990 (June). "The Political Consequences of Electoral Laws 1945-1985." *American Political Science Review* 84(2): 481–96.

Lijphart, Arend, ed. 1992. *Parliamentary Versus Presidential Government.* New York: Oxford University Press.

Lipset, Seymour M. 1960. *Political Man.* Garden City, NY: Doubleday.

Lipset, Seymour M., and Stein Rokkan, eds. 1967. *Party Systems and Voter Alignments: Cross National Perspectives.* Glencoe, IL: Free Press.

Maiz, Ramon and Ferran Requejo, eds. 2005. *Democracy, Nationalism, and Multiculturalism.* NY: Routledge.

Maslow, Abraham H. 1954. *Motivation and Personality.* NY: Harper & Row.

Maslow, Abraham H. 1970. *Motivation and Personality.* 2nd ed. NY: Harper & Row.

Mendelson, Wallace. 1980. *The American Constitution and the Judicial Process.* Homewood, IL: Dorsey Press.

Michels, Robert. 1959. *Political Parties,* transl. Edan and Cedar Paul. New York: Dover. (Originally published by Free Press, Glencoe, IL, in 1915.)

Mitchell, Orenstein. 2001. *Out of the Red: Building Capitalism and Democracy in Postcommunist Europe.* Ann Arbor: University of Michigan Press.

Mueller, Dennis. 1979. *Public Choice.* New York: Cambridge University Press.

Mueller, Edward N., and Mitchell A. Seligson. 1994 (Sept.) "Civic Culture and Democracy: The Question of Causal Relationships." *American Political Science Review* 88(3): 635–52.

Neumann, Sigmund. 1956. *Modern Political Parties.* Chicago: University of Chicago Press.

Nordlinger, Eric A. 1981. *On the Autonomy of the Democratic State.* Cambridge, MA: Harvard University Press.

Nowotny, Thomas. 2004. *Strawberries in Winter: On Global Trends and Governance.* NY: Peter Lang.

O'Kane, Rosemary H.T. 2004. Paths to *Democracy: Revolution and Totalitarianism.* NY: Routledge.

Olson, Mancur. 1982. *The Rise and Decline of Nations: Economic Growth, Stagflation and Social Rigidities.* New Haven, CT: Yale University Press.

Palmer, Monte. 2002. *The Politics of the Middle East.* Itasca, IL: F.E. Peacock Pub., Inc.

Palmer, Monte. 1997. *Political Development: Dilemmas and Challenges.* Itasca, IL: F.E. Peacock Pub., Inc.

Palmer, Monte and Princess Palmer. 2004. *At the Heart of Terror: Islam, Jihadists, and America's War on Terrorism.* Lanham, MD: Rowman & Littlefield Pub., Inc.

Parsons, Talcott. 1977. *Social Systems and the Evolution of Action Theory Glencoe,* IL: Free Press.

The Pew Global Attitudes Project. 2001 (Sept. 19). "Little Support for Expanding War on Terrorism." Online: www.people-press.org/121901rpt.htm.

Putnam, Robert D. 1976. *The Comparative Study of Political Elites.* Englewood Cliffs, NJ: Prentice Hall.

Ranis, Gustav, James Vreeland, and Stephen Kosack, eds. 2005. *Globalization and the National State: The Impact of the IMF and The World Bank.* NY: Routledge.

Ray, James Lee. 1995. *Democracy and International Conflict: An Evaluation of the Democratic Peace Proposition.* Columbia, SC: University of South Carolina Press.

Robertson, David B. 1976. *Theory of Party Competition.* New York: Wiley.

Rogowski, Ronald, ed. 1994. *Comparative Politics in the International Political Economy.* Brookfield, VT: Edward Elgar.

Rorden, Wilkinson. 2005. *Global Governance: Concepts and Issues.* NY: Routledge.

Sartori, Giovanni. 1965. *Democratic Theory.* New York: Cambridge University Press.

Sartori, Giovanni. 1976. *Parties and Party Systems.* London: Cambridge University Press.

Schumacher. Ernest F. 1973. *Small is Beautiful: Economics as if People Mattered.* New York: Harper & Row.

Schumpeter, Joseph A. 1950. *Capitalism, Socialism, and Democracy.* New York: Harper & Row.

Sen, Amartya. 2002 (June 16). "Why Half the Planet is Hungry." *The Guardian-Unlimited Observer,* Online.

Skene, Christopher. 2003 (May). "Authoritarian Practices in New Democracies." *Journal of Contemporary Asia* 33(2): 189–95.

Smith, Adam. 1776. *The Wealth of Nations.* New York: Random House. Republished 1937.

Staniland, Martin. 1985. *What Is Political Economy?* New Haven, CT: Yale University Press.

Steinberger, Peter J. 2004. *The Idea of the State.* NY: Cambridge University Press.

Tetreault, Mary Ann and Robert A. Denemark, eds. 2004. *Gods, Guns, and Globalization: Religious Radicalism and International Political Economy.* Boulder, CO: Lynne Rienner Pub.

Todaro, Michael P. 1997. *Economic Development.* 6th ed. NY: Addison-Wesley.

Tomlinson, John. 1999. *Globalization and Culture.* Cambridge, Oxford: Polity Press.

Truman, David B. 1951. *The Governmental Process.* New York: Knopf.

Vidal, John. 2003. (October 4) "Every Third Person will be a Slum Dweller within 30 Years, UN Agency Warns." *The Guardian Unlimited,* Online.

Vogel, David and Robert Kagan, eds. 2004. *Dynamics of Regulatory Change: How Globalization affects National Regulatory Policies.* Berkeley: University of California Press.

Wallerstein, Immanuel. 1984. *The Politics of the World-Economy.* New York: Cambridge University Press.

Walters, Robert S., and David H. Blake. 1992. *The Politics of Global Economic Relations.* 4th ed. Englewood Cliffs, NJ: Prentice Hall.

Wang, James C. F. 1994. *Comparative Asian Politics.* Englewood Cliffs, NJ: Prentice-Hall.

Weede, Erich. 1983. "The Impact of Democracy on Economic Growth: Some Evidence for Cross National Analysis." *Kylos* 36: 21–39

Weede, Erich. 1984. "Political Democracy, State Strength, and Economic Growth in LDCs: A Cross-National Analysis." *Review of International Affairs* 10: 297–312.

White, Jonathan. 2003. *Terrorism: 2002 Update.* Belmont, CA: Thompson/Wadsworth.

The World Bank. 1992a. *World Development Report, 1992: Development and Environment.* New York: Oxford University Press.

The World Bank. 1992b. "Governance and Development." Washington, DC: The World Bank.

❖

PART II

Politics in Advanced Industrial Democracies

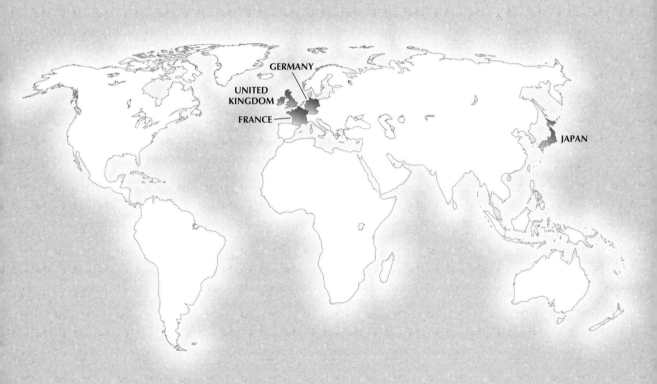

The European Union 2005–2007

2

The European Union

The Evolving Dream

The European Union (EU) is a confederation of 25 European countries who have sought to promote their common interest by voluntarily delegating authority to the EU's governing bodies. Economic issues dominate the EU agenda, but EU regulations also have much to say about social, human rights, and environmental policies.

While it is premature to speak of a European suprastate, the process of European integration has reached the point at which it is no longer possible to discuss the politics of Britain, France, Germany, or other member countries without reference to the European Union. The influence of the EU, moreover, extends far beyond the confines of its member countries. Eastern European and Middle Eastern countries aspiring to join the EU are now attempting to bring themselves in line with EU political and economic standards. Among other things, this has encouraged the establishment of free-market economies and the strengthening of democratic institutions. Even countries far removed from the EU have had to adjust to the presence of an international entity far more formidable than any one of the 25 Western European countries standing alone. A truly unified Europe would also be in a position to challenge the United States for global leadership (Rifkin 2004). That, however, is far from being a reality. Europe does not speak with a single voice on foreign policy.

From a more theoretical perspective, the evolution of the European Union has been of particular interest to scholars interested in nation building, democratization, and the evolution of international organizations. The greater integration of Europe has strengthened stability, democracy, and economic growth throughout the region. Perhaps the EU experience can serve as a model for promoting stability, democracy, and economic growth in other regions of the world as well.

The Evolution of the European Union

The dream of a European Union took shape in the ashes of World War II. The continent lay in ruins and thoughts of yet another European war chilled the most ardent of nationalists. World War II also spelled the end of an old Europe that had dominated world affairs for some three centuries. It was now the Americans and the Soviets who ruled the world. Proud empires were crumbling and the massed armies of the Soviet Union awaited in Eastern Germany. The Soviets were stalled by U.S. threats of nuclear retaliation and a North Atlantic Treaty Organization (NATO) hastily cobbled together of American forces and remnants of Europe's once proud armies. But for how long could the Soviets be held at bay. Western Europe, it seemed, was doomed to become their battle ground. Only a unified Europe, Robert Schuman, the French foreign minister argued, could defend itself and regain its once proud heritage.

The first major step leading to the integration of Western Europe was the creation of the European Coal and Steel Community in 1951 (Vanthoar 2002). The treaty, signed by France, Germany, Belgium, the Netherlands, Italy, and Luxembourg, transferred the regulation of coal and steel production in the six member states to Europe's first supranational authority. In 1957, the Treaty of Rome created the European Economic Community (EEC), thereby establishing the framework for a European common market. In 1965, the governing bodies of the European Coal and Steel Community and the EEC were merged into a single European Community, as were the governing bodies of related organizations such as the European Atomic Energy Commission and the European Economic and Social Council.

Although the integration of Europe began as a largely economic venture, the 1960s also saw the creation of a symbolic **European Parliament,** the first direct elections to which were held in 1979. While representatives to the European Parliament had little power, the framework for a democratic government of Europe was in place.

Britain, long a skeptic, was admitted to the EEC in 1971, and by the mid-1990s, membership in the European Union had expanded to include Spain, Portugal, Ireland, Greece, Sweden, Denmark, Austria, and Finland, bringing the total membership to 15.

The next step in the evolution of a European suprastate was the signing of the **Maastricht Treaty,** the terms of which entered into force on January 1, 1993. *The Maastricht Treaty transformed the European Community into the European Union (EU) and provided the framework for the eventual political unification of its member countries.* Within a transition period of approximately 10 years, according to the Maastricht Treaty, the government of the European Union would create one

Getty Images

Many, but not all, of the countries in the European Union have adopted the "euro" as their common currency. A euro from any participating EU country can be used to purchase goods or services within any other participating EU country.

common European currency—the **euro.** The euro would replace all national currencies and assume broad authority in the areas of foreign affairs, trade, and environmental policy. Wealth would also be equalized among the member states, and a common European citizenship would enable citizens of the EU to work and vote in the region of their choice. Particularly sensitive were negotiations for a "social chapter" that called for uniform standards of health insurance, social security, unemployment benefits, gender equality, and labor relations.

Despite initial skepticism, tremendous progress has been made toward achieving the goals of Maastricht. People and commerce now move among the member countries of the EU with few restraints. January 1, 1999 would see the euro adopted as the common currency of 11 members of the EU. This represented a major delegation of national sovereignty, as the participating states could no longer print generous amounts of money as a means of paying their bills. Monetary decisions are now made by a Central European Bank with powers similar to those of the Federal Reserve Bank in the U.S. Most, but not all, countries have accepted the social chapter of the Maastricht Treaty, a process that has led to common labor and welfare laws throughout much of Europe.

The EU dazzled the world in 2004 by expanding to 25 members, many of whom were former members of the old Soviet Bloc. Once threatened by Soviet invasion, the EU had expanded to the very borders of its former enemy. Russia, the largest successor state to the former Soviet Union, accepted the expansion with scarcely a murmur. Bulgaria and Romania will join the EU in 2007.

The decision to expand to 25 members was made by the heads of 15 member countries. Their logic was compelling. An expanded EU meant a larger internal market, more resources, and a larger work force. It also increased the EU's weight in international circles and strengthened democracy and stability in Eastern Europe, a region still suffering from the scars of its Communist past.

The citizens of the existing member states were not consulted on the enlargement. The leaders of the member countries simply agreed to the enlargement with the powers already at their disposal. The citizens of the EU, however, were very nervous. Their fears, as outlined by the French newspaper *Le Figaro*, were many. Would the wealthy countries of Western Europe be overwhelmed by immigrants from the poorer countries of Eastern Europe? Would crime increase? What about food security and environmental pollution? Could the new Eastern Europe and Mediterranean members (Malta and Cyprus) be counted on to maintain strict border controls (Zielonka 2002)? This was an important consideration in an era of terrorism and illegal immigration. Once in the EU, there are few checks on foreigners. How much money would the wealthy states of Western Europe be forced to pay to improve conditions in the new member states? This too, was a vital concern, because the budgets of EU countries were already strained and welfare benefits were being curtailed. Would the expansion slow economic growth in Western Europe? Would the already ponderous institutions of the EU become paralyzed? Where would the process stop? Would Turkey, a Muslim country be next (*Le Figaro* April 30, 2004, www)?

The above concerns became more pressing with the signing of a draft European Constitution in the summer of 2004. If ratified, yet a larger swatch of national sovereignty would be transferred to the EU. Particularly worrisome were fears that the EU's big three—Germany, France, and Britain—would be outvoted by a coalition of smaller and weaker states. Similar concerns aligned the rich against the poor. Indeed, all the new members to enter the EU in 2004 were far poorer than their Western European counterparts and had a vested interest in voting together.

Once again, the leaders of the EU countries had acted without consulting their citizens. The leaders of France and Britain candidly stated they had no intention of calling a referendum on the new constitution. Both recanted under popular pressure, with popular votes being scheduled for 2005 or 2006. France voted "no" in May of 2005. At least for the moment, hopes for a tighter EU have been put on hold.

For updates, go to http://politicalscience.wadsworth.com/palmer03.

The Institutions of the European Union

The four core institutions of the EU are: the Council of the European Union, the European Commission, the European Parliament, and the European Court of Justice. It is these institutions, along with the member countries, that decide who gets *what, when, and how* in the "new Europe."

The Council of the European Union. The Council officially represents the 25 member countries of the EU. No policies can be adopted without its assent and it alone decides issues in the sensitive areas of foreign and security policy. In most other areas, legislative authority is shared with the European Parliament. If the Council and the Parliament cannot work out their differences, the Council wins.

In most instances, issues before the Council are settled by "qualified majority voting," a pleasant phrase that means most members must agree on a proposal for it to pass. In most cases, a two-thirds majority may suffice. In others, 72 percent of the members must agree. A 100 percent majority is required in sensitive areas such as foreign and security policy, taxation, immigration, and asylum. This means that any member country can veto legislation in these areas. In such cases, the Council attempts to promote cooperation among its member countries. Qualified majority voting was designed to protect the sovereignty of member states and to keep a coalition of smaller and poorer states from imposing policy on the larger and wealthier states of the EU.

Each member country is represented in the Council by a minister of its national government. The minister in attendance depends on the topic under discussion. If the Council is discussing environmental issues, for example, the meeting is attended by the environmental ministers of the member countries. The agenda is prepared well in advance and a minister's vote is binding upon his or her government. On issues of supreme importance such as expansion or the drafting of a constitution, it is the presidents and prime ministers that attend. Such meetings are referred to as "Inter-Governmental Conferences."

Voting on this most powerful of bodies reflects the relative power of the member countries. As indicated in Table 2.1, Germany, France, Italy, and Britain each have 29 votes. Malta, has 3. There are 321 Council votes in all.

The European Commission. The European Commission is the executive of the EU. It proposes legislation and policies to the Council and Parliament and it implements the agreed to policies. The Commission consists of 25 members, each nominated by a member country. This said, all commissioners are required to put aside their national agendas and work for the good of Europe. The president of the Commission is selected by the member states, often after considerable discussion. The Parliament approves the commissioners and can withdraw its support from the Commission by a vote of censure. A new Commission is then selected. This has yet to happen, but a corruption scandal forced the resignation of the Commission in 1999.

The Commission has been very vigorous in forging a new Europe, perhaps too vigorous for some members who complain that the Commission is inclined to overstep its boundaries. It could hardly be otherwise, for members of the Commission are prominent politicians who are accustomed to power. The Commission executes the decisions of the Council and Parliament with the assistance of some 24,000 European civil servants duly tabbed "eurocrats." The bureaucracy of the EU, like most bureaucracies, forms something of a pyramid with directors general heading each branch (directorate) and working closely with the relevant commissioners to develop and execute policy. A preponderance of the eurocrats reside in Brussels, the headquarters of the EU. The Commission has been criticized for the size of its staff, but counters that the number of eurocrats is "fewer than the number of staff employed by most medium-sized city councils in Europe." It notes that they are also selected by very competitive examinations and serve the EU well (EUROPA, "The European Commission," www).

Table 2.1 Distribution of Power Within the European Union

Country	EU Parliament	Council	Commission
Germany	99	29	1
Britain	78	29	1
France	78	29	1
Italy	78	29	1
Poland	54	27	1
Spain	54	27	1
Netherlands	24	13	1
Belgium	24	12	1
Czech Republic	24	12	1
Greece	24	12	1
Hungary	24	12	1
Portugal	24	12	1
Sweden	19	10	1
Austria	18	10	1
Denmark	14	7	1
Finland	14	7	1
Slovakia	14	7	1
Ireland	13	7	1
Lithuania	13	7	1
Latvia	9	4	1
Slovenia	7	4	1
Cyprus	6	4	1
Estonia	6	4	1
Luxembourg	6	4	1
Malta	5	3	1
	732	321	25

SOURCE: Various EU Documents.

The European Parliament. The European Parliament operates much like most legislatures, passing legislation in the areas allotted to it and serving as a watchdog on one EU executive. The Parliament also passes the EU budget, but either must accept or reject it in total. No modifications are permitted. All the Parliament's powers are either shared or exceeded by the far more powerful Council. And yet, the Parliament enjoys the power that comes from being the only body in the EU that is selected by the EU citizens. Its power has increased over the years and will be substantially expanded when, and if, the proposed EU constitution is ratified. In addition to its legislative power, the Parliament must approve the members of the European Commission, the EU's executive.

The 732 members of the European Parliament are elected directly by the citizens of the European Union, albeit using 25 different voting systems. Each country is considered a constituency or voting district and is allocated a number of seats in the Parliament based more or less on the size of its population. Germany, the largest country in the EU, has 99 members of Parliament (MEPs); Malta 5. Tiny Luxembourg has one MEP per 76,000 people; Britain has one per 760,000 (BBC News, July 21, 2004).

The Parliament is located in the French city of Strasbourg, but its members usually meet in Brussels, the headquarters of the EU. All citizens registered to vote in their respective countries are eligible to vote in European elections. Elections are held every five years. A member of the European Parliament is generally referred to as an MEP.

The Court of Justice.   The role of the Court of Justice is "to ensure that EU legislation, technically known as Community Law, is interpreted and applied in the same way in each member state. . . . The court has the power to settle legal disputes between member states, EU institutions, businesses and individuals (EUROPA, "The Court of Justice," www).

Each country appoints one judge to the Court. All are leading jurists in their respective countries and are appointed by joint agreement of member states. This requirement is designed to reduce bias and eliminate justices that might cause tension within the Court. Judges serve six year, renewable for two additional three year, terms. As a practical matter, a Grand Chamber of 11 judges hears most cases. This eases a very heavy workload and prevents important cases from being unduly delayed. A lower court, the Court of First Instance, was introduced for the same reason.

Other Important Units of the EU.   Other key institutions include a Court of Auditors designed to monitor the sound and lawful management of the EU budget, a European Central Bank responsible for managing the euro and establishing monetary power for the EU, a European Economic and Social Council that allows Europe's major interest groups to express their opinions on pending legislation, and a European Ombudsman that helps EU citizens seek redress for errors committed by EU agencies. A detailed description of these and other agencies of the EU exceed the present discussion but are described at length on EUROPA, the information website of the EU (http://europa.eu.int).

How It All Works or Doesn't Work.   Most policies in the EU are initiated by the Commission. Suppose, for example, that the commissioners see a need to prevent further pollution of Europe's rivers. In this case, the director general for the environmental directorate would be requested to make the necessary studies and draft the required legislation. His staff would do so following extensive consultations with the environmental ministers of the 25 states as well as a wide range of business, economic, and environmental groups represented in the European Economic and Social Council. The proposal would then be discussed with all other relevant EU directorates to address their concerns and avoid conflicting legislation. Adjustments would be made as necessary, and the proposed legislation would then be sent to legal services to assure that it conformed to community law. The legislation would be given a final going over by the personal staff of the director general of the environment and then presented to the Commission for its agreement. Further modifications could be made at this time. If the draft legislation were adopted by a simple majority of commissioners, it would be sent to the Council and the Parliament for their approval. If both agreed, the legislation would become part of community law. Aggrieved parties would have the right to challenge the law in the European Court (EUROPA, "The European Commission," www).

Not everything works as smoothly as the EU might wish. The problems are many and involve paralysis in the decision-making process, corruption, and a reluctance to sanction the violations of EU's more powerful members.

The problem of paralysis in the decision-making process focuses directly on the Council of the European Union. The purpose of its members is to protect the national interests of their countries and they do so with a vengeance. Blocks tend to form with Britain and the Scandinavian countries on one side, and France and Germany on the other. The former want less unity, the latter more. National jealousies also enter the picture, with rivalries between Britain and France being particularly bitter. Qualified majority voting makes it relatively easy to block proposed legislation as does the national veto in the key areas of foreign and security policy. Much of the legislation that does escape the Council is watered down to meet the objections of key countries. Expanding the Council to 25 members has not helped the problem. The Commission is also menaced by the daunting task of establishing harmony among 25 different commissioners, each with equal power and each of a different nationality. They all serve Europe, but ideological differences between the left and the right are easily discerned.

Problems of corruption, in turn, focus on the European Commission. The Council and Parliament pass the EU's $134 billion budget. The Commission spends it. It is also the Commission that investigates and enforces regulations. Both provide ample opportunities for corruption and favoritism. In 1999, the Commission was forced to resign due to revelations by a Commission official. He was duly punished, being demoted and docked half of his pay for four months (Edmondson 2004).

It would also seem that the Parliament's role as budgetary watchdog has been less than effective. This, however, may change. The whistle blower who caused the 1999 resignation of the Commission has been elected to the European Parliament. He claims that corruption and mismanagement have cost the citizens of the EU $37 billion. He obviously knows where to look. The EU denies the accusations and says that post-1999 reforms have alleviated the problem (Edmondson 2004).

Finally, the EU finds it difficult to impose sanctions on its members. In 2004, for example, both Germany and France exceeded the debt limit imposed by EU rules to assure fiscal stability throughout the European Union. Both should have been punished with fines, but the issue was dodged by the Commission and the Council. France and Germany were too powerful to punish without creating stress within the EU and most other states welcomed the prospect of higher debt limits. The European Court did not cooperate and decreed that Germany and France would have to be called to order. But what to do next? No one was quite sure.

How Passage of the EU Constitution Would Improve Things. The leaders of the 25 EU member countries met in June of 2004 to put the finishing touches on a draft constitution for the European Union. Up to this point, the EU had operated on the basis of diverse treaties among its member states. Bargaining over the constitution was brutal. The leaders made 80 amendments to the document, 39 by Britain alone. Particularly cumbersome were the issues of states rights and religions. A large block of countries, led by Italy, wanted the constitution to refer explicitly to "Europe's Christian roots." France and Germany led the opposition. The motion was defeated and the constitution merely states that the EU draws its inspiration from "the cultural, religious, and humanist inheritance of Europe." The final draft was a weighty affair of some 325 pages, a far cry from the slim document that guides American politics. Jack Straw, Britain's foreign minister, explains this is precisely because the EU is not a superstate. "Were it a superstate, writing its constitution would be easy, and the result short. You would declare that power resided in its Parliament, government and supreme court and leave those institutions to make and enforce the law. It is precisely because the EU is not a superstate that it needs a more complicated rule-book spelling out, policy by policy, the areas of its competence" (Straw 2004).

Many *euroskeptics,* the name given to those opposed to a stronger union, condemned the new constitution as a ploy to rob the member states of their sovereignty and pave the way for a unified Europe based on the American pattern (Dobson and Follesdal 2004). Not so, said Jack Straw, the British foreign minister. "The constitution dispatches into oblivion any notion that the EU is a federal superstate. It is the member states that confer competences (powers) on the Union. . . . And there is even a streamlined procedure, for the first time, for any member state to withdraw from the EU—proof, if more were needed, that this is an organization of freely cooperating nations" (Straw 2004, 47). He went on to note that the constitution alleviated many of the problems that had dogged the EU to date. Qualified majority voting in the Council, for example, will be reduced to 55 percent on most issues. The Council will also have a president elected for two and one-half years by the member governments. This does away with the present system of a revolving presidency in which each country assumes the presidency for six months. In much the same manner, the size of the Commission would eventually be reduced to 18 members in the name of efficiency. Parliament, it turn, will be strengthened by giving it a veto over policy. All policies will have to pass the Parliament to become law. This is a powerful change, indeed. The constitution also confirms that EU law will be superior to national law in the areas allocated to it (BBC, June 22, 2004).

THE ACTORS IN EUROPEAN POLITICS: COUNTRIES, ELITES, PARTIES, GROUPS, AND CITIZENS

Perhaps the main reason why the institutions of the EU do not work as they might is the behavior of the actors that guide their operation. This includes the member countries, the elites who guide the EU, the political parties that organize its Parliament, the groups who contest for privilege and gain, and the citizens who vote in both national and EU elections. The core of the problem is that the European Union has two sets of each, one at the EU level and one at the national level.

Elites

The elite structure of the EU is separate, divided, joined and unequal. On one side are the EU officials. These include the commissioners and director's general, the judges, the leaders of the Parliament and the heads of EU's myriad committees, agencies, and financial institutions. All play an important role in shaping the operations of the EU. On the other side are the broad array of presidents, prime ministers, cabinet members, senior bureaucrats, generals, jurists, and business leaders who guide the policies of the member countries. The interests of the member countries and their ruling elites are not identical with those of the EU. By and large, they want to benefit from the EU without being bound by it. It is the national elites, through their control of the European Council, who have the larger voice in determining just what the EU can and cannot do (Jennar 2004). It is the competing interests of the member countries and their elites that make EU decision making such an arduous process. Each change in the leadership of a member country, moreover, can have a profound impact on EU policy. The Labour Party in Britain, for example, has been EU friendly. The Conservatives, much less so.

The same duality exists in the political parties that guide the European Parliament. Members of the European Parliament organize themselves by party affiliation rather than national identity, but are never far removed from national issues. It could not be otherwise, for most were elected on the basis of national issues that had little to do with Europe. By and large, European elections are merely a test of party strength within the member countries.

The European Parliament

The 2004 EU elections found the center right (conservatives) to be the largest vote getters with 38 percent of the seats in the Parliament. They were followed by the Socialists with 27 percent, Liberals with 9 percent, the Communists with 7 percent, and the Greens with 6 percent. The remaining 13 percent of the MEPs either belonged to smaller parties or were unaffiliated. As no single party can dominate the Parliament, related parties form alliances to capture leadership positions and pursue their agendas. Some parties such as the Socialists and the Greens possess well-developed European linkages; the Conservatives, less so (Bomberg 2002). As things currently stand, even the most Europeanized parties are merely collections of like minded national parties. None of the EU parties possess a European directorate that can tell the national parties what to do.

This is all more the case because elections to the European Parliament reflect local political issues rather than European issues. Their significance is interpreted in terms of the balance of power within their respective countries rather that in terms of their impact on Europe. The ruling parties in Britain, France, and Germany, for example, all did poorly in the 2004 European elections. This was interpreted as a sign that the ruling parties were losing favor with the voters and could well be defeated in the coming national elections. The impact of the elections on Europe seemed irrelevant.

Citizens

This is not to suggest that citizen participation is irrelevant to the fate of the European Union. It will be the voters who will decide the fate of the proposed EU constitution in France, Britain, and other key countries. Acceptance or rejection of the constitution in these countries will have a profound impact on the future of the EU. Resounding "no's" would lock the EU in its present status, at best. Predictions on how the citizens of the key states will vote are difficult to come by. Past votes in France have been razor thin. Britain has refused to adopt the euro and has opted out of the social charter, both of which were unpopular issues. The 2004 elections also found Europe's voters to be profoundly apathetic, a trend that bode ill for the proposed constitution. Opinion polls indicate that part of the problem is that people just do not understand the proposed constitution (*European Information Services*, July 31, 2004). Supporters of the proposed constitution are hopeful that an information blitz will bring a majority of voters on board. On a broader front, opinion polls indicate that the main concerns of the EU citizens are unemployment 51 percent, terrorism, 34 percent, crime 30 percent, and pensions 29 percent (*Wall Street Journal*, June 9, 2004, A11).

Pressure Groups

Pressure groups, for their part, press their advantage wherever the opportunity presents itself. Sometimes this is at the EU level. Other times it is at the national level. Agricultural groups in France, for example, place tremendous pressure on their national governments to resist EU efforts to trim very generous farm subsidies. They prosper from the subsidies and do not want them altered. To date, they have been quite successful and EU agricultural policy is a shambles. Environmental groups, by contrast, push for EU environmental legislation that will force member countries to clean up their act. Greens have a forceful presence in the European Parliament and also press their case on the Economic and Social Council. Labor and human rights groups have also focused on strengthening their cause via EU legislation. Labor, like the Greens, is well represented in both the European Parliament and the Economic and Social Council.

Business groups, in turn, seek strong representation at both the national and EU levels. They use pressure at the national level to force the EU to adopt policies that are business friendly, and they use pressure at the EU level to support them in their competition with the U.S. and Japan. The United States, for example, complains bitterly that the Air Bus is heavily subsidized in its competition with Boeing for global dominance in the airline industry. Microsoft was also accused of monopolistic practices and forced to make a huge settlement with EU regulators. Unlike labor, business finds it difficult to speak with a single voice. Powerful multinationals favor free trade; smaller and less profitable companies tend to fear free trade. They also fear the competition of the multinationals. This is particularly the case in the poorer countries, and especially those emerging from years of communism. They want the financial support and trade advantages offered by the EU, but not the competition of its stronger members or its environmental regulations.

The losers in group efforts to shape the policies of the EU are the minorities, and especially the immigrants. Some 20 million Muslims in the EU, for example, are becoming a large underclass increasingly estranged from their host countries. Tensions between Muslims and the host countries of the EU have increased in the era of terrorism, much of which has been associated with a small minority of Muslim extremists often referred to as Jihadists. Muslims and other minorities are also blamed for crime and unemployment and have offended European sensibilities by retaining their own cultural and religious traditions (Al Sayyad and Castells 2002). The voice of Europe's Muslims has also been blunted by the absence of effective organization. Part of the problem is that each member country of the EU tends to have Muslims from a different ethnic background. Most Muslims in Britain find their origin in the Indian subcontinent (India, Pakistan, Bangladesh), while those in Germany are largely of Turkish background. France's Muslim community is largely Arabic in background. All share a common faith and heritage, yet cultural and linguistic differences abound. All three communities remained heavily tied to their original communities and feel increasingly estranged from the predominant European community (Ogelman 2003).

As yet, the EU has no common policy on migrants. This is a mistake, for the birth rate of Europe's migrants is far higher than that of its graying European population. With time, 50 years by some estimates, they may achieve parity with their European hosts (Abbasi 2004).

Whether this vast array of competing pressures will impede the closer integration of Europe remains to be seen. If a preponderance of powerful groups benefit from closer integration, the power of the EU will increase apace. If the balance between groups remains ambivalent, closer integration will prove difficult.

THE CONTEXT OF EUROPEAN POLITICS: POLITICAL ECONOMY, POLITICAL CULTURE, AND INTERNATIONAL INTERDEPENDENCE

Just as the effectiveness of EU institutions is shaped by the actors who manipulate them, the affairs of the EU also are shaped by the broader economic, cultural, and international environment in which it exists.

Political Economy

As things currently stand, the European Union is preeminently an economic union. The motivations for the unification were largely economic as the six core members sought to benefit from a broader market and the ability to profit from economies of scale (Talani 2004; Jones and Verdun 2005). Other countries joined the EU for much the same reason. The economic benefits of being in the EU were greater than remaining on the outside.

It is not surprising, accordingly, that the EU's most binding regulations are in the areas of economic and trade policy. The introduction of the euro in 1999 marked a dramatic increase in the integration of Europe by forcing the participating countries to accept the regulation of their monetary policy by the Central European Bank. How could a country be sovereign when it no longer had its own currency?

It was this question that found a number of countries refusing to accept the euro, foremost among whom were Britain and Sweden. A line was thus drawn between those countries willing to accept the ever greater integration of their economies, and those who were not. The future of the EU will obviously hinge on this vital economic issue. For the moment, speculation exists that the EU will evolve along a dual track: an inner circle consisting of the countries in the euro—those countries that have adopted the euro as their currency—and an outer circle of countries that have not (Warleigh 2002). EU officials deny that this process is taking place, but they may have little choice in the matter. Greater economic integration promises greater economic benefits.

Achieving greater economic integration, however, is not the only economic problem that is likely to influence the future of the EU. Unemployment in Germany, France, and many other members of the EU hovers in the 10 percent range. Unemployment causes political tensions within the member countries and within the EU as a whole. France and Germany have both exceeded the debt limits imposed by the EU in order to maintain unemployment and related welfare costs. If France and Germany can violate the rules, why not the less powerful members? If the trend continues, the economic stability of the EU will be weakened and its advantages lessened.

The solution to high unemployment is the increased productivity of the EU countries. The greater the productivity, the greater the demand for workers. Everyone prospers, the firm and the employees. The difficulty is that

European wage, benefits, and welfare costs are so high that European firms are finding it difficult to compete with American, Japanese, and Chinese products. The EU countries also regulate business far more intensely than competing countries. Thus the dilemma: scale back wages, benefits, welfare, and regulations or suffer high unemployment. Whether the EU and its members will be willing or able to make the necessary economic reforms will also have much to say about the future of the EU. A 2004 summit meeting between the leaders of France, Germany, and Britain called the reforms "urgent" (*Guardian,* Feb. 18, 2004, www).

Political Culture

The role of culture in sustaining the EU is less clear. Strong cultural bonds do play a vital role in building solidarity within a political community. They also see it through periods of crisis and economic adversity. Countries that share common values and traditions simply work together better than countries that do not. The political culture of the European Union, however, remains something of a mystery. The EU's draft constitution states that the EU draws its inspiration from the common cultural, religious, and humanist inheritance of Europe. This rich heritage is the material of Western Civilization courses and requires little elaboration. Europe's heritage, however, also includes centuries of religious bigotry, fanatical nationalism, and warfare.

The continued growth of the EU suggests that the conflicts of the past have mellowed and the citizens of the EU are, indeed, coming together as a political community. Leading the charge are France and Germany, the two countries most associated with war and suffering in Europe. It is they who are the driving force in the creation of a truly unified Europe. Britain and the Scandinavian countries are less willing to see their sovereignty slip away. The EU is also becoming a multicultural society, with at least one-fifth of its citizens possessing cultural and religious traditions that differ radically from those of Europe.

The EU aspires to create a unified European political culture that will serve as a balance to its economic focus. Toward this end, it has monitored the attitudes and values of its citizens on a systematic basis since 1973. Key results pertaining to the political culture of the EU are summarized in Table 2.2. As the EU candidly acknowledges that "while one still cannot speak of the existence of a truly European identity, the majority of EU citizens feel to some extent European" (European Union 2001, 10). The EU also acknowledges that tremendous national diversity exists in support for the EU. The countries that show the greatest sense of European identity are Luxembourg, Italy, Spain, France, Belgium, and the Netherlands. The laggards are headed by Britain and include Sweden, Finland, Greece, and Denmark. Austria and Germany occupy the middle ground. Cultural diversity within the EU will obviously increase as it struggles to integrate its 10 new members from Eastern Europe and the Mediterranean.

It is interesting to note that the same countries that rank low on EU political culture are, by and large, the same countries that have resisted the euro and other

Table 2.2 European Political Culture*

Question	High to Medium	Low to Very Low
Feeling attached to the EU	56**	40
European identity	52	45
There is a shared European cultural identity	38	49
Satisfaction democracy in the EU	40	41
Benefit from EU membership	46	31
How much progress has been made toward the integration of Europe over the past 50 years?	55	34
Trust in the EU	39	40
Support for the euro	60	32

*Data based on 15 member countries before the 2004 expansion.

**Figures indicate positive responses. Nonresponses and undecided responses deleted.

SOURCE: Table 2.2 is based on data presented in: European Union, 2001, *How Europeans See Themselves.* Luxembourg: Office for Official Publications of the European Communities. Reproduction authorized.

policies that would lead to the greater integration of the EU. Once again, Britain and the Scandinavian countries have lead the charge against a more integrated Europe.

International Interdependence and Globalization

The EU possesses the size, population, and economic strength to challenge the U.S. for global leadership. Some progress towards that end has been made in the economic sphere, but Europe remains sharply divided over issues of foreign and security policy. Unfortunately for those calling for a greater EU role in world affairs, it is in precisely these areas that individual countries possess a veto. Conflicts over foreign policy came to the forefront during the Iraq war. Britain joined the U.S. in pursuing the war and the subsequent occupation of Iraq. France and Germany led the charge against both. Scars deepened as France and Germany were excluded from reconstruction contracts and it became evident that war had been justified on the basis of faulty intelligence.

This said, the EU does possess mechanisms for coordinating foreign and security policy and has been able to act in a fairly coherent manner when all parties agree. The EU, for example, has played a major role in containing ethnic strife in Bosnia and other areas of the Balkans. Conflict that afflicts any part of Europe, in the EU's view, threatens all of Europe. A "rapid reaction force" of some 60,000 troops has been established to address international crises. It is not an EU army. Rather, the reaction force consists of designated members of national armed forces that can be deployed within 60 days and kept on duty for up to a year. Military coordination and planning are now carried out by the Political and Security Committee, the European Union Military Committee, and the European Union Military Staff, a group composed of national military experts. While these are impressive steps, it is hard to run an army by committee and consensus.

The same problems confront the struggle against terrorism and organized crime—the two greatest threats to European security for the foreseeable future. European police continue to uncover Jihadist cells, and Britain, France, and Italy have all aborted planned terrorist attacks that involved chemical weapons. The March 2004 train bombings in Madrid killed more than 200 people and wounded hundreds more. Train bombs were subsequently found on rail tracks in France. As fear of terrorist attacks mounted, the EU attempted to strengthened its anti-terrorism cooperation and a 2005 deadline was set for boosting the exchange of information on terrorist groups. Efforts were also made to reinforce the Task Force of Member State's Chiefs of Police and other agencies such as Interpol, the European crime fighting agency. It is also hard to fight terrorism by committee and consensus.

In addition to security concerns, the EU is faced with a problem of dealing with neighboring countries. The most pressing concern in this area is the EU's relations with Russia. The 2004 expansion of the EU extended its borders to Russia, the core of the old Soviet Union. Within a few years, all of what was once known as the Soviet Bloc, with the possible exception of Serbia and Albania, will have been incorporated into the EU. But what about Russia itself? A 2002 poll by the Public Opinion Foundation found that 52 percent of Russians favor EU membership. Only 18 percent were opposed (*Financial Times,* May 27, 2002, 15). The question is, as the *Financial Times* asks, is the EU willing to "accommodate a country with a population larger than Germany and France put together and an economy smaller than that of the Netherlands" (Peel 2002, 15)? An alternative question might be: does the EU have an alternative? Russia remains a powerful nuclear power as well as a potentially unstable country capable of posing a serious security threat to the EU. The EU consolidated democracy and stability in Eastern Europe by incorporating the vast majority of its countries. Could it do the same by incorporating Russia?

For the moment, the main sticking point between the EU and Russia is NATO, the U.S. led security alliance directed at the Soviet Union and, by implication, Russia. Efforts have been made to ease Russian concerns by giving it observer status in NATO, but Moscow sees little need for an American alliance on its borders. The EU nations, in Russia's view, should withdraw from NATO as the final step in solidifying the peace and stability of the Europe continent. An increasing number of Europeans share this view.

Another problem confronting the EU are its neighbors across the Mediterranean Sea. All, with the exception of Israel, are predominantly Muslim in faith. Most are poor and have made minimal progress toward democracy and capitalism. The difficulty, from the EU perspective, is that its poor neighbors cannot be ignored. Poverty and political instability in the Mediterranean fuels immigration, legal and otherwise to the EU. Religious extremism in the Mediterranean region has also found expression among the EU's Muslim population, some members of which have been implicated in terrorist activities.

Mediterranean immigrants are also blamed for the lion's share of the EU's criminal activity including drugs. The vast majority are peaceful citizens, but bear the prejudice caused by the few. The EU has sought to ease these and related problems by launching an ambitious partners program designed to speed the economic and democratic development of the Mediterranean region. Turkey is also being considered for membership in the EU, but keeps being rejected on the grounds of insufficient progress in the areas of democracy, human rights, and free market economics. Turks believe that the EU is merely finding excuses for not granting membership to a Muslim country.

Finally, the EU has to decide what to do with the United States. Opinion poll after opinion poll in the EU expresses deep concern with America's cowboy style management of the world (Pew Global Attitudes Project 2001). The polls also express a profound distaste for an American pop culture that has so little in common with Europe's cultural traditions. Not only do Europeans find American culture offensive, they also find it a threat to their own youth. Whatever the case, a divided Europe, even within the loose confines of the EU, lacks the unity to challenge the U.S. in the international arena.

CHALLENGES OF THE PRESENT AND LOOKING TOWARD THE FUTURE

How, then, does the EU score in terms of the United Nations indicators of good development outlined in Chapter 1: democracy, stability, human rights, economic growth, quality of life, and environmental concerns? The answer is, very well thank you.

Democracy and Human Rights

The EU is a bastion of democracy. Britain and France shaped the foundations of world democracy and the authoritarian traditions of Germany have faded into the past. Indeed, Germany has been one of the most forceful advocates of the political integration of the EU. That, in itself, should calm lingering fears that Germany might return to an authoritarianism of the past. The same principle applies to Eastern European countries that joined the EU in 2004. All made the transition from authoritarianism to democracy following the collapse of the Soviet Union in 1991. Membership in the EU is the best guarantee that their revived democratic traditions will continue to grow.

In a curious irony, people are less concerned about democracy in the member states than they are with the democratic practices within the EU itself. The European Parliament is the only democratic EU institution, and it is far weaker than either the Council or the Commission. The members of the Council are elected officials of the member governments, but they represent individual countries and not the EU. The Commission does most of what the

EU does, and it is appointed. The power of the Parliament has strengthened over the course of its history, and should continue to do so as the political integration of the EU progresses. That progression, however, is far from being a certainty.

The EU has taken a particularly strong stand on human rights, a 2001 European Charter of Fundamental Rights upholding the basic freedoms of speech, thought, peaceful protest (subject to national law), and equality before the law. It also stresses the right to education, health care, fair working conditions, equal opportunity, and equal pay for men and women. Its prohibitions include child labor and reproductive cloning. Alas, the European Charter of Fundamental Rights remains advisory. France, Germany, and the Netherlands want to see it incorporated into European law. Others remain skeptical. As a practical matter, the charter already plays a key role in shaping national legislation in the area of human rights.

There are, of course, gaps. The most glaring of these is the treatment of immigrants, most of whom are second class citizens (Morris 2002). Muslims, in particular, find themselves subject to increasingly severe anti-terror legislation. They also resent a growing body of national regulations outlawing the wearing of Islamic dress (head scarves) in schools. Muslims find this to be a flagrant violation of their right to express their religious views. Religious expression is a matter of national law, and is unlikely to find its way into community law. The draft constitution skirted the issue by refusing to stipulate that the EU was founded on Christian traditions.

Stability

The EU is no longer threatened by foreign invasion, although European leaders do keep a sharp eye on Russia. Far more threatening are fears of terrorism. The EU countries have been the target of terrorist attacks, the most vicious of which was the 2004 bombing of Madrid's train stations. The list of near misses adds to the terror and includes a chemical attack on Rome's water supply. Thus far, the Jihadists have concentrated on high profile attacks reminiscent of the September 11th attacks on the U.S. As high profile attacks become more difficult, a high probability exists that the terrorists will shift to lower profile attacks centering on car bombs, the bombing of subways, and suicide attacks (Palmer and Palmer 2004). As ETA, the Basque terrorist group, and radical spin-offs of the IRA have demonstrated, such attacks are virtually impossible to stop.

Perhaps a more threatening source of instability is to be found within the organization of the EU itself. The EU remains a voluntary confederation, the members of which can withdraw at will. The EU has remained stable and expanded because the benefits of membership for the member states outweigh its costs. This could change at any time. It could also be precipitated by a radical change of government within a member country or by efforts to expand the role of the EU. Present support for the EU is high. Support for a more integrated EU is not and varies dramatically from country to country. Even now, talk exists of a two-tiered EU: an inner core focusing on Germany and France, and an outer core focusing on Britain and the Scandinavian countries. How this would play out in reality remains to be seen.

Quality of Life and Environmental Concern

The quality of life within the EU prior to its 2004 expansion was exemplary. Over the course of the past 30 years, some 80 percent of EU respondents rated their quality of life as satisfactory or better (How Europeans See Themselves 2004, 6). Slight variation occurs from year to year, but never by much. The new member countries are poorer than the EU's original members and look to EU membership as the cure for their economic and political woes.

By and large, Europeans worry most about things that are likely to threaten their exemplary quality of life. Heading the list are environmental issues, unemployment, and crime. Some 69 percent of Europeans list the environment as a leading worry, and not without cause. Many EU cities, headed by Paris, have been forced to issue pollution alerts with increasing frequency. Industry produces pollution and the EU is one of the world's primary industrial regions. It is also choked with trucks and automobiles. The EU ranks second in CO_2 emissions, headed only by the U.S. (BBC July 23, 2004). The picture becomes far worse when its new Eastern European members are added to the list, many of whom continue to suffer from old communist era industries known more for their pollution than the quality of their products. Many EU countries continue to be wedded to nuclear energy, a continuing concern of environmentalists. Perhaps the major difference between the EU and the United States in the war against pollution is the greater willingness of Europeans to do something about it (Wurzel 2002). All of the major EU countries ratified the 2002 Kyoto agreement for reduction of greenhouse gases. The U.S. did not.

Worries about unemployment, in turn, are sparked by concern that global competition is forcing EU countries to trim employees, wages, and welfare benefits. Such concerns are easy to understand in a region noted for long vacations, cradle to grave welfare schemes, and government regulations that made it next to impossible to lay off workers. Costs were high, but tariffs reduced external competition. Those tariffs are now collapsing in the face of EU regulations and global pressures. Unemployment in much of the EU hovers around the 10 percent range, and fears of greater unemployment are a source of grave concern to all EU countries. Crime, too, has remained a persistent concern and has been joined by the threat of terror.

LOOKING TOWARD THE FUTURE

The EU remains a confederation of independent countries who have voluntarily delegated authority to the EU's governing bodies. That authority can be withdrawn at any time. Some people would like to see the EU evolve into a sovereign state; others prefer the current arrangement. A few would prefer a reduction in the scope of the EU's authority. Attitudes on the issue also vary markedly from country to country.

The EU has endured and expanded because there is more to gain by being in the EU than staying out. While the most obvious gains have been economic, the EU has also brought its member countries greater security and has the potential to increase European clout in international affairs. Indeed, a more tightly integrated EU would create three centers of world power: the U.S.; an Asian power bloc centering on China, India and Japan; and the EU.

As yet, however, that remains a distant dream. While some 90 percent of European decision makers believe that their countries have benefitted from EU membership, their citizens are less sure. Some 43 percent believe that they have benefitted; 36 percent believe that they have not. The remaining 21 percent do not know (European Union 2001, 51). Such figures are subject to change from year to year, but suggest that the EU must do a better job of selling itself to its citizens. The real test will come with the vote to ratify the EU constitution. If all countries support the draft constitution, dreams of a united Europe will move forward. A sound rejection of the constitution will freeze the EU in its current form and perhaps lead to back sliding. If Germany and France support the constitution and Britain does not, talk of a two-tier union will increase. The core of Europe will move towards greater unity. Britain and the Scandinavian countries will remain on the fringe.

REFERENCES

(Note: The most complete source of basic and updated information about the European Union is the EU website: europa.eu.int).

Abbasi, Nadia Mushtaq. 2004 (Aug. 11.). "Muslims in Europe." *Asia Times* http://atimes.com/atimes/printN.html (accessed 8/11/2004).

Al Sayyad, Nozar and M. Castells, eds. 2002. *Muslim Europe or Euroislam: Politics, Culture and Citizenship in the Age of Globalization.* Lanham, MD: Lexington Books.

Bomberg, Elizabeth. 2002 (July). "The Europeanisation of Green Parties." *West European Politics* 25(3): 29–52.

Dobson, Lynn and Andreas Follesdal, eds. 2004. *Political Theory and the European Constitution.* New York: Routledge.

Edmondson, Gail. 2004 (July 26). "The Fighting Dutchman." *Business Week* (3893): 46.

EUROPA (www.europa.eu.int) is the official website of the European Union. Accessing this address will provide detailed information on all institutions and activities of the EU.

European Information Services, 2004 (July 1). "EU Constitution: One Third of Europeans Feel Well-informed about New Treaty." European Report, 105 (1).

European Union: How Europeans See Themselves. 2001. Luxembourg: Office for Official Publications of the European Communities.

Jennar, Raoul Marc. 2004. *Europe, la trahison des elites.* Paris: Fayard.

Jones, Erik and Amy Verdun, eds. 2005. *The Political Economy of European Integration: Theory and Analysis.* New York: Routledge.

Le Figaro Magazine. L'Europe À 25: Dix questions sur la nouvelle Union, www.lefigaro.com.

Morris, Lydia. 2002. *Managing Migration: Civic Stratification and Migrants Rights.* New York: Routledge.

Ogelman, Nedim. 2003 (Spring). "Documenting and Explaining the Persistence of Homeland Politics Among Germany's Turks." *International Migration Review* 37(1): 163–94.

Peel, Quentin. 2002 (May 27). "Russia Looks to its Future Role." *Financial Times*, 15.

Pew Global Attitudes Project: Views of a Changing World, June 2003; The Pew Center For The People and The Press, Washington D.C.

Rifkin, Jeremy. 2004. *The European Dream*. New York: Jeremy P. Tarcher/ Penguin.

Straw, Jack. 2004 (July 10). "Jack Straw by Invitation." *The Economist* 8383: 47.

Talani, Leila Simona. 2004. *European Political Economy: Political Science Perspectives*. Burlington, VT: Ashgate.

Vanthoor, Willem F.V. 2002. *A Chronological History of the European Union, 1946–2001*. Northampton, MA: Edward Elgar.

Warleigh, Alex. 2002. *Flexible Integration: Which Model for the European Union?* New York: Sheffield Academic Press.

Wurzel, Rudiger. 2002. *Environmental Policy-Making in Britain, Germany, and the European Union*. New York: Manchester University Press.

Zielonka, Jan, ed. 2002. *Europe Unbound: Enlarging and Reshaping the Boundaries of the European Union*. New York: Routledge.

UNITED
KINGDOM

Atlantic
Ocean

SCOTLAND

■ Aberdeen

Glasgow
■

Edinburgh ■

North Sea

NORTHERN
IRELAND

Belfast ■

Liverpool
■

■ Manchester

Dublin ■

Birmingham
■

IRELAND

WALES

Cardiff

ENGLAND

London
■

Cork ■

Bristol ■

English Channel

Population:
60,270,708 (2004 estimate)

Life expectancy at birth:
78 years (total population)
76 years (men)
81 years (women)

Literacy:
99 percent of people age 15
and over can read and write
(2000 estimate)

Capital:
London

Per capita income:
$27,700 (2003 estimate)

The Industrial Revolution, then, added two new elements to the British political equation: the industrial **bourgeoisie,** or *capitalist class,* and the **proletariat,** or *industrial working class.* They would soon become the dominant elements in that equation. The enfranchisement of the working class began with the Reform Acts of 1867 and 1884, acts that extended the right to vote to approximately 28 percent of the British population, all of it male.

In 1918, the right to vote was extended to females over the age of 30, with the proviso that their husbands meet certain minimal property requirements. Finally, the Representation of the People Act of 1928 removed all property restrictions on voting, thereby provided **universal suffrage** to all citizens of the United Kingdom. It was not until 1949, however, that the principle of "one person, one vote" was enacted into law. Prior to this time, business owners and university graduates received two votes apiece: one for their residence, and one for their business or university affiliation.

The expansion of the electorate produced two fundamental transformations in British politics. First, with each expansion of the franchise, the power of the House of Lords, a non-elected body, decreased. Nevertheless, the two houses of the British parliament retained their relative equality until 1911.

The second major change in British politics was the emergence of political parties. By the advent of the seventeenth century, it had become customary for members of Parliament sharing similar views to meet on an informal basis for the purpose of coordinating their strategies. The two main parties of the era were the **Tories** and the **Whigs. Tories** were the "royalists" who supported the Crown, the rights of the landed aristocracy, and the dominant position of the Church of England. The Tories adopted the Conservative label in the nineteenth century following a campaign speech in which a Tory leader declared that the goal of his party was to "conserve all that was good in existing institutions" (Punnett 1988, 74). The popular press continues to refer to the Conservatives as "Tories."

Whigs were the prosperous members of the middle class who advocated less restrictive economic laws and a reduced role for the Crown and the Church of England in the affairs of the country. The Whigs would later evolve into the Liberal Party. Whig is an abbreviation of Wiggammores, a band of Scottish rebels.

There was no need to organize the masses, because the masses could not vote. With the expansion of the electorate, however, the masses took on political relevance, and the two major parliamentary parties of the time—the Conservatives and the Liberals—began to organize local electoral districts in the hope of electing candidates compatible with their views. The Labour Party would emerge in the early 1900s, replacing the Liberals as Britain's second major party.

Over the course of the ensuing years, power would alternate between the Conservative and Labour Parties (Powell 2004). The former championed capitalism and the interests of the business class, while the latter attempted to transform Britain into a socialist democracy. The political system, according to the Labour Party, would be democratic, but the government would run the larger firms and provide its citizens with a broad range of welfare services. Because neither side could dominate the other, the two parties informally agreed to maintain England as a mixed socialist-capitalist economy. Labour curtailed its welfare demands, while the Conservatives resisted efforts to denationalize Britain's heavy industry (Childs 1992). Once the world's leading exponent of free trade, Britain had turned inward.

The Thatcher Revolution

The tacit compromise between Labour and the Conservatives was shattered by the election of Margaret Thatcher in 1979 (Thatcher 1993). During her eleven years as prime minister, Thatcher slashed welfare benefits, denationalized British industries, and did everything within her power to force British firms to become more competitive on a global scale. The Thatcher revolution, while ostensibly economic, also represented a dramatic change in the way the British did politics:

> Most observers, whether supporters or detractors, agreed that "Thatcher's revolution" involved four main changes. The first was in the way Britain was governed. Direction and leadership replaced negotiation and compromise; government by conviction replaced government by consensus. Thatcher re-asserted the authority of the core executive over organized interests and the public sector, and within the executive she stamped her personal authority over the cabinet and the civil service. The second change was in the economy. A broadly corporatist economy was turned into a broadly market economy: Most state-owned industries and services were privatized; subsidies to private industry ceased; economic planning was scrapped; and large swathes of economic activity, notably finance, were deregulated. A third change was social and communal. More people than before, especially in the South and the Midlands, owned their own homes, bought shares, and acquired consumer luxuries; but more people than before, especially in the North and Scotland, were unemployed and in poverty. The fourth change was cultural. Not only in the media but also among ordinary people the old values of class loyalty, national planning, and welfare seemed out of tune with the times; the new accent was on the individual, choice, and "getting on" (King et al., 1993, 1).

Margaret Thatcher was replaced as prime minister by John Major, a less controversial figure who was successful in leading the Conservatives to an upset victory over the Labour Party in the 1992 general elections (Sked and Cook 1993). Major's reign as prime minister was scarred by deep conflict within the Conservative Party, much of it revolving around his efforts to strengthen Britain's participation in the European Union. A hard core of Conservative legislators bitterly opposed closer British ties with the European Union, and their hostility toward Major threw the Conservative leadership into disarray. As the 1997 elections approached, the British press was virtually unanimous in predicting the defeat of a Conservative Party that had ruled the country for 18 consecutive years. They were not to be proven wrong.

On May 2, 1997, Labour swept to a crushing victory, capturing 418 of the 659 seats in the House of Commons (Watkins 1998). John Major moved out of 10 Downing Street, the official residence of the prime minister, on the following day. He was replaced by Tony Blair, the leader of the Labour Party (Butler and Kavanagh 1998). In a brief speech following a formal meeting with the queen in which he was asked to form a Government, Blair, the first Labour prime minister in 18 years and the youngest prime minister in more than a century, announced that Labour had campaigned as New Labour and would rule as New Labour, a stern warning to those who expected a return to Labour's socialist orientation of old. Gone were the slogans of socialism, welfare, and nationalization of industry. Labour, at least as portrayed by Tony Blair, had become a party of the center. Many British commentators, accordingly, referred to the transformation of Labour as a victory for Thatcherism (Kennedy 1998). Not only had Thatcher transformed the British economy, but the success of her reforms had forced Labour to disassociate itself from its socialist past and break its subservience to the unions.

Be this as it may, 2001 would see Blair elected to another five-year term with a crushing majority that raised questions about the ability of the Conservatives, now in total disarray, to survive as one of Britain's two major parties. Blair, himself, suggested that the Conservatives had become irrelevant (*Economist*, Nov. 16, 2002, 54). In August of 2003, he would become Britain's longest, continuous serving prime minister. He also sustained higher popularity ratings than any prime minister since polls on the topic were taken, and could boast of an impressive record of economic growth, reduction in crime, and improvements in health care and education (*New York Times*, July 30, 2003, www).

All, however, was not well. Blair joined the Bush administration in launching a disastrous war on Iraq in the name of fighting terror and stripping the Iraqi dictator of his weapons of mass destruction. In both cases, faulty intelligence was inflated by immoderate claims that had little base in reality (House of Commons 2004). Al Qaeda did not have bases in Iraq and suspected weapons of mass destruction were not to be found. A cover-up followed. The cover of the *Economist*, one of the world's new leading news magazines, featured pictures of Bush and Blair under a magnifying glass and branded them "sincere deceivers" (*Economist*, July 17, 2004). Perhaps the greater sin, from the British perspective, was that a leftist prime minister had blindly followed an arch-conservative American president down the path of folly. By mid-2004, Financial Calculus, a British website that predicts elections based on amalgamating various polls, predicted that Labour's 165 seat majority in Commons would shrink to a mere 24 seats if the elections were held in the summer of 2004 (*Observer*, May 2, 2004, www). Labour's dismal performance in a series of by-elections added to the gloom, party analysts blaming the war. Fifty-two former diplomats and senior officials added to the fray by publically criticizing Blair for his unflinching support of Bush's Iraqi and Israeli policies, claiming that those policies were "doomed to failure" (*New York Times*, April 27, 2004, www). Infighting within the Labour leadership increased apace, forcing Blair to declare he was still in charge (*Guardian*, June 5, 2004, www). Other reports suggested that Blair had considered resigning, but was dissuaded by his colleagues.

Tony Blair called for national elections on May 5, 2005. Labour had dropped in the polls but retained a slim lead over the Tories (Conservatives). Blair publically admitted that he was "an issue" and pledged to end his "I know best" style of leadership (*Observer*, March 6, 2005, www). He stressed that there would be a

Blair, beset by criticism that he lied about the Iraq war, leads Labour
into the 2005 elections.

true partnership with the people, noting that "we can only do it together"
(*Guardian*, Feb 14, 2005, www). He also promised an "opportunity society" in
which all British citizens would prosper. Among other things, this included extended maternity leave, improved child care for working parents, more accessible
health care and drug treatment programs and a ban on religious discrimination,
an issue of preeminent importance to Britain's Muslim community. Nor did
Blair forget the labor unions, assuring Britain's workers of a full 28 days off each
year (*Guardian*, March 28, 2005, www).

    Not all, however, was sweetness and light. Blair refused to back away from
the war in Iraq, despite growing revelations that he had ignored the advice of
British defense and intelligence communities (*Guardian*, March 26, 2005, www).
Adding to the electoral uncertainties was anti-terrorist legislation that would deprive terrorist suspects, including British citizens, of their legal rights. This played
well with the Association of Chief Police Officers, the spokesman of which noted
that, "These are extraordinary times which call for the introduction of extraordinary measures" (*BBC*, March 14, 2005, www). Blair's pro-EU positions were also
of concern, but he had softened these by promising a referendum on the issue.

    The Tories countered by promising to create a special border police that would
keep out illegal immigrants. The idea was popular and emerged as the only issue
on which the Tories led Labour in the polls (*Guardian*, March 29, 2005, www).
The Tories also promised lower taxes, fewer restrictions on business, and a more

cautious approach to the EU. Both parties, however, were divided on the EU issue. The Liberal Democrats were the only party to openly oppose the War in Iraq.

When the dust had settled, it was a humbled Tony Blair that was returned to office. Labour's majority in Commons had shrunk from 160 to 66. Labour was still in power, but had gained only 35.2 percent of the popular vote, the lowest plurality for a winning party in modern history. The popular mandate of the past two elections was no longer. Blair acknowledged that the war in Iraq had been "divisive" and that there were "lots of lessons to learn" (*BBC,* May 6, 2005, www). Key party leaders called upon Blair to set the date that he intended to step down as prime minister. A huffy Blair said he had no intentions of stepping down before the end of his term, but few seemed convinced (*Observer,* May 8, 2005, www). Gordon Brown, the Chancellor of the Exchequer (finance), was broadly credited with creating Britain's strong economy, and was far more popular than the prime minister. It was Britain's strong economy that had compensated for public hostility toward a flawed war, and Brown was demanding his due (*New York Times,* May 7, 2005, www). The "rebel" camp within Labour—those who had opposed Blair on key issues—had also done well. With a reduced majority and facing rebellion in his own party, Blair could no longer steamroll his policies through the Commons (*BBC,* May 6, 2005, www.)

The Conservatives and Liberal Democrats could also take heart from the elections. The Conservatives gained 35 seats in the Commons and garnered 32.3 percent of the popular vote, only three percent less than Labour. The Liberal Democrats also did well, with 22 percent of the popular vote and an additional 8 seats in the Commons. Both proclaimed themselves ready to topple Labor during the next elections.

The evolutionary pattern of British democracy demonstrates that social and economic change can be accomplished peacefully. Nevertheless, the evolutionary nature of political change in Britain has perpetuated the existence of two nondemocratic political institutions, the Crown and the House of Lords. The Crown and the Lords have very little power, but they are part of the political process. The evolutionary pattern of British politics has also resulted in a society that is far more class-conscious than other modem industrial societies. The existence of a monarchy and the House of Lords, at least from the perspective of some members of the Labour Party, perpetuates this sense of class consciousness. In much the same manner, the evolutionary nature of British politics has perpetuated an elitist educational system that provides the upper classes with a superb education while locking the lower classes in mediocrity.

THE POLITICAL INSTITUTIONS OF BRITAIN

The formal institutions of the British government consist of the Crown (king or queen), the House of Lords, and the House of Commons. Collectively, the Lords and the Commons constitute the Parliament. The Crown and the House of Lords give symbolic expression to Britain's aristocratic past but have little influence in shaping public policy.

The House of Commons, by contrast, is the core of British democracy. Bills passed by the House of Commons are the law of the land, and they cannot be vetoed by any other branch of the British government. The authority of the Commons, moreover, is total. There are no inalienable rights reserved for minorities or individuals, nor can a bill passed by the Commons be overturned by the British courts. Indeed, the only restraints on the power of the House of Commons are the informal constitutional restraints of tradition and reasonableness.

Members of the House of Commons are chosen by the British population in elections that are held at least once every five years. The leader of the majority party in the Commons then is requested by the Crown to form a Government. A Government consists of the prime minister, the Cabinet, and other senior political officials who assist the prime minister and the Cabinet in the formulation and execution of policy.

As used herein, **Government** (with a capital G) refers to the prime minister, Cabinet, and other relevant positions selected by the prime minister.

The prime minister is the dominant member of the Government, followed in turn by senior members of the Cabinet, most of whom head a major administrative department. Of these, the Ministers of Foreign Affairs, Defense, and the Treasury (The Chancellor of the Exchequer) wield exceptional power. Some Cabinet positions are also reserved for senior party officials whose responsibilities are purely political. Cabinet members without specific departmental responsibilities are often allocated one of the grand historical titles which, being obsolete, continue to make the nomenclature of British politics impenetrable to outsiders. Foremost among such honorific titles are the Lord President of the Council and the Lord Privy Seal. The Lord Privy Seal is the Government's political manager in the House of Commons, while the Lord President of the Council chairs important cabinet committees in lieu of the prime minister. Both are important political positions (Rose 1989).

Governments rule for as long as they enjoy the confidence of a majority of the members of the Commons or until the five-year term of the Commons expires. Should a majority of the members of the Commons vote to "bring down" the Government—a vote of no confidence—the entire Government must resign, thereby paving the way for new elections. As long as a single party enjoys a majority in Commons, however, a successful vote of no confidence is an unlikely event.

Executive Power in Britain: Prime Ministers and Governments

A British prime minister supported by a strong majority in the House of Commons is more powerful than the American president (Rose 1989). The powers of the prime minister stem from a variety of sources, four of which are of particular importance. *First, the prime minister possesses the prestige of holding the highest political office in the land.* As described by James:

> He is not just leader of the party; he is head of the government. Ministers are not only his colleagues but his subordinates. A few may be rivals; some may dislike him; some will clash with him on policy; but all must accord him

---

Powers of the British Prime Minister

To understand the powers of the British prime minister, four points must be noted.

1. The power of the House of Commons is absolute and cannot be overridden by any other political institution.
2. The power of the majority party in the Commons is absolute and cannot be blocked by the opposition.
3. The power of the Government is absolute because members of the ruling party vote as a cohesive bloc.
4. The prime minister is the dominant figure in the Government. John Smith, the former leader of the Labour Party, used to lament, "We have an elective dictatorship" (Economist, April 18, 1998, 7).

---

the respect due to his office. This attitude is reinforced by civil servants, who have a great respect for No. 10 and its utterances:[1] they may not agree with what the Prime Minister says, but they have a keen nose for where power lies (James 1992, 93–94).

Second, the prime minister is the leader of his or her party. It is the prime minister who has the major voice in determining the legislative program that the ruling party will implement during its term in office. As the leader of the party, moreover, the prime minister selects the members of the Government. Powerful leaders in the party must be accommodated, but prime ministers also use their appointment powers as a means of rewarding friends and punishing enemies. Members of Parliament (MPs) who hope to move up the ranks of the party hierarchy can defy the prime minister only at grave risk to their political careers (Rose 1989; *New Statesman* 1996, 1998).

In much the same manner, the prime minister has the final word in shaping the electoral strategy of the ruling party. Particularly important, in this regard, is the timing of elections. By way of background, it should be noted that it is within the power of the prime minister to call a general election at any time within the statutory five-year term of a Parliament. (The prime minister sets the stage for new elections by requesting the monarch to dissolve the Parliament.) Few Parliaments run their full five-year course, for the governing party is anxious to "go to the people" at a time when it has the best chance of winning a new term in office. Timing can be everything. The best time for calling an election, however, is often a matter of considerable debate within the ruling party, and it is the prime minister who resolves the issue (Smith 2004).

Third, prime ministers derive considerable power from their organizational position as the chairperson of the Cabinet. Cabinets face such a wide range of issues that they can accomplish their tasks only by dividing into committees, often as many as 160 (Hennessy 1991). Prime ministers set the agenda of the Cabinet by determining both the issues to be addressed and the amount of time to be spent on

---

[1]"No. 10" refers to the prime minister's residence at 10 Downing Street, and thus to the prime minister, just as "the White House" often refers to the president of the United States.

each issue. They also decide the membership of the various cabinet committees and chair the committees of their choosing. The organizational powers of the prime minister are strengthened, moreover, by the existence of a personal staff or "Private Office" designed to keep the prime minister in touch with the diverse issues before him or her (Barber 1991).

In addition to the organizational advantages discussed above, it is the prime minister who speaks for the Government. The Cabinet seldom votes on issues, it being the prime minister who "sums up" the discussion and who conveys the "sense" of the Government's decision to Parliament (Punnett 1988). As anyone who has participated in a small-group discussion well knows, a chairperson's interpretation of what transpired may differ markedly from the interpretations of the group's members.

Finally, the power of the prime minister derives from the growing personalization of British politics that has accompanied the advent of television. The prime minister is the focal point of media coverage, and no politician, regardless of party, can compete with a popular and dynamic prime minister (Barber 1991). Popularity, however, is fleeting, and a prime minister lagging in the polls may find the members of his or her cabinet becoming increasingly aggressive (Conley 1990). In the case of Tony Blair, the damage of the Iraq war found one of his supporters noting: "I think he will go. Until that day, everyone will have to keep saying that he intends going on" (MacAskill, Ewen and Maguire, Kevin, "Brown allies plan campaign," *Guardian*, May 1, 2004, www). The battle for succession had already begun.

An important point to be noted in the above discussion is that the powers of the prime minister are largely informal. The British Constitution is an unwritten set of traditions, and there are no formally enumerated powers of the prime minister. Much, accordingly, depends on the skills and the personality of the individuals involved. A skillful and determined prime minister will be far more powerful than a less-experienced prime minister or a prime minister inclined to share large areas of responsibility with his or her peers. Margaret Thatcher's popular label as the "Iron Lady" conveyed a grudging respect for her skill and determination. It was she who dominated the Cabinet. The reign of John Major, by contrast, witnessed a reassertion of ministerial influence. In the words of a senior minister, "John sums up at the end of the meeting rather than the beginning" (Heseltine, cited in Sampson 1992, 22).

While the powers of the prime minister are formidable, they are far from absolute (James 1992). The senior members of the Cabinet each represent powerful wings within the ruling party and, more often than not, their position on the Cabinet is recognition of that power. Prime ministers theoretically are free to choose their Cabinet ministers, but the practical requirements of party cohesion demand that all major wings of the party find adequate representation within the Cabinet. Ideological divisions are a constant source of tension within the Government, as are personality conflicts. Many senior Cabinet ministers also view themselves as potential prime ministers and are not averse to using their Cabinet positions to achieve that end. Gordon Brown, the chancellor of the exchequer (finance) seized upon Blair's woes in Iraq to openly plot his overthrow. Even some of his supporters were taken aback with his aggressiveness, one warning: "It's

scarce resources of the British state are to be allocated.

The dominant role of the prime minister and other senior officials is not a matter of debate. As Anthony Sampson, the dean of British pundits wrote in 2004:

> After all the promises of democratisation and openness, central government has become still more concentrated and impenetrable. . . . And more decisions than ever are concentrated on Number 10. Britain, for all its new diversity at the bottom, has become one of the most centralized of all countries at the top. And in the center a new Establishment has taken over from the old (Sampson 2004).

What is debated is the openness of Britain's political elite. Is political power the preserve of a self-perpetuating ruling class, or is it available to all British citizens regardless of their origins? The answer to this question has much to say about the quality of British democracy.

British scholars are sharply divided on the issue. In the view of some, class rule is a thing of the past (Sampson 1982; Guttsman 1963). The Labour Governments of the post–World War II era, in this view, forced a redistribution of the nation's wealth and shifted political power to the middle class. Indeed, Margaret Thatcher, John Major, and Tony Blair, Britain's three most recent prime ministers, all possess middle-class backgrounds. The House of Lords, the bastion of privilege has been transformed into an honorific debating society. A recent survey of Britain's top 100 political, economic, sport, and academic leaders found a drop in public school (elite private) from 66 in 1992 to 46 in 2002. The Oxford/Cambridge numbers dipped from 54 in 1992 to 35 in 2002. Clearly, the British middle class is making its presence felt ("The Ascent of British Man," *Economist*, Dec. 7, 2002, 53).

Other scholars suggest that the role of Labour in redistributing wealth and power was ephemeral (Scott 1991). Real power, in this view, resides in the hard core of higher civil servants and corporate directors who rule from behind the scenes. The elite can perpetuate its rule because it has received an education far superior to that of the general population and because it has forged a network of political connections based on "old school ties," and because it possesses the wealth to implement its agenda (Scott 1991). With the Thatcher revolution in 1979, moreover, the capitalist elite reasserted its power and rolled back many of the egalitarian programs that Labour had enacted during an earlier era (*Sunday Times,* Mar. 26, 2000, www). They also note that there were only 5 females in the top 100 leaders, and fewer minorities. There may be a new establishment, but it is still white and male.

The debate over the role of class in British politics is unlikely to be resolved in the near future, as each side in the argument emphasizes a different dimension of British political reality. On one hand, the most powerful positions in Britain are held by elected officials drawn largely from the middle class. On the other hand, elitist schools play a far greater role in filling positions of authority in Britain than they do in the United States and most other first world countries, with the possible exception of Japan.

Parties and Politics in Britain

Since the end of World War II, only the Labour Party and the Conservative Party have possessed sufficient strength in Commons to form a Government. A third party, The Liberal Democratic Party, consistently garners some 10 to 20 percent of the popular vote but seldom possess enough votes in any one district to win a seat in the Commons (Peele 2004). The strength of the Liberal Democrats, however, appears to be increasing, and in the 2005 elections, the party won 22 percent of the popular vote.

In addition to its three national parties, Britain also possesses a large number of fringe parties, most of which are of a regional nature. Foremost among these are the Scottish Nationalist Party and the smaller Plaid Cymru, the nationalist party of Wales (Smith 2004). Most recently, a small fascist party, the British National Party (BNP), has gained notice by winning a seat on London's city council. The BNP champions racism and exploits growing hostility toward Muslims and other immigrant groups. It has been joined by the UK Independence Party, a new organization that has emerged to block extended British membership in the EU. A variety of small parties also exist in Northern Ireland, a region largely neglected by the major parties. In 2005, the fringe parties accounted for about 10 percent of the seats in Commons.

Britain's three major parties are **catch–all** political parties: *coalitions of diverse groups held together by the desire to form a Government compatible with their views.* Ideology is important, but it is less important than winning elections. Much as in the United States, most voters identify with a political party without actually joining it.

Britain's major parties are reasonably well organized and operate at three distinct levels: the parliamentary level, the national level, and the local or constituency level. The MPs of each party in the Commons constitute its parliamentary party (Brand 1992). Parliamentary parties meet regularly to discuss strategy, and their members are expected to vote as a bloc. When a party possesses a majority in the Commons, its leaders form the Government.

Each of Britain's three major parties also maintains a national party organization and a vast network of constituency organizations. The national party organization is responsible for fundraising, campaigning, and coordinating local party organizations. Constituency organizations, in turn, nominate candidates from a list of names compiled in cooperation with the national party organization. Should the constituency organization reject its suggestions, the national party organization has the option of withholding its label from the candidate. This has yet to occur in the Conservative Party but does happen from time to time within the ranks of Labour. In such cases, the local candidate may run on a label such as the "True Labour candidate." The national parties attempt to avoid conflict with their constituency organizations, the most probable outcome of which would be an election loss.

The Conservative Party. The Conservative Party, as its name suggests, occupies the center right of the political spectrum (Ball and Holliday 2002). It is the party of big business, small government, and lower taxes. Its detractors would say that it is also the party of privilege and inequality.

The business and middle- to upper-class orientation of the Conservative Party is also reflected in the "public school," Oxbridge background of many of its candidates. The business community is strongly represented in Conservative Governments, as are lawyers. The business community also provides most of the party activists at the constituency level. In spite of its upper- and middle-class orientation, the Conservative Party often receives between 30 and 40 percent of the working-class vote, most of it coming from the prosperous constituencies of southern England. It also won about 50 percent of the lower-middle class vote in the 2005 elections (*BBC,* May 7, 2005, www).

The leader of the Conservative Party is elected by Conservative members of Parliament. The leader of the Conservative Parliamentary Party, in turn, appoints other senior party officials, including the chairman of the party, the chief whip, and the deputy whip. When the party is in power, the dominant members of the Parliamentary Party—the front benchers—form the Government. When the party is not in power, the leader appoints a "shadow cabinet," the members of which lead the party's attack on the Government. The Conservative back benchers, for their part, meet as the "Committee of 1922," a group from which ministers are excluded. Issues are discussed under informal rules, and votes are not taken. Signs of unrest within the Committee of 1922, however, often signal changes in the leadership structure. Reigning confusion within the Conservative leadership has made the Committee of 1922 all the more powerful as they have less to fear from a punitive leader. In 2003, for example, pressure from the backbenchers forced a vote on the leadership of Duncan Smith, the then leader of the Conservative Parliamentary Party. Smith lost, and was replaced by Michael Howard, who resigned following his party's 2005 election defeat.

The strength of the Conservative Party outside of Parliament is its large network of local party organizations, officially referred to as Conservative Constituency Associations. The functions of the local party organizations are to nominate candidates, to support the party's electoral efforts, and to keep the party in touch with local opinion. It is the Conservative Parliamentary Party, however, that makes policy.

The Conservative Party Conference (Convention) meets annually for a period of two or three days and debates a variety of policy issues. Everyone associated with the party and its various constituency, regional, and professional associations is entitled to attend, but only about half of the 6,000 eligible participants actually do so. By and large, the Conservative Conference is a passive gathering, the affairs of which are orchestrated by the Parliamentary leadership.

In a desperate effort to rekindle popular support, the Conservative Party has embarked upon a bold program to double the party's membership by providing members with previously unavailable opportunities to participate in Party decision making. This will be done by a series of periodic ballots distributed to Party members. The leadership has promised a ballot on the party's next electoral platform, a radical departure from past practice in which things were controlled by the Parliamentary leadership of the party. The leadership has also promised that the selection of the next Party leader will be made on the basis of a primary election by Party members, an even more radical departure from the past. The "new" Conservative Party, the leadership promised, would be open to all, not merely the rich. It would also be a party that listened to Britain and dispelled the image of selfishness and sleaze so effectively implanted in voters' minds by Tony Blair and the Labour Party (Willetts 1998; Gamble and Wright 1998). The Conservative's new look proved ineffective in the 2001 elections, but did produce substantial gains in 2005.

The Labour Party. The Labour Party was formed in the early 1900s as an alliance between the labor unions and various socialist groups of the era. Of the latter, the most important were the Fabian Society, the Social Democratic Federation, and the Cooperative Movement. The Social Democratic Federation was a radical Marxist organization that advocated the overthrow of the monarchy and the establishment of a workers' republic. The Fabians, by contrast, were socially concerned intellectuals, not the least of whom was playwright George Bernard Shaw (Piachaud 1993). The Cooperative Movement was a "hands-on" organization that provided low-cost food and clothing via a network of cooperative (worker-managed) shops. All remain within the Labour Party today, but the role of the labor unions is dominant.

The Labour Party was created to force a fundamental change in the allocation of Britain's wealth. Wages were to be increased, jobs made secure, and work rules improved. If this required socialism, so be it.

The financial and organizational power of the unions soon enabled the Labour Party to overtake the Liberal Party as the main challenger to the Conservatives, a feat that was accomplished shortly after the end of World War I. Henceforth, British citizens would have a choice between two fundamentally different views of the world. The Conservatives argued that the primary responsibility of government was to promote the growth of business and industry. The larger the size of the economic cake, from the Conservative perspective, the easier it would be for the government to meet the needs of all its citizens. Labour, by contrast, argued that the primary responsibility of government was to assure an equitable distribution of the nation's wealth and to protect the health and welfare of its citizens. When British citizens cast a ballot for a Conservative or a Labour MP, accordingly, they have a very clear picture of what they are voting for. This is not always the case in the United States.

The leader of the Labour Party is selected at the annual Labour Conference by an electoral college in which one-third of the delegates are chosen by the Labour members of Parliament, including Labour MPs in the European Parliament; one-third by a ballot of the 4.5 million members of Britain's trade unions; and one-third by some 260,000 full members of the party's constituency associations. Policies adopted by the 5,000 eligible delegates to the annual conference are binding upon the Labour Party leadership in Parliament "as far as may be practicable." This escape clause in the party constitution provides the Labour leadership in the Commons with ample room for maneuverability, as does the vague wording of many Conference resolutions. Only about half of the union delegates attend the annual conference, giving the more radical activists sway to launch scathing, if ineffective, attacks on a party leadership dominated by the unions.

The social background of the Labour Party, as one would expect, is quite different from that of the Conservative Party. The majority of Labour voters either have working-class origins or belong to a managerial middle class consisting of bureaucrats, teachers, and people in various other white-collar occupations. The middle class dominates both the constituency associations and the Parliamentary Party. While Labour boasts some 6.26 million members, approximately 6 million of these are affiliate members who belong to the Labour Party by virtue of their union membership. Labour Party dues are automatically deducted from the union dues of British workers unless they specifically opt out. The remainder of the Labour Party membership consists of individuals who have joined Labour constituency organizations or who belong to the socialist and cooperative organizations that originally participated in the formation of the Labour Party. Most union affiliate members of the Labour Party are passive, thereby allowing the members of the constituency associations to play a more vigorous role than their numbers would warrant.

Reflecting its working-class orientation, the Labour Party has traditionally found its strongest support in Britain's industrial centers, particularly the industrial and mining regions of Northern England and Scotland. This has become even more the case since the Thatcher revolution. Labour has also found disproportionately more support among males, younger voters, and non-Anglicans. (Anglicans are members of the Church of England.)

After competing with the Conservatives on an equal basis during the 1950s, 1960s, and 1970s, Labour fell from grace during the 1980s as the Conservatives dominated British politics for eighteen consecutive years. Labour, in the eyes of British voters, particularly the middle class, was too closely tied to Britain's labor unions to adequately address Britain's mounting economic problems. The 1997 general election, then, was to pose a critical test for Labour. If Labour could win the election, it would reestablish itself as one of Britain's two dominant parties. A Labour loss, however, would have excluded Labour from power for another five-year period and called into question Labour's role as a serious challenge to the Conservatives. The Liberal Democrats played upon this theme, suggesting that they, not Labour, were the party of the future.

The stakes of the 1997 election, then, were high indeed. Above all, Labour had to present an electoral manifesto (platform) that would enable it to recapture a large share of the middle-class vote. Indeed, so anxious was Labour to attract the middle-class vote in its 1997 campaign that journalists began referring to the Labour program as "designer socialism."

In the meantime, Labour had undertaken a major reorganization of its own affairs in order to convince the public that it was not the docile tool of the labor unions. An important step in this direction was the 1994 election of Tony Blair as the new leader of the Labour Party. Among other things, Blair pledged to scrap clause four of the Labour Party's constitution, a clause that committed the party to the "nationalization of the means of production, distribution, and exchange"

Table 3.1 British Elections: 1997-2001

Party	Seats in Commons		
	1997	2001	2005
Labour	418	413	356
Conservatives	165	66	197
Liberal Democrats	46	52	62
Other Parties	30	28	30
Total	659*	659	646

*Including the speaker.

SOURCE: Official Statistics.

(McIlroy 1998). Blair has also called for the transformation of Britain into a meritocracy in which hard work and achievement would be rewarded. While such views hardly pleased the unions, they were applauded by a middle class increasingly disenchanted by conservative rule (Whiteley, Seyd, and Richardson 1994).

Blair skillfully coined the term *New Labour* and boldly declared that "Nobody seriously believes in this day and age that the business of the Labour Party is to be the political arm of the trade union movement" (*Observer Review,* Sept. 10, 1995, www). Beyond this, Blair pronounced Labour to be "business friendly," and quietly accepted the main tenets of the Thatcher Revolution including the privatization of state-owned enterprises, the deregulation of industry, and legislation designed to reduce the militancy of the trade unions (Kennedy 1998).

The strategy was successful, and Labour scored a dazzling victory in the 1997 elections, and an even more stunning victory in 2001, the results of which are summarized in Table 3.1. Blair became the prime minister, and much as he had tamed the unions, he began to tame the Labour Party. Accused of being a "control freak," Blair responded by saying that if "control freakery" means "wanting [Labour] to be a modern, disciplined party with a strong center," then he was guilty. He went on to add that "Our party won't return to the factionalism, navel-gazing or feuding of the '70s or '80s, no matter how much a few people long for those heady days of electoral disaster" (*Time International,* Nov. 30, 1998, 25).

Blair extended his control over the party in wake of the party's 2001 landslide victory over the Conservatives. Only a disaster could prevent another Labour victory, and an optimistic Tony Blair hinted at new elections in the fall of 2004. That, however, was before Blair used his extraordinary power to lead Britain into a disastrous war in Iraq, the justifications for which proved both flawed and exaggerated. Buoyed by rebellion in the ranks, Gordon Brown, leaked news that Blair had agreed to relinquish power to him before the coming elections much as Margaret Thatcher had previously relinquished power to John Major. Blair heatedly responded that "deals cannot be done over the position of Prime Minister" (*Observer,* July 18, 2004, www). In the meantime, Blair penciled in elections for May 5 of 2005, presumably hoping that the fury over his handling of the war and subservience to George Bush would have eased by that time. It did not. Labour won the elections, but Blair's leadership was called into question. Gordon Brown awaits in the wings.

The Liberal Democrats. The origins of the Liberal Party parallel those of the Conservative Party. The Conservatives were the heirs of the Tories, while the Liberals were the heirs of the Whigs. The image portrayed by the early Liberals was one of reform, change, and opposition to the Church of England. The Liberals, however, were very much a middle-class party, and conflict between the Liberals and the Conservatives was essentially a conflict within the same social class.

The emergence of the Labour Party in the early 1900s pre-empted the Liberals' position as the party of change and reform, relegating the Liberals to the status of a third party falling somewhere between the more clearly defined positions of the Conservatives and Labour.

The Liberals managed to survive as a third party largely on the strength of a large network of constituency organizations created during their days of glory. Times, however, were difficult, and by 1970, the Liberal representation in the House of Commons had dropped to a low of six (Crewe 1993). Equally problematic were matters of finance. People may have been willing to vote for a losing cause, but they were not willing to pay for it. This was particularly the case among the large pressure groups whose ability to influence policy depended on access to the Government (Rose 1989). As discussed earlier, parties that do not form Governments have little influence in the British scheme of things.

Liberal fortunes were to increase dramatically with the decline of the Labour Party in the 1980s. In 1981, four moderate leaders of the Labour Party broke ranks and formed a new center-left Social Democratic Party. The Social Democrats and the Liberals soon worked out a common electoral strategy, running a joint campaign under the Alliance label. Following a strong showing in 1987, the two parties merged to form the Liberal Democratic Party. The organizational structure of the Liberal Democrats builds upon the strong constituency network inherited from the Liberals and is capped with an annual conference that is far more open and democratic than that of either Labour or the Conservatives.

Despite an optimistic outlook for the future, the Liberal Democrats continue to be stymied by Britain's single-member, simple-plurality election system. Although they garnered some 22 percent of the vote in the 2005 election, the Liberal Democrats received 9.6 percent of the seats in Commons. Both Labour and the Conservatives also possess far more "safe" districts in which they are more or less assured of victory than do the Liberal Democrats, a fact that provides the two larger parties with a critical mass that the Liberal Democrats do not possess.

The best hope for the emergence of the Liberal Democrats as a major force in British politics would be a change in Britain's election laws from single-member, simple-plurality districts to proportional representation. Based on the 2005 results, for example, proportional representation would have given the Liberal Democrats approximately 142 seats in Commons, a far cry from the 62 seats they actually received. No single party would have been able to form a Government, and the Liberal Democrats would almost certainly have been part of a ruling coalition

Government. Proportional representation would also have assured the public that a vote for the Liberal Democrats was no longer a wasted vote. Needless to say, the Liberal Democrats paid close attention to Tony Blair's experiment with proportional representation in the elections for the European Parliament. A change in the British election system, that seems unlikely, is their best hope for the future.

The Functions of British Political Parties

Political parties represent the very essence of British politics. They organize the affairs of Commons; they assure that the Government in power is kept under constant scrutiny; they recruit and train new generations of political leaders; they organize, socialize, and mobilize the British electorate; and they keep the party leadership in touch with grassroots opinion. In this latter function, British political parties provide an important communication link between the Government and the masses. The competition among British parties, moreover, defines the major issues of the day and provides the electorate with a choice between ideological alternatives.

The above functions are common to political parties in most democratic political systems. The genius of the British party system, however, has been its ability to promote political moderation. As only one of the two major parties is in a position to form a Government, all major groups within society are forced to join one party or the other. Competing interests must compromise their differences for the sake of attaining at least a limited degree of political influence. The highly disciplined nature of Britain's major parties also facilitates both political stability and political responsibility by enabling Governments to stay the course of their constitutional term of office. The victorious party has the power to implement its campaign promises, and voters expect it to do so (Hofferbert and Budge 1992; Budge 2004).

Pressure Groups and Politics in Britain

As in all modern industrial democracies, Britain possesses thousands of pressure groups. Of these, the most powerful are the large economic **peak associations** (or umbrella organizations) that aggregate a variety of smaller organizations. Most of Britain's 100-plus labor unions, for example, come together in the Trades Union Congress, and industrial groups find representation in the Confederation of British Industry (Mcllroy 1998). Other peak business organizations include the Retail Consortium, the British Bankers Association, the Association of British Chambers of Commerce, and the National Federation of Building Trades Employers. Approximately 90 percent of British farmers find representation in the National Farmers Union. Other dominant groups include the British Medical Association, the Society of Civil Servants, and the Police Federation.

Not all of Britain's major pressure groups are economic in nature. The Royal Society for the Protection of Birds, the largest of some 1,000 environmental groups in Britain, has more card-carrying members than the three major British political parties combined (*Economist,* Aug. 13, 1994, 49). The membership of the far more radical Greenpeace has passed the 350,000 mark (ibid.). The environmentalists, in turn, are joined by more than 70 animal rights groups and at least

40 groups attempting to alleviate the plight of the poor. In the human rights area, Amnesty International enjoys a membership surpassing 100,000 (ibid.).

Some established groups, by contrast, appear to be in decline. In 2004, a leading Anglican bishop warned that the Church of England may soon become a minority sect. Membership has declined to less than 6 million (*Guardian*, March 20, 2004, www). Only 72 percent of the British people consider classify themselves as Christians, and few of them apparently attend worship services. A prominent Cardinal proclaimed that Christianity had been all but vanquished in Britain. Evangelical and Islamic groups appear to be picking up the slack.

Most members of the social and environmental groups are college-educated individuals from middle-class backgrounds, a voting category of vital interest to British politicians. Indeed, many British citizens now find pressure groups to be more effective in representing their views than political parties (*Economist,* Aug. 13, 1994, 49).

The goal of British pressure groups is similar to that of pressure groups everywhere: to protect and promote the special interests of their members. Most of Britain's larger peak associations work through either the Labour Party or the Conservative Party in the hope of gaining direct access to the Government. When the Labour Party is in power, the ability of the Trades Unions Congress to achieve its objectives is formidable. It was the Labour Governments of the 1950s and 1960s, for example, that nationalized key British industries and legislated sweeping social welfare programs. The influence of the labor union has now weakened considerably as the Labour Party has moved to the center of the political stage. As McIlroy points out, the interests of the union and the Labour Party do not coincide, but they do intersect (1998, 537; *Times,* Sept. 15, 1999). Indeed, 2004 would find a weakened Tony Blair confronted with a spate of strikes ranging from fire fighters (2002), post office employees (2003), and government workers (2004). A brutal 2004 confrontation between the TCU and the Government was avoided at the 11th hour when the Government gave in to TUC demands for a rescue package for workers who lose their pensions due to bankruptcies. More than 200 MP's with TCU connections signed petitions supporting the union (*Guardian*, May 15, 2004,www). British business groups, in turn, find strong representation in the Conservative Party and generally speak though the Confederation of British Industries and other peak associations. It was the strong Conservative Governments of the 1980s that denationalized Britain's key industries, lowered taxes, and scaled back the welfare system. Blair's Governments have been business friendly and furthered the rift between the Labour Party and the TCU. The unions complain, but have nowhere else to turn.

Not all British pressure groups choose to work through a political party, a process that renders them hostage to the uncertainties of a national election. The British Medical Association and the Society of Civil Servants, for example, remain unaffiliated, allowing the major parties to vie for their support.

In addition to their electoral strategies, politically important groups such as the police, the Medical Association, and the Farmers Union work closely with the Government in designing legislation relevant to their respective professions. In many instances, they also have a major say in the regulation of their professions.

Pressure groups unable to reach the ear of a Cabinet minister often use individual MPs to press their cause in the Question Period or to introduce supportive legislation via a private member's bill. Such bills seldom see the light of day but may make their point by stimulating debate on a particular social issue.

A. H. Hanson and Malcolm Walles (1990) cite a particularly bitter commentary on interest politics by James Callaghan, a former minister of the exchequer (Finance):

> When I look at some Member discussing the Finance Bill I do not think of them as the Hon. Member for X, Y or Z. I look at them and say "investment trusts," "capital speculators," or "that is the fellow who is the Stock Exchange man who makes a profit on gilt-edged." I have almost forgotten their constituencies, but I shall never forget their interests. I wonder sometimes whom they represent, the constituents', or their own or their friends' particular interests (Hanson and Walles 1990, 187).

Hanson and Walles go on to note that the power of individual MPs to influence policy is limited by the requirements of party discipline.

Citizens and Politics in Britain

The British population expresses its political views by means of elections, public opinion polls, civic action movements, and a vigorous press. Of the above, the general elections are the ultimate expression of public opinion and portray a population that is increasingly centrist in its political views (Denver 2003). By-elections (replacement elections) and local elections also provide an important sounding board for public opinion, and a rebuff to the ruling party sends a clear signal of public disaffection with the affairs of state. By-elections in the run-up to the 2005 elections, it is interesting to note, revealed a precipitous decline in popular support for Tony Blair and his Labour Government. They proved to be prophetic.

Public opinion polls are a regular part of British life, and rare indeed is the topic that has not been probed by one poll or another. British citizens are concerned with issues of law and order, the economy, unemployment, and health care, the same basic concerns that dominated opinion polls in United States. The war in Iraq has been particularly divisive as has British membership in an increasingly centralized European Union. Tony Blair resisted demands for a national referendum on the EU, but in 2004, was forced by public opinion to promise a referendum that would give the public the final say on the issue (*Guardian*, June 24, 2004, www). Also on the minds of the British is the future of Britain, itself. The Scotts, Welch, and Northern Irish have all achieved devolution (semi-independence) and many English are now demanding special status for England. If present trends continue, Britain could become a federation (*Guardian*, March 29, 2002, www).

Protests, demonstrations, and other forms of civic action are also a regular part of British life and tend to focus on social issues such as AIDS, gay rights, nuclear power, and environmental protection. In 2002, more than 300,000 rural

Britains poured into the streets of London to defend the right to hunt foxes and protest the decline of rural life (*New York Times*, Sept. 22, 2002, www). By and large, the influence of groups on policy is minimal, although the environmentalists have been successful in blocking road-building projects that threaten forests and other "green spaces." Fox hunting was also banned.

How much, then, do the opinions of the British population actually influence public policy? There is no easy answer to this question. All British parties are sensitive to shifts in public opinion, but never more so than at the time of elections. British politicians are also particularly sensitive to issues of widespread concern. For the most part, however, the influence of public opinion is of a temporary nature. Be this as it may, the British public is becoming increasingly involved in community affairs (Marinetto 2003).

THE CONTEXT OF BRITISH POLITICS: CULTURE, ECONOMICS, AND INTERNATIONAL INTERDEPENDENCE

It is relatively easy to describe the general features of the British political system, but it is a much more difficult task to explain why it works the way it does. How have the British managed to achieve such an exemplary blend of democracy, stability, human rights, and economic prosperity? For many observers, the answer to this question lies in the existence of a uniquely British political culture that has evolved over the course of several centuries (Almond and Verba 1965).

The Culture of British Politics

Britain's unique political culture is shaped by several factors. First, there is a strong sense of British identity or "we feeling." The British are very proud of being "British" (Rose 1989; McCrone, Kiely, and Bechhofer 1998). Second, the British population believes in the effectiveness of its political institutions. Their legitimacy is beyond question. Third, British political culture reflects a broad popular consensus concerning the unwritten rules of politics. Central to this consensus is a strong sense of fair play, tolerance, and patience. It is this consensus on the proper way to do politics that provides the essence of Britain's unwritten Constitution. Fourth, British society places a high value on orderliness and self-control. Few manifestations of British culture are more visible to the foreign observer than the British penchant for standing in line. People who willingly stand in long lines must surely be easier to govern than those who do not. Finally, the British population abhors violence (Rose 1989). Ordinary police, or "bobbies," for example, carry nightsticks rather than guns. When people have been properly socialized, guns are unnecessary.

British political culture, it should be stressed, is merely one facet of a more generalized British culture that sets the overall tone of British politics. British culture, has traditionally stressed hard work, innovation, and endurance. It was these cultural characteristics that fueled the Industrial Revolution and enabled Britain to maintain its vast colonial empire. Prosperity does not just occur; it happens because people work hard and take the risks necessary to make it happen.

To say that Britain possesses a unique culture is not to suggest that all members of the British population share in this common culture or that all citizens of the United Kingdom are equally enamored of their political institutions. Northern Ireland's Catholic population has long been at odds with London, and a growing number of British citizens find being Scottish, Welsh, and English more important than being British. For the most part, however, the overwhelming majority of the British population does manifest a strong sense of national identity, does believe in the legitimacy of its political institutions, and does share a common set of expectations about how reasonable people should conduct their political affairs.

The existence of a culture that stresses moderation, fair play, tolerance, and order, then, goes a long way toward explaining why the British political system works the way it does. It is the strength of British culture, for example, that checks the inordinate powers of a British Government and guarantees the civil rights of British citizens (Garrard 2002). The British Constitution is a cultural constitution rather than a legal constitution, but it is just as binding. Indeed, a written constitution unsupported by a cultural constitution is largely meaningless.

Political culture has continuity, but it is also in a constant state of evolution. Each new generation is **socialized** into its political culture, yet each generation must adjust established cultural norms to meet the needs of its own circumstances. It was not until the early twentieth century, it will be recalled, that British culture deemed women fit to vote.

Historically, it was the British family that passed cultural values from one generation to the next. In the modern era, however, schools and the mass media have played an increasingly important role in the socialization process, as have political organizations and professional associations. Particularly important in the evolving nature of British culture has been the rapid expansion of comprehensive schools based on the American pattern. The political values transmitted in a system of mass education must inevitably differ from an elitist system of "public" (private) schools that minister to some 7 percent of the British population (Sampson 2004).

In the aftermath of the Second World War, British political culture was forced to adjust to Britain's declining role as a world power. It must now adjust to a dramatic restructuring of Britain's economic base as the heavy industries that fueled Britain's rise as an industrial power give way to high-tech and service industries. Over time, Britain has also become a multiracial society; today some 7.1 percent of the British population are "nonwhite." Of these, 2.2 are black, 3.4 from the Asian subcontinent (India, Pakistan, Bangladesh, and the Middle East), 1.5 Chinese and other. Government reports suggest that Britain's nonwhites feel unBritish.(*New York Times*, April 4, 2002, www). This is not a matter of small concern, for the 2004 Commission on British Muslims and Islamophobia warned that racial tensions are in danger of "boiling over" (*Observer*, May 30, 2004, www). Accusations of Muslim complicity in Jihadist terrorism add to the problem.

Some observers suggest that these and other changes in Britain's socioeconomic environment have eroded the homogeneity of British culture. The Thatcher revolution, in particular, is seen as having pitted the rich against the poor, undermining traditional sensitivities toward the needs of the community as a whole. Similarly, it has been suggested that Britain is becoming a postmaterialist society in which the traditional British values of innovation, hard work, and sacrifice have given way to a pervasive concern for comfort and environmental harmony.

Political Economy and Politics in Britain

While some observers find the key to British politics in its political culture, others find British politics to be an expression of its political economy. British parliamentary democracy itself, they note, evolved from economic conflict between the Crown and the Barons. It was the Industrial Revolution, moreover, that gave rise to both the bourgeoisie and the working class, each turning to politics as an avenue for advancing its economic interests.

The competing interests of the bourgeoisie and the working class continue to be the defining parameters of political conflict in Britain today. The Conservatives seek to stimulate economic growth by freeing the business community from excessive regulations, while Labour proclaims that the powers of government should be used to achieve a somewhat more equitable distribution of the nation's wealth. New Labour, however, displays none of the fire and brimstone socialism of *Old Labour*. This is one of the keys to its success. The Liberal Democrats, in turn, are attempting to forge a middle ground between the two extremes, a task that makes them not terribly different from New Labour.

British voting behavior over the course of the past several decades also reflects a pervasive sensitivity to economic issues. The swing to Labour during the 1950s and 1960s reflected a widespread belief that a Labour Government would be able to achieve both economic growth and social equity. The move toward socialism, however, proved to be a disappointment as taxes increased and the economy stagnated. The British voters turned away from Labour in 1979, hoping that a Conservative victory would revive Britain's faltering economy. More recently, disenchantment with Conservative economic policies was a strong factor leading to the Labour victories in the 1997, 2001 and 2005 elections. It is also interesting to observe that the battle lines between the Conservative and Labour Parties correspond closely to an economic map of Britain. Labour remains dominant in the depressed areas of Britain, particularly Scotland and the north of England. The Conservatives reign supreme in the high-tech and prosperous south.

International political economists, in turn, suggest that British domestic politics is increasingly being shaped by foreign economic pressure. Intense competition from the Germans and the Japanese, in their view, leaves the British government little choice but to increase the competitiveness of British industry regardless of the social costs entailed therein. An economy that relies on foreign trade for its survival has no other option.

Unfortunately, Britain imports far more that it exports, and 2004 would find that Britain trade deficits reached historical highs (*Guardian*, March 10, 2004, www). British companies, like their American counterparts, are also outsourcing jobs abroad to avoid Britain's high tax and wage structure. Even letters from British hospitals are being typed in India. Again, the old industrial areas of the north are the hardest hit.

International Interdependence and British Politics

Throughout most of its history, Britain was able to forge an international environment that was much to its liking. A vast colonial empire provided British industries with secure markets and a cheap source of raw materials, while a powerful navy protected commercial routes and kept European tyrants at bay. Foreign pressures influenced domestic politics, but they were not determinant.

The end of World War II, however, would find Britain reduced to the status of a secondary power, its colonies in revolt, and its navy powerless to stem the threat of nuclear missiles. British industry, moreover, had been crippled by German bombardments and was patched up to carry on as best it could. The industrial infrastructures of Germany and Japan, by contrast, had been destroyed by the war and were rebuilt using advanced technology. Britain's competitive edge, accordingly, was dulled.

During the period following World War II, the world was divided into two hostile camps: *a democratic capitalist camp under the hegemony of the United States and an authoritarian socialist camp dominated by the Soviet Union.* No longer able to depend on its navy for protection from foreign adversaries, Britain sought security under the nuclear shield of the United States. British forces were also integrated into those of the **North Atlantic Treaty Organization (NATO),** the commander of which was also an American. British policy makers, while uncomfortable with their dependence upon the United States, had little choice in the matter. Not to accept American dominance was to risk the Soviet occupation of Germany and, inevitably, the continent as a whole. British policy, accordingly, focused on creating a "special relationship" with the United States. The United States was sensitive to British interests, and Britain supported U.S. foreign policy initiatives regardless of how ill-advised they found those initiatives to be.

In the economic sphere, the post–World War II era found Britain moving in the direction of a mixed socialist-capitalist economy as labor and industry forged a political compromise that provided job security for workers in outmoded industries while simultaneously offering the private sector protection from foreign competition. This compromise increased the cost of British goods and reduced the ability of Britain to compete with aggressive German, Japanese, and American companies on the world market. Tax revenues fell, as did the funding for Britain's welfare state.

By the mid-1970s, Britain came face-to-face with the hard realities of the world economic system. Countries that wish to remain competitive in the modern world must adopt the practices of their most productive competitors, whatever the costs of those practices may be in terms of domestic politics. This is particularly the case for countries such as Britain that must depend on exports for their survival. Britain could either reassert its capitalist traditions or see its economic base continue to crumble. In many ways, then, the impetus for the Thatcher revolution came from Britain's international competitors.

The vulnerability to external pressures experienced by Britain in the aftermath of World War II pales in comparison to the challenges to British sovereignty posed by the European Union (Forster 2002). Britain reluctantly joined the Economic Community in 1971, shifting the locus of key economic decisions from London to Brussels. The Europeanization of the British economy increased dramatically in 1992 with the creation of the European Union, a broad framework for the eventual unification of Western Europe. (See Chapter 1.) If these trends continue, Britain will be relegated to the status of one province of a larger European state, not necessarily the dominant one. Britain has resisted this process—it did not adopt the common European currency in 1999—and some influential British leaders argue that Britain should join the North American Free Trade Agreement (NAFTA) rather than European Union, although this seems unlikely. The economic benefits, according to this argument, would be equivalent and Britain would retain its sovereignty. The "special relationship" with the U.S. would also be retained. This is not the dominant view in Britain, but the point of view does have its adherents (*Christian Science Monitor,* Aug. 12, 1998, 7).

In the meantime, the economic integration of Britain into the European Union is slowly becoming an accomplished fact. British administrators are guided by European rules in economic and environmental matters almost as much as they are by acts of Parliament. Civil rights activists also use the European "Bill of Rights" to plead their cases in British courts (Oliver 1991; Nicol 2001). Britain has been particularly reluctant to abandon its sovereignty in terms of currency, tax, and foreign policy, but all will be challenged by the proposed EU Constitution. A referendum on the European Union has been promised for sometime in 2005 or 2006. A no vote could well end the British capacity to shape the future of Europe.

Tony Blair, for his part, has talked European unity at the same time that he follows the American lead in foreign policy (Gamble 2003). Britain has consistently followed America's lead in the war on terror, including a disastrous involvement in Iraq. The war was justified in terms of stopping terrorism and stripping Iraq of its weapons of mass destruction. The weapons of mass destruction failed to materialize as did links to bin Laden. Both were analyzed by parliamentary reports as were questionable assertions made by the prime minister (House of Commons, 2003; Butler 2004; Hutton 2004). While the prime minister was absolved of direct complicity, his exaggerations and mishandling of the situation were noted. Britain remains mired in Iraq and the British government has urged its citizens to: "stock up on supplies of tinned food, bottled water and medical kits to help them through a terrorist attack" (*Guardian,* July 19, 2004, www). It was also revealed that an al-Queda attack on Parliament had been thwarted.

Although external pressures play an ever-larger role in determining British policy, it would be a mistake to assume that Britain has ceased to be a major actor

on the world scene. This is not the case. Britain is a permanent member of the
United Nations Security Council, a charter member of the G-8 economic club
that determines world economic policy, and one of three main pillars of the
European Union. Indeed, the British position will have much to say about both
the ultimate shape of the EU and the pace of its evolution. When British colonies
demanded independence, moreover, Britain skillfully fashioned the British Commonwealth, an association of former British colonies that continues to serve
Britain's economic interests.

CHALLENGES OF THE PRESENT AND
PROSPECTS FOR THE FUTURE

In Chapter 1, we outlined six characteristics generally associated with "good government": democracy, human rights, stability, quality of life, economic growth,
and concern for the environment. How well does Britain score on these six measures of good government? The answer depends on one's standard of comparison.
Judged within the world community as a whole, Britain scores exceptionally
well, possessing one of the most democratic, stable, humane, and environmentally
conscious political systems in the world. It also has a political system that provides
most of its citizens with a superior quality of life. When Britain is judged in comparison with other states of the first world, however, the picture is less comforting
(Studlar 1996). Britain is clearly a member of the first world, but it is no longer at
the top of that most privileged grouping.

Democracy and Stability

Britain is the world's oldest and most stable democracy, its lone civil war having
occurred in the mid-1600s. The British, however, have begun to question the
way in which they practice democracy. The prime minister and Government,
in the view of many, are too powerful. Others note that there is too little
opportunity for citizen input between elections (Oliver 1991; Brazier 1991).
The winner-take-all nature of British politics is also criticized for creating dramatic shifts in policy whenever one party replaces another (Jeffery 1998).
Labour, for example, nationalized key industries during the 1950s only to see
the Conservatives denationalize them a few years later. In each case, the minority party was helpless to intervene. Dramatic shifts in social and economic policy, moreover, are carried out by Governments that have received well under 50
percent of the popular vote—hardly a popular mandate. Other criticisms
of British democracy focus on the House of Lords and on the lack of formal
minority rights.

Are political reforms likely to be implemented in the near future? The answer
to this question rests largely with the British electorate. The Hereditary Lords
have been stripped of their voting rights and the Blair Government has experimented with proportional representation voting schemes in the elections for
the European Parliament. An American style supreme court is in the works, but

THOMAS COEX / AFP / Getty Images

Nicknamed the "Chunnel," a tunnel beneath the English Channel speeds travel between England and France, facilitating England's economic integration with Europe.

more radical changes such as a written constitution may be difficult to come by. Most British citizens seem reluctant to change a system that has worked so well for so long.

The stability of Britain is not threatened by rebellion or foreign wars, but it, like the United States, is a prime target of terrorism. The growing strength of nationalistic sentiments throughout the United Kingdom, including England, may find the United Kingdom less united. Stability is not an issue, but the location of power is.

Human Rights

Britain does not have a Bill of Rights, but few countries in the world can match Britain's record in the area of social justice. Critics, however, worry that Britain's tradition of tolerance may be showing signs of erosion.

Until very recently, Northern Ireland was a war zone. British troops openly patrolled the streets, and human rights abuses had become commonplace. As the IRA carried its battle to the streets of London, British security forces came under intense pressure to curb IRA terrorism. The threat of the IRA had hardly declined before Britain found itself the center of Islamic terrorist networks attempting to destabilize friendly countries in the Middle East. The Government responded by rushing out a new set of anti-terrorist laws. As in the Irish case, this pressure has led to growing disregard for the rights of suspects and, in extreme cases, to false arrest and imprisonment (Stevens 2003).

The picture is much the same in regard to the fight against crime. Britain has witnessed a dramatic increase in crime over the past decade, and law and order have become a major concern of the British public. Lord Falconer, the minister in charge of reforming the criminal justice system, frankly stated that most people "have a deep and profound sense that the criminal justice system is failing them." (*Guardian*, June 17, 2002, www).

Human rights have also been strained by the growing multiracial character of British society. Britain's black minority complains bitterly of racial discrimination in employment, housing, education, and health care. They also complain bitterly of police brutality. A 2004 Commission for Racial Equality report similarly reported that all but one of the police authorities in England and Wales are "failing in their legal duty toward ethnic communities (*Observer*, June 13, 2004, www). Violence against minorities has also increased. The police, in turn, have placed the blame on growing immigration. The head of the Association of Chief Police Officers called the number of asylum seekers a "tidal" wave and blamed migrants for everything from crime to terror (*Observer*, May 18, 2003, www).

Critics of Britain's human rights advocates also express concern over the Government's new anti-terrorist legislation, claiming, as did the Law Lords, that it violated traditional British rights. They also fear that the enhanced police powers contained in the legislation will pose a threat to all British citizens, not just to terrorists (*Guardian*, Jan 28, 2005, www).

The above problems noted, Britain remains one of the world's most humane societies. Steps are being taken to address the abuses of Britain's ethnic minorities, and the rights of other groups are also being addressed. Gay marriages are allowed in Britain and a bill outlawing the spanking of minors is likely to be passed in the near future (*Observer*, March 7, 2004, www).

Economic Growth and Quality of Life

Britain has traditionally been one of the wealthiest countries in the world. Labour Governments during the early post–World War II era, moreover, enacted sweeping welfare legislation assuring that all of Britain's citizens, not merely the upper classes, would share in the nation's prosperity. Among other things, the Labour legislation guaranteed all citizens free health care, unemployment insurance, retirement benefits, adequate housing, and free education at newly established comprehensive schools. Wealthier citizens retained the right to send their children to exclusive "public" (private) schools and to consult private doctors.

The Thatcher revolution of the 1980s struck back against a culture of dependency and attempted to create a Britain that was "lean and mean" by cutting back on welfare. Productivity increased, but only in certain sectors. Mining and heavy industry could not compete without state subsidies, and most of Britain's older coal mines and steel mills were forced to close (Taylor 2003). Unemployment rolls swelled. British comprehensive schools also continued to turn out graduates and near-graduates possessing few technical skills, a problem that is equally serious in the United States. Indeed, British public schools entered the millennium faced with a shortage of 10,000 teachers and no end in sight to a worsening crisis (*Sunday Times*, Jan. 3, 1999, www). British universities complain that they are no longer competitive on an international scale because of a lack of funds (*Economist*, Nov. 16, 2002, 51). The picture was much the same in regard to health care, with the National Health Service "falling apart," according to representatives of the British Medical Association. Blair himself has made secret trips to government hospitals in an effort to get a better grip on the situation *(Times,* Jan. 14, 1999, www). Reforms have been proposed in both areas, but the problem is money. British universities now will be allowed to charge increased fees, a policy that threatened a revolt with the ruling Labour Party. Increased fees make it more difficult for students from poor backgrounds to enter universities that are already heavily biased in favor of the middle class (*Observer*, Dec. 7, 2003, www). In another policy at odds with Labour's socialist heritage, the Blair Government is also promoting independent (private) schools modeled on Britain's famous elite private schools in an effort to improve the quality of general education. Independent schools are open to students from all classes providing that they can pay the fees. Britain's private schools show better results than their government counterparts (*Economist*, July 3, 2004, 45).

The Thatcher revolution was softened by successive Labour Governments, but its course was not altered. The middle class has prospered with some 25 percent of the British population now being classified as, "wealthy achievers, up from 19 percent a decade ago. The lower ranks of the middle class 'moderate means' now stands at 37 percent up from 33 percent a decade ago." (*Observer*, Nov.23, 2003, www).

The British quality of life is changing in other ways as well. The number of married women has fallen from 74 percent in 1979 to 51 percent in 2000 (*Guardian*, Dec.12, 2001, www). British women also are having fewer children. As a result, Britain, like most European countries, is becoming a graying society. One hundred years ago, there were five employed people to support each retired person. Today, the ratio is approaching one to one. This would not be a major problem if everyone had a pension or adequate savings. Unfortunately, 40 percent of Britain workers do not (*Guardian*, March 2, 2004, www).

Greater prosperity has also brought a more hectic lifestyle. Rather than bringing happiness, affluence finds a growing number of British people depressed, unhappy in their relationships, and alienated from civic society (*Guardian*, Feb. 22, 2003, www). Drug use has also increased, with recent statistics indicating that "more than 5 million people regularly use cannabis, 2.4 million ecstasy, and 2 million amphetamines and cocaine" (*Observer*, April 2, 2002, www).

Britain, also becoming a **dual society:** *a society of managers and skilled workers who prosper in the more productive environment of the post-Thatcher era, and a society of minimally skilled and unemployed workers who are locked in a culture of poverty (New York Times,* Oct. 5, 1999, www). The minorities are particularly disadvantaged, with unemployment among blacks and Muslims being two and three times the national average, respectively (*Economist*, Jan. 8, 2005, www). Unemployment among youth, particularly minority and working-class youth, is particularly severe.

The Environment

Britain is one of the world's more environmentally concerned countries, but less so than most other states of the first world. Traditionally, Japan, Germany, France, the United States, and Canada all had stronger environmental regulations than does Britain (Weale 1992). Britain's nuclear record has been a particular cause for concern (*New York Times,* Apr. 19, 2000, www). Nuclear power had been curtailed, but is now making a comeback (*Guardian*, May 8, 2005, www).

The reasons for Britain's slower response to its environmental challenges are largely economic in nature. Britain's industrial plant is older than that of most other advanced industrial states, making its cleanup costs proportionally greater. Excessive environmental regulations would also cripple the industrial centers of Northern England and Scotland, areas already suffering from chronic unemployment. The choice between protecting the environment and preserving jobs is difficult.

Britain's membership in the European Union has brought with it a growing body of European environmental legislation, much of it far more rigorous than that implemented by Parliament. It is the European legislation that will shape the future course of environmental legislation in Britain. According to recent surveys, stronger environmental legislation will be welcomed by a majority of the British public (Barr, Gilg, and Ford 2003).

Prospects for the Future

The challenges facing Britain today are manageable. Britain's commitment to democracy is beyond question, and the political debate over constitutional reform merely aspires to make one of the world's oldest democracies even more responsive to the demands of its citizens. The recent uproar over human rights violations, while justified, does not alter the fact that Britain remains one of the most tolerant societies in the world.

Britain's inability to provide a high quality of life for all of its citizens is a more daunting problem. The growing emergence of a dual society, one rich and one poor, is deeply rooted in the structure of British society and does not submit to easy solution.

Ironically, Britain's reluctant entry to the European Union could prove to be an economic boon. Free access to the European market has stimulated the growth of Britain's more productive industries. American and Japanese firms, moreover, have chosen Britain as the preferred point of entry to the EU market. Roughly 40 percent of both American and Japanese corporate investment, for example, is now in England, and approximately one-fourth of all British manufacturing is now in foreign hands. Foreign investors create new jobs and new prosperity, even though they inevitably transform the British way of doing things. Further progress, however, may depend on Britain's acceptance of the euro as the common currency of the European Union.

REFERENCES

Adonis, Andrew. 1990. *Parliament Today.* Manchester, UK: Manchester University Press.

Almond, Gabriel A., and Sidney Verba. 1965. *The Civic Culture: Political Attitudes and Democracy in Five Nations.* Boston, MA: Little, Brown.

Atkins, Burton. 1988–89. "Judicial Selection in Context: The American and English Experience." *Kentucky Law Journal* 77(3): 577–618.

Atkins, Burton. 1990. "Interventions and Power in Judicial Hierarchies: Appellate Courts in England and the United States." *Law and Society Review* 24(1): 71–103.

Ball, Stuart and Ian Holliday, eds. 2002. *Mass Conservatism: The Conservatives and the Public Since the 1880s.* Portland, OR: Frank Cass.

Barber, James. 1991. *The Prime Minister Since 1945.* Oxford, UK: Blackwell.

Barr, Stewart, Andrew Gilg, and Nicholas Ford. 2003 (August). "'Environmentalism' in Britain Today—How do People Value the Environment?" *Town and Country Planning,* 72(7): 216–18.

Benn, A. 1979. *The Case for a Constitutional Premiership.* Institute for Workers' Control. (No city listed, London presumed.)

Blackburn, Robert. 1995. *The Electoral System in Britain.* New York: St. Martin's.

Brand, Jack. 1992. *British Parliamentary Parties: Policy and Power.* Oxford, UK: Clarendon Press.

Brazier, Rodney. 1991. *Constitutional Reform: Re-Shaping the British Political System.* Oxford, UK: Clarendon Press.

Budge, Ian. 2004. *The New British Politics.* Harlow, England: Pearson Longman.

Butler, David, and Dennis Kavanagh. 1998. *The British General Election of 1997.* New York: St. Martin's Press.

Childs, David. 1992. *Britain Since 1945: A Political History.* 3rd ed. London: Routledge.

Churchill, Winston. 1956. *A History of the English-Speaking Peoples.* New York: Dodd-Mead.

Conley, Frank. 1990. *General Elections Today.* Manchester, UK: Manchester University Press.

Crewe, Ivor. 1993. "Parties and Electors." In *The Developing British Political System in the 1990s,* 3rd ed. (pp. 83–111), ed. Ian Budge and David McKay. London: Longman.

Denver David. 2003. *Elections and Voters in Britain* New York: Palgrave.

Forster, Anthony. 2002. *Euroscepticism in British Politics: Opposition to Europe in the Conservative and Labour Parties since 1945.* New York: Routledge.

Gamble, Andrew. 2003. *Between Europe and America: The Future of British Politics.* New York: Palgrave Macmillan.

Gamble, Andrew, and Tony Wright. 1998 (April–June). "The Conservative Predicament." *Political Quarterly* 69(2): 107–9.

Garnett, Mark, and Ian Gilmour. 1998 (April–June). "The Lessons of Defeat." *Political Quarterly* 69(2): 126–27.

Garrard, John. 2002. *Democratization in Britain: Elites, Civil Society and Reform Since 1800.* Basingstoke: Palgrave.

Green Britain. 2001 (July). Environment, 43(6): 7.

Guttsman, William L. 1963. *The British Political Elite.* London: MacGivvon and Kee.

Hanson, A. H., and Malcolm Walles. 1990. *Governing Britain: A Guidebook to Political Institutions.* 5th ed. London: Fontana Press.

Harris, Paul and Hinsliff, Gaby. 2002 (May 26). "Cherie Booth Attacks Sexist Judges." The *Observer,* May 26, 2002, 10.

Hennessy, P., cited in James Barber. 1991. *The Prime Minister Since 1945.* Oxford: Blackwell, p. 77.

Hofferbert, Richard I., and Ian Budge. 1992 (Apr.). "The Party Mandate and the Westminster Model: Election Programs and Government Spending in Britain: 1948–1955." *British Journal of Political Science* 22(2): 151–83.

House of Commons. 2004 (July 14). *Review of Intelligence on Weapons of Mass Destruction*. Report of a Committee of Privy Counselors. Chairman: The Rt. Hon. The Lord Butler of Brockwell KG GCB CVO. London: The Stationery Office.

House of Commons Foreign Affairs Committee. 2003 (July 31). *Foreign Policy Aspects of the War Against Terrorism*. Tenth Report of Session 2002–2003. London: The Stationery Office Limited. HC 405.

Hutton, Lord. 2004 (January 28). *Report of the Inquiry into the Circumstances Surrounding the Death of Dr. David Kelly C.M.G.* HC 247. London: The Stationery Office.

Ichijo, Atsuko. 2004. *Scottish Nationalism and the Idea of Europe*. Portland, OR: Frank Cass.

James, Simon. 1992. *British Cabinet Government*. London: Routledge.

Jeffery, Charlie. 1998 (July–September). "Electoral Reform: Learning from Germany." *Political Quarterly* 69(3): 241–251.

Judge, David. 1993. *The Parliamentary State*. London: Sage Publications.

Keating, Michael. 1998 (Winter). "Reforging the Union: Devolution and Constitutional Change in the United Kingdom." *Publius* 28(1): 217.

Kennedy, Simon. 1998 (February). "New Labour and the Reorganization of British Politics." *Monthly Review* 49(9): 14–26.

King, Anthony B., Ivor Crewe, David Denver, Kenneth Newton, Philip Norton, David Sanders, and Patrick Seyd, eds. 1993. *Britain at the Polls: 1992*. Chatham, NJ: Chatham House.

MacShane, Denis. 1998 (November). "Open Lists Will Give Us Closed Minds." *New Statesman (1996)* 127(4413): 30.

Maor, Moshe. 1998 (July). "The Relationship between Government and Opposition in the Bundestag and House of Commons in the Run-up to the Maastricht Treaty." *West European Politics* 21(3): 187–207.

Marinetto, Michael. 2003 (Feb.). "Who Wants to be an Active Citizen? The Politics and Practice of Community Involvement." *Sociology*, 37(1): 103–121.

Mathews, Jessica Tuchman, ed. 1991. *Preserving the Global Environment: The Challenge of Shared Leadership*. New York: W. W. Norton.

Matthews, Kevin. 2004. *Fatal Influence: The Impact of Ireland on British Politics, 1920–1925*. Dublin: Dublin University Press.

McCrone, Robert Steward, Richard Kiely, and Frank Bechhofer. 1998 (November). "Who Are We? Problematising National Identity." *The Sociological Review*, p. 629.

McIlroy, John. 1998 (December). "The Enduring Alliance? Trade Unions and the Making of New Labour, 1994–1997." *British Journal of Industrial Relations* 36(4): 537.

Mowlam, Mo. 2002. *Momentum: The Struggle for Peace, Politics and the People*. London: Hodder and Stoughton.

Nagler, N. 1979. "The Image of the Civil Service in Britain." *Public Administration* 127–42.

Nairn, Tom. 1994. *The Enchanted Glass: Britain and Its Monarchy*. London: Vintage.

Nicol, Danny. 2001. *EC Membership and the Judicialization of British Politics*. New York: Oxford University Press.

Oliver, Dawn. 1991. *Government in the United Kingdom*. Philadelphia: Open University Press.

Peele, Gillian. 2004. *Governing the UK: British Politics in the 21st Century*. Malden, MA: Blackwell.

Piachaud, David. 1993 (June). "What's Wrong with Fabianism?" *Fabian Society Pamphlet 558*.

Powell, David. 2004. *British Politics, 1910–1935: The Crisis of the Party System*. New York: Routledge.

Punnett, R. M. 1988. *British Government and Politics*. 5th ed. Prospect Heights, IL: Waveland Press.

Richards, Steve. 1998 (November). "The Wars of the Lords Will Go On and On." *New Statesman* 127(4413): 6.

Riddell, Peter. 1998. *Parliament Under Pressure*. London: Victor Gollancz.

Rose, Richard. 1989. *Politics in England: Change and Persistence*. 5th ed. London: Macmillan.

Sampson, Anthony. 1982. *The Changing Anatomy of Britain: Democracy in Crisis*. London: Hodder and Stoughton.

Sampson, Anthony. 1992. *The Essential Anatomy of Britain: Democracy in Crisis*. London: Hodder and Stoughton.

Sampson, Anthony. 2004. *Who Runs This Place? The Anatomy of Britain in the 21ˢᵗ Century*. London: John Murray.

Scott, John. 1991. *Who Rules Britain?* Cambridge: Polity Press.

Sked, Alan, and Chris Cook. 1993. *Post-War Britain: A Political History*. London: Penguin Books.

Smith, Alastair. 2004. *Election Timing*. New York: Cambridge.

Stevens, Sir John. 2003 (April 17). Stevens Enquiry.

Studlar, Donley. 1996. *Great Britain: Decline or Renewal?* Boulder, CO: Westview Press.

Taylor, Andrew. 2003. *The NUM and British Politics*. Burlington, VT: Ashgate.

Thatcher, Margaret. 1993. *The Downing Street Years*. New York: HarperCollins.

Watkins, Alan. 1998. *The Road to Number 10: From Bonar Law to Tony Blair*. London: Duckworth.

Weale, Albert. 1992. *The New Politics of Pollution*. Manchester, UK: Manchester University Press.

White, Michael. 2004 (May 13). "Pressure Grows for Blair to Go." The *Guardian* http://politics.guardian.co.uk/iraq/story/0,12956,121552..., accessed 5/13/04.

Whiteley, Paul, Patrick Seyd, and Jeremy Richardson. 1994. *True Blues: The Politics of Conservative Party Membership*. Oxford: Oxford University Press.

Willetts, David. 1998 (April–June). "Conservative Renewal." *Political Quarterly* 69(2): 110–117.

Woodward, E. L. 1962. *History of England: From Roman Times to the End of World War I*. New York: Harper & Row.

Population:
60,424,213 (2004 estimate)

Life expectancy at birth:
79 years (total population)
76 years (men)
83 years (women)

Literacy:
99 percent of people age 15
and over can read and write
(2000 estimate)

Capital:
Paris

Per capita income:
$27,600

4

France

Politics in the Fifth Republic

Two nations, more than any others, have shaped the political traditions of the Western world: Britain and France. French culture was the preferred culture of the European aristocracy, and the French language long reigned as the international language of culture, commerce, and diplomacy. The French empire spanned the globe, bringing French civilization to broad areas of Asia, Africa, and the Americas, while France's Napoleonic Codes provide the foundation of most legal systems in the world today (Singer and Langdon 1998).

France, moreover, is one of the small handful of states that dictate world economic and social policy. France is a nuclear power and a key member of both the UN Security Council and the G-8 club of industrial powers. France is also one of the core states in the European Union and has been a driving force in efforts to create a European suprastate. Little happens in the world arena without the participation of the French.

To study France simply because it is a major power, however, would be short-sighted. One studies France because it possesses one of the most innovative political systems of recent history. While the British have remained wedded to the past, the French have treated their political institutions with a disdain that other countries find disconcerting.

Beyond politics, one studies France for its art, its music, its language, its cuisine, its philosophy, its science, and its quality of life. It is doubtful that the citizens of any other nation squeeze more personal enjoyment out of life than do the French (Zeldin 1982).

The opening of Euro Disney, an American-style theme park near Paris, met with mixed responses from French citizens. To critics, it was seen as another example of foreign encroachment on French culture.

Despite their country's power and exceptional quality of life, the French find themselves in something of a malaise. Once the most powerful nation in Europe, France now is overshadowed by the United States, Japan, and Germany. France remains a major power, but not a power of the first rank. French culture, moreover, is under siege. English has replaced French as the international language of culture, commerce, and diplomacy, and France's leading scientific research is now published in English as well as French. Even the French cinema, long Europe's most innovative, is struggling to survive in a pop culture dominated by Hollywood.

In the ensuing discussion of French politics, we will trace the evolution of French political traditions and describe the institutions that give expression to those traditions today. Next, we will examine the elites, political parties, pressure groups, and citizens who give life to French politics, as well as the cultural, economic, and international context in which those politics take place. Special emphasis will be placed on the evolution of democracy in France, an evolution that has been far more conflictive than that of Britain (described in the preceding chapter). While British political traditions have stressed tolerance and compromise, those of France have been characterized by revolution and violence.

FRANCE IN HISTORICAL PERSPECTIVE

France possesses two contradictory political traditions: an authoritarian tradition and a democratic tradition. The latter has sometimes bordered on anarchy (Brubaker 1992; Hazareesingh 1994).

Efforts to reconcile these conflicting political traditions have not been easy for the French, but they have made for interesting politics.

France's emergence as an independent power is generally traced to the rise of Charlemagne, King of the Franks, in approximately 800 A.D. Britain would not be unified for another two centuries and the German states would remain divided among themselves well into the nineteenth century.

The evolution of the French state, like that of the British state, began with efforts by feudal kings to extract ever-greater financial sacrifices from their subjects. In Britain, the monarch's need for money led to power sharing, first with the Lords and eventually with the Commons. In France, the need for money led to authoritarianism and to the establishment of a centralized bureaucracy that would tax the masses with ruthless efficiency.

French kings ruled with the support of the Catholic Church and the landed aristocracy, the latter having received huge land grants in return for their service to the crown. The Church legitimized the monarchy by preaching the divine right of kings. In return, it received absolute control of religious life in France. The aristocracy, for its part, subsidized the monarchy and maintained order in the countryside, its sons staffing the ever-expanding bureaucracy. The Church, too, provided the state with skilled administrators, the most illustrious of whom was Cardinal Richelieu (1624) (Wright 1987). Richelieu modernized the state apparatus and laid the groundwork for a modern standing army.

Over time, a "haute bourgeoisie" (big businessmen) of rich commoners replaced France's self-indulgent aristocracy in the upper echelons of the political structure and used its wealth to buy hereditary titles (Popkin 1994). Unlike their British counterparts, however, the French bourgeoisie did not serve as a counterweight to the monarch. Rather, they chose to glory in their association with royalty. Supporting this grand edifice of royalty, aristocracy, church, and bourgeoisie were the French masses. By the end of the eighteenth century, the masses had been reduced to famine and had nothing more to give. The state, for its part, was bankrupt.

On May 5, 1789, King Louis XVI convened the "Estates General" in a desperate attempt to raise new taxes for his faltering regime. The Estates General was an irregular parliamentary body that had evolved to give expression to the three estates of the nation: the nobility (First Estate), the clergy (Second Estate), and the commoners (Third Estate). The king, standing above the three

In this depiction of the plight of the French peasant, an old farmer is bowed down by the weight of the privileged aristocracy and clergy. Meanwhile, birds and rabbits, protected by unfair game laws, nibble away at his crops.

estates, considered himself the embodiment of the nation. The nobility were represented in the Estates General by 330 deputies, the clergy by 326 deputies, and the common people by 661 deputies. Voting was to be by estate or order, a procedure that made the voice of the nobility and the clergy equal to that of the masses. The deputies of the Third Estate protested, demanding that voting be "by head" rather than by order. The king refused, and on July 14, 1789, Paris erupted in revolution. The king, disguised as a servant, was seized in flight two years after the revolution. The Cathedral of Paris was seized and renamed the Temple of Reason.

A newly proclaimed National Assembly declared France to be a democratic republic, issuing the *Declaration of the Rights of Man and Citizen,* a document that stands beside the American *Declaration of Independence* as one of the world's fundamental statements of human liberty (Popkin 1994). France's revolutionaries, however, had little experience with either democracy or human rights, and the National Assembly soon fell under the sway of extremists demanding vengeance for centuries of aristocratic oppression. In a wave of mass hysteria, churches were sacked and aristocrats were hunted as animals. Having destroyed the monarchy, the revolution then turned upon itself, finding traitors in every shadow. Tens of

party in shambles following their 2002 debacle now was looking forward to the 2007 elections with renewed optimism.

The single-member, simple-majority format of French elections has encouraged French political parties to coalesce into two reasonably well-defined blocs—the left and the right. As there can be only one winner, like-minded parties must come together if an ideologically acceptable candidate is to have any hope of victory. Nevertheless, the single-member, simple-majority format of French elections also allows France's diverse political factions to retain their identity during the first round of the electoral process. Only when the relative strength of the various parties and factions has been determined does the bargaining process begin in earnest. Thus, France's single-member, simple-majority electoral system forces fragmented political groups into grand coalitions, or "party families," but it does not force them into cohesive political parties on the pattern of the British Conservative or Labour Parties (Rae 1967; Schlesinger and Schlesinger 1998).

Executive Power in France:
The President and the Prime Minister

The de Gaulle Constitution presented to the French voters in the summer of 1958 was designed to provide France with an executive capable of taking decisive and sustained action. The president, not the parliament, was to become the centerpiece of the new political system (Quermonne 1993; Massot 1993).

Although he created a strong presidency, de Gaulle was reluctant to transform France into a presidential system on the American pattern. Rather, he chose to create a hybrid political system in which France would possess both a president and a prime minister. The president would establish the broad parameters of public policy; and the prime minister, who had been nominated by the president, would guide the president's program through the parliament (Elgie 1993).

The President. The president is by far the most powerful player in French politics. Some of the president's powers are enumerated in the Constitution, while others have been "implied" from a generous interpretation of its articles. Still other presidential powers have been established by precedent or have resulted from the broader informal context of French politics.

The enumerated powers of the French president are sweeping, but they are not without limits. The president names the prime minister and Cabinet and can, presumably, change both at will (Stevens 1992). The National Assembly can force a prime minister to resign by means of a vote of no confidence, but the president is not forced to honor that resignation. As a practical matter, the president has little to gain by retaining a prime minister who lacks the confidence of the National Assembly, the latter merely destroying the program of the former. Should the prime minister and the National Assembly become deadlocked, the president has the option of dissolving the National Assembly and calling for new elections. The president cannot veto legislation but can force the National National Assembly to reconsider legislation. This, given the divisiveness of the National Assembly, is often enough to kill legislation the president opposes. Treaties calling for the expenditure of funds must be ratified by Parliament.

The president is also the commander-in-chief of the armed forces and may negotiate and ratify treaties. These provisions have provided French presidents with total dominance in the areas of defense and foreign policy. Beyond this, Article 5 of the Constitution calls upon the president to "see that the Constitution is respected" and to "ensure by his arbitration, the regular functioning of the governmental authorities." While the exact meaning of this article has been subject to considerable debate, it is certainly sweeping in its potential implications.

The Constitution of the Fifth Republic goes on to state that it is the president who shall make appointments to the civil and military posts of the state. This clause, in itself, assures that the president will be the state's primary distributor of patronage. Chirac and the UMP now control all major and political positions in France and have created what the French newspaper *Le Monde* call the Chiracan state (*Le Monde,* July 7, 2004). The term of the presidency, moreover, is five years, thereby providing French presidents with sufficient time to pursue long-range policies that might otherwise be avoided by politicians required to go to the electorate on a more frequent basis. Finally, de Gaulle provided the president with the power to rule by decree during states of emergency. The emergency powers of the president were very much on de Gaulle's mind in drafting the constitution, for as noted above, he was brought to power by the threat of civil war. These emergency powers were used to quell the revolt of the generals in Algeria but have not been used since.

The enumerated powers of the French president exceed those of the American president. The framers of the American Constitution were intent on avoiding the tyranny of the executive. De Gaulle crafted his Constitution to counter the tyranny (and immobilization) of the legislature. Indeed, de Gaulle would write to his son that he viewed the president as being a "popular monarch" (Hayward 1993).

The presidential powers explicitly enumerated in the Constitution are not open to serious challenge. This is less the case in regard to the president's implied powers and the presidential powers derived from precedents established by de Gaulle during the formative years of the Fifth Republic (Massot 1993).

In this regard, it should be noted that the French Constitution is a particularly vague document that invites interpretation. As mentioned previously, Article 5 calls upon the president to "ensure by his arbitration, the regular functioning of the governmental authorities," a passage that continues to stir heated debate among French jurists.

In point of fact, de Gaulle interpreted all of the clauses of the constitution in an imperial fashion. De Gaulle, for example, left little doubt that the decision to dissolve both Governments and Assemblies rested squarely with the president. De Gaulle also forced his prime ministers to "resign in advance," thereby establishing the precedent that it was within the president's power to change Governments at will (Massot 1993).

Many of the powers of the president are "shared" between the president and the prime minister, the naming of the Cabinet ministers and the nomination of senior administrative officials being cases in point. In these and other instances, de Gaulle considered the countersignature of the prime minister to be little more than a formality and acted accordingly (Massot 1993).

De Gaulle established the tradition of an imperial presidency, a tradition maintained by his successors (Duhamel 1991). As a frustrated leader of the opposition, François Mitterrand, would complain of then-President Valery Giscard d'Estaing:

> [The] president of the republic can do anything, the president of the republic does everything, the president of the republic substitutes for the government, the government for the parliament, thus the president of the republic substitutes himself for parliament. The president of the republic takes care of everything, even the gardens along the Seine (Tiersky 1994, 53).

President Mitterrand would later comment, however, that "the institutions were not of my intention, but they serve me well" (Massot 1993, 38).

The formal and implied powers of the French president are further augmented by a variety of informal powers. If the party of the president controls the National Assembly, it is the president and not the prime minister who determines the legislative program. The prime minister will undoubtedly be an important member of the president's party or coalition, but his or her position will be secondary to that of the president. This means, in effect, that a president supported by a majority in the Parliament controls both of the major branches of government, the legislative and the executive. *It is only when the president does not have the support of a majority of the deputies in the National Assembly that a clear division of power between the president and prime minister exists.* This occurred for the first time in the two-year period between 1986 and 1988, a period known as the **cohabitation.** It occurred again during the years from 1993 to 1995 and 1997 to 2002. Indeed, nine years of cohabitation have made it a regular feature of French politics. During a period of cohabitation, the powers of the prime minister equal those of the president, a topic to be discussed shortly.

The president's informal powers include the ability to mold French public opinion (Perry 1998). The president is the centerpiece of French media coverage, and French presidents have used their domination of the media to cultivate an image of paternal aloofness that places them above the petty squabbles of ordinary politicians (Stevens 1992). De Gaulle's imperial grandeur gave birth to this style, but it was refined, if not extended, by his successors (Giesbert 1990).

The Prime Minister and Cabinet: The Council of Ministers. What powers, then, accrue to the prime minister? This is not an easy question to answer. In contrast to its lengthy elaboration of presidential powers, the Constitution of the Fifth Republic merely stipulates that "the Government shall determine and direct the policy of the nation" (Article 20) and "the prime minister shall direct the operation of the Government" (Article 21). Clearly, the role of the prime minister did not weigh heavily on the mind of Charles de Gaulle. Be this as it may, the power to "determine and direct the policy of the nation" would seem to rival the powers of the presidency itself (Wright 1993). As noted above, moreover, the appointment of Cabinet ministers and senior officials also requires the approval of the prime minister.

In constitutional terms, then, the division of powers between the president and the prime minister is characterized by considerable ambiguity. As a practical matter, the balance of power between the two executives depends on which coalition of political parties controls the National Assembly. If the president's coalition controls the National Assembly, the role of the prime minister is that of "floor manager" for the president. The president selects most of the members of a "friendly" Government (Council of Ministers) and presides over their meetings. Indeed, Mitterrand selected his first Cabinet upon being elected the president of France before naming the prime minister who was to head that Cabinet (Giesbert 1990). Senior ministers, moreover, have direct access to the president and often bypass the prime minister entirely. The picture is much the same in regard to public opinion and the media. Not only do the media focus primarily on the president, but much of the media attention that does accrue to the prime minister is negative. When things go well, presidents assume credit for their programs. When things go poorly, presidents change prime ministers.

Cohabitation: Who Rules France? The first two decades of the Fifth Republic were characterized by strong presidents supported by clear majorities in the National Assembly. Prime ministers were secondary figures, changed at will by the president. This precedent was shattered with the initiation of the first period of cohabitation in 1986. President Mitterrand, a socialist, was confronted with a National Assembly overwhelmingly dominated by the parties of the political right. The strongest of these was the Gaullist RPR led by Jacques Chirac (the current president of France). It was within Mitterrand's power to name a prime minister from within the ranks of the socialists, but little was to be gained by the appointment of a socialist Government that lacked the votes required to implement its program (Stevens 1992). The people, moreover, had spoken.

Chirac, supported by a majority coalition in the National Assembly, wasted little time in fulfilling his constitutional charge to "determine and direct the policy of the nation." The cornerstone of Chirac's program was the liberalization of the French economy, including the privatization of key government-owned industries. Chirac also rolled back several of the welfare programs that the socialists had put in place upon assuming power in 1981. Mitterrand continued to dominate the areas of foreign policy and defense, but not without some pressure from Chirac in these areas as well.

In spite of its brevity, the initial period of "cohabitation" demonstrated the extent to which de Gaulle's imperial presidency depended on the ability of the president to maintain a majority in the National Assembly. Mitterrand was the first president of the Fifth Republic to face a hostile majority in the National Assembly, and he responded by allowing the opposition to form a Government. More importantly, he allowed a hostile Government to implement its programs. In setting these precedents, Mitterrand enabled the Constitution of the Fifth Republic to evolve into an instrument that promoted both democracy and stability (Ardagh

1990). Not to have done so would, in all probability, have spelled the end of the Fifth Republic.

In addition to redefining the powers of the prime minister, the first period of cohabitation also illustrated the problems inherent in having dual executives of equal authority. As described by Tiersky:

> At a meeting of heads of government, would Mitterrand or Chirac represent France? When heads of government and foreign ministers met, would Chirac sit with his foreign minister, Jean-Bernard Raimond, or would Mitterrand? At the first G-7 meeting to face the French cohabitation regime, an additional chair was found. But another time Chirac gave way to the president, and yet another time the foreign minister, Raimond, was made to give up his place to the prime minister, so that Chirac could sit at the table alongside Mitterrand. Throughout these humiliating shenanigans, Mitterrand and Chirac both repeated solemnly and unconvincingly to the international press that "France speaks with a single voice" (Tiersky 1994, 57).

The second experiment in cohabitation was to occur between 1993 and 1995, a period that coincided with the final years of the Mitterrand presidency. As in the earlier case, Mitterrand allowed the leaders of the right to form a Government while he returned to a position of critical aloofness. Unlike Chirac, Mr. Balladur, the new rightist prime minister, went out of his way to work in cooperation with the socialist president. While harmony would be too strong a word to describe France's second experiment in cohabitation, the easy relationship between the two leaders demonstrated that cohabitation could work effectively. Balladur, in retrospect, was also preparing for the 1995 presidential elections and spared no effort to demonstrate his centrist credentials. The strategy was not successful, and Balladur finished behind Jacques Chirac, a member of his own party, in the first-round elections.

Having crushed the left in the 1993 National Assembly elections, the right, led by Jacques Chirac, captured the presidency in 1995. Chirac would thus have three years to re-establish the imperial presidency and implement the program of the right before the next round of mandatory legislative elections in 1998. Chirac, however, dissolved the National Assembly in April of 1997, hoping to retain his legislative majority for an additional five years. This proved to be a disastrous gamble, for the left swept to a dazzling victory in the 1997 elections, crippling the program of the right, and forcing Chirac to share power with a socialist prime minister, Lionel Jospin (Szarka 1997). Cohabitation had become a standard feature of French political life. To add insult to injury, Chirac also saw control of his own party pass to one of his main adversaries.

Stunned by the magnitude of the disaster that he had brought upon himself and his party, Chirac seemed to go into retreat while the socialist prime minister tackled the affairs of state (Lawday 1998). Indeed, it was not until 1999, midway through his term, that Chirac began to counterattack and reassert his authority, a move that the French newspaper, *Le Monde,* interpreted as Chirac's attempt to lay the groundwork for the 2002 presidential election (*Le Monde,* Jan. 2, 1999, 2). The ploy was successful and Chirac scored a dazzling victory in the 2002 elections. The imperial presidency had returned (Grunberg 2003).

In sum, then, the balance of power between the president and prime minister during periods of cohabitation is still evolving (Patrait 2002). In many ways, it is as if France has two political systems: one system when the same party family controls both the presidency and the National Assembly, and another when power is split between the left and right. While others find this arrangement confusing, the French, always skeptical of politicians, seem to relish their discomfort (Duhamel and Mechet 1998). Be this as it may, many French political analysts have increasingly blamed cohabitation for immobilizing the French political process. To paraphrase *Le Monde,* "Everything demonstrates that cohabitation is a deceptive system that accentuates the risks of blockage, paralyzes the (popular) will, and stifles initiative (*Le Monde, les dossiers en ligue,* 1998). The tensions between the prime minister and the president, moreover, show no signs of easing (*Le Monde,* Feb. 27, 2000, www).

The Parliament versus the President.   The Constitution of the Fifth Republic and the Constitution of the United States provide an interesting study in contrasts. The Constitution of United States delineates in great detail what the American executive can and cannot do. The French Constitution, by contrast, stipulates in great detail what the French parliament can and cannot do. The French Constitution, for example, stipulates that all "laws" must be passed by Parliament. Having said this, the Constitution goes on to establish a clear distinction between "laws" and "regulations." Regulations do not require parliamentary approval.

De Gaulle had little respect for legislatures, the members of which, in his view, placed self-interest before the greater interests of France. In framing the Constitution of the Fifth Republic, he sought to assure that the Parliament would not be in a position to jeopardize the effective functioning of the state.

Parliamentary approval is required for legislation in the areas of civil rights, criminal and civil law, finance, taxation, nationalization of private property, employment, health, education, welfare, the organization of local government, and the declaration of war (Article 34, Title 5). In areas not specifically designated as "law," the executive has established the precedent of ruling by decrees that carry the full weight of the law (Safran 1991). The areas of defense and foreign policy, while often debated by Parliament, have been the almost exclusive domain of presidential decree (Safran 1991). Should the Parliament fail to reach a decision on a finance bill within 70 days, moreover, "the provisions of the bill may be enforced by ordinance" (Constitution, 5–47).

Parliament has been weakened in other ways as well. Issues on which Parliament is unwilling to act can be taken directly to the people in the form of a referendum (Brechon 1993). If approved by the majority of the electorate, they become law. It is the Government, moreover, that sets the agenda of Parliament. Unlike the United States Congress, the French parliament cannot avoid an issue simply by ignoring it. The Government can also force the Parliament to accept "blocked" legislation, in which Government bills must be accepted or rejected

---

Chambers of the French Parliament

National Assembly
- 577 members
- Maximum five-year terms
- Elected by universal suffrage
- Determines final version of legislation
- Dominant chamber of Parliament

Senate
- 321 members
- Nine-year terms
- Elected by electoral college
- Formal powers—to delay and obstruct legislation

---

without modification. A critical dimension of "blocked bills" is the requirement that the prime minister submit his or her resignation to the president if the legislation fails. Placing the fate of a Government on the line raises the stakes of political debate, for the collapse of a Government could well lead to the dissolution of the National Assembly and new elections. This prospect is relished by few deputies, and most blocked bills do succeed (Emeri 1993).

The weakness of Parliament is also evident in the fact that it is the president, not the National Assembly, who names the prime minister.[1] The National Assembly may bring down a Government by forcing a vote of no confidence (census in French parlance), but the President is not forced to honor that vote.

The National Assembly and the Senate.   The French parliament consists of two chambers, the National Assembly and the Senate. The 577 members of the National Assembly are elected by universal suffrage for terms not to exceed five years. The president of the Republic has broad latitude in dissolving the National Assembly, but its dissolution must be followed within three weeks by the election of a new National Assembly (Stevens 2003). The 321 members of the Senate are elected for nine-year terms by an electoral college that consists of the vast majority of France's elected politicians, including the members of the National Assembly, some 3,000 members of departmental (provincial) councils, and more than 100,000 members of city councils. The dominance of departmental and city councils in the selection of senators provides the Senate with a strong provincial orientation. French citizens residing in France's overseas territories also find representation in the Senate. The Senate cannot be dissolved by the president.

All bills are considered by both chambers. If both approve a bill, it is sent to the president for signature. Should the National Assembly and Senate pass conflicting versions of a bill, three procedures are used to reconcile their differences: (1) a period of shuttle diplomacy (*navette*) may take place in which informal efforts are made to work out the differences between the two versions of the bill; (2) the Government may request that a formal conference committee be con-

---

[1] Members of the Parliament, moreover, may not serve in the Government. To do so, they must resign their seats in Parliament.

THOMAS COEX / AFP / Getty Images

Representatives in the National Assembly are elected for terms of up to five years. The National Assembly is the dominant chamber of Parliament, with the Senate's powers consisting mainly of delay and obstruction.

vened to work out a compromise bill; or (3) the Government may request each chamber to reconsider the legislation. Of these procedures, the conference committee is the most common (Safran 1991). If it proves impossible to reconcile the differences between the National Assembly and the Senate, it is the National Assembly, upon the request of the Government, that determines the final version of the legislation. In this instance, the passage of a bill requires an absolute majority of all members of the National Assembly, not merely those members present and voting (Constitution 5–44).

The National Assembly, then, is the dominant chamber of Parliament, with the formal powers of the Senate being those of delay and obstruction. By and large, the obstructive power of the Senate is inversely proportional to the size and cohesion of the dominant coalition in the National Assembly. The less cohesive the National Assembly, the stronger the voice of the Senate. The Senate is also particularly sensitive to issues that influence local finance (*Le Figaro*, June 1, 2004, www).

How a Bill Becomes a Law. Both the Government and individual legislators have the right to introduce legislation. The former are referred to as Government bills (projects), the latter as private-member bills (propositions). As might be expected, Government bills fare much better in the legislative process than private-member bills. Among other things, it is the Government that determines the order in which legislation is considered. Once a Government bill is introduced into the National Assembly, it is sent to the Council of State for an advisory opinion on its legality. The bill may also be sent to the Economic and Social Council for its opinion. The Economic and Social Council provides French pressure groups with a formal mechanism for expressing their views on pending legislation.

Bills then are assigned to the appropriate committee. The committee studies the bill to examine its compatibility with existing legislation, often making minor amendments. Such amendments tend to be of a technical nature and often have the prior approval of the Government. Unlike American practice, committees cannot change the intent of the bill. The bill then is scheduled for debate by the full National Assembly. That debate will be vigorous, but its influence in shaping the final version of the bill will depend largely upon the strength of the Government's coalition in Parliament. The stronger the ruling coalition, the fewer amendments will be tolerated (Prost and Jacout,1993; *Le Figaro,* July 17, 2004, www). In the case of a "blocked bill," no amendments are permitted and the National Assembly either must accept or reject the Government bill as it stands. Once a bill passes in the National Assembly, it is sent to the Senate and the process repeats itself. If the Senate version of the bill differs from that of the National Assembly, the two versions of the bill are reconciled by the techniques discussed above. Once passed in the National Assembly and the Senate, a bill is sent to the Government for the necessary signatures and then to the president for his or her signature.

If a president disapproves of the legislation—a likely circumstance during periods of cohabitation—three options are available.

1. *First, the legislation can be returned to the Parliament for reconsideration.* This may be an effective strategy in killing bills that lack a firm majority, but it can do little to alter the will of a determined Parliament.

2. *Second, the president can refuse to sign the legislation.* This does not stop the legislation from becoming law, but it does disassociate the president from the legislation. Mitterrand, for example, did not sign the legislation denationalizing many of France's major industries. By withholding his signature, he reaffirmed his socialist credentials and distanced himself from a process that caused many workers to lose their jobs.

3. *Finally, the president can challenge the constitutionality of the legislation in the Constitutional Council* (Massot 1993). As will be discussed in the ensuing section, the Constitutional Council has become a major actor in the legislative process.

Parliament as a Watchdog. The Parliament is also expected to keep a watchful eye on the activities of ministers and bureaucrats. Special committees are formed from time to time to investigate the improprieties of a particular minister, but such committees are partisan in nature and are reluctant to embarrass the Government (Emeri 1993).

Members of Parliament also have the right to question the Government on a wide range of issues of concern to their party or their constituents. Questions may be presented either orally or in writing, but the presentation of oral questions is organized by the Conference of Presidents, which goes out of its way to spare the Government undue embarrassment (Hofstein 2004).

The weakness of the National Assembly in relation to the executive has created a sense of futility among many deputies, and absenteeism has become a problem of critical proportions. Traditionally, less than 60 of the 577 members of the National Assembly were present for all but the most pressing debates, with those in attendance voting on behalf of their absent colleagues (Prost and Jacout 1993, 17). This process, referred to as the "dance of the crabs," has now been outlawed (Jarreau 1993). Absenteeism is also increased by the tendency of many deputies to serve as mayors or to occupy other political positions. The low salaries of French legislators often leave them little choice but to seek a second position. Staff support is also minimal. For all of the above reasons, French legislators are less effective than their counterparts in the United States, Britain, and Germany (Tiersky 1994).

Law and Politics in France: The Constitutional Council and the Council of State

One of the most innovative dimensions of de Gaulle's Constitution was the establishment of a Constitutional Council or supreme court. Unlike most other provisions of the Constitution, virtually all of which found precedence in one or another of France's political traditions, the concept of a supreme court was alien to France. French courts had traditionally been prevented from interference in the legislative process, it being unthinkable that a small group of appointed judges would have the power to set aside the laws passed by the elected representatives of the people (Rosseau 1993). Equally problematic was the transitory nature of French Constitutions. In sharp contrast to the American experience, the French did not view constitutions as divine law. Rather, constitutions were practical documents that embodied the prevailing consensus on the best way to decide "who gets what, when, and how." They certainly were not inviolable, a sentiment that de Gaulle expressed with great clarity:

> Three things count in constitutional matters. First, the higher interest of the country . . . and of that I alone am the judge. Second, far behind, are the political circumstances, arrangements, tactics. . . . Third, much further behind, there is legalism. . . . I have accomplished nothing in my life except by putting the welfare of the country first and by refusing to be entrapped by legalisms (Stone 1989, 30).

It is probable that de Gaulle included a supreme court in his Constitution as yet one more device for curbing what he considered to be the legislative tyranny of the Third and Fourth Republics (Rosseau 1993). As indicated by the comments cited above, he did not, himself, intend to be bound by its dictates.

The Constitutional Council consists of nine judges, with three of its members being appointed by the president, three by the president of the National Assembly, and three by the president of the Senate (Constitution VII–56). Terms are staggered, with the composition of the Council changing at three-year intervals. The president of the Constitutional Council is appointed by the president of the republic and votes only in the case of ties. In sharp contrast to the practice of the United States Supreme Court, the Constitutional Council rules on the constitutionality of laws prior to their promulgation by the president.

In addition to declaring proposed legislation unconstitutional, the Constitutional Council has the option of declaring only one part of the proposed bill unconstitutional. In this instance, it either may kill the entire bill because of the "centrality" of its unconstitutional elements or allow passage of the bill devoid of its offending elements. In this situation, the Constitutional Court is exercising a line-item veto, keeping what it likes and rejecting the rest—a powerful role, indeed.

As originally instituted, the Constitutional Council could only rule on the constitutionality of legislation brought to it by the president or the prime minister. As such, the Council was just one more weapon in the arsenal of the executive (Rosseau 1993). Ordinary citizens did not have access to the Council, nor did members of Parliament. This was to change in 1974, when a joint session of Parliament amended the Constitution to read that a petition signed by 60 deputies or 60 senators could also force the Council to review pending legislation. By allowing 60 members of either the National Assembly or the Senate to test the constitutionality of pending legislation, this amendment allowed a small minority in Parliament to obstruct the will of the majority by sending a bill to the Constitutional Council for review. A new hurdle thus had been added to the legislative process, and not a hurdle of minor import. Approximately 25 percent of the laws submitted to the Council between 1975 and 1981 were declared at least partially unconstitutional. By 1990, that figure would jump to 50 percent (Stone 1989; Emeri 1993). By and large, the increased use of the Constitutional Council reflects its utility as a means of blocking Government legislation. Council rulings, for example, were used by the parties of the political right during the early 1980s to slow Mitterrand's efforts to transform France into a welfare state. They have subsequently been used by the political left to slow the dismantling of the welfare state.

In sum, then, the legalisms so abhorred by de Gaulle have now become a central element in the French political process (Chagnollaud 1993). To make matters worse, pressures now are building to allow individual citizens to contest the constitutionality of laws.

The Council of State is the Government's official legal advisor. Government bills introduced into the Parliament are sent first to the Council of State for an opinion on both the bill's constitutionality and its "goodness of fit" with existing laws and projects. The Council of State's opinions are advisory and may be ignored by the Government, but there is little to be gained by pushing through Parliament a bill that is destined to be declared unconstitutional (Stone 1989).

The Council of State also heads France's system of administrative courts, playing an important role in resolving disputes between various administrative departments and agencies (*Le Monde,* May 12, 2004, www). The Council of State may also initiate studies of pressing social and administrative problems, making appropriate recommendations to the Government (Safran 1991).

Bureaucracy and Politics in France

The bureaucratization of France paralleled the concentration of power by French kings. The greater the centralization of the state, the greater the need for bureaucrats. Napoleon rationalized the structure of the bureaucracy, his Grandes Ecoles drawing France's best and brightest into the service of the state. France, in Napoleon's design, was to be "managed" by a dedicated technocracy that placed the interest of the state above the petty squabbles of its politicians (Stevens 1992; Armstrong 1973).

The power of the bureaucratic elite expanded during the Third and Fourth Republics as fragmented Parliaments granted the bureaucracy sweeping powers to make policy, only the bare outlines of which had been approved by Parliament (Safran 1991). It was the competence and dedication of the senior bureaucracy that kept the affairs of state on an even keel while the elected politicians of the era devoted more energy to destroying Governments than they did to running the country. In time, both the Parliament and the population grew accustomed to rule by administrative decree (Quermonne and Rouban 1986; Sardan 1993).

The elitist nature of the senior bureaucracy was further increased with the establishment of the Ecole Nationale d'Administration, or ENA (National School of Administration), in 1946. The ENA was a new "Grande Ecole" created to provide senior administrators with advanced training in economics, planning, and public administration. As described by Pierre Birnbaum,

> These senior bureaucrats, utterly different from the professional politicians, cut off in every way from the deputies—office workers, teachers, doctors, and lawyers—and ministers of similar background, were by this time all trained by a single school, the ENA, which imparted a uniform view of the world, superb competence, and an acute awareness of their own effectiveness, which they looked upon as something politically neutral . . . these officials lived in a world apart and were distrustful of the political process, which they often regarded as reflecting the power of special interests (Birnbaum 1982, 40–41).

As noted previously, French parliaments have traditionally delegated broad and sweeping powers to the bureaucracy, a practice that continues today (Rouban 2004). Senior bureaucrats also shape policy by controlling the information that ministers require to make informed decisions. This is not a minor consideration, for members of the Government are heavily dependent upon the bureaucracy for technical expertise. Finally, the bureaucratic elite often uses its control of the administrative process to determine when and how policies will be executed. Those programs that it supports are facilitated, those that it opposes find an endless series of obstacles in their path. Ministers have the power to force the issue but are usually too busy to do so.

The ENA now is considering full admission to students from Germany and other EU countries, and already offers a short course to students from a variety of third world countries. Going European would be a step toward extending

French influence within the European Union, a step very much on the minds of France's leaders (*Le Figaro,* March 17, 2004,www).

The strong policy-making role played by France's enarques has called into question precisely who it is that rules France (Hofstein 2004). Is it France's elected representatives or its bureaucratic elite? This question becomes all the more pertinent when one realizes that 15 of the Fifth Republic's 16 prime ministers have been civil servants, as have 249 members of the National Assembly elected in 1997 (Banks 1998).

In terms of organizational structure, the French bureaucracy—some 2,500,000 strong—is divided into 4 broad classes: administrative, executive, clerical, and custodial. Of these categories, some 10,000 senior members of the administrative class are considered to be an elite service that stands above the ordinary civil service. Heavily weighted in favor *of graduates of the ENA,* or "enarques," it is they who control the bureaucratic apparatus. Of these, a very small group, the "grands fonctionnaires," is preeminent. Its members possess inordinate power and represent a key element in the French political elite.

While France's bureaucratic elite is renown for its creativity and efficiency, the average French bureaucrat is not. French bureaucrats are also under attack as global pressures to ease regulation and cut costs have resulted in reform plans that will reduce both the size and scope of the bureaucracy (*Le Monde,* July 28, 2004, www).

THE ACTORS IN FRENCH POLITICS: ELITES, PARTIES, GROUPS, AND CITIZENS

As noted throughout this text, political institutions represent the arena of politics, but the actors in the political process play a critical role in deciding who gets what, when, and how. In this section, we will look at four broad categories of political actors in France—elites, parties, groups, and citizens.

Elites and Politics in France

Despite its revolutionary traditions, France is a profoundly elitist society (Rioux 1991). The core of France's elitism is its system of Grandes Ecoles, the graduates of which monopolize senior positions in both government and business. Entrance to the Grandes Ecoles, while open to all French citizens on the basis of competitive examinations, is heavily weighted in favor of the upper classes. Indeed, only 5 percent of the "enarques," the ENA graduates who dominate the government, come from "modest means" (Denni 1993, 419). French universities educate the masses, but they are inferior to the "Grandes Ecoles." Mitterrand sought to reverse this trend by infusing both the Cabinet and bureaucracy with leftist academicians, but the elitist orientation of the government remains pronounced. Elitism also exists at the local and regional levels, with political families tending to pass mayorships and other senior positions from one generation to the next (Denni 1993).

The focal point of France's political elite is the presidency. Presidents wield enormous power, and they wield that power for a five-year term. The more an individual has direct access to the president, the more influential that person is likely to be.

Prime ministers and senior Cabinet ministers also rank high in the elite hierarchy, as do top business leaders, senior members of the president's office (personal staff), generals, and labor leaders. All have a voice in shaping how the scarce resources of the French state will be allocated.

In many ways, France possesses two distinct political elites: an elected elite that sets the direction of public policy and an administrative-business elite that determines how policies will be executed. Until the Mitterrand presidency, both elites shared a common vision of a strong French state guided by a partnership between business and government. The enarques served both, often *beginning their careers in government service and then jumping to the private sector,* a process the French refer to as **pantoflage.** Indeed, the heads of almost half of France's major companies are graduates of the ENA or one or another of the Grandes Ecoles (*Economist,* May 6, 1995, 70).

It would be a mistake, however, to draw too sharp a line between the elected elite and the administrative elite. As Denni points out, all of the presidents of the Fifth Republic, with the exception of Mitterrand, were career public servants. That trend now has been continued with the election of Chirac; both he and Lionel Jospin, the defeated Socialist Party candidate in the 2002 elections, are graduates of the ENA.

Parties and Politics in France

The fluidity of France's political institutions has been paralleled by the fluidity of its political parties. Much like a kaleidoscope, French political parties emerge on the political scene only to splinter and reconstitute themselves in differing forms.

The Concept of Party Families. Given the fluidity and complexity of French politics, no attempt will be made to trace the historical antecedents of today's parties—a daunting task for even the most ardent student of French politics (Evans 2003). Rather, our discussion will focus on the two major tendencies in French politics: the political left and the political right. While far from unified, the left and the right constitute *party families,* the members of which cooperate with each other on most occasions. The concept of **party families** is an important one, for most French parties tend to be composed of several wings, as well as a variety of "clubs" and various personality groupings, any one of which could splinter into a separate political party or join forces with an opposing party (Wilson 1989; Hanly 2002).

In order to appreciate the bitterness of conflict within party families, it is necessary to understand that a French president, once elected, does little consulting with party leaders other than those of his own party. In point of fact, consultation is thin even within the president's party. Being a partner in the winning coalition, accordingly, does not provide party leaders outside of the president's inner circle with a great deal of influence. It merely assures them that the reigning president is closer to their point of view than to the point of view of the opposition. For most politicians, that is not enough.

The Center Right: The Rally for the Republic (RPR) and the Union for French Democracy (UDF). The decade of economic and colonial turmoil following France's liberation by the Allied forces in 1944 culminated in the intense polarization of French society. The political right sought salvation in the return of Charles de Gaulle, the proverbial man on horseback, while the left coalesced around the Communist Party and its socialist allies.

As originally constituted, the Gaullists were a melange of business, military, Catholic, and related groups unified by the charisma of de Gaulle and a fear of communism. They also drew upon a deeply embedded sense of French nationalism, reflecting justifiable pride in France's historical, cultural, and scientific accomplishments (Baudouin 1993).

By the mid-1970s, however, the party's future was in doubt. Its problems were many: de Gaulle was gone, fears of a Communist takeover had diminished, personality conflicts were sapping the party's strength from within, and big businesses and small businesses were finding it difficult to work within the confines of the same party. More fundamentally, the party was losing its identity. Was it a party of the center or a party of the far right?

Divided among themselves, the Gaullists would split into two separate parties: a new party of the center right named the **Union for French Democracy** or *1'Union pour la democratie français* (UDF) and the **Rally for the Republic** or *Rassemblement pour la republique* (RPR).

The restructuring of the French right would find the Gaullist RPR championing the interests of *small merchants, artisans, farmers, retirees,* and other members of France's **petite bourgeoisie** (Chariot 1993). Its goals would be those of the traditional French right: law and order, morality, low taxes, and high tariffs. The RPR also had reservations about moving too rapidly toward the integration of Europe, fearing that many of France's older industries would find it difficult to compete on a European scale.

The UDF, by contrast, attempted to build a centrist coalition that would unite the interests of big business with those of France's large white-collar class (Ysmal 1993). Ideologically, the UDF would become the party of economic liberalism and European unity. The sooner the free market was allowed to weed out the weaker segments of the French economy, from the UDF's perspective, the better off France would be. Workers losing jobs by the closure of inefficient plants, according to the UDF, would soon find work via expanded production in those industries that were competitive on a world scale.

The UDF's economic liberalism was matched by a strong emphasis on individual freedom. It was not the responsibility of the government, from the UDF's perspective, to legislate morals (Ysmal 1993). The UDF's emphasis on personal freedom was designed to appeal to a salaried middle class that had been pushed to the left by the moral inflexibility of the right. The ideological differences between the two parties, while significant, were not beyond compromise. Personality differences between the leaders of the RPR and the UDF have proven more difficult to overcome and, in all probability, led to the defeat of the "right" in the

1988 presidential elections. By 1995, reason prevailed and a union of the two parties enabled Chirac to capture the presidency, then seven years, in 1995. The alliance was short lived (Duhamel and Mechet 1998). The UDF ran its own candidates in the 2002 elections for the presidency and National Assembly, but lost in both. Chirac swept to the presidency with 82 percent of the second round vote and his party gained an absolute majority in the National Assembly. The UDF was left out in the cold.

Alas, French voters became disenchanted with Chirac's imperial use of power and particularly his efforts to scale back France's generous health, welfare, and labor legislation, including the 35-hour work week. The socialists swept the 2004 regional elections, the last before the 2007 presidential and National Assembly elections. Chirac's party was in crisis (*Le Monde,* Apr. 12, 2004, www). Adding to the confusion has been an abiding power struggle over succession as the Chiracian era moves to a close. The closer 2007 becomes, the less power Chirac will have to keep the party in line. The leader of the UDF again called for unity of the right, but on the basis of mutual respect and a willingness of the president to listen to all currents within the alliance (*Le Monde,* March 25, 2004, www).

The Far Right: The National Front. The history of the Fifth Republic has witnessed the transformation of France from a country of political extremes to a country in which the political center of gravity resides firmly in the middle. Nevertheless, extremist parties continue to receive some 20 percent of the first-round popular vote on a consistent basis. The *dominant extremist party of the left* is the **Communist Party,** while the *dominant extremist party of the far right* is the **National Front.** The Communists are declining in influence, but support for the National Front has stabilized and may be increasing (Maniere 2002).

By the early 1900s, the National Front could claim 3 councilors general, 33 mayors, 239 regional councilors, 1,666 municipal councilors, and 10 deputies in the European parliament (Birenbaum 1992). The National Front also polled some 15 percent of the first-round ballots in both the 1988 and 1995 presidential elections and almost 17 percent in the 2002 presidential elections. This was sufficient to propel Le Pen, the party's leader, into a run-off with Chirac in the second round of the elections.

Although the National Front has done well in the first-round elections, its extreme positions have precluded it from achieving any second-round victories. Its performance in the second round of the 2002 elections was a dismal 18 percent of the vote as opposed to 82 percent for Chirac. It fared no better in the 2004 regional elections, with a strong showing in the first-round elections producing minimal results in the second and final round.

As with most French political parties, it is prone to fragmentation and internal conflicts (*Le Monde,* Apr. 30, 2000, www). Nevertheless, more than 3,000,000 French citizens typically voted for the National Front during the first-round elections, a figure that has not gone unnoticed by the other parties of the political right.

The platform of the National Front is strikingly simple. France, according to the National Front, suffers from record unemployment, exorbitant taxes, terrorism, escalating crime, and an epidemic of drug use. All could be solved, according to the National Front, by reducing France's large immigrant community, most of which comes from North Africa. The party has also benefitted from the charisma of its leader, a strong organizational structure and the very effective use of the Internet.

Both the UDF and the RPR have disavowed any ties with the National Front, with Chirac publicly denouncing the National Front as "a racist and xenophobic" party that is "unworthy and dangerous" *(Economist,* Mar. 28, 1998, 46).

Be this as it may, some 25 percent of the people who voted for Chirac in 1995 favor closer cooperation with the National Front (Duhamel and Mechet 1998). There have even been calls for a new party of the right that would incorporate the National Front, although this is unlikely to occur *(International Herald Tribune,* Apr. 25, 1998, 2). Clearly the French right has an identity crisis. Is its center of gravity on the center right or the far right? Until it resolves this issue, unity will be difficult to achieve.

The Political Left: The French Communist Party and the Socialist Party.
The French Communist Party (PCF) emerged from the Second World War as one of the strongest political parties in France, having been in the vanguard of the resistance forces (Baudouin 1993). Communist doctrine, moreover, found broad appeal in a society characterized by low wages, inferior working conditions, and a widening gap between rich and poor. Many French citizens also voted Communist to indicate their displeasure with a political system seemingly bent on self-destruction (Wright 1987; Wilson 1993). Finally, the Communist Party benefited from a strong party organization that included control of France's largest labor union, the CGT. All in all, support for the PCF would peak at 28.2 percent of the vote in the 1946 elections, a figure that would remain stable throughout the Fourth Republic (Becker 1988; Furniss 1960). The size of the Communist vote destabilized the Fourth Republic, raising very real fears that the Communists would "vote" themselves into power.

The Socialist Party, by contrast, was a much smaller party which, while advocating the nationalization of French industry and greater social equality, was less radical than the Communists. It was the Communists, however, that set the tone for the French left.

The rise of de Gaulle marked a slow but unrelenting decline in Communist fortunes (Jensen 1991). Unemployment decreased in the wake of economic reforms, and Gaullist social legislation eliminated the worst inequities of French society (Baudouin 1993). The Constitution of the Fifth Republic also weakened the Communist Party by shifting political power from the legislature to a popularly elected presidency. The Communist Party was guaranteed representation in the National Assembly by virtue of its strong support in working-class districts, but its programs were too radical to enable it to compete effectively for the presidency (Wilson 1989).

The Communist Party thus was faced with a choice between popularity and ideological purity. Broader electoral appeal could be achieved by championing the doctrine of **Euro-communism,** *a democratic version of communism that presented social welfare and the socialist economic policies as desirable alternatives to the inequities of capitalism* (Antonian 1987; Schwab 1978).

The French Communist Party, however, was dominated by resistance leaders who chose to maintain its ideological purity (Gaffney 1989; Hazareesingh 1991). Electoral support, according to the Communist leaders of the era, was to be achieved by using the smaller Socialist Party as a front. The Socialists could steal the electoral limelight, but the Communists would remain the power behind the throne (Godt 1989). This strategy was formalized in a 1971 "Common Program" worked out between the Communist Party and the newly reconstituted Socialist Party of François Mitterrand. In retrospect, this was a mistake. The center of gravity of the French left, buoyed by an improving economic environment, shifted from the Communists to the Socialists. The shift was sealed by Mitterrand's election to the presidency in 1981, an election that saw the Communists capture a meager seven percent of the vote in the first-round elections. The Communists continue to poll between five percent and seven percent of the first-round vote in French elections. Belatedly, 1999 would see the Communist Party drop the hammer and sickle from the masthead of its 95-year-old paper, *l'Humanité (International Herald Tribune,* March 19, 1999, www). They have also been beset by internal conflict (*Le Monde,* Apr. 23, 2000, www).

The 1988 elections saw Mitterrand transform the Socialist Party from a Marxist Party into a broad-based Social Democratic Party advocating a mild form of socialism that amounted to little more than capitalism with a conscience. He was rewarded with a second seven-year term of office. Ideological purity, once the hallmark of French socialism, had given way to the expediency of winning elections. Indeed, many Socialists now find the extremism of the Communists to be something of an embarrassment. The Communists screamed betrayal but had little choice but to support the Socialists.

The 1990s, however, were unkind to the Socialists. Again, the problems are many. French voters had swung to the right, yet many of the party's most ardent supporters remained loyal to their Marxist traditions (Wilson 1989; Safran 1991; Gaffney 1998; Clift 2003). It is they who were the workhorses of the party, and it was difficult for the party to prosper without their support.

The Socialists, moreover, had experienced severe financial problems. The Socialist Party maintained a large network of constituency organizations but lacked the funds to exploit them to maximum benefit. The position of the Socialist Party was also weakened by the absence of a direct link with France's highly fragmented labor movement. In France, unlike many other European countries, union support for the Socialists cannot be taken for granted (Portelli 1993). The unions, moreover, were themselves losing membership, a trend that bodes ill for the left in general.

Despite all of its problems and despite its defeat in the 1995 presidential elections, the Socialists rebounded in 1997 with an overwhelming victory in the National Assembly elections of that year and entered a five year period of cohabitation with Chirac. While Chirac receded to the background, it was the socialists who asserted their power. The victory of the Socialists in 1997 reflected a new pragmatism that saw the program of the Socialists closer than ever to the political center. The days of radical socialism were over (Krause 1997). This diluted their traditional support among the left and the party suffered an ignominious defeat in 2002, losing both the presidency and the National Assembly.

All, however, was not lost. Buoyed by a stunning sweep of the 2004 regional elections, the French left is attempting to prepare for the 2007 elections by building upon the unaccustomed unity that played a crucial rule in its 2004 victory. The Communists will probably go along. The choice for the Communists "is very simple, if one goes it alone, one is dead. . . . .If one chooses union with the Socialists, one disappears" (Roger 2004).

The Greens. Over the course of the past three decades, the Greens have emerged as an important force on the center left of the French political spectrum, capturing some 10 percent of the first-round vote in the 1993 legislative elections. They are particularly strong at the local levels, having polled almost 15 percent of the vote in the 1992 regional elections. This trend continued in the 1997 elections with the Greens capturing eight seats in the National Assembly, and participating in the Government for the first time. The Greens now believe that they can replace the Communists as the second party of the left in a few years (*Le Monde,* Sept. 13, 1998, 6). The Greens remain largely a first-round party, however, being too small to challenge the larger parties of the left and right in the more important second-round elections (Deleage and Saul 1997).

This situation is unlikely to change in the near future, as the Greens are a loosely knit organization that is divided into two competing branches. One branch of the party identifies strongly with the Socialists and advocates a broad range of social welfare issues. The other, in contrast, prefers to focus strictly on environmental issues, thereby allowing the Greens to enlist support from environmentally concerned citizens of all persuasions (Boy 1993). The party has also been fragmented by personality conflicts and constrained in its operations by a lack of resources (*Le Monde,* Apr. 27, 2000, and Apr. 16, 2000, www).

As environmentalism has become popular, France's major parties, especially the Socialists, have attempted to capture the Green vote by appearing to be environmentally concerned. Mainline candidates masquerading as environmentalists— "false Greens"—siphoned off much of the Green vote in the 1993 legislative elections (Boy 1993), and the Socialists picked up 35 percent of Green voters in the first round of the 1995 presidential elections (*Le Monde, L'Election presidentielle: 23 avril–7 mai, 1995*). Both suffered in the 2002 elections and both revived in the 2004 regional elections. The Greens, like the Communists, face a critical choice of how closely to embrace the Socialists in the 2007 elections. To go it alone, is to forego influence. To embrace the socialist is to sacrifice the purity of their message.

As in most European countries, the Greens find their major support among young professionals, as well as among teachers, social workers, and students (Boy 1993; Burchell, 2002). This base, while articulate, is too narrow to challenge France's larger parties in the second-round elections.

The French Party System: An Assessment. For all of its diverse parties and factions, it seems quite probable that the French party system will continue to solidify around two broad coalitions: a right-of-center coalition centering on the UMP and UDF, and a left-of-center coalition dominated by the Socialists.

The increasing stability of party families has allowed the French party system to sustain Governments over the life of their term, something that was largely impossible during the Third and Fourth Republics. It has also eliminated much of the post-election horse trading that characterized the Third and Fourth Republics. The French electorate is now confident that the National Assembly either will be dominated by a moderate party of the center left or a moderate party of the center right. While the range of electoral options has been reduced, the consequence of electoral choices has been clarified. French parties, accordingly, are also becoming increasingly responsible; that is, the French electorate can reasonably expect them to carry out their campaign promises.

While the evolution of two large party families has contributed to the growing stability and moderation of French politics, French parties do not serve as an effective check on the powers of the executive. Elected leaders are minimally constrained by their party organizations, and personalities dominate parties, not the contrary (Schain 1989).

Pressure Groups and Politics in France

Pressure groups play such an active role in French politics that the distinction between party factions and pressure groups is often difficult to discern. The Constitution of the Fifth Republic established a special Economic and Social Council that provides France's major pressure groups with the opportunity to comment on relevant legislation before it is passed into law. More specialized consultative councils also exist in most administrative departments. Groups, then, are vitally important to the political process in France.

The Economic and Social Council consists of some 231 members, slightly more than half of whom are appointed by the government. The remainder are elected by the members of France's diverse labor unions, trade associations, and professional groups. Labor unions receive the largest representation on the council (69 members), followed in turn by business associations (27 members) and agricultural associations (25 members). Other interests represented on the Council are cooperatives, mutual societies, renters' and savers' associations, public enterprises, artisans, and various professions including doctors and lawyers (Mouriaux 1993). Special councils also give representation to France's major religious groups including Jews and Muslims. The Muslim group was added in 2003 in the face of growing unrest among France's large Islamic population.

The influence of the Economic and Social Council on the legislative process is a matter of some debate. With so many interests represented, it is not easy for the members of the Council to speak with a common voice; even then, their voice is merely advisory. Be this as it may, those groups represented on the Council *enjoy direct and formalized entry to the legislative process. In return, they are expected to be moderate in their demands and to work in harmony with government agencies.* This arrangement is referred to as **neocorporatism.** Not all groups in French society, it is important to note, find representation on the Economic and Social Council, the most glaring exceptions being immigrants and women. There are also calls to rejuvenate the Council by making it less lethargic (*Le Monde,* Sept. 1, 2004, www).

Labor. Labor is represented by at least six major unions, each reflecting a different ideological position. Of these, the most important are the General Confederation of Labor (CGT), a labor union closely linked to the Communist Party; the French Confederation of Christian Workers" (CFTC), a labor union linked to the Catholic Church; and the Work Force (FO), a moderate labor union that inclines toward the Socialist Party.

Labor is well aware of the problems caused by its disunity, but attempts to unify the movement succeed for the moment, only to collapse in the face of disputes over strategy, ideology, or personality (*Le Monde,* Apr. 29, 2000, www; *Le Monde,* May 1, 2004, www). All in all, the power of the French unions peaked with the general strike of 1968 and has declined since that time (Mouriaux 1993). The situation remains much the same today, with only 8 to 14 percent of France's workers and white collar employees being represented by unions, depending on how one counts. The unions won't say (*Le Figaro,* 10, May, 2004, www). Whatever the case, France's rate of unionization is the most feeble in Europe.

The declining position of French labor has also paralleled the decline of France's "rust belt" industries. The economy of France, like that of the rest of the first world, is becoming a high-tech and service-oriented system. The pool of industrial workers, the core of the French union movement, has simply shrunk. A persistent unemployment rate of more than 10 percent has also made workers fearful that joining a union will jeopardize their employability. The same logic has depressed their willingness to engage in "industrial action." Although strikes by truckers, civil servants, and transportation workers continue to be part of the French political scene, most are short lived (Singer 1997).

Business. Business in France is better organized than labor but is also divided among itself. The National Council of French Employers (CNPF) serves as the peak association for several hundred specialized business associations and more than 900,000 individual firms. The CNPF is dominated by France's larger corporations and has a pronounced "big business" orientation. As such, it often finds itself in conflict with the General Confederation of Small and Medium Enterprises (CGPME), many members of which are threatened by the expansionist tendency of France's larger firms. The spread of supermarkets is of particular concern to the CGPME, for small food shops have traditionally been the mainstay of France's petite bourgeoisie.

The conflict between the two organizations also finds political expression, with the CNPF supporting the moderate UDC while CGPME inclines toward the Gaullist RPR . The CGPME also criticizes the CNPF for its "cozy" relationship with the bureaucracy and unions (Jones 1993).

The Catholic Church. The Catholic Church, once the bastion of conservatism and conformity, has also seen its power eroded by factionalization and public disinterest. As described by John Ardagh:

> The Church, from being a central pillar of society, has come more to resemble a loose network of semi-autonomous groups, militants in the midst of a largely irreligious nation, and priests and laity alike are splintered into

Table 4.2 The Concerns (Values) of French Youth

Elements	Very Important/Indispensable
A successful family life	91%
An interesting job	91%
To be among good friends	84%
To be of service to others	57%
To have a long life	36%
To have a spiritual life	24%

SOURCE: Based on data presented in Olivier Duhamel and Philippe Mechet. *L'Etat de l'opinion* (pp. 238–239) by SOFRES © Editions du Seuil, 1998. Data adapted from a poll presented by Pelerin magazine, July 15, 1997. N=40, Youth between the ages of 15 and 25.

highly varied tendencies. While some priests flirt with Marxism, others return to the purest dogmas of integrism, insisting on the Mass in Latin. While some preach and even practice sexual freedom, others fiercely denounce the abortion reforms (Ardagh 1990, 430).

Be this as it may, France remains a profoundly Catholic country in which 90 percent of the population is statistically classified as Catholic and 80 percent of the population identifies itself as Catholic (Tiersky 1994). While only 10 percent of the population admits to being "practicing" Catholics, most French citizens are not hostile to the Church (*New York Times,* June 18, 1994, 5). Indeed, a 1984 bill placing greater restrictions on public assistance to Catholic schools was withdrawn by Mitterrand in the face of the largest public outcry since the protests of 1968 (Tiersky 1994). At least in some areas, then, the Church retains a significant political voice. Catholics voted for Chirac more heavily than did members of other religions (Protestants, Jews, Muslims), with the figure for practicing Catholics reaching 74 percent.

Students and Intellectuals.   Students and intellectuals, long the revolutionary vanguard of French politics, are heavily oriented toward the political left. France's two largest student organizations are the Marxist *Solidarité etudianté,* or student solidarity, and the more socialist-oriented *Independent democratique.* Students continue to protest Government policies, but their influence on policy making is minimal. As Tiersky laments,

> Young people in France, like industrial workers and nostalgia, are also not what they used to be politically and culturally. Whereas a French student of the 1950s or '60s could be found or at least easily imagined arguing politics and philosophy in a cafe, today students at a *fac* (a public university), a *lycee* or a *collège* (a lower secondary school) want to be tied into international fads more than existentialists and trendsetters of political engagement.
>
> Urban, upwardly mobile French youth are no longer even sure to know the difference between political "right" and "left," or worse still, to think that it matters much (Tiersky 1994, 30).

Nevertheless, student protests in the spring of 1994 forced the Government to abandon its proposal to exclude "youth" from France's minimum wage law (*New York Times,* Mar. 29, 1994, 1). So shaken was the Government by the protest, estimated to involve 200,000 students, that it sent a questionnaire to all French youth between the ages of 15 and 25 asking their views on topics ranging from school to social welfare (*New York Times,* June 18, 1994, *5; Le Monde,* Oct. 20, 1998, www). Among other things, the results suggested that the majority of French youth have little confidence in the future and believe their educations will be of little utility in helping them find jobs. Such responses are hardly surprising, given the fact that unemployment confronts one-fourth of France's citizens between the ages of 18 and 25 (*New York Times,* Oct. 6, 1994, A7).

More than 500,000 Lycée students also poured into the streets of some 350 French cities during 1998 protesting the degeneration of French education marked by a shortage of teachers, inadequate facilities, overstuffed classrooms, and excessive course loads (*Le Monde,* Oct. 17, 1998, 1). The protests were poorly organized, amounting to what *Le Monde* referred to as "joyous anarchy" (*Le Monde,* Oct. 15, 1998, www). It was not, however, a joyous event for socialist Prime Minister Lionel Jospin, who was desperately struggling to match his promises of social reform with the realities of the French budget (*Le Monde,* Nov. 3, 1998, www). French youth may have lost their interest in the grand ideological debates of the past, but they do expect their political leaders to provide them with jobs. The prospects for reduced unemployment among youth, however, are not bright (*Le Monde,* Apr. 21, 2000, www).

The same decline in ideological debate and political activism has become increasingly apparent among France's teachers and professors, with membership in the FEN dropping off sharply in recent years.

Over the course of the Fifth Republic, then, the violent group confrontations of an earlier era have given way to a responsible pluralism that provides a strong foundation for French democracy. Particularly interesting, in this regard, has been the evolution of civic action groups or "new social movements" designed to give expression to the rights of those lacking a voice in the traditional channels of French politics. In February of 1997, for example, more than 100,000 people filled the streets of Paris to protest planned legislation designed to impose further restrictions on illegal immigration. Other movements have arisen to protest the Fascist tendencies of the extreme right, to champion the rights of women, and to urge support for victims of AIDS (Waters 1998).

Citizens and Politics in France

The power of the bureaucratic elite in shaping public policy raises serious questions about the role of elections and public opinion in the French political equation. Just how important is citizen politics in France? The answer to this question is straightforward. French citizens have little to say about the day-to-day affairs of their government, but they play a profound role in shaping the long-term direction of public policy. Mass protest, it will be recalled, signaled the end of the Fourth Republic, just as the mini-revolution of 1968 spelled the end of the de

Gaulle regime. The French electorate also brought the Socialists to power in 1981, only to temper socialist rule with right-of-center Governments in 1986 and 1993, a trend consolidated by the election of a right-of-center president in 1995. By 1997, however, the public mood had again shifted, and the Socialists recaptured the National Assembly. It is the growing moderation of the French electorate, moreover, that has forced French parties to move to the center of the political spectrum. Conversely, public concern over unemployment, crime and terrorism has forced the Government to take a hard line on immigration.

The responsiveness of France's elites to public opinion depends on a variety of factors. All democratic leaders, French or otherwise, find it difficult to resist views that are shared by a broad cross section of the public. They also find it diffi-cult to resist opinions of great intensity held by an articulate segment of that pub-lic. Hostility toward foreign immigrants currently falls in both categories. Much, of course, also depends on the nearness of elections.

French public opinion is expressed largely in three ways: elections, public opinion polls, and demonstrations. The second round of presidential and legisla-tive elections are taken very seriously by French voters, while first-round elec-tions are often used as a protest vote to express dissatisfaction with current policies (Grunberg 1993). Both the Greens and the National Front, for example, have done very well in the first-round elections but have found it difficult to elect members to the National Assembly. Their large first-round vote, however, has not gone unnoticed by France's larger parties. The Socialists have become increas-ingly Green, while the RPR has moved to capture the National Front vote by sponsoring stringent anti-immigration laws.

Public Opinion in France

Public opinion polls captured the imagination of the French electorate in 1965 by accurately predicting that Charles de Gaulle would be forced into a second-round runoff in the presidential elections of that year. Since that time, the French have become among the most polled individuals on earth. Recent polls indicate an abiding concern for unemployment (71 percent), quality of life (48 percent), social security (retirement) (40 percent), social inequalities (40 per-cent), quality of education (36 percent), costs of health insurance (32 percent), and the environment (31 percent) (*Le Figaro,* March 30, 2004, www). These figures have been fairly consistent over the past several years and suggest that the French public is overwhelming concerned with economic issues (Chariot 1993; Duhamel and Mechet 1998).

Public opinion polls take on added importance in as much as paid advertising is prohibited three months before elections. This has forced politicians to place heavy reliance on opinion polls in shaping their electoral strategy (Maarek 1997).

Protests and demonstrations continue to be a viable expression of French public opinion, although their numbers have decreased markedly in recent years. Aside from the students, the most visible demonstrators have been truckers, farm-ers, and fishermen protesting increased foreign competition. In 2004, more than 2,000 French scientists took to the street to protest cut-backs in research funding.

The same year would see 6,000 power workers take to the streets of Paris to protest the proposed privatization of France's electric utilities. Strikes occur, but they tend to be of short duration and are designed to cause maximum embarrassment to the Government. Truckers snarl traffic, and the 2004 protest of the electrical workers resulted in black-outs in France's major cities. Taken collectively, the three avenues of French public opinion portray a society that is increasingly centrist in orientation, that places issues above ideology, and that is primarily concerned about economic issues.

THE CONTEXT OF FRENCH POLITICS: CULTURE, ECONOMICS, AND INTERNATIONAL INTERDEPENDENCE

In addition to the influence of institutions and actors, the political process in France is also shaped by the broader context in which it occurs. Accordingly, in this section we will examine how French politics is influenced by its political culture, its political economy, and its interactions with the rest of the world.

The Culture of French Politics

Historically, France possessed a fragmented political culture (Almond and Verba 1963). While some French citizens embraced revolutionary ideals, others embraced the values of authoritarianism and state dominance (Gaffney and Kolinsky 1991; Gemie 1998; Parry 1998). Traditional French culture was also characterized by high levels of interpersonal distrust, each family being an island unto itself and each looking to the state to protect it from its neighbors (Wright 1987; Crozier 1964). Groups and parties formed, but they seldom endured.

The political **immobilisme** of the Third and Fourth Republics was, from the culturalist perspective, the result of a nation fragmented by conflicting political values. If French politicians seemed to do little but bicker, it was because the gulf separating the political left and the political right was too vast to be bridged. There was nothing else they could do but bicker (Hoffman 1963).

The France of today is more unified than at any time in the past, a fact reflected in the growing centrism of French voters. This growing centrism, from the culturalist perspective, is the result of changes in French society. Culture changes slowly, but it does change. The deep scars of the Second World War and the de Gaulle era are far less relevant to new generations of French citizens than they are to their parents. The younger generation of French citizens, moreover, has matured in an environment of stability and prosperity. They are also the product of MTV and the popularization of international youth culture (Tiersky 1994). In line with the general trend toward post-industrial values throughout the first world, French citizens are more concerned with quality of life and environmental issues than they are with the fine points of ideology (Inglehart 1990). Be this as it may, the French retain a healthy skepticism of politics and politicians, with more than one-third of French citizens finding politics to be a less than honorable profession, and an even larger number suggesting that democracy does not function well in France.

We would be remiss if we failed to mention that France is also becoming a multicultural society with a large Muslim community, most from Algeria, Morocco, and Tunisia, France's former North African colonies (Safron 2003) While many Muslims have assimilated into French culture, a growing number have remained faithful to their cultural traditions including the wearing of head scarves by female Muslim students. This has increased tension between the Muslim community and French authorities intent on maintaining France's secular and cultural traditions. Laws banning head scarves have increased tensions and led to open conflict. Fears that France's Muslims have supported terrorist operations has added to the bitterness as have accusations that France's Muslim and African ghettos have become centers of crime and drugs.

A 2004 study by the French government attempted to identify neighborhoods (quartiers) with a potential for violence on the basis of a long list of criteria including: the number of families of immigrant origin, the increase of ties to the Muslim religion, the practice of oriental traditions, the prevalence of anti-Semitic and anti-western graffiti, and number of schools with recent arrivals who do not speak French (*Le Monde,* July 5, 2004, www). Some 300 quartiers were identified as problem areas with a combined population of some 1.8 million inhabitants. Ghetto youth are particularly alienated from French society.

A special Islamic Council was established in 2003 to better express the concerns of France's Muslim community. Radical imams (religious leaders) are being expelled from France and French authorities are also starting to train French imams (preachers) who better understand and respect French traditions (*Guardian,* April 23, 2004, www).

Political Economy and Politics in France

Virtually all major events in French history, from a political economic perspective, are economic in character. Feudalism was as much an economic system as it was a political system, and the French Revolution, whatever its romantic overtones, was a confrontation between wealth and poverty. The same confrontation between wealth and poverty, from the political economic perspective, continues to define the basic parameters of political conflict in France today. The French left draws a preponderance of its support from the working class, while the center of gravity on the right is found in the bourgeoisie. Even the divisions within party families are economic in nature. The Communists are more hard-core working class than the socialists, and the RPR inclines toward the petite bourgeoisie while the UDF gives expression to the interests of big business.

As in most countries, then, France's major political parties are essentially coalitions of economic interests. Particularly vivid is the correlation between unemployment and support for the neo-Fascist National Front. While much of the growing French middle class is moving toward the political center, the economically disadvantaged are moving toward the extremes of the political spectrum,

and related tensions have fueled support for the National Front and other extremist movements, but there is little indication that extremism poses a serious threat to a mature democracy that has become increasing centrist in its political outlook.

REFERENCES

Almond, Gabriel, and Sidney Verba. 1963. *The Civic Culture*. Boston: Little, Brown.

Antonian, Armen. 1987. *Toward a Theory of Eurocommunism: The Relationship of Eurocommunism to Eurosocialism*. New York: Greenwood Press.

Antoine, Rector. 1968. "Les Etudiants et la nouvelle université." *Realités* 274: 70–81.

Ardagh, John. 1990. *France Today*. London: Penguin.

Armstrong, John A. 1973. *The European Administrative Elite*. Princeton, NJ: Princeton University Press.

Banks, Howard. 1998. "A Giant Kick in the Pants." *Forbes* 161, 11: 80–81.

Baudouin, Jean. 1993. "Le parti communist français." In *La Vie politique en France* (pp. 292–307), ed. Dominique Chagnollaud. Paris: Editions du Seuil.

Becker, Jean-Jacques. 1988. *Histoire politique de la France depuis 1945*. Paris: Armand Colin Editeur.

Besson, Jean-Louis. 1988. *Le Livre de l'histoire de France*. Paris: Gallimard.

Birenbaum, Guy. 1992. *Le Front National en politique*. Paris: Editions Balland.

Birnbaum, Pierre, trans. 1982. *The Heights of Power*, by Arthur Goldhammer. Chicago: University of Chicago Press.

Borella, Francois. 1993. "Le system des partis." In *La Vie politique en France* (pp. 223–42), ed. Dominique Chagnollaud. Paris: Editions du Seuil.

Boy, Daniel. 1993. "Les ecologists." In *La Vie politique en France* (pp. 310–27), ed. Dominique Chagnollaud. Paris: Editions du Seuil.

Brace, Richard, and Joan Brace. 1965. *Algerian Voices*. Princeton, NJ: D. Van Nostrand.

Brechon, Pierre. 1993. "Elections et referendums." In *La Vie politique en France* (pp. 367–84), ed. Dominique Chagnollaud. Paris: Editions du Seuil.

Brubaker, Rogers. 1992. *Citizenship and Nationhood in France and Germany*. Cambridge, MA: Harvard University Press.

Burchell, Jon. 2002. *The Evolution of Green Politics: Development and Change Within European Green Parties*. London: Earthscan Pub.

Célestin, Roger, Eliane DalMolin, and Isabelle de Courtivron, eds. 2003. *Beyond French Feminisms: Debates on Women, Politics, and Culture in France, 1981–2001*. New York: Palgrace Macmillian.

Cerny, Philip G. 1989. "From Dirigisme to Deregulation? The Case of Financial Markets." In *Policy-Making in France: From de Gaulle to Mitterrand* (pp. 142–64), ed. Paul Godt. New York: Pinter.

Cesari, Jocelyne, ed. 1998. *Musulmans et republicains: Les jeunes, 1'islam et la France*. Paris: Complexe, Les Dieux dans la cité.

Chagnollaud, Dominique, ed. 1992. *Etat politique de la France*. Paris: Quai Voltaire.

Chagnollaud, Dominique. 1993. "Droit et politique sous Cinquieme Republique." In *La Vie politique en France* (pp. 11–23), ed. Dominique Chagnollaud. Paris: Editions du Seuil.

Chariot, Jean. 1993. "Le Rassemblement pour le Republique." In *La Vie politique en France* (pp. 243–54), ed. Dominique Chagnollaud. Paris: Editions du Seuil.

Clift, Ben. 2003. *French Socialism in a Global Era: The Political Economy of the New Social Democracy in France*. New York: Continuum.

Cook, Don. 1983. *Charles de Gaulle: A Biography.* New York: G. P. Putnam's Sons.

Crozier, Michel. 1964. *The Bureaucratic Phenomenon.* Chicago: University of Chicago Press.

Deleage, Jean-Paul and Mahir Saul. 1997 (Winter). "The Fragile Victory of French Ecologists." *Environmental Politics* 6(4): 159–165.

Denni, Bernard. 1993. "Les elites en France." In *La Vie politique en France* (pp. 418–31), ed. Dominique Chagnollaud. Paris: Editions du Seuil.

Derbyshire, Ian. 1990. *Politics in France: From Giscard to Mitterrand.* Paris: Chambers.

Duhamel, Alain. 1991. *De Gaulle–Mitterrand: La Marque et la trace.* Paris: Flammarion.

Duhamel, Olivier. 1986. "L'hypothese de la contradiction des majorites en France." In *Les Regimes semi-presidentielles* (p. 271), ed. Maurice Duverger. Cited in *De Gaulle to Mitterrand: Presidential Power in France,* ed. Jack Hayward. London: Hurst and Company.

Duhamel, Olivier, and Philippe Mechet. 1998. *L'etat de l'opinion: 1998.* Paris: Editions du Seuil.

Elgie, Robert. 1993. *The Role of the Prime Minister in France: 1981–91.* New York: St. Martin's.

Emeri, Claude. 1993. "Le Parlement." In *La Vie politique en France* (pp. 53–82), ed. Dominique Chagnollaud. Paris: Editions du Seuil.

Evans, Jocelyn. 2003. *The French Party System.* Manchester, UK: Manchester University Press.

Furniss, Edgar S. 1960. *France: Troubled Ally: De Gaulle's Heritage and Prospects.* New York: Praeger.

Gaffney, John. 1989. *The French Left and the Fifth Republic.* London: Macmillan.

Gaffney, John. 1998. "Socialism in France: An Appraisal." *West European Politics* 21(3): 208–213.

Gaffney, John, and Eva Kolinsky, eds. 1991. *Political Culture in France and West Germany: A Comparative Perspective.* London: Routledge.

Gemie, Sharif. 1998 (April). "Octave Mirbeau and the Changing Nature of Right-Wing Political Culture: France, 1870–1914." *International Review of Social History* 43(1): 111–135.

Giesbert, Franz-Olivier. 1990. *Le president.* Paris: Editions du Seuil.

Godt, Paul, ed. 1989. *Policy-Making in France: From de Gaulle to Mitterrand.* New York: Pinter.

Grunberg, Gerard. 1993. "Le comportment electoral des français." In *La vie politique en France* (pp. 385–401), ed. Dominique Chagnollaud. Paris: Editions du Seuil.

Grunberg, Gerard. 2003 (Fall). "Le systeme politique français apres les elections de 2002 in France." *French Politics, Culture and Society,* 21(3): 91–108.

Guelaud, Claire. 2004 (Jan. 9). "Le Conseil economique et social renouvelle, mercrdi, ses 231 membres." *Le Monde.fr.* http://www.lemond.fr/web/imprimer_article/0,1@2-3224,36-377402,0.html.

Hanley, David. 2002. *Party, Society, and Government: Republican Democracy in France.* New York: Berghahn Books.

Hayward, Jack. 1993. "The President and the Constitution: Its Spirit, Articles, and Practice." In *De Gaulle to Mitterrand: Presidential Power in France* (pp. 36–75), ed. Jack Hayward. London: Hurst and Company.

Hazareesingh, Sudhir. 1991. *Intellectuals and the French Communist Party: Disillusion and Decline.* Oxford: Clarendon Press.

Hazareesingh, Sudhir. 1994. *Political Traditions in France.* New York: Oxford University Press.

Hewlett, Nick. 2003. *Democracy in Modern France.* New York: Continuum.

Hoffman, Stanley. 1963. "Paradoxes of the French Political Community." In *In Search of France* (pp. 1–117), ed. Stanley Hoffman. Cambridge, MA: Harvard University Press.

Hofstein. 2004 (May 7). "Pour un 'spoil system' a la française." *Le Figaro.fr* http://www.lefigaro.fr/cgi/edition/genimprime?cle.2004.

Howorth, Jolyon. 1993. "The Presidents, the Parties, and Parliament." In *De Gaulle to Mitterrand: Presidential Power in France* (pp. 150–89), ed. Jack Hayward. London: Hurst and Company.

Inglehart, Ronald. 1990. *Culture Shift in Advanced Industrial Society.* Princeton, NJ: Princeton University Press.

Jarreau, Patrick. 1993. "Elections legislatives." *Le Monde,* 21 mars–28 mars 1993, pp. 5–7.

Jensen, Jane. 1991. "The French Left: A Tale of Three Beginnings." In *Searching for the New France* (pp. 85–112), ed. James F. Hollifield and George Ross. New York: Routledge.

Jones, H. S. 1993. *The French State in Question: Public Law and Political Argument in the Third Republic.* Cambridge, MA: Cambridge University Press.

Krause, Axel. 1997 (July–Aug.). "Jospin's Socialist Team: Lean, Feminine, and Pro-Europe." *Europe* 368: 16.

Lawday, David. 1998. "Chirac Shrinks the Presidency." *New Statesman* 127(4394): 20–21.

Le Monde. 1995. "L'election presidentielle: 23 avril–7 mai, 1995." Paris: Numero special, Dossiers et documents.

Maarek, Philippe J. 1997 (July). "New Trends in French Political Communication: The 1995 Presidential Elections." *Media, Culture & Society* 19(3): 357–368.

Maniere, Philippe. 2002. *La vengeance du peuple: les elites, Le Pen et les français.* Paris: Plon.

Massot, Jean. 1993. "Le president de la Republique et le premier ministre." In *La Vie politique en France (pp.* 53–83), ed. Dominique Chagnollaud. Paris: Editions du Seuil.

Matlack, Carol. 2004 (March 29). "France is Shooting Itself in the Pied: Its Rigid Labor Policies are Driving Out - Desperately Needed Foreign Investment." *Business Week,* (3876): 28.

Maus, Didier. 1998. *Les Grands Textes de la practique constitutionnelle de la V Republique.* Paris: La Documentation française.

Mendras, Henri, and Alistair Cole. 1991. *Social Change in Modern France: Towards a Cultural Anthropology of the Fifth Republic.* Cambridge, MA: Cambridge University Press.

Miguet, Arnauld. 2002 (October). "The French Elections of 2002: After the Earthquake, the Deluge." *West European Politics* 25(4): 207–221.

Moisi, Dominique. 1998. "The Trouble with France." *Foreign Affairs* 77(3): 94–104.

Mouriaux, Rene. 1993. "Les Syndicats sous la Cinquième Republique." In *La vie politique en France* (pp. 344–63), ed. Dominique Chagnollaud. Paris: Editions du Seuil.

Parry, D. L. L. 1998 (March). "Political Culture, Political Class, and Political Community." *The Historical Journal* 41(1): 311–315.

Patriat, Claude. 2002. *Voter Cohabitation? 1986–2002: la fin de la monarchie republicaine.* Paris: Le Pre Aux Clercs.

Popkin, Jeremy D. 1994. *A History of Modern France.* Englewood Cliffs, NJ: Prentice-Hall.

Portelli, Hughes. 1993. "Le Parti Socialist." In *La Vie politique en France* (pp. 272–91), ed. Dominique Chagnollaud. Paris: Editions du Seuil.

Price, Roger. 2004. *People and Politics in France, 1848–1870.* Cambridge, UK: Cambridge University Press.

Prost, Dominique, and Pierre Jacout. 1993. *Un Deputé ca sert á quoi.* Lony: Editions Prost.

Quermonne, Jean-Louis. 1993. "Genèse et évolution du régime." In *La Vie politique en France* (pp. 24–52), ed. Dominique Chagnollaud. Paris: Editions du Seuil.

Quermonne, Jean-Louis, and Luc Rouban. 1986. "French Public Administration and Policy Evaluation: The Quest for Accountability." *Public Administration Review* 46(5): 397–406.

Rae, Douglas. 1967. *The Political Consequences of Electoral Laws.* New Haven, CT: Yale University Press.

Rioux, Jean-Pierre. 1991 (Sept.). "Ces Elites qui nous gouvernent." *L'histoire* 147: 48–57.

Rioux, Jean-Pierre. 1998 (Sept. 27–28). "La Vie Republique Plebiscitée." *Le Monde,* 12.

Roger, Patrick. 2004 (March 31). "Apres la 'divine surprise' des regionales, le PC s'interroge sur sa strategie." *Le Monde* http://www.lemonde.fr/web/article/l0,1-0@2-3224,36-3.... access 4/01/04.

Rosseau, Dominique. 1993. "Le conseil constitutional." In *La Vie politique en France* (pp. 109–32), ed. Dominique Chagnollaud. Paris: Editions du Seuil.

Rouban, Luc. 2004. "Politicization of the Civil Service in France: From Structural to Strategic Politication." In Guy Peters and Jon Pierre, eds. *Politicization of the Civil Service in Comparative Perspective: The Quest for Control.* New York: Routledge.

Rumpala, Yannick. 2003. *Regulation publique et environement: questions econlogiques, reponses economiques.* Paris: Harmattan.

Sabine, George H. 1961. *A History of Political Theory.* 3rd ed. New York: Holt, Rinehart and Winston.

Safran, William. 1991. *The French Polity.* 3rd ed. New York: Longman.

Safron, William. 2003 (Fall). "Pluralism and Multiculturalism in France: Post-Jacobin Transformations." *Political Science Quarterly,* 118(3): 437–67.

Sardan, Pierre. 1993. "L'administration." In *La lie politique en France* (pp. 148–67), ed. Dominique Chagnollaud. Paris: Editions du Seuil.

Schain, Martin A. 1989. "Politics at the Margins: The French Communist Party and the National Front." In *Policy-Making in France: From de Gaulle to Mitterrand (pp. 73–90),* ed. Paul Godt. New York: Pinter.

Schlesinger, Joseph, and Mildred Schlesinger. 1990 (Dec.). "The Reaffirmation of a Multiparty System in France." *American Political Science Review* 8(4): 1077–102.

Schlesinger, Joseph and Mildred S. Schlesinger. 1998 (Feb.). "Dual-ballot Elections and Political Parties: The French Presidential Election of 1995."

Comparative Political Studies 31(1): 72–97.

Schwab, George, ed. 1978. *Eurocommunism: The Ideological and Political-Theoretical Foundations.* Westport, CT: Greenwood Press.

Singer, Barnett, and John Langdon. 1998 (May). "France's Imperial Legacy." *Contemporary Review* 272 (1588): 231–237.

Singer, Daniel. 1997 (July–Aug.). "The French Winter of Discontent." *Monthly Review* 49(3): 130–139.

Sowerwine, Charles. 2001. *France Since 1870: Culture, Politics and Society.* New York: Palgrave.

Stevens, Anne. 2003. *The Government and Politics of France.* 3rd ed. New York: Macmillan.

Stevens, Anne. 1992. *The Government and Politics of France.* London: Macmillan.

Stone, Alec. 1989. "Legal Constraints to Policy-Making: The Constitutional Council and the Council of State." In *Policy-Making in France: From de Gaulle to Mitterrand (pp. 28–41),* ed. Paul Godt. New York: Pinter.

Suzzarini, M. F. 1986. *L'etat c'est vous!* Alleur, Belgium: Marabout.

Szarka, Joseph. 1997 (Oct.). "Snatching Defeat from the Jaws of Victory: The French Parliamentary Elections of 25 May and 1 June 1997." *West European Politics* 20(4): 192–199.

Tiersky, Ronald. 1994. *France in the New Europe: Changing Yet Steadfast.* Belmont, CA: Wadsworth.

Waters, Sarah. 1998 (July). "New Social Movement Politics in France: The Rise of Civic Forms of Mobilisation." *Western European Politics* 21(3): 170–186.

Williams, Ann. 1968. *Britain and France in the Middle East and North Africa, 1914–1967.* London: Macmillan.

Wilson, Frank L. 1989. "Evolution of the French Party System." In *Policy-Making in France: From de Gaulle to Mitterrand* (pp. 57–72), ed. Paul Godt. New York: Pinter.

Wilson, Frank L. 1993. *The Failure of West European Communism: Implications for the Future.* New York: Paragon House.

Wright, Gordon. 1987. *France in Modern Times.* 4th ed. New York: W. W. Norton.

Wright, Vincent. 1993. "The President and the Prime Minister: Subordination, Conflict, Symbiosis or Reciprocal Parasitism?" In *De Gaulle to Mitterrand:* *Presidential Power in France* (pp. 101–19), ed. Jack Hayward. London: Hurst and Company.

Ysmal, Colette. 1993. "Centristes et liberaux." In *La Vie politique en France* (pp. 257–71), ed. Dominique Chagnollaud. Paris: Editions du Seuil.

Zeldin, Theodore. 1982. *The French.* New York: Pantheon.

Denmark

North Sea

Baltic Sea

Hamburg ■

■ **Bremen**

Poland

Hanover ■

■ Berlin

GERMANY

**FORMER
EAST GERMANY**

Netherlands

■ **Düsseldorf**

Dresden ■

Belgium

■ **Bonn**

Czech Republic

Frankfurt ■

Slovakia

France

Nürnberg ■

■ Stuttgart

Munich ■

Austria

Hungary

Switzerland

Slovenia

Croatia

Italy

**Bosnia and
Herzegovina**

Population:
82,424,609 (2004 estimate)

Life expectancy at birth:
78 years (total population)
75 years (men)
82 years (women)

Literacy:
99 percent of people age 15
and over can read and write
(2000 estimate)

Capital:
Berlin

Per capita income:
$27,600

5

Germany

The Dominant Power
in Europe

Germany is the dominant economic power of Europe. This was true before the unification of East and West Germany in the fall of 1990, and it will be the case for the foreseeable future.

Germany's mounting economic power has given rise to fears of a German military revival (Geipel 1993). Such fears are not easily discounted, for German aggression produced two world wars during the twentieth century, the second of which resulted in the systematic killing of more than 6 million Jews. The Second World War also destroyed much of Europe, with the Soviet Union alone suffering 27 million deaths as a result of the German invasion (Nove 1992).

Could it happen again? Most scholars say no. Conradt bluntly states that "Germany and the Germans have changed" and chides Americans for watching too many old war movies on television (Conradt 1986, xviix). Edinger similarly states that the "haunted have departed" (Edinger 1977). Their views are supported by the resounding success of German democracy over the course of the past five decades. Few states in the world today are as democratic as Germany.

Nevertheless, doubts remain. In 1990, Nicholas Ridley, a member of the British Cabinet, created a crisis in Anglo-German relations by proclaiming that Germans were "authoritarian and expansionist by nature," a recurring theme in the political science literature of the 1950s and 1960s (Almond and Verba 1965). The Minister duly resigned, but his views are shared by many Europeans. Opinion polls conducted in 2004 indicated that one-third of Americans and Russians still associated Germany with Hitler (FAZ, June 12, 2004, www).

For those who question the depth of Germany's commitment to peace and democracy, the revival of a small neo-Nazi movement during the 1990s served as a reminder of things past. Fueled by a permanent unemployment rate of more than 10 percent, the neo-Nazis launched violent attacks against immigrant workers, often bombing the apartment complexes in which they resided. By the end of 1993, then-Chancellor Helmut Kohl was forced to admit that neo-Nazis posed a "serious problem." More than 10,000 hate crimes were attributed to Nazi groups in 2002, most involving the defacing of synagogues or Jewish cemeteries (*Christian Science Monitor*, May 6, 2003, 16). Some 342 suspects were investigated in 2004 for posting songs by skinhead bands on the Internet, the new venue for the propagation of racial hatred. Such crimes are punishable by imprisonment in Germany (Haaretz.com, March 25, 2004, www). This said, Germany's neo-Nazi movement is embryonic in form and remains smaller than similar movements in France and most other European nations (Eatwell and Mudde, 2004). It is Germany's past that makes it seem so frightening.

Despite lingering fears concerning a revival of German authoritarianism, most political observers find the German population to be fully committed to the principles of liberal democracy. They also note that Germany has put aside its extreme nationalism and become one of the main pillars of the European Union, Europe's emerging superstate (Edinger and Nacos 1998).

In the pages that follow, we will examine how the German population decides "who gets what, when, and how." Special focus will be placed on Germany's successful transition from an authoritarian dictatorship into a liberal democracy. Perhaps the lessons of the German experience will benefit Russia and other states that are making similar transitions.

GERMANY IN HISTORICAL PERSPECTIVE

The First Reich (936–1870)

The emergence of Germany as a historical entity is frequently traced to the breakup of Charlemagne's empire in approximately 843 AD, an event that saw Otto the Great (936–973) establish his domain over many of the German-speaking areas of Central Europe. Otto's empire was subsequently referred to as the Holy Roman Empire, a misleading title honoring the defeat of Rome by German tribes. Placed in historical perspective, the Holy Roman Empire represents the first German **Reich,** or *empire.*

The Holy Roman Empire was not a state in the modern sense of the word, representing little more than a loose confederation of tribes and principalities, the cohesion of which varied with the power of the emperor. By the end of the thirteenth century, the Empire existed in name only, having been fragmented into hundreds of principalities and free cities (Detweiler 1976).

Germany was to remain fragmented well into the eighteenth century. While Britain and France used their growing industrial might to forge powerful empires, the Germans, divided by petty squabbles, remained largely pastoral. By British and French standards, Germany possessed all of the characteristics of a "developing area." It was not industrial, it had yet to evolve a large and politically conscious middle class, and it lacked "national" political institutions.

Napoleon invaded Germany in 1806, forcing the smaller German states to merge with their larger neighbors. Full unification, however, would not be achieved until 1871, a date marking the defeat of France by a confederation of German states under the leadership of Otto von Bismarck, Chancellor of Prussia. With the war's end, Prussian dominance left its allies little choice but to accept Bismarck's demands for the creation of a unified Germany (Hucko 1987). The Second Reich was born.

The Second Reich (1871–1918)

Economically, the Second Reich represented a period of accelerated industrialization that would place Germany on a par with England and France. Industrialization, in turn, sparked the urbanization of German society and led to a rapid expansion of both the middle and working classes. Unlike the British and French experiences, however, Germany's industrial revolution was not matched by a political revolution. Rather, German politics under the Second Reich was dominated by an aristocratic coalition of industrialists, landed nobility, and generals (Schonhardt-Bailey 1998). The middle class, content with its growing wealth, was largely swept along by the tide of German nationalism, as was much of the working class (Grunberger 1971).

The Second Reich dissolved in the ashes of World War I. The war, launched by Kaiser Wilhelm II to establish German primacy in Europe, was to have been the crowning demonstration of German military genius (Scheele 1946). Plans had even been made to invade the United States. Sixty ships laden with troops were to have seized Boston while heavy cruisers bombarded Manhattan (*Guardian,* May 9, 2002, www). The Kaiser's dreams, however, evaporated in the trenches of France. With support for the war crumbling and victory beyond hope, the Kaiser abdicated his throne, proclaiming Germany to be a republic. A republic, he reasoned, would be in a stronger position to negotiate a "just peace" with the Allied Powers than a discredited monarchy (Tuchman 1962).

Hopes for a "just peace" were to remain unfulfilled. Indeed, it has been argued that the origins of the Second World War are to be found in the harsh conditions imposed upon a defeated Germany by the Allied Powers at the termination of World War I.

The French provinces of Alsace and Lorraine, which had been seized by Germany in the Franco-Prussian war of 1871, were returned to France. In one fell swoop, Germany was deprived of 15 percent of its arable land and 10 percent of its population. Germany was also stripped of all of its foreign colonies, as well as much of its merchant navy and railway stock. Adding insult to injury, the Allied Powers demanded billions of dollars in reparations for the damage wrought by the German armies.

The bitterness of defeat found direct expression in fragmentation of the German population. The military condemned liberal politicians for deserting the war

Proclamation of the German Empire, Second Reich, at Versailles in 1871 (based on a painting done by Anton von Werner in 1885).

effort, insinuating that they had "stabbed the military in the back" (Hucko 1987, 60). Liberals, in turn, derided the conservative alliance of industrialists, generals, and landed aristocracy for its misplaced dreams of national grandeur. Communist movements, fueled by the harsh working conditions that had accompanied Germany's belated industrialization, mushroomed throughout the country. Power was seized for a brief period in the German province of Bavaria (Grunberger 1971), giving an ominous warning of things to come.

The Weimar Republic (1919–1933)

It was in this environment that a constitutional assembly was convened in 1919 to draft a new Constitution for the German republic. Meeting in the town of Weimar, the delegates to the assembly attempted to design a Constitution so democratic that it would forever preclude a return to power by Germany's military-industrial elite (Broue 2004). Toward this end, the new Germany was provided with both a popularly elected president and a prime minister elected by the lower house of the parliament (Reichstag), each possessing the power to check the other. Germany was to have a bicameral parliament, with the Reichstag elected by direct universal manhood suffrage and the Bundesrat (upper house) by the Lander (states). Representation in the Reichstag, moreover, was to be on the basis of proportional representation. If a party received 2 percent of the popular vote, it would receive 2 percent of the seats in the Reichstag. No political group in Weimar Germany, according to the framers of the Constitution, would be without a voice in parliament.

By attempting to preclude a return to authoritarianism, the framers of the Weimar Constitution had created a political system that was unable to take decisive action in times of crisis. Unfortunately, the Weimar Republic was to have no shortage of crises. Politically fragmented by its defeat in the war and crippled by punitive reparations, the German state would soon find itself in the throes of a world economic depression. By 1932, Germany had become a country without hope as roughly one-half of its population was touched in one way or another by unemployment.

Fueled by despair, extremist parties proliferated. An attempted military coup or "putsch" was put down in 1920, only to be followed by an abortive communist coup in the state of Saxony (1923) and an abortive Nazi coup in Munich (1923). The system of proportional representation, moreover, assured that extremist groups of all varieties would find representation in the Reichstag, including a powerful Communist Party that advocated class warfare and world revolution. The communists had seized power in Russia in 1917, and many observers felt that it was only a matter of time before they seized power in Germany as well.

By 1932, the Nazis had become the largest party in the Reichstag, their major opponents being the Communists. The Social Democratic, Liberal, and Catholic parties, the core of German democracy, controlled only 30 percent of the seats in the Reichstag. This was less than half of their representation in 1919. With parliamentary government having become impossible, the German president—the aging General Paul von Hindenburg—invoked the Constitution's emergency provisions and ruled by decree (Grunberger 1971). The government, however, was becoming irrelevant as pitched battles between opposing Nazi and Communist militias pushed Germany to the brink of civil war.

The history of the Weimar Republic testifies to the fact that structural (organizational) arrangements alone cannot guarantee either democracy or human rights. Constitutions and other structural arrangements can facilitate the exercise of democracy, but they cannot compensate for the absence of a population dedicated to democratic principles. The history of the Weimar Republic also raises interesting questions concerning the fragmentation of political power. It is dangerous to concentrate excessive power in the hands of a narrow oligarchy. It is equally dangerous to deprive the government of the capacity to rule.

Hitler and the Third Reich (1933–1945)

Hitler's meteoric rise to power has been recounted so many times that it requires little retelling. Formed in Munich in 1919, Hitler's **Nazi Party** was one of a multitude of fringe parties that appealed to the marginal elements in German society. Under normal circumstances, the Nazi Party would probably have remained a fringe party of little consequence. Circumstances, however, were far from normal. By 1930, German society was in a state of collapse, and the government was losing its capacity to rule. Germany's social and economic institutions were also disintegrating, creating a condition that sociologists refer to as **anomie,** or *normlessness.* A German population long noted for its disciplined adherence to rules found itself with few rules to follow.

When the rules of society collapse, observed the German sociologist Max Weber, the masses will seek a charismatic leader to lead them to salvation.

The term **charisma,** according to Weber, can be applied to *"a certain quality of an individual's personality by virtue of which he is set apart from ordinary men and treated as endowed with supernatural, superhuman, or at least specifically exceptional powers or qualities* (Weber 1947, 328).

The Hitler of 1920 bore little resemblance to Weber's superhuman prophet, Hitler's virulent message of anti-Semitism and Aryan superiority appealing largely to a handful of misfits living on the margins of society. As the economic and political structure of German society collapsed, however, virtually all segments of German society had become marginalized (Anheir, Neidhardt, and Vortkamp 1998). The size of Hitler's following increased apace, a process described by Hans Gerth:

> Persons whose career expectations are frustrated or who suffer losses in status or income in the intensive vocational competition of modern capitalism should be especially likely to accept the belief in the charismatic leader. Those placed on the disadvantaged side of life always tend to be interested in some sort of salvation which breaks through the routines associated with their deprivation. Such "unsuccessful" persons were to be found in every stratum of German society. Princes without thrones, indebted and subsidized landlords, indebted farmers, virtually bankrupt industrialists, impoverished shopkeepers and artisans, doctors without patients, lawyers without clients, writers without readers, unemployed teachers, and unemployed manual and white collar workers joined the movement. National Socialism as a salvationary movement exercised an especially strong attraction on the "old" and "new" middle classes, especially in those strata where substantive rationality is least developed and will be most highly represented among those seeking salvation by quasi-miraculous means—or at least by methods which break through the routines which account for their deprivation (1940, 526–27).

Nazism was also embraced by Germans who feared a communist revolution or who dreaded the prospect of civil war (Brustein 1998). This included members of the middle class and the conservative aristocracy of landowners, generals, and industrialists that had long dominated German politics (Grunberger 1971; Lipset 1960). Hitler, in their view, was a tool to be used for the moment and discarded when the crisis had passed. As it turned out, it was they who were discarded.

The 1933 elections saw Hitler and his allies gain 51 percent of the popular vote, and Hitler was duly proclaimed chancellor (Grunberger 1971; Flint 1998). The communists were crushed and the Third Reich was born. Hitler's authoritarian methods would transform Germany from a bankrupt nation on the brink of civil war into a military and industrial power that came within a hairsbreadth of world domination. It would also establish the doctrine of fascism as one of the dominant political philosophies or "isms" of the modern era.

Keystone/Getty Images

During World War II, Hitler's Nazi forces systematically slaughtered millions of Jews and other "non-Aryans" in concentration camps. In this photo taken shortly after the war, General Dwight D. Eisenhower views a cluster of corpses while visiting a former concentration camp in Ohrdruf, Germany.

Fascism. Fascism, as preached by Hitler and the Nazi Party, was *a fanatical blend of racism, extreme nationalism, and paranoia.* The Germans, according to Hitler, were a **master race,** historically destined to rule the world. The German state was the logical expression of German racial superiority, its role being to fulfill Germany's historical mission of world conquest.

In Hitler's demented mind, the Jews had engineered Germany's socio-economic decline as part of a broader international conspiracy designed to deny Germany its rightful place in the world (Smith 1998). Germany could not achieve its historical mission, according to Hitler, until the Jews had been exterminated. Fascists also preached **Social Darwinism,** or the *survival of the fittest.* There was no room for the handicapped in Nazi Germany; the purity of the Aryan race was not to be diluted (Sargent 1987; Reich 1990).

The Two Germanys (1945–1989)

With the unconditional surrender of Nazi Germany in May 1945, the victorious Allied Powers divided German territory into American, British, French, and Soviet occupation sectors, coordination among which was to be achieved by a Supreme Allied Command located in Berlin.

The unity of the wartime allies collapsed shortly after the German surrender, and in 1948, defeated Germany was divided into two independent countries: the

Richard Peter sen./Getty Images

Rebuilding Germany after the war was a massive undertaking. This photo was taken in the city of Dresden, located in what would become East Germany, shortly after the city was bombed by allied forces.

German Democratic Republic (East Germany) and the Federal Republic of Germany, or West Germany. The Cold War had begun in earnest.

A constitutional convention was convened shortly after the merging of the American, French, and British zones into West Germany. Delegates to the constitutional assembly, however, displayed little enthusiasm for drafting a Constitution that would give permanent expression to the division of their country into two separate entities. It was decided, accordingly, that they would draft a **"Basic Law"** to serve in place of a Constitution.

The Basic Law was not imposed by force, but the occupying powers left little doubt that the Federal Republic of Germany was to be a democratic and demilitarized country in which former Nazis would have no voice. As if to underscore the differences between the new Germany and its predecessors, the capital of the Federal Republic was located in Bonn, a sleepy college town that possessed neither the imposing elegance of Berlin nor its symbols of imperial grandeur (Bertram 1998).

For the next four decades, each of the two Germanys would go its own way. West Germany pursued a path of democracy and capitalism, becoming one of the wealthiest states in the world. East Germany, by contrast, had merely traded one form of totalitarianism for another and languished in socialist mediocrity.

While East Germany and West Germany had become independent countries, the Allied Powers continued to maintain their occupation zone in Berlin, a city

Meeting with little resistance from authorities, East Germans made history in November 1989 with the destruction of the Berlin Wall.

that was totally encircled by East Germany. East Germans soon found this Western enclave in the middle of their country to be a convenient avenue for defecting to the West. In 1961, accordingly, the communist authorities encircled West Berlin with a fortified prison wall (the **Berlin Wall**), shooting defectors on sight. East Germany's land mass was approximately 40 percent the size of West Germany, with about 25 percent of its population. Its economic production, however, was less than 15 percent of West Germany's.

As the Soviet Union began to crumble in the late 1980s, its puppet regime in East Germany found it increasingly difficult to prevent its citizens from defecting to the West (Wallach and Francisco 1992). On November 9, 1989, the citizens of East Berlin took matters into their own hands, smashing the wall that had imprisoned them for some forty years. The East German regime had collapsed.

Both the West and the U.S.S.R. were stunned by the speed with which the East German regime had fallen. For the U.S.S.R., it signaled the end of communism in Eastern Europe, if not the Soviet Union itself. The West rejoiced, but its euphoria was soon tempered by the realization that the reunification of the two Germanys was inevitable. Indeed, the reunification agreement was formally signed on October 3, 1990, less than twelve months after the breach of the Berlin Wall. East Germany was simply absorbed by West Germany, agreeing to accept the Basic Law as well as all West German social and economic legislation.

While allowing the unification of Germany, Western countries remained apprehensive about the status of a reunified Germany in the world community.

Would the new Germany continue on its path of democracy, or would it revert to its former authoritarian traditions? World War II had ended more than four decades earlier, but its scars ran deep.

The Incomplete Reunification (1990–)

The reunification of the two Germanys occurred in a rush of euphoria and optimism. West Germans understood that economic sacrifices would have to be made, but most assumed that the period of adjustment would be relatively short. East Germany had been the most productive area of the communist bloc and Germans, after all, were Germans.

The optimism that preceded the reunification of the two Germanys was soon to be shattered. Few West Germans had understood precisely how much the East German economy had deteriorated.

As the costs of reunification continued to mount, West Germans began to question the enormous subsidies that were being paid to East Germans in an effort to ease the pain of the transition from socialism to capitalism (Pond 1993; Pickel 1997). East Germans, in the West German view, were not pulling their weight. Matters were made all the more difficult by the onset of a broader European economic recession that would find West Germans suffering economic hardships unknown since the end of the Second World War. These sentiments found expression in a 2004 survey suggesting that one-fifth of the West German population preferred a return of the Berlin Wall.

Bitterness, however, was not reserved for the West Germans. East Germans faced the brunt of the reunification process, as former state-run factories were either closed by the German government or streamlined by their new owners. By 1993, hundreds of thousands of East German jobs were lost. Some of the displaced workers found new jobs, but others did not, and unemployment figures for the unified country soon exceeded the 12 percent level, with unemployment figures for the area of the former East Germany exceeding 16 percent, a figure that continues to haunt the region today.

Whatever the case, 15 years of reunification and the expenditure of $1.52 trillion have failed to provide the states of eastern Germany with more than the most rudimentary economic infrastructure. Cash transfers to the East are guaranteed through 2019, but the decline of the German economy has made them ever more painful (FAZ, April 9, 2004, www). Even that date now appears optimistic (Wisenthal 2003).

THE POLITICAL INSTITUTIONS
OF GERMANY

As we have seen in the preceding chapters, a country's political institutions provide the arena for its political process. In this section, we will look at the formal structures of German government and how they were designed to prevent a return to authoritarianism. The experience of Germany in providing a legal framework for democracy is now being applied in Iraq and other countries embarking on a transition to democracy. Whether they can duplicate the German experience remains to be seen.

The Basic Law (Constitutional Document) of Germany

The framers of Germany's Basic Law attempted to design political institutions that would be strong enough to provide effective leadership yet remain responsive to the will of the masses. They distrusted a strong executive but feared that a weak and divided government would be unable to solve the massive problems confronting the war-torn nation. Weak governments, as the experience of the Weimar Republic had well demonstrated, were an invitation to tyranny.

It was thus determined that the Federal Republic would be governed as a parliamentary democracy in which executive power would be vested in a chancellor responsible before a popularly elected **Bundestag** *(lower house of Parliament)*. Germany would also have a largely symbolic president who played a role similar to that of the monarch of England. The chancellor would serve at the pleasure of the members of the Bundestag and could be removed at their will. To further guard against the resurgence of an authoritarian regime, Germany was to become a federation. Laws affecting the states, or **Lander,** were to require the approval of the **Bundesrat,** or *upper house of Parliament,* the members of which were selected by the Lander. Laws affecting the Lander would also be administered by the Lander, thereby assuring a maximum of "home rule." Finally, as one last impediment to the return of authoritarianism , the acts of the federal government were subject to the review of an independent judiciary headed by a "Supreme" Constitutional Court. Merely issuing rules, of course, offers no guarantee that the "players" will abide by those rules. Nevertheless, the framers of the Basic Law clearly attempted to compensate for the structural problems of the past.

Elections and Politics in Germany

In an electoral system that is among the most complex in the world today, German voters cast two ballots (James 2003). The first ballot is for a member of the Bundestag to be elected on the basis of single-member, simple-plurality districts. The candidate who receives the most votes in a district wins the seat in the Bundestag. The second ballot designates the voter's political party of choice. It is this second, or party, ballot that determines the actual number of seats that a party will receive in the Bundestag. If the Christian Democratic Union wins 50 percent of the party vote, for example, it is assured 50 percent of the seats in the Bundestag. The occupants of CDU's seats in the Bundestag will be determined first by the results of the district elections and secondly by the "party list." In this instance, the CDU's 50 percent of the popular vote now entitles it to 336 (or one-half) of the 672 seats in the Bundestag. Assume also that CDU candidates won 290 seats in the district elections. To reconcile the results of the two elections, the 290 seats won in the district election would be subtracted from the CDU's allocated total of 336 seats. The remaining 46 seats would be filled in numerical order from the names on the party list. The CDU's representation or "fraction" in the Bundestag, accordingly, would consist of the 290 party candidates victorious in the district elections, as well as the top 46 names on the CDU's electoral list.

This system of voting is sometimes referred to as a personalized proportional representation system. It is a proportional voting system because a party is guaranteed a number of seats in the Bundestag equivalent to the percentage of its popular vote. It is a personalized system because the German voters are provided with the opportunity to select most of their representatives in district elections.

The only proviso to this system is that a party must receive at least 5 percent of the popular vote. Barring this, its votes are wasted. The 5 percent provision was a reaction to the experience of the Weimar Republic and was designed to prevent the legislative process from being obstructed by an excess of minor parties, most of which were little more than narrow pressure groups. It was also designed to keep small radical groups from using the Parliament as a political forum.

The order of names on a party's election list is determined by the party leadership. Party leaders are thus assured a seat in the Bundestag in the unlikely event they should lose their district elections. The list system also provides the party leadership with the ability to "discipline" its members by removing them from the party list.

The German electoral system, then, represents an attempt by the framers of the Basic Law to gain the benefits of both single-member districts and proportional representation. As we saw in the discussion of British politics, single-member, simple-plurality districts promote stability by limiting the number of viable political parties. As the party with the most votes wins the single seat available, like-minded groups must combine their efforts if they are to have any hope of victory. The disadvantage of single-member, simple-plurality systems is that votes are wasted. The losers, often a majority, have no influence on policy. The advantages and disadvantages of proportional representation, by contrast, are exactly the opposite. Allocating seats in Parliament in proportion to the popular vote provides an accurate reflection of the popular will but often leads to political instability by creating too many parties in the legislature, none of which has the capacity to lead.

The framers of the Basic Law were vitally concerned with assuring the stability of the new state, but they also wanted to create a political system that would be as democratic as possible. By combining single-member districts and proportional representation, they hoped to achieve both objectives (Jeffery 1998).

Executive Power in Germany: Chancellors, Governments, and Presidents

Germany possesses both a chancellor and a president. The **chancellor** is Germany's *chief executive*, his role being parallel to that of the British prime minister. The German **president** is the symbolic head of state and plays a role similar to that of the British monarch.

The Chancellor and Cabinet (Government). Executive authority in Germany is vested in a chancellor (prime minister) elected by the Bundestag from among its members. In practice, the chancellor is usually the head of the dominant party or dominant coalition of parties in the Bundestag. The chancellor, in turn, selects the members of the Cabinet. Collectively, *the chancellor and the Cabinet* are referred to as the **"Government."** The Government is responsible before the Bundestag and can be forced to resign by a "positive" vote of no confidence, a topic to be discussed shortly. The Government, however, stands and falls as a whole, and the Bundestag cannot remove individual ministers.

Technically speaking, chancellors possess the authority to appoint and remove Cabinet ministers as they see fit. In reality, however, most Cabinet positions are filled by powerful politicians who represent important wings of the chancellor's party. Their removal, if not threatening the collapse of the Government itself, would surely trigger a crisis within the dominant party.

The chancellor is precluded by law from intervening in the day-to-day affairs of the respective ministries. Each minister is a powerful policy maker who is supreme in his or her domain. The exact line between the independent responsibility of the ministers and the chancellor's power to set "the general guidelines for governmental policy" remains imperfectly defined, with much depending on the relative power of the individuals involved (*New York Times,* Mar. 22, 1999).

It would be a mistake, however, to overstate the power of individual ministers, as the chancellor possesses the constitutional authority to override ministerial decisions that are contrary to his or her general policy guidelines. Individual Cabinet ministers, moreover, are precluded from making major policy statements without the prior clearance of the chancellor, and they must also keep the chancellor informed of the activities of their ministries. Overall, German ministers are somewhat less powerful than their British counterparts (Conradt 1986).

Also falling in the realm of executive authority is the Chancellor's Office. Consisting of more than 400 individuals, the Chancellor's Office represents his personal staff and is organized into departments paralleling the various Cabinet ministries. Each is headed by a senior official possessing the expertise to "keep tabs" on the activities of his or her ministerial counterpart. The "head" of the Chancellor's Office is a member of the Cabinet without portfolio; that is, he doesn't head a major administrative agency (Conradt 1986, 2005).

The formal powers of the German chancellor are also strengthened by a variety of informal powers. The chancellor is usually the head of his or her political party and, as such, will have much to say about how names will be ordered on the party electorate lists. The chancellor is also the focal point of the German mass media, a position that facilitates the manipulation of public opinion. While others respond to policy, it is the chancellor who sets the policy agenda.

The President. The German president is the symbolic head of Germany. The president must sign all bills passed by the Parliament, and it is also the president who dissolves the Bundestag prior to new elections. These roles, much like those of the monarch of England, are pro forma—the real power lies with the chancellor. Nevertheless, past presidents have often played forceful moral roles in German society by speaking out against racism. Horst Kohler, Germany's current president, has continued this tradition by using his inaugural speech to suggest that German politicians "have gotten tired" and that they have lost sight of the concerns of the German public (FAZ, April 9, 2004, www).

The German president is elected for a five-year term by an electoral college consisting of all parliamentary representatives at the federal and Land level, some 1,338 in all. German presidents are limited to two terms in office, and candidates for the office are respected political figures.

Legislative Power in Germany: The Bundestag and the Bundesrat

Legislative authority in the Federal Republic of Germany is divided between the Bundestag and the Bundesrat. The Bundestag is the popularly elected lower house of the German Parliament, while the Bundesrat (or upper house) represents the Lander (states).

The Bundestag. The heart of German politics is the Bundestag, consisting of 672 members elected by the German population. They are the only individuals at the national level elected directly by the population. The deputies of the Bundestag, in turn, elect the chancellor (prime minister). Elections to the Bundestag must be held within a four-year period, the exact timing of the elections being determined by the chancellor and the dominant members of his coalition. By and large, most elections in Germany run their full four-year cycle.

As in most parliamentary systems, the Bundestag can bring down the Government by a vote of no confidence. It must, however, be a "positive" vote of no confidence in which the fall of the old Government is contingent upon the election of a new Government within fourteen days. The word *positive* means that in Germany, unlike most parliamentary systems, the country cannot be left without a majority government for a long period of time. Again, the requirement for a positive vote of no confidence was designed to avoid the instability that had undermined the Weimar Republic. There have been only two successful votes of no confidence in the history of the FGR, both in the mid-1970s.

The Bundestag also keeps in touch with the Government by means of a "Question Hour" and a "Current Hour." Adopted from the British practice, the **Question Hour** allows members of the Bundestag to question the Government on issues ranging from matters of national policy to the personal grievances of constituents. The Question Hour, being alien to German practice, was used less than 400 times during the four-year period of the first Bundestag. The practice was soon to catch on, however, and by the seventh Bundestag (1972–1976), the Government found itself compelled to answer some 19,000 queries, a figure that has remained steady through the 1990s (Dalton 1993). The Current Hour was added in 1965, and it allows deputies to force a question period on issues of particular importance.

In addition to helping the Bundestag keep tabs on the Government, the Question Hour provides opposition parties with an active forum for criticizing

Government policy. In the final analysis, the effectiveness of the Question Hour as a political forum for the opposition probably outweighs its utility as a mechanism for controlling the activities of the Government.

The Bundestag also possesses the power to investigate Government officials, but the process is a cumbersome one and is seldom used. The Bundestag's investigative capacity is also limited by its inadequate staff support, not to mention the reluctance of the majority party to investigate its own leaders.

The primary function of the Bundestag is legislation (Maor 1998). All bills must receive a majority vote in the Bundestag before they can become law. While individual members of the Bundestag possess the right to introduce legislation, most legislation originates with the Government.

As in most parliamentary systems, Government bills fare much better than private bills. Indeed, the strong cohesion of German political parties makes the passage of Government bills a near certainty. Those bills, moreover, are unlikely to be amended by committee deliberations or by subsequent debate within the Bundestag. Amendments do occur, but they are of a technical nature and usually have the support of the Government.

The dominant position of the Government in the legislative process rests upon the cohesion of *German parliamentary parties* or **Fraktionen.** A Fraktionen consists of all of a party's deputies in the Bundestag, with the leader of the majority Fraktionen becoming the chancellor. The British would refer to it as a parliamentary party. If the members of the majority party or coalition do not vote as a cohesive unit, they will lose their majority and the Government will fall. This, in most cases, would result in the formation of an opposition Government or in a call for new elections, neither of which would serve the interests of the dominant party.

The German electorate, moreover, expects the majority party or coalition to carry out its platform. The dominant vote in German elections, it will be recalled, is a party vote. Deputies are expected to represent local interests, but they are also expected to support the Government.

Finally, the leaders of Germany's political parties use their control of party finances to impose party discipline. German elections are very expensive and far exceed the resources available to the average candidate for state or national office.

The German government subsidizes the electoral process by allocating funds to the parties in rough proportion to their success at the polls (Kloss 1991, 49–50), but this money is also allocated by the party leadership. This is not a minor consideration, for by the mid-1980s, these subsidies amounted to approximately one dollar per vote (Conradt 1986). Pressure groups also contribute generously to Germany's major parties, but again it is the party leadership that largely determines how those funds will be allocated.

At the broader level, the chancellor's dominance of the Bundestag is also a function of information. The meager staff support provided to the members of the Bundestag is no match for a Government supported by both the federal bureaucracy and the chancellor's personal staff.

The tradition of a strong chancellor, moreover, possesses deep roots within German culture. While Germany's commitment to democratic government is not in doubt, public opinion polls suggest little desire for a weak executive.

German Parliament

Bundestag (Lower House)

- 672 members
- Elected by German population
- Up to four-year terms
- Members elect chancellor
- Power of vote of no confidence legislation

Bundesrat (Upper House)

- 69 members
- Selected by Land governments
- Provides German Lander with active voice in federal policy
- Majority vote required for passage of legislation
- Considers most federal legislation not directly related to foreign policy and national defense

---

The Bundesrat and German Federalism. The Bundesrat, or upper house of the German parliament, was expressly designed to provide the German Lander with an active voice in federal policy making. It consists of 69 members selected by the Land governments (Gunlicks 2003). A majority vote in the Bundesrat is required for all legislation of direct relevance to the rights and responsibilities of the Lander, the nature of which are either specified or implied by the Basic Law. Education, the police, local finance, most transportation issues, land use, and boundary disputes between the Lander all fall within the purview of the Bundesrat, as do national emergencies and amendments to the Basic Law. Bills that do not receive the approval of the Bundesrat in these areas are effectively vetoed and cannot become law. On all other bills, the opposition of the Bundesrat can be overridden by either an absolute majority or a two-thirds majority in the Bundestag, depending upon the circumstances.

As in the United States, the precise line between the powers of the federal government and the powers retained by the German Lander remains fluid and subject to judicial interpretation. In sharp contrast to the American experience, however, the power of the German Lander has increased rather than decreased over the course of the past four decades. According to some estimates, the framers of the Basic Law assumed that the Bundesrat would possess "veto power" over about 10 percent of the legislation considered by the Bundestag. In current practice, however, approximately 60 percent of federal legislation requires the approval of the Bundesrat (Conradt 1996, 2005).

In large part, the expanded power of the Bundesrat is the result of a liberal interpretation of the *Doctrine of Co-Responsibility* by the Constitutional Court. This doctrine makes the Lander responsible for the administration of federal laws. In additional to their own primacy in the areas of education, internal security, and justice, moreover, the state bureaucracies also collect federal taxes and share "joint responsibility" with the federal government in the areas of higher education, regional planning, and agrarian reform. In one way or another, then, the Bundesrat has asserted its right to consider most federal legislation not directly related to questions of foreign policy and national defense.

The 69 members of the Bundesrat are apportioned among Germany's 16 Lander on the basis of population. The most populous Lander receive six seats in the

Bundesrat, while the others receive between three and five seats each, depending on their size. The delegates to the Bundesrat are instructed by their Land governments on the policies to be pursued and on the votes to be cast.

Many members of the Bundesrat are ministers in Land governments and, as such, have a major voice in determining the policies of their own Land. Their role in the Bundesrat enhances their ability to see that the policies of their Land are implemented and also enables them to play an effective role in coordinating the affairs of the national and Land governments (Dalton 1993).

In keeping with the general tenor of German government, relations between the Bundesrat and the Bundestag tend to be more cooperative than conflictual. Nevertheless, some conflict is inevitable when the Bundesrat is controlled by the parties of the opposition. Although Government legislation is sometimes rejected by the Bundesrat, it is far more common for the Government to work informally with members of the Bundesrat's leadership to shape legislation that will be acceptable to the parliament as a whole. Bundesrat rejection of Government legislation does not constitute a vote of no confidence, but it is a source of considerable embarrassment.

Law and Politics in Germany: The Federal Constitutional Court and the Judicial System

The Federal Constitutional Court is similar in function to the Supreme Court of the United States. It reviews the constitutionality of both federal and state (Land) legislation, interprets the various articles of the Basic Law, settles disputes between Land governments, adjudicates conflicts between the Land governments and the Federal Government, and serves as the final guarantor of those civil rights enumerated in the Basic Law. In addition to the above functions, the Federal Constitutional Court has the special responsibility of protecting the constitutional and democratic character of the German state. In this role, the Court has the right to outlaw nondemocratic political parties attempting to use democratic procedures for the purpose of reestablishing an authoritarian regime in Germany.

The Constitutional Court consists of 16 members elected in equal proportions by the Bundestag and the Bundesrat. A two-thirds majority of the respective chambers is required for the election of justices, a stringent requirement that has contributed to the high quality of the Court's members. The Court is divided into two chambers, one specializing in issues related to civil rights and the other in issues involving the constitutionality of legislative acts and intergovernmental relations.

The concept of a Supreme Court empowered to review the acts of the Government was an innovation adopted from the American experience in the hope of placing yet another obstacle in the path of authoritarianism. With little prior experience to draw upon, no one was quite sure how much vigor the Federal Constitutional Court would display in executing its constitutional responsibilities.

After a slow start, the Federal Constitutional Court has emerged as a major actor on the German political scene (Vanberg 2005). By 1990, the Constitutional Court had considered some 80,000 cases, more than 75,000 of which involved an interpretation of the Basic Law. Only 2 percent of the challenges to the Government's interpretation of the Basic Law were allowed, making the Court a very conservative force in German politics.

The influence of the Court, moreover, is increasing. The use of German troops in United Nations peacekeeping missions had to be approved by the Court, as did Germany's ratification of the Maastricht Treaty. The Constitutional Court has also been playing a major role in sorting out problems resulting from the reunification of the two Germanies. The untangling of property rights in East Germany is a particularly knotty issue, as is the resolution of differences in "moral" legislation between the two Germanies. The East German policy of providing free abortions, for example, was struck down by the Court as contrary to the Basic Law *(New York Times,* May 29, 1993). More recently, the Court threw out the Government's liberal immigration law on the grounds that it was "steam-rolled" through the Parliament *(Guardian,* December 19, 2002, www). The following year it struck down attempts to ban the neo-Nazi National Democratic Party. The Court's logic was that the incriminating acts had been committed by government intelligence agents who had infiltrated the party *(Guardian,* March 19, 2003). This, in turn, was followed by the Court's rejection of tenure for professors who didn't publish (FAZ, July 20, 2004).

The Federal Constitutional Court is a separate branch of the German government. As such, it possesses its own budget and is fully independent of the federal bureaucracy. The German judiciary, by contrast, is administered by the Lander, with more than 17,000 Land judges administering both local and federal law (Kloss 1991). While the German legal system is controlled by the Lander, the law they administer is the uniform legal code of the Federal Republic. In contrast to the American experience, the law on key issues such as criminal offenses, divorce, and custody is the same throughout the German Republic. Also, unlike the American experience, the German court system operates quickly, cheaply, and with minimal complexity. One reason for this is that Germany employs approximately nine times more judges than the United States on a per capita basis (Conradt 1986).

Bureaucracy and Politics in Germany

The German civil service personifies the ideals of efficiency, precision, and dedication (Paterson and Southern 1991). It was the efficiency of the German (Prussian) bureaucracy that enabled Bismarck to transform a confederation of feudal principalities into the dominant military power of Europe (Smith 1990). It was the same efficiency that enabled Hitler to launch his quest for world domination. Today, the efficiency of the German bureaucracy supports the economic prosperity of the Federal Republic.

The efficiency of the bureaucracy has contributed to the legitimacy of the Federal Republic by providing its citizens with a remarkably high standard of public services (Smith 1990). German trains run on time, as does almost everything else in Germany. It could be argued, of course, that the German bureaucracy is *too* efficient and that this same dedication to order has taken precedence over humanistic and moral concerns. The heart of this criticism was the remarkable efficiency of the German bureaucracy in implementing the programs of Hitler's Third Reich.

Senior bureaucrats are also important decision makers. The Government provides the broad guidelines for policy, leaving the details to be worked out by the senior bureaucrats. To some extent, political decision makers have little choice but to delegate large areas of decision-making authority to senior bureaucrats, for it is the senior bureaucrats who possess most of the information and expertise required to implement government policy. Senior bureaucrats, however, are also highly respected for their expertise, and their views are actively sought by the political leadership (Goetz 1997).

As decision makers, the German bureaucrats represent a very conservative force in German politics. Efficiency is a function of order and regimentation. Change, by contrast, is disruptive, shattering routine and forcing officials to take unwanted risks. If changes are to occur, from a bureaucratic perspective, they should be incremental changes that are easily incorporated into the system (Conradt 1993).

The conservative orientation of the German bureaucracy has created something of a paradox. On one hand, the efficiency of the German bureaucracy has few peers in today's world. On the other hand, the conservative orientation of the bureaucracy makes it poorly suited to the task of providing creative solutions to Germany's growing environmental, educational, and social problems, not to mention the problems associated with the reunification of the two Germanies and the integration of Germany into the European Union.

To some extent, this paradox has been resolved by creating a variety of planning agencies external to the bureaucracy. Most ministries now have planning staffs independent of the bureaucracy, as does the Chancellor's Office. Planning, however, remains a difficult task. Not only does tension exist between the planners and the bureaucracy, but federal planning is also beset by the multiple checks and balances of Germany's political system (*Economist,* Aug. 30, 2003, 35).

THE ACTORS IN GERMAN POLITICS:
ELITES, PARTIES, GROUPS, AND CITIZENS

The political institutions reviewed above represent the core of the German political system. They are the formal mechanisms for deciding who gets what, when, and how. Political institutions, however, do not exist in a vacuum. In order to understand the functioning of the political process in the Federal Republic of Germany, accordingly, it is necessary to examine the elites that run the government, the political parties and groups upon which elites rely for their power, and the broader pattern of popular attitudes toward the government.

Elites and Politics in Germany

German history has been characterized by elitism (Dahrendorf 1959). Elites made policy, competent bureaucrats executed policy, and the masses obeyed policy.

The elites of the Federal Republic differ from earlier German leaders in two critical ways. *First, unlike Bismarck and Hitler, the leaders of modern Germany have demonstrated an unwavering commitment to democracy.* Indeed, during the early years

Chancellor Gerhard Schroeder represents the post–World War II generation that has come to power in Germany.

of the Federal Republic, Germany's political elites were probably more democratic than the population as a whole. This argument is supported by the results of a 1951 opinion poll which indicated that 42 percent of the West German population and 53 percent of the West German population over the age of 35 considered the pre-war years of the Third Reich to be the best that Germany had experienced during the twentieth century (Conradt 1986). Elite commitment to democracy, then, played an important role in building support for democracy among the German masses.

This said, Germany possess a tradition of very strong individuals. Konrad Adenauer, the Federal Republic's first chancellor (1949–1963), set the tone for his successors by totally dominating the Cabinet, the Bundestag, and the national bureaucracy. Subsequent chancellors have continued to dominate Germany's elite structure, albeit in a somewhat less imperial manner than Adenauer. Willy Brandt (1969–1974) was a dazzling intellect who dominated both Germany and the international stage. Helmut Kohl (1982–1998) dominated German policy-making for 16 years and forged the unification of the two Germanies. Gerhard Schroeder, Kohl's successor, inherited the problems of reunification and a declining economy and his power has suffered accordingly. In 2004 a party revolt stripped him of chairmanship of the Social Democratic Party while allowing him to remain as chancellor. In the view of some observers, Schroeder's decline is a plus for democracy and heralds the end of the "imperial chancellor" (Reutter 2003).

A second critical difference between the elite structure of the Federal Republic and the elite structure of the Second and Third Reichs lies in its pluralistic nature (Dalton 1993). Hitler had consolidated all sources of political power under his personal control. Political power in the Federal Republic, by contrast, is divided among a wide variety of institutions, parties, and groups.

The *dominant political decision makers* or **elites** in the Federal Republic of Germany are the chancellor and the members of the Cabinet. Other members of the inner circle of political decision-makers include the ranking members of the majority party in the Bundestag and their coalition partners. Members of the Constitutional Court are also included among the political elite, as are top-level bureaucrats and ranking members of the various Land governments. The presidency of a Land government often serves as a springboard to Federal leadership, with half of the Federal Republic's six chancellors having served as president-ministers of Land governments prior to becoming chancellor.

Leaders of the opposition party, although far less influential than the leaders of the governing party, also qualify as political elites. They play a major role in the policy-making process by publicizing the weaknesses of Government programs and proposing viable alternatives. Opposition leaders also derive considerable power from the closely contested nature of German elections. The opposition of today could well be the dominant party of tomorrow. More tangibly, the opposition party invariably controls important Land governments, thereby giving its leaders an active voice both at the Land level and in the Bundestag. Should the opposition party control the Bundesrat, its leaders possess the ability to block Government programs that fall within the purview of state's right.

The political elites of the Federal Republic are closely linked to the German party system. Party leaders are assured safe positions on the party lists in both the federal and the Land elections. If their party is victorious, it is they who become members of the Government and otherwise dominate the policy-making process.

Given the dominant role of political parties in German politics, members of Germany's political elite have typically served a long apprenticeship in the party hierarchy (Dalton 1993). Most enter politics at the Land level before moving to the federal arena, and most have demonstrated both competence in office and loyalty to the party. By the time German politicians reach elite status, then, they are seasoned veterans with broad experience in the administrative and political realms. In the process of working their way up within the party hierarchy, moreover, most senior members of Germany's political elite have also established a strong base of popular support including links with a major pressure group such as the German Federation of Labor (GDB) or the Federation of German Industry (BDI) (Hancock 1989).

German elites continue to be committed to democracy. This said, they were sharply rebuked by Johannes Rau, Germany's outgoing president, for being "greedy" and "selfish." "Egoism, greed and self-righteousness in parts of the so-called elite are weakening people's trust in institutions," Rau said (FAZ, May 14, 2004, www).

Parties and Politics in Germany

German political parties are of three varieties (Padgett 1993). At the first level are the **Christian Democratic Union** (CDU) and **Social Democratic Party** (SPD), Germany's two large **catch-all parties.** Collectively, they garner more than 75 percent of the popular vote. The CDU and SPD also dominate the Land elections, and thereby the Bundesrat. It is either the CDU or the SPD that forms a Government, although the support of a smaller party is often required for either to achieve an absolute majority in the Bundestag.

At the second level of the party structure one finds the Free Democratic Party and the Greens. Both generally possess enough support to meet the 5 percent rule for representation in the Bundestag, but neither is large enough to contend for power. As the major parties are seldom able to gain a clear majority in the Bundestag, a coalition with one of the smaller parties is often necessary to form a government. The role of balancer had traditionally been played by the Free Democrats, but following the SPD's victories in the 1998 and 2002 elections, it was the Greens that played this role.

At the third level of the party structure one finds a small Communist Party as well as a spate of neo-Nazi parties. Neither the Communists nor the neo-Nazi parties are major players in German politics, but they do appeal to an extremist fringe. The Communists, reconstituted as the Democratic Socialists, are particularly strong in Eastern Germany, often receiving sufficient votes for symbolic representation in the Bundestag and state parliaments. The neo-Nazi parties have not been strong enough to enjoy sufficient popular support to surpass the 5 percent rule required for representation in the Bundestag.

Both the various neo-Nazi parties and the Communist Party could be banned at the discretion of the Constitutional Court should their activities pose a potential threat to the regime. Indeed, rallies of some neo-Nazi groups are now being banned (FAZ, Jan. 25, 2005, www). Whether the banning of the authoritarian parties would cripple or enhance their political influence is open to debate. On one hand, the outlawing of authoritarian parties deprives them of the opportunity to manipulate democratic procedures for authoritarian ends. On the other hand, merely outlawing an authoritarian political party does little to address the social forces that gave rise to its existence in the first place. Indeed, the very act of banning a political party may have the adverse effect of increasing its symbolic importance.

German political parties, as noted earlier, are very cohesive and disciplined. Once a party position has been decided upon, members of the Bundestag are expected to support the party leadership regardless of their personal views. Members of the Bundestag vote their conscience only on issues that the party leadership has declared to be a "free vote."

The Christian Democratic Union. The Christian Democratic Union and its Bavarian counterpart, the Christian Social Union, emerged in the late 1940s as a broad coalition of centrist groups dedicated to the establishment of liberal democracy in Germany (Smith 1990). The Christian label was designed to unite

Germany's Protestant and Catholic communities within the confines of a single party as well as to lend a moral tone to the political process. The Christian label was also designed to draw a clear line between the new party and its leftist counterparts, all of whom were manifestly anti-religious.

Victorious in Germany's first post-war election (1949), the CDU was soon forced to choose between a course of mild socialism on one hand and free enterprise on the other. Under the strong leadership of Conrad Adenauer, the CDU chose the path of free enterprise. Germany prospered and the CDU, in alliance with the smaller Free Democrats, would rule Germany for much of its existence as a democratic republic.

Once the CDU had made the decision to become the party of the center right, both its identity and that of its rivals took on greater clarity. The CDU was to become the party of business, proclaiming that a productive Germany would be a prosperous Germany. The CDU has also championed German participation in both a unified Europe and NATO, and it led the charge for German reunification. The achievement of unification transformed the image of Chancellor Kohl from that of a competent if unimaginative bureaucrat into a national hero. Ironically, the costs of digesting East Germany would quickly undermine his fleeting popularity, leading him to the brink of defeat in the 1994 elections. The costs of unification in conjunction with a staggering rate of unemployment—11 percent in the former West Germany; 16 percent in the former East Germany—spelled final defeat in 1998. The CDU came close to regaining power in 2002 and appears poised for victory in 2006. (For updated elections results log on to http://politicalscience.wadsworth.com/palmer03/.

The CDU has traditionally drawn its support from practicing Catholics, the business community, women, older voters, and residents of Germany's smaller cities and rural areas (Smith 1990). In order to broaden its religious appeal, a number of seats on the CDU list are reserved for Protestants. In spite of its "big business" orientation, the CDU has also gone out of its way to accommodate German labor, many members of which vote for the CDU.

Although the CDU has dominated German politics throughout most of the Federal Republic's history, the growing urbanization of German society and Germany's persistently high rate of unemployment have strengthened the position of the SPD and the Greens.

To make matters worse, Helmut Kohl and most of those in key leadership positions in the CDU were implicated in a massive fundraising scandle that shook the Party to its core. In a bold move to regain its credibility, the Party selected Angela Merkel, an East German, to be its new leader, a dramatic move indeed.

The Social Democratic Party. The Social Democratic Party (SPD) emerged during the Second Reich as a Marxist-oriented socialist party that was only slightly less radical than the communists. The SPD survived the persecution of the Hitler years with its leadership more or less intact, and was widely favored to win Germany's first post-war election (Paterson and Southern 1991; Berghahn 1987).

The 1949 elections, however, were won by the CDU. Germany prospered, and SPD appeals for the nationalization of German industry seemed antiquated, if not dangerous. Catholic workers were also offended by the hostility of the SPD to organized religion, and the Marxist orientation of the party raised lingering doubts about the ultimate loyalty of its members. Did their loyalties lie with Germany, or were they the unwitting tools of a Soviet Union committed to world domination?

Receiving only 30 percent of the popular vote in the 1957 elections, the SPD faced a critical choice. It could maintain its ideological purity and be relegated to the status of a minor party, or it could disavow Marxism and become a large catch-all party capable of challenging the CDU for the right to rule. It chose the latter course (Paterson and Southern 1991).

In 1959, the SPD dropped its demand for the nationalization of German industry, calling instead for a reasonable balance between economic growth and social welfare. The SPD also affirmed its support for NATO and pronounced socialism and Catholicism to be compatible doctrines. Marx was dead.

By 1966, the SPD had gathered sufficient public support to force a "Grand Coalition" with the CDU. The Grand Coalition, an unwieldy affair headed by the CDU, was to give way three years later (1969) to the first of several SPD Governments. The SPD would rule Germany without interruption for the next 16 years (1969–1985).

Upon assuming power in 1969, the SPD moved rapidly to reassure the German business community that it was not hostile to capitalism. Labor was given an expanded role in corporate decision making, but Germany remained a bastion of capitalism. In point of fact, the German business community prospered under SPD rule. For all intents and purposes, the SPD had become a slightly left-of-center catch-all party, the major thrust of which was to offer voters a somewhat "kinder and gentler" approach to the business of government than the CDU. The 1998 elections and 2002 elections, for example, saw the SPD platform call for gender equality, tax cuts for a large percentage of the German population, mild environmentalism, and a variety of government programs to solve Germany's unemployment problem by creating new jobs. They were successful in both elections, forming a coalition government with the Greens. Much like Tony Blair and the Labour Party in Britain, then, the SPD had become a member of the **new left,** *a moderate, slightly left-of-center ideology* that at the turn of the century would be the dominant force in 13 of the 15 EU countries.

The SPD, however, has been unable to solve Germany's economic and social problems, the most pronounced of which are high unemployment, a declining economy, and the failed economic integration of East Germany (Thompson 2004). Tensions within the party have increased apace and, in 2004, Schroeder was forced to step down as party chairman. He remained prime minister, but his power had been weakened. German business, once accepting of Schroeder, has criticized him for imposing excessive rules that make business difficult. The unions, Schroeder's support base, have threatened to form a new party (FAZ, March 12, 2004, www). All in all, the approach of the 2006 elections found the SPD in disarray.

Like the CDU, the SPD remains a pragmatic party whose policy positions are dictated largely by the desire to win elections (Markovitz and Gorski 1993).

Placed in a comparative perspective, the SPD would be less doctrinaire than the British Labour Party, yet far clearer in its promotion of social justice than the Democratic Party of the United States.

As the position of the SPD would suggest, it finds a preponderance of its electoral support among younger, urban voters. The Party also draws considerable support from union members, and particularly from union members of secular orientation. The SPD, however, is not "owned" by the unions, and relations between the two groups often reflect considerable tension (Paterson and Southern 1991). Finally, the Party also attracts a disproportionate share of the Protestant vote.

The Free Democratic Party.   The **Free Democratic Party (FDP)** attempts to occupy the middle ground between the Christian Democrats and the Social Democrats, but its positions are not always easy to define on a left-right spectrum. In recent years, for example, the FDP has been to the left of the CDU on foreign policy issues but has moved to its right on domestic issues involving social welfare. The members of the FDP are drawn disproportionately from the Protestant middle class and from farmers. Although small in size, never having garnered more than 13 percent of the popular vote, the FDP has traditionally played a pivotal role as a balancer between the larger CDU and SPD. Indeed, the FDP has served in more governments than either the CDU or SPD.

Unfortunately, from the perspective of the FDP, the middle ground between the CDU and the SPD has become increasingly narrow as each of the two major parties vies to dominate the political center. By the late 1980s, the FDP was struggling to surmount the 5 percent barrier, and did so largely on the willingness of CDU voters to split their ticket to keep the FDP alive (Paterson and Southern 1991). The FDP also faced growing competition from the Greens, the success of which in the 1998 and 2002 elections suggested it was they, not the FDP, who had become Germany's "third party."

The Greens.   The **Greens** emerged in the late 1970s in response to the growing deterioration of the German environment. Peace activists soon gravitated to the party, providing it with a dual focus: peace and the environment. Both issues commanded a vocal following in Germany.

To be concerned about the environment, however, was not necessarily to be opposed to a strong defense. While many students and intellectuals tended to support both issues, a large portion of the general population did not. As a result, many middle-class voters who were genuinely concerned about the environment found the Greens too radical for their liking (Kitschelt 1989; *International Herald Tribune,* March 8, 1999). Following the unification of the two Germanies, the environment has again dominated the Greens' agenda.

The Greens received 7.3 percent of the vote in the 1994 elections, a showing that forced the major parties, and especially the SPD, to place greater emphasis on environmental issues. While the dominant parties have shown greater sensitivity to environmental issues in recent years, neither could qualify as the party of the environment. The Greens did well in the 1998 and 2002 elections, forming and formed coalition governments with the dominant SPD. While the two parties have worked well together, tension remains over what the Greens consider to be Schroeder's lukewarm commitment to a strong environmental package. Particularly knotty is the Greens' demand for the abolition of Germany's program of nuclear energy. Schroeder has agreed in principle, but said that it will have to be worked out over the next 20 years. As things currently stand, the Greens are attracting new members; the SDP is not (FAZ, June 25, 2004, www).

Germany as a Party and Partisan State: The Role of Political Parties in the Political Process.   The influence of political parties on German political life is so pervasive that Germany is often referred to as a "party state" (Smith 1990). In order to better understand this point, it may be useful to examine the diverse functions that the German party system performs.

First, as noted earlier, the party system plays a crucial role in recruiting and "educating" Germany's political elites. Before individuals assume leadership positions at the federal level, their mettle has been thoroughly tested. As a result of this process of political apprenticeship, Germany's leaders have generally displayed outstanding competence. Moreover, as democratic parties tend to select democratically inclined leaders, the recruitment process has provided the nation with almost five generations of political leaders committed to the democratic process.

Second, political parties provide a counterweight to the power of the chancellor. The chancellor is the party leader, but he or she is just one of several key party figures, all of whom possess an independent base of support. A chancellor who fails to keep in touch with the leadership core of his or her party risks a party rebellion or, in extreme cases, a vote of no confidence. In a parallel situation in England, it will be recalled, Margaret Thatcher was forced to resign by an internal revolt of the party leadership.

Third, the existence of two large and disciplined political parties lends responsibility to the German political process. The dominance of Germany's two major parties virtually assures that either the Christian Democrats or the Social Democrats will have sufficient votes in the Bundestag to form a Government, albeit with some assistance from the Free Democrats or the Greens. The majority party does possess the capacity to implement its electoral platform, and the German electorate expects it to do so.

Fourth, the cohesiveness of Germany's major political parties promotes coordination and harmony among the diverse units of a very complex political system (Paterson and Southern 1991). German federalism and the checks and balances inherent in the Basic Law were designed to fragment political power and, thereby, to preclude a return to authoritarian rule. The price of fragmenting power, however, is often confusion, indecision, and scapegoating as each branch of the government blames the others for its failings. The cohesion of German political parties helps to overcome these problems by providing members of the same party at all levels with a strong incentive for cooperation. This is not to suggest that party cohesiveness totally eliminates friction between the various units and levels of government, but it does make that friction considerably less evident than is the case in the United States.

Fifth, German parties provide the electorate with a meaningful choice of candidates and issues. Cynics might argue with this proposition, suggesting that the preoccupation of the two major parties with capturing the political center has blunted their role in providing the public with new options. Both major parties, they correctly point out, have become advocates of the status quo.

Sixth, the German party system provides citizens with an avenue of political participation that goes well beyond the regularly scheduled elections. German political parties encourage their members to get involved in all dimensions of the political process. Such political involvement, from the perspective of many political scientists, has strengthened German democracy by providing German citizens with a sense of political efficacy, that is, a belief that the average citizen can make a difference. In this regard, it is interesting to note that actual membership in the two major parties has increased steadily over the course of the post–World War II era, a trend that bodes well for the future of German democracy.

Seventh, the German party system represents an important channel of communication between the political elites and the masses. Both of the major parties maintain a strong network of constituency organizations that enables their leadership to keep in touch with grassroots sentiment. In much the same manner, party meetings provide the leadership with the opportunity to explain the logic of its positions to the party faithful. This two-way communication process is an important element in German democracy.

Finally, the German party system plays an important stabilizing role in German society. If parties are to win elections, they cannot adopt extreme positions (Jeffery 1998). The integrating role of German parties is particularly critical in the post-unification era, an era that finds many former East Germans attempting to cope with an alien political system in which they are treated as second-class citizens.

Pressure Groups and Politics in Germany

Germany possesses essentially the same array of economic, political, and social interest groups that exist in most Western democracies. As we shall see, however, the relationship between pressure groups and the government in Germany is very different from that in the United States.

Business. The German business community is represented by three large associations: the Federation of German Industry (BDI), the Federation of German Employment Associations (BDA), and the German Industrial and Trade Conference (DIHT). The BDI represents some 90,000 German firms, occupying a position roughly equivalent to that of the National Association of Manufacturers in the United States. The BDI is the most politically visible of the three business organizations and, as one might expect, maintains close ties with the Christian Democrats. The DIHT is the preferred organization of small businesses and independent craftsmen, and its members often have interests that differ from those of the industrial giants. The BDA serves as the business community's watchdog on wage policies and attempts to forge a unified policy toward labor.

Labor. Labor, for the most part, expresses its views through the German Federation of Labor (DGB), Germany's major labor organization. Unlike the ideological unions of the Weimar era, the DGB follows the American pattern of placing economic goals above ideological concerns. Much of its activity in recent years has focused on *increasing worker participation in management decisions,* a process Germans refer to as **co-determination** (Kloss 1991). The DGB has also been increasingly concerned with protecting German workers from displacement by the influx of East European and Turkish "guest workers."

German unions have been extraordinarily successful in pressing their demands, with German workers being the most highly paid of any of the major industrial powers. Many German workers also work 35-hour weeks and receive up to 40 days of vacation and sick leave per year, as well as generous pensions.

As in most countries of Western Europe, however, German labor is on the defensive *(Sunday Times,* Feb. 7, 1999, www; *Time International,* Aug. 4, 2003, 51). Only 40 percent of the labor force was unionized before unification, a figure that is being tested as the DGB attempts to reconcile the conflicting demands of workers in the two Germanies.

Germany's Social Democratic Governments, moreover, have demanded givebacks by the unions, citing the need to keep Germany competitive in the world economic arena. This has caused a rift between the unions and the Social Democratic Party, with the unions threatening to form their own party (FAZ, July 3, 2004, www). The threat has yet to materialize, but militancy has increased apace. In 2002, the unions launched their first major strike in seven years. Lesser strikes have followed. Whatever its woes, the DGB continues to bargain for the wages of most German workers (unionized or not)—but the reality of Germany's economic plight has weakened its once-powerful position. In 2004, for example, Germany's powerful IG Metall union agreed to scrap its hard-won victory for a 35-hour work week. The alternative was to see more jobs exported outside of Germany (FAZ, July 6, 2004, www).

Institutional and Social Groups. German bureaucrats also constitute an important pressure group. German officials are encouraged to run for public office and are provided with six weeks of unpaid leave to do so. With about one-third of the members of the Bundestag being drawn from the ranks of the civil service, it is unlikely that the prerogatives of the German bureaucracy will soon be in jeopardy.

The Catholic and Protestant churches also possess formidable political influence, a fact well illustrated by the "church tax." Unless instructed otherwise, the government allocates 10 percent of an individual's income tax to a church. Religion also finds political expression through the Christian Democratic Party, a political organization expressly designed to integrate religion into the political process. Clearly, German citizens are less concerned with the separation of Church and State than are their American counterparts.

All of the associations surveyed in the above discussion are **peak (or umbrella) associations,** which incorporate a multitude of smaller, more specialized organizations. All in all, Germany possesses more than 20,000 associations, a figure that testifies to the strength of its civil society.

Most large peak associations find representation on a broad array of governmental councils and committees that enables them to review preliminary legislation before it is enacted into law. Most of Germany's professional organizations are also self-regulating. The German medical association, for example, licenses doctors and oversees the ethics of the medical profession.

In addition to their representation on semi-official councils, the dominant pressure groups are also well-represented on the electoral lists of the two major parties, each of which trades "safe" positions on their lists for financial and electoral support. Indeed, some 50 percent of the Deputies in the Bundestag are employed in one capacity or another by a pressure group (Dalton 1993).

The CDU, quite logically, possesses stronger representation from the business community; the SPD, from labor. Both parties, however, strive to win at least some support from all of Germany's major groups. The CDU has successfully wooed the more moderate elements of the labor movement, particularly practicing Catholics.

Corporatism and Neocorporatism. The quasi-official role of German pressure groups stands in sharp contrast to the far more conflictive pattern of pressure group activity in the United States. To understand this difference, it is necessary to look at the differing group traditions of the two countries. American traditions have long stressed individualism and individual representation. German traditions, by contrast, have historically stressed group representation, or **"corporatism"** (Reich 1990). German craftsmen of the middle ages were organized into guilds that regulated the affairs of both the craft and its members. Entrance into a craft was closely regulated, as were ranks and wages. Eventually many guilds also took on the role of social organizations, attempting to care for the broader health and welfare of their members. The feudal leaders of the era soon found it convenient to provide the guilds with a self-regulating legal status in return for their political and financial support. Church leaders played similar roles, as did many labor groups in the era following Germany's belated industrialization.

Corporatism facilitated Hitler's rise to power by allowing him to win the support of large organizations by promising them that their interests would be secure. Following Hitler's 1933 victory, for example, the civil service and teaching professions joined the Nazi Party en masse (Grunberger 1971). The labor unions, in particular, were pressed into the service of the Nazi Party, trading their right to independent action for extravagant promises of a worker's paradise.

With the end of the Second World War and the emergence of the Federal Republic, authoritarian corporatism gave way to a democratic **neocorporatism** based upon voluntary cooperation between the Government and Germany's major pressure groups (Hancock 1989). Rather than the conflict that characterizes the pluralistic pattern of group representation in the United States, the emphasis in German politics is on finding broadly acceptable solutions to Germany's economic and social problems. German pressure groups articulate the interests of their members, but they do so in a manner that facilitates compromise. While some groups must ultimately win more than others, the emphasis is on precluding the alienation of any important segment of the population.

Neocorporatism remains an inherently conservative force in German society. Traditional corporate groups are "locked into" the system and possess far greater opportunity to shape legislation affecting their members than do the newer political interests that have emerged in the postwar era. Women, youth, environmentalists, and foreign workers, for example, all represent important segments of the German population that have been *"locked out"* of the established corporatist network.

Responding to their under-representation, women, youth, and environmentalists have forged a variety of "citizen action groups" as a means of achieving their political objectives (Rucht 2003). These groups represent a new and expanding dimension of German politics that uses demonstrations, petitions, and marches to express their views on a broad variety of issues ranging from the environment and nuclear power to kindergarten reform and transit fares. Whether citizen action groups can compensate for the conservative nature of Germany's corporatist traditions remains to be seen. Neocorporatism remains a powerful force in German politics but, like the once-dominant power of the chancellor, shows signs of weakening (Vail 2003).

Citizens and Politics in Germany

German citizens are among the most politically active in the world. Election turnout often exceeds 80 percent, a figure that dwarfs the 50 to 55 percent of the United States population that typically participates in presidential elections. Germans are also more likely to be members of political parties, interest associations, and "citizen action" groups than are their American counterparts.

In addition to the formal avenues of political participation, the opinions of the German population are assessed on a regular basis by a variety of polling organizations (Brettschneider 1997). Recent polls indicate the major concerns of German citizens are high unemployment, crime among children and adolescents, the lack of adequate training positions, the rising criminal rate, and the high immigration rate. Far more disconcerting is the sense of malaise that has descended on German society. Various polls conducted in 2003 and 2004 suggest that upwards of 47 percent of Germans believe that their country has major problems, with 38 percent speaking of a severe crisis. Some 69 percent believe that the next generation will be poorer than they are (*Economist,* March 27, 2004, 50). Some 70 percent of Germans are annoyed at being held responsible for the Holocaust. Some 60 percent are inclined to believe that "many Jews try to use Germany's Third Reich past to their advantage and want to make Germans pay for it" (*Guardian Unlimited,* Dec. 12, 2003).

Election results and opinion polls also indicate a relentless movement of German public opinion toward the center of the political spectrum. While fringe parties have enjoyed a brief revival in the post-unification era, the center of gravity of German politics has clearly shifted to the middle (Fuchs and Rohrschneider 1998).

Citizens of the former East Germany have yet to become full participants in German prosperity and remain somewhat distrustful of the federal government. It is they, more than any other segment of German society, who have been swayed by the appeals of the extremists. The Party of Democratic Socialism, the remnants of the old Communist Party that ruled East Germany, threatens to become the second-most popular party in the region (FAZ, Aug. 20, 2004, www).

This then, brings us to the question of mass influence on German politics. Does mass participation really make a difference? As in most Western democracies, public opinion matters most at election time. The primary goal of Germany's main parties is to win elections, and they can ignore public opinion only to their own detriment. Beyond question, it has been the force of citizen opinions that has pushed the locus of German politics to the political center (Jones and Retallack 1992).

THE CONTEXT OF GERMAN POLITICS: CULTURE, ECONOMICS, AND INTERNATIONAL INTERDEPENDENCE

Politics is a reflection of a nation's institutions and the individuals and groups that give life to those institutions, but it is also influenced by the broader environmental context in which the political process occurs. As discussed in Chapter 1, political events are profoundly affected by the culture of the participants as well as by economic and international factors. This is certainly the case in Germany.

The Culture of German Politics: From the Authoritarian State to the Post-Industrial Society

It is the underlying cultural values of German society, according to cultural analysts, that are likely to provide the best guide to German politics over the long haul (Inglehart 1990). If the German masses are truly committed to human freedom and democracy, it would be difficult for a new dictatorship to emerge and survive. By contrast, if the German masses are primarily concerned with order and nationalism, the German government could well move in the direction of greater authoritarianism.

Sociological studies following the end of World War II found the German population to possess an abiding concern with authority. Many scholars questioned the compatibility of German culture with democracy (Smith 1990). The German population also displayed a far stronger devotion to rules and regulations than was evident in Anglo-American culture. Rules were rules, and they were to be obeyed. The German sociologist Dahrendorf (1959) also suggests that Germans possessed a low tolerance for ambiguity and social conflict. If problems exist, according to Dahrendorf, Germans attempt to resolve them immediately and then codify that resolution into law. This tendency, Dahrendorf continues, has resulted in the intense legalism and rigidity of German society. Once rules have been codified, they are difficult to change. Indeed, much of the German legal code is still based upon the laws of the Second and Third Reichs.

Not all Germans, of course, act or feel the same way, any more than all Americans act or feel the same way. Stereotypes are dangerous. **Political culture** merely suggests that certain values are more prevalent in some societies than in others. It would be difficult, for example, to argue with the observation that Germans, on average, tend to manifest a greater respect for rules and regulations than Egyptians or Nigerians, a topic to be explored in Chapters 11 and 12.

Socialization and Cultural Change.   Cultural values are passed from one generation to the next, but they also change in response to new environmental realities (Inglehart 1990). The vast majority of today's Germans were either not yet born during Hitler's Third Reich or were in their infancy. Unlike their parents and grandparents, they have grown up in an environment of democracy and prosperity. The newer generations of German citizens are also far more educated and far more urban than prewar Germans, and they have been intensely socialized (indoctrinated) to believe in democratic values (Shafer 1991). One cannot, accordingly, assume that the values of today's Germans are the same as the values that predominated during the Second or Third Reich (Inglehart 1990).

What, then, are the dominant features of German political culture today? Until the advent of unification in 1990, both public opinion polls and election results indicated a persistent increase in democratic values over the course of the post-war era. While pockets of authoritarianism remained, the data indicated a commitment to democratic values equalling that of most other Western democracies.

The unification of East and West Germany put a temporary cloud on this otherwise rosy horizon (Minkenberg 1993). The former citizens of East Germany did not grow up in an environment of democracy and prosperity, and their political socialization continued to stress authoritarianism and compliance (Friedrich 1991). The economic burdens of reunification have done little to erode these values (Dun 1992). The reunification of Germany, then, involves far more than the collapse of the Berlin Wall. It also involves taking down a cultural wall that will remain for some time (Yoder 1998).

Questions of democracy and legitimacy aside, Germans do seem to manifest a stronger commitment to rule compliance than do the citizens of many other societies. Other frequently cited traits of German political culture would include a strong sense of cultural identity, a high regard for organization and efficiency, and a belief that the good of the collective should come before the rights of the individual (Dalton 1993; Paterson and Southern 1991). Indeed, few countries in the world share the United States' pervasive concern for the rights of the individual. There has also been a persistent trend to throw off the guilt of the Nazi era and reassert pride in being German. Chancellor Schroeder joined the debate by proclaiming himself "a German patriot, who is proud of his country." These are strong words, indeed, for a former leftist radical (*New York Times,* Mar. 20, 2001, www). His foreign minister, also a former leftist radical, disagrees and warns of a persistent racism (*International Herald Tribune,* Aug. 28, 2000, 5).

German politics, moreover, is also influenced by the broader social and economic dimensions of German culture. Particularly important in this regard is the strong achievement orientation of German society. Germans, by and large, work very hard. They also place a premium on thrift and savings, as well as on organizational efficiency (Kloss 1991). Achievement is an economic trait rather than a political trait, but there can be little doubt that the strong performance of the German economy in the decades following World War II played a central role in consolidating the legitimacy of the Federal Republic (Inglehart 1990).

Some German business leaders, however, now fear that Germany's famed work ethic has begun to fade as younger Germans are less willing to accept a deteriorating environment and the psychological stress of competition for the sake of a marginal increase in their paychecks. Individual freedom, equality of the sexes, and grassroots democracy have also begun to rival efficiency as core social values. Prosperity remains an important concern, but not necessarily the most important concern (Fuchs and Rohrschneider 1998; Mayer and Hillmert 2003). Suggestions also abound that the German image for quality and precision has begun to tarnish. German magazines have increasingly raised the issue of declining quality control, and *Consumer Reports* now regularly gives German cars low marks for reliability (*New York Times,* May 9, 2004, www; *Consumer Reports,* June 2004, 52–53).

Germany, like much of Europe, has also become multicultural. Not only does Germany have a large Muslim population, but at least a portion of that population has resisted integration into German culture. Tensions between the two groups has increased apace, with Germany issuing a ban against wearing Islamic dress (head scarves) in public schools (Ogelman 2003).

Political Economy and Politics in Germany

For political economists, the evolution of German politics has far more to do with the economy than with culture. The rise of Hitler, from the perspective of political economists, was the result of the collapse of the German economy during the Weimar era. Germans, in this view, were driven to authoritarianism by the inability of democratic political institutions to meet their basic needs. Hitler's program of re-armament and military expansion sparked an economic revival, lifting Germany from the depths of economic depression to the pinnacle of world domination (Borchardt 1991).

The success of German democracy in the post–World War II era, from the political economic perspective, is a function of German prosperity. Prosperity doesn't guarantee democracy, but it does build support for democratic regimes that provide that prosperity. Had the economic circumstances of the Weimar Republic been more favorable, from the political economic perspective, the devastation of the Hitler era might well have been avoided.

West Germany achieved its phenomenal record of economic success by a version of state capitalism that it refers to as **social market economy.** Under the system of social market economy, *government, business, and labor all cooperate to achieve two goals: growth and equity.* The Weimar Republic had been undermined by intense class conflict that pitted workers against the bourgeoisie in a drama straight from the pages of Marx. The social market economy was designed to assure that West German democracy would be free of class conflict. It has succeeded admirably.

Germany's social market economy possesses three basic components: (1) strong government regulation of the economy; (2) cradle-to-grave welfare programs;

and (3) government-mandated cooperation between labor and industry. The German government also provides German industry with a technically trained labor force, something that is sadly lacking in the educational systems of both Britain and the United States. The famed German work ethic is matched by a high level of vocational competence.

As positive as the German experience has been, four clouds loom on the horizon. Of these, the first is *the escalating cost of the social welfare system*. Half of the West German population will soon be past retirement age and entitled to generous pensions. A falling birth rate, moreover, places increased pressure upon younger workers to fund the welfare system, something they have been increasingly reluctant to do, as German taxes are already among the highest in the first world. The unemployment rate in Germany also continues to hover around the 12 percent mark (16 percent in the former East Germany) and shows little sign of falling. The Government is now in the process of scaling back the welfare package.

The second cloud on Germany's economic horizon concerns *the unexpected and as yet incalculable costs of reunification*. The cost of bringing East Germany's infrastructure of roads, communications, and factories on par with those of West Germany will be staggering, and the stress of reunifying the two Germanies will mar the political landscape for several years to come.

The third cloud on Germany's economic horizon is *the pressure of competition from Asia and the newer members of the European Union*, all of which have labor costs that are far lower than those of Germany. Indeed, German labor costs are currently the highest in the first world. To remain competitive, German factories are attempting to hold the line on salaries and scale back the number of their employees. Labor unrest has increased apace.

Finally, the future of the German economy has been clouded by *excessive regulation*. Germany ranked 47th out of 49 major countries in terms of economic flexibility and its ability to adapt to new economic developments (*International Herald Tribune,* Sept. 10, 2002, www). A 2004 survey of 859 German companies said that they could take on new workers only if laws on hiring and firing were relaxed (FAZ, April 23, 2004, www). Many are simply relocating to cheap-labor areas. Chancellor Schroeder called the relocation of jobs "unpatriotic," but business leaders responded that they can no longer survive in an economic environment they characterize as a "regulatory straitjacket"(FAZ, Mar. 26, 2004, www).

To make matters worse, the four crises confronting the social market economy are occurring simultaneously. The crowning achievement of the West German government was its ability to provide both economic growth and a high level of social welfare under a democratic system. That may no longer be possible. Germany's democracy is not in doubt, but the long peace between labor and business that played such a crucial role in Germany's political stability may soon be a thing of the past. Germany's large guest-worker population is bearing the brunt of Germany's economic frustration. Hate crimes have risen, and no less of personage than former Chancellor Helmut Schmidt warned that Germany was in danger of "being stuck" with a multicultural society. The former leftist chancellor didn't blame the immigrants. Rather, he suggested that they couldn't be assimilated because his countrymen were "racist down deep"(*Guardian,* March 29, 2002, www).

International Interdependence and the
Politics of Germany

Germany, in many ways, is the creation of international forces. It was Napoleon's consolidation of the German principalities at the turn of the nineteenth century that stimulated the process of German state building. It was similarly the Franco-Prussian War of 1871 that facilitated the final unification of the German state. The harsh conditions of the peace treaty imposed upon Germany by the Allied Powers at the conclusion of World War I encouraged the rise of the Third Reich by undermining the economic viability of the Weimar Republic. Whatever chance the Weimar Republic may have had for success, moreover, was crushed by the Great Depression, control of which was far beyond the capacity of a single country. The rise of Hitler was also facilitated by the passivity of the Western powers. The British and French sought to buy peace by capitulating to Hitler's demands, while the United States was locked in an isolationist stupor (Churchill 1948).

External influence, moreover, was paramount in shaping the structure of the Federal Republic. The Basic Law was drafted under the watchful eye of the Allied Powers, as were educational and labor reforms designed to reshape German political culture (Dalton 1993).

Responding to the outbreak of the Cold War, the Western powers went out of their way to assure the economic and political stability of the Federal Republic. The stationing of Allied troops in West Germany, far from being the act of an occupying power, provided West Germany with a security umbrella under which its economy and its democracy could prosper. A West Germany unprotected from attack by Soviet troops stationed in Eastern Europe could not have become the economic and technological superpower that exists today.

More recently, the reunification of East and West Germany was made possible by the collapse of the Soviet empire. That collapse has also provided Germany with a new window of economic opportunity as the states of Eastern Europe seek German cooperation in the rebuilding of their shattered economies. On the negative side, the collapse of the Soviet bloc has resulted in Germany being inundated with refugees and migrants from all areas of Eastern Europe. How well Germany can cope with its refugee problem while struggling to integrate its East German population remains to be seen.

The European Union also exerts a profound influence on German politics. The euro has now replaced the mark as Germany's currency, a clear sign that the management of German economic policy is shifting from Berlin to the European Union. The more the integration of Europe progresses, the less freedom Germany's leaders will have in charting their own economic course. Germany remains a key pillar of the European Union, but enthusiasm has begun to lag.

Germany has also been deeply involved in the war against terror. Jihadist (Muslim terrorist) cells are well established in Germany and played a critical role in both the September 11, 2001, attacks on the United States and the March 11, 2004, Madrid attacks that killed more than 190 and wounded more than 1,800.

The Spanish attacks prompted suggestions that the German military be used to beef up anti-terrorist security within the Federal Republic. Peter Struck, the Minister of Defense, downplayed the idea, suggesting that it would probably necessitate a constitutional amendment, a difficult process that requires ratification by Germany's 16 Lander. He did not downplay the terrorist threat to Germany, noting that "We have troops in Afghanistan, the home base of Al Qaeda. As a result of this mission, terrorists could hit here any day. We have to expect that this will happen" (FAZ, Apr. 9, 2004, www). The German president also ended a trip to Africa prematurely as a result of terrorist threats on his life.

Finally, it should be recalled that the economic foundation of German politics is being threatened by growing competition from Asia, the poorer countries of the European Union, and North America. German industry is being forced to trim its labor costs in order to remain competitive, and such cutbacks have resulted in mounting tensions between labor and the government.

Germany and the World. While German domestic policy is profoundly influenced by international forces, Germany also possesses a determining voice in shaping the broader contours of the international community. Germany is an economic superpower, its economic clout in world circles being surpassed only by that of the United States and Japan. Indeed, World Trade Organization figures for 2003 found Germany to account for 10 percent of the world's merchandise exports, followed by the United States at 9.7 percent and Japan at 6.3 percent. Germany's size , economic power, and central location also make it the heart of the European Union. Whether the EU could survive without German participation is a matter of some debate (Jeffery and Patterson 2003).

The influence of German economic policy on the states of Eastern Europe is profound (Miller and Templeman 1997; Wood 2004). Remittances from guest workers in Germany are vital to the economies of many Eastern European states and Turkey. If Germany continues to reduce its dependence upon guest workers, it will exact a heavy toll from an Eastern Europe struggling to recover from five decades of Soviet domination.

Concentrating on Germany's position as an economic superpower makes it easy to lose sight of the link between economic power and military power. While precluded by law from having a large military force independent of NATO, Germany maintains one of the largest military establishments in Europe, being eclipsed only by France and Russia. German firms have also been in the forefront of those states exporting nuclear, chemical, and missile technology to the less stable states of the third world, including Iraq, Iran, and Libya. There is no question of Germany's technical capacity to reestablish itself as the dominant military force in Europe should it choose to do so. Such an eventuality, of course, is forbidden by both law and treaty. Ironically, Germany now finds its former wartime adversaries calling upon it to play a greater military role in sustaining the "new world order." It has begun to do so by sending troops in support of UN peacekeeping efforts to both the Balkans and Afghanistan. Germany refused to send troops to Iraq, a reflection of its intense opposition to what it considered to be a profoundly misguided war (Szabo 2004).

that guide Western practice, a circumstance that often has led to cross-cultural misunderstandings.

A second important difference between Japanese and Western cultures lies in their differing views of the role of the individual in society. Western society, perhaps because salvation is a personal matter, tends to be intensely individualistic. The rights of individuals, as enshrined in documents such as the American *Declaration of Independence* or the French *Declaration of the Rights of Man and Citizen,* are considered inviolable and stand on par with the rights of society.

The Japanese, by contrast, often place the rights of the group above the rights of the individual. It is social harmony, from the Japanese perspective, that allows the individual to prosper. Individuals are expected to subordinate their own interests to those of the group.

The pervasive influence of culture on Japanese politics will be discussed throughout this chapter. The link between culture and politics, moreover, is not accidental. Emperor worship was added to Shinto rituals in the fourth century AD as the political leaders of that era sought to legitimize their rule by appeals to divine authority. Confucianism was added to Japanese culture in the fifth century in an effort to promote hard work and to enhance respect for hierarchical order. Buddhist doctrines stressing social obedience followed in the sixth century. *The Japanese practice of adapting foreign doctrines to fulfill political needs, then, has very deep roots* (Earhart 1982).

Japan's cultural traditions were nurtured by a geographic isolation so complete that Japan's first sustained contact with the West would not occur until the middle of the nineteenth century. While Japan would eventually borrow Western technology and many of the overt characteristics of Western society, it would also remain supremely confident of the superiority of its own culture. This point is essential to understanding Japanese politics.

The political history of Japan is far too complex for easy recounting. Suffice it to say that the seventeenth century found Japan to be a loosely integrated state, the citizens of which were intensely proud of their ethnic uniqueness. Japanese religious beliefs reinforced this pride by placing Japan at the center of the universe. Racial purity continues to be cited by Japan's political leaders as one of the main reasons for Japanese economic dominance in the world today.

However much the Japanese population shared a common cultural identity, the Japan of the seventeenth century did not constitute a state in the modern sense of the word. Rather, the political system of the era was based on feudal arrangements not unlike those of medieval Europe. Under these arrangements, a **shogun,** or *military warlord,* ruled Japan in the name of an emperor who had long ago become a symbolic figure (Duus 1976). The shogun directly ruled the central region of Japan. The remainder of the country was divided into approximately 250 **daimyo,** or *feudal fiefdoms,* the leaders of which swore allegiance to the shogun. Both the boundaries of the shogun state and the allegiance of the daimyo would ebb and flow with the power of the shogun.

Feudal Japan also boasted *a large aristocracy of warriors* called the **samurai** (Wilson 1992). Much like the knights of medieval Europe, the samurai served their daimyo in exchange for land and financial allowances. Over time, they

Brown Brothers

Commodore Matthew Perry is depicted meeting the Japanese imperial commissioners at Yokohama. In 1854, to the outrage of the Japanese public, the government signed a treaty permitting foreign vessels to obtain provisions in Japanese territory and allowing American ships to anchor at Shimoda and Hakodate.

evolved into a hereditary military aristocracy that constituted some 6 percent of the Japanese population (Duus 1976). Not all samurai, however, were treated equally. While some enjoyed immense wealth and prestige, others found it difficult to survive on the allowances provided by the daimyo. As Japan approached the end of the feudal era, the samurai, as a class, had fallen on hard times.

The Meiji Restoration (1868–1912)

The Japan of the early nineteenth century shared few of the Western advances in the areas of education, science, and industrialization. Political loyalties, while acknowledging the emperor as a deity, also remained localized.

The gap between the strong sense of Japanese nationalism and the inherent weakness of the Japanese state was of little consequence as long as Japan remained an isolated kingdom (Milward 1979; Arnason 2002). In July of 1853, however, that isolation was shattered when a fleet of American warships entered Edo Bay and demanded that Japan open its ports to trade with the United States. The Japanese government, finding itself unable to resist the military power of an industrial state, capitulated. The outrage of the Japanese public was so great that the country was pushed to the brink of civil war (Duus 1976). On January 3, 1868,

military units from three of the larger daimyo seized the government and proclaimed the "restoration" of imperial rule. Popular support for the restoration was
rallied under the slogan, "Restore the Emperor and Drive Out the Barbarians!"
The Emperor Meiji issued a decree abolishing both the daimyo and the samurai
as the first step toward building a new court capable of challenging the West
(Duus 1976). The feudal period in Japan had come to an end. The daimyo received government bonds in exchange for their landholdings, while the more aggressive samurai became administrators in the new, modernizing bureaucracy.
Many samurai also became involved in business organizations that were to become Japan's great corporations.

While the Emperor was rehabilitated as the symbol of political authority, all
real power resided with the oligarchy that had seized power. This group included
the daimyo who had overthrown the shogun, the more enlightened samurai, and
educated commoners who were familiar with the West (Duus 1976). Although
drawn from different backgrounds, the oligarchy was united by an all-consuming
desire to transform Japan into a modem industrial country (Wilson 1992;
Gordon 2003). Never again, they swore, would Japan be humiliated by a foreign
power.

Under the Meiji reforms, every dimension of Japanese life was harnessed to
the goal of modernization. The Japanese army was reorganized along Western
lines, and the Japanese educational system was revamped to stress the Confucian
virtues of obedience, loyalty, hard work, and patriotism. Japan's feudal bureaucracy was also modernized, becoming a skilled technocracy capable of transforming Japan into a modern industrial power.

Finally, and much later, the Meiji oligarchy would provide Japan with a **Diet,**
or *parliament*. Although the Meiji oligarchy continued to rule in the name of the
emperor, democracy had established a presence within the Japanese political consciousness (Duus 1976).

The Meiji reforms led to economic power, and economic power led to military power and expansionism. Japan began its occupation of Korea in 1887, and
the colonization of China would follow in less than a decade. Far more dramatic,
from the Western perspective, was the Japanese victory in the Russo-Japanese War
of 1904–1905, a victory that shattered the myth of Western invincibility. The slogan "strong army, strong nation" became the order of the day.

The Era of Two-Party Government (1912–1931)

By the early twentieth century, Japan was a country far different from what it had
been on the eve of the Meiji restoration. Firmly established as an economic and
military power, Japan had also made some progress, however limited, toward the
establishment of parliamentary government.

Japanese politics, moreover, had begun to reflect the changing structure of
Japanese society. Japan's industrial revolution had created a powerful business class,
the influence of which soon rivaled that of the Meiji oligarchy. Particularly important was the emergence of **zaibatsu,** or *large business conglomerates controlled by
a single interlocking directorate*. In time, the large zaibatsu would grow into integrated

networks of mining, manufacturing, commercial, and banking firms, all under the control of a single board of directors.

The industrial revolution also transformed Japan's traditional class structure. A middle class consisting of bureaucrats, white-collar workers, and merchants entered the political fray as did an industrial working class increasingly enamored of Marxist philosophy. The middle class formed political parties and the proletariat took to the streets. Reflecting the altered structure of Japanese society, the years between 1912 and 1931 would see Japan transformed into a quasi-democracy in which civilian political parties would share power with an emerging military-industrial elite.

The era of quasi-democracy was profoundly unstable, with the Japanese economy alternating between periods of boom and bust. The gap between rich and poor was stark, as was the gap between the cities and the countryside. Marxism had become a popular force, and rioting and political violence were commonplace. Further complicating matters was the advent of the Great Depression. Japan required far-sighted and decisive leadership, but its quasi-democratic regime could provide neither.

Japan Prepares for War

The collapse of party government was precipitated by the escalating tension between the party bosses and the military. The military, arguing that Japan's economic problems were best solved by expanding its colonial empire, urged preparation for total war against any power that stood in the path of its colonial expansion. The party bosses, by contrast, attempted to ease Japan's economic woes by slashing the military budget. The conflict came to a head on September 18, 1931, when the Japanese military launched an unauthorized invasion of Manchuria. Divided among itself, the Government remained passive.

Government indecisiveness during the Manchurian crisis shifted the balance of power from Japan's civilian leadership to the Japanese military. By 1936 the military had become the dominant force in Japanese politics and began its preparation for total war. The early phases of the war effort would transform much of the Far East into what the Japanese would euphemistically call their "Asian co-prosperity sphere." Having consolidated its position in the North Pacific, Japan launched a brutal attack on Pearl Harbor on December 7, 1941. Only the United States, in the Japanese view, stood in the way of its unchallenged mastery of the Pacific basin.

Japan's preparation for total war was both psychological and economic. Psychologically, the military inflamed nationalist sentiments by transforming the emperor-god into a war god who would accept nothing less than total sacrifice from his subjects. The new cult of the emperor was referred to as State Shintoism (Earhart 1982).

Economically, the mobilization for total war saw the Japanese economy brought under the control of government planners, a pattern well established during the Meiji restoration. The military also intensified the transformation of Japanese business firms into paternalist organizations that provided their employees with lifetime job security and generous welfare benefits. The employees, in

The port city of Hiroshima was almost totally destroyed when the
United States dropped an atomic bomb on the city on August 6, 1945.
Nagasaki was bombed by the United States three days later.

turn, were expected to sacrifice for the firm much as they would for their own
families. Political indoctrination sessions became as common in the workplace as
they were in the schools. In the present era, the large Japanese zaibatsu (business
conglomerates) have refined the "company family" into something approaching a
cult (van Wolferen 1990). The transformation of firms into families had been pio-
neered during the turn of the century by the Ministry of Communications as a
means of increasing the productivity and solidarity of the railroad workers. By
1920 the process had become widespread but voluntary. During the military period, it became government policy (Milward 1979).

Despite Japan's military dominance, Japanese politics during the Second World
War remained divided and conflicted. The zaibatsu resisted state control, and both
the party bosses and the aristocracy retained considerable influence in political
affairs. Conflict between the army and navy was particularly intense, as each
sought total command of the war (Duus 1976).

Japan's wartime leadership was able to mobilize the nation for war, but it was
not able to prosecute the war with a single voice. The tragic consequence of this
situation was that no one was able to stop a war that had been lost long before
the dropping of atomic bombs on Hiroshima and Nagasaki in August 1945 (Duus
1976). Even then, it was the emperor, in a rare exercise of personal authority, who
declared the war to be at an end.

American Occupation and the Framing of
a New Constitution

The Japanese political system as we know it today was largely dictated by General MacArthur and American occupation authorities following the end of World War II (Herzog 1993). As in the case of Germany, the United States faced a critical choice. Many argued for the creation of a weak and fragmented Japan that would be incapable of further aggression. Others cautioned that a weak state would merely invite authoritarianism by falling prey to violence and instability (Kataoka 1992). There was also the Soviet threat to consider, not to mention the growing power of the communists in China.

In the end, Japan was provided with a political system that resembled the parliamentary systems of Europe. Executive power resides in a prime minister responsible before the popularly elected House of Representatives, the lower house of the Diet, or parliament. An upper house, the House of Councillors, is also popularly elected and serves as a check on the more powerful House of Representatives. A supreme court, although alien to Japanese culture, possesses the power to declare acts of the Diet unconstitutional and serves as Japan's final arbitrator of individual rights. The emperor, now stripped of his status as a deity, serves as the symbol of national unity, performing a role similar to that of the British monarch.

American efforts to engineer an institutional foundation for Japanese democracy were matched by equally pervasive efforts to reshape Japanese political culture, a process described by Joy Hendry:

> ... textbooks in use before the Second World War were banned by the Occupation Government because they helped to propagate the nationalistic fervour which led Japan into defeat. They taught Japanese mythology as history, encouraging all Japanese people everywhere to think of themselves as belonging to branch lines of the imperial line and thus descended ultimately from the imperial ancestress Amaterasu. Shinto ideology was also banned from schools in the immediate post-war period, and the values which were subsequently taught were for a while very Western, mostly American, with the lives of heroes such as Benjamin Franklin being held up as models for the children. Gradually, the courses have become more "Japanese" in content, and suitable Japanese heroes have been brought in to localise the value system being advocated. However, the content of school textbooks remains a topic of considerable controversy (Hendry 1991, 88-89).

The early years of the post-war era proved to be a violent free-for-all in which a conservative alliance of businessmen and bureaucrats vied with leftist unions for control of the political system. Wary of the growing radicalism of the left and stunned by the 1949 victory of the communists in China, the occupation authorities turned a blind eye as Japan's conservative politicians, many of whom had played a prominent role in the military regime, used less than democratic procedures to consolidate their power (Yakushiji 1992). Indeed, the CIA spent "millions" to keep the Japanese rightists in power during the 1950s and 1960s (*New York Times,* Oct. 9, 1994, 1).

By the advent of the 1960s, Japanese politics had stabilized and the Japanese economic miracle had begun to take shape. Democratic attitudes also appeared to be taking root. All of these trends would continue to strengthen over the ensuing decades, transforming Japan into one of the world's leading democracies.

The only shadow on this otherwise serene picture is the fact that the Liberal Democratic Party (LDP), an alliance of conservative politicians, business leaders, and senior administrators has been the only party to govern Japan since the end of the U.S. occupation with the exception of a 9-month period in 1993. The LDP is credited with orchestrating Japan's economic miracle. It is also blamed for its collapse.

The similarity of Japanese political institutions to those of the West suggests that the political process in Japan is not markedly different from the political process in any other advanced industrial democracy (Richardson and Flanagan 1984). The Japan of today, it is argued, resembles the states of the West far more than it resembles the Japan of the prewar era. Japan's commitment to democracy has also been demonstrated by more than 40 years of constitutional government.

Japan's similarity to the West has been challenged by Karel van Wolferen in a recent book entitled *The Enigma of Japanese Power*. Van Wolferen writes:

> The Japanese have laws, legislators, a parliament, political parties, labor unions, a prime minister, interest groups and stockholders. But one should not be misled by these familiar labels into hasty conclusions as to how power *is* exercised in Japan.
>
> The Japanese prime minister is not expected to show much leadership; labor unions organize strikes to be held during lunch breaks; the legislature does not in fact legislate; stockholders never demand dividends; consumer interest groups advocate protectionism; laws are enforced only if they don't conflict too much with the interests of the powerful . . . (van Wolferen 1990, 25).

Japan's political system "works" when a high level of consensus exists among its political, administrative, and business leaders, an alliance often referred to as **Japan Inc.**

The Japanese system falters when consensus is not present. This, unfortunately, occurs most often during times of crisis, as each power bloc within the ruling alliance vetoes the suggestions of the others. The present economic crisis, for example, has found the Japanese leadership paralyzed by internal conflict. Everyone recognizes the need for reform, but the dominant groups in the LDP and the Diet cannot agree on what should be done. Much in line with our earlier definition of politics as who gets what, when, and how, each group or faction wants its opponents to bear the brunt of reform while it protects its own turf (Hiwatari 1998).

The Japanese political system, then, has yet to achieve the elusive goal of decisive leadership. The prime minister is at the helm, but he lacks the ability to force his programs upon either his own ruling coalition or the administrative and business elites that provide the foundation of that coalition. *Some American and Japanese observers, accordingly, characterize Japan as an intensely centralized state with a vacuum in the middle* (van Wolferen 1990; Asada 1989).

It is the vacuum problem that Japanese leaders are confronting in their effort to reform the Japanese political system. Politics as usual is not working and Japan desperately needs decisive leadership during times of crisis. Important steps have been made in this direction. Election procedures have been revised, the power of the prime minister strengthened, campaign contributions limited, corruption outlawed, and Japan's semilegal criminal gangs restricted. All these reforms will be discussed at later points in the chapter. Whether they have been bold enough to provide the strong leadership Japan requires to solve its economic problems is a matter of debate (McCreedy 2004).

THE POLITICAL INSTITUTIONS OF JAPAN

In the pages that follow, we will discuss continuity and change within the Japanese political system. We will examine the forces that hold the system together, as well as those that are most likely to transform Japanese politics during the coming decade. Our discussion will begin with an examination of Japan's political institutions.

Elections and Politics in Japan

Until very recently, Japan possessed a complex electoral system that allowed any group able to garner 10 to 15 percent of the vote in an electoral district to elect its own member to the House of Representatives. Given the intense loyalty that Japanese workers feel toward their firms, many of the larger conglomerates were able to elect several members to the House of Representatives, most of whom were nominally affiliated with the LDP. The electoral system also strengthened the power of local political bosses who, as a result of their ability to control 10 percent or 15 percent of the vote in their respective districts, could literally sell a seat in the House of Representatives to the highest bidder (Cox and Theis 1998).

All dimensions of the Japanese electoral system, then, encouraged the lavish outlay of money. By the 1980s, the cost of running for office in Japan had become so prohibitively expensive that the average campaign for junior politicians cost some $2 million (*Christian Science Monitor,* Apr. 18, 1994, 22). Under these circumstances, it was difficult to run a successful campaign without illegal campaign contributions.

Between 1989 and 1991, for example, construction companies alone made more than $1 billion in illegal campaign contributions (*New York Times,* June 30, 1993, A4). Particularly troublesome was a growing dependence on campaign contributions from Japan's well-organized and quasi-legal crime syndicates. In early 1992, the magnitude of criminal involvement came to light when one of the LDP's most powerful leaders was forced to resign for accepting an illegal campaign contribution of $4 million from criminal elements. He publicly apologized and was fined $1,700 for his indiscretion (*New York Times,* Oct. 15, 1992, A3).

Japan's leaders understood that escalating incidents of corruption and scandal were undermining their public support, but in line with the vacuum theory outlined previously, found it difficult to take decisive action until the situation had reached crisis proportions.

Eventually, the LDP's failure to address electoral reform fragmented the party and led to its first defeat at the polls.

Japan's first post–LDP Government created a new electoral system by dividing Japan into 300 districts, each of which elects a single member of the House of Representatives. An additional 200 members of the House of Representatives, however, continue to be elected by 11 proportional representation districts. Each voter thus has two votes: one for the single-member district to be cast for a candidate of choice, and one for the proportional-representation district to be cast for the political party of choice. The new electoral procedures were designed to force Japan's diverse political factions to come together for the sake of electing a single candidate who embodied their shared interests. It was also hoped that the new procedures would reduce the number of financial scandals by making it difficult for factional groups to buy seats in the House of Representatives. The factions are somewhat less powerful today and Japan shows signs of moving toward a two-party system. Aside from 9 months in 1993, however, the LDP has remained in power. Things do change in Japanese politics. They just do not change very rapidly.

Electoral procedures in the House of Councillors (HC) are also complex. Of the 252 members of the HC, 152 are elected in one of 47 multimember districts that correspond to Japan's prefectures or provinces. The remaining 100 members are elected by proportional representation on a national basis (Baerwald 1986). In this instance, Japanese voters cast two ballots: one for a national political party and one for a district candidate, each district being allocated from one to four members of the HC, depending on the size of the district. Members of the HC are elected for fixed six-year terms, with half of the chamber being elected every three years.

Executive Power in Japan: The Prime Minister

The Japanese prime minister is elected by the members of the Diet and serves for as long as he or she retains the confidence of the House of Representatives (HR) or until the four-year term of the HR expires. Between 1955 and 1993, the Liberal Democratic Party dominated the House of Representatives, with the cohesion and discipline of its "Dietmen" assuring that the president of the LDP would automatically become the prime minister.

Under these circumstances, the Japanese prime minister should have been among the strongest leaders in the first world. Like so much else in Japanese politics, however, executive authority in Japan does not conform to Western patterns. Rather than being the strongest prime minister in the first world, the Japanese prime minister was the weakest. Japan possesses a parliamentary political system, but the operation of that system is uniquely Japanese.

The weakness of the Japanese executive during the four decades of LDP rule found its origins in the fragmented nature of the ruling party (Ishida and Krauss 1989). Despite sharing a common vision of a stable and prosperous Japan, the competing factions of the LDP were intensely jealous of each other. The slightest policy disagreements threatened to fragment the party and jeopardize its control of the Government. The prime minister, accordingly, was expected to be a coalition builder who would craft policies upon which the diverse factions of the LDP could agree. Policies lacking consensus were to be delayed until a consensus could be achieved. Relations within the LDP were so sensitive that approximately one-half of the members of the Cabinet were changed on an annual basis as prime ministers scrambled to keep their coalitions intact. Prime ministers, moreover, were rarely elected for a second term, it being essential that each of the dominant groups in the LDP get its day in the sun (Hayes 1992). There were exceptions to this rule, but those exceptions were rare.

The temporary fall of the LDP in 1993 offered a chance for stronger political leadership in Japan, but instead the situation became even more confused. While LDP prime ministers had forged coalitions within a family of groups committed to a common principle, post-LDP prime ministers now were forced to forge ruling coalitions that spanned the breadth of the political spectrum (Shinoda 1998). The first post-LDP government, for example, was an eight-party coalition that was voted out of office a few months after its formation. A subsequent coalition government consisted of a Socialist prime minister supported by the Conservative LDP, two parties of diametrically opposing philosophies. Japan continued to pursue policies that were in place, but its ability to alter those policies decreased.

The LDP reasserted its dominance after Japan's 1993 experience and all subsequent prime ministers have been members of one of the LDP factions. There have, however, been changes. Rather than emerging from opaque bargaining among faction heads in smoke-filled rooms, the process for nominating the prime minister was thrown open to something approaching a primary election among the members of the party. While the details are too complex for easy recounting, suffice it to say that the final selection of candidates is made by a combination of branch representatives and the LDP's members in both houses of the Diet. Factions within the party remain important—all LDP Dietmen belong to one faction or another—but they are easily out maneuvered by a popular contender. Prime Minister Koizumi, for example, assumed office in 2001 despite the fact that he was a member of a minor faction and had irritated the party elders by demanding sweeping changes in this most venerable of party organization. The votes of the party branches proved critical and Koizumi led the party to victory. Far more threatening to the party elders was his determination to serve his full four-year term and run for a second term in 2004.

Japan, or at least the LDP, has prepared the groundwork for the selection of strong leaders capable of addressing its pressing economic problems. And yet, the power of Japanese prime ministers rests less on their ability to dictate policy than on their ability to broker between competing factions and parties within their ruling coalition. Prime ministers must also "broker" between different administrative agencies as well as between competing business interests. The success of a Japanese prime minister, then, is measured by his or her success as a political broker (Baerwald 1986).

The power of the prime minister and Cabinet also resides in their ability either to ratify or block policy initiatives generated by administrative agencies or powerful business interests. Policies must have the support of the prime minister and the inner circle of Cabinet if they are to see the light of day. Dietmen are also under increasing pressure to be supportive of the prime minister if they want to see their districts receive their fair share of state construction projects.

Legislative Power in Japan: The Diet

The Japanese Diet (Parliament) consists of two houses: the House of Representatives (HR) and the House of Councillors (HC). The prime minister and Cabinet—the Government—are elected by the Diet and serve at its pleasure. Should the HR and the HC disagree on the selection of a prime minister, a joint committee of the two chambers is given 30 days during which to work out a suitable compromise. Failing this, the candidate of the HR becomes the prime minister. The prime minister is responsible before the HR, a vote of no confidence among its members serving to bring down a Government. Legislation requires the approval of both houses of the Diet, but an HC veto of an HR bill can be overridden by a two-thirds majority in the latter. Clearly, then, the House of Representatives is the dominant house of the Diet. The most powerful of Japan's politicians are to be found in its ranks.

The House of Representatives. The 480 "Dietmen" of the House of Representatives (HR) are elected for four-year terms by the complex procedures discussed previously. Most bills are introduced by the Government, having been prepared in advance by the bureaucracy or the ruling coalition. Once introduced into the HR or the HC, they are sent to a standing committee for review. Committees do little to change the nature of a bill before sending it back to the floor for full debate.

Debate in the HR is vigorous, and the passage of Government legislation is far from automatic. Indeed, roughly one-half of the Government bills introduced into the Diet receive at least some modification. Others are withdrawn simply on the basis of a threatened fight by the opposition. This situation differs markedly from Western parliamentary practice in which Governments use their parliamentary majority to ram-rod bills through a hostile opposition. Why is this the case?

A partial answer to this question is to be found in Japan's historical and cultural heritage. *Conflict and individualism are accepted elements of Western culture and, ipso facto, of Western parliamentary practice. Japanese culture, by contrast, places enormous emphasis on harmony, accommodation, and collectivism.* Conflict is as common in Japan as it is in the West, but the Japanese go to extreme lengths to avoid direct confrontation. Battles are fought in private and losers are allowed to save face. In parliamentary practice, this cultural norm results in far greater emphasis on accommodation than occurs in the West. Consensus, not conflict, is the norm (Baerwald 1986).

Accommodation, however, also has a practical side. Coalitions are things of many parts, and most are exceptionally fragile. The Government reflects the dominant view within the ruling coalition, but each new bill also generates its own temporary coalition of Dietmen based on regional and group interests. The cohesion and discipline of the ruling coalition, accordingly, is dependent upon the leadership's willingness to accommodate a broad array of entrenched interests, some of which may not be to its liking (Cox and Rosenbluth 1993). Cardinal to this dimension of Japanese politics is the concept of **fair share.** Japanese political leaders have traditionally promoted political stability by portraying Japan as one large family, all members of which are entitled to their fair share of the nation's wealth.[1] Important groups who can demonstrate they are not receiving their "fair share" will generally be accommodated in order to perpetuate this myth (Hayes 1992, 2001).

In addition to its legislative function, the HR serves as a check on the powers of the Government, investigating political malfeasance and using the question period to force ministers to justify their policies. Neither has been effective in bringing ministers to heel.

This pattern, while still the norm, has also begun to change. Younger Dietmen are joining informal groups that cross party lines to pursue a particular policy. Most noteworthy in this regard was a group of young Dietmen who came together to force a more balanced view of a Japanese defense policy that was essentially passive and dependent on the United States (Samuels 2004). The Government is also becoming less inclined to seek a consensus for its policies. Indeed, 2004 would see a brawl erupt in the House of Councillors as opposition members physically protested the "strong arm" tactics of the Government (*Asahi*, June 4, 2004, www). The Japanese find these and similar events to be significant, if disquieting, indicators of change.

The ultimate power of the HR, of course, lies in its ability to withdraw its confidence from the Government. This is difficult as long as the LDP remains dominant, but that too may be changing.

The House of Councillors. The **House of Councillors** (HC) was designed to restrain the Government without actually crippling its ability to rule. As such, the 252 members of the HC can reject bills passed by the HR, but the HR can reassert its will by a two-thirds majority. The organizational structure and procedures of the HC parallel those of the HR.

While there can be little question that the HR is the dominant chamber of the Japanese Diet, the role of the HC is far from negligible. Three points, in this regard, are of particular importance.

1. It is not always easy for the Government to gain the two-thirds majority in the HR required to override a veto by the HC. This is particularly the case since the LDP has found its monopoly of power weakened.

2. The HC sometimes is controlled by a coalition different from that controlling the HR. In such circumstances, the Government must temper its legislation if a veto in the HC is to be avoided.

3. An HC veto near the end of an HR session may stick for the simple reason that the HR does not have time to override it. Pending legislation is not carried over from one session to the next.

---

[1]Japanese mythology maintains that all of Japan's citizens emanated from the same tribes.

In the final analysis, then, *the power of the HC is inverse to the power of the ruling party or coalition in the HR*. Strong Governments override the HC with ease. Weak Governments bow to its demands. With the weakening of the LDP, the HC has become a far more significant factor in the Japanese political equation than it was in the past.

Bureaucracy and Politics in Japan

The structure of Japan's bureaucratic apparatus mirrors that of other Western democracies. Layers of clerks are supervised by a hierarchy of functionaries who reach their apex in a senior service of permanent secretaries and senior managers who work directly with Cabinet ministers in the formation of public policy. All bureaucratic positions are filled on the basis of merit.

Japan's bureaucratic elite is filled almost exclusively with graduates of the Tokyo University Faculty of Law and other prestigious institutions of higher learning. As such, it is largely indistinguishable from Japan's business and political elites, most of whom have also graduated from the same handful of elite institutions.

Bureaucratic elitism exists in many Western societies, but not to the degree that it exists in Japan. Neither the Oxbridge network in Britain nor the "enarques" of France approach the exclusiveness of the Japanese bureaucratic elite.

Japan also differs from its Western counterparts in the degree of power wielded by its bureaucratic elite. Senior administrative officials are part and parcel of Japan Inc., the three-way alliance of business leaders, bureaucrats, and conservative elites who have ruled Japan since the mid-1950s. *More than merely serving the power structure, Japan's bureaucratic elite is one of its major components* (Kato 1994).

Indeed, some authors suggest that politicians do little more than pump money into their constituencies while the senior bureaucrats make policy and manage the economy. In this view, it was the bureaucracy that orchestrated Japan's economic miracle. It has also been the inflexibility of the bureaucracy that has led to Japan's current economic woes (Hartcher 1998). Particular blame is placed on the Ministries of Finance and International Trade and Industry.

The Diet, moreover, generally sketches the broad outlines of policy, leaving the bureaucrats to work out the technical details. While this is the case in many countries, few can rival Japan in the level of discretion left to its senior bureaucratic officials. Even when legislation is relatively specific, the bureaucracy can resist policies that it opposes by simply out-waiting Governments, the average life of which is two years (Hayes 1992; Muramatsu 2004).

In addition to their considerable role in the drafting and implementation of legislation, Japan's senior bureaucrats derive tremendous power from their role as economic managers. It was Japanese bureaucrats who orchestrated Japan's industrialization following the Meiji Restoration, just as it was bureaucrats who mobilized the country for total war during the era of military rule. Japan is not a "closed" or "command" society in the authoritarian sense of the word, but the Japanese economy is far more "managed" than its Western counterparts (Johnson 1989). Key ministries such as the Ministry of Finance and the Ministry of

International Trade and Industry are particularly powerful, using their control over licenses, clearances, loans, and other fiscal instruments to force compliance with the national economic plans that played such an instrumental role in orchestrating Japan's economic growth. Officials also manipulate the intense competition that exists among Japan's large business conglomerates by playing one firm off against another. *Because of the strong influence of the bureaucracy in managing the economy, Japan's economic system is often referred to as* **state capitalism.** Rather than being a passive bystander, the Japanese government is an active participant in the economic process.

The power of senior bureaucrats also emanates from "old-boy" networks that permeate the entire elite establishment, be it the bureaucracy, the LDP and its off-shoots, or the business conglomerates. In order to appreciate the critical importance of the "old-boy" networks, it is necessary to understand that Japan is simultaneously the most formal and the most informal of societies. Economic relationships in Japan are complex, legalistic, and rigid. If all of the rules and regulations were followed to the letter, the Japanese economy would probably stop. The rules, however, are not followed to the letter. Rather, *most economic transactions in Japan take the form of informal agreements among elites sharing a common background—a* system that works to Japan's advantage in dealing with foreign competitors. While the "old boys" work things out informally, the foreigners are left to storm the castle of Japanese legalism (van Wolferen 1990). It is the bureaucrats who are the guardians of the rules.

The power of the bureaucratic elite also emanates from the "pork barrel" nature of Japanese electioneering. Politicians get elected by providing jobs, facilities, and related benefits to their constituents. Just as bureaucrats are the guardians of the rules, they are also the guardians of public spending on schools, roads, public buildings, and related projects. The goodwill of a highly placed bureaucrat can do wonders for the career of a Japanese politician. The recent electoral reforms may have reduced the pork barrel power of the bureaucracy, but they have not eliminated it.

The formal powers of Japanese bureaucrats are more than matched by their informal powers. Senior administrators constitute an integral part of the ruling elite. Many prime ministers and senior members of the Cabinet have come from **bureaucratic** backgrounds, and bureaucrats are the dominant occupational group in the Diet, a position generally occupied by lawyers in the West. The "descent from heaven," as the jump of bureaucrats to senior positions in large economic firms is referred to, tends to be of three varieties: former regulatory bureaucrats are hired by large companies and industrial associations, former finance bureaucrats join major economic think tanks, and former police officers, according to some sources, join yakuza (criminal) dominated companies (Socrates.com, June 17, 2004). During the past 5 years, some 2,597 former bureaucrats have accepted jobs with the firms that they formerly regulated. The line between politics and administration in Japan is fine, indeed.

Finally, the power of bureaucratic elites is a function of Japanese culture. Acceptance of bureaucratic rules finds strong roots in Japan's Confucian and collectivist traditions (Drucker 1998). The Japanese are an orderly public that accord great respect to senior bureaucratic officials.

Perhaps because of their dominance, the power of the administrators now is being challenged by both politicians and business leaders, both of whom would like greater freedom from bureaucratic controls. Even intellectuals have joined the fray by questioning the competence of Japanese bureaucrats (Taichi 1998; Atsushi 1998). Recent surveys of Japan's bureaucratic elite finds them demoralized by their decreasing power (Muramatsu 2004). For the moment, however, it is they who fill the leadership vacuum in Japan (Nakano 1998; Kato 2004).

Law and Politics in Japan: The Supreme Court

The Japanese legal system reflects the same intriguing blend of Western and Japanese traditions as the parliament and the bureaucracy. *In structure, it is very Western, but in practice, it is inherently Japanese.*

The Japanese Constitution provides for an American-style Supreme Court with the power to declare acts of the Diet unconstitutional. This power, however, is seldom used, and it does not constitute a major constraint on the power of the Government. The 15 justices of the Supreme Court are appointed for life, with the provision that their appointments be ratified by popular referendum at 10-year intervals. Ratification is largely pro forma, but the ratification process represents an interesting variation on American practice. In further variation from the U.S. practice, only one-third of Japan's Supreme Court justices are drawn from the ranks of the lower courts, the remainder being mostly senior bureaucrats who have passed the retirement age of 55. Membership on the Japanese Supreme Court is also far more fluid than in the United States, with many justices retaining their positions for only a few years.

The elite complexion of the Japanese Supreme Court makes it very much part of the system, and acts of the Diet are rarely overturned (Hayes 1992). The Supreme Court is also inclined to sustain the power of the Government in the face of challenges to its authority launched in the lower courts.

The Supreme Court heads a highly centralized legal system that includes a variety of high courts, district courts, and summary courts (courts of first instance). In a uniquely Japanese innovation, the legal system includes a broad network of **conciliation commissions** *designed to facilitate the out-of-court settlement of disputes whenever possible.* The conciliation commissions, in combination with the general Japanese abhorrence of public conflict, have resulted in a caseload for Japanese courts that is less than one-tenth that of courts in the United States and Europe (van Wolferen 1990). Japan is also preparing to experiment with a limited jury system for serious crimes, the number of which averages about 2,800 per year. This is not a large number by American standards, but is shocking to the Japanese. It also has caused a decline in Japanese confidence in their police (Curtin 2004).

Lawyers' fees are inordinately high in Japan, as entrance to the legal profession is highly regulated. In some years, less than 3 percent of the applicants pass the bar exam, as compared to some 70 percent in the United States *(International Herald Tribune,* Feb. 15, 1996, 4). This now is changing as new law schools are opening to meet the demand created by the gradual deregulation of Japan's economy and the gradual opening of Japan's economy to foreign competition. Nevertheless, supply remains far behind demand (Fuyuno, Ichiko, "Japan Grooms New Lawyers," *Wall Street Journal,* April 13, 2004, A-16). More applicants are also being allowed to pass the bar exam (*Daily Yomiuri*, Mar. 2, 2005, www).

Aside from having a clear bias in favor of the political establishment, the legal system in Japan appears to work quite well. It is interesting to note that Japan has the lowest reported crime rate among the states of the first world. Perhaps Japan's low crime rate is related to its legal system or to aspects of Japanese culture. It might also be result of a Japanese reluctance to report petty crimes.

THE ACTORS IN JAPANESE POLITICS: ELITES, PARTIES, GROUPS, AND CITIZENS

Political institutions are the arena of politics, but the actors in the political process give life to those institutions. In this section, we shall examine the four main types of political actors in Japan: elites, political parties, groups, and citizens. Each plays a critical role in determining who gets what, when, and how in Japan.

Elites and Politics in Japan

Japan is an intensely elitist society that is ruled by the conservative political, administrative, and business leaders who form the inner core of Japan Inc. (Rothacher 1993). As the three groups overlap, it is difficult to say which is dominant (Koh 1989). Although much power is exercised behind the scenes, participation in the Cabinet is a visible sign of elite status. To be named prime minister is the ultimate recognition of success. The heads of Japan's large conglomerates are also exceptionally powerful individuals, as are its senior bureaucrats. The power of senior bureaucrats, as noted in the preceding section, is also enormous. "Diet-men," most of whom speak for powerful interest groups, rank among the lower echelon of the elite, as do provincial governors and the mayors of the larger cities, the latter positions being stepping stones to higher office.

Japan is not unique in the fact that most of its policy decisions are made by a political elite. What is unique about Japan is the exceptionally narrow base from which its political elite is selected and the extraordinary ability of that elite to maintain itself in power (Johnson 1994).

Japan's political, administrative, and business leaders are recruited almost exclusively from a handful of elite universities headed by the Tokyo University Faculty of Law (Japan Access.com, "Issues in Japanese Education," 2001). In recent years, some 60 percent of the LDP members in the House of Representatives have attended one of Japan's top 5 universities, a full 32 percent having attended Tokyo University Faculty of Law. Exceptions to this dominance, while rare, have occurred when successful entrepreneurs from outside of the political circle have used their wealth and talents to build powerful political machines.

The picture is much the same in regard to Japan's administrative elites. The Ministry of Education frankly admits that a university's name is of vital importance in determining future employment prospects and that "competition for top level schools is 'unbelievably intense'" (Japan Access.com, "Education, Schools and Curricula," 2001).

The tightness of Japan's ruling elite provides its members with an "old-boy" network that is virtually impenetrable. Tensions exist, but communications within the elite are open and fluid, allowing problems to be sorted out before they threaten the system (van Wolferen 1990). The elite club is also very close to becoming a distinct social class, as the rich are better able to afford the elite prep schools and pre-schools required for access to the elite universities. Japanese society, accordingly, is something of a paradox. Everything is based on merit examinations, but the rich and famous are better able to afford the elite training required to pass these tests. Some grants, however, are provided to merit scholars from poorer backgrounds.

Parties and Politics in Japan

Japan's first era of party rule (1912–1931) was a tumultuous one in which strikes and riots were commonplace (Duus 1976). Party politics was also riddled with corruption as party leaders pandered to special interests and used the public treasury to finance local political machines. One observer of the era likened the Diet to a bull ring and its members "to whores running after money and patrons" (Duus 1976, 172). Many Japanese recoiled from the electoral process, finding it abhorrent to Japan's traditions of harmony, decorum, and order (Duus 1976). All in all, Japan's first venture into Western-style democracy left much to be desired. It was, however, a beginning.

Party rule collapsed with the ascendance of the military but was revived during the United States occupation. The party map in the immediate post-war period included parties of every conceivable political persuasion, none of which were able to control more than a minority of the seats in the Diet (Calder 1988). Although the conservatives were the dominant force in the country, they were hopelessly divided among themselves. A pragmatic left, if cohesive, could easily have established itself as a powerful force in Japanese politics. The left, however, was also fragmented.

The conservatives chose the path of pragmatism, coming together in 1955 to form the Liberal Democratic Party (Masumi 1992). The parties of the left had earlier closed ranks to form the Japanese Socialist Party (JSP), but the JSP retained a strong Marxist orientation that was distrusted by a large segment of the Japanese population. This, among other things, allowed the LDP to rule Japan without interruption from 1955 until 1993. The LDP would reassert its dominance following a brief fall from grace, but the electoral reforms enacted during that period appear to be pushing Japan in the direction of a two-party system, each of which is a collection of factions and smaller parties. The LDP remains the more dominant of the two parties, but the recently formed Democratic Party of Japan (DPJ) may soon challenge that dominance.

The Liberal Democratic Party. For all intents and purposes, the leadership of the LDP is the political leadership of Japan. The two entities remain virtually inseparable and one cannot understand the growing complexity of Japanese politics today without reference to the leadership of the LDP. It is they who continue to have the major voice in determining who gets what in Japan.

The Internal Politics of the LDP. The LDP is a large **catch-all party** that *aggregates a broad spectrum of business, administrative, and political interests often referred to as Japan Inc.* The LDP's conservative philosophy differs little from that of the Conservative Party in Britain or the Christian Democratic Party in Germany. Business is good for Japan, and the LDP is good for business. The pragmatic orientation of the LDP reflects a need to accommodate the three main elements that dominate the party: the business community, the professional politicians, and the administrative elite, each of which must receive its due.

Big business demands strong support from the government in terms of tax breaks, subsidies, and protected markets. These are granted by LDP politicians who thrive on the lavish campaign contributions provided by the business community. Both business leaders and politicians, in turn, submit to rule by a powerful administrative technocracy that uses its vast spending and regulatory powers to promote the prosperity of its partners.

Beyond being a three-way alliance between big business, senior administrators, and conservative politicians, the LDP is also a party of personalities and factions, each of which vies for domination of the party apparatus. Each of the LDP's five to eight factions resembles a self-contained political party, and each is headed by a senior politician with a strong power base among the LDP's members in the Diet. Indeed, the fall of the LDP Government in 1993 occurred when several LDP factions simply declared themselves to be independent parties and withdrew their support from the LDP prime minister. The recently formed Democratic Party of Japan also contains a long list of former LDP leaders.

Some of the dissident factions would later rejoin the LDP; others would form coalition governments with the LDP. So fluid is the formation and dissolution of LDP factions that in a single month of 1998, one new faction formed and four others merged. In the meantime, two of the smaller opposition parties had also merged to strengthen their position against the LDP (*Japan Times,* Nov. 7–13, 1998). Some observers have likened the growing struggles within the LDP to a civil war (Nagata 1998).

The formal organization of the LDP is topped by its president, followed in turn by the secretary general, the chairman of the General Council (executive committee), and the chairman of the Policy Research Council. Next in line are the chairmen of the Committees of National Organizations, Public Relations, Finance, Diet Affairs, and so on (*Liberal Star,* Nov. 15, 1991). The secretary general is selected by the president to manage the party, the president himself becoming the prime minister when the party is in power (Flanagan et al. 1991). The LDP holds an annual convention, but its role is largely symbolic.

The occupants of the leadership positions reviewed above, along with the leaders of the party's diverse factions, form its inner core. Chairs of lesser party committees have generally served as vice ministers and will form the next generation of party leaders. All have served long apprenticeships in the Diet and are exceptionally skilled politicians.

The formal leadership positions within the LDP are filled after tense and protracted bargaining among factional leaders. The same tense bargaining determines which factions will make party policy and what the "fair share" of Cabinet positions allocated to each group will be when the party is in power. Under this arrangement, ambitious "Dietmen" jockey to join a faction that will be strong enough to name a prime minister (party president) or stake a claim to important Cabinet positions. This, however, can be risky business as the fortunes of each faction ebb and flow with the course of events (Yakushiji 1992).

Even in the heat of battle, however, care is taken to assure that all factions receive at least minimal representation on the Cabinet when the party is in power. This reflects the traditional Japanese concern with harmony. It also makes good political sense. Who knows what tomorrow will bring?

In years past, it was common for LDP prime ministers to allocate cabinet positions to "five-term" politicians on the recommendation of their faction leader. The current prime minister suspended this practice in an effort to weaken the faction system (*Daily Yomiuri,* Sept. 5, 2004, www).

LDP factions are welded together by **patron-client networks** in which *the party's junior members in the Diet are promoted to ever-higher positions within the party in return for their support of a faction leader,* a process described by Brian Reading:

> The young politician starts by receiving help from his seniors. As he progresses up the political ladder, he is expected to raise more money himself. In time, it becomes his turn to help his juniors. Once he has been in the Cabinet, he is expected to make a significant personal contribution to his faction's funds. The faction leaders themselves must raise billions of yen each a year (sic), part of which are distributed to their younger followers. At oseibo, New Year, before elections and at other gift-giving times such as chugen in July, faction leaders hand out money to their followers, several million yen to each, nominally for "rice cakes" (Reading 1992, 238).

The electoral clout of a faction within the LDP, as the above passage suggests, depends on its access to financial support and bureaucratic largess. More than any other factor, Japanese elections are determined by the candidate's ability to finance a powerful local machine and to provide its constituents with subsidies, construction contracts, and related pork barrel projects (*Japan Times,* Apr. 25, 2000). It should come as little surprise, accordingly, that Japanese elections are among the most expensive in the world.

As elections became increasingly expensive, LDP factions sought to strengthen their relative positions by turning to illegal sources of funding, sources that included kickbacks on government contracts, rigging of the stock market, and contributions from Japan's quasi-legal crime syndicates. In one scandal, for example, no less than 130 members of the HR received an estimated $80,000,000 in illegal payoffs (Sterngold 1992). The *Japan Times* even featured a regular column entitled "Scandal Du Jour" (*Japan Times,* Mar. 25, 2000). A new electoral law is attempting to make Japanese politics less money-driven, but scandals continue. In 2003, 150 "fast track" officials—younger bureaucrats being groomed for stardom—were accused of making secret donations to the LDP to assure that they stayed on the fast track (*Daily Yomiuri,* Sept. 10, 2004, www). Later revelations disclosed huge secret contributions being made to the LDP and other parties by a variety of business and professional groups including: the Japan Dental Association, the Japan Nursing Association, the Federation of Health Insurers Societies, the Real Estate Association, and the Pharmacutical Association, to mention but a few (*Daily Yomiuri,* Sept. 11, 2004). The LDP has employed a public relations firm to clean up its image (*Daily Yomiuri,* Jan. 10, 2005, www).

How the LDP Rules, and Why it May Lose Power (Again). The dominance of the LDP is based upon three key factors.

1. *The LDP has been very flexible in accommodating potential challenges to the party's dominance.* Any issue that reflects a broad base of voter support is embraced by the LDP. This has been true of environmental and welfare issues, both of which were initially championed by the Japan Socialist Party. All in all, the party's conservative ideology is secondary to staying in power. The LDP 's alliance with Japan's administrative and business elites enables it to outspend its opponents. Money and "pork barrel" are the driving forces of Japanese electoral politics, and the LDP controls both.

2. *The factions within the LDP, while fiercely competitive and often hostile, have been held together by the confidence that each will get its fair share of influence.* Being part of the LDP power structure is far more advantageous than attempting to attack it from the outside. This message has been brought home time and time again as break-away factions reunite with the LDP.

3. *The LDP is recognized as the party that built Japan's phenomenal prosperity.* Even now, Japanese voters seem reluctant to change a system that worked so well for so long. Scandals, while unfortunate, have been tolerated as long as they do not alter the capacity of the system to operate effectively.

Unfortunately for the LDP, each of the pillars of its power are beginning to erode. Japan is midstream in its second decade of recession, and Japan's voters are no longer convinced that the system is meeting their economic needs. Electoral reforms have also reduced the confidence of the LDP's factions that they will receive their fair share of positions and influence. Prime Minister Junichiro Koizumi has appointed ministers without consulting faction leaders and has used the support among the party's branches to remain in office far longer than the normal two-year term. This, as Shin'ichi Kitaoka writes, is causing severe tension within the LDP.

> By the same token, the prime minister's tenure must be short. For the sake of simplicity, suppose there are five factions of the same size. . . . if Prime Minister A wishes to hold his position for longer than one term (in most cases two years), then the second faction leader must wait four years. The third faction leader has to wait six to eight years (Kitaoka 2004).

Other problems also abound. Japan Inc., the three-way alliance between politicians, business leaders, and bureaucrats, is starting to unravel. Business leaders are rebelling against bureaucratic control and politicians are less willing to give the bureaucracy carte blanche in drafting legislation. New campaign finance laws also restrict business contributions to candidates, although it is not clear that they are being rigorously enforced.

The Democratic Party of Japan. It is these realities that have led a mélange of opposition parties and disaffected LDP factions to believe that a strong second party that occupied the political center of Japanese politics could dethrone the LDP. The thought is not new. The spring of 1992 would see one of the LDP's major factions announce that it was rejecting the "putrid politics" of the LDP and forming its own political party, the Japan Renewal Party. The fact that leaders of the Japan Renewal Party possessed long records of political corruption was seemingly irrelevant. All major factions of the LDP possessed long records of corruption (*European,* July 15-18, 1993, 7). Other factions soon followed suit and eventually united with the New Frontier Party. The platform of the new party called for electoral reform, an end to corruption, an enhancement of urban life, better trade relations with the United States, and a reduction in the power of Japanese bureaucrats (Ozawa 1993).

The leaders of the New Frontier Party proclaimed its formation to be the most significant event in Japanese politics since the end of World War II. Pundits predicted the birth of a two-party system in Japan was at hand. In reality, the new entity varied little from the LDP. Decisions required consensus among diverse factions, each of which was, at least for a brief moment, an independent political party. If anything, the differences between the factions of the New Frontier Party were greater than those between the factions of the LDP. Also problematic was the absence of a clear ideological difference between the New Frontier Party and the LDP (Hiwatari 1998). These and related problems were too great for the new party to overcome, and it collapsed in December of 1997, giving way to six minor parties.

The logic of a strong alternative to the LDP, however, remained compelling and many groups of the now defunct New Frontier Party regrouped as the Democratic Party of Japan in the late 1990s. One commentator described it as an "election cooperative" rather than a political party. The majority of DPJ members elected to the Diet (parliament) are refugees from other parties, including a large number from the LDP (*Asia Times,* Sept. 25, 2002, www).

Be this as it may, the DPJ did well in the 2003 elections, forcing the LDP to form a ruling coalition with two minor parties, one of which subsequently merged with the LDP. The leaders of the DPJ were euphoric, proclaiming that the era of the two-party democracy was at hand. This is not yet the case, but Japan is moving in that direction (Reed 2003).

Pressure Groups and Politics in Japan

Japan possesses the same array of business, labor, and social pressure groups that are found in all modern industrial societies. In common with other features of Japanese politics, however, Japanese pressure groups are Western in form but Japanese in substance. Most pressure groups in the West, for example, are practical in nature, their members coming together to achieve a specific set of economic or social objectives. Individuals in the West seldom value pressure group membership as a social experience, and they often belong to several groups with competing objectives. As a result of such *conflicting group loyalties,* the cohesion of Western pressure groups is often weak.

The Japanese also form groups to achieve specific economic and social objectives. Unlike the situation in the West, however, pressure group participation in Japan is valued as an important social experience. The same intense loyalties that accrue to the family or the firm also accrue to the pressure group. The Japanese are also less likely to join groups with conflicting interests, a fact that makes Japanese groups far more cohesive than their Western counterparts.

Group leaders, moreover, command great respect in Japan. Decisions, once made, are generally obeyed by the rank and file. Translated into the broader political equation, this means that the political leaders of Japan are in a far stronger position to control and mobilize their population by making deals with their country's large pressure group associations than would be the case in the West, particularly in the United States.

Business Associations. *Business associations are the most powerful of Japan's pressure groups.* They include a variety of large peak associations such as the Federation of Economic Organizations, the Japan Committee for Economic Development, the Japan Chamber of Commerce, and the Japan Iron and Steel Federation (Fukushima 1989). The Federation of Economic Organizations and the Japan Federation of Employers merged in 2002 to create one of the most powerful pressure groups in Japan. Before the 2002 merger, the Federation of Economic Organizations alone possessed some 800 large corporate members. The Chamber of Commerce represents a broad spectrum of business interests, regardless of size. Organizations also exist to express the specific interests of medium-sized and smaller businesses—interests that may or may not conflict with those of the industrial giants (Lamont-Brown 1995).

The National Federation of Cooperatives (NFC), in turn, represents a vast network of agricultural cooperatives, agrarian associations, and agri-business organizations. The NFC delivered the rural vote for the Liberal Democratic Party during its formative years and was rewarded for its support with protective measures that made Japanese produce the most costly in the world.

The farm lobby continues to be among the most powerful groups in Japan, but it has lost strength as a result of urbanization. Today, farmers amount to only 10 percent of the Japanese population (Mulgan 1997). The exorbitant cost of food, moreover, has become increasingly burdensome to Japan's urban population, making continued price supports politically unpopular. Also problematic have been demands from the United States for greater access to the Japanese food market, an area in which American products are more than competitive with their Japanese counterparts. Japan's large business corporations do not want to engage in a trade war with the United States over the question of agricultural subsidies, and they have begun to turn on their former allies (Calder 1988). Conflict over support for agriculture was one of the major issues leading to the fragmentation of the LDP.

Nevertheless, the farm lobby has been able to play a key role in blocking Japan's much-needed economic reform (*Asia Times,* Oct. 1, 2003). In this they have been joined by Japan's massive construction industry and its large bureaucratic agencies. The former fears a curtailment of lucrative government construction contracts, while the latter fear a diminution of their massive regulatory power (Leblanc 1998).

Most of the associations discussed above are large peak associations that possess a multitude of group and corporate members. Doctors, lawyers, the police, and other professions are also represented by powerful peak associations, the leaders of which have figured prominently in the circles of the LDP and its conservative spin-offs. As a reward for their support of Japan Inc., professional associations have been allowed to regulate both their work rules and the ethics of their members. Not surprisingly, doctors' and lawyers' fees in Japan are astronomical, even by United States standards.

Labor Unions. Japanese labor emerged from the Second World War as one of the best organized forces in Japanese society and was expected to play a central role in Japanese politics. The failure of Japanese labor to live up to this expectation is attributable to a variety of factors. Japanese unions, like the socialist movement in general, remained preoccupied with questions of ideological purity. In line with their Marxist ideology, energies were spent on promoting class conflict rather than wage and benefit packages that would provide material benefits to Japan's workers. Problematic, also, was the cradle-to-grave embrace of Japan's larger firms, the comprehensiveness of which reduced the need for unions. The large conglomerates also viewed union membership as an act of disloyalty and usually provided their workers with a company union designed to solidify their loyalty to the firm. Finally, union activities were hampered by the large percentage of Japanese workers who found employment in small firms. In such cases, personal ties to the owner often precluded union participation (van Wolferen 1990). Given the above circumstances, it is not surprising that Japan loses fewer days to strikes than any other advanced industrial country (Hayes 1992). The number of strikes, moreover, has been declining.

In one way or another, then, Japanese unions have been deprived of the critical mass required to achieve political dominance. A labor movement that had unionized approximately 55 percent of the industrial labor force in 1949 would speak for only half of that number, 28 percent, by the mid-1980s (Hayes 1992, 2001).

Japanese unions have also been weakened by the recent privatization of the nation's railroads and telecommunications, two large public-sector organizations that employed many of Japan's unionized workers. Dealing with private organizations may prove far more difficult for Japan's unions than dealing with government corporations (Woodiwiss 1992).

The driving force in the Japanese labor movement is **Rengo,** a large umbrella organization created in 1987 to give focus to the labor movement. Rengo now speaks for approximately 65 percent of organized labor, or approximately 20 percent of the Japanese labor force. The Rengo strategy is to pursue a pragmatic, non-ideological approach to labor relations and to strengthen cooperation between the Japanese Socialist Party and other smaller parties of the center-left. As yet, this strategy shows little sign of being successful.

Women. By Western standards, Japanese women appear to be the most oppressed females of the first world. The post–World War II years have witnessed the economic emancipation of Japanese women, but economic liberation has not been matched by gains in the social and political arenas. Some 40 percent of Japanese women now work outside the home, but they are expected to work for less money than do men and to occupy minor positions. Japan possesses an "equal employment" law, but there are few serious penalties for noncompliance (Leblanc 1998). Working wives are expected to assume primary responsibility for child rearing and to serve their families in the traditional Japanese manner. Women have also been systematically excluded from the inner circle of Japanese politics. The situation is improving, but women's parliamentary participation in Japan is the lowest of the major industrial democracies. Cabinets generally have between 1 and 3 women. (Japan Access.com, "Women's Issues," 2001).

Lacking direct access to the political system, feminists have launched a variety of civic action groups, the largest of which is **Chifuren,** *an association of Japanese housewives* (Pons 1998). Chifuren, which claims to represent some 6 million consumer-oriented housewives, focuses largely on economic issues such as fair product labeling.

Women are also forcing a change in Japanese society by more subtle means, not the least of which is the tendency of educated Japanese women to delay marriage or avoid it altogether. Some indication of the changing role of Japanese women is provided by Jane Condon:

> Although young Japanese women are still renowned for being *yasashii* (tender, kind, gentle), the days of total obedience are over. Young wives are less disposed to being nurses and maids at home. They want their husbands to help around the house, at least a little. They want the whole family to go out to eat at least once a month, if not once a week (hence the rise in the number of family restaurants). They are less likely to pack away their high fashion Japanese clothes when they marry. They buy new clothes less often, but they still want to look as nice as they did when they were *dokushin kizoku* (single aristocrats). They insist that their husbands talk with them more. And although young husbands may still be number one in the family, the idea of walking behind them strikes young wives as absurd (Condon 1985, 298).

It is not clear, however, that Japanese women are as vulnerable as Westerners believe. As discussed by Sumiko Iwao (1993):

> Today it is, in a sense, the husbands who are being controlled and the ones to be pitied. The typical Japanese man depends heavily on his wife to look after his daily needs and nurture his psychological well-being. The Confucian ethic of the three obediences formerly binding women could be rewritten today as the three obediences for men: obedience to mothers when young, companies when adult, and wives when retired. Recent television dramas have depicted the plight of salaried-worker fathers as their presence and power in the home fades; such men are estranged from their families by extended absences

(e.g., work assignments abroad or in other cities) and suffer from a syndrome known as "involuntary incapacity to go home [kitaku kyohil]." Their plight is only intensified by the stronger position of women in the home. These recent phenomena lead us to wonder whether it is not men, instead of women, who are being exploited in Japanese society today. The vast majority of men, however, remain largely unaware of their own vulnerability as they cling to the illusion that they are the respected superiors of society and belittle women's voices as nothing but emotional, unrealistic "female logic" (7–8).

Organized Crime As a Pressure Group. Particularly interesting is the political role played by *Japan's large and quasi-legal crime syndicates,* the **yakuza**. During the 1990s, the syndicates claimed some 90,000 members, approximately one-half of whom were members of Japan's three largest gangs. A 1992 law has sought to integrate the gangs more directly within the "system" by allowing district governments to register them as official **boryokudan** or *violence groups.*

Organized crime presents the political leaders of all countries with three choices: to wage an expensive and endless war against the crime barons, to legalize everything, or to make organized crime a self-regulating part of the system (Nagashima 1990). The Japanese have opted for the third alternative, preferring to deal with organized crime rather than disorganized crime.

Japan's large criminal organizations are expected to regulate the activities of their members in the same manner as the Japanese Medical Association or any other professional group. A magazine published by one of Japan's foremost crime syndicates, accordingly, calls upon its members to do the following:

1. preserve harmony in order to strengthen the group;
2. love and respect people outside the group and remember what is owed to them;
3. always be courteous and always be aware of senior-junior relationships;
4. learn from the experience of seniors and work for self-improvement; and
5. show restraint in contacts with the outside world (van Wolferen 1990, 104).

The strategy of treating criminals as part of the Japanese family apparently works, for Japan has a lower reported crime rate than any other state of the first world (Sessions 2005; Kitching 2005). This strategy, however, is not without its dangers. Massive amounts of crime money has subverted the electoral process and Japan's large crime families are merging with legitimate economic enterprises. Recent estimates suggest that as many as 30,000 "business suit yakuza" who operate like ordinary businessmen (Socrates.com, June 17, 2004). Perhaps belatedly, authorities now are beginning to assert themselves against organized crime and especially extortionists who target large companies (*New York Times,* Aug. 11, 1999, www). These measures, along with a declining economy, have taken their toll on the yakuza. As Socrates writes, "Consolidation is typical in any maturing or declining sector, and the proportion of yakuza in the three largest umbrella gangs has increased markedly: in 1995, for example, the three largest groups accounted for just 24.8 percent of total members, compared with around 77 percent in 2002 (Socrates.com, June 17, 2004).

Citizens and Politics in Japan

Japan is a democracy, and the Japanese electorate possesses the ability to alter its political system if it chooses to do so. To date, however, the electorate has been reluctant to do so. Despite electoral reforms, the LDP continues to monopolize all vestiges of political and economic power in Japan.

It would be a mistake, however, to suggest that the Japanese public either was totally passive or without influence. One of the main reasons for the LDP's long domination of Japanese politics was its willingness to listen to public opinion and to respond accordingly. In this regard, three indicators of public opinion are of particular importance: elections, public opinion polls, and civic action protests. Of these, election results are the most important, as they have a direct and immediate impact on the composition of the Diet (Flanagan et al. 1991).

When the electorate supported candidates favoring stronger environmental regulation during the 1960s and 1970s, for example, the LDP became the party of the environment, attacking Japan's environmental problems with characteristic Japanese vigor. Not only did the elite listen, but it acted. In the same manner, when voters demanded better care for the aging, the LDP became the party of the elderly. Treatment of the elderly, unlike the environment, did not stay a hot issue, and welfare programs for the elderly were scaled back (Campbell 1992). More recently, the LDP has accepted political reform and wooed public opinion by fielding younger and more popular candidates.

Current public opinion polls indicate a preeminent popular concern with economic prosperity. They also indicate a growing concern with the intense pressures of Japanese life as well as the manifest corruption of the Japanese political system (Leblanc 1998). In addition to economic considerations, recent polls suggest that some 40 percent of the Japanese citizens fear for the security of their country, and some 84 percent fearing that Japan could find itself at war. They also remained intensely proud of their long tradition of their country (*Japan Today*, April 29, 2004 and March 28, 2004).

By far the most visible expressions of Japanese public opinion are the civic action protests, sometimes violent, that have become an accepted part of Japanese politics. As with most other aspects of Japanese life, political protests are highly organized affairs (Steinhoff 1989).

THE CONTEXT OF JAPANESE POLITICS:
CULTURE, ECONOMICS, AND
INTERNATIONAL INTERDEPENDENCE

What makes the Japanese system work? Why do Japanese voters maintain a conservative elite in power in spite of repeated and ever-worsening scandals? Why is Japanese society so self-regulating? Why are Japanese elites able to "trust" each other to honor informal agreements despite intense competition between groups? Why does the Japanese population trust bureaucrats to run things? Why are the Japanese so productive and their goods of such high quality?

Answers to these and similar questions tend to fall into two categories: culture and economics. We first examine the cultural bases of Japanese politics, and then turn to Japanese political economy. Both perspectives offer compelling explanations of "what makes Japan tick." We will also examine the extent to which Japanese politics is shaped by the country's interdependence with the other members of the world community.

The Culture of Japanese Politics

Cultural explanations of Japanese politics center on four themes: nationalism (racism), harmony (collectivism), acceptance of hierarchical authority, and an intense dedication to hard work. Each of the four themes finds its origins in the unique evolution of Japanese culture discussed in the introductory sections of this chapter.

Nationalism. The Japanese are intensely proud of being Japanese (Hendry 1991). They also have an infinite faith in their ability to succeed. To some observers, Japanese national pride borders on racism (van Wolferen 1990).

Japan's conservative leaders have used two nationalistic themes to build a broad base of popular support for their programs: pride and vulnerability. The Japanese have ample reasons to be proud of their accomplishments. In a few short decades, Japan has been transformed from a defeated ruin into an economic superpower. Paralleling nationalist pride, however, is a profound sense of vulnerability, a pervasive fear that Japan is too small to maintain its economic dominance and that its competitors are dangerously jealous of its success (Calder 1988). Japan's conservative elites have used this sense of vulnerability to solidify their control of Japanese politics, arguing that a radical change of leadership would jeopardize the nation's hard-won prosperity by aiding its adversaries.

The most recent manifestation of Japanese nationalism is a movement to rewrite the history of Japan's colonial expansion in the years leading up to World War II. The revisionist movement attempts to portray Japan's colonial expansion as a response to Western imperialism designed to protect the values of Asian culture. Revised manuals of history have sold over 250,000 copies since 1996, and their popularity is growing (Leblanc 1998).

Harmony. *The cornerstone of Japanese political culture is its emphasis on collective harmony, or wa.* Western culture idealizes individualism, while Japanese culture idealizes the group. To be ostracized from the group is to lose one's sense of identity. More than that, it means losing one's entire system of social and psychological support. Ideal citizens in Japan are citizens who merge their identities with that of the group and who place group interest above self-interest (Moeran 1986). Interpersonal conflicts are often intense, but they are "brokered" to maintain the cohesiveness of the group (Nakane 1970).

The Japanese emphasis on social harmony provides the cultural underpinning for the concept of "fair share" that is so prominent in Japanese politics. Japan is viewed as one large family, all parts of which must, in some way or another, be kept within the system. The Japanese emphasis on collective harmony helps to explain the ability of Japan's political, economic, and administrative elites to "network" so effectively. Again, they are all part of the same family.

As demonstrated by these elementary school students in Tokyo, Japanese students are responsible for keeping their schools clean. This is one of many practices that produce an orderly, safe, and rigorous, if regimented, educational system.

The cultural emphasis on harmony further underlies the self-effacing style of Japanese politicians, a style that makes it difficult for Western negotiators to pin down precisely who controls what. Everyone denies having power, and no decision can really be taken without the consensus of the larger group. Even when promises are made, these promises are contingent upon group approval.

Pressures for social conformity also strengthen the cohesion of Japanese pressure groups. Group members are under intense pressure to vote as a group, and conflicting group memberships (cross-cutting cleavages) are discouraged (Richardson and Flanagan 1984). Work groups also tend to become political groups. To accept employment in one of Japan's large conglomerates is to make a decision that will regulate the individual's economic, political, and social behavior for the remainder of his or her life. Japanese employees seldom change jobs and are expected to internalize the economic and political interests of their firms. It is the collective thing to do.

The Confucian Ethic: Hierarchical Authority and Hard Work. *Japanese political and economic culture also builds upon* **Confucian culture,** *four dimensions of which are particularly important: hard work, respect for hierarchical authority, rule by merit, and devotion to the group* (Hendry 1991 and 2003; Dore and Sako 1989). These tenets of Confucian culture underscore the very foundation of Japan's political success in the post–World War II era. The Japanese are orderly, they follow the dictates of their leaders, most of whom are selected on the basis of merit, and they work hard. In so doing, they assure that the state will have ample resources to meet the economic needs of its people. Indeed, a recent survey reported that three out of four Japanese would prefer to work with a fever, rather than take sick leave (*Japan Times*, Jan. 11, 1999, www).

Culture also permeates the way Japanese do business. Table 6.1 outlines the profound differences between Eastern and Western management techniques.

Political Socialization and Cultural Change. Because Japanese cultural patterns are an important element in the Japanese political equation, they are carefully nurtured by Japan's political leaders. School curricula actively reinforce all of the cultural patterns cited above, downplaying cultural trends that the ruling elite deems "anti-Japanese." The socialization process is further reinforced by a mass media that is very much part of the "system". The intellectual community, too, seems to have been lulled into passivity by economic prosperity, being described as "disturbingly quiet and vacant" (Miyoshi and Harootunian 1989, ix–x).

Even after a decade and one-half of economic adversity, Japan's press remains reluctant to criticize the government. Scandals are noted, but attacks on major leaders soon fade (*New York Times,* May 19, 2004, www).

Be this as it may, Japan is no longer an isolated community in which a narrow oligarchy can choose the values to which its subjects will be exposed. Two million foreigners now enter Japan on an annual basis, a figure that has been more than matched by the number of Japanese traveling abroad (Sugiyama 1992). In 1985, for example, approximately 4,000,000 Japanese citizens traveled abroad for reasons of business or tourism, a number that would approach the 9,000,000 mark by 1988 and nearly 14,000,000 by 1994 (Sugiyama 1992; *New York Times,* Aug. 23, 1994, A3). By 2004, almost a million Japanese were residing abroad on a long-term basis, about one-third of them in the United States (*Japan Today,* April 6, 2004, www).

Particularly worrisome to Japanese leaders is the fear that Japan is becoming, however slowly, a post-industrial society. The pace of Japanese life is staggering, and many younger Japanese executives are "dropping out" of the rat race (Noguchi 1992; Leblanc 1998). Also new to Japan are the "furita," some 2,000,000 unmarried people under 35 years of age who only engage in casual work that suits their needs. The number is not large, but Japanese officials fear that its will grow and create yet another burden for Japanese society (Socrates.com, June 17, 2004, www). The Japanese population that created the economic miracle is also becoming older, giving way to a generation of Japanese workers that may be less imbued with the work ethic of its elders. This, however, remains to be seen. No one expects radical changes in Japanese culture in the near future, but business leaders are nervous.

Also worrisome to Japan's business leaders is the low emphasis on innovation in Japanese culture. Toward this end, schools now display signs saying "Let us all be individuals," to which The *Economist* quipped, "All together now, repeat after me" (*Economist,* Mar. 21, 1998, 21).

Table 6.1 The Business Characteristics: A Comparison of American and Japanese Management Practices

Characteristics of American Business	Characteristics of Japanese Business
I. Game Concept	**I. Mutual Trust**
1. Business is a game in pursuit of profits under the rules of laws and contracts. ■ more arguments, documents, litigation, and trials ■ high acting ability ■ precedence of logic ■ clear agreement and expression ■ willingness to confront	1. Business is based on trusting relationships among people rather than on the rules of the game. ■ fewer arguments, documentation, litigation, and trials ■ low acting ability ■ precedence of relationships among people ■ ambiguous agreement and expression ■ avoidance of confrontation
II. Individualism—Dignity as the Highest Priority	**II. Human Relations—Oriented**
2. The dignity of individuals and self-assertion ■ active self-assertion ■ individual decisions over consensus	2. "In the same boat" sensibility and mutual trust ■ weak self-assertion ■ dependence on consensus
3. Individual work	3. Teamwork
4. Refusal of individuals to be placed at a disadvantage	4. Reluctance to say "no"
5. A society excelling in creativity and versatility	5. Uniform society
6. An economy within which entrepreneurs with a high level of creativity are important	6. An economy in which entrepreneurs are less important
7. The existence of excellent professionals and their important social functions	7. Less important social functions for professionals
8. Priority of customer's benefit in sales	8. Salesperson loyal to employer
9. Exceedingly high mobility of labor	9. Exceedingly low mobility of labor
10. Lack of mutual dependence between employers and employees	10. Mutual dependence between employers and employees
III. Efficiency-Oriented—Simplicity, Clarity, and Speed	**III. Precision-Oriented—Dependence on Human Awareness**
11. Heavy dependence on machinery and technology versus dependence on human resources	11. Heavy dependence on human resources
12. Binary way of thinking ■ quick decision of yes or no, white or black ■ increased efficiency and less precision	12. Decimal scale way of thinking ■ consideration of various possibilities and careful decision making ■ increased precision and decreased efficiency

(Continued)

Table 6.1 The Business Characteristics: A Comparison of American and Japanese Management Practices (*Continued*)

13. Vertical way of thinking
  ■ pursuit of efficient management and teamwork through quick decisions
  ■ danger of low precision
	13. Horizontal way of thinking
	  ■ adoption of bottom-up management
	  ■ careful decisions based on diverse considerations

14. A business-oriented stance
  ■ realistic, straightforward, self-interested, and less consistent
	14. Nonbusiness consideration taken into account
	  ■ heavy dependence on consistency

15. Approximate accuracy	15. Perfectionism
16. Limited loyalty and incentive-oriented work ethics	16. High loyalty and less incentive-oriented

17. Pursuit of profit accountability and operations
  ■ short-term performance evaluation
	17. Pursuit of profit accountability from mid-/long-term viewpoint
	  ■ mid-/long-term performance evaluation

18. Low service quality
  ■ mechanical-service oriented
	18. High service quality
	  ■ service with human touches

19. Easy dismissal of employees and selling of business	19. Lifetime employment and less selling of business
IV. Top-Down Management	**IV. Participation-Oriented Management**

20. Top-down management techniques by excellent managers
  ■ management by forcing employees through authority rather than motivation
	20. High degree of employee participation
	  ■ management by motivating employees through participation rather than forcing them

SOURCE: *World Link*, "Special Report: Japan," vol. 5, no. 1, 1992, p. 61.

Political Economy and Politics in Japan

The link between economics and politics in Japan is symbolized by the expression Japan Inc., the once affectionate name given to the Liberal Democratic Party that has ruled Japan for 50 years give or take a few months in 1993 (Amyx and Drysdale, 2003). It was this combination of business, political, and administrative leaders that used the levers of state power to create an economic miracle. State capitalism, as practiced by the LDP , used the power of the government to identify those areas in which Japan enjoyed a competitive advantage in terms of resources, technology, and labor. A combination of loans, tax breaks, and import restrictions then was used to encourage Japanese firms to expand in these areas. Japanese firms competed abroad, but foreign firms found it difficult to compete in Japan.

This does not mean that the Japanese were not capitalistic or that they were unconcerned with the need for economic competition. That was not the case. Once the government had targeted an area of designated growth, Japan's fiercely jealous conglomerates competed for domination of that area. The automobile industry, for example, has long been favored by government incentives. Nevertheless, competition among Japanese automobile firms is intense. That competition has resulted in a product that is among the most efficient and the most reasonably priced in the world. The same is true of consumer electronics, optics, and an array of other products too numerous to mention.

As Japan prospered, the LDP prospered. Scandals became a way of life, but nobody seemed terribly concerned as long as prosperity reigned. Opposition parties cried foul, but to no avail.

Japan, however, is no longer prospering. More than a decade and one-half of stagnation and recession have called into question both the LDP and the concept of state capitalism. It is this decline, according to political economists, that is forcing the transformation of the Japanese political system. It also may force a viable two-party system in Japan.

If the LDP is to maintain its power, from the political-economic perspective, it must solve the problems that led to the burst of Japan's economic bubble which have persisted well into the twenty-first century. Some of Japan's economic woes are global in nature. The United States and Europe are no longer willing to accept massive Japanese exports without access to the Japanese market. This has led to increased competition within Japan itself and many less efficient firms, once protected by the government, now are facing bankruptcy. That, however, is only part of the international problems. Japan's hold on mass produced hi-tech goods now is being lost to China, Taiwan, and South Korea, all of whom have cheaper labor. Indeed, many of the larger Japanese companies have shifted production to neighboring countries. Japanese technology has gone with them and has been pirated by other local firms. Japan's economic bureaucrats have put intense pressure on Japanese companies to keep their advanced technology at home, but this is a hard sell (*Economist,* April 10 2004). Business is business. Tensions between corporate leaders and bureaucrats within the LDP have increased apace.

Other problems are cultural in nature. Marika Sugahara, a former senior official in the prime minister's office is quoted by The *Economist* as listing five key elements in what The *Economist* refers to as the Japanese disease. The elements are: "a weakening of the Japanese work ethic; excessive homogeneity and conformity; a loss of creativity; a diminishing sense of public spirit; and a huge resistance to tapping the productive potential of women and the elderly" (*Economist,* March 21, 1998, 21).

Still other problems are political. The nerve centers of Japan's system of state capitalism are the Ministry of Finance and the Ministry of International Trade and Industry, the senior administrators of which have the determining voice in deciding which areas are to be targeted for development (Johnson 1982; Bingman 1989). Once praised as the authors of the Japanese miracle, both agencies have come under scathing criticism for being inflexible, excessively theoretical, and heavy-handed. They have also been accused of propping up weak companies and being more concerned with their own power than the good of the country (*Economist,* March 21 and June 28, 1998). As the Japanese economy stagnated, banks were urged to make low interest loans to unprofitable firms, few of which will ever be repaid. By 2002, Japanese banks found themselves some $418 billion in debt and they, themselves, had to be bailed out by the government at great cost to the Japanese taxpayers. Some now have been sold to foreign investors, a thought unthinkable only a few years ago (*Asia Times,* Oct. 8, 2002, www).

Solving Japan's economic problems requires strong leadership, something that remains in short supply. As one of America's leading Japanese scholars has summed up the problem, "the ministries are discredited, the Liberal Democratic Party (LDP) is transparently inept, and the business elite is unwilling to step forward to fix whatever is broken" (Samuels 2004, 16). Japan's political and economic systems are sinking in tandem. It is doubtful that one can be reformed without the other.

International Interdependence and the Politics of Japan

Two dimensions of Japan's international environment have a profound impact upon its politics. *First, Japan lives by trade.* Any sustained diminution in its ability to export its goods and services will undermine a political system that bases legitimacy upon economic growth. As noted in the preceding section, Japan's economic and political woes are largely the result of external pressures. Industrial democracies are demanding that the Japanese stop protecting domestic industries, and China and other neighboring Asian countries are exporting a wide range of products that were formerly stamped "made in Japan." The cold war is long over, and the U.S. is far more concerned with reducing its staggering trade deficit with Japan than it is with mopping up the final vestiges of world communism (Krauss and Pempel 2004). Japan either must change or suffer further economic reverses.

Second are concerns of external aggression. Japan is a demilitarized country surrounded by powerful neighbors, not the least of which are China and Russia. Indeed, Article 9 of the Japanese Constitution explicitly prohibits Japan from maintaining a military force capable of threatening its neighbors. Any sustained threat by Russia or China, accordingly, must inevitably cause a political crisis in Japan. Added to the fray has been the threat of global terrorism and the increasing aggressiveness of North Korea. Bin Laden's September 11, 2001 attacks of the United States were to have been followed by a massive attack on the 2002 Olympic Games in Japan. The attacks failed to materialize because Al Qaeda found it difficult to get the necessary operatives in place. Japanese police have also uncovered some one billion yen linked to Al Qaeda accounts (*Japan Today,* May 28, 2004, www). High on the list of worries are chemical and biological weapons, dirty bombs, electromagnetic pulses (EMPs), agroterrorism, trains and theme parks (*Japan Today,* April 8, 2004, www). North Korea, for its part, now possesses nuclear weapons. It has also test fired rockets over Japan. If the Japanese feel insecure, it is not without reason.

Japan is a densely populated country and well understands the impact of weapons of mass destruction.

Many people argue that Japan's politics change only when it is faced with insurmountable pressure from abroad (Leblanc 1998). The Meiji Restoration was triggered by the frigates of Admiral Perry, just as the foundations of Japanese democracy were put in place by the U.S. victory in World War II. The changes taking place in Japan today are less dramatic, but they are occurring. In addition to the gradual reform of its political and economic systems, pressure is building for an amendment to the Japanese Constitution that would allow Japan to develop a full fledge military. Noncombatant troops were sent to Iraq, and Japan now is contemplating a missile defense shield similar to that being contemplated by the United States. Nuclear weapons may also be in the offing (Kase 2003). In 1994, the Japanese prime minister shocked the world by inadvertently mentioning that Japan possessed the capacity to build nuclear weapons (*New York Times,* June 21, 1994, A5). The comment was later disavowed, but secret reports leaked from the Japanese foreign ministry confirm that Japan has possessed a nuclear capacity for some time, perhaps since the 1970s (*SCMP,* Aug. 6, 1994, 9; *Japan Today,* June 19, 2004, www). The United States, for its part, admitted that it had been secretly supplying Japan with bomb grade plutonium for at least seven years prior to the 1994 disclosure (*New York Times,* Sept. 9, 1994, A5).

Japan is also looking to China as an alternate to the United States as the foundation of its economic and security arrangements (DiFilippo 2002). Indeed, the upswing in the Japanese economy that occurred shortly after the turn of the century has had more to do with massive exports of hi-tech equipment to China than it does with reform of the Japanese economy (*Economist*, March 26, 2005).

Looking to China as a solution to its economic problems is fraught with danger. China's imports of hi-tech equipment are designed to improve China's position in the hi-tech market, not to place it in a position of permanent dependency. Economic competition between the two Asian economic powers will increase a pace. China is also Japan's competitor in the political sphere, each aspiring to the leadership of the East Asian region. China has blocked Japanese efforts to gain a permanent seat on the United Nations Security Council. Tension has also flared over crimes committed by Japan during its occupation of large parts of China from 1931 to 1945. The spring of 2005 would see tens of thousands of protestors storm the Japanese Consulate in Shanghai. The Chinese government looked on in silence, a sure sign that it approved of the demonstrations. Many observers interpret this as a sign of China's displeasure over Japan's support for Taiwan, a topic to be discussed in our review of Chinese politics. China also fears a US–Japanese alliance designed to block China's growing influence in the Pacific region (*Washington Post,* March 19, 2005, www). The Japanese prime minister hurried to China to ease the tensions and reiterated his "deep remorse" for the wartime crimes of his country. He did not apologize for Japan's growing cooperation with the United States in the management of Pacific affairs.

CHALLENGES OF THE PRESENT AND
PROSPECTS FOR THE FUTURE

The international community has increasingly defined "good government" in terms of six criteria: democracy, stability, human rights, quality of life, economic growth, and environmental concern. Japan is the only non-Western state to score in the top group in each of these six areas. Japan is a stable, prosperous, and egalitarian democracy whose citizens enjoy a broad range of human rights. Japan has also become a world leader in environmental legislation.

Even more remarkable than Japan's record in the six areas of good government is the fact that this record was largely achieved in the five decades following the end of World War II. Japan had industrialized well before the war, but its industrialization had brought little prosperity to the average Japanese citizen and had been orchestrated by authoritarian governments without regard for human rights, the quality of Japanese life, or the environment. Japan has experienced an economic miracle, but it has achieved a political miracle as well. The Japan of today bears little resemblance to the authoritarian Japan of an earlier era.

For all of Japan's accomplishments, critics suggest that Japan's political miracle is less miraculous than it seems. In particular, they argue that the Japanese view of democracy and human rights is far different from that of the West (Reading 1992; Herzog 1993). These and related topics will be discussed in the remainder of this chapter as we examine the challenges that confront Japan in each of the six areas of good government outlined above.

Democracy and Stability

Japan meets all of the procedural requirements for stable democracy discussed in the introductory chapter. Free elections are conducted at specified intervals; voters are provided with a meaningful choice of issues and candidates; issues are freely discussed; winners take office; and once in office, they rule. If voted out of office, political leaders step down without threat of revolution or violence.

Criticisms of Japanese democracy focus not on its procedures but on its practices. A single political party, the LDP, ruled Japan from 1955 until 1993. The LDP was finally voted out of office in 1993 but returned to power a few months later. The overwhelming dominance of a conservative elite does not, by itself, make Japan undemocratic. The escalating cycle of election scandals, however, does speak to the existence of a ruling elite that is more than willing to flout democratic procedures for the sake of remaining in power.

However entrenched Japan's conservative elite may be, it is well within the capacity of the Japanese electorate to "vote the rascals out." They have done so rarely. In the view of some observers, popular acquiescence in conservative rule represents a clear sign that Japan has yet to develop a democratic political culture (Dale 1990). Acceptance of this criticism, however, is far from universal. As Louis Hayes put it, "To their critics, the Japanese are not really happy; they just think they are" (Hayes 1992). Whether a continuing economic crisis will change things remains to be seen.

Human Rights

The Japanese Constitution delineates the rights of Japanese citizens in great detail. The concept of human rights in Japan, however, differs considerably from the concept of human rights in the United States and many other Western countries (Hendry 1991). Japanese culture stresses collectivism rather than individualism, viewing the rights of individuals as a set of reciprocal obligations within the group context (Hendry 1991). The group cares for the individual, but the individual is expected to subordinate his or her interests to those of the group.

Four dimensions of Japanese human rights practice are particularly worrisome to human rights groups in the West.

1. *The level of bureaucratic control is far greater in Japan than it is in most Western countries.* The government controls everything, and Japanese citizens find it very difficult to challenge the government. Japan, moreover, does not possess a freedom of information act. For the most part, Japanese citizens are ignorant of the content of their police dossiers. The Japanese legal system also provides few rights for defendants, but this would seem to be a matter of minor concern in a penal system that is one of the most forgiving in the world.

2. *Foreign minorities are severely disadvantaged in Japanese society* (Sellek and Weiner 1992; *Japan Times,* Apr. 11, 2000, www). The 700,000 members of Japan's long-established Korean community, its largest ethnic minority, enjoy few rights. They have, however, become increasingly organized and are seeking closer integration into Japanese political life (*Japan Today,* March 28 2004, www).

3. *The constitutional rights of Japanese women are not enforced with vigor.* While the Japanese Constitution expressly states that "there shall be no discrimination in political, economic, and social relations because of race, creed, sex, social status, or family origin," the reality, as noted previously in this chapter, is quite different (Article III, Constitution). Japanese women, by Western standards, are the least liberated in the first world and some 90 percent of the Japanese firms acknowledge problems with sexual harassment. Few have done much about it (*Christian Science Monitor,* Apr. 14, 1998). Hiring of female graduates also lags behind that of men, a practice justified by the assumption that they are less dedicated to their careers than males (*Japan Times,* Jan. 1, 1999 and Jan. 5, 1999). Japan's prolonged recession has not helped. Some law makers also worry that greater gender equality will result in fewer children, a category in which Japan leads the world. Indeed, 2004 would find the number of Japanese children declining for the 23rd year in a row (*Japan Today,* May 5, 2004, www).

The Basic Law on Gender-equal Society was enacted in 1999, but the results have yet to be apparent. Things are changing for Japanese women, but they are changing very slowly. The courts could alter this situation, but they have been reluctant to counter traditional practices. Ironically, it may be the aging of Japanese society that propels women to the forefront in economic affairs. With its workforce shrunk by retirement and a declining birth rate, Japan finds itself in desperate need of new workers. There may be little choice but to give women a greater

Associated Press/AP

A prominent Japanese political leader has referred to Japan's "salary-men" as "commuter slaves in a commuter hell." The country's intense work ethic has been blamed for strained family relationships and increased rates of alcoholism.

role in economic affairs. It is unlikely, however, that this will translate into political rights.

The Japanese government is sensitive to criticisms of its human rights policy and has vowed to address all the issues raised above. New laws emphasize accelerated processing of civil rights cases. Greater emphasis is also being placed on sexual harassment, domestic violence, and violations of Internet privacy (*Japan Today,* March 26, 2004, www).

Economic Growth and Quality of Life

Japan's economic miracle has made it the world's second-largest economy after that of the United States. Economic prosperity, however, has not brought the average Japanese citizen a quality of life equivalent to that of the average citizen in the United States or Western Europe. Japanese workers earn as much as their Western counterparts, but the cost of living in Japan is so exorbitant that their money does not go as far as it would in the West. Indeed, the cost of living in Tokyo is more than twice as great as the cost of living in New York or London. Perhaps more damning is the fact that Japan's famed system of providing employees with a job for life is showing signs of strain as the unemployment rate has passed the 4 percent level, an acceptable figure for the U.S. but a disastrous figure for the Japanese. Be this as it may, the quality of life ranks 14th among the world's industrial democracies (*Japan Today,* April 3, 2004, www).

Economic growth has also had its psychological costs. The intense work ethic that has driven Japan's rise to economic dominance has also transformed Japan into a socio-psychological pressure cooker. The leader of one of Japan's political parties recently referred to Japanese "salarymen" as "commuter slaves in a commuter hell." Family life is strained, and alcoholism has become a national problem. Not unexpectedly, many younger Japanese are starting to question the "growth at any cost" philosophy preached by Japan's conservative elite.

On the positive side, Japan's wealth is equitably distributed, and Japan boasts the longest life expectancy and the most highly educated population in the world (Hendry 1991). Japanese education also places an increasing emphasis on equality among individuals, albeit an equality that stresses uniformity and conformity (Cummings 1980; Hendry 1991; *Japan Times*, Mar. 23, 2000, www). By and large, Japan's students are being socialized to fit into an industrial system that will find them spending their entire lives working for a single employer. The sustained economic crisis that began in the 1990s has called Japan's famed job security into question as the wave of bankruptcies continues to mount along with the rate of Japanese joblessness (*Look Japan* 2002). This, plus an aging society, have put inordinate strain on Japan's social security system. The gap between rich and poor has increased apace (*Daily Yomiuri,* July 24, 2004, www). Too few people are being expected to pay for too many. Benefits are being lowered and premiums increased. Adding insult to injury was a 2004 scandal revealing that many of Japan's high ranking politicians had not paid their social security (pension) fees for years, not the least of who were the prime minister and the leader of the leading opposition party. The latter resigned in disgrace. The prime minister did not.

The Environment

Japan's environmental regulations are among the most stringent in the world, but this does not mean that Japan is an environmental paradise. It merely means that Japan, like the United States and other major industrial countries, has begun to attack its very substantial environmental problems. Emissions of toxic gases and other problems have been severely reduced, but Japanese industries, like those in other industrial countries, have difficulty in meeting government environmental standards (Allan 2003).

From the perspective of environmental activists, two major problems remain.

First, Japan is heavily dependent on nuclear energy. Nuclear plants pose the threat of radiation leaks for both Japan and it neighbors. They also require the storage of nuclear waste and the transnational shipment of lethal plutonium. The accidental sinking of a plutonium ship would be an unmitigated catastrophe for the regions affected. The Japanese have countered foreign criticism by stressing the exemplary safety record of their nuclear facilities. This record, however, was shaken in December 1995 by a "mishap" at an experimental "fast breeder" nuclear reactor. The mishap was all the more damaging to the government's nuclear program because of a botched attempt to hide it from the press (*Christian Science Monitor,* Dec. 29, 1995, 7). Other "mishaps" have followed in rapid succession, and in 1999 Japan suffered the worst nuclear disaster in its history, and was forced to seek technical assistance from the U.S. and Russia. More nuclear related deaths followed in 2004 and resulted in revelations of sloppy enforcement of safety procedures. Several plants were closed pending further inspections (*Guardian,* Aug.14, 2004, www). Nevertheless, it is unlikely that such setbacks will deter Japan's plans to become the world's first all-nuclear country.

The second area in which the Japanese have displayed a marked lack of environmental concern involves whales and other forms of marine life that figure prominently in the Japanese diet. With whales becoming an endangered species as a result of over-fishing, the International Whaling Commission has imposed a temporary ban on most whaling. The Japanese maintain that the ban on whale hunting has more to do with Western emotions than with the number of whales being harvested, and they have been pushing to have the ban lifted. Thus far, they have failed.

Prospects for the Future

Does the above discussion suggest that Japan is somewhat less of a first world state than the United States and its Western allies? Not at all. What it does suggest is that Japan, like all states of the first world, is still a long way from meeting the ideal standards of good government expressed in the UN charter and related documents. The Japanese experience also suggests that countries possessing cultural and historical traditions different from that of the West will tend to approach concepts such as democracy, equality, and human rights from non-Western perspectives.

Japan is changing in the face of the domestic and external pressures outlined in this chapter, but the process of change is slow and evolutionary in character. The key question facing Japan is the ability of the Japanese government to address the pressures for change in a timely manner. (Tadashi 1998). Japan's leaders believe that they are. Others are not so sure.

REFERENCES

Allan, Phillip. 2003 (March). "Japan Relationship with the Environment," *Geography Review,* Vol. 16, I4, 35C3.

Amyx, Jennifer and Peter Drysdale, eds. 2003. *Japanese Governance: Beyond Japan Inc.* New York: RoutledgeCurzon.

Asada, Akira. 1989. "Infantile Capitalism and Japan's Postmodernism: A Fairy Tale." In *Postmodernism and Japan,* ed. Masao Miyoshi and H. D. Harootunian. Durham, NC, and London: Duke University Press.

Arnason, Johann Pall. 2002. *The Peripheral Centre: Essays on Japanese History and Civilization.* Melbourne: Trans Pacific Press.

Atsushi, Yamada. 1998 (Jan.–Mar.). "Change-Proof Finance Ministry." *Japan Quarterly* 45(1): 37–41.

Baerwald, Hans H. 1986. *Party Politics in Japan.* Boston, MA: Allen and Unwin.

Bingman, Charles F. 1989. *Japanese Government Leadership and Management.* London: Macmillan.

Calder, Kent E. 1988. *Crisis and Compensation: Public Policy and Political Stability in Japan, 1949–1986.* Princeton, NJ: Princeton University Press.

Campbell, John C. 1992. *How Policies Change: The Japanese Government and the*

Aging Society. Princeton, NJ: Princeton University Press.

Condon, Jane. 1985. *A Half Step Behind: Japanese Women Today.* Tokyo: Charles E. Tuttle Co.

Cox, Gary W., and Frances Rosenbluth. 1993 (Sept.). "The Electoral Fortunes of Legislative Factions in Japan." *American Political Science Review* 87(3): 577–89.

Cox, Gary W., and Michael F. Theis. 1998 (June). "The Cost of Intraparty Competition: The Single, Nontransferable Vote and Money Politics in Japan." *Comparative Political Studies* 31(3): 267–292.

Cummings, William K. 1980. *Education and Equality in Japan.* Princeton, NJ: Princeton University Press.

Curtin, Sean. 2004 (Aug. 27). "In Japan, The Crime Rate Also Rises." *The Asia Times*, online.

Dale, Peter N. 1990. *The Myth of Japanese Uniqueness.* London: Routledge.

DiFlippo. 2002. *The Challenges of the US–Japan Military Arrangement: Transitions in a Changing International Environment.* Armonk, NY: M. E. Sharpe.

Dore, Ronald P., and Mari Sako. 1989. *How the Japanese Learn to Work.* London: Routledge.

Drucker, Peter F. 1998. (Sept.–Oct.). "In Defense of Japanese Bureaucracy." *Foreign Affairs* 77(5): 68–81.

Duus, Peter. 1976. *The Rise of Modern Japan.* Boston, MA: Houghton Mifflin.

Earhart, H. Byron. 1982. *Japanese Religion: Unity and Diversity.* Belmont, CA: Wadsworth.

The Economist. 1997. "A Survey of Japanese Finance."

The Economist. 2004 (April 10). "Special Report: Manufacturing in Japan." 57–59.

Eisuke, Sakakibara. 1998 (Feb.). "Moving Beyond the Public Works State." *Japan Echo* 25(1): 31–36.

Flanagan, Scott, Bradley Richardson, Joji Watanuki, Ichiro Miyake, and Shinsaku Kohei, eds. 1991. *The Japanese Voter.* New Haven, CT: Yale University Press.

Fukushima, Glen S. 1989. "Corporate Power." In *Democracy in Japan* (pp. 255–80), ed. Takeshi Ishida and Ellis S. Krauss. Pittsburgh, PA: University of Pittsburgh Press.

Gordon, Andrew. 2003. *A Modern History of Japan.* New York: Oxford University Press.

Government of Japan, Environment Agency. 1990. *Quality of the Environment in Japan: 1990.*

Hartcher, Peter. 1998. *The Ministry.* Cambridge, MA: Harvard Business School Press.

Hayes, Louis D. 1992. *Introduction to Japanese Politics.* New York: Paragon House.

Hayes, Louis. D. 2001. *Introduction to Japanese Politics.* Armonk, NY: M. E. Sharpe.

Hendry, Joy. 1991. *Understanding Japanese Society.* London: Routledge.

Hendry, Joy. 2003. *Understanding Japanese Society.* New York: RoutledgeCurzon.

Herzog, Peter J. 1993. *Japan's Pseudo-Democracy.* Sandgate, Kent, England: Japan Library.

Hiwatari, Nobuhiro. 1998 (Oct.). "Adjustment to Stagflation and Neoliberal Reforms in Japan, the United Kingdom, and the United States: The Implications of the Japanese Case for a Comparative Analysis of Party Competition." *Comparative Political Studies* 31(5): 602–633.

Ishida, Takeshi, and Ellis S. Krauss. 1989. *Democracy in Japan.* Pittsburgh, PA: University of Pittsburgh Press.

Iwao, Sumiko. 1993. *The Japanese Woman: Traditional Image and Changing Reality.* New York: Free Press.

Jain, Purnendra. 1997 (Nov.). "Media and Politics in Japan." *Australian Journal of Political Science* 32(3): 481–82.

Johnson, Chalmers. 1982. *Miti and the Japanese Economic Miracle.* Stanford, CA: Stanford University Press.

Johnson, Chalmers. 1989. "MITI, MPT, and the Telecom Wars: How Japan Makes Policy for High Technology." In *Politics and Productivity: The Real Story of Why Japan Works* (pp. 177–239), ed.

Chalmers Johnson, Laura D. Tyson, and John Zysman. New York: Ballinger.

Johnson, Chalmers. 1994. *Japan: Who Governs? The Rise of the Developmental State.* New York: Norton.

Johnston, Eric. 1999 (Jan. 6). "Century of Change: Foreign Press Find Japan Tough to Figure." *Domestic News,* p. 5.

"Just the Job." 2002 (Nov.). *Look Japan,* 48(560): 24–6.

Kase, Yuri. 2003 (Winter). "Japan's Nonnuclear Weapons Policy in the Changing Security Environment: Issues, Challenges, and Strategies." *World Affairs* 165(3):123–32.

Kataoka, Tetsuya, ed. 1992. *Creating Single-Party Democracies.* Stanford, CA: Hoover Institution Press.

Kato, Junko. 1994. *The Problem of Bureaucratic Rationality: Tax Politics in Japan.* Princeton, NJ: Princeton University Press.

Kitaoka, Shin'ichi. 2004 (Jan.). "Japan's Dysfunctional Democracy." *Japanese Political Reform: Progress in Process.* Asia Program Special Report, 117. Washington D.C.: Woodrow Wilson International Center for Scholars.

Kitching, Leslie. 2005 (Feb.). Interview with author.

Koh, B. C. 1989. *Japan's Administrative Elite.* Berkeley, CA: University of California Press.

Krauss, Ellis S. 1989. "Politics and the Policy-Making Process." In *Democracy in Japan* (pp. 39–64), ed. Takeshi Isheda and Ellis S. Krauss. Pittsburgh, PA: University of Pittsburgh Press.

Krauss, Ellis S. and T. J. Pempel, eds. 2004. *Beyond Bilateralism: US-Japan Relations in the New Asia-Pacific.* Stanford, CA: Stanford University Press.

Lamont-Brown, Raymond. 1995 (April). "Japan's Quartet of Important Advisors." *Contemporary Review* 266(1551): 196–99.

Leblanc, Claude. 1998. *Le Japoscope 98.* Paris: Editions Ilyfunet.

Masumi, Junnosuke. 1992. "The 1955 System: Origin and Transformation." In *Creating Single-Party Democracies* (pp. 34–54), ed. Tetsuya Kataoka. Stanford, CA: Hoover Institution Press.

McCreedy, Amy. 2004 (Jan.). "Introduction" in Asia Program Special Report #117, *Japanese Political Reform: Progress in Process.* Washington, DC: Woodrow Wilson International Center for Scholars, pp 1–5.

McMillian, Charles J. 1985. *The Japanese Industrial System.* New York: De Gruyter.

Milward, R. S. 1979. *Japan: The Past in the Present.* Kent, England: Paul Norbury.

Miyoshi, Masao, and H. D. Harootunian, eds. 1989. *Post-Modernism and Japan.* Durham, NC: Duke University Press.

Moeran, Brian. 1986. "Individual, Group and *Sishin:* Japan's Internal Cultural Debate." In *Japanese Culture and Behavior* (pp. 62–79), ed. Takie S. Lebra and William P. Lebra. Honolulu, HI: University of Hawaii Press.

Mulgan, Aurelia G. 1997 (Dec.). "Electoral Determinant of Agrarian Power: Measuring Rural Decline in Japan." *Political Studies* 45(5): 875–900.

Muramatsu, Michio. 2004 (Jan.). "An Arthritic Japan? The Relationship between Politicians and Bureaucrats." *Japanese Political Reform: Progress in Process.* Asia Program Special Report, 117. Washington D.C.: Woodrow Wilson International Center for Scholars.

Nagashima, Atsushi. 1990. "Criminal Justice in Japan." In *Crime Prevention and Control in the United States and Japan,* ed. V. Kusuda-Smick. Dobbs Ferry, NY: Transnational Juris Publications.

Nagata, Jiro. 1998 (Sept.–Oct.). "LDP Civil War." *The International Economy* 12(5): 29–32.

Nakane, Chie. 1970. *Japanese Society.* Berkeley, CA: University of California Press.

Nakano, Koichi. 1998 (March). "The Politics of Administrative Reform in Japan, 1993–1998: Toward a More Accountable Government?" *Asian Survey* 38(3): 291–310.

Nimura, Kazuo. 1992. "The Trade Union Response to Migrant Workers." In *The Internationalization of Japan* (pp. 246–68), ed. Glenn D. Hook and Michael A. Weiner. London: Routledge.

Noguchi, Yoshi. 1992 (Mar. 1). "Dropping Out of Tokyo's Rat Race." *New York Times,* p. F11.

Ohsumi, Haruyasu. 1992. "The Business Characteristics." *World Link* 1: 61.

Ozawa, Ichiro. 1993 (Spring). "My Commitment to Political Reform." *Japan Echo* 20(1): 8–12.

Pons, Philippe. 1998 (Mar. 22–Sept.). "Le Japon dans la Lumíere des Femmes." *Le Monde,* 17.

Reading, Brian. 1992. *Japan: The Coming Collapse.* London: Orion Books, Ltd.

Richardson, Bradley, and Scott Flanagan. 1984. *Politics in Japan.* Boston: Little, Brown.

Rothacher, Albrecht. 1993. *The Japanese Power Elite.* New York: St. Martin's.

Reed, Steven, ed. 2003. *Japanese Electoral Politics: Creating a New Party System.* New York: RoutledgeCurzon.

Sage, Junichi. 1991. *Confessions of a Yakuza.* Tokyo: Kodansha Int.

Samuels, Richard J. 2004. "Generational Change and Japanese Leadership" in Asia Program Special Report #117, *Japanese Political Reform: Progress in Process.* Washington, DC: Woodrow Wilson International Center for Scholars, pp. 16–19.

Sellek, Yoko, and Michael A. Weiner. 1992. "Migrant Workers: The Japanese Case in International Perspective." In *The Internationalization of Japan,* ed. Glenn D. Hook and Michael A. Weiner. London: Routledge.

Sessions, Dillon David. 2005 (Feb.). Interview with author.

Sheridan, Kyoko. 1993. *Governing the Japanese Economy.* Cambridge, England: Polity Press.

Shinoda, Tomohito. 1998 (July). "Japan's Decision Making Under the Coalition Governments." *Asian Survey* 38(7): 703–24.

Steinhoff, Patricia G. 1989. "Protest and Democracy." In *Democracy in Japan* (pp. 171–98), ed. Takeshi Ishida and Ellis S. Krauss. Pittsburgh, PA: Pittsburgh University Press.

Sterngold, James. 1992 (Feb. 23). "Another Scandal in Japan." *New York Times,* E3.

Stockwin, J. A. A. 2003. *Dictionary of the Modern Politics of Japan.* New York: Routledge.

Sugiyama, Yasushi. 1992. "Internal and External Aspects of Internationalization." In *The Internationalization of Japan,* ed. Glenn D. Hook and Michael A. Weiner. London: Routledge.

Tadashi, Nakamae. 1998 (March 21). "Views from 2020." *Economist* 346(8060): 25–27.

Taichi, Sakaiya. 1998 (Feb.) "The Myth of the Competent Bureaucrat." *Japan Echo* 25(1): 25–31.

Thurow, Lester. 1993. *Head to Head: The Coming Economic Battle Among Japan, Europe, and America.* New York: Warner Books.

van Wolferen, Karel. 1990. *The Enigma of Japanese Power.* New York: Vintage Press.

Wilson, George. 1992. *Patriots and Redeemers in Japan.* Chicago, IL: The University of Chicago Press.

Woodiwiss, Anthony. 1992. *Law, Labour and Society in Japan: From Repression to Reluctant Recognition.* London: Routledge.

World Link. 1992 (Jan./Feb.). "Special Report: Japan." *World Link* 5(1): 50–69.

Woronoff, Jon. 1981. *Japan: The Coming Social Crisis.* Tokyo: Lotus Press.

Yakushiji, Taizo. 1992. "Japan's Political Change Towards Internationalization." In *The Internationalization of Japan,* ed. Glenn D. Hook and Michael A. Weiner. London: Routledge.

Stalin was also denounced, giving hope for a more humane political environ-ment. Khrushchev, however, was unable to revive a moribund Soviet economy, and his efforts to reform the Party apparatus resulted in his removal from office. Few Party members at any level were willing to have their security jeopardized by the magnitude of reform that would have been necessary to truly revitalize the Soviet system (Kelley 1987). Khrushchev was not executed, but he became a "nonperson" whose existence was purged from the Soviet history books.

The Brezhnev Era (1964–1982). Khrushchev was followed in office by Leonid Brezhnev, a Politburo member less enamored of radical reform than his predeces-sor. Brezhnev offered Party bureaucrats increased job security in exchange for in-creased performance. The compromise failed (Kelley 1987).

All in all, the Brezhnev era was a time of remarkable stability. The Khrushchev reforms were pushed aside and business within the mammoth bureaucracy con-tinued much as usual (Kelley 1987). That stability, however, was illusory. The So-viet economy continued to deteriorate and the Soviet population became increasingly alienated from a system that had trouble meeting their basic needs (Hauslohner 1989; Lapidus 1989; Bahry and Silver 1990).

The Gorbachev Era (1985–1991). By 1985, the balance of power in the Politburo and Central Committee had shifted to the side of the reformers, paving the way for the appointment of Mikhail Gorbachev as general secretary. Opposition to Gorbachev's appointment was intense, but the time for reform had arrived (Bialer 1989).

The Gorbachev reforms began with a call for *greater openness and democracy within the Soviet system,* a process conveyed by the Russian term **glasnost.** The logic of glasnost, according to Gorbachev, was simple. The terror of the Stalinist era and the administrative suffocation of the Brezhnev years had created a pop-ulation that was alienated from its political system. Mass apathy, moreover, had led to the stagnation of the Soviet economy. The situation had now reached crisis proportions and could be reversed only by energizing the Soviet masses and renewing their faith in the system. To accomplish this, the masses would have to be empowered, regardless of what that might mean for the Party and its bureaucratic apparatus (Bialer 1989). These were powerful words for an ardent communist, but the salvation of the Communist Party, in Gorbachev's view, re-quired no less.

Glasnost was part of a broader process called **perestroika,** or *structural reform. The goal of perestroika was to break the grip of the government and party bureaucracies on the Soviet economy* by giving factory managers increased flexibility in the manage-ment of their plants (Hewett and Winston 1991). Managers, in turn, were ex-pected to make a profit and to increase the quality of their products. Changes in the political system were equally sweeping, with elections to government coun-cils at all levels featuring multiple candidates elected by secret ballot following an extended period of free and open discussion. Experimentation with small-scale capitalism was also encouraged (Spulber 1991).

Gorbachev declared the cold war to be over and pledged world peace in exchange for Western cooperation in rebuilding the Soviet economy. Matching his words with deeds, Gorbachev relaxed Soviet controls over its client states in Eastern Europe, allowing each to form its own government independent of Moscow. Some former communist regimes collapsed in the face of popular revolts, while others moved toward greater democracy of their own accord. No symbol of the end of the Cold War, however, was more poignant than the collapse of the Berlin Wall in 1989 and the subsequent reunification of Germany, a country that had been responsible for some 27 million Soviet deaths during the Second World War.

Gorbachev's reforms, however profound by Soviet standards, came too late to save a system well on its way to collapse (Mandel 1992; Duch 1993). Hardline conservatives scuttled Gorbachev's reforms from within, while the leaders of the "nationalities" used the new democracy to press for ever-greater autonomy (Willerton 1992). Lithuania and the other Baltic states forcibly annexed by the U.S.S.R. during World War II proclaimed their independence from the U.S.S.R. in 1991, but Gorbachev was reluctant to crush the Baltic revolts for fear of jeopardizing promised economic aid from the West. He may also have been apprehensive about using the army against Soviet citizens, as it had become increasingly clear that the Marxist state was withering away.

The Commonwealth of Independent States (CIS). On December 8, 1991, Russia, the Ukraine, and Belorussia proclaimed their independence as sovereign states and signed a treaty forming the Commonwealth of Independent States (CIS). Most other former Soviet Republics would follow suit (Willerton 1992). The Soviet Union had ceased to exist. The new states created by the breakup of the U.S.S.R. are illustrated in Figure 7.1.

The Commonwealth of Independent States was a voluntary association formed to preserve the benefits of economic and military integration that had existed under the Soviet system (Diller 1992). The Commonwealth Treaty remains in place, but its effectiveness is limited at best. Economic agreements are honored in the breach, and conflict over the control of former Soviet weapons has shattered any serious hope of forging a unified military command.

Hopes for an effective commonwealth have also been dampened by ethnic conflicts within and between the newly independent republics. Several countries erupted in civil war as competing nationalities attempted to create ethnically pure states. Other republics attacked their neighbors in the hope of resolving boundary disputes. The reconstitution process will take decades to sort itself out.

The Soviet Union: A Postmortem and a Legacy. Why did a superpower as overtly successful as the Soviet Union simply collapse? It is doubtful that the debate surrounding this question will ever be fully resolved, yet certain factors hold particular importance. Of these, four are remarkably similar to the factors that led to the collapse of the tsarist empire (Smith 1992).

First, the Soviets, like their tsarist counterparts, had failed to solve the "nationalities" problem. The Soviet Union had been integrated economically, but it had not been

FIGURE 7.1 Independent countries created by the collapse of the former Soviet Union.

integrated either culturally or politically. Indeed, most of the Soviet Union's more than 100 ethnic groups retained a strong sense of "national" identity and resented Russian dominance (Bremmer and Taras 1993). In the words of one senior Russian official, there was a common perception "that the USSR is an empire in which Russia is the metropolis and the national republics the colonies" (Kux 1990, 17). Once the Soviet system began to weaken, the pressure for greater "national" autonomy became irresistible.

A second similarity between collapse of the tsarist empire and the collapse of the U.S.S.R. is to be found in the alienation and passivity of the Soviet masses. The totalitarian regime

---

The Western Response to Gorbachev

The United States and its allies were not casual bystanders in the reform process. Gorbachev pleaded for Western assistance in his reform effort, but the Western response was as confused as Gorbachev's reforms themselves. Gorbachev was honored as a hero, but little aid was forthcoming, the West being unsure of how to assist a decaying economic system that remained largely socialist in orientation. While some Western leaders urged massive loans for the Gorbachev regime, others cautioned that it made little sense to pour money into a sinking ship. Still others argued that it was best for the ship to sink; why should capitalist powers attempt to salvage a communist regime? Whatever the reasons, Gorbachev was left to dangle in the wind.

---

could force the Soviet population into submission, but it could not force them to embrace the system.

A third area of similarity between the collapse of the tsarist empire and the collapse of the U.S.S.R. is to be found in the rigid and parasitic nature of their respective bureaucracies (McAuley 1992). As discussed by Hillel Ticktin, there was little that Gorbachev could do to alter the situation:

> Gorbachev . . . embarked on wholesale dismissals of ministers, the closing down of entire ministries, the merging of ministries, and the devolution of tasks down to enterprises. The simple effect of removing the old corrupt bureaucrats and replacing them with new, dynamic corrupt bureaucrats undoubtedly stirred people up and compelled management to find ways of forcing workers to work better, but this could only last a short time. Workers and managers became increasingly tired of exhortations and threats. Gorbachev could not imprison the large numbers incarcerated under Stalin in order to increase production; he was compelled simply to rant along about "making life harsh for those who do not work" (Ticktin 1992, 155).

A fourth similarity between the collapse of the tsarist empire and the collapse of the U.S.S.R. is to be found in "the Western problem." The U.S.S.R., like the tsarist empire before it, labored under a pervasive fear that its survival was threatened by the technological superiority of the West. The longer the arms race continued, the greater the technology gap between the two power blocs became. America's "star wars" initiative, however fanciful, threatened to put the technology race out of reach. The economic burden of the arms race with the West placed excessive strains on a weak Soviet economy and deprived its population of basic necessities.

It would be a mistake, however, to draw too close a parallel between the collapse of tsarist Russia and the collapse of the Soviet Union. The essence of the Soviet system was **socialism:** the belief that state ownership of the means of production could provide a more rational allocation of a society's resources than capitalism. The most fundamental reason for the collapse of the U.S.S.R. was that socialism, at least as practiced in the U.S.S.R., did not result in the rational allocation of the Soviet Union's resources. Control of the economy was placed in the hands of a massive, centralized bureaucracy that lacked the capacity to address the complex needs of the largest country on earth (Campbell 1992). Delays, confusion, and shortages became the norm as managers of factories and collective farms struggled to meet unrealistic production goals established by State planners in Moscow (Nove 1992). Managers also responded to pressure from Moscow by placing quantity above quality, a problem that had existed from the earliest days of the Soviet regime.

The collapse of the U.S.S.R. was also hastened by the decay of the Communist Party, the leadership of which had become immobilized. Wedded to the past, Soviet leaders were reluctant to chart a new course for the future. This was particularly the case during the Brezhnev era. The problem, however, was not merely one of leadership. Seventy years of unchallenged rule had dulled the zeal of Party members and transformed one-time revolutionaries into self-serving bureaucrats (Kelley 1987).

Finally, many observers place the blame for the breakup of the Soviet Union on the reform process itself. Gorbachev was committed to reforming the Soviet system, but there is little evidence that he had a clear plan in mind or that he appreciated the severity of the U.S.S.R.'s economic woes (Nove 1992; Bialer 1989). The first two years of the reform effort were a period of trial and error. In some instances, reforms that met strong resistance were replaced by others of a less threatening nature. In other instances, cautious reforms were strengthened to increase their effectiveness. The result was a confusion of half-hearted and sometimes contradictory policies that sought a middle ground between socialism and capitalism and between democracy and authoritarianism (Dowlah 1992; Kux 1990). Such middle ground, however, was not to be found (Nove 1992).

Russia Reborn

If Mikhail Gorbachev presided over the collapse of the U.S.S.R., it would be Boris Yeltsin, his one-time supporter, who would guide the rebirth of the Russian state (Morrison 1991).

Yeltsin, a mining engineer by training and the First Secretary of a regional Party organization, was brought to Moscow as part of Gorbachev's effort to instill new life in the Party apparatus. Yeltsin soon became a key figure in the Central Committee, being a tireless worker and an outspoken advocate of Gorbachev's reforms. Gorbachev made Yeltsin a candidate member (junior member) of the Politburo in 1986, using him to lead the charge against his conservative opponents. Yeltsin's commitment to reform, however, far outpaced that of an unsure Gorbachev, and his thinly veiled attacks on Gorbachev's "hesitancy" weakened Gorbachev's position within the Politburo. Gorbachev responded by removing Yeltsin from the Politburo in 1987, a move that, under normal circumstances, would have spelled the end of Yeltsin's political career. Circumstances, however, were far from normal, and 1991 would see Yeltsin become the first democratically elected president of the Russian Republic (province).

Yeltsin would use his position as president of the Russian Republic to accelerate the pace of reform within the Soviet Union and to demand ever-greater independence for the Soviet Union's 15 republics (provinces). Yeltsin's efforts brought him tremendous popularity, and his personal stature quickly surpassed that of Gorbachev. They also spelled the end of the U.S.S.R.

The Transition to Democracy and Capitalism. With the breakup of the Soviet Union later in 1991, Boris Yeltsin would proclaim the newly independent Russian Federation (Russia's formal designation) to be a democratic republic. Russia's socialist economy, Yeltsin said, would be transformed into a free-market economy within the broader framework of a world capitalist system. Gorbachev's reforms, in Yeltsin's view, had failed because they sought a compromise between Party control and democracy and between socialism and capitalism. The new Russia, he said, would not make the same mistake.

The transition to democracy and capitalism, however, would prove difficult. No one was absolutely sure what should be done or how to go about it. Theories abounded, but theories are often wrong, and much would depend on the results of trial and error. Russia may have been reborn, but it was not starting with a clean slate. The leaders of the new Russia were reformed communists, and the best-organized groups in the new Russia were the remnants of the old Communist Party. The citizens of the new Russia, moreover, had been socialized into politics under the Soviet system, and nothing in their prior experience had prepared them for either democracy or capitalism. In addition, citizens in the Soviet Union were brought up under an economic system that, whatever its failings, provided them with a great deal of economic security. Their standard of living was below that of the West, but people did have jobs and enough food to eat. It was not clear that the Russian electorate would be willing to jeopardize that security for the vague promise of capitalist prosperity somewhere down the road. This was not an insignificant worry, for the transition to capitalism promised to be extremely painful. The transition process, then, was not starting from zero. Much of what had been done under the communist regime would have to be undone by its successors.

Under socialism, providing jobs was more important than making a profit, and most Soviet factories had far more workers than they needed. If a factory didn't make a profit, the government merely provided subsidies to keep it afloat. Few Russian firms showed a profit in the Western sense of the word. Soviet workers also had little incentive to work hard; their wages were low, and raises and other benefits were more or less automatic. With the transition to capitalism, Russian firms would need to become profitable. Excess employees would be laid off and unprofitable firms closed down. Job security and a cradle-to-grave welfare system would also become relics of the past. The harsh side of capitalism, then, was a source of grave concern to many Russians who, while welcoming a capitalist lifestyle, were reluctant to jeopardize the economic safety net provided by socialism. Indeed, as rational actors, it would be logical for the Russian electorate to use its new democratic freedom to vote for a continuation of socialism. Capitalism would have to prove its utility in a hurry or suffer the consequences.

Institution Building in Democratic Russia. Russia emerged from the breakup of the U.S.S.R. with a political system that was as bewildering to the politicians as it was to the general public (Hahn 1992). By and large, its new leaders made up the rules as they went along (Bremmer and Taras 1993). As long as Yeltsin's popularity remained intact, there was little the Parliament could do to oppose his policies. Indeed, the Parliament granted Yeltsin the power to rule by decree during Russia's first year of independence. They had little choice, for without a strong leader, Russia would have dissolved into chaos. *Yeltsin used his emergency powers to implement a sweeping program of capitalist reforms suggested by his American advisors. Often referred to as "shock therapy," the reforms were designed to dismantle the old socialist economy in the shortest time possible.* The sooner Russia embraced capitalism, the American argument went, the sooner it would be placed on the path to economic growth and prosperity. There would be hardships for Russia's workers, but that was the price of cleaning up the economic mess created by 70 years of socialism. Proceeding slowly would merely prolong the pain.

The rapid pace of Yeltsin's economic reforms soon encountered strong opposition throughout Russian society. It was one thing to talk about reform, but quite another to do it. *While a minority of Russians prospered under the capitalist reforms, the majority feared losing the social safety net that they had long taken for granted.* After one year of reform, Yeltsin himself would be forced to admit that things were getting worse rather than better (*New York Times,* Dec. 2, 1992, A8).

The stage was thus set for a confrontation between the forces of political and economic reform embodied in the person of Boris Yeltsin and the forces of resistance embodied in the Parliament.

Irregular forces loyal to the Parliament stormed key government buildings in a move that was broadly interpreted as an attempted coup. Army divisions loyal to the Parliament were also rumored to be on the outskirts of Moscow. They failed to materialize, and Yeltsin ordered the Parliament evacuated. The conservative deputies, however, refused to leave the Parliament building and challenged Yeltsin to evict them by force (*New York Times,* Sept. 29, 1993, A6). Supporters of both sides poured into the streets, and Yeltsin, perhaps fearing civil war, ordered the army to shell the Parliament. It did so, albeit reluctantly, bringing the crisis to an end on October 5, 1993. Yeltsin would rule by decree until the convening of the new Parliament, or Duma, in January 1994 (*New York Times,* Oct. 6, 1993, A4).

Elections in the New Russia. Elections were duly held on December 12, 1993, with Russia's voters being asked to elect a new Parliament and to approve a new Constitution that had been designed by Yeltsin a few months earlier. As a democratic exercise, Russia's first post-Soviet election left much to be desired. Electoral procedures were not agreed upon until a few days before the election, making electoral strategy rudimentary at best. The draft Constitution itself would not be presented to the voters until thirty-three days before the election, hardly adequate time for serious debate in a country as large and diverse as Russia.

Vladimir Putin, Russia's enigmatic president.

The electoral system that evolved was similar to that of Germany, with half of the 450 seats in the lower house, now renamed the State Duma, being elected by single-member districts and the other half being elected by party lists. This was confusing stuff for a nation with little experience in democratic practice. Few of the parties involved in the election, moreover, were more than a month or two old, and voters were unfamiliar with the programs and the candidates.

Approval of the Constitution was a victory for Yeltsin, but the results of the parliamentary election were not. The Russia's Choice Party, the main party supporting Yeltsin's economic reforms, remained a minority in a Duma dominated by anti-reform parties ranging from the very conservative to the profoundly anti-democratic. The most startling result of the parliamentary elections was the emergence of the neo-fascist "Liberal Democratic Party" as the second-largest party in the Duma. Vladimir Zhirinovsky, the party's leader and an announced candidate for the 1996 presidential elections, was widely referred to as the Russian Hitler (*Christian Science Monitor,* Jan. 10, 1994, 2).

Yeltsin won the 1996 presidential election, but serious questions remained concerning his health and his ability to rule. Because of this uncertainty, the remainder of Yeltsin's term in office would be characterized by profound **immobilism.** Yeltsin would collapse in illness only to reassert his power by sacking those whom he had appointed to key positions during earlier periods of lucidity. Meanwhile, the Russian economy neared collapse as banks folded and workers and soldiers remained unpaid for months. Yeltsin surprised the world community by resigning on New Year's Eve, 1999. Vladimir Putin, prime minister and Yeltsin's personal choice to succeed him, became acting president the following day.

One of Putin's first acts was to grant Yeltsin immunity from prosecution. Simultaneously, he began removing Yeltsin's cronies, including his daughter, from positions of influence. To a large extent it was they who had been running things during Yeltsin's long periods of incapacity.

Chechnya: A Nasty Little War. Shortly after the proclamation of the Russian Federation as an independent country, one of its component parts, the small Muslim state of Chechnya, declared its independence from the Russian Federation. The turmoil of the era precluded Yeltsin from taking action against the breakaway state, and the event went largely unnoticed outside of Russia. From Yeltsin's perspective, however, the secession of Chechnya, if left unchallenged, would trigger similar action by other states dominated by non-Russian minorities. It was not merely the loss of one minor state that was at stake, but the continued viability of the Russian Federation as a whole (*Economist,* Jan. 14, 1995, 43).

With the 1993 elections behind him and his power consolidated, Yeltsin turned his attention to the Chechnya problem. Dispatching troops to the border of the breakaway republic in the autumn of 1994, Yeltsin demanded that the Chechnyan leaders end their secession. They refused, and Russian troops began a halfhearted and erratic march toward the Chechnyan capital of Grozny. Once the battle was joined, Chechnyans fought with uncommon valor, while the Russian forces hardly fought at all (*New York Times,* Dec. 25, 1994, 1). Indeed, confusion reigned as the Russian army seemed incapable of crushing a rebellion sustained by a few thousand poorly equipped Chechnyan forces with no air cover.

With Yeltsin's victory in the 1996 elections, a tentative peace was reached with the Chechnyan forces, a peace that was generally considered a defeat for the Russian forces. The problem, however, continued to fester, and in the summer of 1999, rebels in the neighboring province of Dagestan proclaimed their independence. Much of their support came from Chechnya. Russian troops would enter Chechnya a few months later, blaming Islamic groups in Chechnya for a series of terrorist attacks in Russia and reasserting Russia's position that Chechnya remain part of the Russian Federation. In the meantime, Russian security officials arrested some 20,000 suspects, mostly from Chechnya and its neighboring provinces, in an attempt to stem the wave of terrorist bombings. Vladimir Putin, who served as prime minister during the final months of Yeltsin's reign and then became acting president with Yeltsin's surprise resignation, gained tremendous popularity by pursuing the war with a brutality reminiscent of Joseph Stalin. Chechnya was recaptured but only at a horrific cost that saw the province's major cities obliterated. Even then, most of the resistance fighters merely retreated to their mountain hideaways, and launched a fierce guerrilla war against Russian forces that continues unabated. Indeed, terror spawned by the war has extended its battlefields to Moscow.

Who Is Vladimir Putin? The illusion of Russian victory in Chechnya was tremendously popular in Russia, and Putin, a totally unknown individual prior to being named prime minister by Yeltsin in the final months of 1999, was catapulted into the political limelight. Other than his brutal suppression of the Chechnyan rebellion, Putin's few months in office had done little to indicate the direction of his political and economic views. Indeed, all that was known of him was that he was young (47 years old) and tough, an ex-KGB spy, and the former director of the Federal Security Service, the successor to the KGB. Putin's decisive action in Chechnya, however, was credential enough for a population reeling from the near chaos of Yeltsin's final years in office, and Putin scored a first-round victory in the 2000 presidential elections with approximately 52.5 percent of the popular vote (*New York Times,* Mar. 28, 2000, www). Putin had also bolstered his image as a "tough guy" by flying his own jet to inspect the situation in Chechnya and by publicizing his expertise in judo. No one was entirely sure of the direction he intended to take Russia, but he spoke elegantly of pursuing Russia's transition to democracy and capitalism.

Putin was elected for a second term in office in the spring of 2004 with an amazing 71 percent of the popular vote. Perhaps embarrassed by the size of his victory, he vowed to share power with Russia's other democratically elected elites and reaffirmed his commitment to democracy and capitalism. There could be little doubt of Putin's commitment to capitalism. Putin's first term in office had seen a major restructuring of the Russian economy. While much remained to be done, the U.S. added Russia to its list of capitalist countries. Russia's transition to democracy, by contrast, appears to have stalled. The democratically elected governors of Russia's regions have been shorn of their power, the press crippled, and the Parliament weakened. Some 70–80 percent of Putin's senior administrators and policy advisors are former colleagues in the KGB, the Soviet secret police (*Moscow Times,* Sept. 8, 2004, 7). The secret service has been rechristened the FSB, but it is not clear just how much its policies have changed. Russian commentators speak despondently of the end of the liberal era. Putin has said that his actions are necessary to fight the war in Chechnya and to crush the terror that now engulfs Russia.

Putin himself has remained an enigma. He describes himself as a democrat. Others have been less kind, labeling him the glacial chameleon, the Teflon president, or the new tsar. President George W. Bush said he looked into Putin's soul and pronounced him to be an "honest and straightforward man" (*Atlantic Monthly,* October 2003, 48). Many see Putin as a Russian nationalist dedicated to the restoration of Russia's much battered glory (Arian-King 2004). If this requires a dose of authoritarianism, so be it. Optimists see Putin's authoritarian tendencies as a transitional adjustment designed to curb the excesses of the Yeltsin era. Putin's "guided democracy," they hope, will give way to full democracy once Russia's rush to capitalism has been completed.

All of this is compatible with Russia's transition to capitalism. It would seem to be far less compatible with Russia's transition to democracy. Russia's Freedom House ranking of world democracies has declined with each year that Putin has been in power. In the pages that follow we shall examine the various dimensions of Russia's political system and their role in shaping Russia's future.

THE POLITICAL INSTITUTIONS OF RUSSIA

Political institutions are the arena of politics. It is the executives, legislatures, courts, bureaucracies, and other agencies of government that authoritatively allocate the resources of the state. In this section, we shall examine the political institutions of Russia, of which the executive is by far the most important.

The Constitution of Russia

The Yeltsin Constitution has much in common with the Constitution of France, upon which it is patterned (Belyakov and Raymond 1994). Its centerpiece is a very strong president, a bicameral parliament called the **Federal Assembly,** and a Constitutional Court. The 450 members of the *lower house of parliament* **(Duma)** are elected directly by the populace, while the **Federation Council,** or *upper house,* consists of 178 members (two apiece from each of the 89 regions that constitute the Russian Federation). The president shares executive power with a chairman (prime minister) named by the president with the consent of the Duma. The new Constitution also provides Russia's citizens with a broad array of civil rights, including freedom of thought, speech, and religion. A free press is also guaranteed, as is the right to form groups and parties. In addition to these and other rights taken for granted in the United States, the Constitution guarantees all Russian citizens the right to housing, education, health care, and an old-age pension (Constitution, Articles 39–43).

Popular support for the Constitution remains a matter of conjecture, inasmuch as it was ratified under extraordinary circumstances. But then, so was the Constitution of France, both constitutions having been dictated by strong leaders in countries on the brink of civil war. The French, however, possessed deeply rooted democratic traditions. The Russians do not.

Putin has expressed strong support for the Constitution, as well he should. The powers of the president border on the dictatorial, the major limits on Putin's power being a limit of two terms in office. Even that, however, is not an insurmountable obstacle. The constitution can be amended by a two-thirds majority of the Duma and Putin's party, United Russia, possesses a two-thirds majority in that body.

Executive Power in Russia:
The President and the Prime Minister

Much like the Constitution of France, the Russian Constitution creates a dual executive. Unlike France, however, the dominance of the Russian president is unlikely to be challenged by his or her prime minister.

The President. The formal powers accorded to the Russian president by the Yeltsin Constitution are awesome. The president is the commander-in-chief of the armed forces and is charged with protecting both the Constitution and the integrity of the State. If either is endangered, the president is empowered to declare a state of emergency and to rule by decree. He also nominates the prime minister and must approve the members of the Cabinet. The president, moreover, is Russia's chief legislator, possessing the right to introduce legislation and to veto acts of Parliament. Beyond this, the president may also issue presidential decrees that have the force of law if they are not declared unconstitutional by the Constitutional Court or overruled by the Parliament (Remington, Smith, and Haspel 1998). If the Parliament does pass new legislation overriding a presidential decree, that legislation is also subject to a presidential veto and must be overridden by a two-thirds majority in both houses. The president can also bypass Parliament altogether by taking his case directly to the people via a referendum. And, if all else fails, he can dissolve the Duma, thereby initiating a new round of legislative elections.

The president, moreover, is Russia's chief bureaucrat. In this capacity, he nominates and removes heads of government departments. Putin has carried out both tasks with a vengeance in an effort to make the state bureaucracy more responsive to his wishes. The president also nominates judges, including those of the Constitutional Court.

The formal powers of the Russian president, then, are profound, perhaps taxing the limits of democratic practice. Were it not for a constitutional provision limiting presidents to two four-year terms of office, the powers of the Russian president would rival those of the latter tsars.

The informal powers of the president are also formidable, three of which are of particular importance. First, because the president dominates both the legislative and administrative processes, interest groups must curry his favor if they are to achieve their objectives. Very little gets done in Russia without presidential approval. Second, because the president is Russia's chief dispenser of patronage, it is his supporters who will dominate Russia's administrative and legal structure. Legislators wanting programs for their constituents will also be under intense pressure to join the president's team. Finally, the president is the focal point of public opinion. He is the mover and shaker in Russian politics, and everything he does is noteworthy. The ability of the Russian president to control the media also appears to be far greater than it is in most Western democracies, a fact that became evident during the 2004 presidential campaign.

The Russian president is surrounded by a massive support team, replete with its own militia (Presidential Guard) and an airline. The presidential telephone book runs some 227 pages (Meier 1995).

The president's combination of formal and informal powers provides him with extraordinary influence over the future of Russian politics. Although the new Russian Constitution embodies many of the theoretical checks and balances of the United States Constitution, it has yet to be demonstrated that those checks pose a serious obstacle to a determined president. If Russia's social and economic circumstances continue to deteriorate, Putin could well be tempted to cross the thin line that separates Russian democracy from dictatorship. Many feel that he already has. The *Moscow Times* speculates that he intends to stay in office beyond his constitutional term (*Moscow Times*, March 17, 2005, www).

The Prime Minister and Cabinet. The president names the prime minister (Chairman of the Duma) with the approval of the Duma. If the Duma rejects three candidates nominated by the president, or if it withdraws its confidence from a sitting prime minister, the president has the option of dissolving the Duma and calling for new legislative elections. The prime minister presides over the Cabinet, most members of which have also been selected by the president. Indeed, the most powerful members of the Cabinet, including the Ministers of Defense, Interior (Police), and Foreign Affairs, report directly to the president rather than to the prime minister, as do special intergovernmental committees on espionage, frontier guards, information, and the media. Yeltsin had no intention of creating a prime minister who could challenge his authority in any way, a view clearly endorsed by Putin.

The Cabinet consists of approximately 25 ministers, most of whom supervise large bureaucratic departments and are responsible for drafting policy in their domains. Cabinet ministers represent a core element in the new Russian elite, but given the uncertain nature of Russian politics, their power is often fleeting.

Legislative Power in Russia: The Federal Assembly

The Federal Assembly consists of two houses: the State Duma, a name adopted from the abortive parliaments of the tsarist era, and the Federation Council (Hahn 1995). The Duma is the popularly elected house of the Russian Parliament; the Federation Council is designed to provide representation for Russia's 89 regions, each of which is accorded two seats. Both chambers must approve legislation for it to become law. A two-thirds majority in each chamber is also required to override a presidential veto—a daunting task indeed.

The Duma. While both houses of the Federal Assembly must approve legislation before it can become law, the Duma alone has the power to force the resignation of a Government (prime minister and Cabinet) via a **vote of no confidence.** Votes of no confidence have been frequent, but no government has fallen. The Duma also confirms the presidential nominations for the head of the central bank as well as many other senior positions.

The Duma's ability to bring down a Government makes it the focal point of partisan conflict in Russia. This is all the more the case because half of the 450 members of the Duma are elected on the basis of party lists, a procedure that makes the Duma a barometer of party support among the Russian electorate. The other half of the Duma's members are elected in single-member districts, a process that often finds partisan identification being clouded by local and ethnic considerations. Nevertheless, most of the members of the Duma elected in single-member districts soon affiliate with the party that best reflects their ideological views.

The main strength of the Duma lies in the budget-making process. To date, parliamentary squabbling has resulted in budgets that have been both delayed and confusing. The Duma, moreover, seldom votes a major piece of legislation up or down. Rather, the legislation is introduced in different guises until a reasonable consensus can be reached. The 1995 budget, for example, went through 13 votes before it was finally passed by the Duma (*New York Times,* Dec. 28, 1994, A4). Subsequent budgets under the Yeltsin regime were equally traumatic (*Le Monde Economie,* Sept. 8, 1998). Putin, with near-dictatorial powers, has found the budgetary process to be less arduous. Everyone, it seems, wants to be his friend.

Indeed, some elements of the Communist Party openly attempted to jump on Putin's bandwagon in the final days of the 2000 election campaign despite the fact that the Communist candidate was Putin's main challenger (*New York Times,* Mar. 21, 2000, www). The public is not pleased, with only 3 percent of no respondents in a 2005 survey giving the Duma positive marks (*Moscow Times,* Feb. 1, 2005, www).

The Federation Council. The Federation Council participates in all phases of the legislative process except the naming and censure of Governments. Its special powers include confirmation of a state of emergency, approval of the use of Russian troops on foreign soil, and acceptance of presidential nominations for judges and the public prosecutor. The Federation Council must also approve boundary changes within the Russian Federation. Given the ethnic complexities of Russia's diverse regions, the latter task may prove challenging. The early experience of the Federation Council suggests that it is more inclined to cooperate with the president than is the Duma. If this trend continues, Russian presidents should be able to weaken further the powers of the Parliament by playing one chamber against the other.

The powers of the president and the Parliament, then, are far from equal. The Parliament plays an important role in the legislative process, but that role is largely a passive one of responding to presidential initiatives. There is little that the Parliament can do to force legislation on a reluctant president. There is also little the Parliament can do to check the powers of the president, short of outright impeachment. Impeachment, however, requires the participation of both houses of the Federal Assembly and is a long and complicated process. Because of the dominant role of the presidency, much of the burden of building democracy in Russia will rest with its president.

Law and Politics in Russia: The Constitutional Council

The **Constitutional Council** (Supreme Court) consists of 19 judges appointed for life by the president. The Council is empowered to review the constitutionality of laws and presidential degrees, and it must consent to the initiation of impeachment proceedings against the president. The Constitutional Council also arbitrates disputes between the president and the Parliament and may hear cases brought by the member states of the Russian Federation and by individual citizens.

The concept of judicial review, which states that courts can declare acts of government unconstitutional, is totally foreign to Russian practice (Butler 1992). The Soviet Union possessed a Constitutional Court, but its role was to regulate a subservient legal system rather than to pass judgment on the wisdom of Soviet leaders. In the confusing days following the collapse of the Soviet Union, however, the old Constitutional Court was placed in the position of arbitrating the conflict between Yeltsin and his opponents. Leaning first toward one side and then the other, the Court did establish the precedent of declaring the acts of both Parliament and the president unconstitutional (Sharlet 1997). Be this as it may, it is unlikely that the new Constitutional Council will soon be in a position to check the power of Putin or his successors. Indeed, in 2004 the parliament extended Putin's ability to control the legal system at all levels (*Washington Post*, Oct. 2, 2004, www).

While its power may be far from absolute, the Constitutional Council will not suffer from a lack of business. Russia's commercial law is being totally rewritten, and boundary disputes between Russia's 89 states (republics), the demarcation of which was often arbitrary, will also crowd the Council's agenda. Also to be resolved are disputes arising from the reform of Russia's criminal justice system, including the institution of jury trials. This will not be an easy task, for both Russian law and Russian jurists are holdovers from the Soviet Union.

Federalism in Russia

The Yeltsin Constitution divides Russia into 89 republics or states, each of which sends two members to the Federation Council, the upper house of the Russian Parliament. (Two of the 89 republics are being merged in the name of greater economic and social development.) Of the 89 republics, 21 are ethnic republics that give special autonomy to a particular minority group. The remainder are administrative republics. Many of Russia's smaller ethnic groups are also demanding special status as ethnic republics.

As the Chechnyan conflict illustrates, the potential for ethnic conflict in Russia remains very high and, if left unchecked, could lead to the fragmentation of the Russian Federation. Ethnic Russians are a minority in approximately half of the Federation's republics and can be outvoted in local elections by ethnic minorities, most of whom resent Russian domination (Diller 1992). Most ethnic republics (states) have used their autonomy to press for ever-greater independence from Moscow, and many have also passed legislation prejudicing the rights of ethnic Russians (Theen 1993; Dowley 1998). Moscow has relied on legal maneuvers to curb both tendencies but may eventually be compelled to maintain the integrity of the Russian state by force. This was certainly the message of the war in Chechnya. Strained relations between the central government and the republics, then, represent yet another obstacle that must be overcome if the reformers are to lead Russia to the promised land of democracy and capitalism (McAuley 1997; Tolz and Busygina 1997).

Putin has responded to the challenge posed by the growing independence of Russia's 89 regions by creating seven larger "presidential districts." He has also suggested replacing the 89 regions with 28 "beefed up" regions (*Moscow Times,* June 7, 2004, 9). Federal supervision of the republics has increased apace as has the growing centralization of the Russian government. As one of Putin's top aids described the struggle with Russia's regional governors:

> This is a serious battle. Putin was hesitating. My position was that it had to be done. Russia cannot exist as a confederation with 89 regional autocrats. Now they have accepted the primacy of the federal center. Of course, they're not happy. Many of them are hiding their irritation. But as in metallurgy, the process works by pressure. So if you can keep on the pressure, then the body can change its form. We believe that they will change their outlook (Surkov 2002).

That struggle is now over. Russia's governors are no longer elected by the citizens of their region. They are appointed by Putin. The change was justified in the name of fighting terror. Whatever the case, Russia is becoming a federation in name only (*New York Times,* Sept. 13, 2004).

The Military and Politics in Russia

The Soviet Union was ruled by the Communist Party and sustained by the Soviet military. The Soviet military was a highly professional military that occupied a powerful and privileged position within Soviet society (Garthoff 1966; Garthoff 1992).

After the collapse of the U.S.S.R., efforts were made to transform the Soviet military into the collective military of the Commonwealth of Independent States (CIS), thereby providing the members of the CIS with an element of stability during a period of profound uncertainty in both regional and international affairs. The breakaway states, however, distrusted Russian dominance of the old Soviet military, and cooperation gave way to conflict as each new country, however poor, established its own army.

Russia's share of the Soviet military became the Russian military, much of it stationed in Eastern Europe and the former Soviet republics. Finding itself the object of fear and scorn, the military began a slow withdrawal into the Russian heartland, retreating from a war that it had not lost. Russia, moreover, had few facilities for its returning forces, the housing for which had been provided by the "host countries" of Eastern Europe. Compounding matters was the collapse of the Russian economy. Military spending fell from $246 million in 1985, the beginning of the unraveling of the U.S.S.R., to some $40 million in 1992 (*New York Times,* Nov. 26, 1993, 3).

Reflecting the changing role of the Russian military, the massive tank formations of the past are being dismantled and replaced by a greater reliance on rapid development capabilities and "smart" weapons.

Even more problematic was the military's loss of a mission. With the cold war at an end, Russia no longer needed a Soviet-type military. Sensing a military in disarray, few conscripts bothered to show up for duty. Some estimates placed the level of draft-dodging at more than 90 percent, while others suggested that the Russian military would soon have more officers than enlisted men (Schmemann 1993). Both trends were aggravated by the Chechnya War. Indeed, Army Day in 1995 was marked by a Yeltsin warning that the Russian military was on the verge of disintegration (BBC, Feb. 23, 1995).

The situation continued to deteriorate during 1996 as Alexander Lebed, then Russia's security chief, warned that the army was "on the brink of mutiny" as a result of unpaid wages (*International Herald Tribune,* Oct. 7, 1996, 11). The quasi-victory in Chechnya provided a boost in army morale, but not to the extent of stemming the tide of draft dodgers that has become a torrent (*International Herald Tribune,* Apr. 13, 2000, 4). Not only was the army short of recruits, but those who chose to honor their draft notices were poorly educated and lacked the technical skills of which the army was in urgent need (ibid.).

The Russian military is now in the process of redefining its role in the new Russia. This involves changes in both the military's mission and the relationship between the military and Russia's civilian leaders.

The process of redefining the military's mission began late in 1993 when Yeltsin, after extensive consultation with military leaders, announced a new military doctrine that declared Russia to be free from the threat of foreign invasion. Henceforth, the role of the military will be to insulate Russia from the regional conflicts that have engulfed the former states of the U.S.S.R. In line with its new mission, the military will concentrate on developing rapid deployment forces rather than relying on the massive tank formations that were its hallmark during the Soviet era. Decreases in troop strength will be balanced by increased technological sophistication and by greater reliance on smart weapons (*New York Times,* Nov. 3, 1993, A6). While the mission of the military has been redefined, it will take years to complete the transformation process. It will also take time to rebuild the military's badly shaken morale (*Christian Science Monitor,* Oct. 15, 1993, 1).

Putin, it is interesting to note, did not challenge the power of the military until he had firmly consolidated his power in the 2004 election. Now confident of his power, he forced a law through the Duma that severely restricts the power of the General Staff, the power center of the military command (*St. Petersburg Times,* May 21, 2004). The General Staff exists, but its role is largely that of a planning body. Orders come from the Kremlin. The shift was designed to speed up the modernization of the military. It was also designed to reduce the role of the General Staff as a competing center of power.

An article in *Russian Life,* a publication of the Russian Information Services, describes the Russian army, as presently constituted, as "a diminutive, one-third-sized copy of the Soviet Armed Forces. Yet this copy is useless for the defense of the state. In fact, it endangers it. . . . Of course, modern Russia, given all its imperfections, cannot support such an army. As a result, the army is disintegrating. Draft evasion has become a national sport" (Glots 2003, 30–31). The navy is in little better shape—its chief ordered the decommissioning of an entire series of nuclear submarines that had been described by a Russian admiral as Russia's most powerful vessels (*Moscow Times,* May 25, 2004, www).

In the meantime, the morale of a military bogged down in Chechnya continues to sink and Russian youth continue to avoid the draft. The Russian Information Services announced that in the first two weeks of the 2003 draft, "some 40,000 young men dodged the draft after getting their call-up notices; 50,000 could not even be found to be presented their call up notices" (*Russian Life,* July/August 2003, 34). Those inducted often desert. Putin has promised an end to the draft by 2007. He has also escalated the transition to a very high-tech army.

Bureaucracy and Politics in Russia

No matter what happens within Russia's decision-making institutions, the country's day-to-day affairs continue to be managed by the huge state bureaucracy inherited from the U.S.S.R. Privatization may eventually reduce bureaucratic control of the economy, but the process will be slow. Russia has not had a private sector for more than 70 years, and it will take at least a decade to develop a new class of capitalist managers capable of transforming Russia's antiquated state enterprises into effective private-sector firms.

Continued dependence upon a large state bureaucracy poses two major threats to democratic and economic reform in Russia. First, the Russian bureaucracy is the same corrupt and self-serving bureaucracy that contributed to the stagnation of the Soviet Union (Mellor 1997). Indeed, Putin has blamed corruption for the upsurge in terror spawned by the war in Chechnya (*Washington Post,* Sept. 4, 2004). There is little reason to believe that the behavior of the bureaucracy will change any time soon. Second, it appears that most segments of the bureaucracy are opposed to economic reform. It could hardly be otherwise, as government officials possess a vested interest in maintaining a bureaucratic regime.

Yeltsin made little secret of his frustration with the bureaucracy, referring to it as an "army of rapacious and bumbling officials" (*New York Times,* Feb. 25, 1994). Putin is of a similar view, but has given hefty raises to Russian officials in the hope of increasing efficiency and reducing corruption. Twenty percent of the federal bureaucrats are simultaneously being cut with the same goals in mind. Unfortunately, it may take a long time to alter the situation. Russia continues to be a bureaucratic state and, aside from removing a few senior officials, it has little option but to rely on the bureaucracy to carry out its programs. The Russian bureaucracy, moreover, is a seamless web of patron-client networks, each level receiving support from another. The more a president attacks the bureaucracy, the more rigid and uncooperative it becomes (Afanasyev 1998). Corruption is also so deeply rooted in the bureaucracy that it has become part of the bureaucratic ethic (*Moscow Times,* April 19, 2004, www). Adding to Russia's bureaucratic woes is the need to compete with the private sector for top talent. Putin, to put the picture in perspective, doubled his own salary to about $5,000 a month. Before the increases, government Ministers were making about $400 a month (*Moscow Times,* April 19, 2004, www).

THE ACTORS IN RUSSIAN POLITICS: ELITES, PARTIES, GROUPS, AND CITIZENS

Political institutions are the arena of politics, but the actors in the political process mold and shape those institutions. They are the "human" element in the political process. In this section, we shall examine the four main types of political actors in Russia: elites, parties, groups, and citizens. Each plays a critical role in determining how Russia's scarce resources are allocated.

Elites and Politics in Russia

Russia inherited the elite structure of the Soviet Union (Steen and Gel'man 2003). As such, virtually all members of the new elite were former members of the Communist Party. Some, including Boris Yeltsin and his followers, became advocates of democracy and capitalism. Others remained faithful to the ideals of communism or embraced Russian nationalism with a fervor that bordered on fascism. Putin is committed to the rebuilding of a strong Russia. He believes that this is best achieved through capitalism and a strong central government. How democracy fits in this picture remains a matter of conjecture. He seems to have little interest in recreating the stifling autocracy of the Soviet era. By the same token, he seems to have little interest in allowing democratic procedures to fragment the country or abet his enemies.

The centerpiece of the Russian elite structure is the presidency created by the Yeltsin Constitution. No other political institution in Russia, singly or in concert, can effectively challenge the decision-making power of the presidency. Putin has amply demonstrated that he intends to use the full extent of his constitutional powers to achieve his vision of a powerful and prosperous Russia. He has also demonstrated a willingness to go beyond those powers should the need arise. No sooner was he elected to a second term in office in 2004 than speculation began that the constitutions would be amended to allow more than two terms in office. Should this prove to be the case, Putin will be Russia's leader for a long time to come.

The next rung on the elite hierarchy is occupied by the president's inner circle of policy advisors. The more one has the president's ear, the greater one's influence in shaping policy. Defined in these terms, the inner circle of the Russian elite would certainly include presidential confidants in the Cabinet, the Duma, the presidential staff, and the military as well as the president's informal policy advisors. The security services, and especially the FSB, the successor to the KGB, are particularly well represented in this group.

Not included in the core groups are the oligarchs, a less-than-affectionate name given to the six tycoons who played a major role in keeping Yeltsin in power (Freeland 1998). As *Newsweek* quipped, they "made their money the old-fashioned way—through sweetheart deals, buying up state assets at bargain prices not available to others and then receiving more state property in exchange for short-term loans to the government" (*Newsweek,* Sept. 7, 1998, 31). Some are in exile; others in prison on fraud and tax evasion charges. Their major sin was challenging the power of Putin, a fate that has also befallen many of Yeltsin's military favorites.

At the secondary level, the Russian elite structure includes the leaders of the Federal Assembly, senior bureaucrats, senior military officers, managers of Russia's huge public-sector factories, and powerful regional and ethnic leaders (Hughes 1997). These secondary elites have little to say about the formation of public policy, but they have been very effective in dragging their feet on programs that they oppose.

Putin has instituted a three-prong program to bring competing elites at all levels under control. First, powerful individuals who pose a direct challenge to his authority are being purged, whatever the cost. This was clearly the case of the oligarchs. Western investors were stunned, but Putin made it clear that politics came before economics. It also illustrated Putin's use of the Soviet strategy of punishing the few to remind the many. The same strategy has been prevalent in Putin's "reform" of the military and the bureaucracy. Second, powerful individuals who have bent to Putin's will have been allowed to remain in power for the time being. That time may be limited, for the third element in Putin's game plan is vertical integration. All people at all levels are to be loyal supporters of Putin and his vision of Russia's future. This includes political leaders and it also includes economic, bureaucratic, and military leaders. Under the old Soviet regime, it was the Communist Party that served as the vehicle for vertical inte-

Mass participation, however, is not limited to elections and public opinion polls. Strikes and protests have become more frequent, sometimes threatening to turn violent. Mothers' marches dog the war effort in Chechnya, and demonstrations of all varieties have increased. Finally, it should be noted that the masses do not have to be politically active in order to influence the political process. Mass apathy undermined the power of both the tsarist empire and the Soviet Union. It may also undermine Russia's fragile democracy.

THE CONTEXT OF RUSSIAN POLITICS: CULTURE, ECONOMICS, AND INTERNATIONAL INTERDEPENDENCE

While the actors in Russian politics play a vital role in determining who gets what, when, and how, the behavior of those actors is often influenced by the broader environmental context in which Russian politics occurs. In this section, we examine three dimensions of Russia's environmental context: political culture, political economy, and the influence of the international arena.

The Culture of Russian Politics

Russia inherited the political and economic institutions of the Soviet Union. It also inherited Soviet political culture. It is relatively easy to craft new institutional structures, but the task of reshaping the values, attitudes, and predispositions of the individuals who give life to those institutions is a far more difficult task (Smith 1991; Kolst and Blakkisrud 2004).

In this regard, observers of Russian politics have noted a variety of *cultural traits likely to slow Russia's transition to democracy and capitalism,* many of which originated during the era of tsarist rule (Gorer and Rickman 1962). It is not suggested that all Russians share these traits, but only that their prevalence makes them politically relevant. Russians, for example, have traditionally displayed *an intense concern for order and stability* (Brown 1985).

Russians are also said to be predisposed toward authoritarianism, a trait that could well find them seeking salvation from their political and economic woes in a charismatic father figure (Brown 1985; Rainone 1998). Support for Boris Yeltsin clearly fits this mold, as does the now-fleeting popularity of Vladimir Zhirinovsky (Finifter and Mickiewicz 1992). The socialization programs of the Stalin era, moreover, actively sought to inculcate Soviet youth with the virtues of authoritarianism. The official Stalinist guide to child-rearing provides interesting insights into this process:

> In relation to children, parents must be unremittingly vigilant, exacting, and consistent in disciplinary demands and in the imposition of duties; no relaxation of effort on the parents' part is permissible for fear that the child may fall under bad influences and be controlled by antisocial elements. While parents should show warmth, affection, and understanding, they should not

permit excessive intimacy, which might undermine their authority. Parents must not be all-forgiving, for conduct deviations in children cannot be tolerated (Calas 1955, 107).

Still other prominent features of Russian culture include *apathy and a sense of psychological disengagement from the political system*. As stated previously, widespread political apathy played a key role in undermining both the tsarist empire and the Union of Soviet Socialist Republics (Tucker 1987). In both instances, political apathy was reinforced by a profound mutual distrust between the elites and the masses. The masses resented the capriciousness of a harsh political system, and the political elites feared the hostility of the masses (Brown 1985).

Although they may be ambivalent toward their political institutions, *Russians are intensely nationalistic* (Tolz 1998). They resent Russia's decline as a world power and remain suspicious of the West and its motives (Dunlop 1993).

Many also retain the culture of dependence created by Soviet cradle-to-grave welfare policies. Russians will accept capitalism if it improves their standard of living, but they will find it difficult to accept a reduction in personal welfare. In short, the Russian population is likely to expect the best features of both capitalism and socialism (Alexander 1998). For the moment, it has neither.

Further complicating matters is *the persistence of a socialist work ethic that saps the productivity of Russian workers.* This negative work ethic evolved in response to the Soviet practice of giving all workers more or less the same salary, regardless of how hard they worked or the quality of their output. The lack of incentives, combined with a guaranteed job, resulted in a work force that was sluggish, at best. The socialist work ethic also found strong cultural support in the traditional peasant emphasis on equality: better that all suffer than only one succeed. Whatever the case, productivity lagged, innovations were few, quality was poor, and upkeep of facilities was neglected (Smith 1992). Perhaps capitalism and the profit motive will alter this situation, but culture changes slowly. It will take time to generate an achievement ethic similar to that which has promoted the tremendous productivity of Germany and Japan.

Finally, Russians must cope with the stress of collapsing social, political, and economic institutions, a situation often referred to as **anomie.** People can adjust to new rules if they know what the rules are, but the rules in Russia continue to be in a state of turmoil. No one is quite sure where to turn or what the future will bring. Simply stated, *Russia is currently suffering from a crisis of authority.* Laws are passed in Moscow, but they are often ignored by those in outlying regions. Gangs and local "bosses" have emerged to fill the vacuum. In many areas, local police officials have become petty warlords.

Escalating levels of crime, drug abuse, and drunkenness reflect this state of social disorganization. Alcoholism, for example, increased dramatically during the latter Brezhnev years, with the average Soviet citizen consuming three times more alcohol than a resident of Western Europe (Diller 1992). It continued to increase during the Yeltsin years, with one commentator suggesting that Yeltsin used cheap vodka as a means of muting public dissent (Ivanov 1998). Crime, moreover, has become so pervasive that it is now threatening Russia's transition to capitalism.

Business people have become the preferred targets of Russia's proliferating gangs. They are the ones who have the money.

The main themes of Russian culture, then, are nationalism, apathy, distrust, authoritarianism, alienation, and uncertainty, themes that are not conducive either to democracy or to rapid economic development. Cultural predispositions change, but they change slowly, sometimes over the course of several generations. Dramatic cultural change, moreover, will require an active and far-reaching program of resocialization. The old "cultural map" must be redrawn and Russia's educational curriculum must be totally revamped to forge a political culture based upon democratic and capitalistic values (Frost and Makarov 1998; Urban 1998). These values must also be stressed by the media, labor unions, youth groups, political parties, parents, and other agents of political socialization. To date, steps in this direction have been minimal and haphazard.

Political Economy and Politics in Russia

Cultural analyses of Russian politics focus on the values, attitudes, and predispositions of the average Russian citizen. Political economists, by contrast, are more inclined to focus on their economic motivations. The collapse of the Tsars, from the political economy perspective, was the result of old Russia's rush to industrialization. Peasants thronged to the cities in search of prosperity but found only misery and despair. Despair and the harshness of factory life brought class awareness and broad worker support for the Communists. It was they, more than any other group, who offered the workers a solution to their economic woes. The fall of the communists, from the political economy perspective, was the failure of the communists to meet the economic demands of the population. The basic needs of the population were met, but the communist regime could not keep pace with mass demands for an economic quality of life similar to that of the West. Capitalism became the new panacea and Yeltsin swept to power on a surge of misplaced optimism. The Yeltsin years produced wealth for the few, but not for the many and his popularity crumbled. Putin read the mood of the masses and established his power by promising an orderly transition to capitalism that would benefit all Russians. His attack on the oligarchs, the fat cats, was immensely popular and spawned renewed hope for a better economic future.

Russia's future, from the political economy perspective, will also be dictated by economics. If individuals benefit from capitalism, they will support capitalism. If they do not, they will not. The same logic applies to Russian democracy. If democratic institutions can solve Russia's mounting economic problems and improve the economic well-being of the average citizen, they will be embraced by the Russian electorate. Optimism fueled by five years of sustained economic growth, from the economic perspective, fueled Putin's crushing victory in the 2004 presidential elections. If economic growth continues, political economists argue, it will build the tolerance upon which democracy depends and ease the nondemocratic tendencies of Russian culture reviewed above (Gibson 2002). The uneven nature of Russia's headlong transition to capitalism—the rich are getting richer, the poor are not—will be sorted out with time. Once Russia is on a firm economic foundation, political economists argue, the transition to democracy will follow suit.

It is not clear, moreover, that the Russian economy will continue to grow. Russia's economic success is not built upon a broad-based economic diversification that will lead to prosperity among all sectors of society. Rather it is based upon the export of oil, natural gas, and other natural resources. This fills the state coffers when oil prices are high and enables the Russian government to buy its way out of poverty and create the air of prosperity. It is a disaster when oil prices fall. Unless Russia builds a broad-based economy, the future of both Russia and democracy could be shaky, indeed. This, at least, is the view of the administrator of the United Nations Development Program in Russia (*St. Petersburg Times,* March 24, 2004, www). Even minor economic shocks make the Russian populace nervous and trigger a run on the banks, many of which have now closed (*Moscow Times,* July 8, 2004, www).

International Interdependence

Russia's transition to capitalism and democracy have been matched by an equally dramatic transition in its international affairs. The cold war is a thing of the past as is the vast empire fashioned by the tsars and their communist successors. Many former puppet states in Eastern Europe have joined the European Union. Some have even joined the North Atlantic Treaty Organization (NATO), the western alliance forged at the end of World War II to prevent further Soviet incursions into Europe. Vladimir Putin has vowed to build a powerful Russia that plays an equal role in the world community. Some suspect that Russian nationalists want a more than equal role. The problems, however, are many.

- The Russian military, aside from its nuclear arsenal, no longer poses a credible threat to the West. This is all the more the case with the expansion of NATO and the European Union to Russia's borders.

- Putin's dream of a building a powerful and prosperous Russia cannot be achieved without cooperation by the West. Russia requires massive infusions of both money and technology. Military power requires economic power.

- What began as a minor rebellion in Chechnya has been transformed into a jihad pitting Russia against Islamic extremists and their supporters. While most of the fighting is carried out by Chechnyan rebels, money, arms and jihadist fighters have poured into the breakaway republic from all areas of the Islamic world. Terror related to the Chechnyan wars has also struck at the heart of Russia as jihadists have bombed Moscow subways and theaters. In 2004, more than 300 children and teachers were killed when Russian security forces charged a rural school held by jihadist militants.

Putin has forged a foreign policy that addresses all of the above issues. He acquiesced in the expansion of NATO and the European Union to Russia's borders in exchange for accelerated Western cooperation in rebuilding the Russian economy. In reality, he probably had little choice in the matter and made the best of a bad situation. He has also signed major arms reduction treaties with the United States. The United States could afford the costs of a continued arms race.

(BBC, July 20, 1999, www). These, in turn, are divided into some 27 military districts, more than 200 subdistricts, a nearly equal number of garrison commands, and more than 2,000 departments (Godwin 1988, 45). Each military region, district, and sub-district is headed by both a military commander and a political commissar. Each also possesses its own Communist Party replete with an executive committee and party organization. The role of the political commissar is to assure that military commanders conform to the party line. They also keep party officials abreast of military affairs via a special political department that spans all levels of the military establishment (Godwin 1988). In most instances, the role of the political commissar is filled by the first secretary of the appropriate party organization (Liu 1986). The intricacies of the Chinese military are poorly understood in the West, and their exact structure and their operation is the subject of considerable uncertainty. The important point to be noted is that the party has spared no effort to assure that the command of the PLA remains firmly under party control (Jencks 1992) This, too, was a major theme of the 2002 Party Congress.

The relationship between the military and the party remains complex. Five dimensions of this relationship are particularly important to the shaping of China's future.

1. *China's military leaders are dedicated party members.* As such, they possess a vested interest in the survival of the system.

2. *Factionalism within the party extends to the military.* Indeed, each party faction has sought to bolster its position by recruiting military allies. The military, then, does not speak with a single voice (Jencks 1992; Lee 2003).

3. *The military leadership appears to be less factionalized than the party leadership.* As such, it has been able to shape policy by arbitrating between party factions. It was military support for Deng, for example, that allowed his economic reforms to continue. The same remains true today.

4. *The military has displayed signs of "warlordism" as regional commanders carve out personal fiefdoms.* Warlordism is a contravention of party discipline and poses a clear threat to party dominance.

5. *The military represents a corporate pressure group.* Like other pressure groups, the members of the military are united by a common interest in extending their power, benefits, and social status. The military also is vitally interested in attaining modern weapons.

The multifaceted relationship between the military and the party makes it difficult to predict how relations between the two pillars of Communist authority will unfold under Hu as China continues its course of dramatic change. Depending on the circumstances, each one of the five factors outlined above could play a determining role in shaping the behavior of China's military leaders. This said, present trends suggest that the military, like the party itself, is becoming better educated, more professional, and less involved in politics than earlier generations. It is also far better paid. The threat of political involvement, however, is never far beneath the surface. China's leaders well understand this fact of political life in the middle kingdom. Jiang, himself, promoted 500 generals in a single year (Dittmer 2003).

THE ACTORS IN CHINESE POLITICS: ELITES, GROUPS, AND CITIZENS

Political institutions are the arena of politics, but it is the actors in the political process that give life to those institutions. To a great extent, it is these actors who determine who gets what, when, and how. In this section, we will look at three main groups of political actors in China: elites, groups, and citizens. (China's single political party, the Chinese Communist Party, has already been discussed extensively.)

Elites and Politics in China

The elite hierarchy in China is topped by the members of the all-powerful Standing Committee of the Politburo, many of whom also serve on the Central Military Commission. They are followed in order of importance by the lower-ranking members of these key party organs. Provincial first secretaries, the commanders of the Grand Military Regions, and the leaders of the state apparatus are also powerful individuals. Most are members of the Central Committee, a sure sign of elite status. Ironically, Deng Xiaoping occupied no formal positions during the final years of his rule, choosing instead to rule through his protégés. Hu has rapidly consolidated his hold on the presidency and clearly occupies the top rung in the hierarchy of Chinese elites.

Two aspects of China's elite structure have been particularly visible. First, a very small number of individuals wielded extraordinary power. Second, those individuals were very old. On the eve of the Fourteenth Party Congress (1992) Deng Xiaoping was 87; Chen Yun, his arch foe, was 86; and Yang Shangkun, the president of the Republic, was 85 (*Economist,* Feb. 1, 1992, and Mar. 21, 1992). Even the new generation of party elites is old by Western standards.

This, however, now may be changing as Hu, now the forth generation of Communist leaders, characterizes a changing elite that has few if any ties with the great revolution. All 25 members of the politburo now possess college educations as opposed to 9 members of Deng's Politburo. Most are also in their 60s and, on average, some 10 years younger than Deng's associates. All have matured in an era of peace and most have technical rather than purely political backgrounds. These generational differences, presumably, give them a view of the world that differs from that of China's earlier leaders (Wang 2003). This is certainly reflected in the rapid transition to capitalism and the halting steps toward democracy. As so much in China, however, this remains a matter of some conjecture. There is also a great deal of continuity. Commitment to party dominance has not eased nor has China's insistence that Taiwan remains part of China.

The appeal of Marxism to the young Chinese intellectuals of the early twentieth century is easy to understand. China was a backward society on the verge of collapse. Its masses lived in squalor and its elite was preoccupied with its own luxury. Marxism offered both modernity and social equality. Marxism also placed Mao and other members of the Communist Party in the vanguard of a powerful movement. It was they who would lead revolutionary China. Once in power, Mao followed Marxist doctrine to the extreme. Industries and commercial establishments were nationalized, farms were collectivized, capitalism gave way to centralized planning, and heavy industry replaced agriculture as the cornerstone of the Chinese economy.

What went wrong? Why is China now turning to capitalism in order to cure its economic ills? The explanations are many. In part, China's economic woes of today can be traced to Mao's erratic economic policies, not the least of which was the Great Leap Forward. Attempts to terrorize the workers into greater productivity merely produced inflexibility and routinization (Teiwes and Sun 1998).

The CCP, moreover, does not distinguish between economic leadership and political leadership. Political leaders make all of the major economic decisions, regime survival being considered more important than economic development. Deng Xiaoping emphasized economic reform, but as the tragic events of Tiananmen Square illustrated, not to the point of jeopardizing party supremacy. Economic reform would gain new momentum in the post-Tiananmen era, but not until the party had reasserted its political authority.

Neoclassical political economists attribute China's economic problems not merely to Mao but to Marxism in general. Any governmental distortion of the free market, in their view, reduces productivity. The more the Chinese leadership interfered with the natural operation of the market, the worse things became. Empirical support for this argument is striking. The relaxation of government economic controls produced the fastest-growing economy in the world.

Marxist-oriented political economists acknowledge that bureaucratic rigidity and cults of personality crippled China's economic growth (Gregor 1995). These, in their view, were vestiges of China's inadequate preparation for socialism, but were not attributable to Marxism itself. Marxist-oriented political economists also blame China's economic failure on the West's refusal to provide the Communist state with the markets and technology required for its economic development.

Whatever the case, it is difficult to underestimate the influence of economics on Chinese politics. To meet the basic needs of China's masses, its leaders were forced to turn to capitalism. In the dictum of Deng Xiaoping, "It doesn't matter if the cat is black or white as long as it catches mice." The success of China's capitalist experiment has provided stability to the country precisely because it has helped the party meet the needs of its people. For many Chinese, however, these needs are not being met. Expectations are also rising. China's citizens expect far more from their government than they did even a decade ago. This represents a potential danger for the future, for China must generate 12 million new jobs a year, perhaps more, just to keep pace with population growth. The process of pursuing capitalist growth, moreover, is changing the Chinese political system itself. Capitalists have become a powerful pressure group in China and China's Communist leaders have become ardent capitalists. Perhaps this will lead to greater democracy. For the moment, however, it is merely transforming China into a capitalist dictatorship that has little to do with the regime's Communist origins.

International Interdependence and the Politics of China

With the shattering of China's isolation in the mid-1800s, its domestic politics would increasingly be shaped by the pressures of the outside world. Of these, none was greater than the West's reaction to the victory of the Communists in 1949.

The United States responded to the Communist victory by encircling the Chinese mainland with a ring of military bases that stretched from Japan to the Philippines. It also rebuilt Chiang Kai-shek's forces on Taiwan, thereby presenting the Communist regime with the constant threat of renewed war. China turned to the Soviet Union for protection but found its alliance with the U.S.S.R. to be a difficult one. Indeed, tensions between the two Communist states soon rivaled those between China and the United States.

The hostility of China's international environment played upon Mao's "siege mentality," a trait deeply ingrained during the formative years of revolutionary struggle. China became a garrison state, a "bamboo curtain" isolating the middle kingdom from the modern world. Relations with the West improved with the passing of Mao, but the Chinese leadership remains cautious. The U.S. Department of Defense Annual Report on the Military Power of the People Republic of China (2003) notes that China views the U.S. as a long-term threat. The reasons for China's concerns are not difficult to understand. China continues to be encircled by hostile forces in Japan, Taiwan, South Korea, and, perhaps, Russia (Kornhberg and Faust 2004). More immediate, is the U.S. military support for Taiwan. It is that support, in the Chinese view, that has prevented the reunification of the two Chinas. China has repeatedly threatened to invade Taiwan, but lacks the military sophistication to counter anticipated U.S. support for the island nation. That balance may soon change as China continues to upgrade the technical capacity of its massive army. Indeed, China is now the world's largest importer of foreign weapons, most of which are hi-tech in nature. Some estimates suggest that China has imported some $10 billion in sophisticated weapons over the course of the past decade with no end in sight (Fisher 2004). China's own assessments rank it fourth in world military power after the United States, Japan, and the United Kingdom (Lee 2003) It is not a matter of matching the military strength of the U.S., but of being able to force the U.S. to take unacceptable losses in a minor war thousands of miles from the U.S. homeland. China has a long way to go in its modernization drive, but as early as 2004, China's watchers were predicting that 2006 would be the year of China (*Asia Times,* April 10, 2004, www). Taiwan, moreover, is merely symbolic of a broader Chinese belief that it should

Shambaugh, David. 2003. *Modernizing China's Military: Progress, Problems, and Prospects.* Berkeley, CA: University of California Press.

Sivin, Nathan. 1990. "Science and Medicine in Chinese History." *In Heritage of China* (pp. 164–96), ed. Paul S. Ropp. Berkeley, CA: University of California Press.

Taylor, Ian. 1998 (June). "China's New Prime Minister." *Contemporary Review* 272 (1589): 291–94.

Teiwes, Frederick C., and Warren Sun. 1998. *China's Road to Disaster: Mao, Central Politicians, and Provincial Leaders in the Unfolding of the Great Leap Forward, 1955–1959.* New York: M. E. Sharpe.

Urban, George, ed. 1971. *The "Miracles" of Chairman Mao.* Los Angeles, CA: Nash Publishing.

Wade, Robert. 1990. *Governing the Market: Economic Theory and the Role of Government in East Asian Industrialization.* Princeton, NJ: Princeton University Press.

Walder, Andrew G. 1991. "Social Structure and Political Authority: China's Evolving Polity." In *Two Societies in Opposition: The Republic of China and the People's Republic of China After Forty Years* (pp. 358–59), ed. Ramon H. Myers. Stanford, CA: Hoover Institution Press, Stanford University.

Wandi, Jiang. 1998 (March 16). "Fostering Political Democracy from the Bottom Up." *Beijing Review* 41(11): 11–14.

Wang, T.Y. 2003 (Dec.). "China after the Sixteenth Party Congress: Prospects and Challenges." *Journal of Asian and African Studies* 38(4–5): 323–30.

Wasserstrom, Jeffrey N. and Elizabeth J. Perry, eds. 1992. *Popular Protest and Political Culture in Modern China: Learning From 1989.* Boulder, CO: Westview Press.

Watson, James. 1992. "The Renegotiation of Chinese Cultural Identity in the Post-Mao Era." *In Popular Protest and Political Culture in Modern China: Learning from 1989* (pp. 67–83), ed. Jeffrey N. Wasserstrom and Elizabeth J. Perry. Boulder, CO: Westview Press.

Watts, Jonathan. 2004 (April 17). "China and USA Row over Human Rights." *Lancet* 363(9417): 1287.

Wedeman, Andrew. 2001 (Winter). "Incompetence, Noise, and Fear in Central-Local Relations in China." *Studies in Comparative and International Development* 35(14): 59–88.

Wei-Ming, Tu. 1990. "The Confucian Tradition in Chinese History." *In Heritage of China* (pp. 112–37), ed. Paul S. Ropp. Berkeley, CA: University of California Press.

White, Gordon. 1987. "Riding the Tiger: Grassroots Rural Politics in the Wake of Chinese Economic Reforms." *In The Re-Emergence of the Chinese Peasantry,* ed. Ashwani Saith. London: Croom Helm.

White, Tyrene. 1998 (Sept.). "Village Elections: Democracy from the Bottom Up?" *Current History* 97(620): 263–68.

Winckler, Edwin A. 2002 (Sept.). "Chinese Reproductive Policy at the Turn of the Millennium: Dynamic Stability." *Population and Development Review* 28(3): 379–412.

Wo-Lap Lam, Willy. 1993. "Beijing in Bid to Overhaul Unions." *South China Morning Post International Weekly,* July 10–11, 1993, 7.

Wo-Lap Lam, Willy. 1994. *China After Deng Xiaoping: The Power Struggle in Beijing Since Tiananmen.* Hong Kong: P. A. Professional Consultants.

World Bank. 1992. *World Bank Report, 1992: Development and The Environment.* New York: Oxford University Press.

Yu-lin, Yu. 1991. "Change and Continuity in the CCP's Power Structure Since Its Thirteenth National Congress: A Line Approach." In *Two Societies in Opposition: The Republic of China and the People's Republic of China After Forty Years* (pp. 57–73), ed. Ramon H. Myers. Stanford, CA: Hoover Institution Press, Stanford University.

Zhibin, Gu. 1991. *China Beyond Deng: Reform in the PRC.* Jeffrey, NC: McFarland and Co.

Zhong, Yang. 2003. *Local Government and Politics in China: Challenges from Below.* Armonk, NY: M. E. Sharpe.

Zweig, David. 2002. *Democratic Values, Political Structures and Alternative Politics in Greater China.* Washington, DC: United States Institute of Peace.

PART IV

The Politics of Development

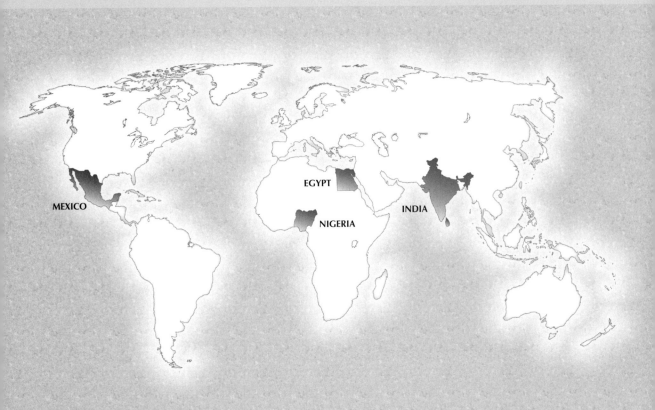

Aghanistan

China

Pakistan

New Delhi ■

Nepal

Bhutan

■ Kānpur

■ Ahmadābād

INDIA

Calcutta ■

Bangladesh

Burma

Bombay ■

■ Hyderābād

Bay of Bengal

Arabian Sea

Bangalore ■

■ Madras

Indian Ocean

Goa ⏤

Sri Lanka

Population:
1,065,070,607 (2004 estimate)

Life expectancy at birth:
64 years (total population)
63 years (men)
65 years (women)

Literacy:
59 percent of people age 15
and over can read and write
(2003 estimate)

Capital:
New Delhi

Per capita income:
$2,900 (2003)

9

India

Democracy in Turmoil

India is the world's largest democracy. With a population of more than 1 billion, its electorate is larger than that of the United States, Canada, Great Britain, France, Germany, Italy, and Japan, *combined*. The most remarkable aspect of India's democracy, however, is not its size but its very existence. Political scientists have long maintained that democracy requires a literate electorate and a substantial level of economic development (Lipset 1960). India, however, began its existence as an independent country without meeting either of these conditions. India's first task, said its first prime minister, would be "to free India through a new constitution, to feed the starving people, and to clothe the naked masses" (Shah 1988, 263). India has made tremendous strides in education and economic development in the six decades since it achieved its independence. Nevertheless, it remains among the poorest countries in the world.

For the most part, theories suggesting that democracy requires an educated and reasonably prosperous electorate would seem to be valid. Among the major countries of the third world, India alone has succeeded in maintaining a democratic political system throughout the course of its history as an independent country. While much of the third world is now moving toward greater democracy, India's democracy is beginning to show signs of strain. The most consistent themes in current analyses of Indian politics are "institutional decay" and the "crisis of governability" (Kohli 1990; Vanaik 1990; Rudolph and Rudolph 1987).

The special focus in this chapter will be on India's unique ability to maintain a democratic political system under social and economic conditions that have fostered dictatorship elsewhere.

The Taj Mahal stands in testimony to the artistic brilliance of pre-colonial India.

INDIA IN HISTORICAL AND RELIGIOUS PERSPECTIVE

The richness of India's early history defies easy summary. By the advent of British rule in 1818, the Indian subcontinent, an area that includes the current countries of India, Pakistan, Bangladesh, Burma, Nepal, and Tibet, had witnessed the rise and fall of some 100 major dynasties (Mansingh 1986). The last of the great empires, the Mughal Empire, began in the early 1500s and lasted, at least in name, until the mid-1800s. By that time, however, the Indian subcontinent had long since fragmented into a mosaic of princely mini-states, some 562 of which were allowed to retain quasi-independent status within the context of British rule. Not only did the fragmentation of India make it easier to rule, but the British found the principalities to be "a pleasant backwater of feudalism and flattery, of pomp and circumstance" (Mansingh 1986, 43).

Two legacies of India's early history are of particular importance to the study of modern India. The first was the emergence of a distinctively Indian culture that found Indians having more in common with each other than they did with their neighbors. The second was the adoption of the Hindu religion by approximately 80 percent of the Indian population.

Hinduism

The major religions of the West teach that the souls of the righteous will reside in heaven. Hindus also believe that the souls of the righteous will reside in heaven, but their version of heaven is substantially different from that depicted in the Torah, Bible, or Koran. For Hindus, heaven is a cosmic soul that embodies the true harmony of the universe. Eternal peace for the human soul can be achieved only by *uniting with the cosmic soul,* a process referred to as attaining **nirvana.** The goal of salvation is not to remain an individual soul but to become part of a greater soul.

Attainment of nirvana demands such an exceptional level of purity and religious knowledge that it can be achieved only after a prolonged cycle of birth and rebirth in different life forms. Believing that the reincarnation of the soul often occurs in animal form, many Hindus refrain from eating meat. Cows maintain a special status in the Hindu religion, symbolizing motherhood, fruitfulness, and exceptional purity. To injure a cow is to commit a major transgression against Hindu beliefs (Fuller 1992).

Souls reborn in human form enter one of five levels, depending upon their record of knowledge and purity: the **Brahman,** or *priestly caste;* the **Kshatriya,** or *warrior caste;* the **Vaishya,** or *trader caste;* the **Sudra,** or *artisan caste;* and the **untouchables,** *individuals who lack standing in one of the four castes.* Untouchables are expected to clean sewers and execute other "impure" tasks, thereby allowing members of the four castes to maintain their ritual purity (Deliege 1999).

The four castes are further broken down into *more than 2,000 sub-castes,* or **jati,** the members of which share a common occupation and station in life. It is now possible for individuals to escape from the social and economic limits of their caste and jati, but most do not (Nyrop 1986).

According to Hindu doctrine, each soul possesses **karma,** *the predisposition for good or evil.* Karma is a particularly difficult concept to pin down, being described as everything from a cosmic force to luck or destiny (Benderly 1986). Wise individuals use their karma to increase their purity and their cosmic knowledge.

Hinduism contains an incredibly rich pantheon of gods and goddesses, the role of which is to inspire individuals to strive toward ever-greater purity and cosmic knowledge (Fuller 1992). Of these, the three dominant gods are **Brahma,** the *god of creation;* **Vishnu,** the *god of preservation;* and **Shiva,** the *god of destruction.* These gods are joined by innumerable lesser gods and goddesses, the nature of which varies from region to region. The holy books of Hinduism describe the deeds of the major deities as a means of providing guidance in the attainment of nirvana.

Because Hindu gods and goddesses are viewed as "guides to knowledge" rather than as the central force in the universe, Hinduism has been able to incorporate a far greater range of religious beliefs than monotheistic religions such as Islam, Christianity, and Judaism (Benderly 1986; Bayly 1999).

Hinduism, as the above discussion suggests, is far more than a religious system. It is also a social system, a political system, and an economic system.

- As *a social system,* Hinduism divides societies into specific classes and assigns a prescribed role to each class.
- As *a political system,* Hinduism specifies which classes are to rule and which are to serve.
- As an *economic system,* Hinduism establishes a highly complex division of labor and provides a religious justification for the unequal distribution of wealth.

For all of its venerable traditions, many scholars now view Hinduism as an obstacle to India's modernization. The problems are twofold. *First, the caste system perpetuates inequality between individuals and groups. As* such, it conflicts with modern notions of democracy and human rights. *Second, the caste system restricts the types of economic activity in which groups can engage.* In so doing, it restricts mobility between groups and forces individuals to pursue the same occupation as their parents. For traditional Hindus, economic activity is not a matter of merit and energy, but of birth.

In India, as in all societies, some people are more religious than others. The caste system has been eroded by some six decades of secular rule dedicated to economic equality and social justice. Many untouchables have also converted to Buddhism and Christianity, religions that advocate equality. Nevertheless, Hinduism remains a strong component of India's political culture.

The Religious Minorities

Islam, India's second religion, was discussed at some length in Chapter 1, and requires little elaboration at this point. Suffice it to say that Islam shares much in common with Christianity and Judaism. According to Islam, the fate of humanity is determined by a single, all-powerful God, and there is no concept of reincarnation. A particularly interesting aspect of Islam is the belief that pigs are impure, if not a manifestation of the devil.

Islam and Hinduism, then, represent opposing religious systems with little scope for compromise (Varshney 2002). In times of communal passions, the cow and the pig have become highly charged political symbols; Muslims have taunted their adversaries by killing cows, while Hindus have thrown pigs into mosques (Muslim houses of worship).

Muslims represent only 12 percent of the Indian population (see Table 9.1), but that percentage translates into 128 million citizens, most of whom are concentrated in India's northern states. The geographical concentration of India's Muslims increases their political influence and has led to persistent demands for greater regional autonomy. Besides Hinduism and Islam, India also contains sizeable Christian, Sikh, and Buddhist communities.

In addition to its diverse religions and castes, India is further fragmented into hundreds of linguistic groups, fifteen of which have been recognized as official languages. Not only is India divided into a vast mosaic of religions, castes, and ethnic and regional groups, then, but each tends to speak its own language.

Table 9.1 The Religions of India

Religious Affiliation	Percent	Millions
Hindu	81.3	865.9
Muslim	12.0	127.8
Christian	2.3	24.5
Sikh	1.9	20.2
Other	2.5	26.6

SOURCE: *The CIA Factbook,* 2000.

British India

The **British East India Company,** *a private British corporation, established trading posts in India during the early 1600s.* Over the course of the next 250 years, it would transform the Indian subcontinent into a private colony (Judd 2004). Huge fortunes were made in India, most of which found their way back to England. In the view of some historians, it was the wealth of India that financed Britain's industrial revolution (Thompson 1980).

As the British East India Company expanded, it became inevitable that the British government would be drawn into the governance of the subcontinent. In part, government involvement was triggered by Company demands for financial assistance in ruling a geographic area several times larger than the British Isles.

The involvement of the British government in Indian affairs was also precipitated by a public outcry over the Company's inhuman exploitation of the Indian population. The Company's goal was to make money, and it pursued that goal with ruthless efficiency.

Far greater than its concern for the Indian masses was the British public's outrage over the "heathen" practices of the Indian population. Of these, none was more offensive to the British population than the practice of **sati,** or *wife-burning at funeral ceremonies.* Given the logic of the day, the wife's spirit was sent to join that of her departed husband (Hardgrave and Kochanek 1993). Vivid portrayals of this and other alien customs were provided to the British public by returning missionaries, who, unswerving in their belief in the superiority of the Christian faith, demanded that the British Government join their struggle against the devil.

Public revulsion against the greed of Company directors and the heathenism of the Indian population led to the India Act of 1784, a law that imposed a British-style legal system on those areas of the subcontinent controlled by the Company. It also called for the creation of an Indian Civil Service based upon merit examinations. A tradition was thus established in which the best and brightest of the British middle class would pursue a career in the Indian Civil Service (ICS). In so doing, they would attain a lifestyle of power and splendor normally reserved only for royalty (Collins and Lapierre 1975).

The transition from Company rule to colonialism was triggered by the Sepoy Rebellion of 1887, a rebellion ignited by rumors that newly introduced British artillery shells had been sealed with a mixture of cow and pig fat (Mansingh 1986). Sepoys were native soldiers employed by the British East India Company. The underlying causes of the Sepoy Rebellion, of course, were far more complex. The Indian population had been increasingly impoverished by the exploitive practices of the British East India Company, and Government reforms had only confused an unstable situation by undermining the authority of local rulers. Anti-British sentiments were also fueled by the clash of Christian and Hindu cultures and the overzealous activities of Christian missionaries (Mansingh 1986). Whatever the case, the rebellion of the Sepoys was crushed by British forces, and India became the crown jewel of the British Empire. Three-fifths of the subcontinent was placed under direct British rule, while the remainder was ruled indirectly through some 562 princes and maharajahs. British rule would remain in effect until 1947.

Colonialism and Its Consequences

The advent of direct colonialism accelerated a process of social change that had begun with Company rule. Some of these changes made a positive contribution to India's emergence as a modern country. Others would condemn the new nation to decades of conflict and poverty.

On the negative side, the Indian economy was restructured to meet the economic needs of England (Tomlinson 1992). India provided Britain with raw materials, and Britain used India as a protected market for its manufactured products. British industries flourished while India's industrial development was stunted. The colonies were designed to serve Britain, not to compete with its industries (Mansingh 1986).

Colonial rule also unleashed a Pandora's box of social problems that continue to plague Indian society today. Foremost among these problems was an explosion of the Indian population. Traditionally, a large family was vital to survival in India, providing hands for the field, power within the local community, and security in old age. Indian culture, accordingly, glorified large families. A woman's status depended upon her ability to bear children, particularly male children. The "real" man was a man who could produce a large family. The cultural emphasis on childbearing was made all the more urgent by the fact that disease killed most babies before they reached adulthood. Colonialism revolutionized Indian health practices by introducing modern medicine and sanitation procedures, but it did not alter the cultural emphasis on large families. People lived longer, but they also continued to have large families. The result was a population explosion that continues today.

British rule also disrupted traditional social and cultural patterns by imposing British law upon a society that had little in common with British traditions. This was particularly the case in regard to land ownership and inheritance. Land and property in India were often owned collectively by an extended family or clan. British commercial law, by contrast, stressed individual ownership based upon written deeds. Efforts to force the British tenure system upon India, as a British official of the era would admit, were catastrophic:

> Our rigid and revolutionary methods of exacting land revenue have reduced the peasantry to the lowest extreme of poverty and wretchedness, and the procedures of our settlement courts have been the means of laying upon

them burdens heavier than any they endured in former times (Mansingh 1986, 38).

As a result of the population explosion and the disruption of established agricultural practices, famine became commonplace. India could not produce enough food to support its rapidly expanding population.

While some Indians embraced British values, many more clung to their traditional ways. A large segment of the Indian population, however, found themselves torn between the two extremes. The security of traditional ways was collapsing, yet the laws and customs of the British were difficult to grasp. In many instances, they seemed profoundly inappropriate. In sociological terms, a large segment of Indian society, particularly in urban areas, was becoming **marginalized,** *its members belonging neither to the old world nor to the new.* Caught in the conflict between two cultures, their primary goal became one of survival. India today remains very much a **transitional society,** *a society in which a large segment of the population is struggling to find security among the conflicting demands of tradition and modernity* (Naipaul 1990).

Colonialism, for all of its exploitive characteristics, also gave much to India. British colonialism strengthened the unity of India by providing the subcontinent with *a powerful cadre of administrators,* the Indian Civil Service (ICS). It also provided India with an *infrastructure of roads, railroads, currency, and communications* far superior to that found in most of the third world. Perhaps more importantly, India was provided with *a language that would transcend the linguistic boundaries that isolated its diverse groups.* That language was English.

The colonial experience was also to provide India with a *Westernized political elite.* Acknowledging that India was too vast to be ruled by the British alone, the British East India Company soon determined "to form a class who may be interpreters between us and the millions whom we govern; a class of persons, Indian in blood and color, but English in taste, in opinions, in morals, and in intellect" (Mansingh 1986, 40). Over time, the members of this Westernized political elite began to guide India's struggle for independence.

Finally, the colonial era provided India with *almost fifty years of democratic experience.* Popular elections, however limited in scope, introduced the Indian population to the principles of democracy and facilitated the development of modern political organizations. Of these, the most prominent were the Congress Party and the Muslim League.

The **Congress Party** began in 1885 as a regular gathering of Westernized intellectuals from various parts of the Indian subcontinent. Over the course of the next four decades, the Congress Party evolved from a loose debating society concerned with securing greater Indian representation on provincial councils into a highly sophisticated political organization capable of mobilizing mass opposition to British rule throughout the subcontinent. The Congress Party, however, was to become far more than a mere political party. It was to become India's independence movement: its symbol of hope, democracy, and development (Sisson and Wolpert 1988). Indeed, the Congress Party would be the subcontinent's only "all-India" political organization.

A nineteenth-century painting from Punjab depicts a European leaning to shoot a tiger that is clawing an elephant.

The rise of the **Muslim League** paralleled that of the Congress Party, albeit in predominantly Muslim areas of the continent. The Muslim League, like the Congress Party, consisted largely of Westernized intellectuals from upper class backgrounds. Both organizations pressed for self-government and occasionally cooperated for the achievement of that end. Each increase in self-government, unfortunately, sparked growing conflict between the two communities. The Muslims, then some 25 percent of the population, feared domination by the Hindu majority (Gilmartin 1998). By the dawn of independence, communal conflicts had become so intense that civil war could be averted only by dividing the subcontinent into two independent states, India and Pakistan. Even with the partitioning of the subcontinent, millions of Muslim and Hindu refugees would die in the desperate struggle to reach safe borders. In spite of the creation of Pakistan as an independent Muslim state, many Muslims chose to remain in India. For them, as for the Hindus, India was their home and the home of their ancestors.

How then, does one evaluate India's colonial experience? Was India helped or hindered by its colonial heritage? The answer depends upon one's point of view. The British emphasize colonialism's legacy of democracy, national unity, and infrastructure development. Many Indians, by contrast, believe that colonialism locked them in a cycle of poverty and economic dependence from which they have yet to escape. They also blame today's ethnic and religious tensions on a colonial strategy that stressed the principle of "divide and rule." Britain did not create India's ethnic tensions, but its colonial policy clearly exacerbated them. Whatever one's point of view, today's India is very much a product of its colonial past.

Forging the Indian State

Of India's Westernized elite, two individuals would leave an indelible stamp on India and on the world as a whole. These individuals were Mahatma Gandhi and Jawaharlal Nehru.

Mahatma Gandhi. Mahatma Mohandas Karamchand Gandhi was born into a devoutly Hindu family in 1869, shortly after India's emergence as a British colony. His Hindu upbringing would be tempered by the study of law in Britain and South Africa and by an insatiable interest in philosophical currents as diverse as Christianity on one hand and Thoreau and Tolstoy on the other (Mansingh 1986). In many ways, Gandhi embodied the intellectual turmoil of an Indian population torn between the spiritual superiority of India's past and the material superiority of the West. The challenge for Gandhi, as for India itself, was to use Western advances in the areas of health and education to build a new India that embraced the best of both worlds, the traditional and the modern. The first step in meeting that challenge, in Gandhi's view, was to end the exploitive colonial system that was destroying the inherent goodness of traditional India.

Gandhi returned to India in 1915, having spent more than twenty years in South Africa. He assumed the leadership of the Congress Party shortly thereafter, setting himself the herculean task of liberating India from British rule while simultaneously improving the health and welfare of the Indian population. While much attention has been devoted to Gandhi's hunger strikes, far less mention is made of his tireless campaigns to introduce sanitary health practices to rural India, campaigns that often found Gandhi and his entourage lugging a portable toilet from village to village in order to teach rural villagers the principles of modern sanitation (Collins and Lapierre 1975).

The four pillars of Gandhi's political philosophy were *tolerance, human dignity, self-reliance, and nonviolence.* Colonialism, in his view, was inherently wrong, but so was the plight of the untouchables or "scheduled" classes. Hoping to spare India the devastation of class warfare, he called upon the rich to give generously of their wealth and the poor to be moderate in their demands.

Gandhi preached that human violence could be attributed to seven causes (*Christian Science Monitor,* Feb. 1, 1995, "Interview with Arun Gandhi," 14):

1. Wealth without work
2. Pleasure without conscience
3. Knowledge without character
4. Commerce without morality
5. Science without humanity
6. Worship without sacrifice
7. Politics without principles

Gandhi's political strategy, in turn, focused on three fundamental points: *transforming the Congress Party from a debating society into a mass-based political organization, teaching the masses to oppose colonialism by nonviolent means, and using himself as a model of sacrifice and self-denial.* Gandhi's policies of nonviolence were a combination of passive resistance, protests, boycotts, noncooperation, and tax avoidance, depending upon the needs of the moment. When the British increased the tax on salt, for example, Gandhi called for a boycott on salt purchases and taught his followers how to extract salt from sea water. Gandhi's moral appeals were reinforced by a policy of self-denial that often found him wearing little more than a loincloth and going on hunger strikes that riveted the world's attention on the plight of Indian masses and their struggle for independence (Fischer 1954).

As Gandhi's program took root, Gandhi himself acquired almost saintly stature among the Indian masses. The name *Mahatma,* literally translated, means "Great Soul." The British government, as might be expected, cared little for Gandhi and his tactics. Winston Churchill referred to him as "a half-naked fakir" (Tully and Mansani 1988).

Some flavor of Gandhi's campaign of noncooperation is provided by Louis Fischer's description of Gandhi's "spinning wheel" campaign, a campaign directed against the purchase of British-made clothes. Indians, Gandhi preached, should become self-reliant by spinning their own clothes, however crude they might appear. The spinning wheel would subsequently become the symbol of Gandhi's movement.

> Gandhi's long propaganda journey for noncooperation. . . had all the attributes of religious revivalism. He told audiences they must not wear foreign clothing, and when they applauded he asked them to strip off all wearing apparel made abroad and pile it in front of him. To this heap of shirts, trousers, coats, caps, shoes, and underwear Gandhi then set a match, and as the flames ate their way through the imported goods, he begged everybody to spin and weave their own clothing.
>
> During those strenuous seven months of travel all of his meals, three a day, were the same and consisted of sixteen ounces of goat's milk, three slices of toast, two oranges, and a score of grapes or raisins (Fischer 1954, 69).

Jawaharlal Nehru. Jawaharlal Nehru, the son of a prominent Congress Party leader, was born in 1889 into the Brahman or aristocratic caste. Educated in the finest of British schools, he was assured a successful career in law or business. Nehru, however, chose to become a disciple of Gandhi, embracing his views on equality and nonviolence. He was also deeply influenced by the social views of the British **Fabians,** *a group of British intellectuals who advocated democratic socialism as the means of achieving a just and democratic society.* Human misery, in the Fabian view, was the result of tyranny and economic inequality. A democratic political system was the remedy for tyranny and a socialist economic system the antidote to inequality.

Although he was devoted to Gandhi, Nehru's vision of a modern India was to diverge markedly from that of his mentor. Gandhi advocated a fusion of traditionalism and modernity, glorifying the Indian village as the model of social harmony. Nehru, while retaining the essence of Gandhi's message of tolerance and nonviolence, visualized a modern, industrialized, and totally secular India. The India of the past, in Nehru's view, had little choice but to give way to the India of the future.

Nehru worked tirelessly for independence, his exceptional oratorical skills and his vision of a prosperous and modern India transforming him into a charismatic figure whose popularity would eventually rival that of Gandhi himself. If Gandhi was the spiritual force of the independence movement, Nehru would become its symbol of hope.

In spite of their differing visions of India's future, the personal bond between the two men remained unshakable (Fischer 1954). As independence approached, Gandhi urged the Congress Party to name Nehru as his successor. It was Nehru who would head the new nation. Gandhi, tragically, was assassinated by a Hindu fanatic in 1948 during the communal strife that accompanied the partition of the subcontinent into Hindu and Muslim countries (Tully and Masani 1988). In the view of many, it was the horror of Gandhi's death that quelled the will to violence. In death, he had performed one last service for his country (Tully and Masani 1988).

Nehru assumed the leadership of India with a vision of democracy, mild socialism, secularism, equality, and neutrality in international politics (Tharoor 2003). Universal suffrage was proclaimed, expanding the Indian electorate from some 14.2 percent of the population to all adult citizens (Tully and Mansani 1988). The free-market economic policies of the colonial period were overlaid by socialist economic planning. While some capitalism remained, government policy dictated a path toward self-reliant industrial development. *Locally produced goods were to replace foreign imports, even if the quality of local goods proved to be inferior.* The important thing was for India to develop its own industrial base and its own core of technical expertise. This policy is referred to as **import substitution.**

India's new Constitution proclaimed India to be a secular country. Discrimination on the basis of caste or religion was banned, and a quota system was introduced to assure that the untouchables and other "scheduled" or disadvantaged classes received fair access to educational and employment opportunities (Shah 1988). At the international level, Nehru proclaimed that India would follow a

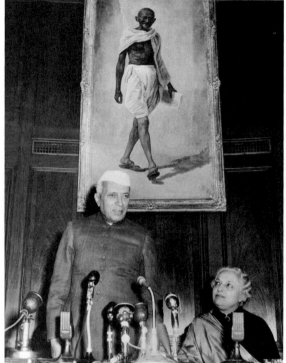

Jawaharlal Nehru's vision of India's future differed from that of
Mahatma Gandhi (shown in painting behind Nehru), but Nehru shared
Gandhi's belief in the value of tolerance and nonviolence.

policy of nonalignment, preaching nonviolence at the international level much as
Gandhi had preached nonviolence to the Indian masses.

Nehru's policies were the policies of India's Westernized elite, but they did
not necessarily reflect the views of the masses (Embree 1990). The majority of
India's population remained locked in the isolation of their rural villages,
poverty-stricken and illiterate. Traditional ways were the only ways that
they knew. The situation was little better in the sprawling slums of urban India
(Mamoria and Doshi 1966).

The masses accepted Nehru's policies more out of faith than understanding.
The Congress Party had liberated India from British rule, and its leaders were
not to be doubted. The rhetoric of the independence struggle, moreover, had
painted a glowing picture of an independent India that offered prosperity to
all. It was a time of great optimism. Finally, Nehru's policies were accepted for
the same reason that government policies had always been accepted: docility
and passivity. As later events would indicate, however, acceptance did not mean
commitment.

Despite Nehru's personal popularity, opposition to his policies came from all fronts. Many Westernized intellectuals doubted the wisdom of allowing illiterate peasants to vote. In the words of Nehru's cousin, B. K. Nehru:

> And now 100 percent of the adult population has suddenly got the vote. The consequence is that the representatives they send to parliament or the state legislatures have no idea of how the British constitution, which we regard as the model for our behavior, functions, or what the rule of law involves, or what the position of the permanent civil services is in a modern state. . . . That being lacking, the institutions themselves get eroded (Tully and Mansani 1988, 24).

Religious and regional tensions also remained intense, with mass protests forcing Nehru to redraw the boundaries of India's states to reflect the linguistic and religious backgrounds of their inhabitants. Nehru's hopes of making Hindi the unifying language of the Indian state were also to fade. Hindi was the language of the northern elite, and its dominance was resented by inhabitants of India's other regions. While Hindi retained its premier position, 14 additional languages also received sanction as official languages (Brass 1992). English continues to be India's "common" language, although it is spoken mostly by the educated classes.

Nehru was also to experience reverses in the economic sphere. Socialism proved to be a disappointment as economic development got bogged down in bureaucratic red tape and failed to keep pace with mass expectations. As a result, the optimism of the independence era began to give way to disillusionment, eroding popular support for the Congress Party and its programs. Within a decade of independence, the Communist Party would win sweeping victories in Kerala, a key industrial state, while regional parties were increasing their strength throughout the country.

Particularly disappointing to Nehru were his failures in the international arena. Nehru had hoped to transform the "nonaligned" movement of newly independent countries into a "moral force" that would ease cold war tensions and bring the superpowers to their senses (Gordon 1992). The nonaligned movement was a coalition of third world states that met periodically to discuss common strategy in dealing with the United States and the Soviet Union. They pledged to avoid joining alliances with either nation. Nehru also hoped that the nonaligned movement would become a strong moral force in world politics. This, however, was not to be. War flared with Pakistan, and the situation along India's poorly demarcated border with China became increasingly tense. Nehru had hoped that the border disputes between the two countries could be resolved within the framework of the nonaligned movement, but this was not to be. War erupted in 1962, and the Indian military suffered a humiliating defeat at the hands of the Chinese.

Nehru suffered a stroke in 1964, passing away a few months thereafter. His close associates believed that his spirit had been broken by the war with China, a war that had shattered his belief in the capacity of the third world to resolve its own problems in a peaceful and cooperative manner (Tully and Mansani 1988).

Indira Gandhi sits beneath a portrait of her father, Jawaharlal Nehru, about three years after his death.

Indira Gandhi. Worried by the steady erosion of its popular support following Nehru's death, the inner core of the Congress Party, the "Syndicate," sought a candidate who would be both popular and pliable. There was only one logical choice who met both criteria: Nehru's daughter, Indira Gandhi. Indira Gandhi was not related to Mahatma Gandhi but had taken her husband's last name. Gandhi is a common name in India.

The Syndicate had accurately assessed Gandhi's popularity. The Congress Party won the ensuing election (1967), and Indira Gandhi was sworn in as India's third prime minister. The Syndicate, however, had grossly misjudged Indira's pliability. She kept her own counsel and largely excluded the Syndicate from the decision-making process.

By 1969, tensions between Indira Gandhi and the Syndicate had reached the breaking point. The Syndicate stripped Gandhi of the party leadership and called upon the Parliamentary Congress Party (the Congress Party's Members of Parliament) to elect a new prime minister. They refused to do so, thereby splitting the Party into two factions: the Congress (R) and the Congress (O). The situation remained ambivalent until the 1971 general elections, in which Gandhi's Congress (R) scored a resounding victory. The Congress (R), for all intents and purposes, was the Congress Party.

The 1971 elections placed Indira Gandhi firmly in control of both the Congress Party and the Parliament, the masses having reaffirmed the magic of the Nehru legacy. Her personal popularity further increased with the crushing defeat of Pakistan in the third Indo-Pakistan war. Gandhi seized the moment to place her close supporters in key positions, not the least of which was the position of Chief Justice of the Supreme Court.

The more powerful Indira Gandhi became, however, the more her problems seemed to mount. The thrill of independence had worn off, and inflated hopes of sudden prosperity had been dulled by a stagnating economy. Rampant corruption in high places fostered mass cynicism and tarnished the image of the Congress Party. Even nature seemed to turn against Indira as droughts caused mass famine. In mid-1973, the army was called in to crush food riots.

Gandhi's problems were also of her own making. Nehru had used the Congress as a sounding board for diverse opinions. Things got worked out and tensions were kept in check. Gandhi, by contrast, ruled the Congress (R) with an iron hand, alienating key figures in the Party's state and local organizations (Manor 1992). Equally disconcerting was the growing political influence of Sanjay Gandhi, Indira Gandhi's youngest son and heir apparent to his mother's power. Many observers believed that it was Sanjay, not Indira, who was ruling the country. Whether or not this was the case, Sanjay and his "friends" were at the core of the mounting corruption scandals. Some flavor of the situation is provided by the following conversation between Indira Gandhi and Romesh Thapar, one of her close friends and supporters.

> I began a series of collisions with Mrs. Gandhi over all this corruption. She used to get very indignant and say: "You know that I don't do anything like this, and it's absurd." I said: "Well, if you're not prepared to accept what people are feeling, then we'll call it a day." "No, no," she said, "I'm not saying that. I'm just saying that you must discipline yourself and think of all the problems I have to face." So I said: "Well, I'm just telling you that people think you're corrupt." She said: "I am not." I said: "They say you're the queen bee that sends them out to make the collection." She was very upset, and so we started meeting less frequently (Tully and Mansani 1988, 117).

The crisis came to a head in June 1975, when an Indian court convicted Indira Gandhi of minor election fraud and ruled that she was to be replaced as prime minister. Gandhi denounced the court decision as a conspiracy against Indian democracy and invoked the "emergency powers" of the Constitution. The elections were postponed, and the press was placed under strict censorship. More than 100,000 opposition leaders were also "detained" by the police.

Presumably under Sanjay's influence, Gandhi also used her emergency powers to introduce sweeping social reforms including slum clearance, reforestation, the abolition of dowries, literacy programs, and mass sterilization (Seekins 1986). In many ways, the reforms were precisely what the stagnating country required to regain its momentum. India was being denuded of its forests, dowry conflicts fueled bride-burning, slums perpetuated subhuman living conditions, illiteracy depressed development, and overpopulation precluded India from breaking its cycle of poverty and despair.

However appropriate Sanjay's reforms may have been in theory, the result was chaos. Traditional Hindus (and other sects) resented the abolition of dowries, slum dwellers were evicted from their hovels merely to become homeless, and sterilization programs were directed largely at untouchables and Muslims. The clash between Nehru's vision of secular modernity and the reality of traditional values had become the cutting edge of Indian politics. Rumors that Gandhi would soon assume dictatorial powers swept the country.

Just as hope for democracy faded, Gandhi declared the emergency to be at an end. Among other things, she was upset by Western portrayals of herself as a dictator and the corresponding implication that India had ceased to be a democracy. The emergency powers, in her view, had been invoked to save Indian democracy, not destroy it. She also believed that she was far more popular than was actually the case and that her decision to impose emergency rule would be vindicated by the electorate. The illusion of popularity was propagated by advisors anxious to curry favor and could not be contradicted in the press because of the emergency decrees. Whatever the case, elections were scheduled for March 1977. Indira Gandhi and the Congress (R) were defeated.

For the next two years, India was ruled by a fractious coalition Government headed by Morarji Desai of the Janata Party. It was the first non-Congress Government in India's history. The transition from the Congress to the Janata was carried out in the best of democratic traditions.

The Desai coalition was a patchwork of diverse parties and individuals unified solely by their opposition to Gandhi's rule. Lacking common political values and wracked by personality conflicts, the Desai coalition collapsed of its own weight in 1979, and new elections were scheduled for June of the following year.

Indira Gandhi, in the meantime, had been rebuilding the shattered Congress (R), now rechristened the Congress (I) or Congress Indira. The Congress (I) swept to victory in 1980, returning Indira Gandhi to the prime ministership. Sanjay, his influence now dominant, waited in the wings (Manor 1992). A Sanjay reign, however, was not to be. He was killed in an airplane accident later the same year, and Rajiv, his elder brother, reluctantly became the heir apparent of the Nehru dynasty.

The next four years would see Indira Gandhi face a crisis of center-periphery relations as religious, regional, and linguistic minorities throughout India pressed for greater autonomy from the central government (Manor 1992). Particularly knotty were Sikh demands for a "Sikh Autonomous Region" loosely attached to the Indian state. The central government, if the Sikhs had their way, would retain responsibility for defense, currency, communications, and foreign affairs, but little more (Seekins 1986).

When Gandhi refused, extremist elements within the Sikh community launched a campaign of terror against the regime, killing government officials and destroying government facilities. The government responded with overwhelming military force, forcing the extremists, now fearing annihilation, to take shelter in the Golden Temple, the holiest shrine in the Sikh religion.

The situation had become critical. To violate the sanctity of a holy shrine would risk inflaming political tensions among India's religiously sensitive population. Capitulation to Sikh demands for a Sikh Autonomous Region, however, would invariably provoke similar demands among other communal groups. The crisis came to a head in 1984 when the army assaulted the temple with force, perhaps excessive force, causing hundreds of casualties and severely damaging the Golden Temple (Dua 1992). Indira Gandhi was assassinated by her Sikh bodyguards in November of the same year.

Rajiv Gandhi. Rajiv Gandhi assumed the leadership of the Indian government following the assassination of his mother, and he led the Congress (I) to a sweeping victory in the national elections held later that year. His margin of victory was the largest in Indian history, possibly reflecting a large sympathy vote resulting from the assassination of his mother. Be this as it may, the campaign was also the most expensive in Indian history (Noorani 1990).

Rajiv Gandhi seemed to be the right person at the right time. He was more a technocrat than a politician, and his reputation for honesty restored popular confidence in the government. He was also far more flexible than his mother and used his persuasive powers to rebuild the party organization at the state and local levels (Seekins 1986).

Rajiv Gandhi's rule was marked by a turn toward increased capitalism as taxes were reduced and the door was opened to limited foreign investment. The economy flourished, as did the Indian business class, raising hopes that India would soon "take off" on the path to rapid economic growth.

All, however, was not well. Gandhi's reforms were timid, leaving control over most areas of the economy in the hands of the bureaucracy. The upsurge in private-sector investment, while benefitting the business community, broadened the gap between rich and poor and triggered an inflationary spiral that crippled the lifestyle of India's salaried middle class. Regional and religious tensions also mounted as extremist groups of all varieties tested the resolve of the Government.

Faced with the need for decisive leadership, Gandhi proved indecisive (*Economist,* "A Survey of India," 1991 and 1995). His image of honesty had also been scarred by the blatant corruption of his close supporters (Noorani 1990). Rajiv Gandhi and the Congress were voted out of office in 1989 and two years later, Rajiv would fall to an assassin's bullet.

Perhaps in reaction to the assassination, the Congress was returned to power in 1991, but was again defeated in 1996 with the Congress Party receiving the lowest percentage of the popular vote in its illustrious history. Power passed to the hands of the pro-Hindu Bharatiya Janata Party, but the BJP was unable to secure a majority in the lower house of Parliament and resigned after 13 days.

Power then passed to the leftist-oriented United Front, a coalition of some 13 parties. The reign of the United Front lasted less than two years and saw the Indian political system thrown into even greater confusion as no Government could hold the unwieldy coalition together for more than a few months. The return of the BJP, following the 1998 general elections, represented India's fourth Government in 22 months (*International Herald Tribune,* Mar. 30, 1998, 4). The return of the BJP in 1998 did not offer much greater hope for stability. With only 178, or

33 percent, of the 540 seats in the Lok Sabha, the lower or popular house of the Indian parliament, the BJP could rule only by piecing together an 18-party coalition, fragile stuff indeed (Kohli 1998). Even then, it lacked a clear majority in the Lok Sabha (*Economist,* May 2, 1998, 39). A new round of national elections took place in the fall of 1999, with the BJP and its allies receiving a clear majority. The Congress Party had suffered its third successive loss (*Times of India,* Oct. 11, 1999, www).

The BJP downplayed its religious agenda and set itself the task of unshackling the Indian economy from the suffocating regulation of the bureaucracy . The BJP, its leaders proclaimed, was an "all India party," and it openly courted the Muslim vote (*Hindustan Times,* March 22, 2004, www) The BJP's strong tilt toward capitalism was rewarded with a surge of economic growth that had global financial institutions applauding, albeit with admonitions that much remained to be done. A rush of optimism seized middle-class India that prime Prime Minister Atal Behari Vajpayee promptly dubbed "the feel-good factor." Indeed, Vajpayee was so impressed with the feel-good factor, that he advanced the date of India's elections by several months in order to capitalize on his peaking popularity before the mood changed. "India Shining" became the BJP's banner. With luck, the BJP could capture an outright majority. The issue was not whether the BJP would win, but by how much. Adding to the feel-good effect was the endorsement of a dazzling parade of Bollywood stars, all singing the praises of Vajpayee and the BJP. Bollywood is the popular name for India's Hollywood like cinema complex in Bombay.

The Congress, led by Sonia Gandhi, the Italian widow of Rajiv Gandhi, was largely written off. The Congress and its allies had captured only 22 seats in the 1999 elections, and seemed doomed to the same fate in 2004. India was shining. The Congress was not.

As in the past, the 2004 elections were conducted in four stages over the course of one month to assure maximum security for the voting process. This was not an easy task for a country with 660 million registered voters, many living in states wracked by religious, ethnic, caste, political, and criminal violence. Violence occurred, but India's voters were not deterred. Some 400,000 police and military troops were deployed to protect 400 million voters, candidates, and polling personnel. As the headline of the *Times of India* declared, "Ballot power triumphs over bullet power" (*Times of India,* April 24, 2004, www).

The elections were generally fair, although re-polling was required in hundreds of polling places. Voter turnout was higher, on average, than the typical voter turnout in the United States. The BJP lost, and the Congress and its allies won. It was not an overwhelming victory, but the Congress and its allies carried the day with about 40 percent of the vote. The Congress, as the leading party of the alliance, was asked to name India's next prime minister.

Sonia Gandhi had led Congress to victory and was selected by the party and its 19 allies to be India's next prime minister. She declined the offer, but continued to serve as president of the Congress Party and chairperson of the Congress Parliamentary Party, a group consisting of the party's members of parliament.

After prolonged negotiations within the Congress Party and consultations with the party's coalition partners, Manmohan Singh, a Sikh and former minister of finance credited with initiating India's capitalist reforms, was selected as prime minister. An unpopular choice for prime minister would have made a coalition Government impossible. Singh was duly appointed to the post by India's largely symbolic president.

Why did the BJP suffer such a humiliating loss? Almost every pundit had a different explanation. Many focused on the fact that not all of India was "shining." The urban middle class and the educationally advantaged were feeling good, but the poor were not. The feel-good factor had not reached the approximately one-third of India's population that lives below the poverty line on the equivalent of $1 per day. Indeed, India had become a prime example of a dual society. One modern and prosperous, the other tradition-bound and locked in poverty.

Added to the BJP's problems was a profound distrust of its fundamentalist religious ideology. Indeed, the Congress and its allies had billed the campaign as a struggle between religious fundamentalism and India's secular tradition. Muslims were particularly reluctant to see a party dedicated to Hindu extremism entrench itself in power for years to come, as were many of India's disadvantaged classes and castes. The BJP would subsequently add to Muslim hostility by suggesting that the Muslim population was growing too rapidly (*Hindustan Times,* Sept. 7, 2004, www).

The leader of the BJP, for his part, accused the party of being complacent (*Hindustan Times,* June 1, 2004, www). They too had read the press reports assuring victory and declaring the Congress Party dead.

Other factors also contributed to the BJP's defeat. Sonia Gandhi, aided by a new generation of Gandhis, revived the Nehru charisma. The BJP's coalition partners also dragged their feet. Perhaps they were afraid that a crushing victory by the BJP would leave them out in the cold. With a strong BJP, there would be little need for coalition partners. Local power brokers, too, had found negotiations with the BJP to be difficult and shifted their support to the Congress.

The Congress had reasserted its charisma, but only as the head of an unwieldy coalition that may find it difficult to stand the test of time. Its vote totals were hardly a mandate, and it faces the challenge of leading India into the global capitalist economy while simultaneously providing jobs, equality, and welfare for India's poor. Equally daunting are India's endemic violence and the infusion of crime into politics. No less than four of Singh's prospective Cabinet appointees were under criminal indictment.

The Political Institutions of India

In crafting the political institutions of independent India, Nehru and the leaders of the Congress Party were guided by five overriding considerations. First, *India was to be a democracy.* This point was nonnegotiable. Second, *India required a government strong enough to tackle the massive problems confronting the new state,* not the least of which was the growing threat of civil war between the subcontinent's Hindu and Muslim populations. Third, *the rights of India's citizens had to be protected* from the whims of a strong government. Fourth, the new political institutions had to *correct the ravages of the caste system* and other inequities of Indian society. Finally, India's political institutions had to *be responsive to the profound regional and cultural diversity* of the subcontinent.

The resulting government structure was a complex blending of British and American practice, the heart of which was a British-style parliamentary democracy. India's leaders had profound respect for the British system. They believed that a prime minister supported by a strong majority in Parliament would give them the power they needed to tackle the herculean problems confronting the new state. (As mentioned in Chapter 3, a prime minister supported by a majority in Parliament has virtually unlimited power.)

The leaders of the Congress Party, however, well understood that India was not Britain and that communal tensions posed a constant threat to the rights of India's citizens. India, accordingly, was provided with a written constitution that enumerated the rights of its citizens and created a system of checks and balances.

The Constitution of India

The checks and balances provided by the Indian Constitution include the fragmentation of power between the prime minister and a president; the creation of two houses of Parliament—the **Lok Sabha** *(House of the People)* and the **Rajya Sabha** *(Council of States)*; the establishment of a Supreme Court empowered to declare acts of parliament unconstitutional; and the implementation of a federalist system that divides power between the central government and the states. The Constitution also addressed the inequities of Indian society by abolishing untouchability and by reserving seats in the Parliament for members of the scheduled minorities (untouchables and primitive tribes) in proportion to their share of the population. Bureaucratic positions were also reserved for the "scheduled classes" consistent with the requirements of efficiency.

While impressive in scope, India's political institutions were alien to Indian culture. They had evolved in England to meet the needs of a culture radically different from that of the Indian subcontinent. India's institutional development, accordingly, has witnessed constant tension between the ideals of Nehru's secular democracy and the reality of India's social, religious, and economic environment. The political system envisioned in the constitution of 1950 is far different from the Indian political system today. The form remains, but the substance is evolving to meet the realities of Indian life.

Many observers find the India of today to be far more chaotic than the India of the Nehru era. In their view, India's political institutions are decaying. Others see changes in the way India does politics as a process of adjustment. India, in their view, is India, not Britain. Its political institutions must reflect its own cultural traditions. Whatever the case, Nehru's vision of a secular and socialist India is being severely tested, a theme to be examined throughout the remainder of this chapter (Rudolph and Rudolph 1987 and 1998; Tully and Mansani 1988; Ganguly 1998).

Executive Power in India:
The President and the Prime Minister

Executive power in India is divided between the president and the prime minster. The president is elected indirectly by an electoral college consisting of both houses of the Indian parliament and all state legislatures. The prime minister is elected by a majority vote in the Lok Sabha, the popularly elected house of Parliament.

The President. By custom, the role of India's president is largely symbolic, often being compared to that of the German president or the British monarch. Unlike the British monarch, however, the Indian president possesses formidable constitutional powers. The president appoints the prime minister in accordance with the will of the Lok Sabha. If one party possesses a majority in the Lok Sabha, the appointment of its leader as prime minister is purely pro forma. If the Lok Sabha is deadlocked, however, the president may play a determining role in the appointment process. The president also appoints the governors of India's states and territories, the justices of the Supreme Court, and most other high officials. The president serves as the commander-in-chief of India's armed forces and, in times of emergency, can suspend the Government and rule by presidential decree. The president can also suspend state governments if, in his or her view, the state government has lost the power to rule effectively.

The Constitution requires the president to *seek* the "aid and advice" of the prime minister and Cabinet in the exercise of the above powers, a provision that was amended in 1976 to read that the president *will seek the advice of the prime minister and act in accordance with that advice*. Much of the president's theoretical power, accordingly, now resides with the prime minister. As the president of India declared bluntly in granting Indira Gandhi the right to rule by emergency decree, "India is Indira, and Indira is India" (Tully and Mansani 1988, 119). Nevertheless, the situation could easily change. With the power of India's major political parties on the wane, it has become increasingly difficult for prime ministers to dominate parliament. This could well force the president to play a more decisive role in Indian politics.

The Prime Minister. The formal role of the Indian prime minister is to propose legislation to the Parliament, to guide that legislation through the parliamentary process, and to administer the programs approved by the Parliament. In practice, if not in theory, the prime minister also exercises most of the powers reserved for the president, including the power to appoint governors, Supreme Court justices, and most other major officials. It is also the prime minister who determines when a national state of emergency should be declared or when state governments should be removed for violating the Constitution. The appointment powers usurped from the presidency provide the prime minister with abundant patronage at both the national and state levels. Friends and supporters fill key positions; opponents find their careers truncated.

The formal powers of the prime minister, then, are formidable. As the experience of Indira Gandhi well illustrated, no other single branch of the Indian

Chronology of Indian Prime Ministers

1947   India is granted its independence. Jawaharlal Nehru becomes India's first prime minister.

1948   Mohandas (Mahatma) Gandhi is assassinated.

1964   Nehru suffers a stroke and passes away shortly thereafter. Lal Bahadur Shastri becomes prime minister.

1966   Indira Gandhi is sworn in as prime minister upon the death of Lal Bahadur Shastri.

1967   Indira Gandhi leads the Congress to victory in national elections, reaffirming her position as prime minister.
       Indira Gandhi and the "Syndicate" are locked in a power struggle for control of the Congress. The party will split two years later.

1969   The Congress Party splits into two factions: an Indira Gandhi faction, Congress (R), and an opposition faction, Congress (O). Indira Gandhi remains prime minister.

1971   In March Indira Gandhi and the Congress (R) win a two-thirds majority in national elections (lower house).

1973   Indira Gandhi strengthens her hold on the Indian political system by appointing a loyal supporter as the Chief Justice of the Indian Supreme Court. Her move breaks tradition and undermines the independence and impartiality of the Supreme Court.

1975   In June Indira Gandhi is found guilty of corrupt electoral practices and activates the emergency provision of the Constitution, ruling by decree.

1977   Elections are held. Indira Gandhi and the Congress (R) are defeated. The Congress is out of office for the first time since independence.
       Morarji Desai of the Janata Party becomes India's first non-Congress prime minister.

1979   The Janata Government falls. A caretaker Government is formed.

1980   Indira Gandhi is reelected prime minister. Sanjay Gandhi, Indira Gandhi's son and heir apparent to the position of prime minister, is killed in an airplane accident.

1984   On June 5, Indira Gandhi orders the Indian army to attack the Golden Temple, the holiest site of India's Sikh minority.
       On October 31, Indira Gandhi is assassinated by her Sikh bodyguards. Her son, Rajiv Gandhi, assumes leadership of the Congress (I) Party.
       Rajiv Gandhi and the Congress (I) win the largest majority in Indian history. The Party begins a gradual move away from socialism.

1989   National elections deprive the Congress (I) of a majority in Parliament. In November Rajiv Gandhi resigns as prime minister.
       V. P. Singh of the Janata Dal Party forms a minority government.

1989/ Chandra Shekhar, the leader of a small
1990   factional party, becomes prime minister with the support of Rajiv Gandhi and the Congress (I).

1991   Conflict between Shekhar and Gandhi precipitates the collapse of the Shekhar Government and a call for new elections. Rajiv Gandhi is assassinated.
       The Congress (I) wins a marginal victory in national elections. On June 1 Narasimha Rao is sworn in as prime minister. The Nehru dynasty ends.

1996   The BJP emerges from the 1996 elections as the largest party in the Lok Sabha. Its leader, Atal Bihari Vajpayee, is asked to form a Government. Unable to garner a majority in the Lok Sabha, he resigns after 13 days. A 13-party coalition referred to as the United Front rules for almost two years but changes prime ministers every few months.

1998   The BJP wins a plurality in the 1998 elections and Vajpayee heads a coalition Government consisting of 18 diverse parties.

1999   The BJP (and allies) win a clear majority in the 1999 elections. Vajpayee returns as prime minister.

2004   Manmohan Singh of the Congress Party heads a broad coalition Government.

government can long resist the will of a powerful prime minister. Indira Gandhi weakened the presidency, undermined the authority of the Supreme Court, and crushed state governments hostile to her programs (Moog 1998). It was during the reign of Indira Gandhi that the "decay" or "adjustment" of India's political institutions began in earnest.

The formal powers of the prime minister, moreover, are augmented by a variety of informal powers. The Nehru Dynasty, for example, derived extraordinary powers from both the organizational dominance of the Congress Party and the charisma of the Nehru-Gandhi name. The prime minister is also the focal point of the mass media and is better positioned to shape public opinion than any other agency of the Indian government.

With the passing of the dynasty, one would expect Indian politics to be less influenced by issues of charisma and personal popularity, but this may not be the case. Personality continues to play a profound role in the electoral process, as do charismatic religious movements, not the least of which is a resurgent Hindu fundamentalism (Tully and Mansani 1988). The Congress Party, itself, made Sonia Gandhi, Rajiv Gandhi's Italian-born wife, president of the Party in an effort to recapture the magic of the Gandhi name (Ganguly and Burke 1998). The strategy proved to be an asset in the 2004 elections.

The Council of Ministers (Government). The prime minister heads the Council of Ministers, the Indian equivalent of Britain's "Government." The Council of Ministers consists of three layers: the Cabinet, non-Cabinet ministers, and deputy ministers. The Cabinet usually consists of approximately 20 of the ruling party's most senior politicians, and it is they who advise the prime minister on key issues of public policy. Of these, the holders of prestige ministries such as Foreign Affairs, Finance, and Defense are the most powerful. Non-Cabinet ministers are individuals waiting to work their way into ministerial positions.

The Council of Ministers (Government) as a whole may have more than 100 members, as each incoming prime minister uses appointments to the Council as a means of building parliamentary support. Coalition governments are under even greater pressure to make large numbers of appointments to the Council, for each segment of the coalition must have its share of the spoils (*Times of India,* Jan. 15, 1999, www).

As the size of the Council of Ministers makes it too unwieldy to meet as a collective body, most work is done by committees in consultation with the prime minister. This increases the power of the prime minister, for only the prime minister possesses a complete picture of what is going on.

During the era of the Nehru Dynasty, prime ministers dominated the Cabinet, leaving its members little scope for independent action. The experience of India's coalition governments has been exactly the opposite, with prime ministers being elected only after exhaustive negotiations among coalition partners, all of whom were well represented on the Cabinet. As the slightest affront to a coalition partner risked bringing down the Government, prime ministers were reluctant to take decisive stands on key issues. The result was frustration and conflict as each faction in the coalition blamed the others for the Government's failings

(*Times of India,* Jan. 7, 1999, www). If the tendency toward coalition governments continues, the most fundamental challenge to Indian democracy may be finding a pattern of leadership that is both decisive and stable.

Legislative Power in India: The Indian Parliament

Legislative power in India is divided between two houses of parliament, the Lok Sabha, or lower house, and the Rajya Sabha, or upper house. Both houses of parliament are important to the political process, but the Lok Sabha is dominant.

The Lok Sabha. The Lok Sabha is the focal point of parliamentary democracy in India. Much as in England, voters in each of India's 543 single-members, simple-plurality electoral districts elect one member to the Lok Sabha. The members of the Lok Sabha elect the prime minister who, in turn, forms a Government (Council of Ministers). Once appointed, the Council of Ministers serves at the pleasure of the Lok Sabha. A vote of no confidence "brings down" the Council of Ministers. This forces either the dissolution of the Lok Sabha or the reconstruction of a new Council of Ministers that is capable of winning a majority therein.

Parliamentary procedures leading to the passage of a bill are similar to those of Great Britain (see Chapter 3), with each bill receiving several readings before being sent to the president for the official stamp of approval. During the four decades of the Nehru Dynasty, the prime minister dictated both the content and priority of legislation. Opposition parties used debates and the Question Hour to embarrass the Government, but such tactics, while often animated, had little influence on policy.

Reflecting this tradition of domination by the prime minister, the Indian Parliament now epitomizes the decay of India's political institutions and especially the scourge of corruption (*Times of India,* Dec. 24, 1998, www; *Asia Times,* April 20, 2004, www).

The Rajya Sabha. The upper house of the Indian Parliament, the Rajya Sabha, is elected by the state legislatures. The Rajya Sabha is roughly equal to the Lok Sabha in its legislative authority, but it cannot bring down a Government. The prime minister and Council of Ministers (Government) are responsible before the Lok Sabha alone. The members of the Rajya Sabha, much like senators in the United States, are elected for six-year terms, with a third of the membership standing for election at two-year intervals. The 250 seats of the Rajya Sabha are allocated in rough proportion to the population of India's states and territories, with smaller states faring slightly better than their larger counterparts. Twelve of the members of the Rajya Sabha are nominated by the Indian president for meritorious service to the state.

If the Lok Sabha and the Rajya Sabha pass differing versions of a bill, the bill is shuttled back and forth between the two chambers until agreement is reached. If a mutually acceptable bill cannot be reached by this process, the president may call a joint session of Parliament to work out the differences.

During most of the past five decades, the Congress Party dominated both the Lok Sabha and the Rajya Sabha, thereby limiting conflict between the two houses. This pattern is now changing as the growing strength of regional and communal parties has made the Rajya Sabha the focal point of efforts to re-assert state rights. The ability of a revitalized Rajya Sabha to reverse the decay of India's political system remains open to question. On the positive side, an as-sertive Rajya Sabha would breathe new life into both the Indian Parliament and India's federal system. On the negative side, a strong Rajya Sabha could cripple the ability of the Indian government to take decisive actions against re-ligious and regional groups intent on destroying the unity of the Indian politi-cal system.

Law and Politics in India: The Supreme Court

The Indian political system represents a fusion of British and American practice. India's leaders preferred a parliamentary system patterned after that of Great Britain, but they were fearful that Britain's "unwritten" constitution would be unworkable in the tumultuous environment of Indian politics. India's citizens, ac-cordingly, were provided with a broad array of constitutionally guaranteed rights, all of which were protected by an American-style Supreme Court empowered to declare acts of parliament unconstitutional. A fundamental tension was thus es-tablished between the British concept of parliamentary supremacy and the Amer-ican concept of constitutional/judicial supremacy.

The inherent tension between the Supreme Court and the Parliament came to a head when the Supreme Court declared many of Indira Gandhi's social pro-grams unconstitutional. The battle was an unequal one, as Indira Gandhi, sup-ported by large majorities in the Parliament, merely amended the Constitution to gain her objectives. This was a relatively simple process, for an amendment to the Indian Constitution generally requires little more than a majority vote in the two houses of Parliament.

The real weakness of the Supreme Court, however, proved to be political rather than legal. Faced with the prospect of the Supreme Court's continued op-position to her policies, Indira Gandhi merely "stacked" the court with friends and supporters. The 1977 defeat of Indira Gandhi found the Supreme Court "restacked" by the Janata Party, only to be again restacked by Gandhi following her return to office in 1980.

The Supreme Court survived, but its integrity had been severely compro-mised. The Court is now attempting to reestablish a position of impartiality and independence, a goal that may be easier to achieve in the era of weak coalition governments (Moog 1998). In point of fact, India's elected politicians have begun to complain of the Supreme Court's growing activism, claiming that it is attempt-ing to become a third house of Parliament (*India World,* Jan. 17, 1999, www).

The broader India court system is best described as overwhelmed, a fact that legal experts say is destroying the justice system. On average, Indian courts now take 6.6 years to process a case, perhaps more (*Times of India,* Apr. 3, 2000, www; *Washington Post,* March 2, 2003, www).

Federalism in India

In addition to the existence of a Supreme Court, American influence on the Indian Constitution is also evident in the federal structure of the Indian political system. Powers such as defense, foreign affairs, currency regulation, and other matters of overriding national importance are reserved for the federal government. Education, welfare, and police security are largely controlled by the states. In areas such as economic planning, the federal and state governments enjoy concurrent authority. The states also possess direct representation in the Parliament via their ability to appoint members to the Rajya Sabha.

Although power is divided between the federal and state governments, the powers of the federal government are clearly superior to those of the states. The Constitution empowers the federal (Union) government to override state legislation on issues requiring national uniformity and to remove state Governments (governor and cabinet) that violate the Constitution. Prime ministers have used this constitutional provision to remove antagonistic state Governments on several occasions, often for political rather than constitutional reasons (Hardgrave and Kochanek 1993). As things currently stand, the powers of the states have been weakened so much that they can do little without the approval of the central government (Manor 1998; Dua and Singh 2003).

Bureaucracy and Politics in India

India entered independence with a core of senior civil servants who were among the finest in the world (Braibanti 1966). It was the Indian Civil Service, variously referred to as the "steel frame" or "permanent government," that enabled India to make a smooth transition from colonialism to independent rule. India, thus, was twice blessed. It was blessed with an experienced political elite committed to democracy, and it was blessed with an exceptionally qualified administrative elite capable of executing government policies in an efficient manner.

With the pressures of independence, the quality of the ICS, now renamed the Indian Administrative Service (IAS), began to erode. As a colonial service, the responsibilities of the ICS were largely those of collecting taxes and maintaining law and order (Tummala 1982). With independence, the IAS was suddenly expected to provide the Indian population with a full range of health, education, and welfare services, not to mention the management of a complex socialist economy. The task of the IAS was made all the more difficult by the mediocre nature of the lower levels of the Indian bureaucracy. Unlike the elite senior service, the rank-and-file members of the Indian bureaucracy had not been trained in Britain, nor did they necessarily accept Nehru's ideal of a Westernized India. Most were merely intent on personal survival. No matter how talented they may have been, the elite core at the top of the administrative pyramid could not compensate for weaknesses at the pyramid's base.

The IAS was to suffer other problems as well. Many Indians resented the elitist, upper-caste, "Anglo" nature of the IAS. A democratic state, in the view of many, should have a democratic bureaucracy that was open to all (Dharia 1969).

Much as in the case of the Supreme Court, a tension soon developed between the ideological goals of India's political leaders and the "efficiency" goals of the IAS. Political leaders wanted to relax the standards for entrance to the IAS, but the IAS resisted, arguing that a lowering of entrance standards would open the civil service to less qualified and less politically neutral applicants. The choice between efficiency and democracy is not an easy one, and as in the case of the Supreme Court, efficiency was sacrificed to politics. Entrance standards to the IAS were relaxed, and performance declined (*Times of India*, Dec. 1, 1998, www).

Much of the political pressure on the IAS took the form of pure bullying, a process described by Nehru's cousin, B. K. Nehru:

> Suspension, denial of promotion and transfer are the three powers that have been used to bend civil servants to the Minister's will. What does a married man with children do if he's told to do something and says "I won't"? So the next day he finds himself transferred. Now his children can't get admission to schools, he can't get a house; it causes complete dislocation to his life. So it's not surprising that so many have succumbed to these pressures (Tully and Mansani 1988, 49).

Despite strong movement toward a free market economy, the Indian bureaucracy continues to serve as a brake on economic development (*Economist*, "A survey of India," Feb. 21, 2004). It could not be otherwise, for the bureaucracy remains one of the most powerful forces in Indian politics (Chakrabarty and Bhattacharya 2003). The Indian bureaucracy also continues to grow (*India Times*, Apr. 20, 2000, www).

THE ACTORS IN INDIAN POLITICS: ELITES, PARTIES, GROUPS, AND CITIZENS

Political institutions are the arena of politics, but the actors in the political process play a critical role in determining who gets what, when, and how. In the present section, we shall examine the four main types of political actors in India: elites, parties, groups, and citizens.

Elites and Politics in India

The transformation of India's political institutions is often attributed to the changing nature of India's political elites. This argument is both simple and persuasive. India is an elite-directed society in which the masses, most of whom are poorly educated, follow the path outlined by their leaders. If the elites are democratic, the masses will be democratic. If the elites incline toward fragmentation and demagoguery, the masses will offer little opposition. One way or the other, it is the elites who determine the direction of the Indian political system.

Over the course of the past six decades, the Indian elite system has progressed through three stages: the independence stage, the nationalist stage, and the professional politician stage (Rudolph and Rudolph 1987). *The elite structure during the independence stage was dominated by Mahatma Gandhi, Nehru, and other leaders of exceptional vision.* That vision was one of a secular and democratic India. It was Gandhi and Nehru who created the Indian political system, and it was Nehru, supported by an elitist Indian Civil Service, who made the system work during its formative years.

The nationalist stage in the evolution of the Indian elite structure featured Indira Gandhi and other "second-generation" leaders of the Congress Party. Indira Gandhi's vision of India focused squarely on the creation of a strong centralized government in which overwhelming power would reside with the prime minister. As the dominance of Indira Gandhi increased, the creativity and resourcefulness of other leadership positions decreased proportionally. Leaders became survivors.

The present elite structure of India, the professional politician stage, is increasingly dominated by a class of professional politicians who attained office by virtue of their close association with the Nehru Dynasty and its successors (Guru 1991). India's current generation of professional political elites, according to its critics, lacks the vision, commitment, and energy of either the independence or the nationalist elites. Their primary interest appears to be perpetuating a status quo from which they are the primary beneficiaries.

Pedigree has also become the name of the game in Indian politics, and the children of India's political elite are now poised to move into positions of power (*Times of India,* March 21, 2004, www). Of these, the most prominent are the children of Rajiv and Sonia Gandhi: Rahul Gandhi and Priyanka Gandhi Varda. Rahul declined a cabinet position in the Singh Government of 2004.

An elite structure drawing its power from politicians and the higher civil service, moreover, is now finding its authority increasingly challenged by a new wave of business, religious, and regional elites. Powerbrokers and leaders of regional parties have also moved to the fore as coalition politics has forced India's dominant parties to seek their support in building winning alliances. Most are demanding that Nehru's vision of a secular, socialist democracy give way to the religious traditions of Indian culture and the capitalist pressures of a new world order dominated by the United States.

Parties and Politics in India

The Indian political system was long classified as a single-party-dominant democracy. The Congress Party, with the exception of two brief experiments in coalition rule, ruled India for almost 50 years. Congress dominance, however, is a thing of the past and India is rapidly becoming a multi-party democracy in which the Congress is but one of several major players (Hasan 2002).

The Congress Party. The early dominance of the Congress Party had four sources: the charisma of Gandhi and Nehru, the prestige that accrued to the Party as the vehicle of the independence movement, the Party's broad base of local and regional organizations, and the Party's flexibility in absorbing a broad range of ideological, regional, and communal groups. Most groups simply found that some influence within the Congress was preferable to no influence outside of the

Congress. From time to time, groups would leave the Congress, only to return to the fold at a later point (Weiner 1957).

Those, however, were the early days of independence. The Congress Party remains one of the dominant political forces in Indian politics today, but the foundations of its power are rapidly being eroded. The stalwarts of the Dynasty have passed into history and the optimism of the independence era has given way to an awareness of the harsh realities of Indian life. Whether Rahul Gandhi and his sister Priyanka Gandhi Varda can capture the charisma of old remains to be seen.

The problems besetting the Congress (I), moreover, are not limited to the loss of a charismatic leader or to the weakness of its organizational structure. The Party is also developing a split personality. The Congress has traditionally championed Nehru's vision of a secular socialist state that stressed equality for all religions and social classes. This made its appeal particularly strong among the Muslims, Sikhs, Christians, the scheduled castes, and the other "disadvantaged" groups that constitute some 40 percent of the Indian electorate. Bearing in mind that slightly more than 40 percent of the vote is sufficient to secure a majority in the Lok Sabha, a strong minority vote could almost guarantee dominance of the Congress. The importance of the "secular" vote was also heightened by the tremendous diversity that existed within the broader Hindu community. Minorities tended to vote as a bloc, but Hindus were less likely to do so.

Six decades of secular politics, however, have increasingly galvanized India's Hindu majority into a politically conscious voting bloc, and the pro-Hindu Bharatiya Janata Party now represents the fastest-growing political movement in India (Thakur 1998).

The Congress Party is also having difficulty deciding if it is the party of socialism and equality or the party of capitalist growth. Thus far, the party has vacillated on both issues, conveying the image of a party without a clear vision of India and its future. It is also increasingly perceived as the party of the rich.

The Bharatiya Janata Party.   The party most likely to challenge the Congress during the coming decade is the pro-Hindu Bharatiya Janata Party (Hansen and Jaffrelot 2001). Prior to the 1991 elections, the BJP ranked second in strength to the Congress, with 86 seats in the Lok Sabha. The BJP doubled its popular vote in the 1991 elections and emerged as the largest party in the Lok Sabha following the 1996 elections. While the BJP's victory was impressive, the Party fell well short of a majority in the Lok Sabha and failed in its bid to form a ruling coalition. It achieved this goal in 1998 and again in 1999 but suffered an unexpected defeat in the 2004 elections. (See Table 9.2.) The appeal of the BJP is quite simple. To paraphrase BJP statements:

> The two major components of the BJP's ideology are Hinduism and a strong commitment to transforming India into a capitalist economy. This means clipping the wings of the bureaucracy and scaling back India's traditional commitment to social welfare.

In spite of the BJP's recent successes, the realities of India's communal mosaic make it unlikely that the BJP will be able to win elections without the support

Huge posters of historical leaders overshadow a meeting of India's Congress Party, which ruled the country for more than half a century.

of a broad coalition of minor parties. Non-Hindus and the disadvantaged classes (untouchables and tribes) constitute almost 40 percent of the electorate. This, when added to the 25 percent of the electorate that belong to the lower castes, makes a total of 65 percent of the population that would likely be disadvantaged by BJP rule. This is all the more the case because the so-called "backward castes," a group composed largely of farm workers and small artisans, has begun to generate their own leadership rather than following the lead of the BJP. Money is becoming more important than subservience to the higher-caste elites.

The BJP is now attempting to portray a more populist image, hoping to convince lower-caste Hindus that a BJP victory would not jeopardize their rights. It is also working hard to establish alliances with regional parties in an effort to strengthen its electoral base. Judging by the results of the 2004 election, it has a long way to go.

Other Parties. The decline of the Congress Party over the past several decades was accompanied by the rise of a variety of socialist parties advocating greater equality of opportunity and increased taxation of the rich (Crossette 1992). The unity of the left was fleeting, however, and, more often than not, brief electoral alliances were shattered by personality conflict and internal bickering. Indian opposition parties also tend to be fluid and ephemeral, emerging to meet the needs of one election, only to fade or reconstitute themselves before the next. Even

Table 9.2 Seats in the Lok Sabha

Party	1999	2004
BJP and allies (The National Democratic Alliance)	298	188
Congress (and allies)	135	219
Others	110	132
Vacant or Pending	6	5
TOTAL	**549**	**544**

India's communists have found it difficult to form a single party. The original Communist Party of India split into two factions, one—the CPM—more Marxist than the other. They, in turn, have been joined recently by a Communist Party Marxist-Leninist (CPML) (*Times of India*, Jan. 8, 1999, www). The Maoists, for their part have now created a "red zone" in India consisiting of some 156 districts in 13 states. The Maoists, referred to as Naxalites, rule by "brute force and terror" (*Hindustan Times*, Jan. 21, 2005, www).

As a practical matter, India's diverse parties tend to coalesce into three blocs or alliances: a center alliance dominated by the Congress Party, a rightist alliance dominated by the BJP, and a leftist alliance sometimes referred to as the United Front. The leftist bloc advocates socialism and higher job quotas for minorities and the disadvantaged classes, while the rightist alliance stresses greater capitalism and the transformation of India into a Hindu state. The Congress and its allies are desperately seeking middle ground between these two irreconcilable extremes. The task is a daunting one.

India's party system, moreover, has been made all the more complex by the emergence of increasingly strong regional parties. Regional parties gained more than 15 percent of the national vote in 1989 and some 12 percent of the national vote in 1991. This trend continued in 1996 and 2004, with the United Front drawing much of its support from regional parties (*India Today*, June 15, 1996, 25; Chandra 2004). The strongest of the regional parties are those associated with regional and religious movements demanding greater autonomy from New Delhi (India's capital).

Groups and Politics in India

India possesses a more complex group structure than any other country on earth. All of India's groups, moreover, are politically relevant. In order to understand this point, it is necessary to recall that the traditional social order of India was based upon a system of castes and sub-castes, each of which possessed specific rights and obligations depending upon its hierarchical position within the Hindu religion.

The Muslim invasion added complexity to India's communal mosaic by introducing a religion that stressed social equality and the worship of a single, all-powerful God. Lesser challenges to Hindu dominance would also be posed by India's smaller Christian and Buddhist communities. In a country as populous as India, however, few groups are truly small.

Both caste and religious communities, in turn, are fragmented by linguistic differences. *Indians speak some 1,652 diverse languages, of which Hindi is the most prominent* (Krishna 1992). Large segments of the country, however, do not speak Hindi and resent persistent efforts to make Hindi the national language. The issue is far more than a matter of pride, for imposing Hindi as the national language would give Hindi speakers a political and economic advantage over Indian citizens who do not speak Hindi.

The British occupation further fragmented Indian society by pitting Western values against traditional Hindu and Muslim values. It thus became common to speak of "forward-looking" groups and "backward-looking" groups (Frankel 1988). *Foremost of the forward-looking groups were the new elites created by the British, elites that would eventually form the Congress Party. The backward-looking groups, by definition, were any groups that opposed the Westernization of the subcontinent.*

The British occupation also witnessed the emergence of Western-style interest groups ranging from business associations and labor unions to student groups and human rights organizations. Conflict between economic classes, once clouded by religious dogma, was also brought into sharper focus by the colonial experience (Shah 1988; Vanaik 1990).

As things stand today, the list of politically relevant pressure groups includes castes, jati, social classes, religions, tribes, linguistic groups, business and labor organizations, peasant movements, student groups, women, regional movements, and institutional interests such as the bureaucracy and the military (Shah 1990).

Business and Labor.   The Indian Chamber of Commerce (FICCI), the main peak organization of Indian business, was founded in 1927, a full two decades before the granting of Indian independence in 1947. The FICCI is well financed and uses both formal and informal procedures to lobby for its policies (Misquitta 1991). At the formal level, the FICCI and its component organizations are represented on an endless array of official advisory boards and commissions designed to reconcile differences between the public and private sectors of the Indian economy. The councils are also designed to build harmony between business and labor. At the informal level, the FICCI makes its point by lavish campaign contributions (Misquitta 1991).

As is true of most Indian organizations, the effectiveness of the FICCI has been undermined by internal conflict. In part, this conflict is the result of competition between India's large industrial families. It is also the result of growing dissension between exporters who favor free trade and local industrialists demanding continued protection from foreign competition. Tensions have also emerged between the giants of India's industry and their smaller competitors, a problem that led to the creation of rival business organizations such as the Indian Merchant Chamber (Misquitta 1991). Whatever its internal strains, the business community is rapidly becoming a dominant force in Indian politics. The continued liberation of the Indian economy can only increase this trend.

Labor unions, like business organizations, are deeply rooted in the colonial era. Indeed, the eve of independence would find India with no fewer than 457 labor unions of one form or another (Misquitta 1991). The Indian labor movement has sought to press its demands through a combination of strikes and collective bargaining, but neither strategy has enjoyed much success. It is very difficult to bargain effectively or to conduct a sustained strike in an environment of severe unemployment. Those strikes that do occur are usually crushed by the Government. As labor leaders would lament, "The wind in the country has shifted. It is no longer in our favor" (Roychowdhury 2003). The wind of which this leader was speaking was India's surge toward capitalism. Even the Congress, once a staunch ally of labor, has jumped on the capitalism bandwagon, albeit capitalism with a conscience. Finally, the effectiveness of the Indian labor movement has been undermined by its lack of unity. Rather than confronting business and government as a unified front, Indian labor has allowed itself to be fragmented into a variety of conflicting regional and ideological units, not the least of which are the All India Trade Union Congress, All India Council of Central Trade Unions, Bhartiya Mazdoor Sangh, Centre of India Trade Unions, Hind Mazdoor Sabha, and others too numerous to mention (*Times of India,* March 14, 2002, www). Despite its limited success, one would expect the pace of labor unrest to increase as India continues to scale back its huge and largely unprofitable state-owned industries. It is jobs in these industries, after all, that are the core of India's labor movement. And yet, that has not happened. India's unions appear to be on the defensive rather than the offensive (Roychowdhury 2003).

Students. More than 4 million strong, India's students are at the forefront of most political demonstrations. Not all students are politically active, but those who are active are very active. Student protests have brought down state Governments on several occasions and have often forced the federal (union) Government to change course on politically sensitive issues. India's colleges and universities are routinely closed down as a result of student activism (Hardgrave and Kochanek 1993). Needless to say, politicians attempt to exploit the students to suit their own purposes (*Times of India,* Dec. 26, 1998, www).

Student protests are motivated both by the idealism of youth and by frustration with a political system that will doom many students to either unemployment or a low-paying government job. Unfortunately, the latter may be the lucky ones.

The effectiveness of student protests is a function of several factors. Student protests are loud and noisy and have also become increasingly violent. Perhaps more importantly, student protests serve as the catalyst for broader mass protests, the growing volatility of which is an unwelcome prospect for any Government, state or national. Despite their effectiveness in stimulating protests, students are too fragmented by class, caste, religious, or other differences to stay the course. They also manifest a profound lack of discipline, personality often being more important than ideology.

Women. Women's groups have become increasingly active in Indian politics, and not without cause. Women remain second-class citizens. They are also subject to wife-beating and more extreme forms of violence.

The main flash point of violence against women is the dowry. Even when women meet the demands of their prospective husbands, demands for dowry supplements may continue long after marriage (*Washington Post*, March 27, 2005, www). Abigail Haworth suggests that noncompliance results in beating and, in some cases, death: "Between 6,000 and 7,000 women are murdered each year by dissatisfied husbands and in-laws. Most victims are set on fire, to disguise the killing as a 'kitchen accident.' Others are poisoned, thrown over balconies, or pushed out of moving vehicles" (Haworth 2004, 77–82).

Dowries were banned by law in 1961, but the law is ignored as being part of Indian culture. Indian women are not only fighting political injustices. They are also fighting cultural norms that severely undervalue the importance of women. Women's organizations tend to be divided between groups attempting to fight political injustice and groups that provide support for battered and abused wives. Those groups attempting to fight political injustice face a particularly difficult task, for India's laws already stress the equality of all citizens, male and female. This was part of Nehru's vision of a modern secular India. Those laws, unfortunately, are rarely enforced with vigor, as neither the government nor the police are inclined to alter practices that are broadly accepted by society. In the final analysis, political oppression and cultural oppression are difficult to separate.

The effectiveness of the women's movement in India is further undermined by the same caste, class, regional, and political differences that fragment most pressure groups in India. The position of educated, upper-class women is far superior to that of poor women and particularly women living in rural areas. In gender relations, as in most everything else, India is becoming a dual society: a society of abundance and increasing opportunities for the rich, and a society of scarcity and increasing despair for the poor.

While much of the writing on Indian women focuses on violence and political rights, it is important to stress that those issues will be difficult to address without a far greater emphasis on the broader feminist problems of inferior education, health care, and economic opportunity. All continue to lag. Also distressing is the growing trend to abort female fetuses. The director of the Indian census estimates that the number is is the millions (*New York Times,* Oct. 6, 2003, www). The Indian government has taken notice as the ratio of females to males continues to decline.

The Disaffected: Secessionists and Peasants.   Groups that have found the Indian Government unresponsive to their demands have turned to violence. Sikh extremists in the Punjab are in open rebellion, as are the Muslims in Kashmir and the Tamils in the south of India. Several Indian provinces are either currently or have recently been under direct military control. The rural poor, lacking a responsive ear in Delhi and the state capitals, have also turned to violence (Karna 1989).

Are Group Loyalties Becoming Stronger or Weaker?   Most Indians are members of an organized religion, a status group within that religion, a linguistic group, a professional group, a social class, and a region. With so many attachments pulling in so many different directions, it is difficult for any single group to claim the total allegiance of most of India's citizens. Middle-class bureaucrats spar with middle-class businessmen over the pace of economic reform. Poor Hindus are torn between religious obligations that stress the rewards of the hereafter and the opportunity to

---

Five Axes of Political Conflicts in India

In spite of the existence of *multiple memberships* **(cross-cutting cleavages),** political conflict has increasingly polarized the Indian electorate along five axes: rich/poor, centralization/decentralization, socialist/capitalist, Western/traditional, and Hindu/minority.

- The rich/poor axis is manifest in the growing gulf between India's rich and poor. Indeed, it has become commonplace to speak of two Indias: the dynamic and prosperous India of the middle classes and the destitute India of slum dwellers and landless peasants. As in most countries, it is the poor who are the least successful in making their voices heard.
- The centralization/decentralization axis pits the bureaucracy, the Government, and most other elements of the national political establishment against a bewildering array of religious, regional, and linguistic groups demanding greater autonomy from Delhi rule. Only the most extreme groups advocate outright secession, but all demand a shift of power from the center to the periphery.
- The socialist/capitalist axis places the bureaucracy, labor unions, and welfare organizations in conflict with business interests. India's business leaders, although divided on the issue, increasingly view economic liberalization (capitalism) as the path to prosperity and

development. Bureaucrats, labor groups, and welfare recipients, by contrast, fear that greater capitalism will lead to unemployment and the dismantling of India's social welfare network.
- Political conflict in India also continues to revolve around a Western/traditional axis. The Indian Constitution, as discussed earlier, imposed a British-style political system on a society with radically different cultural traditions (Embree 1990). The conflict between those competing traditions continues today, finding its most visible expression in religious fundamentalism of several varieties, Sikh and Muslim fundamentalism as well as Hindu fundamentalism (Singh 1998).
- Finally, political conflict in India continues to be shaped by a Hindu/minority axis. The divide between the Hindus and Muslims, always problematic has been sharpened by a growing Hindu assertiveness. India, in the view of Hindus, is a predominantly Hindu society and should reflect Hindu values. This view is not limited to Hindu fundamentalists but has been fueled by broad-based resentment over the sweeping affirmative action programs designed to improve the socioeconomic status of India's disadvantaged groups. All parties, however, are playing the religious card.

---

achieve a better life in the present (Gould 1990). Caste and religious attachments, accordingly, are no longer adequate to assure political dominance.

Citizens and Politics in India

One of the major criticisms of the elitist perspective of politics is that it assumes an almost mindless pliability among the masses. This model may have been valid during the era of independence when India was overwhelmingly rural and illiterate, but it is less applicable today. India possesses an educated, highly politicized, and prosperous middle class that now constitutes as much as 30 percent of the Indian population. Indeed, it is the urban middle classes that now form the bulwark of Western democracy in India (Dubey 1992). India's lower classes, moreover, are also becoming politicized, placing ever-increasing demands for social justice on a political system that, despite its socialist rhetoric, has done little to meet their needs.

The growing politicization of the Indian population is partially attributable to increased education and urbanization. It is also a function of an Indian press that

Citizens in Calcutta line up to cast their ballots in the 1995 federal election. The Indian electorate has become increasingly politicized in recent years as a result of educational attainment, urbanization, and frustration with the country's social and economic problems.

is as "vivid" as it is intense. Except for a few premier papers, the line between fact and conjecture in India's more than 4,000 newspapers is often difficult to distinguish. Politicization, however, has also been increased by mass frustration over corruption, violence, and the failure of India's leaders to come to grips with the country's pressing social and economic problems. A majority of India's population is "hurting," and they want solutions to their problems.

Election studies provide two diverse views of Indian public opinion. The first view is provided by the platforms and campaign rhetoric of India's political parties, and the second by the voting patterns of the Indian electorate. Both suggest that the issues of primary concern to the Indian public are violence, rising prices, poverty, corruption, and economic growth. Similar concerns are reflected in public opinion polls. Each of the five issues has reached crisis proportions in India, and each touches the lives of most Indian citizens.

The expression of public opinion, however, encompasses far more than elections and public opinion polls. Public opinion is also reflected in the escalating cycle of communal violence and crime that continues to erode the fabric of Indian society. The use of violence as a form of political expression is also increasing. Leading the fray are Hindu fundamentalist attacks on India's Christian and

Muslim minorities. Following the 2002 BJP electoral victory in the Gujarat, the state's chief minister (governor) called upon his supporters to "teach a lesson" to those who did not support the party (Marshall 2004). More than a 1,000 Muslims were killed in the ensuing violence. Hindu violence is followed in short order by criminal violence and Jihadist (Muslim extremist) violence, not the least of which have been the downing of an Indian airliner and the subsequent 2001 bombing of the Indian parliament. Added to the mix are regional secessionist movements and extremist political parties.

For all of their problems, Indians scored remarkably high on the "happiness barometer," a survey of 22 countries. The U.S. led the list with 46 percent of American citizens saying they were "very happy," with India's 37 percent being not far behind and well ahead of the French and the British (*Times of India,* Apr. 14, 2000, www).

THE CONTEXT OF INDIAN POLITICS: CULTURE, ECONOMICS, AND INTERNATIONAL INTERDEPENDENCE

India has remained a democracy throughout its almost six decades of independence. As we have seen in the preceding discussion, this impressive record has been achieved in the face of overwhelming odds. India's democracy, however, is showing signs of strain, and an increasing number of observers now speak of a crisis of governability (Kohli 1990).

Why has India become so difficult to govern? Some explanations are cultural in nature, suggesting that many Indians have yet to embrace Nehru's vision of a secular, democratic state. Other explanations are economic, suggesting that the roots of India's political crisis lie in its inability to meet the basic needs of its people. Still other explanations focus on the existence of an international system that places India at a disadvantage in its dealings with the first world. Each offers important insights into India's crisis of governability.

The Culture of Indian Politics

Cultural analyses of India's crisis of governability tend to focus on the concept of a **civic culture** (Almond and Verba 1963). The concept of a civic culture suggests that the citizens of a democratic state must do more than merely follow their leaders. They must *be committed to democratic values, understand how their political institutions work, and believe in their ability to influence those institutions.* Barring this, it will be impossible for citizens of a state to assure the accountability of their leaders. A civic culture also implies that *loyalties to the state are stronger than loyalties to ethnic, religious, and other parochial groups and that the good of the state will take precedence over the good of its parts.* A state in which loyalties to parochial groups are stronger than loyalties to the state is doomed to a nightmare of communal conflict. This at least has been the message of Bosnia, Lebanon, Northern Ireland, the states of the former Soviet Union, and much of Africa.

India did not possess a civic culture at the time of its independence. Its largely rural and illiterate population possessed little understanding of modern democratic practice, and most individuals lived and worked within the confines of their jati or related groups. Not only was their personal identity a product of the group, but it was also an identity that they could not escape. They were what their group was. Under such circumstances, it was only to be expected that group attachments would surpass loyalties to the state or to the concept of a united India. Tolerance of other groups was minimal, at best.

The challenge of Nehru and the Congress Party, then, was to create a civic culture in India by making the lofty ideals of the Indian Constitution part of India's political culture. Their successes were many. Indians vote, participate in political campaigns, and discuss politics with a ferocity seldom found in the democratic states of the first world. They are also intensely conscious of being Indian and are justifiably proud of their democratic traditions.

Does this mean that India has evolved into a civil society in which communal and other group loyalties give way to a greater concern for India? Perhaps the answer to this question depends on which India we are speaking about. If we are speaking of an India that is shining, to use the BJP's 2004 election slogan, the answer could well be yes. India's growing and increasingly prosperous middle class resembles that of the west in its attitudes and aspirations. India, however, is a dual society, much of which remains locked in the traditions of the past. Loyalties are shaped by ethnic, religious, regional, and tribal concerns rather than an overriding loyalty to the concept of a united India (Jodhka 2001; Sivaramakrishnan and Agrawal 2003). It would also be naive to suggest that communal loyalties did not permeate the more prosperous classes as well. The BJP, after all, is essentially a political organization devoted to Hindu supremacy.

Political Economy and Politics in India

Political economists find India's crisis of governability to be essentially an economic crisis. It is unrealistic, in their view, to expect people to support a political system that cannot meet their basic needs (Roy and James 1992). The growing conflict between communal groups that has become endemic to Indian politics, from the political economic perspective, is a struggle for scarce resources. The greater the disparity between the wealth of groups, the greater the violence. India's rich states are getting richer; the poor states are getting poorer. At the very least, the gap between them is growing (*Asia Times,* Feb 27, 2004, www). The same principle applies to India's varied secessionist movements. In the view of their leaders, there is more to gain as an independent country than there is by remaining part of India. The slogans are often ethnic and religious, but the core of the matter is economic. Prosperity seldom leads to revolt. Electoral conflict is also viewed as being largely economic in nature, with the more prosperous upper-class/caste Hindus voting for the BJP and the minorities and the disadvantaged groups voting for either the Congress or the parties of the left (*Asia Times,* May

13, 2004, www). A robust economy, moreover, is not keeping up with India's equally robust birthrate, and the projections suggest more unemployment and not less (Slater 2004). Indians, like most other people, tend to be rational economic actors.

While political economists agree that India's crisis of governability is economic in origin, they disagree violently on the cure. Neoclassical economists urge a total liberalization of the Indian economy. They would clip the wings of the India's powerful bureaucrats (often referred to as the "License Raj") and allow Indian businesses to operate free of government regulation. The massive Indian bureaucracy would be radically downsized, and state subsidies on food and other necessities would be curtailed. Curtailed, too, would be social legislation that precludes employers from firing employees for poor performance (Tomlinson 1992).

In support of their argument, **neoclassical economists** point to the rapid growth in the Indian economy that has accompanied the country's growing shift to capitalism. With a truly capitalist economy, they argue, India would more than keep pace with the economic miracles of South Korea and Taiwan. To be sure, economic disparities between advantaged and disadvantaged groups would increase in the short run. Inefficient government enterprises would have to be trimmed of excess workers, and the weaker government firms would probably have to be closed. The gap between rich and poor would also increase as capitalists reaped the benefits of their investments. Capitalists, however, create jobs. In the long run, all groups would be better off than they are today.

Leftist economists reject the capitalist argument, pointing to the inequalities that accompany economic liberalization. More than ever, from their perspective, India would be transformed into a dual society in which a modern, technologically advanced India would coexist with an India of backwardness and poverty. Leftist political economists also point with pride to the tremendous economic progress that India has made in recent decades, arguing that it is possible for India to develop economically while simultaneously caring for the health and welfare of its population. While some tightening up of bureaucratic laxity may be in order, they say, socialism has not been a failure (Vanaik 1990).

A third group of political economists, generally referred to as **"growth with equity" economists,** seeks a balance between the goals of rapid economic growth and social welfare. (Growth with equity is one of several versions of state capitalism.) Free-market capitalism would be encouraged, but the state would continue to assure that all major elements of society were cared for (Todaro 1989). As expressed by former Prime Minister Rao, "Governments do not have the right to go overboard and plunge large amounts of people into mass misery" (*New York Times,* Jan. 15, 1995, 4).

India's politicians are moving toward the "growth with equity" position more out of necessity than conviction ("Chidambaram unveils please-all Budget," *Hindustan Times,* July 8, 2004). They understand that increased capitalism is necessary to stimulate a faster pace of economic growth, but they fear that a rapid transition to capitalism would strain the fabric of Indian politics beyond the breaking point. They also understand that broad coalition governments require that the economic interests of all members of the coalition are cared for. In typical Indian fashion, India's politicians have sought a midpoint between the two extremes. The Government, for example, has reduced the bureaucratic red tape that has traditionally choked capitalist activity in India. It has also eased the barriers to foreign investment in India. By the same token, it maintains a broad range of public-sector industries, most of which are noncompetitive on the world market and survive by the grace of protective tariffs and government subsidies (Roychowdhury 2003). Some 50 percent lose money, a combined $61.7 billion in 2001 (*Asia Times,* Aug. 26, 2003, www).

This blend of reform and protectionism has been sufficient to stimulate an upswing in the Indian economy, but it has not produced the economic miracle that has occurred in South Korea, Taiwan, Malaysia, and India's other neighbors that have taken the fast track to capitalism. Ironically, even China, a presumably communist state, seems to be embracing capitalism with greater zeal than India (*Economist,* Mar. 5, 2005, www).

The difference between India and her neighbors, of course, is democracy. South Korea, Taiwan, and the other rapidly industrializing states of Asia carried out their transitions to capitalism under the auspices of authoritarian or quasi-authoritarian regimes. They did not have to worry about being voted out of office by an electorate fearing unemployment or distraught by the removal of subsidies on food, rent, and other necessities. Once capitalism was in place, these states moved, however grudgingly, in the direction of greater democracy. India, by contrast, is a democracy, and the proponents of economic reform must face the wrath of voters worried by an environment of growing economic insecurity.

International Interdependence and the Politics of India

The above discussion has focused on the domestic underpinnings of India's political crisis. Many Indians believe that their political and economic woes also have much to do with an unfavorable international environment. This point of view, generally referred to as dependency theory, argues that the major economic powers of the first world have little interest in stimulating economic development in India or in any other state of the third world.

While the merits of dependency theory continue to be debated, it is difficult to dispute the dominance of rich states in establishing the terms of trade with their less-developed counterparts. In what has come to be known as the North-South Dialogue, the poorer states of the world, most of which lie in the Southern Hemisphere, are demanding that the wealthy states of the Northern Hemisphere commit themselves to the economic and social development of the third world. In particular, they want favorable terms of trade with the countries of the North. The North or first world has shown willingness to do so, but only at a price.

In the case of India, the price of that help has been the scaling back of its vast network of government-owned enterprises, curtailing the suffocating Indian bureaucracy, and opening the Indian economy to multinational corporations. India has made great strides in liberalizing its economy, but it has yet to become as open as the West would prefer (Nayar 2003). Be this as it may, India has now surpassed China as the preferred location of first world countries seeking to shift production to the third world, due to a strong mix of low costs and high-tech resources (*Hindustan Times,* May 4, 2004, www). Indeed, India has become one of the world centers of information technology. Many Americans may be stunned to learn that 1-800 calls to the Social Security Administration and many other U.S. government agencies are being answered in India. As the *Hindustan Times* reports, even religion is being outsourced to India. "Faced with a shortage of priests in the West, European and American clergy are outsourcing 'mass intentions'— requests for services, such as Thanksgiving and memorial masses for the dead—to priests and congregations with time on their hands" (*Hindustan Times,* April 28, 2004, www).

India's relations with the United States were long strained by India's strong ties with the Soviet Union. India was not hostile to the United States, but it was hostile to Pakistan, a key component of America's global strategy. America armed Pakistan and India gravitated toward the U.S.S.R. in self-defense.

With the collapse of the Soviet Union in 1990–1991, India's ties with the United States began to thaw and have now reached the point at which India may become a "major non-NATO ally of the United States." The ties between the two countries have been strengthened by trade, by India's strong cooperation in American's war on terror, and by India's growing stature as a military power. Both Pakistan and India possess nuclear weapons and both have threatened to use them against the other (Nizamani 2000). India has eased its rhetoric and the United States has been appreciative. The United States also finds it awkward to be at odds with the world's largest democracy. India has also turned the other cheek to U.S. diplomatic affronts, not the least of which was the strip-searching of the Indian Minister of Defense on an official visit to the United States (*Hindustan Times,* July 13, 2004, www).

The problem, from the Indian perspective, is that the United States has retained its strong ties with Pakistan. Pakistan does enjoy the status of being a "major non-NATO ally of the United States." It is also one of the vital components in America's war on terror. This is somewhat ironic in as much as Pakistan long encouraged Jihadist attacks against Indian targets in Kashmir, a predominantly Muslim region that was awarded to India in 1947 (Zutshi 2004). Failing to regain the territory by military force, Pakistan turned to terror. The Jihadists carried out the attacks; the Pakistani government denied responsibility. During the 1990s, the United States also encouraged the development of Jihadist terrorists in Pakistan for deployment against Soviet forces in Afghanistan (Gunaratna 2002; Ali 2002). It made sense at the time, but now haunts both the United States and India (Palmer and Palmer 2004). General Musharraf, the Pakistani president, has vowed to crush the Jihadists in Pakistan, but results have been minimal. In the meantime, the Jihadists have begun to strike within India's major cities. Pakistan and India are attempting to reconcile their differences, but neither appears willing to give up their claims to Kashmir.

India's Muslims and Christians, in turn, warn of a growing number of Hindu terrorist groups and have asked the United Nations to include them on its list of world terrorist organizations.

CHALLENGES OF THE PRESENT AND
PROSPECTS FOR THE FUTURE

In Chapter 1 we outlined six standards of good government that find wide acceptance among the nations of the international community: democracy, stability, human rights, quality of life, economic growth, and environmental concern. Nehru's vision of a modern India personified these six standards. India was to be a stable democracy that guaranteed the human rights of all its diverse citizens. It was also to be a country that provided its citizens with an improving quality of life. Although India was a poor state, all Indians would have an equal opportunity to share in its development. Economic growth required no less. Although Nehru spoke little of environmental concern, the logic of his philosophy projected an India that would live in harmony with its physical universe.

To what extent, then, has India lived up to Nehru's vision of a stable democracy committed to human rights, an equitable quality of life, economic growth, and environmental harmony?

Democracy and Stability

There can be no ambiguity about India's status as a democracy. Free and fair elections are held at regularly scheduled intervals, and the winners of those elections take office and rule. Political parties and pressure groups abound, and the Indian press is free and vigorous. India's political elites also remain overwhelmingly committed to democracy. Unlike the situation in neighboring states, democracy is not being forced upon a reluctant leadership by a restive population.

While meeting all of the established criteria of a democratic state, India's practice of democracy has often differed from that of the West. Until very recently, India was a one-party democracy in which several parties contested for power but only the Congress Party ruled (Chhibber and Kollman 1998). Indian democracy is also a rough-and-tumble democracy in which the fine points of electoral decorum are not always observed (Austin 1995). Voting is conducted on different days in different regions in order to assure the maximum deployment of security forces. Four Indian states remain under virtual military rule.

India is now evolving into a multiparty democracy, a process which, while making India appear more democratic to Western observers, risks the destabilization of the Indian political system. Also undermining India's democracy is the decay of its political institutions. India's citizens once had faith in the fairness of their political institutions, but this faith has since been eroded. As discussed by Atul Kohli:

> India is still, of course, a functioning democracy, but increasingly it is not well governed. The evidence of eroding political order is everywhere. Personal rule has replaced party rule at all levels—national, state, and district. Below the rulers, the entrenched civil and police services have been politicized. Various social groups have pressed new and ever more diverse political demands in demonstrations that often have led to violence. The omnipresent

but feeble state, in turn, has vacillated; its responses have varied over a wide range: indifference, sporadic concessions, and repression (Kohli 1990, 5).

Ramakrishna Hegde echoes these sentiments:

The present system, especially during the past 20 years, has moved the country close to disintegration. The parliamentary system gives unlimited scope for horse-trading, floor-crossing and corruption. It is also responsible for the emergence of casteist (sic) and regional forces. It has led to political instability because of frequent elections (Hegde 1998).

In the final analysis, the success of India's democracy will depend upon the ability of its leaders to stem the violence, economic stagnation, and institutional decay that have become endemic to Indian politics (Austin 1995). In attempting to achieve this goal, India's democratic leaders have sought a compromise that will reconcile the widely divergent positions of the left and the right. To date, these efforts have produced timid policies that border on immobilization. In the meantime, India's social and economic problems continue to escalate. Because of these problems, there have been proposals to transform India into a presidential rather than a parliamentary system (*Times of India,* Feb. 2, 2000, www).

Human Rights

The Indian Constitution enumerates an impressive list of civil rights including the rights of free speech, religious expression, and assembly. All Indian citizens are equal before the law, regardless of race, creed, color, language, or gender. The Constitution addresses past grievances by reserving jobs, educational opportunities, and seats in Parliament for members of India's scheduled classes and tribes. In so doing, the Indian Constitution addresses group rights as well as individual rights. Ironically, the guarantee of group rights often contradicts the guarantee of individual rights. The Constitution, for example, gives preference to religious law in areas such as marriage, divorce, and inheritance. Muslim women are governed by more restrictive personal statutes than their Hindu counterparts, a clear violation of their individual rights as Indian citizens.

The situation of the disadvantaged groups is also problematic. The enforcement of group rights has fared much better than the enforcement of individual rights. Disadvantaged groups do receive enhanced educational and employment opportunities, but the picture is far from perfect. Most members of the disadvantaged groups find employment at the lowest levels of the bureaucracy, a fact that is attributable to a high rate of illiteracy among these groups (Madan 1989). Progress, however, is being made.

Rural workers also enjoy few rights in Indian society, with many in the more traditional states such as Bihar living in conditions of near-servitude. As local governments are controlled by the landowners, little has been done to alter that situation. The courts have sided with the landowners, citing the constitutional right of private property.

Growing religious and ethnic violence have placed a particular strain on India's attempts to guard the civil rights of minorities, with violence against them being endemic and attacks on Christians becoming pronounced in recent years (*Times of India,* Apr. 20, 2000, www). Illegal searches and seizures are becoming commonplace, and in extreme cases, soldiers have fired upon civilian crowds. Such atrocities have been particularly frequent in Government efforts to control the Sikhs in the Punjab and Islamic extremists in Kashmir. Prime Minister Singh, a Sikh, has vowed to stamp out sectarian violence, but this, of itself, requires the heavy hand of the law. The persistent threat of terror has also made it difficult for the Government to restrict emergency legislation that allows the army and the police to carry out mass arrests free of normal constitutional constraints (*Asia Times,* May 29, 2004, www). The Indian government acknowledges unfortunate excesses by its security forces, but generally views them as an exception to an otherwise strong record on human rights. The plight of Indian women is also acknowledged.

Economic Growth and Quality of Life

Nehru viewed economic growth and the provision of an equitable quality of life as part of the same package. Both were to be achieved by a socialist economic system in which India's resources, however meager, would be allocated in a rational and just manner. As India developed, so would the prosperity of all of its citizens.

The six decades since independence have seen dramatic improvements in the quality of Indian life. Its transition to capitalism, when complete, could make India the new economic tiger of Asia. Even in mid-transition from socialism to capitalism, India ranks as one of world's largest economies and manufactures everything from cars and buses to nuclear weapons. By its own calculations, it ranks eighth in a world power index that includes military, economic, and human resources (*Times of India,* March 29, 2004, www). Its green revolution has also assured self-sufficiency in grains for a country that long suffered from famine. The Indian middle and upper classes, moreover, are both highly skilled and prosperous. For them, India is shining.

The quality of life enjoyed by the middle and upper classes, unfortunately, is not shared by India's poor, a group that includes some 28–35 percent of the Indian population, depending on how one defines poverty. The poor, by and large, are illiterate, poorly fed, have little access to medical attention, and live in conditions of squalor. While all of India's poor live in penury, the rural poor are truly the wretched of the earth. The more India seems to develop, moreover, the greater the apparent gap between the two Indias. Despite all of its accomplishments, the Indian economy lags behind that of its Asian neighbors, including the People's Republic of China. Violence, crime, and political extremism are all fueled by the gap between the two Indias: the India that is shining and the India that is suffering.

Other quality of life issues also abound. HIV/AIDs has reached epidemic proportions (*Guardian,* Aug. 14, 2004, www). The aborting of female fetuses has created a crisis for India's bachelors. Demands for dowries, once a source of abuse, are becoming less stringent as the parents of daughters are becoming more choosy. Some are even requesting a bride price. At the very least, they are holding out for grooms with enhanced wealth and social standing. Life in India's major metropolitan areas is a struggle. Even here, however, there has been progress. In 2002, the Quality of Life Survey ranked New Delhi 177th among the 215 cities surveyed. By 2004 it had moved up to 154 (*Times of India,* March 14, 2004, www). Education is also suffering, as India has stressed high-tech universities and institutes to the detriment of primary education. This doesn't impact the middle and upper classes, but it does pose severe mobility problems for the poor (*Asia Times,* March 2, 2004, www). Poor Indians are becoming literate, but they are not becoming educated. A growing population also suggests that many of India's problems will remain for some time to come. India is expected to overtake China as the world's largest country in 30 years (*Guardian,* July 12, 2004, www).

The Environment

India's environmental record mirrors the duality of its record in regard to quality of life and human rights. Its environmental legislation is exemplary, but the enforcement of that legislation often leaves much to be desired (Khator 1991).

In part, India's environmental crisis finds its origins in the same tension between economic development and environmental concern that exists in most countries of the third world. Rapid economic growth, although it is destructive to the environment, provides much-needed jobs. It also provides the monies that the state requires to provide its citizens with an acceptable quality of life. Enforcement of environmental legislation slows economic growth. To date, the cruel choice between rapid development and environment has been settled in favor of economic development.

As with so much else in India, poor environmental enforcement is also a function of political expediency and bureaucratic laxity. Politicians are more concerned with stimulating growth than with controlling its side effects. Bureaucrats can't be bothered, especially when bribes are involved. Adding to the fray are escalating auto emissions, as India's growing wealth has been translated into a surging automobile sales. Human sanitation also lags. According to some estimates, some 690 million people have no access to proper sanitation. Some 150,000 die from water-related diseases on an annual basis (*Guardian,* Dec. 30, 2002, www).

The phenomenal growth of India's population makes the choice between economic growth and protecting the environment all the more difficult. An India of 360 million in 1947 has become an India of more than one billion today. A vigorous birth control program has slowed the rate of population growth to 1.8 percent per annum, but that figure translates into 16 million new citizens each year. Most will be born into poor and illiterate families.

Prospects for the Future

As India has moved grudgingly in the direction of greater capitalism, Western economists have begun to speak of an awakening Indian tiger whose economic muscle will rival that of its Asian neighbors. As the Indian economy grows, in their view, all Indians will benefit. The rich will get richer, but the increased wealth will "trickle down" to even the lowest rungs of Indian society. India's democracy will strengthen and its social problems lessen.

Such optimism rings hollow to those familiar with the depths of India's political and social woes. Increased capitalism has produced increased wealth, but that wealth has yet to trickle down to a third of India's population. If the violence and political instability caused by India's social problems continue to increase, both Indian democracy and the integrity of the Indian state will be placed under increasing strain.

Pessimism, however, is nothing new in India. Prophecies of despair have accompanied each stage of India's political evolution, yet Indian democracy has continued to survive despite formidable odds. More than likely, this strength and resilience will continue to sustain India in the years to come.

REFERENCES

Ali, Tariq. 2002. *The Clash of Fundamentalism: Crusades, Jihad, and Modernity.* London: Verso.

Almond, Gabriel, and Sidney Verba. 1963. *The Civic Culture.* Princeton, NJ: Princeton University Press.

Anderson, Walter. 1992. "Lowering the Level of Tension." In *India Briefing, 1992* (pp. 13–46), ed. Leonard A. Gordon and Philip Oldenburg. Boulder, CO: Westview Press.

Austin, Dennis. 1995. *Democracy and Violence in India and Sri Lanka.* New York: Council on Foreign Relations Press.

Basu, Alaka Malwade. 1992. *Culture, the Status of Women, and Demographic Behaviour: Illustrated with the Case of India.* Oxford: Clarendon Press.

Basu, Amrita. 1992. *Two Faces of Protest: Contrasting Modes of Women's Activism in India.* Berkeley, CA: University of California Press.

Baxter, Craig, ed. 2004. *Pakistan on the Brink: Politics, Economics, and Society.* Lanham, MD: Lexington Books.

Bayly, Susan. 1999. *Caste, Society and Politics in India from the Eighteenth Century to the Modern Age.* NY: Cambridge University Press.

Benderly, Beryl Lieff. 1986. "Religious Life." In *India: A Country Study* (pp. 131–76), ed. Richard F. Nyrop. Washington, DC: U.S. Government Printing Office.

Bonner, Arthur. 1990. *Averting the Apocalypse: Social Movements in India Today.* Durham, NC: Duke University Press.

Braibanti, Ralph, ed. 1966. *Asian Bureaucratic Systems Emergent from The British Imperial Tradition.* Durham, NC: Duke University Press.

Brass, Paul R. 1992. "Language, Religion and Politics." In *Foundations of India's Political Economy* (pp. 60–92), ed. Subroto Roy and William E. James. New Delhi: Sage.

Calman, Leslie J. 1992. *Toward Empowerment: Women and Movement Politics in India.* Boulder, CO: Westview Press.

Chakrabarty, Bidyut and Mohit Bhattacharya, eds. 2003. *Public Administration: A Reader.* NY: Oxford University Press.

Chandra, Kanchan. 2004. *Why Ethnic Parties Succeed: Patronage and Ethnic Head Counts in India.* Cambridge: Cambridge University Press.

Chaube, S. K. 1992. "The Campaign and Issues." In *Lok Sabha Elections 1989: Indian Politics in the 1990s* (pp. 72–85), ed. Mahendra Prasad Singh. Delhi: Kalinga Publications.

Chhibber, Pradeep K., and Ken Kollman. 1998 (June). "Party Aggregation and the Number of Parties in India and the United States." *American Political Science Review 92(2):* 329–342.

Chhibber, Pradeep K., and John R. Petrocik. 1990. "Social Cleavages, Elections and the Indian Party System." In *Diversity and Dominance in Indian Politics* (pp. 105–22), ed. Richard Sisson and Ramashray Roy. New Delhi: Sage.

Collins, Larry, and Dominique Lapierre. 1975. *Freedom at Midnight*. New York: Simon and Schuster.

Crossette, Barbara. 1992 (May 19). "India's Descent." *New York Times Magazine*.

Deliege, Robert. 1999. *The Untouchables of India*. Trans. by Nora Scott. London, England: Berg Pub., Ltd.

Deolalikar, Anil. 1992. "Nutrition and Health." In *Foundations of India's Political Economy: Towards an Agenda for the 1990s* (pp. 242–73), ed. Subroto Roy and William E. James. New Delhi: Sage Publications.

Dhadve, M. S. 1989. *Sociology of Slum*. New Delhi: Archives Books.

D'Souza, Victor S. 1990. *Development Planning and Structural Inequalities: The Response of the Underprivileged*. New Delhi: Sage.

Dua, Baghwan D. 1992. "Problems of Federal Leadership." In *Foundations of India's Political Economy: Towards an Agenda for the 1990s* (pp. 91–111), ed. Subroto Roy and William E. James. New Delhi: Sage.

Dua, B.D., and M.P. Singh, eds. 2003. *Indian Federalism in the New Millennium*. New Delhi: Manohar Pub.& Dis.

Dubey, Susan. 1992. "The Middle Class." In *India Briefing, 1992* (pp. 137–64), ed. Leonard A. Gordon and Philip Oldenburg. Boulder, CO: Westview Press.

Economist (The). 2005 (March 5). "The Tiger in Front: A Survey of India and China."

Embree, Ainslie T. 1990. *Utopias in Conflict: Religion and Nationalism in Modern India*. Berkeley, CA: University of California Press.

Fischer, Louis. 1954. *Gandhi: His Life and Message for the World*. New York: Mentor Books.

Frankel, Francine R. 1988. "Middle Classes and Castes in India's Politics." In *India's Democracy* (pp. 225–63), ed. Atul Kohli. Princeton, NJ: Princeton University Press.

Fuller, C. J. 1992. *The Camphor Flame: Popular Hinduism and Society in India*. Princeton, NJ: Princeton University Press.

Gandhi, Indira. 1972. "On Environmental Politics in India." Speech at the opening session of the United Nations Conference on Human Environment, Stockholm.

Ganguly, Meenakshi, and Greg Burke. 1998 (March 2). "That Gandhi Magic." *Time International* 150(27): 28.

Ganguly, Sumit. 1998 (Feb.). "India in 1997: Another Year of Turmoil." *Asian Survey* 38(2): 126–134.

Gilmartin, David. 1998 (July). "A Magnificent Gift: Muslim Nationalism and the Election Process in Colonial Punjab." *Comparative Studies in Society and History* 40(3): 415–36.

Gordon, Sandy. 1992. "Domestic Foundations of India's Security Policy." In *India's Strategic Future: Regional State or Global Power?* (pp. 6–34), ed. Ross Babbage and Sandy Gordon. London: Macmillan.

Gould, Harold A. 1990. *The Hindu Caste System, Vol. 3: Politics and Caste*. Delhi: Chanakya Publications.

Gunaratna, Rohan. 2002. *Inside Al Qaeda: Global Network of Terror*. NY: Columbia University Press.

Guru, Shyama Prasad. 1991. *Political Socialization of the Urban Political Elites*. New Delhi: Discovery Publishing House.

Hansen, Thomas Blom and Christophe Jaffrelot, eds. 2001. *The BJP and the Compulsions of Politics in India*. NY: Oxford University Press.

Hardgrave, Robert L., and Stanley A. Kochanek. 1993. *India: Government and Politics in a Developing Nation*. 5th ed. New York: Harcourt Brace Jovanovich.

Haworth, Abigail. 2004. (June.) *Marie Claire*, 77–82.

Hasan, Zoya, ed. 2002. *Parties and Party Politics in India*. NY: Oxford University Press.

Hegde, Ramakrishna. 1998 (Dec. 1). "Partisan of Good Politics." *The Times of India* 1–3, www.

Inoue, Kyoko. 1992. *Industrial Development Policy of India*. Tokyo: Institute of Developing Economies.

Jannuzi, F. Tomasson. 1989. *India in Transition: Issues of Political Economy in a Plural Society*. Boulder, CO: Westview Press.

Jodhka, Surinder S., ed. 2001. *Community and Identities: Contemporary Discourses on Culture and Politics in India.* Thousands Oaks, CA: Sage Pub.

Judd, Denis. 2004. *The Lion and the Tiger: The Rise and Fall of the British Raj.* Oxford: Oxford University Press.

Karna, M. N. 1989. "Studies in Peasant Protests and Agrarian Relations in India: A Trend Analysis." In *Peasant and Peasant Protests in India* (pp. 1–20), ed. M. N. Karna. New Delhi: Intellectual Publishing House.

Khator, Renu. 1991. *Environment, Development and Politics in India.* New York: University Press of America.

Kohli, Atul. 1990. *Democracy and Discontent: India's Growing Crisis of Governability.* Princeton, NJ: Princeton University Press.

Kohli, Atul, 1998 (July). "Enduring Another Election." *Journal of Democracy 9(3):* 7–20.

Krishna, Sumi. 1992. "The Language Situation: Mosaic or Melting Pot? In *Federalism in India: Origins and Development* (pp. 64–86), ed. Nirmal Mukarji and Balveer Arora. New Delhi: Vikas Publishing House PVT, LTD.

Kumar, Arun. 1991. *The Tenth Round: Story of Indian Elections 1991.* Calcutta: Rupa Co.

Kux, Dennis. 1992. *India and the United States: Estranged Democracies, 1941–1991.* Washington, DC: National Defense University Press.

Lipset, Seymour M. 1960. *Political Man.* New York: Doubleday.

Madan, N. L. 1989. *Indian Political System: Socio-Economic Dimensions.* Jawahar Nagar, Delhi: Ajanta Books International.

Mamoria, C. B., and S. L. Doshi. 1966. *Labour Problems and Social Welfare in India.* Delhi: Kitab Mahal Private.

Manor, James. 1992. "The State of Governance" In *Foundations of India's Political Economy: Towards an Agenda for the 1990s* (pp. 37–59), ed. Subroto Roy and William E. James. New Delhi: Sage Publications.

Manor, James. 1998 (July). "Making Federalism Work." *Journal of Democracy 9(3):* 21–35.

Mansingh, Surit. 1986. "Foreign Relations." In *India: A Country Study* (pp. 459–502), ed. Richard E Nyrop. Washington, DC: U.S. Government Printing Office.

Marshall, Paul. 2004. (June–July.) "Hinduism and Terror" *First Things: A Monthly Journal of Religion and Public Life,* (144): 10–14.

Mishra, Sachida Nand. 1980. *Political Socialization in Rural India: Social Change and Leadership Patterns in a Bihar Gram Panchayat.* Delhi: Inter-India Publications.

Misquitta, L. P. 1991. *Pressure Groups and Indian Democracy.* New Delhi: Sterling Publishers.

Mittal, S. P. 1986. "Perspectives of New Peasant Movements in India." In *The Peasant Movement Today* (pp. 135—45), ed. Sunil Sahasrabudhey. New Delhi: Ashish Publishing House.

Moog, Robert. 1998 (April). "Elite-Court Relations in India." *Asian Survey* 38(4): 410–423.

Naipaul, V. S. 1990. *India: A Million Mutinies Now.* New York: Viking Press.

Nayar, Baldev Raj. 2003. (July.) "Globalization and India's National Autonomy." *Commonwealth & Comparative Politics,* 41(2): 1–35.

Nizamani, Haider. 2000. *The Roots of Rhetoric: Politics of Nuclear Weapons in India and Pakistan* Westport, CN: Greenwood Publishing Group, 167.

Noorani, A. G. 1990. *Indian Affairs: The Political Dimension.* Delhi: Konark Publishers.

Nyrop, Richard F. 1986. *India: A Country Study.* Washington, DC: U.S. Government Printing Office.

Palmer, Monte and Palmer, Princess. 2004. *At the Heart of Terror: Islam, Jihadists, and America's War on Terror.* Lanham: MD.: Rowman & Littlefield Pub., Inc.

Roy, Subroto, and William E. James, eds. 1992. *Foundations of India's Political Economy: Towards an Agenda for the 1990s.* New Delhi: Sage.

Roychowdhury, Supriya. 2003 (Feb.) "Public Sector Restructuring and Democracy: The State, Labour, and Trade Unions in India." *Journal of Development Studies*, 9(3): 29(22).

Rudolph, Lloyd I., and Susanne H. Rudolph. 1987. *In Pursuit of Lakshmi: The Political Economy of the Indian State.* Chicago: University of Chicago Press.

Rudolph, Lloyd I., and Susanne H. Rudolph. 1998 (March 16). "Organized Chaos." *The New Republic* 218(11): 19–20.

Sahasrabudhey, Sunil. 1986. *The Peasant Movement Today.* New Delhi: Ashish Publishing House.

Seekins, Donald. 1986. "Government and Politics." In *India: A Country Study* (pp. 375–458), ed. Richard F. Nyrop. Washington, DC: U.S. Government Printing Office.

Sekhar, Chandra, and Mohan Dharia. 1969. "Committed Bureaucracy." *Hindustan Times* (New Delhi, December 1, 1969), cited in "Higher Civil Service in India" in *Administrative Systems Abroad* (pp. 96–126), ed. Krishna K. Tummala. Washington, DC: University Press of America.

Shah, Ghanshyam. 1988. "Grass-Roots Mobilization in Indian Politics." In *India's Democracy* (pp. 225–63), ed. Atul Kholi. Princeton, NJ: Princeton University Press.

Shah, Ghanshyam. 1990. *Social Movements in India.* New Delhi: Sage.

Shahin, Sultan. 2004. (May 11.) "Democracy, India's Newest Faith." *Asia Times*, http://www.atimes.com/atimes/South-Asia/FE11Df04.html.

Singh, Gurharpal. 1998 (April). "India's Akali–BJP Alliance." *Asian Survey* 38(4): 398–409.

Singh, Mahendra Prasad, ed. 1992. *Lok Sabha Elections 1989: Indian Politics in the 1990s.* Delhi: Kalinga Publications.

Sisson, Richard, and Stanley Wolpert, eds. 1988. *Congress and Indian Nationalism.*

Berkeley, CA: University of California Press.

Sivaramakrishnan, K. and Arun Agrawal, eds. 2003. *Regional Modernities: The Cultural Politics of Development in India.* NY: Oxford University Press.

Slater, Joanna, 2004 (May 5). "In India, a Job Paradox," *The Wall Street Journal,* May 5, 2004 pA12.

Thakur, Ramesh. 1998. "A Changing of the Guard in India." *Asian Survey* 38(6): 603–623.

Tharoor, Shashi. 2003. *Nehru: The Invention of India.* NY: Arcade Pub.

Thompson, Edward. 1980. *The Making of the Indian Princes.* Columbia, MO: South Asia Books.

Todaro, Michael. 1989. *Economic Development in the Third World.* New York: Longman.

Tomlinson, B. R. 1992. "Historical Roots of Economic Policy." In *India's Political Economy* (pp. 275–305), ed. Subroto Roy and William E. James. New Delhi: Sage.

Tully, Mark, and Zareer Mansani. 1988. *From Raj to Rajiv: 40 Years of Indian Independence.* London: BBC Books.

Tummala, Krishna K. 1982. "Higher Civil Service in India." In *Administrative Systems Abroad* (pp. 96–126), ed. Krishna K. Tummala. Washington, DC: University Press of America.

Vanaik, Achin. 1990. *The Peaceful Transition.* London: Verso.

Varshney, Ashutosh. 2002. *Ethnic Conflict and Civic Life: Hindus and Muslims in India.* New Haven, CN: Yale University Press.

Weiner, Myron. 1957. *Party Politics in India.* Princeton, NJ: Princeton University Press.

Zutshi, Chitralekha. 2004. *Languages of Belonging: Islam, Regional Identify, and the Making of Kashmir.* NY: Oxford University Press.

Population:
104,959,594 (2004 estimate)

Life expectancy at birth:
75 years (total population)
72 years (men)
78 years (women)

Literacy:
92 percent of people age 15
and over can read and write
(2003 estimate)

Capital:
Federal District (Mexico City)

Per capita income:
$9,000

10

Mexico

The Long Road to Democracy and Beyond

STEPHEN D. MORRIS

On December 1, 2000, Vicente Fox Quezada[1] of the **National Action Party (PAN)** was sworn in as Mexico's president, ending over seven decades of one-party rule by the **Institutional Revolutionary Party (PRI)**. This monumental change did not come suddenly, but capped a long political transition marked by the gradual erosion of support for the PRI, incremental reforms of the electoral system, and the steady rise of opposition parties like the PAN. Nor could this democratic breakthrough be attributed to any one person or group, but rather to the struggle of thousands of individuals working within political parties, labor unions, human rights and other civic organizations, working through both systemic and anti-systemic channels, to pressure the one-party authoritarian regime for change. Though most observers now label Mexico as democratic, the 2000 defeat of the PRI did not mean that the country had overcome the legacies of authoritarianism or that it had succeeded in erecting a fully functioning democracy. Much remained to be done. Indeed since taking office, Fox has faced challenges in his efforts to broaden and deepen democratic reform, to refashion the old while crafting the new. Recent changes offer hope, however, Mexico continues to face an uncertain political and economic future.

Once referred to as "one of the seven political science wonders of the world" (Blum 1997, 34), the Mexican political system has long puzzled observers.

---

[1]Latin Americans formally use two last names, the paternal followed by the maternal last name. In general usage, it is the paternal last name that is used.

Because the political system that emerged from the violent Revolution of 1910–1917 fused characteristics of pluralist democracy (a progressive constitution, formal division of powers, and elections) with authoritarian practices (extreme concentration of power in the presidency, single-party dominance, repression, and electoral fraud) it was difficult to label the system as either democratic or authoritarian. Indeed, the Mexican system seemed unique. Unlike other Latin American countries known for political instability, military coups, brutal repression, and democratic-authoritarian cycles, under the PRI Mexico enjoyed stable, civilian-controlled institutions for most of the twentieth century. The unique system kept the military on the political sidelines, and never relied extensively on repression to control the population. Also unlike other authoritarian regimes, Mexico's PRI-led system was inclusive, not exclusive, incorporating a broad spectrum of societal interests. In addition, the regime transferred political power regularly and peacefully by using elections that combined fair (opposition parties) and unfair (fraud) tactics to legitimize the PRI's rule.

Mexico's unique road to democracy continues to set the country apart from other democratic transitions in two fundamental ways. First, how it got to this point is distinct. In contrast to the elite negotiated transitions in many Latin American countries that put an end to military rule and established new elections, or in contrast to the collapse of the communist-led regimes in Eastern Europe, in Mexico change came gradually. Over a number of years, the tightly centralized PRI-led system that had evolved from the Revolution slowly, but steadily unraveled. The PRI lost more and more of its support at the polls and seats in government, the once omnipotent president slowly ceded power to other governmental institutions, the scope of freedom gradually expanded, and the ideological pillars that once helped legitimize the authoritarian edifice slowly withered. Even electoral fraud and repression, used strategically to help keep the PRI in power, gradually lost their capacity to stem the tide of change.

In addition to the protracted transition, there is a second important distinction between the democratic transition in Mexico and the road followed by other countries. It centers on the nature of the current regime and the unique challenges it faces. Whereas most recent new democracies started with virtually a clean slate with new actors and new institutions, the slow and incremental change in Mexico has meant that the old institutions, interests, and actors (like the PRI itself) have remained largely intact, providing the framework for the day-to-day political dynamics and many of the challenges facing President Fox. Thus the 2000 election becomes a step in the broader process of democratization.

The political uniqueness of Mexico—the longest authoritarian regime in modern history, the protracted democratic transition, and the combination of the old with the new—makes the study of Mexican politics exciting, and the country has attracted considerable scholarly attention over the years as a result. But the country's salience to the U.S. and the world further bolsters the country's importance. Mexico shares a porous 1,952-mile border with the U.S.—the longest border bridging a first and **third world** country. Thanks in large part to the 1994 North American Free Trade Agreement (NAFTA) that inaugurated a free trade zone linking Mexico, the U.S., and Canada, Mexico now ranks as the second-largest trading partner of the U.S. behind Canada.[2] Everyday about $65 million worth of goods cross the busiest border in the world. Mexico also is the largest source of immigrants to the U.S. with an estimated 20–25 million people of Mexican origin currently residing in the U.S.—a trend that is transforming the demographic and cultural landscape of both countries.[3] And with an estimated 75 percent of the illegal drugs entering the U.S. passing through Mexico's arid and mountainous terrain, the country also figures prominently in the U.S. war on drugs.

But Mexico is also important in its own right notwithstanding its salience to the U.S. Mexico is the largest Spanish-speaking nation in the world. It is the thirteenth largest country by area—roughly the size of the United Kingdom, France, Spain, Italy, and Germany combined—and the eleventh most populous (104.9 million in 2004). It has the twelfth largest economy based on purchasing power ($648.5 billion in 2002), ranks as the eighth largest producer of crude oil, the second largest recipient of foreign investment among developing countries, and a diplomatic leader among third world nations. Though poor when compared to developed countries (U.S. per capita income is approximately 6 times that of Mexico and Mexico ranks 80th globally), Mexico is classified as a high income developing country. Moreover, Mexico was the first developing country to ever host the Olympic games. It has given the world Nobel winners in literature (Octavio Paz), chemistry (Mario Molina), and peace (Alfonso Garcia Robles), and has made notable contributions to the worlds of art (Frida Kahlo, Diego Rivera, Rufino Tamayo), cinema (Selma Hayek, Mario Moreno, Anthony Quinn), music (Plácido Domingo, Augustin Lara, Luis Miguel), literature (Carlos Fuentes, Octavio Paz), and sports (Oscar Chávez, Esteban Loaiza, Fernando Valenzuela).

Our exploration of Mexican politics will highlight the system's unique features and recent changes. We begin with a brief overview of the nation's history: a history marked by a rich indigenous past, political instability and revolution, foreign invasion, the fracturing and loss of territory, and the unique PRI-led system. Next, we will examine the country's main political institutions as they developed since the Revolution and as they have evolved in recent years with the onset of democracy. Our next focus of attention will be the main actors in the political drama. We will examine the "informal" rules that structured the elite-dominated political game under the PRI, the ability of the PRI-system to hold onto power for so long, the major political parties and the nature of elections, the politics of groups and citizens, and the changing roles of the various political actors in recent years. Shifting our focus somewhat, we will explore the broader context of Mexican politics with brief discussions of Mexican political culture, economic policy, and the country's all-important relationship with the U.S. In the concluding section we will look at Mexico's political challenges and prospects for the future, raising a series of critical questions: Will NAFTA and the neoliberal economic reforms of the past decade pave the way for sustainable and equitable growth? Despite ongoing political problems, will Mexico be able to

---

[2]NAFTA is a lengthy accord designed to lower tariffs and trade barriers between Mexico, the U.S., and Canada. The agreement went into effect January 1, 1994, and will eliminate virtually all tariffs on trade by 2009.

[3]In 2004, Mexicans in the U.S. will remit an estimated $14 billion to family inside Mexico—an amount second only to the exportation of oil in dollar earnings and more than foreign direct investment.

construct a functioning democratic system and extend the protection of basic human rights to all?

MEXICO IN HISTORICAL PERSPECTIVE

Pre-Columbian History

As most visitors to the country soon realize, Mexico is an archeological treasure, featuring a rich history dating as far back as 10,000 BC and incorporating an array of indigenous cultures. The Olmecs, best known for their colossal carved stone heads and cult of the jaguar, were among the first groups, flourishing in the eastern-central region of the country around 1200 BC. The classic period, stretching from 200 BC to AD 1000, featured the resplendent cultures of the Teotihuacán in the valley of Mexico, the Monte Albán in what is today the southern state of Oaxaca, and the Maya in the Yucatan peninsula. Perhaps better known are the groups that thrived in the post-classic period, such as the Toltecs, the Zapotecs, and later the Mexica or Aztecs whose empire spanned most of the central and southern portions of the country by the sixteenth century.

The numerous archeological sites and anthropological museums dotting the landscape and attracting millions of tourists each year bear witness to the nation's rich indigenous heritage. Mexico's indigenous past informs popular legends, beliefs, and practices. For the majority of Mexico's **mestizo** or mixed Spanish-Indian population, their indigenous roots serve as a source of pride and a component of personal and national identity—a sentiment nurtured by the government's promotion of the ideas of *mexicanidad* and *indigenismo* in the 1920s and 1930s. Even today, according to the 2000 census, about 7.3 million indigenous people remain culturally distinct from the mestizo mainstream, speaking one of among one hundred different indigenous languages heard across the country. Most of the indigenous Mexicans live in the southern regions and sadly, suffer the worst levels of poverty, social discrimination, and political repression of any social group—an irony given the important place of indigenous peoples in the nation's history and psyche. The deplorable conditions of the present-day indigenous helped trigger the guerrilla uprising in 1994 by the Ejército Zapatista de Liberación Nacional (EZLN) (Zapatista Army of National Liberation) in the southern state of Chiapas and their struggle since then, through more peaceful and political means, to assert the political and cultural rights of indigenous peoples.

Conquest and Colonization

The great Aztec city of Tenochtitlán (see box) —now the site of Mexico City—fell to the Spanish *conquistadores* led by Hernán Cortez in 1520, making him Mexico's greatest villain and ushering in three centuries of Spanish colonial rule. The legacies of colonial rule over what was then called New Spain are many. The Spanish imposed a strong, centralized authoritarian state upon indigenous Mexico, with power concentrated in the hands of the viceroy. They imposed an all-powerful and privileged Catholic Church that instilled Christianity, the Spanish language, and attitudes of intolerance toward those who disagreed with the

The Aztec Founding of Tenochtitlán

Legend has it that the Aztecs set out from the north sometimes after AD 1100 to establish a city on the site where, according to prophecy, they were to find an eagle perched atop a cactus in the middle of a lake devouring a snake. After years of wandering, their search ended when they entered the valley of Anahuac and gazed out upon Lake Texcoco. After years battling rival tribes, they established on that site the glorious city of Tenochtitlán: a city rivaling the great municipal centers of Europe by the time of the conquest. Since then, Tenochtitlán, now known as Mexico City, has been the political, economic, and cultural center of Mexico, while the symbol of the eagle atop the cactus adorns the Mexican flag. The Aztecs or Mexicas also provided the country with its modern-day name, while words from the náhuatl language, including chocolate, coyote, and many others, inform more than just Mexican Spanish.

Church's teachings. The Spanish colonial rulers erected an economic order that turned Mexico's abundance, particularly its rich mineral resources, into Spanish wealth. And through miscegenation, the Spanish created the bronze race of the mestizo. The colonial system rested atop a strict racial and cultural hierarchy. Those of Spanish descent enjoyed the highest positions; the mestizos were relegated to an ambiguous legal–social status, and the indigenous, at the lowest rung, provided the physical labor. Though the crown officially abolished Indian slavery in the 1550s, systems of forced labor prevailed long afterwards. Colonialism even fostered a legacy of corruption. Because laws were made in distant Spain and not only took time to reach the colony but failed to reflect local conditions, a culture of disrespect for the law and corruption took hold.

In many ways, Mexico's three hundred years of colonialism transformed the land and its people. The Spanish built mining camps to extract Mexican silver; introduced European crops, draft animals, and technology; altered production and trade; and developed ranching on huge estates, particularly in the drier northern regions of the country, taking land from the indigenous communities. But among the many transformations wrought by the Spanish, none was more devastating than the introduction of diseases such as smallpox and measles against which the indigenous population had virtually no defense. Though estimates vary widely, Mexico's indigenous population fell drastically from around 30 million at the time of the conquest to fewer than 1 million less than a century later. Mexico would not reach the 30 million population mark again until the middle of the twentieth century.

Independence and Instability: The Nineteenth Century

As in other Latin American countries, Napoleon and war in Europe triggered Mexico's struggle for independence. Stretching from 1810 to 1821, Mexico's independence movement left a unique legacy of popular, mass-based uprisings that failed to achieve their objectives, but that produced some of the nation's most important heroes and ideals. Initiating the *Grito de Dolores* (Cry from the town of Dolores in the state of Guanajuato) on September 16, 1810 (recognized as Mexico's independence day), the priests Miguel Hidalgo and later Jose Maria Morelos (the fathers of Mexican independence) led peasant/indigenous-based mass

Schalkwijk/Art Resource, NY

Shown here is a detail from a Diego Rivera mural of the ancient Aztec city of Tenochtitlan, on the site of present-day Mexico City.

uprisings under the banner of the Virgin of Guadalupe (see box p. 423). Demanding liberty, an end to slavery, and modest social reforms, Hidalgo and Morelos' peasant armies attacked Spanish citizens and property. But both leaders were captured by royal forces and executed. The decapitated heads of Hidalgo and his cohorts were put on public display in the city of Guanajuato. Only after years of intermittent struggle in 1821 would Mexico finally attain its independence, but not in a mass-based popular movement, nor for such progressive goals as those inspired by Hidalgo and Morelos. Instead, a conservative general from the colonial army, General Augustin de Inturbide, would switch sides to join other reformist rebels to expel the Spanish rulers and establish himself as Mexico's first emperor, a post that lasted only a year and a half.

Throughout much of the nineteenth century, political instability, foreign intervention, and economic turmoil engulfed Mexico, scarring the country permanently. In the aftermath of the bloody independence struggle, and with the economy in ruins, conflict erupted between two main elite factions: the Conservatives and the Liberals. The Conservatives favored centralized authority, respect for traditional Spanish values, and protection of the position and privileges of the Catholic Church. Liberals, influenced by the ideals of the French and American Revolutionaries, rejected Spanish traditions, embraced republican and free-market ideals, and sought to curtail the overwhelming economic and political power of the Church. The deep split led to almost constant conflict,

The Virgin de Guadalupe

The Virgin of Guadalupe is the most important religious and cultural symbol of Mexico. According to legend, the dark-skinned Virgin appeared to the Indian peasant Juan Diego on December 9 and 12, 1531, on the hill of Tepeyac outside Mexico City, a site where Indians had always worshiped Tonantzin, the mother of gods. Unable to convince the bishop of the apparition, Juan Diego returned to the site, where the Virgin called out his name. This time the Virgin gave Juan Diego roses, a rarity to the region, and instructed him to carry the roses in the fold of his shirt to the bishop. When Juan Diego unfurled his peasant shirt to present the roses, the shirt bore the likeness of the Virgin. In her honor, a shrine was erected on the site. The legend hastened the Christianization of the indigenous population, and the Virgin of Guadalupe became the nation's symbol. Just as Fathers Hidalgo and Morelos fought for Mexican independence under the banner of the Virgin of Guadalupe, her image today adorns the homes of millions of modern-day Mexicans and millions flock to visit the Basilica built in her honor. During his 1998 visit to Mexico, then Pope John Paul II recognized the importance of the Virgin of Guadalupe to Mexico and all Hispanics. A few years later, the Church canonized Juan Diego.

and the periodic emergence of military strongmen who could provide a semblance of order. It also set the stage for foreign intervention.

During the early decades of the nineteenth century, Mexico was larger geographically than the U.S. But holding the huge, sparsely populated country together amid such political turmoil proved particularly difficult. Soon after independence, the country confronted the fracturing of its territory in the north and in the Yucatan peninsula. Though the government put down the quest for independence in the Yucatan, it was unable to prevent American settlers in the north from establishing an independent Texas in 1836. Eleven years later when Texas joined the American union, the U.S., long desirous of Mexican land and drunk on the ideas of Manifest Destiny (the belief that God had destined the U.S. to conquer and civilize the western frontier), launched an all-out war against Mexico. When the fighting ended with the U.S. invasion of Mexico City (hence the line in the U.S. Marine Hymn: "From the Halls of Montezuma"), Mexico was forced to relinquish half its territory to its northern neighbor, ceding the lands of current-day California, Arizona, New Mexico, Nevada, and parts of Colorado. No country in modern times has lost as much territory to a foreign invader. The event wounded the nation's pride, feeding a sense of anti-Americanism that has held for years. Indeed, the *niños heroes* or child heroes—the young cadets who leaped to their death at Chapultepec Castle in Mexico City rather than surrender to invading U.S. forces—still rank as important national heroes officially recognized on September 13.

But the war with the U.S. was not the only episode of foreign invasion and instability during the period. Following the victory of the Liberals behind Benito Juarez[4] in the War of the Reform (1858–1861), Spanish, French, and British forces

---

[4]Benito Juárez served as president of Mexico from 1858 to 1872. He is popularly viewed as the greatest Mexican president in history.

took control of the Gulf port of Veracruz in 1861 to collect on past loans. England and Spain withdrew following negotiations, but the French, encouraged by Mexico's Conservatives, launched a war of occupation. Though defeated temporarily in the battle of Zaragoza on May 5, 1862—the famous Cinco de Mayo celebration of today—Napoleon III's troops eventually gained control of the country in 1864 and placed the Austrian duke Maximilian on the throne. Civil war ensued as the Liberals, exiled in the U.S., struggled to overturn the monarchical order and re-establish republican rule. In 1867, after years of struggle and aided by the U.S., Benito Juárez defeated the French and returned to power.

Historians Michael Meyer and William Sherman (1995) cite the victory of Juarez in 1867 as the beginning of modern Mexico. During his three terms as president, Juárez—and Sebastian Lerdo following Juárez's death in 1872—re-instituted liberal policies that stripped the Church of its political and economic power, opened a free internal market, broke up the communal landholdings of the Indians to encourage private land ownership, strengthened the power of the state, and promoted secular education and development. But divisions within the liberal ranks led to revolt in 1871 when General Porfirio Díaz, in what would become one of Mexico's greatest historical ironies, assailed the practice of indefinite re-election. He rose up in rebellion and took control of the nation in 1876.

The Porfiriato and the Mexican Revolution

Stressing order as necessary for development, Díaz consolidated his grip on political power and ruled Mexico for more than three decades, a period known as the **Porfiriato**. During this brutal authoritarian period, Díaz promoted the development of agricultural exports by large landowners—foreign and domestic—who pushed peasants off the land, leaving millions landless. He opened the country to foreign businesses and oversaw the construction of the nation's first railroads, the revitalization of the mining industry, and the drilling of vast oil fields. Maintaining a sham of democracy that selected a string of powerless presidents, Díaz ruled from behind the throne with a combination of political mastery and an iron fist, relying on the army and the rural police to keep order. By the turn of the century, Mexico could indeed point to many achievements under Díaz: political stability, economic growth, an increase in the population, improvements in health and sanitation, the beginnings of industry, and a boom in the nation's cultural and intellectual life. Yet Mexico remained basically a rural society with land concentrated in the hands of a few and a mass peasant population living in conditions worse than those of their ancestors. Under the system of haciendas, for example, fifteen of the richest Mexican landowners owned more than three hundred thousand acres each.

Despite the economic advances under Díaz, by the first decade of the twentieth century the dictator faced strong opposition. In a dramatic call to arms, Francisco Madero, the leader of the Anti-Re-electionist Party,[5] spearheaded a

---

[5]Recall that Díaz 's rise to power was also based on the idea of no re-election.

revolt on November 20, 1910 celebrated today as the Day of the Mexican Revolution. This opened one of the bloodiest chapters in the history of the nation and the first social revolution of the twentieth century. Rebel armies sprang up in towns throughout the country and by May 1911, Díaz resigned and fled to Europe. Madero then was elected president in what most considered to be a relatively free election. But Madero was killed two years later in a military coup led by Victoriano Huerta and supported by the U.S. Once again, the revolutionary generals, some of whom had continued to fight despite Madero's victory, rose up in arms against Huerta's reactionary government. The major protagonists included Generals Venustiano Carranza and Alvaro Obregon of the Constitutionalist army in the north, Pancho Villa from the northern state of Chihuahua, and Emiliano Zapata in the state of Morelos just south of Mexico City. By 1915, anarchy reigned as civil war engulfed large parts of the country. By 1917, more than a million and a half Mexicans were dead (over 10 percent of the population), many more were left homeless, and the economy lay devastated. Within a few years, those who would eventually become the nation's Revolutionary heroes— Madero, Carranza, Villa, Zapata, and Obregon—would all meet violent deaths.

Upon gaining the upper hand militarily, Carranza organized a constituent assembly that met in the city of Querétaro in 1917 to draft a new constitution. The document, which despite many changes remains in force today, gave meaning to the Mexican Revolution and shaped Mexican political thought for years to come. Designed to satisfy as many political interests as possible, the document contained strong anti-clerical language, greatly restricting the role of the Church in politics and society; it promised land to the peasants in response to the abuses under the Porfiriato and the demands of Zapata's agrarian guerrillas; it granted the state exclusive rights to exploit the subsoil in contrast to Díaz's policy of turning mines over to foreigners; it provided extensive rights to workers, including an eight-hour work day, a minimum wage, and equal pay for equal work; it established an array of political freedoms; and, reflecting perhaps the primary problem of the Díaz period, it banned re-election.

But despite the new constitution and the Carranza victory, conflict continued to rack the country. Carranza was ousted and killed by his once-trusted advisor Alvaro Obregon, who himself was gunned down years later by a lone assassin upset over the government's anti-Church policies. In a bid to quell such violent conflict, consolidate power, and provide for an orderly transfer of power among the Revolutionary elite, President Plutarco Elías Calles (1924–1928) brokered an agreement among the elite to establish the Party of the National Revolution (PNR) in 1929—the forerunner of today's PRI. Established from the seat of political power, the young party demonstrated during the 1929 presidential election its capability to mobilize the electorate and, according to some, even use fraud to garner victory. Though Calles ruled from behind the scenes for more than a decade—a period known as the Maximato—the PNR became the nation's preeminent political vehicle, incorporating and channeling the aspirations and demands of the nation's political elite. As such, it brought needed political stability to the country and ended the violence of the Revolutionary period.

General Porfirio Díaz ruled Mexico with an iron fist for more than three decades, promoting industrialization at the expense of indigenous peasants.

The term of Lázaro Cárdenas (1934–1940), one of Mexico's most popular presidents, brought to an end what is referred to as the Revolutionary Phase in Mexican politics. During this period, Cárdenas greatly strengthened the power of the presidency and the state. He forced former President Calles into exile and incorporated the nation's major labor and peasant organizations into the dominant party, turning these organizations into "official" and privileged sectors of the party. Known at the time as the PRM (Party of the Mexican Revolution), the dominant party not only monopolized political power, but also represented both ideologically and organizationally the nation's major labor and peasant groups. At the same time, Cárdenas began to implement with unprecedented vigor the more radical, socialistic components of the Constitution, further broadening the power and scope of the state. He took land from wealthy landowners and gave it to peasants organized into state-controlled cooperatives known as *ejidos*. He nationalized the foreign oil companies following a labor dispute, creating the state-owned oil company Pemex (Petróleos Mexicanos). And he promoted the state's role in developing infrastructure, particularly in the countryside, providing a foundation for the nation's subsequent industrial growth. Building on Calles's accomplishments, he also promoted a strongly nationalistic and socialistic ideology rooted in the ideals of the Mexican Revolution, a glorification of the nation's indigenous past, and a cultural renaissance.

In response to the abuses of the *Porfiriato,* Mexican revolutionaries sought to improve conditions for workers aned peasants. Political conflict continued for years, leading to the formation of the Party of the National Revolution (PNR) in 1929.

The Institutionalized Revolution

The unique political edifice built in the aftermath of the Revolution provided the foundation for an unprecedented period of political stability and economic prosperity in Mexico that stretched from the 1940s to the early 1980s. The president's authority was largely unquestioned, and the dominant party—which by 1946 became known as the PRI—channeled popular demands, mobilized the vote, and distributed political spoils and the rewards of economic growth. Meanwhile, the constitutional prohibition on re-election ensured presidential authority and fluidity of leadership. With such political stability in effect, the government downplayed many of the more radical, socialist ideals of the Revolution and focused its energies on developing the country along more capitalist lines. Like other governments of the region during this time, the Mexican government rejected the notion that free trade and free markets alone could pull the country out of its poverty and underdevelopment and thus took the lead in promoting economic development by using its extensive powers to build infrastructure, encourage local industry and foreign investment, and restrict foreign competition.

In many ways the strategy of development paid off. For more than 30 years, the economy grew at an average annual rate of over 6 percent, transforming Mexico from a predominantly rural, agrarian-based, and illiterate society into an urban, largely industrial, and literate country. Clearly the lives of millions improved during these years. And for the first time in its history, Mexico enjoyed a large increase in its population, which skyrocketed from 22 million in 1945 to more than 70 million by 1980.

The relationship between political stability and economic development is complex. On the one hand, Mexico's decades of economic growth, known as the "Mexican Miracle," clearly contributed to its remarkable political stability. Growth supplied real benefits that could be distributed to those incorporated into the PRI, particularly the privileged labor, peasant, and bureaucratic organizations; it kept the nation's business elite satisfied and thus "out of politics"; and it provided sufficient spoils to reward government officials who chose to play by the rules of the PRI-dominated political game. Economic growth also fostered a measure of popular legitimacy that led many to overlook the lack of true democracy, the corruption, the electoral fraud, or the selective repression of the regime's opponents. Yet, on the other hand, economic growth and development also set the stage for eventual political change by giving rise to new social organizations and interests that would increasingly stand outside of the PRI-dominated political framework, thereby straining the political system. With growing prosperity, demands by workers, students, business, and the growing educated middle class for greater autonomy, liberty, and free elections grew more and more insistent, often triggering repression. In 1968, for example, weeks prior to the opening of the Olympic Games in Mexico City, students, joined by middle-class citizens and workers, staged massive protests against the authoritarian government. They carried signs protesting government repression, the denial of basic rights, and the massive poverty of the people. The government responded brutally, killing hundreds of protesters and arresting thousands more. The event—a watershed in Mexican political history—revealed some of the failings of the political system and underscored the need for fundamental political change.

Crises and Change

The stability of the *institutionalized period* flowed perhaps as much from the capacity of the regime to overcome crisis as from the absence of crisis. Events in the 1980s and 1990s severely tested this reformist capacity. Facing growing budget deficits and balance-of-payment problems, the government incurred significant debt during the 1970s and early 1980s. Part of the debt resulted from the more populist governmental efforts to respond to the social problems championed by the students and the left in 1968. Though oil exports provided a surge of economic growth from 1978–1981, global economic conditions turned sour in 1981 when oil prices dropped and interest rates rose. By August 1982, the Mexican government was bankrupt, unable to meet its obligations to foreign banks. Economic growth, long the source of regime legitimacy, plummeted. Recovery proved difficult as the country embarked on a rocky road spiked with the multiple challenges of economic and political crisis and change. In response to the deep economic crisis, Presidents Miguel de la Madrid (1982–1988), Carlos Salinas de Gortari (1988–1994) and Ernesto Zedillo (1994–2000) downplayed the more progressive tenets of the revolutionary ideology and began to dismantle the economic model of the "Miracle" years. They removed trade restrictions, joined the General Agreement on Trade and Tariffs (GATT—currently the World Trade Organization), negotiated free trade agreements with the U.S., Canada (NAFTA), and many others, privatized hundreds of state-owned industries, opened the economy to foreign investment, and cut back drastically on social programs and government spending. In a period of about a decade, Mexico would go from a closed economy to one of the most open economies in the world.

In the midst of economic crisis and reforms, pressures for political change mounted. Opposition parties, once pacified by being allowed minor representation in Congress, pressed harder for free and open elections, gained popular support, and thus challenged the PRI's hold on power at the polls. Many new social organizations, human rights groups, indigenous groups and others, together with existing business and labor organizations, became more active, clamoring for a greater role in the system while challenging the state's and the PRI's controls over society. And as the government struggled to pay off its massive foreign debt to international commercial banks, it found that it had few spoils to distribute to help shore up support. Even once tolerable levels of political corruption among political leaders began to draw a firestorm of criticism in the wake of economic crisis, further undermining the legitimacy of the PRI-controlled government. By the late 1980s, such pressures created divisions within the ranks of the PRI itself as Cuauhtémoc Cárdenas (and many others) quit the party of his famous father to challenge the PRI's contender, Carlos Salinas, in the 1988 election. Although election officials declared Salinas the victor with barely 50 percent of the vote, the election was so marred by fraud that the outcome further robbed the regime of its legitimacy (the true results of that election may never be known). It was clear that politics as usual had become untenable and that political reform was inevitable.

Salinas (1988–1994) took office at a difficult time. Fearing the rise of the newly formed **PRD**, he brokered a political deal with the PAN, consolidated power through such measures as a new and massive social program known as Solidarity, and continued to deepen the economic reforms. While providing the PAN with some new political space (recognizing the first loss of a PRI gubernatorial candidate in 1989), the Salinas government used repression and electoral fraud to keep the PRD at bay. Combined with the restoration of economic growth in the early 1990s, such measures helped Salinas overcome or at least forestall fundamental political change. But political conflict reached new heights in the mid-1990s just as Salinas was preparing to depart from office. On January 1, 1994, coinciding with the beginning of NAFTA, a group of indigenous rebels seized control of a series of small towns in the southern state of Chiapas. Two months later, Salinas's handpicked presidential candidate for the PRI, Luis Donaldo Colosio, was gunned down in open daylight in Tijuana. Though the fighting in Chiapas soon gave way to prolonged negotiations, the EZLN nonetheless challenged the PRI's hold on power in the state, raised questions about indigenous rights, and increased the popular pressures on the government to make true democratic reforms. And despite the fact that President Salinas handpicked a replacement candidate who was able to win the August 1994 election, divisions among the political elite would continue to fester.

Soon after President Zedillo (1994–2000) took office, the economy once again fell into a deep recession. Thousands of businesses went bankrupt, personal and public debt skyrocketed, the middle class shrank, and poverty climbed. Among the many effects, the crisis produced a major split between President Zedillo and former President Salinas as well as further divisions within the PRI: a split made complete when the government jailed Salinas' brother for the 1994 murder of PRI leader Francisco Ruiz, prompting former President Salinas to flee the country. More critically, the economic crisis strengthened the appeal of the opposition parties and forced the government to agree to a series of electoral reforms that placed elections in the hands of an independent entity. This made elections freer and campaigns more equal, and thus set the stage for the opposition to register important electoral gains, including the presidency in 2000. Though Fox would inherit the institutions of the past and face many of the same policy challenges as his predecessors, he would inherit a distinct political setting and face a new balance of political forces. Getting things done, however, as we will see, would prove very difficult for the new president.

THE POLITICAL INSTITUTIONS OF MEXICO

To understand Mexican politics during and after the PRI's long reign in power, it is useful to distinguish between the system's formal rules and the way it actually operates. The gap between the ideal and the reality not only provides a partial explanation for the confusion over the nature of Mexican politics noted at the outset, but also adds to the tension that shapes political developments today. As we will see, the incremental reforms during the long transition center largely on efforts to push the system closer to the way it is supposed to operate and away from the way it had functioned in the past.

The Constitution

Mexico's is a highly legalistic society, a trait it inherited from Spain and the medieval period. This means that government acts must be justified and grounded firmly in the written law, and that dealing with the government usually entails a mountain of legal paperwork and regulations. The Mexican Constitution, drafted in 1917 and amended frequently since then, lays out the basic parameters of the political system and serves as a guide to the legitimizing ideals and goals of the system (if not its operation). The Constitution may not define what actually happens, but it at least specifies what "should" happen. The Mexican Constitution resembles the U.S. Constitution in several ways. It establishes a democratic form of government and divides power between the executive, legislative, and judicial branches; it enshrines the principle of popular sovereignty through elections; it creates a federal system whereby each of the nation's 31 states operates under its own constitutional framework, exercising certain powers; it mandates a clear separation of church and state; and it provides for individual freedoms and rights. The Mexican Constitution differs from the U.S. document, however, in two fundamental ways. First, the Mexican Constitution mandates a strong governmental role in the economy and society. Article 27, for instance, grants the government exclusive rights over the exploitation of the subsoil, which broadly interpreted sanctions the state's right to determine the limits and functions of private property and, specifically, the government's ownership of the oil sector. Article 123 establishes the state's role in protecting the rights of workers, going so far as to mandate a system of profit-sharing and to specify the number of paid vacation days. A second difference with the U.S. Constitution is in the electoral arena. Here, the Mexican document creates a mixed system of proportional representation and district seats and, most importantly, prohibits re-election. Rooted in the revolution's opposition to Porfirio Díaz's long reign in power or *continuismo*, the ban on re-election applies not just to the executive, as might be expected, but to all elected officials at the federal, state, and local levels. Legislators may repeat in office, but not consecutively. With the defeat of the PRI monopoly, this now has become a matter of intense debate because the ban cripples the ability of the legislative branch to balance the power of the executive.

Executive Power in Mexico

As set out under the Constitution, the executive branch of the Mexican government is headed by the president, who is elected for a six-year term with no re-election. Today, the executive branch includes nineteen cabinet-level departments, numerous semi-autonomous or autonomous entities such as the Social Security Institute (IMSS), the Central Bank (Banxico), the National Development Bank (NAFIN), the Banco Nacional de Comercio Exterior (BancoMext), the national human rights commission (CNDR), the **Federal Electoral Institute (IFE)**, and state-owned firms like the large Petróleos Mexicanos (PEMEX), Comisión Federal de Electricidad (CFE), and several others.

Like the U.S. Constitution, the Mexican Constitution separates powers and creates a system of checks and balances. Under the PRI's dominance, however, the Mexican president enjoyed almost unlimited powers, prompting literary comparisons with dictators, Spanish viceroys, and Aztec chiefs. In fact in relation to other institutions of government or society, under the PRI the president truly "ruled," maintaining tight controls over budgetary and policy matters. Until 1997 when the PRI lost its majority in the **Chamber of Deputies**, the president totally dominated the legislative branch, naming congressional leaders, dictating the agenda, and gaining routine approval of his legislative proposals. The president held similar control over the judiciary, the federal bureaucracy, and even state and local governments. And given the extensive power of the state over the economy and the PRI's control over societal organizations for most of those years, the power of former presidents reached even further and deeper. For years, this awesome presidential power went so far as to include the power to hand-pick a successor. This was accomplished by the outgoing president naming the PRI's presidential candidate.

As recent events have made clear, however, much of the extraordinary power once enjoyed by Mexican presidents stemmed from the PRI's political/electoral

dominance in a context of no re-elections and a weak to nonexistent civil service system. As political head of the PRI, the president had long held the authority to determine the party's nominations for the vast number of elected
seats at the federal and state levels including the presidential candidate as noted,
a prerogative that helped ensure party discipline and personal loyalty. The PRI's
long-time control of federal and state legislatures not only enabled the president to dictate to basically rubber-stamp congresses, but also permitted the
president to count on the number of votes needed to alter the Constitution, or
remove judges or state governors. Few, at least within the PRI, ever dared to
challenge presidential authority or initiatives because their political future depended on his goodwill, thereby making meaningless the institutional checks
on the power set out in the Constitution. Even beyond the formal branches of
government, the PRI's incorporation of peasant, labor, and other social organizations placed the president at the center of power, enabling him to determine
leadership in these critical organizations, reward loyalty, and punish opponents.
As might be expected, the absence of checks on presidential authority also facilitated corruption and the abuse of power within the executive and bureaucratic ranks.

Though the president still remains the most important political actor, recent
reforms and developments have severely eroded presidential authority. In contrast
to their predecessors, President Zedillo from 1997 on, and President Fox throughout his administration, have had to deal with divided government. Since 1997 no
party has enjoyed a majority in the lower house of Congress. This has strengthened the power of the legislature at the expense of the presidency. Fox in particular has had to work with a Congress where the PRI continues to hold the largest
number of seats. Even beyond Congress, and again unlike his PRI predecessors,
Fox has encountered the growing autonomy of the Central Bank (BANIXO),
the electoral authority (IFE), the judiciary, and state and local governments, not
to mention major divisions within the political parties and a more active and as-
sertive cast of civic organizations. Whereas past presidents from the PRI possessed
the power to discipline everyone from union leaders and local politicians to
judges, and controlled substantial majorities in Congress, Fox's power by comparison is strikingly limited. This has severely tested his ability to push through his
priority reforms, which often have been blocked by Congress (fiscal reforms), the
Supreme Court (energy reforms), civic protests (plan to build a new airport), or
others.

Legislative Power in Mexico

The bicameral Mexican Congress includes the Chamber of Deputies and the
Senate. The Chamber is composed of 500 members elected for a term of three
years: 300 deputies represent electoral districts in a winner-take-all electoral system, and 200 are party representatives elected through a system of proportional
representation. The Senate, in turn, has 128 members, or 4 from each of the nation's 31 states and the Federal District (Mexico City) elected to a 6-year term:
3 are elected "at-large" in the state, and 1 seat is given to the runner-up party in

by the PRD since 1997, the Mexico City government represents an important base of support for the party. The situation has also led to intense political battles between the PRD and President Fox. In 2004, for instance, in a highly controversial move, the Fox government sponsored a constitutional reform that stripped the Mexico City government of its federal education funding. The measure, which many saw as a way to weaken the Mexico City mayor's presidential ambitions, prompted members of the city government to storm the congress building in defense of education funding.

To summarize, extensive political changes have occurred within Mexico's institutional setting in recent years. Though the presidency is still the most powerful institution, it has relinquished much of its power to increasingly assertive and autonomous legislative and judicial branches, and state governments. But the decline of the all-powerful presidency has also created power vacuums and uncertainty as the details of executive-legislative, executive-judiciary, and intergovernmental relations in this new era have yet to be worked out. Today, these institutional ambiguities provide much of the fodder of political conflict.

THE ACTORS IN MEXICAN POLITICS:
ELITES, PARTIES, GROUPS, AND CITIZENS

Elites and Political Recruitment

From the Revolution until Mexico's democratic breakthrough, Mexican politics had been an exclusive game among a relatively homogenous political class (PRI) whose members were loosely organized into informal networks and who bowed to a set of informal political guidelines. As a general rule, patterns of political recruitment in any country reflect the way the political system operates, and in Mexico this long centered on the power of the presidency, the electoral dominance of the PRI, and the absence of re-election. Recruitment to the powerful cabinet and even the weaker, rubber-stamp Congress centered around the president. Candidates for public office were formally selected by the party rather than voters through primaries, but the president always played the dominant role. Many of the individuals selected to run on the PRI's ticket for office came from the party's many affiliated organizations. Officials of major labor unions or other organizations tied to the PRI who had demonstrated their abilities to maintain order among the rank-and-file, their capacity to deliver support to the PRI and, above all, their loyalty, were rewarded with political office. Rarely, given the absence of re-election, did PRI candidates have strong local bases of support outside the party or their organizations so their loyalty was directed clearly toward the president. The power of the president in recruitment under the PRI-controlled system extended all the way to the presidency itself, as noted earlier where in a process known in Mexico as the **dedazo** (literally "big finger"), the outgoing PRI president was able to hand-pick his successor.

Studies of recruitment patterns in Mexico from 1884 to 1991 by Roderic Camp (1996) showed the nation's top political officials during that time to have been somewhat of a homogenous bunch, though changes occurred over the years. Military backgrounds predominated during the early years, but by the 1950s this was no longer the case and a true political class began to emerge. The majority of the country's top officials during the institutionalized period were middle-class males, mainly from the Mexico City region, who had attended the national university and had climbed the ranks of the Mexican bureaucracy. Few of the top leaders followed electoral routes to power through either Congress or state and local governments—a clear indication of where "true" power in Mexico rested. During the last few PRI governments, the top officials, often referred to as technocrats, came disproportionately from the Mexico City area, pursued graduate degrees abroad, spent time in the financial/economic agencies of the federal government, and had very limited electoral experience. In fact, none of Mexico's last three PRI presidents prior to 2000 had any electoral experience prior to running for the nation's top post.

One distinctive feature in the workings of the political elite in Mexico is the **camarilla**. As Camp describes it, a camarilla is a "group of people who have political interests in common and rely on one another to improve their chances within the political leadership" (1996, 114). Camarillas are essentially informal teams or networks of politicians who work together to pursue their political objectives and careers. The links extend well beyond one government agency and encompass generations of politicians. All successful politicians are members of a camarilla, and these networks provide much of the fluidity of recruitment and continuity that has long characterized Mexican politics. Loyalty holds these elite teams together as politicians carry their groups of supporters with them from one position to another.

Like other features of Mexican politics, recruitment methods and other rules of the game have changed in recent years, though slowly and in often unpredictable ways. Since being tapped as the PRI's candidate for public office is today no longer a guarantee of victory, the party has taken greater care in recent years to select individuals who are not only faithful to the system, but can mount an effective campaign and compete in more meaningful contests. Facing a decline in the party's appeal, reforms within the PRI in the 1990s actually restricted the president's role in recruitment and established requirements to become the party's presidential nominee. Though no pattern has been firmly established among the states, the PRI has experimented with using party conventions and even open primaries to select their candidates, although in many cases the results have left some party members claiming fraud and actually dropping out of the party in protest, often running on the tickets of opposition parties. At the national level, for the first time the party conducted a national primary to select its 2000 presidential candidate. Though the process ran relatively smoothly, it nonetheless exposed internal divisions within the party and, to be sure, failed to produce the next president. Within this context, it is clear that internal turmoil has replaced much of the stable elite game that once characterized the PRI.

Among what were once called the "opposition parties," including the PAN, whose members now occupy key positions in the government, recruitment patterns have been somewhat different from those historically found within the PRI. Reflecting their key constituencies, PAN representatives tend to have backgrounds in the world of business or the ranks of the middle class. Prior to getting involved in politics in the early 1990s, for instance, President Fox was as an executive with the Coca Cola Company in Mexico, the owner of a vegetable processing company, and a rancher. His cabinet includes a combination of long-time PAN politicians, many from Guanajuato, business executives, and even former officials of past PRI administrations. The PRD leadership, by contrast, traces its roots to the PRI or to the array of social organizations constituting the base of PRD's support. Many members of the PRD are teachers, leaders of independent unions, or activists of NGOs (non-governmental organizations). Historically, the candidate selection procedures of the opposition parties have been more open than those of the PRI. The PAN, in particular, has a long tradition of conducting democratic party conventions to select their candidates. Throughout the years the PAN touted these as "lessons in democracy" for the PRI. The PRD has also experimented with conventions, local primaries, and even allowing non-party members, or social candidates, to run on the PRD ticket, though factional divisions and accusations of fraud have long plagued the PRD. Neither party, however, has fully embraced primaries to select their candidates.

For most of the twentieth century, the nation's economic elite remained separate from the political class. The distinctions began to blur only somewhat in the 1980s when the PAN began to incorporate small business owners and a portion of the professional middle class. Because of the extreme levels of inequality and the structure of Mexican business, the nation's economic elite includes a relatively small cohort of the leaders of large economic groups with vast industrial and financial holdings throughout the country. Respecting an unwritten accord with the PRI-led government, the economic elite shied away from the political limelight and sought to influence policy from behind the scenes. For decades, the government kept its side of the bargain by ensuring stability and a propitious business climate. Though big business still works from behind the political scenes, business organizations have become much more local and public in articulating their demands on the government.

Political Parties and Elections

The PRI and One-Party Rule. Political parties have clearly played the central role in the political life of Mexico under both the lengthy authoritarian period and the new democratic framework (see box p. 442). Unlike parties operating within a democracy, the PRI (known originally as the National Revolutionary Party, the PNR) was created by President Calles in 1929 as a means to resolve disputes among the revolutionary elite and ensure their continuation in power. The PRI, in other words, was not established to compete for power like most parties but rather to protect it. And so it did quite successfully for over seven decades, totally dominating the nation's political life.

Political Parties of Mexico

Major Parties

PRI (Institutional Revolutionary Party).
Founded in 1929 as the PNR (National Revolutionary Party), the PRI became an all-encompassing, umbrella party incorporating a broad range of interests, ideas, and individuals. Yet, because of its subordination to the president, the PRI lacked true independence and autonomy despite its hold on power. Officially, the PRI represents the ideals of the Mexican Revolution, though each president has tended to stress certain ideals while downplaying others. The party's corporatist structure encompasses large segments of the nation's poor, while the stability the party guaranteed for decades helped it maintain the support of much of the nation's economic elite. Despite its defeat in 2000, the PRI still holds the greatest number of seats in Congress and a majority of governorships. The party is currently led by Roberto Madrazo.

PAN (National Action Party).
Founded in 1939 in opposition to the leftist policies of President Cárdenas, the PAN posed the strongest challenge to the PRI over the years. Though incorporating principles of Christian democracy in its early days, the party came to consider itself a center-right organization emphasizing democratic political reform and a pro-business economic platform. The party draws particularly well among the middle class, business, and conservatives, and enjoys its greatest levels of support in the northern and western states. The PAN registered important electoral gains beginning in the 1980s culminating in Fox's presidential victory in 2000.

PRD (Party of the Democratic Revolution).
The PRD was formed in 1989 in a political alliance that brought together an array of small independent leftist parties and dissident members of the PRI. A large part of its success stems from the popularity of Cárdenas who, along with others, broke from the PRI in 1987. The PRD classifies itself as center-left, opposes the government's neoliberal economic policies, seeks to reform parts of NAFTA, though the party does not support a Socialist platform. The party draws support from the nation's poor and working-class sectors and enjoys its greatest base of support in Mexico City and the poorer states of the south. The party is led today by the popular mayor of Mexico City, Andrés Manuel López Obrador.

Minor Parties

PT (Workers Party).
The PT was formed in 1990 by local political groups primarily in the states of Chihuahua, Durango, and Zacatecas. It promotes popular mobilization, and its platform calls for a socialist, pluralist, and democratic society. It has regional strength in the central state of Durango and has worked in coalition with the PRD at times.

PVEM (Mexican Ecologist Green Party).
Beginning as the Mexican Green Party (PVM) in 1986, the PVEM was founded in 1993. The PVEM represents an ideological movement with a social base interested in the preservation of nature and the environment. It draws much of its support from the Mexico City area. The Greens formed part of a coalition with the PAN in support of Fox in 2000, though it broke from the coalition less than a year later.

A number of factors contributed to the PRI's incredible tenure in power (Morris 1995). First, the party strove to be inclusive and to incorporate key groups within society, offering them a vehicle to express their demands in exchange for the opportunity to partake in the spoils of power. This meant that the PRI was not a true party of individuals exercising their freedom of association, but rather a party of affiliated organizations grouped together since 1946 into three broad sectors: the labor, peasant, and popular wings. Until the reforms in the 1990s officially (though not unofficially) eliminated the practice, workers, for instance, who would have to join the labor union where they worked, would become a part of the PRI by virtue of belonging to the union. This framework not only expanded the party's representation or inclusiveness, but also undercut the ability of other political parties or organizations to mobilize these interests against the government or the party. From this corporatist arrangement, leaders of the hundreds of affiliated organizations (like union leaders) in turn represented a pool from which the party selected its candidates for public office, relying on their organizations to help mobilize the rank-and-file to vote for the PRI. To keep the rank-and-file happy, the government also used these organizational channels to distribute the fruits of economic prosperity and to implement public policy. The leaders, of course, not only enjoyed the perks of public office, but also the many opportunities to enrich themselves through corruption.

A second ingredient in the PRI's long success was the party's ideology. An outgrowth of the ideals of the Mexican Revolution, the PRI stressed the progressive principles of social justice, equality, the struggle of labor against capital, land reform for peasants, and nationalism. With historic strands of anti-Church, anti-business, and even anti-U.S. sentiments included, the PRI's ideology virtually defined and embodied the interests of the nation. Indeed, the PRI was the only party to brandish the colors of the Mexican flag, helping blur the distinction between party and nation. And even if the government failed to realize the lofty goals of the revolution, the party nonetheless embodied those ideals and reinforced them. The sheer ideological strength and nationalist charm of the PRI put on display during every electoral campaign and lavish government ceremony conveniently undercut the appeal of other parties or the regime's opponents, whom the PRI usually labeled as anti-revolutionary and, hence, anti-Mexican.

A third factor promoting the PRI's ability to maintain power for so long derived from the party's unique relationship to the government. Of course technically, politicians from the PRI controlled the government at all levels. But through a variety of mechanisms, the government crafted and manipulated policy to favor the PRI, helping to ensure its continued electoral dominance. The government, for instance, backed the founding and the funding of small "opposition" parties in the 1950s and 1960s that supported the PRI in presidential elections (referred to as satellite parties) to help give the appearance of democracy and to water down the presence of the true opposition like the PAN. The government routinely dismissed allegations of fraud directed at the PRI and drew (gerrymandered) electoral districts in ways that played on the PRI's strengths. Similarly, the government favored and rewarded PRI-affiliated organizations, such as labor unions, while repressing and making life difficult for any "independent" unions. This usually made PRI affiliation more beneficial to those abiding by the rules of the game, despite the lack of autonomy or internal democracy. The government also provided substantial financial, human, and material resources, as in its relationship to the media, to enable the PRI to run massive and effective campaigns. This, of course, gave the PRI a further edge over any competitor.

Though the government favored the PRI and the PRI provided the personnel for the government, it is important to distinguish "rule by the party" from "rule over the party" in the old Mexican authoritarian system. In contrast to the former Soviet Union or China, in which Communist parties effectively controlled the government and determined policy ("rule by the party"), Mexico's PRI never truly controlled the Mexican government, or made policy, or selected the nation's leaders. Instead, the PRI was controlled by the Mexican president, who used the party as an electoral machine to discipline the political elite and to mobilize popular support for the government during elections ("rule over the party"). In short, it was the president, rather than the PRI, who shaped policy and picked the nation's leaders. So while the PRI dominated the electoral scene in Mexico, it lacked true autonomy and always remained weak vis-à-vis the president.

Just as the PRI was not exactly a political party, elections were not exactly elections under the PRI-led system. Elections were designed not so much to select the nation's leaders as to celebrate and legitimize the PRI's rule. Of course, this created quite a paradox—a dominant party participating in a democratic game—and raised questions for the various players. For opponents, why compete in a game that was largely rigged? For citizens, why vote if the outcome was a foregone conclusion? And even for members of the PRI itself, how could they bow to the ideals of democracy and yet participate in a system that was anything but democratic? In considering these questions it is important to recognize the underlying tensions this basic paradox created in Mexico. Whereas the opposition faced the dilemma of whether to promote change from within the system or from outside it (to participate in fraudulent elections or boycott them), the PRI-led government had to balance the need for "democratic" legitimacy against the need to maintain "control."

Elections and the Opposition. Because the Constitution officially set up a democratic system and the PRI-led government called itself "democratic," elections were always held, and opposition parties were always allowed to participate. This made the Mexican authoritarian regime different from many other authoritarian systems that either banned elections or opposition parties. But even though the opposition was allowed to participate in Mexico, to enjoy some semblance of representation, it was really not allowed to win power. Similarly, the people were allowed to vote, but not to choose. This meant that opposition parties had to struggle on two fronts. Politically, they sought to push the government to abide by the rules of democracy, to create truly competitive and fair elections, and to respect the outcome. Meanwhile on the electoral front the parties recruited candidates, conducted campaigns, and sought the support of the voters on election day.

Among the first parties to carve out an independent course and truly contest the PRI and the government was the PAN: the party that in 2000 would finally unseat the PRI from Los Pinos (the Mexican version of the "White House") (see box p. 445). Founded in 1939 in opposition to the left-leaning and anti-clerical policies of President Cárdenas, the PAN attracted some support among the emerging middle class, small business owners, and traditional Catholics, particularly in the northern and western parts of the country where an historic anti-government and conservative sentiment had long existed. Since its inception, the

---

Outfoxing the PRI: How Did Fox and the PAN Win in 2000?

The political and institutional changes of the 1990s set the stage for the stunning Fox victory, but the outcome was not a foregone conclusion. In fact a few months prior to the contest, polls showed the PRI candidate, Francisco Labastida, with a sizable lead. Even pre-electoral polls pointed to a PRI victory. So what happened? According to a team of researchers led by Jorge Dominguez and Chappell Lawson (2003) "the campaign mattered." On the one hand, the PRI's Labastida ran an ineffective campaign. His message of stability and reform did not connect with voters and he failed to jumpstart the party's traditional electoral machine. By contrast, the charismatic Fox, who had already been campaigning for the office for three years, ran a very successful campaign. He not only succeeded in turning the election into a referendum on the PRI's rule, but also in casting himself as the candidate offering the best hope for change. Even his negative campaigning against Labastida and the PRI connected well with the voters who turned out in force to cast their vote for change. Even disaffected PRI voters and many PRD voters threw their support behind Fox.

---

staunchly pro-democratic PAN mounted public campaigns challenging the government to make elections fair and eliminate fraud and to teach democratic values to the nation. The party staged numerous protests designed to expose the regime's failings and to raise questions about the system's democratic credentials. At various points during the PRI's long reign in power, the PAN boycotted elections, boycotted Congress, organized marches and blocked bridges to expose electoral fraud, some of which even turned violent, and filed complaints with international institutions like the Organization of American States. In some cases in the 1990s, the PAN and other parties would stage massive public protests over electoral fraud that effectively prevented the declared "victors" from taking office or governing, thereby forcing the government to call for new elections or to negotiate a solution.

Besides facing pressures from the PAN, the PRI-led government also faced the problem of abstentionism. Again, why should people vote if the outcome was known beforehand and the process unfair? In fact as early as the 1960s many citizens failed to see a reason to vote, and more stayed home on election day than voted. Since this, too, weakened the PRI and the government's legitimacy, the government dealt with this problem by changing the electoral rules to ensure greater participation by opposition parties (helping to give the appearance of competition). Among the many changes, in 1963 the government established seats in Congress specifically for the opposition parties based on a system of proportional representation. This ensured parties a minor say in government and more importantly their participation in the elections, while providing voters an outlet to express their political emotions. The competition, in turn, gave greater meaning to the government's claims of being democratic, but without really threatening the PRI's hold on power.

Over the years, efforts by the government to balance "democratic" legitimacy and authoritarian "control" amid such pressures forced the PRI-led government to agree to reforms that would gradually open the electoral system and make way for the opposition to win more and more races. Among the various reforms, the political/electoral reform of 1977 legalized a number of independent leftist parties. The measure not only helped the government bolster its democratic credentials but it did so while also diluting the opposition from the PAN: a simple strategy of divide and conquer. Though the emergence of the new parties provided a legal and peaceful channel for leftist opponents, thereby weakening the appeal of guerrilla or terrorist routes to change that had emerged in the early 1970s in response to the 1968 student movement, such parties drew only minimal support until 1988 when much of the left united behind the candidacy of Cuauhtémoc Cárdenas following his dramatic split with the leadership of the PRI. One year later, Cárdenas, along with much of the PRI's left wing, established the PRD, formally uniting an array of leftist factions, former members of the PRI, and leaders of civic organizations into a national party.

This process whereby popular pressures led to electoral reforms and in turn to opposition wins became much more intense and rapid throughout the turbulent 1980s and 1990s. During the 1980s, and amidst widespread discontent over the economic crisis, the PAN won (was allowed to win!) a number of state and local elections, particularly in the northern states. Many believed that the de la Madrid government made the decision to respect the results to help ease some of the popular pressures. But when the government realized that the growing movement actually threatened their control, widespread and blatant electoral fraud was used in the latter part of the 1980s to block the PAN, leading to large public protests, conflict, and even violence. By the 1990s, and particularly in the wake of the fraudulent election of 1988, the government ceded further electoral reforms to create the IFE, thereby handing over the responsibility to register voters, train poll workers, monitor the spending of the parties and press coverage, and, most importantly, to count the votes. By the late 1990s as the IFE became autonomous, professional, and legitimate, elections became cleaner, parties and campaigns more transparent, and the results more reliable.

The rise of the opposition and the decline of the PRI that took place alongside these electoral reforms can be illustrated in a number of ways. Figure 10.2 depicts the electoral trends in the presidential races since 1964. With the exception of 1976 when internal bickering left the PAN without a candidate, support for the PRI steadily declined over the years. Marred by fraud, even the official results of the fraudulent 1988 election showed the PRI candidate receiving just barely a majority of the national vote.

Table 1 also demonstrates the growing competitiveness of the elections by showing the number of competitive electoral seats for the Chamber of Deputies. As indicated, as late as 1979, 242 of the 300 electoral districts were firmly controlled by one party—the PRI. Though the PAN by then had been struggling for democratic change for four decades, it was only competitive in 53 of the 300 districts. Most of these districts were located in large urban areas, leaving most of the country with no effective competition. Since 1979, however, the majority of electoral districts have gone from being controlled by the PRI to being competitive so by 2003, only 23 seats could be considered "safe" seats, with 16 controlled by the PRI. But as Joseph Klesner indicates, Mexico does not yet have a three-party

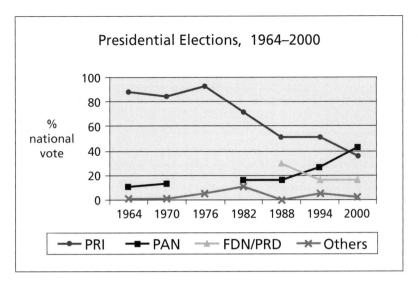

FIGURE 10.2 *Due to internal disputes, the PAN did not run a presidential candidate in 1976.

SOURCE: CEDAC.

system featuring the PAN, PRI and PRD, but rather a segmented two-party system (2004). The PRI and PAN compete in certain parts of the country, while the PRI and PRD battle in other parts. Generally, the PAN enjoys its greatest strength in the northern and western states and in the Yucatan, while the PRD draws well in the south and Mexico City area. (Figure 10.1 of the gubernatorial seats in 2004, offers one indication of the parties geographical strength).

As the data suggests, despite the rise of opposition parties, even in 2004 the PRI remains the strongest political party nationwide and is still the only party that effectively covers the entire nation. Table 10.2, showing the distribution of seats within the 2000–2006 Congresses, provides a final look at the distribution of power among the parties. Note that in both the 2000–2003 and 2003–2006 Chamber of Deputies, the PRI enjoyed the largest delegation, but not a majority. This is certainly a far cry from the rubber-stamp Congresses in the 1950s and 1960s when the PRI held over 90 percent of the seats. Today, the PAN has the largest number of Senators, but similarly lacks a majority. Such a divided government has made it difficult for Fox to pass what he sees as much needed reforms.

The three major political parties—the PAN, PRI, PRD—differ not only in their geographic and social bases, but also in their ideals (see box p. 449). Though historically the PRI had represented a position on the center-left emphasizing nationalism and supporting the interests of peasants and workers, the party shifted in the mid-1980s to champion free market reforms, a dismantling of the state, the promotion of business interests, and economic integration with the U.S. The ideological shift at the time created serious divisions in the party, prompting many of the party's left-wing to leave the party to join the ranks of the PRD.

Table 10.1 The Rise of Competition in Mexico, 1979–2003

Federal Electoral Districts Categorized by Number of Parties

Number of Parties (NP Index)	1979	1982	1985	988	1991	1994	1997	2000	2003
Hegemonic (1.0–1.5)	242	205	199	130	187	73	25	29	23*
Pure Bipartisan (1.5–2.0)	53	70	71	43	92	89	107	100	100**
Plural Bipartisan (2.0–2.5)	5	24	27	38	20	105	112	101	114**
Tripartite (NP > 2.5)	0	1	3	89	1	33	56	70	66

* 16 of the 23 hegemonic districts belonged to the PRI.
** Of the bipartisan districts, PRI-PAN competition existed in 146 and PRI-PRD competition in 50.

SOURCE: Klesner (forthcoming) with data from Instituto Federal Electoral.

Table 10.2. Composition of Congress, 2000–2006

Party	Chamber of Deputies						Senate
	2000–2003			2003–2006			2000–2006
	District Seats	PR	Total	District Seats	PR	Total	Total
PAN	136	70	206	80	71	151	60
PRI	132	79	211	161	63	224	46
PRD	24	26	50	56	41	97	16
PVEM	6	11	17	3	14	17	5
PT	2	6	8	0	6	6	0
Others	0	8	8	0	5	5	1
TOTAL	300	200	500	300	200	500	128

SOURCE: Instituto Federal Electoral.

Ideologically the PAN has long emphasized the principles of democracy and good government, calling for an end to political corruption and authoritarian rule. Like the PRI of the 1980s and 1990s, the PAN also favors free-market economics, economic openness, and integration with the U.S., but combines these with staunch conservative values. The PRD, by contrast, occupies the center-left position along the ideological spectrum. It stresses capitalism with a human face, emphasizing the issues of social justice, equality, and the interests of the "popular class" (a term that refers to the large working and poor classes in Latin America).

Among the other minor political parties are the Partido Verde Ecologista de Mexico (PVEM) and the Partido de los Tabajadores (PT), or Workers Party. Founded in 1986 as the Ecological Party of Mexico, the PVEM supports the preservation of nature and the environment and draws much of its support from the Mexico City area. Many environmentalists, however, do not follow the party

A Sample of Public Opinion

- 76% "very proud" of being Mexican; 73% "willing" to fight for the country.[1]
- 53% consider democracy preferable to any other form of government.[2]
- "Much" or "some" confidence in:[3]

Police 33%	Government 30%
Press 29%	Parties 28%
Schools 64%	Army 45%
Congress 64%	

- 76% disagreed with the idea of priests talking politics during religious services.[4]
- Principle problem facing the country.[5]
  Public Security 29%; Unemployment 21%; Economy 10%; Corruption 9%

- What has been the principle success and failure of the Fox government?[5]
  Success: having removed the PRI from the presidency—40%
  Failure: lack of political accords—24%
- How many in government are corrupt?[3]
  42% almost everyone; 34% many; 9% few; 2% almost no one
- 20% expressed "trust" in the U.S.; 50% "distrusted" the U.S.[6]
- 76% opposed the U.S. war in Iraq.[7]

SOURCES: [1] Gutiérrez Vivo (1998); [2] Latino barómetro (2003); [3] Klesner (2001); [4] Beltran, et al. (1997); [5] La Reforma, September 1, 2004, 9A); [6] Inglehart, et at. (1996), [7] La Reforma, October 26, 2004.

and see it as merely a tool of its leader, Jorge Gonzalez. The PVEM entered into a coalition with the PAN in 2000 to support the candidacy of Fox, but broke with the PAN a short time later. Since then the PVEM has entered similar coalitions with the PRI in state elections. The PT was formed in 1990 by local political groups primarily in the states of Chihuahua, Durango, and Zacatecas. The center-left PT supports a mildly socialist program and often allies with the PRD as it did for the 2000 presidential election. The party is particularly strong in the central state of Durango.

Mexican Parties Under Democracy. Fox's victory and the PRI's defeat in 2000 have fostered new challenges for Mexico's political parties. The PAN in particular wrestles with the problems associated with its rapid growth and its transition from opposition to governing party. According to a recent study by Yemile Mizrahi (2003), however, the historically closed, elitist, and sectarian party has largely failed to expand its organization, forge a mass base while in office, solidify the support of voters, or win re-election. While generally good at managing the government, the PAN has proved unable to translate those deeds into political support. The PRI has faced perhaps an even more formidable task in adapting to the new political environment. Though still relatively well organized, it confronts the challenge of arresting its declining popularity, maintaining the support of the traditional corporate sectors, financing its operations without relying on illegal government funds, and of course, competing in freer and fairer elections. As a result of these pressures, serious divisions have erupted within the PRI and internal discipline has eroded as competing factions battle for control of the party. Critical of the PRI's shift to the right that began in the mid-1980s—a shift that paralleled the party's decline—the party's new leadership has sought to reassert the historic party's more traditional ideological roots.

Pressure Groups and Politics in Mexico

Pressure groups provide much of the raw material of politics. Under authoritarian rule, most Mexican organizations were tied to the system through official or unofficial mechanisms—a feature that added to the system's authoritarian credentials. Such organizational links may have been with the PRI, with the government, or both; but the corporatist structure allowed the government to restrict the freedom of social organizations and control social mobilization. This limited pluralism, of course, is what made the system authoritarian. Yet, as in other areas, recent political changes have spawned new groups and actors, new rules and procedures, and new issues and problems. Part of the growing opposition to the PRI and the gradual erosion of presidential power over the years reflects the growing pluralism of Mexican society.

Groups Historically Controlled by the PRI and the Government. Corporatism refers to a formalized system of bargaining between the state and state-designated or controlled social organizations. As part of this arrangement, organizations exercise control over their particular social domains but lose a degree of autonomy. We saw this in our discussion of the PRI and its inclusion of labor, peasant, and popular organizations. Such a pattern also existed at another level where the government (rather than the PRI) incorporated privileged organizations into policy-making circles. The government, for example, placed representatives of the major labor confederations on local labor arbitration and conciliation boards and similar agencies that implemented labor and social policy. Such agencies not only ruled on the legality of strikes, internal union politics, and the distribution of funds for housing and other social programs, but they also acted in ways that favored and hence rewarded organizations that supported the president and the party.

For years, labor unions and popular organizations coalesced within the PRI, while groups outside the PRI's organizational reach were tied to the government through a variety of techniques, usually enhancing government control. Government-mandated entities such as the CONCANACO (Confederation of National Chambers of Commerce), CANACINTRA (National Chamber of Industries of Transformation),[6] CONCAMIN (Confederation of Chambers of Industry), and the ABM (Mexican Bankers Association), for instance, offered a framework for government-business bargaining, while the government's extensive controls over the economy provided it with the wherewithal to discipline the demands of the business sector. Facing the need to secure government licenses for virtually everything or a market structured by government-controlled enterprises, most businesses recognized the importance of cooperating with the government. Indeed, the government often used these corporatist channels and controls to discipline and repress individuals. Such government controls (sometimes subtle, sometimes not) over

---

[6] "Transformation" normally referred to industries that enjoyed government assistance in some way or were beneficiaries of the government's industrialization policy.

social organizations could also be seen with respect to the press. Though the Constitution mandates a free press, the PRI-led government historically limited that freedom through a variety of mechanisms. For the visual media, the government was in charge of granting the concessions, thus ensuring that the nation's major television stations were held by supporters of the PRI. The major television network, Televisa, for instance, still a virtual private monopoly, was created by a government concession in the 1950s to two families with close ties to the ruling elite. Even Televisa's main competitor today, Television Azteca, emerged as the result of a government auction in the 1990s. Though perhaps more subtle, governmental controls over the written press were equally effective for decades. This included everything from the placement of government advertisements (a critical source of revenue for the press) and the government's subsidized sale of imported newsprint, to under-the-table payments to journalists for favorable coverage. Such controls historically nurtured self-censorship within the press and a symbiotic relationship, but the government occasionally applied more strong-arm tactics to remove recalcitrant editors or outright repression to destroy forays into opposition journalism.

"Independent" organizations such as "unofficial" labor unions, like opposition parties, were permitted to exist during the PRI's rule, but because they did not enjoy the "favors" from the government, their ability to provide benefits to their members remained limited. If they became a real threat to the government or stability, such organizations were repressed. A wave of strikes in the late 1950s, led by the railroad and electrical workers unions, for example, ended with the military arresting the strikers. The government used a similar tactic to cripple the massive protests led by students in 1968 and teachers in the 1970s. Historically, such repression was used to discourage the creation and activities of "unofficial" organizations that would seek influence outside the normal corporatist channels or against individuals who sought to instill democratic reforms within the PRI-controlled organizations. Labor's struggle to democratize the official unions tied to the PRI, for instance, has proved particularly difficult over the years.

As with other aspects of the system, political changes in recent decades have opened significant political space for social organizations while at the same time raising the political costs to the government of outright repression. The nation's major labor organizations, though some still swear allegiance to the PRI, have largely broken free of the party and government control, though repression and a denial of basic rights continues. Business organizations have similarly become more active politically since the 1980s, exerting their political independence and influence. Facing economic decline and economic policies detrimental to their interests, big business created the independent CCE (Coordinating Council of Enterprises) and COPARMEX (Employers Council) to better represent their interests before the government. Breaking the nonpolitical pattern of the past, these organizations actually began to channel some support to the PAN during the 1980s and 1990s. Presidents de la Madrid, Salinas, and Zedillo were able to stem this trend somewhat by embracing economic measures favorable to big business. The press has also become much more independent and critical in recent years, as described by a recent study by Chappel Lawson (2002). Though continuing to favor the PRI throughout most of the

1990s, by the 2000 election press coverage became much more balanced and even critical of the government.

The Rise of NGOs. During the 1980s and 1990s, many societal organizations came onto the scene in Mexico, hastening the nation's move from authoritarian corporatism to pluralist democracy. Certainly, NGO's (non-governmental organizations) are not unique to Mexico. But fueled in particular by the economic crises of the period, the 1985 earthquake, and the fraudulent election of 1988, a range of NGO's formed to mobilize citizens, channel demands for change, and assert vigilance over government. Beginning in 1991, for example, organizations such as Civic Alliance lobbied the government for electoral reforms, monitored polling places on election day, coordinated quick counts to help expose "unbelievable" or fraudulent results, and collected and disseminated data on the media's biased treatment of the parties. In 1994, Civic Alliance coordinated more than 83,000 election observers, including 900 foreign observers. Similar social organizations operated in the area of human rights, exposing abuses and effectively pressuring the government to establish the independent National Human Rights Commission. By the mid-1990s, more than 200 human rights organizations operated throughout the country. Such organizations have played a critical role in raising citizen consciousness and activism, and strengthening accountability.

One particularly high-profile organization that burst onto the scene in 1994 was the Zapatista Army of National Liberation (EZLN). Composed of indigenous guerillas, the EZLN took control of a handful of local towns in the impoverished southern state of Chiapas. The violence soon gave way to a cease-fire and negotiations, but the talks broke down in 1996 when the government backtracked on a deal brokered by its own congressional delegation. Other groups like the Ejército Popular Revolucionaria (EPR) also emerged during the period, carrying out a series of attacks on official targets in the states of Oaxaca and Guerrero. For years, the presence of these groups led to the growing militarization of these areas, the emergence of paramilitary organizations, and heightened repression. Clashes among supporters of the indigenous organizations, often in alliance with the PRD, and supporters of the PRI became common. Though a PRD alliance won the gubernatorial election in Chiapas in 2000, the deep-seated social and economic problems underlying the uprising have remained largely unaddressed. In 2001, the EZLN staged a massive march to the capital. The leaders spoke at the national Congress. Soon afterwards, the Congress and the Fox administration passed an indigenous rights bill granting the communities greater autonomy. But because the bill had been watered down by Congress, the accord was eventually rejected by the indigenous community. Subsequent efforts by the EZLN to become a major political force and create parallel municipal administrations in their strongholds have met with limited success. Still, the political situation remains tense and potentially explosive.

Drug Traffickers. A different type of challenge comes from drug businesses and organized crime in Mexico. According to estimates by the U.S. State Department, the portion of cocaine entering the U.S. through Mexico climbed from around 10 percent in the mid-1980s to about 70 percent a decade later particularly as Colombian cartels turned to Mexico as a major port of entry. It is also estimated that 20 to 30 percent of the heroin consumed in the U.S. and 80 percent of the imported marijuana comes from Mexico. Estimates of Mexico's earnings from the drug trade range from $7 billion to $30 billion a year. Through corruption, violence, and the threat of violence, drug trafficking organizations have come to enjoy significant influence over government and society, operating with virtual impunity in some parts of the country. By the 1990s, Mexicans and others actually began to use terms such as "narco-democracy," "narco-politicos," and "narco-violence" to describe the political situation. The drug trade weakens the nation's political institutions and seriously undermines social order. The existence of these organizations breeds corruption and creates vast security problems. Journalists in particular have suffered violence at the hands of organized crime.

Citizens and Politics in Mexico

Given the unique nature of the Mexican political system, citizens have been politically active historically, but usually in tightly controlled government or PRI-sponsored activities. In the early years, the PRI-led government, for instance, actually supported the formation of peasant organizations and labor unions, sponsoring marches and mobilizing the rank and file to manifest their support for government policy. Even in the face of opposition pressures during late 1980s and early 1990s, the Salinas government organized citizens in the Solidarity program to tackle development problems. The government donated materials, while the local organizations provided the labor (and presumably votes for the PRI in appreciation). Extensive inclusion of citizens in the government and the PRI helped ensure a degree of social control and arguably even reduced the need for repression. At the same time, the hegemonic government-PRI alliance left individual citizens with few means to protect themselves against political abuse. Repression, abuses, and impunity dominated the political scene, and individuals confronting repression or extortion by police usually had no effective recourse. Even when clear evidence of governmental wrongdoing surfaced, whether in terms of corruption or repression, those responsible for the abuse were rarely prosecuted.

Recent political changes have opened the way for greater citizen involvement, though abuses continue to occur. Citizens now actively participate in opposition parties and social organizations, they are better informed, and they are far more likely today to challenge the government and stand up for their rights. Yet, perhaps because of the heightened conflict and the power vacuums hastened by the erosion of old institutions, the abuse of human rights by the government continues, and security problems in society have grown worse. As documented by national and international organizations, torture, other abuses, impunity, and corruption continue. At the same time, according to numerous polls, the lack of security has become the most important issue to society. Kidnapping and robbery have become a major concern throughout the country and especially in Mexico

In an Italian-owned garment factory in central Mexico, a Mexican worker assembles designer clothing.

City. A massive citizen march in Mexico City in the summer of 2004 brought national and international attention to the wave of crime and kidnappings, and the public's demand for change.

Women in Mexico. Generally, official or formal politics continues to be a male-dominated game in Mexico. The country has never had a female president. Only four women have ever served in the cabinet (one in the Fox administration) and just four as state governors. Women are better represented in Congress holding 116 of the 500 seats in the 2003–2006 Chamber (23 percent) and 28 of the 128 Senate seats (22 percent). Such presence in the legislative branch stems in part from the political parties use of a quota system requiring that women receive a certain percentage of the nominations for Congress. Though marginal in formal politics, women are often involved in social movements and popular organizations, particularly in organizations that seek to provide support to the poor. In many indigenous communities, women also play a major role in running commerce and public affairs. Although women enjoy legal and constitutionally mandated equality, many civil codes still maintain male marital power, and the general culture continues to view the family as the woman's primary responsibility. In most areas, the culture of Machismo remains firm. Even so, the drop in the average number of children per family from six to fewer than three during the past two decades, combined with economic crisis, has prompted more women to enter the workforce in recent years. Mexican women now constitute 35 percent of the workforce, though they are paid less than males and work overwhelmingly in the service sector, particularly in education, health services, and family care. Women continue to constitute a slight majority of the workforce in the maquiladora or assembly-plant sector of the economy located largely in the north, where they receive low wages and face various types of discrimination such as forced pregnancy exams (Fernandez Poncela 1996). In terms of education, gender differences have been greatly reduced in recent years. In 2000, 27 percent of females compared to 29 percent of males above 15 years old had completed high school, although in 2001 48 percent of undergraduate students and 43 percent of graduate students were women (Inegi 2004).

THE CONTEXT OF MEXICAN POLITICS: CULTURE, ECONOMICS AND INTERNATIONAL INTERDEPENDENCE

The Culture of Mexican Politics

Mexican Nationalism. Prior to the Mexican Revolution, one could hardly speak of a Mexican nation. No common identity or sense of belonging existed; rough terrain and limited communications separated vast regions of the country; indigenous communities were isolated from the mainstream *mestizo* society; and strict class and racial divisions were well defined. Nothing really united the people together as one. But the tumultuous revolution and the cultural programs that followed in the 1920s and 1930s changed much of that. In what President Calles dubbed a "cultural revolution," the government sponsored extensive public education programs, commissioned public murals by artists such as Diego Rivera, and developed a nationalistic rhetoric that instilled a sense of unity and a common ideology throughout the country. Since that time, Mexicans have felt a strong sense of national identity and pride. Much of that common identity is rooted in shared ethnic/religious/cultural values and manifests itself in a sense of pride in *mestizaje*, or the people's mixed European/indigenous ancestry. Part of this, as noted earlier, involves positive images of the nation's indigenous past and a deep reverence for the Virgin of Guadalupe. Identity rooted in ethnicity ensures unity by downplaying class differences. Mexican nationalism also incorporates a civic/historical component represented by the social and economic ideals and principles of the revolution. This includes beliefs in the rights of peasants to own the land they work and workers to share in the fruits of their labor, a preference for an activist state charged with the task of defending the rights of the nation against foreigners, and strong feelings that the Church, business, and foreigners should stay out of politics.

A critical component informing Mexico's political culture and the ideology of the Mexican Revolution is the perception of mistreatment and threat from the U.S. History has taught Mexico to remain cautious and suspicious of its extremely powerful neighbor to the north, a posture reflected in the popular Mexican saying attributed to Porfirio Díaz: "Poor Mexico, So Far from God, So Close to the US." This defensive attitude has long shaped Mexican foreign policy and strengthened the imperative for national unity. According to analysis by Jorge Castañeda (Pastor and Castañeda 1989, 28), the prime lesson contained in Mexico's history textbooks is that "the nation is lost, easily dominated by the Americans, when it is divided."

For years, most Mexicans shared these views, creating a strong sense of identity and unity. Although the government failed to realize its revolutionary objectives, as we have seen, at least the populace agreed on what the objectives should be. But as in other areas, recent changes have challenged some of the foundations of the nation's identity and many of the tenets of the revolution. Economic reforms since the 1980s have not only replaced the more revolutionary economic programs designed to protect the workers and the peasants, but have strengthened ties to the U.S. and business—groups previously excluded from the ideological equation. By challenging past thinking, NAFTA and the sale of state-owned enterprises have raised questions about the nature of Mexican nationalism and the goals and objectives of the state. Consequently, some see the current leadership as "selling out" the country, while others express concerns that closer ties to the U.S. threatens the nation's cultural identity. In a similar vein, the rise of the Zapatista guerrillas in the mid-1990s raised questions about the situation of the nation's indigenous. Current-day Indians are demanding that their languages and cultures be respected, thereby challenging past notions of national unity and traditional perceptions of what it means to be Mexican. The idea of multiculturalism promoted today seems oddly out of place in a country that has long considered itself unified both racially and culturally. By exposing new divisions and debates and by weakening the foundations of political agreement and cooperation, these cultural trends further complicate the current political transition.

Beyond issues of national identity, Mexican political culture is also noted for deep seated attitudes of mistrust and cynicism toward the government and politicians. While institutions such as the family and the Church enjoy positive ratings, few trust the government. Popular evaluations of unions, Congress, and the police are particularly negative (see box p. 449). The lack of trust and respect for political institutions suggest that the country still has a long way to go to make democracy work.

Mexico's Social Values.   On a broader plane, Mexican culture stresses the importance of personal relationships, the family, hierarchy, and Catholicism. Mexicans attach an almost spiritual importance to the nurturing of human relationships and to downplaying materialism. As a result, needs involving human relations generally take precedence and greater emphasis is placed on the humanistic pursuits of philosophy, literature, and the arts than on other subjects. Mexicans consider the bonds of family sacred, and family members tend to rely upon one another for personal advancement. Within both the family and society as a whole, Mexicans also stress hierarchy. Authority and respect in Mexico are usually tied to one's position, and titles are used frequently to indicate prestige and status. Finally, Mexicans are culturally Catholic, though fewer attend church on a regular basis. Owing to the historic conflict and the resulting constitutional restrictions, the Church has played a very limited political role in the country, though it has occasionally spoken out against human rights abuses and electoral fraud. In 1991, President Salinas reformed Church-State relations, extending diplomatic relations to the Vatican and allowing Catholic Church officials to participate more actively in politics. Some more liberal Church officials in the southern part of the nation have become particularly important figures in promoting political change. Bishop Samuel Ruiz, for instance, played a critical role mediating the conflict with the Zapatistas in Chiapas.

Political Economy

In Mexico, as in most developing countries, the economy greatly influences politics. And just as it has undergone changes politically, Mexico has also undergone significant economic changes over the years. From the 1940s to the mid-1970s, the PRI ruled over a stable period of strong economic growth known as the Mexican "Miracle." During this time the country moved from being an illiterate agrarian society relying on the exportation of basic products such as silver, cattle, and coffee to an urban, literate society producing a range of industrial goods for domestic consumption. With an average growth rate of six percent per year for more than three decades, standards of living rose, and people began to enjoy opportunities and wealth unknown to their parents. A policy package known as import substitution industrialization guided this long period of prosperity. To promote industrialization, the government imposed high tariffs to discourage imports and competition, channeled funds through state-controlled development banks into infrastructure, offered incentives to encourage foreign companies to set up operation in Mexico, kept taxes low to promote the growth of business, and even controlled the demands of labor to help reduce the costs of doing business. As a complement to the large and growing private sector, the government owned and operated numerous companies: oil and gas, electric power, transportation, telephone, and eventually even steel, chemicals, and vehicle producers, often providing their products at subsidized prices to the private sector. This period of economic prosperity and stability certainly facilitated the dominance of the PRI over the nation.

By 1976, however, this prosperity and the state-business-labor alliance that had helped sustain it began to crumble, giving rise to periodic economic crises that would weaken the support for the PRI and the government and fuel political conflict and change. Facing huge trade deficits and growing demands to attend to poverty, the Mexican government borrowed heavily internationally during the 1970s to finance an expansion of the size and scope of the state. This debt-led strategy maintained economic growth for a few years, bolstered in large measure by the government's discovery of significant reserves of petroleum in the Gulf region that it sought to develop at an almost break neck pace using even more foreign loans. But global economic conditions turned sour in the early 1980s and the bottom fell out of the Mexican economy. With skyrocketing interest rates and global recession, Mexico announced in August 1982 that it was bankrupt, unable to meet its financial obligations to international commercial banks. The announcement sent shock waves throughout the world and triggered Latin America's debt crisis. It began what would become known throughout the region as "the lost decade" (Lustig 1998).

Saddled with a massive foreign debt, high interest rates, low petroleum prices, and international banks reluctant to lend more money, Mexico faced hard choices and hard times. Under pressure from the U.S. and international financial institutions such as the IMF, the government slashed government spending on everything from infrastructure to social programs, cut real wages by holding unions in check and allowing inflation to outstrip wage increases, and tightened monetary policy. As the economy slipped further and further into recession, the government fully abandoned the import substitution model of the "Miracle" years and in its place embraced a program of neoliberalism. It auctioned off ("privatized") or closed state-owned enterprises, reducing the number of such entities from 1185 in 1982 to 185 by 1997. It eliminated or cut tariffs, removed restrictions on trade, and opened the economy to foreign investment. The percentage of products controlled and forbidden fell from 100 percent of imports in 1983 to 10.4 percent in 1985 and to 0.8 percent by 2000 and 13.9 percent of exports in 1983 to 8.4 percent in 1985 and 1.4 percent by 2000 (Jaime 2004, 40). In addition, the government removed price controls, reduced or eliminated subsidies to the poor and middle class, and slashed industrial promotion programs.

The dramatic policy shift transformed the structure of the Mexican economy within a relatively short period of time. Within a decade or so, Mexico would go from a relatively closed economy to one of the most open economies in the world. Trade increased from $40 billion or 13.1 percent of GDP in 1980 to over $200 billion or 35.6 percent of GDP in 1999. At the same time, with the boom in maquiladoras (assembly operations mainly along the U.S. border), because of reductions in the costs of labor and the growth of the auto industry, Mexico would significantly reduce its reliance on the exportation of oil to become a major exporter of manufactured goods. The maquiladora industry would climb from $15 billion in exports and 465 thousand jobs in 1991 to a peak of $79 billion and 1.3 million jobs in 2001 before slowing in response to the U.S. recession and growing competition from China (*Mexico: 2004 Country Review*). Though to date oil remains the nation's largest export item, manufactured goods now make up more than 80 percent of total exports.

Part of this dramatic economic opening came with the signing of numerous free trade agreements. Among the most celebrated and intensely debated accord is the North American Free Trade Agreement (NAFTA) with the U.S. and Canada that took effect in 1994. Though the name is not entirely accurate to describe the more than 800-page document, NAFTA eliminated tariffs and other restrictions on most goods, thus facilitating trade, investment and the economic integration of Mexico with the U.S. economy. In many ways, Mexico has become the new industrial belt for the U.S., providing its northern neighbor with autos and auto parts, electrical machinery, electronic equipment, and textiles. Though almost 90 percent of Mexico's trade is with the U.S., Mexico has also signed numerous trade agreements with other countries. Table 10.3 lists the many agreements as of 2004 and the resulting increases in trade.

But despite the structural transformation of the Mexican economy (from closed to open, from public to private), the dramatic increase in exports, the taming of inflation and monetary and fiscal discipline in recent years, the overall results have

Table 10.3 Mexico's Free Trade Agreements

Country	Implementation Year	Total Trade 1993 (millions $)	Total Trade 2002 (millions $)	% Change
Chile	1992	329.8	1,268.9	285%
United States	1994	88,145.5	249,719.2	183%
Canada	1994	2,744.0	7,292.9	165%
Bolivia	1995	33.3	43.9	33%
Costa Rica	1995	121.4	760.4	528%
Colombia	1995	322.8	908.1	181%
Venezuela	1995	455.0	1,118.8	146%
Nicaragua	1998	32.0	118.1	269%
EU	2000	10,587.4	21,659.4	105%
Israel	2000	149.1	301.4	102%
El Salvador	2001	127.1	302.0	138%
Guatemala	2001	266.0	631.0	137%
Honduras	2001	44.8	233.1	420%
Japan	2004	na	na	na

SOURCE: Gereffi and Martinez (2005).

been mixed and short of expectations. Though the country enjoyed modest levels of economic growth in the late 1980s and early 1990s, by 1995 the government was forced once again to devalue the currency and the economy plummeted into a deep recession. With the help of a U.S. brokered $40 billion bailout (a loan Mexico paid back a few years later) and a deepening of neoliberal reforms and austerity, the economy recovered in the late 1990s only to stall once again during the U.S. economic slowdown of the early 2000s. Overall, economic growth under neoliberalism has been less than that enjoyed during the period of import substitution. And under the first three years of the Fox administration (2001–2003) the economy grew at an average annual rate of barely more than 1 percent.

Underlying this sluggish pattern of growth, Mexico continues to face high rates of poverty, low wages, a lack of jobs, and growing inequality. Data from the Bank of Mexico reveals that in 2002, 20.3 percent of the population lived in extreme poverty, including 65 percent of the rural population. With an average education level of just 7.3 years, workers have few opportunities and receive low pay. Adjusted for inflation, maquiladora workers in 2002, for instance, received about the same in real terms as they did in 1993 and about 1/6 of what workers in similar jobs in the U.S. earn. That same year the minimum wage was just $120 a month. Social spending on anti-poverty programs has increased in recent years, though progress has been slow. In 2003, the government's major anti-poverty program OPORTUNIDADES provided an average monthly support of $25 to 2.6 million families (Pardinas 2004, 66). At the same time, evidence suggests that income inequality has grown alongside the neoliberal reforms and reoccurring economic crises. According to the World Bank, from 1980 to 2000, the portion

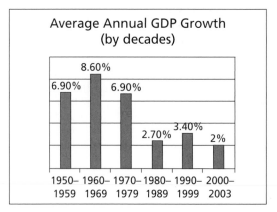

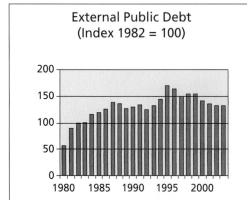

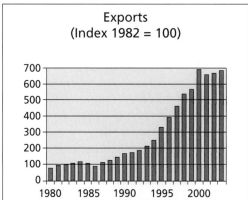

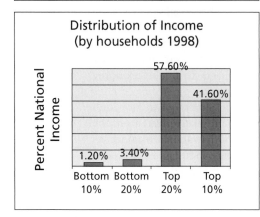

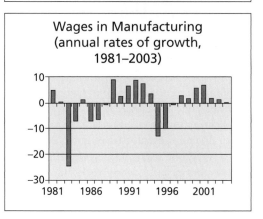

FIGURE 10.3 Economic Indicators: Trends Since the 1980s

SOURCES: Lustig (1998); Nadal (2003); Pastor and Wise (1998); Human Development Report (2004); and IENEGI.com.

of income going to the poorest 20 percent of the population fell by 1.2 percent, while the share accruing to the wealthiest 10 percent increased by 7.8 percent.

NAFTA certainly facilitated many of the structural changes noted earlier. It spurred the growth in exports, foreign investments, and the integration of the Mexican and the U.S. economies. Though the impact of the trade agreement has been sharply debated, many studies show that it has failed to address a range of problems effectively. An assessment of the impact of NAFTA after its initial decade by the Carnegie Endowment, for example, offered the following conclusions (Audley et al. 2003):

1. NAFTA has not helped the Mexican economy keep pace with the growing demand for jobs.

2. Real wages for most Mexicans today are lower than they were when NAFTA took effect.

3. NAFTA has not stemmed the flow of poor Mexicans into the United States in search of jobs.

4. The fear of "a race to the bottom" in environmental regulation has proved unfounded. Some elements of Mexico's economy are dirtier and some are cleaner.

5. Mexico's evolution toward a modern, export-oriented agricultural sector has also failed to deliver the anticipated environmental benefits of reduced deforestation and tillage.

Mexico faces a number of economic challenges besides poverty. First, there is a clear need for fiscal reform given the low level of state revenues compared to industrialized countries and the government's continued dependence on oil revenues. From one-quarter to one-third of government revenues come from the sale of oil. In addition, certain sectors of the economy lack real competition. Private monopolies like Telmex, public ones like PEMEX, or the electrical companies remain inefficient and bloated resulting in high energy and communication costs for consumers. With most of its profits going to the state, PEMEX suffers from a severe lack of capital investment and low productivity. Investment in infrastructure, the rural countryside, and education are particularly low. At the same time, the government continues to struggle to provide for the most basic of public goods like legal security and the protection of property rights. Unfortunately, Fox has failed to address these challenges effectively. His fiscal reform initiative suffered a major defeat in Congress during his first year in office and his inability to pull together a congressional consensus to promote energy or labor reforms has weakened the economy.

International Interdependence:
Relations with the United States

Mexico's proximity to the powerful and wealthy U.S. has affected tremendously all aspects of the nation's life, from national identity to economic policy and even the country's unique political experiment. Indeed, the country's relationship with its northern neighbor dominates Mexico's foreign relations.

Living in the shadow of the U.S. has never been easy for Mexico, presenting the country with a complex mix of risks and opportunities (Morris 2005). Generally, the Mexican government has sought to balance a genuine concern about U.S. influence with a pragmatic policy of engagement. On the one hand, Mexico has suffered historically at the hands of the U.S. It has been invaded by the U.S. on multiple occasions spanning two centuries, lost more than half its territory to U.S. expansionism, and has often felt the meddling presence of the U.S. in its internal affairs. For good or ill, the Mexican economy has long been dominated by U.S. interests, whether by U.S. companies, trade, or financial bailouts. Even today, almost 90 percent of Mexican trade is with the U.S. and many key industries are held by U.S. investors and U.S.-based multinational corporations. Even in the field of culture, U.S. companies provide extensive programming for television, radio, and theaters—compromising, according to some, the nation's distinct cultural identity. At the same time, Mexicans living and working in the U.S. suffer discrimination and abuse, some owing to their status as "illegals," while those going to the U.S. in search of a better life risk their lives at the hands of organized smugglers and the scorching heat of the southwestern deserts. As a result, Mexicans have tended to distrust the U.S.—something often interpreted as an anti-U.S. sentiment.

Consistent with these concerns toward their northern neighbor, the government has long stressed the basic principles of international law, such as a country's right to self-determination and the principle of nonintervention in the affairs of other countries, and has pursued a path independent of the U.S., both in its rhetoric and reality. Contrary to other countries of the region, for instance, Mexico rebuked the U.S. lead in breaking relations with Cuba in the 1960s, maintaining a close political relationship with the Castro regime ever since—despite some recent problems—often denouncing the U.S. embargo in the international arena. During the 1980s when conflict racked Central America, Mexico led the way in opposing U.S. policy, seeking a peaceful, negotiated solution to the conflict. And like many countries of the world, Mexico opposed the U.S.-led war in Iraq in 2003. Even Mexico's domestic economic policy has historically ensured a certain distance from the U.S., with constitutional provisions, regulations, and policies restricting foreign ownership of Mexican properties, particularly in the cultural industry. Throughout the 1960s and 1970s, for instance, Mexico had one of the most restrictive policies toward foreign investment, requiring foreign firms to partner with domestic firms in order to establish operations in the country. In addition, Mexico protected national control of publishing, television, and education.

And yet, together with these views and policies, Mexicans have also held a positive image of the U.S. and the governments have pursued a peaceful, pragmatic, and constructive relationship, even taking advantage of the country's proximity to promote economic development through means unavailable to other countries. Just as polls show a lack of trust toward the U.S., they also show that Mexicans like the U.S.'s economic and political system. And despite critical views of the U.S. government and U.S. policy, most Mexicans are open and have a favorable opinion toward U.S. citizens. After all, because of cultural and demographic trends, many Mexicans now have family in the U.S. and/or have visited

ants) into the strongest army of the Middle East, Mohammed Ali was able to conquer much of the region that now constitutes the Sudan, Israel, Jordan, and Saudi Arabia (Goldschmidt 1988, 19). On two occasions, he threatened to conquer Turkey itself, but both efforts were stymied by the British and French (Lawson 1992).

The line of Mohammed Ali proved to be an undistinguished one. The royal family, supported by an aristocracy of large landowners, lived in oriental splendor while the Egyptian peasants were reduced to lives of servitude (Ayrout 1962). The political and economic structure of Egypt during this period was remarkably similar to the feudalism of medieval Europe, with an aristocracy of large landowners providing financial support to the monarchy in exchange for the right to rule their fiefdoms as they saw fit. How they achieved these objectives was of little concern to the royal family (Lane 1954).

The profligate lifestyle of the royal family soon exhausted Egypt's meager financial resources. The completion of the Suez Canal in 1869 provided the Egyptian government with royalties from canal traffic, but even this new source of revenue could not satisfy the appetites of the monarch. Short of cash, the king sold Egypt's 44 percent share in the Suez Canal to British and French investors. Britain and France now controlled 100 percent of the shares of the Suez Canal. When the money had been squandered, the heirs of Mohammed Ali turned to deficit financing (Longgood 1957). Possessing little in the way of new resources, Egypt defaulted on its loans. England and France responded by seizing the Egyptian custom houses, depriving the king of Egypt's most reliable form of taxation and sparking a brief rebellion (1882) that led to the British occupation of Egypt.

By the early 1920s, hostility to British occupation would find expression in two political movements. The first was the **Wafd Party,** *a broad coalition of nationalist groups dedicated to liberating Egypt from British rule* (Berque 1967). The Wafd would remain Egypt's major political party throughout the era of the monarchy. The second organization was the **Muslim Brotherhood,** *a secret religious organization dedicated to the creation of an Islamic state in Egypt* (Husaini 1956). The Muslim Brotherhood remains one of the strongest political forces in Egypt today. There was considerable overlap between the two movements, as the Muslim Brotherhood was also violently opposed to the British presence in Egypt.

The British granted Egypt independent status in 1922 but retained the right to station troops on Egyptian soil. Egyptian politics throughout the inter-war period would remain a three-way struggle between the British Embassy, King Farouk I, and the Wafd (Hassan Pasha Youssef 1983; Arab 2000).

The end of World War II ushered in a period of profound political instability as the British sought to remain a key force in Egyptian politics while Farouk, a particularly corrupt and inept leader, struggled to rule as an absolute monarch. The Wafd continued to press for greater democracy, but the party had lost much of its nationalist zeal, becoming the party of the wealthy (Berque 1967). The influence of the Muslim Brotherhood had been weakened by the assassination of its founder.

The Egyptian Revolution of 1952

It was in this environment in 1948 that Farouk sent his army to war against the newly proclaimed country of Israel, in the misguided belief that the Jews couldn't fight. Once victory had been assured, the king would rule Jerusalem from Cairo (Hassan Pasha Youssef 1983). Poorly led and poorly armed, the Egyptian forces suffered huge losses, liberating only the Gaza Strip, a sparse coastal area adjacent to the Egyptian border.

Smarting from their defeat at the hands of the Jews and frustrated by the ineptness of their political leaders, a small group of junior army officers headed by Gamal Abdel Nasser formed the Free Officers, a secret military organization dedicated to the modernization of Egyptian society. The group seized power in July 1952 (ElDin 1995).

Their task would not be an easy one. The Egyptian population, largely illiterate, was mired in poverty and disease and was growing at a rate that outpaced Egypt's meager resources. More people meant more starvation. The security of the revolution, moreover, was threatened by both a narrow aristocracy of large landowners and a large contingent of British troops who continued to be stationed on Egyptian territory. The presence of foreign troops was particularly worrisome for the new regime, as the United States and Britain threatened to overthrow any Arab regime that posed a direct threat to Western interests.

The first two years of the revolutionary era were relatively uneventful as Nasser and the Free Officers remained in the background, allowing formal power to be exercised by General Mohammed Naguib, a respected military leader with moderate political views. The appointment of a figurehead president was designed to reassure both the West and Egypt's established elite that the new regime did not pose a threat to their interests. Nasser and the Free Officers, moreover, needed time to figure out how best to modernize Egypt and its population. None of Egypt's new leaders possessed broad experience in either government or economics; they would have to learn by trial and error. Efforts were also made to work with the Wafd and other political groups in order to place Egypt on the path to democracy, but these efforts went poorly. The military demanded unity and sacrifice, while Egypt's civilian politicians sought little more than a continuation of the corrupt and divisive policies of the old regime. The experience left Nasser with a profound distrust of political parties and the politicians who led them. Egypt needed sacrifice and discipline, not chaos (Dekmejian 1975).

Naguib chafed under the figurehead role assigned to him and challenged Nasser for leadership of the revolution. He was removed from office in 1954, some two years after the July revolution, and Nasser ascended to the presidency (Woodward 1992).

The Political Revolution Becomes a Social Revolution:
Nasser (1954–1970)

The Nasser who replaced General Naguib possessed a far clearer picture of Egypt and its future than the younger officer who had deposed the hapless King Farouk some two years earlier. Egypt's future, in Nasser's view, required a program of rapid industrialization that would bring the country and its population on par with the nations of the West. The West was invited to cooperate in Egypt's modernization, but only on the condition that Egypt be treated as a sovereign and independent country. Foreign troops would no longer be welcome on Egyptian soil.

The centerpiece of Nasser's modernization plan was to be the Aswan Dam, a towering structure that would span the narrows of the Nile River in a sparsely populated region not far from the Sudanese border. Electric power generated by the dam would fuel an economic miracle, providing jobs for Egypt's masses and transforming Egypt into a modern industrial state. The dam would also control the Nile's floods, thereby producing a dramatic expansion of Egyptian agriculture. The Aswan Dam, however, was to be more than an economic venture. It would also symbolize hope and progress, legitimizing the revolutionary regime and eliciting popular support for its programs.

The West applauded Nasser's goal of economic development and promised support for the construction of the Aswan Dam. The honeymoon between Nasser and the West, however, was to be short-lived. Nasser demanded the evacuation of British troops from Egyptian soil, a demand reluctantly agreed to by a Britain still clinging to dreams of empire. Clashes between Israeli forces and Palestinian refugees seeking shelter on Egyptian soil soon escalated into clashes between Israeli forces and the Egyptian army. Nasser asked the West for arms to resist Israeli incursions, but the West refused. Nasser responded by purchasing arms from the Soviet bloc, a move that shattered the West's monopoly of power in the Middle East. For the first time in its history, the Soviet Union had gained entree into the Middle East and the Mediterranean basin. Fearful that Western security would be placed at risk, the United States demanded that Nasser rescind the communist arms deal. When he refused, the United States cancelled its aid for the Aswan Dam (Gorst and Johnman 1997). Nasser, in turn, responded by nationalizing the Suez Canal.

It was at this point that Israel, fearful of Nasser's escalating popularity in the Arab world, conspired with Britain and France to bring down the Nasser regime. Israeli forces stormed the Suez Canal in October 1956, while Britain and France demanded the right to occupy the canal under the pretext of protecting international shipping (McNamara 2003). The second Arab-Israeli war had begun. When Egypt refused to cede the canal, it was occupied by British and French forces. The three conspirators, however, had failed to consult with an American administration that was attempting to counter Soviet influence in the third world by stressing America's history as a revolutionary, anticolonial power (Brands 1993). Eisenhower sided with Egypt, forcing French, British, and Israeli forces to withdraw from Egyptian territory. Nasser reigned victorious.

In a period of two brief years, Nasser had evicted British troops from Egyptian soil, shattered the Western arms monopoly in the Middle East, nationalized the Suez Canal, and defeated (albeit politically) the combined forces of Israel, France, and Britain. In the eyes of Egypt and the entire Arab world, Nasser had become a charismatic hero of towering proportions, well fitting Weber's description of a charismatic leader "endowed with supernatural, superhuman . . . powers" (Weber 1947).

Arab Nationalism. Nasser's near-defeat in the Arab/Israeli war of 1956 convinced him that Egypt would never be free from external threat as long as his Arab neighbors remained subservient to the West. His resentment of foreign domination, moreover, was shared by thousands of students, military officers, and intellectuals throughout the Arab world. Indeed, Arab nationalism was rapidly becoming the dominant political ideology of the region.

The message of Arab nationalism was both simple and powerful (Farah 1987; Doran 1999): The Arabs are one people united by a common history, a common culture, a common language, and for the most part, a common religion. Once powerful, the Arabs now find themselves fragmented into a multitude of petty countries manipulated by Western imperialists and Israel. All that is required for a resurgence of Arab power is the reunification of the Arab people into a single country.

However potent its message, the Arab nationalist movement had historically lacked a dominant leader capable of marshaling its diverse and conflicting wings (Gershoni 1981). Nasser provided that leadership.

A union of Egypt and Syria was forged in 1958. Pro-Nasser coups also overthrew the pro-Western monarchs of Iraq, Yemen, and Libya. Nasser's supporters also came within a hairsbreadth of toppling pro-Western regimes in Saudi Arabia, Jordan, and Lebanon. As soon as the Arab world was united, Nasser vowed, the humiliation of 1948 would be redressed and Israel would be returned to the Palestinians.

On the domestic front, Nasser transformed Egypt's political system into a military dictatorship. The quasi-parliamentary institutions that had evolved under the monarchy were abolished. Abolished too, were the Wafd and other political parties of the era. The Muslim Brotherhood was driven underground and remained dormant throughout much of the Nasser era. All effective power would reside in Nasser and the Revolutionary Command Council, a group of Nasser's most trusted associates among the Free Officers. Nasser would later create a single political party, the Arab Socialist Union, in an effort to mobilize popular support for his regime and its objectives.

Changes in the economic and social arena were equally dramatic. Egypt's largest farms were expropriated by the government and their lands redistributed among the peasants. All banks, insurance companies, factories, and large commercial establishments were also nationalized, transforming Egypt into a predominantly socialist economy. Only small firms employing a handful of employees were allowed to remain in the private sector. Schools and health clinics mushroomed as the government sought to eliminate the scourges of illiteracy and poverty. Graduates of the new schools and universities were guaranteed a job with the government.

Egypt, however, was not a communist state. Its ideology was Arab nationalism. Nasser's goal was the creation of an Egypt that was as equitable as it was prosperous. Socialism and military rule were merely the means to that end (Hosseinzedeh 1989). Capitalism and party politics, in the view of Nasser and his colleagues, had brought Egypt little more than poverty, inequality, and conflict. Egypt's military leaders would use their authority to assure that Egypt's scarce resources were allocated in a just and productive manner. Once economic and social development

Egyptians pour into Cairo for the funeral of Gamal Abdel Nasser, Egypt's president from 1954 to 1970. Nasser's popularity extended beyond the borders of Egypt, with his supporters proclaiming, "We Arabs are all Nasser."

had been achieved, Egypt would become a true democracy in which educated and prosperous Egyptians could make wise and judicious choices.

Both Arab unity and economic development, however, were to prove elusive. The union with Syria was short-lived, and pro-Western regimes in Lebanon, Saudi Arabia, and Jordan were stabilized by the United States and Britain. The 1960s also found Egypt embroiled in the Yemeni Civil War, a disastrous involvement that paralleled the American experience in Vietnam. Egyptian forces controlled the major cities but could not subdue the tribes that dominated Yemen's impenetrable countryside. The morale of the Egyptian forces sank as defeat became inevitable. The collapse of the Yemeni venture was followed in short order by the outbreak of the third of the Arab-Israeli wars, in June 1967. Israel would rout the Egyptian forces in less than six days.

The domestic situation was equally bleak. Dramatic progress had been made in the areas of education and public welfare, but Egypt's economy lagged as funds that might have been used for economic development were sapped by war and the quest for Arab unity (Abdel-Fadil 1980; Beattie 1994). Efforts to provide all Egyptians with employment, moreover, were overwhelmed by Egypt's continuing population explosion. There were simply too many people for too few jobs. The shift to socialism, for its part, served only to swell the size of an unproductive bureaucracy (Waterbury 1978; Ayubi 1980).

The Revolution Changes Course: Sadat (1970–1981)

Nasser, long in ill health, died in 1970, bringing to an end the most dramatic era in modern Arab history. Nasser was succeeded in office by Anwar Sadat, his vice-president and a charter member of the Free Officers (Heikal 1975). The picture facing Sadat was bleak (Baker 1990). Egyptian forces faced the Israelis across the Suez Canal, the economy was depressed, and the Egyptian population was demoralized. The military, once viewed as the savior of Egypt, was in disgrace (Abdul-Hamid 1992; Kechichian and Nazimek 1997). Arab nationalism and socialism were equally victims of the war. Both had proven to be false gods.

Anwar Sadat, moreover, possessed none of Nasser's charisma. Many Egyptians believed him to be a weak individual who had been placed in office as a figure-head president until more powerful forces could sort out the course of the revolution (Heikal 1983). The Soviet Union also distrusted Sadat, preferring that the Egyptian presidency go to an Egyptian military leader with communist leanings. Even American officials had little faith in Sadat, assuming, as others did, that his tenure in office would be a brief one (Heikal 1983).

Sadat, however, proved to be a remarkably resilient individual. He crushed an attempted coup in 1971, expelled Soviet military advisors in 1972, and temporarily drove the Israelis from the Suez Canal in the October War of 1973. That war, the fourth Arab-Israeli war in a quarter of a century, saw Egyptian forces score dazzling victories against an Israeli army that had humiliated the Egyptian army some five years earlier (Bar-Joseph 2005; Jamasi 1993). The outcome of the war was inconclusive, with Israeli forces (backed by strong support from the United States) regaining lost territories. The October War, referred to as the Yom Kippur War by the Israelis, made Sadat a hero in his own right. He had masterminded the first Egyptian military victory of the modern era. Sadat was now the unquestioned ruler of Egypt.

The course of Egyptian policy under Sadat was to bear little resemblance to that of the Nasser era. Sadat had little interest in either Arab unity or world revolution, a position that gained him the strong support of both the United States and Saudi Arabia. Neither the United States nor its oil-rich allies wanted to contend with a new Nasser. The cornerstone of Sadat's foreign policy, moreover, was to be peace with Israel. The October War was followed during the mid-1970s by a negotiated withdrawal of Israeli troops from the Sinai Peninsula. The Camp David peace accords between Egypt and Israel were agreed to in 1978, bringing Israel peace with the most powerful of its Arab neighbors. The Arab world felt betrayed. The headquarters of the Arab League was moved from Cairo to Tunisia, and Arab financial assistance to Egypt was terminated. Egypt, now severed from its natural base of support, became dependent upon economic and military assistance from the United States.

Policy changes on the domestic front were equally dramatic. In 1974, Sadat launched his **infitah,** or *shift to capitalism* (Gillespie 1984). Henceforth, Egypt would possess a mixed economy in which private-sector firms were free to compete with the public sector. American aid and Western investment, Sadat promised, would make Egypt the economic hub of the Middle East (Fahmy 1988). Egypt, moreover, had traded guns for butter. The "peace dividend" would

Gamal Abdel Nasser (left) pushed for rapid industrialization, seeing it as Egypt's key to a prosperous future. Anwar Sadat (center), who advocated economic and political reforms, was killed by Muslim extremists. Hosni Mubarak (right) maintained Sadat's reforms and strengthened Egypt's ties with the Arab world.

allow Egypt to scale back its military expenditures and concentrate on economic development. Prosperity was assured. Economic reforms were matched by halting steps toward democracy. Although Sadat remained the absolute leader of Egypt, political parties re-emerged and the Egyptian Parliament was allowed to debate issues of minor importance.

Sadat's dream of capitalist prosperity fared little better than Nasser's vision of a socialist utopia. The newly revived capitalist sector concentrated on quick-profit projects that did little to strengthen the overall economy, while huge sums of money found their way into the pockets of Sadat's friends and family (Springborg 1989). Although a minority of Egyptians prospered, the majority sank deeper into poverty (Gillespie 1984). Egypt's economic and social problems continued to multiply, as did its population. Democratic reforms were cancelled as Sadat's popularity plummeted. Many of the disaffected joined the Muslim Brotherhood and more extreme Islamic groups. In September 1981, Sadat ordered the arrest of more than 1,500 political activists, many of them Muslim Fundamentalists of one stripe or another. He was assassinated a month later by Muslim extremists within the military.

The Revolution in Retreat: Mubarak (1981–)

Sadat was succeeded as president of Egypt by then-Vice President Hosni Mubarak. Mubarak, a leader with a reputation for honesty and caution, has extended Sadat's reforms in the areas of democratization and capitalism and maintained Sadat's policies of friendship with the United States and Israel. Mubarak, however, has also reestablished Egypt's ties with the Arab world. The headquarters of the Arab League has returned to Cairo, as has foreign assistance from Saudi Arabia and the oil-producing states of the Arab/Persian Gulf. Egypt has once again become the center of the Arab World.

The Egypt of today bears little resemblance to the Egypt of the Nasser era. Revolutionary Councils have given way to a constitutional structure not dissimilar to that of France. Executive power is divided between a strong president and a weak prime minister selected by the president. Legislative authority resides in a Parliament elected in a quasi-fair election; a Constitutional Council (Supreme Court) possesses the power to declare acts of the Government unconstitutional. It has done so on several occasions but usually with the implicit agreement of the president. The single-party apparatus of the Nasser era has been replaced by a multiparty system, albeit a multiparty system in which the government party always wins. The Egyptian press is freer than at any time since the Nasser Revolution of 1952, and the rigid socialism of the earlier era has been challenged by a growing private sector.

Nevertheless, the Egypt of today is very much the product of the Nasser era. The president of the Egyptian Republic is still a military officer, as are his major advisors. The Parliament and the Court, while vigorous in the execution of their responsibilities, pose little challenge to the presidency. Despite some progress toward privatization and economic reform, the Egyptian economy continues to be micromanaged by a massive bureaucracy (Harik 1997).

The Egypt of today has also inherited the problems of the past (McDermott 1988). The population explosion continues, with the 20 million Egyptians of the revolutionary era having become nearly 80 million today. That figure, moreover, is expected to reach 125 million by the year 2020. Poverty continues, although few Egyptians are threatened with starvation. Housing shortages are critical, as are levels of unemployment and underemployment. Official estimates place the unemployment figure in the 10 to 13 percent range, but unofficial estimates are much higher. From one-third to one-half of all working Egyptians, moreover, are underemployed, a euphemistic term for disguised unemployment.

The capitalist reforms of the Sadat and Mubarak eras have also created new problems. While a minority of the Egyptian population enjoys unparalleled prosperity, most Egyptians find life increasingly difficult. Many Egyptian intellectuals also feel that Egypt is in danger of becoming dependent on the United States. While this may or may not be the case, the $2 billion in foreign aid that the United States provides to Egypt on an annual basis does assure that American views will receive a careful hearing in Cairo. The growing strength of the Islamic extremists also threatens to undermine the viability of Egypt's quasi-democratic political institutions.

Adding to the mix has been the confusion surrounding Egypt's 2005 presidential elections. "Enough" (of Mubarak) emerged as a spontaneous group of students and intellectuals demanding that Mubarak amend the Egyptian constitution to allow more than one candidate to run for the presidency (*Al Jazeera*, March 30, 2005, www). The Muslim Brotherhood issued similar demands. Mubarak rejected the demands out of hand. Then, in a sudden about-face, he announced that the constitution would be amended and that multiple candidates would be allowed. Even the leaders of the National Democratic Party were taken by surprise. No indication was given of the procedures to be followed.

The possibility of an opposition victory was virtually nil. The opposition parties, to be discussed shortly, were intellectual affairs with little organization and minimal capacity to mobilize the masses. Active campaigning by opposition candidates was out of the question. The right of assembly was outlawed by the prevailing "emergency laws." Just to be on the safe side, potential candidates were intimidated, some being placed under house arrest on technicalities. The NDP, by contrast, regularly returned presidential majorities in the 90 percent range and was free to campaign as it saw fit. Why would it be any different this time?

and are generally free of political influence. Politically sensitive issues are more problematic, as the Constitutional Court's power to review government decisions can be overridden by the president's emergency powers.

The president has the option of sending issues of state security to military courts rather than to civilian courts. Islamic Fundamentalists charged with attacks on foreign tourists, for example, have been tried by military courts, a procedure that deprives them of their constitutional rights. The military has its own legal system and is not subject to civilian law.

These limitations aside, the Constitutional Court has played a vigorous role in strengthening Egyptian democracy. Unfair election laws have twice been declared unconstitutional by the Court, and the Court has also played a vigorous role in blocking Government attempts to restrict the activities of political parties. The Constitutional Court cannot rival the presidency as a source of political power, but it has developed at least some precedents for independent action. The president has also allowed unpopular policies to be overridden by the Court as a means of saving face. Rather than backtracking in the face of popular opposition, he can claim to be strengthening Egyptian democracy. Recently, for example, the Court invalidated a very controversial law prohibiting female students from wearing Islamic dress to schools. The government capitulated in the name of democracy, thereby freeing itself from a policy that would have been difficult, if not dangerous, to enforce. More recently, the courts have been in the forefront of attacking corruption in the People's Assembly, a fact that has created tension between the two branches of government (*Al-Ahram,* Sept. 4, 1999, 16). Egyptian judges are also beginning to enter the political fray by demanding greater independence from executive interference (*Al-Jazeera,* April 15, 2005, www). Over 1200 judges also vowed to abstain from supervising presidential and parliamentary elections unless their demands for independence were met (*Al-Ahram Weekly,* April 21, 2005, www).

Bureaucracy and Politics in Egypt: The Emergence of a Bureaucratic State

The Egyptian bureaucracy, in common with most bureaucracies of the third world, performs two basic functions:

- First, it maintains an ever-increasing array of services essential to the day-to-day operation of the state.

- Second, it bears primary responsibility for the economic and social development of Egyptian society.

If one is to judge by the comments of President Mubarak, the Egyptian bureaucracy has failed on both counts. In a 1985 address to the Egyptian Parliament Mubarak complained that

We had before us (upon assuming office) the prospect of crumbling public services and utilities. The situation was the result of years of accumulated paralysis and neglect. Citizens complained of the situation from the moment they opened their eyes in the morning until they returned from work. The flow of water was inadequate and irregular. Electric current fluctuated, and extended blackouts were common. Communications moved at a snail's pace. Roads were impassable. Television was limited. The decay of the sewer system turned some streets and quarters into swamps. . . .

Medical equipment in public hospitals is old and in short supply. Public services (bureaucracy) oppress the citizens with routine and delay. Free education has lost much of its effectiveness, and the expense of college education is oppressive to Egyptian families. Then there are the problems of housing shortages, rising prices, vanishing goods, and of houses collapsing on their inhabitants. The list of problems our people complain of is endless, yet they are forced to put up with them (*Al-Ahram,* Nov. 14, 1985).

The situation is little better today. Indeed, the Egyptian bureaucracy is now viewed as a major obstacle to the economic and social development of Egyptian society (Palmer, Leila, and Yassin 1988; *Al-Ahram,* Sept. 2, 1999, 11).

The criticisms of the Egyptian bureaucracy are numerous and varied. Government employees in Egypt are said to be self-serving, lazy, corrupt, rigid, lacking in creativity, insensitive to the public, and fearful of taking responsibility (Allam 2002). One study estimated that the average Egyptian official "works" somewhere between twenty minutes and two hours per day (Ayubi 1982). Unless bureaucratic performance improves dramatically, the quality of life of the average Egyptian will continue to slide. Political stability and hopes for democracy will deteriorate apace.

The International Monetary Fund (IMF), USAID, and the World Bank have all demanded that Egypt scale down the size of its bureaucracy. Egyptian intellectuals and the Egyptian press have joined the chorus, blaming the bureaucracy for most of Egypt's social and economic woes. As yet, however, reform remains elusive (*Al-Ahram Weekly,* Dec. 2003) The Mubarak government, as the Nasser and Sadat governments before it, depends upon the bureaucracy to provide a safety net to the ever-increasing number of unemployed graduates. The ruling party also needs a patronage system to reward supporters of the regime.

THE ACTORS IN EGYPTIAN POLITICS: ELITES, PARTIES, GROUPS, AND CITIZENS

Political institutions are the arena of politics, but it is the actors in the political process who determine who gets what, when, and how. In this section we will look at the "human" element of Egyptian politics by examining the political influence of Egypt's elites, parties, groups, and citizens.

Elites and Politics in Egypt

Political power in Egypt is concentrated in the hands of the president. Parliaments and political parties exist, but their ability to constrain the authority of the president is largely symbolic. Elite status in Egypt, accordingly, is determined by access to the president.

The concentration of political authority in the hands of the Egyptian president makes the decision-making process inordinately dependent upon the values, style, and personality traits of a single individual. The concerns of one president, moreover, are not necessarily those of the next (Kassem 2004). In a period of a few years, for example, Egypt was transformed from Nasser's vision of Egypt as a socialist state allied with the Soviet Union and dedicated to the cause of Arab unity into Sadat's vision of Egypt as a mixed socialist/capitalist state allied with the United States and disparaging of Arab unity. Mubarak, in turn, has tried to stake out a middle ground between the two extremes. Should Egypt's gradual march toward democracy lead to a victory for the Islamic forces, the transformation of Egyptian politics would be total.

Predicting the course of Egyptian politics, then, has much to do with analyzing the personality style of the man in power. In this regard, Salwa Gomaa suggests that the personality styles of Egypt's three presidents have been radically different (Gomaa 1991). Nasser, for example, saw himself as a guide and teacher. Sadat's self-image, by contrast, was that of the patriarchal father. He viewed Egypt's citizens as his children and felt it was his duty to take care of them. Others have suggested that Sadat viewed himself as something of an English gentleman, smoking his pipe while shaping the course of world history (McDermott 1975). Both Nasser and Sadat, according to Gomaa, had large egos. Both felt that they could change the course of history and were anxious to do so. Mubarak, by contrast, appears to view himself as a senior bureaucrat assigned the responsibility of guiding the ship of state through troubled waters.

Differences in self-image are paralleled by differences in decision-making styles. Sadat gloried in the element of surprise, making sweeping decisions with blinding speed. He hated details, and he made many decisions on the basis of oral reports and poorly documented information. He also seemed to place greater faith in foreign advisors than in his own people. This was particularly true in the area of foreign affairs. Mubarak, by contrast, is far more cautious than his predecessor. He proceeds slowly, making careful, step-by-step decisions based upon consultations with a wide variety of groups. He also tends to read reports in great detail and doesn't like surprises. Nasser fell between the two extremes. He was careful by nature but reacted swiftly to external events. Mubarak's personality style, then, lends itself to moderation. It is not clear, however, that his incremental mode of decision making is conducive to solving Egypt's massive social and economic problems. Massive problems often require radical solutions.

As powerful as the Egyptian president may be, he ultimately shares power with a variety of sub-elites or secondary elites who assist in the formulation and execution of his policies. This group includes senior military commanders, vice-presidents (if they exist), senior members of the presidential office, senior Cabinet ministers, and the leadership of the NDP. The elite circle would also include governors of Egypt's most populous provinces, a growing number of business leaders, and Egypt's senior religious authorities.

Increasingly, the elite circle is making room for Mubarak's son Gamal, an investment banker and head of the ruling National Democratic Party (Weaver 2003). Accusations that Gamal is being groomed to replace his father have been heatedly denied by Mubarak and his son, but to no avail. Why else, people ask, would Gamal be made head of the NDP? A senior member of the NDP has even written a book eulogizing Gamal Mubarak as "the most qualified" man for the job (*Al-Jazeera,* March 9, 2004, www). It is now his pictures that adorn the billboards of Cairo (*BBC*, Sept. 10, 2004, www).

In his early forties, Gamal Mubarak is generally viewed as being too young for the job, but this would be less of a problem if President Mubarak accepts a fifth term in office in 2005, a likely event. The ascension of Gamal Mubarak to the presidency would rupture Egypt's long tradition of military rule and could well be overruled by generals, not the least of whom is the chief of Egyptian intelligence, General Omar Suleiman. Apparently the generals have reached a consensus on the issue (Weaver 2003).

The secondary elites, in turn, head a cadre of "influential" military officers, party leaders, and senior bureaucrats that forms the backbone of Egypt's presidential system. Although not qualifying as an elite in the grand sense of the term, they clearly represent a privileged "political" class. As such, they coexist with both the new entrepreneurial class spawned by the infitah and the older aristocratic class, both of which also enjoy privileged status in Egyptian society.

Parties and Politics in Egypt

Mubarak's era of quasi-democracy has witnessed a proliferation of political parties. Some have deep roots in Egyptian society, while others are little more than empty shells left over from the Sadat era. The picture is made even more complicated by the fluidity of Egyptian parties. Parties merge in an effort to make a stronger electoral showing, only to splinter as a result of personality conflicts or ideological differences.

For all its complexity, the Egyptian party system is dominated by four distinct tendencies: the left, the center, the capitalist right, and the Islamic (Muslim) right.

The parties of the left, now dominated by the Nasserites and the Tagumma (Communists), advocate a return to the socialism of the Nasser era, albeit a socialism administered in a more efficient and less corrupt manner. The parties of the capitalist right, and the **New Wafd** in particular, call for a complete break with Egypt's socialist past, including the privatization of the public-sector enterprises that constitute a large percentage of the Egyptian economy. The religious right, of which the Muslim Brotherhood is the quasi-legal representative, would transform Egypt into an Islamic theocracy but is not opposed to capitalism. Spanning the middle of these seemingly irreconcilable tendencies is the ruling National Democratic Party. Its ideological position, such as it is, calls for some socialism, some capitalism, and some religion. However vague its ideology, the NDP is the only party that counts. Aside from the Muslim Brotherhood, to be discussed shortly, the other parties are ephemeral to the political process. They are scrambling to form a United Front in the run-up to the 2005 elections, but can

Egyptian Party System		
Tendency	*Dominant Party*	*Type of Government*
Left	Nasserites, Tagumma	Socialism
Center	National Democratic Party	Guided democracy
Capitalist right	New Wafd	Free-market democracy
Religious right	Muslim Brotherhood	Islamic state

agree on little other than the need for greater democracy in Egypt. That is not likely to happen in the near future.

Despite its democratic trappings, the NDP is a highly centralized organization controlled by President Mubarak. Its role is to provide Egypt's quasi-military regime with resounding majorities in the Parliament, a role accomplished by the lavish use of "wasta" (political patronage). The NDP is the regime's primary dispenser of patronage, and its members enjoy preferential access to government jobs. Members of the NDP also find it easier than ordinary individuals to wend their way through the obstacles of Egypt's all-pervasive bureaucracy. Both concerns are of vital importance in a country where little can be accomplished without "connections" of one form or another.

The NDP also assures its dominance by co-opting local landowners, businessmen, and other notables into the Party apparatus. The notables use their considerable influence to encourage voting for the NDP. The NDP reciprocates by assuring that the interests of the notables are taken care of and by providing them with patronage to reward their supporters. The stronger the base of the notables, the stronger the position of the NDP.

Finally, election laws have been manipulated in favor of the NDP. Until recently, for example, election laws required that a party receive 8 percent of the vote to be represented in the Parliament. The votes of parties receiving less than 8 percent automatically went to the majority party—the NDP. The huge electoral victories of the NDP result from other factors as well. Many Egyptians feel that opposing the NDP is useless, so they refrain from voting. This has made voter turnout in Egypt among the lowest in the world.

The NDP's domination of the People's Assembly has enabled Mubarak to rule under the guise of parliamentary democracy without fear of serious opposition to his policies (*Middle East Times,* 2000, Issue 7, www). Indeed, the NDP maintains an array of specialized committees, the membership of which is remarkably similar to the membership of the legislative committees in the People's Assembly. What the party committees decide is essentially what the parliamentary committees recommend. Although opposition delegates can (and do) chastise Government policy, the Government's position is never in doubt (*Middle East Times,* 2000, Issue 14, www).

Islam and Politics in Egypt

To understand the role of the Islamic right in Egyptian politics, it is important to recall that Islam does not recognize a clear distinction between church and state. The Koran (the holy book of Islam) is the law of God as revealed to the Prophet Mohammed. The Koran speaks of a world of peace and a world of war (Khadduri 1955). Muslims, the adherents of Islam, live in the world of peace. As such, they constitute an Islamic nation to be guided by Islamic law. Western notions of nationalism are contrary to the concept of a unified nation of believers, for loyalty to a state contradicts loyalty to God.

Egypt is a predominantly Islamic country, with approximately 90 percent of its citizens adhering to the Islamic faith. Divorcing Islam from Egyptian politics is a virtual impossibility (Murphy 2002). The political influence of Islam manifests itself in at least five ways.

First, Islam provides the moral underpinning of Egyptian society. Egyptian politicians are very careful not to offend Islamic sentiments. Even in the heady days of revolutionary nationalism, every effort was made to find an Islamic justification for Nasser's policies. Egyptian socialism was not Marxist socialism. Rather, it was Islamic socialism, legitimized by the principles of social equity contained in the Koran.

Second, much of the current political debate in Egypt centers on the extent to which Islamic law should be incorporated into Egyptian secular law. Islamic groups are pushing hard to have the Koran implemented as the legal Constitution of Egypt. At the minimum, they demand a sharp curtailment of bars, imprudent dress, and other Western practices offensive to Islamic law.

Third, the mosque provides a focal point of Islamic opposition to the Mubarak regime. The Government can ban the Fundamentalists from forming political parties, but it cannot close the mosques. Sermons in the mosque are often political, suggesting indirectly or not so indirectly that Egypt's problems would be fewer if the Government followed Islamic principles. Informal conversations before and after the prayers also provide Islamic Fundamentalists with ample opportunity to proselytize in support of their goal of an Islamic state. Sadat made an abortive attempt to bring Egypt's mosques under government control, but he was assassinated for his efforts. The Mubarak regime has now renewed this endeavor (Zaqzug 1999). As the Minister of Religious Endowments charged with implementing the policy explained, "The Friday sermons are not a political broadcast" (Zaqzug 1999). Whether it will succeed or not remains a matter of conjecture, for it is estimated that Egypt possesses some 60,000 mosques, many beyond the control of the state. The government also lacks a sufficient number of "qualified" preachers to service the vast numbers of nongovernmental mosques (Mustafa 1995). (Nongovernmental mosques are operated by private individuals, while government mosques are owned and operated by the Egyptian government.)

Fourth, Islamic groups now control the "street." In Egypt, as in most other countries of the third world, street demonstrations often turn violent, testing the Government's resolve and threatening to trigger broader religious and class violence. More often than not, such demonstrations begin in the universities and spread to

© Sandro Vannini/ CORBIS

Tens of thousands of Muslims kneel in prayer in front of Cairo's
Mosque of Amr during Ramadan. Nine out of ten Egyptians are
Muslim.

labor unions and other groups. The Jihadist have now gone far beyond street
demonstrations, assassinating government officials, and foreign tourists. In 1995
an attempt was made to assassinate Mubarak, but it failed. Jihadist violence has
eased for the moment as Jihadist groups attempt to go mainstream, but has made
a resurgence in 2005.

Finally, Islam stands as an alternative to the established model of a Westernized state.
The Islamic Fundamentalists are minimally concerned with reforming the Egyptian political system. Their goal is the destruction of the present system and the
creation of an Islamic state, a process that occurred in Iran in 1979. The creation
of an Islamic state has considerable appeal to many Egyptians. Since the present
system isn't working, what do they have to lose?

The Islamic forces in Egypt, although formidable, do not speak with a single
voice. Rather, one finds three separate claimants to the Islamic mantle: the traditional Islamic religious establishment, the Muslim Brotherhood, and the Jihadists
(Mustafa 1995).

The Islamic Establishment.   The most important figures in Egypt's formal
Islamic establishment are the Minister of Religious Endowments, the Grand
Mufti or Judge, and the Rector of Al-Azhar, Cairo's renowned Islamic university

(Barraclough 1998; Ismail 1998). These, in turn, are surrounded by a variety of religious leaders collectively referred to as the Ulema. The government plays a dominant role in the appointment of senior religious officials, thereby assuring that the religious establishment is headed by men whose positions are compatible with the views of the president. Under Nasser, the Islamic establishment was headed by religious scholars who shared the regime's reformist views. Under Sadat and Mubarak, it has become more conservative. Despite their differences, all Egyptian governments have sought the blessing of the Ulema for their policies.

The Muslim Brotherhood.   The Muslim Brotherhood is the oldest and largest of Egypt Islamic Fundamentalist groups. It is also the largest Islamic Fundamentalist group in the world. Created in the 1920s by Hassan Al-Banna, the Brotherhood preached a message that was both simple and poignant. Egypt's plight, according to the Brotherhood, was caused by the decadence of the ruling elite and by the foreign influences that sustained that elite. God's word, as revealed by the Prophet Mohammed, was both clear and unequivocal. To follow the word of God was to achieve eternal salvation; to ignore it was to court damnation. It was the duty of all Muslims to forge a government based on Islamic principles. The main tools of the Brotherhood were teaching and preaching, providing welfare service for the poor, and violence (Husaini 1956).

Anwar Sadat and many other Free Officers were members of the Muslim Brotherhood before seizing power in July 1952 (Abdula 1990). Indeed, relations between the Free Officers and Brotherhood were not to become fully clarified until the Brotherhood attempted to assassinate President Nasser in 1954. Nasser's revenge was swift and brutal. The Brotherhood was driven into remission, but its organizational roots remained intact. Sadat revived the Brotherhood in 1971 in an effort to curb the growing influence of his leftist opponents.

Sadat's tactic was successful. The failures of the Nasser regime and the humiliation of the 1967 War fueled an Islamic revival that would see the Muslim Brotherhood emerge as the dominant political movement in Egypt. The international expansion of Muslim Brotherhood proceeded apace, with the Brotherhood strengthening its branches in the Arab World and establishing an international network that now spans 70 countries including the United States, Canada, Russia, and the countries of the European Union (Nada 2001, 2002; Palmer and Palmer 2004). Every time the Nasserites or Communists took to the street they found their demonstrations crushed by the Brotherhood and other Islamic groups. It was now the Muslim Fundamentalists who controlled the street.

It was a chastised Brotherhood, however, that emerged from the ashes of the 1967 War. Terror was renounced as being counterproductive. Civilian militias, however well armed, the Brotherhood concluded, could not challenge the firepower of modern armies. Henceforth, the Brotherhood would concentrate on its teaching, preaching, and welfare services to strengthen Muslim values in Egyptian society.

The tacit acceptance of the Brotherhood as a quasi-legitimate political organization provided it with increased scope for political activity. Electoral alliances were forged with the New Wafd and other parties of the capitalist right. More recently, the Brotherhood has simply incorporated the Socialist Labor Party and the much smaller Liberal Party. The Brotherhood also dominates Egypt's most important student and professional unions and has deepened its mass base by opening a vast network of Islamic schools, clinics, and investment companies (Aly 1989; Fahmy 1998). Some estimates now suggest that as much as 10 percent of the Egyptian population uses the services provided by the Brotherhood and related organizations (Mustafa 1995). In many ways, the Islamic elements are creating a social infrastructure parallel to that of the state. The Egyptian government is now attempting to curb the activities of the Muslim Brotherhood, a dangerous proposition that could plant the seeds of civil war.

Jihadist Terror. The new moderation of the Muslim Brotherhood was rejected by its more radical members, who believed that the only way to achieve their goal of an Islamic state was to declare war, a jihad, against the Egyptian government. The ideology of the Jihadists, the name now associated with Muslim extremists who advocate terror, was clear and direct: One does not achieve religious goals, they argued, by cooperating with the devil. The Brotherhood, they said, claims to be reforming the Egyptian government from within. In reality, it is strengthening a corrupt and oppressive government by making it appear religious in the eyes of the Egyptian people. Rather than making better Muslims, the Jihadist critique continued, the Brotherhood was cooperating with an Egyptian government controlled by the United States, the great Satan. Far from instilling Islamic morality, it was exposing Muslim youth to the seductive evils of Western culture. Terror, they concluded, was the only path to the achievement of an Islamic state. The morally corrupt government of the Islamic world were to be overthrown by force, as were the Western governments that occupied the Islamic world. All, including Israel, would be the target of a violent Jihad.

The Jihadists, too, were blessed by Sadat in his efforts to crush the leftist radicals who were attempting to overthrow his regime. In retrospect, this was a mistake. The Jihadists flourished and eventually assassinated Sadat. Their terrorist activities continued through 1980s and 1990s, being marked by attacks on Mubarak himself and the slaughter of tourists (Orr 2003). Tourism, a major source of Egypt's budget, plummeted and the government openly declared that it was in a state of war against the Jihadists.

The Jihadists also spread their poison throughout the Islamic world and became one of three pillars of a global Jihadist movement that replaced the Soviet Union as the major threat to the United States and world stability. The other pillars of the Jihadist movement were Pakistan and Iran (Palmer and Palmer, 2004). Osama bin Laden's September 11, 2001 attacks on the United States brought the Jihadist war to the United States, but bin Laden and Al Qaeda are not the only game in town. Indeed, Al Qaeda is fragmenting into a multitude of Jihadist groups, each with the capacity of wrecking havoc in the free world.

Ironically, the Islamic Group, the largest of Egypt's Jihadist groups, has made its peace with the Egyptian government, as have several lesser groups. A "truce" was declared in 1997 and tacitly accepted by a Mubarak regime that declared victory. Thousands of Jihadists have now been released from prison and encouraged to return to a normal life. Mubarak attributes his victory to the greater effectiveness of Egyptian security forces and improved international cooperation in the war against terror. The Jihadists say that the truce was the result of confusion within the Jihadist movement and a loss of public support. Self-criticism by the Jihadists acknowledged that violence had become an end in itself and that coordination among Jihadist groups had been poor (al-Zayat 2002). It was particularly difficult for the Jihadists to overcome Koranic injunctions against killing Muslims and innocent civilians. Even government clergy, however, acknowledge that terror is a legitimate weapon in the Palestinian war of liberation against Israel. They ask: Do not Israeli civilians pay the taxes that sustain the occupation of Islamic territory? Are not Israeli children the soldiers of the future? While the Jihad against Israel is used as a special case, bin Laden used the same logic to justify his attacks against the United States.

A curious question remains. If Mubarak has conquered the Jihadists, why has he allowed them the opportunity to rebuild? This question troubles the United States and its allies especially with the revival of Jihadist terror in Egypt in recent years (*Middle East Times*, April 8, 2005, www). Also curious is Mubarak's continued harassment of the Muslim Brotherhood, an organization that he once supported in an effort to weaken the Jihadists. While peaceful, the Brotherhood would probably sweep to power in fair elections. Perhaps Mubarak fears the Brotherhood more than he fears the Jihadists.

Pressure Groups and Politics in Egypt

In addition to political parties and Islamic organizations, a variety of other groups exercise varying degrees of influence on Egyptian politics. We will look at several of these groups, including workers and peasants, business associations, the military, and social groups.

Workers and Peasants.   The latter years of the monarchy had witnessed the emergence of a wide variety of labor unions, business organizations, professional associations, and other Western-type pressure groups in Egypt. With the advent of revolutionary socialism in the early 1950s, the business groups disbanded, while the labor, peasant, and professional associations were tied to the government in a corporatist arrangement similar to that described in the discussions of German politics (Beinin and Lockman 1987; Binder 1978). Egypt's unions, weak by European standards, supported the Nasser regime in the hope that the new corporatist arrangements would result in improved wages, job security, and welfare benefits for their members (Bianchi 1989).

Similar efforts were made to mobilize Egypt's peasants by organizing them into state-managed cooperatives, but the peasants were of less concern to Egypt's military leaders than were the labor unions (Bianchi 1989). Organized labor was an urban phenomenon that, if left unchecked, could challenge the authority of the regime. Peasants, by contrast, were isolated from the center of power and lacked either the organizational capacity or group consciousness required to pose a sustained threat to the regime (Ayrout 1962; Johnson 2004).

Egypt's professionals were also organized into a variety of government-sponsored syndicates with a view toward better controlling their activities and assuring their subservience to the regime. Of these, the most prominent were the syndicates of journalists, lawyers, teachers, and engineers (Bianchi 1989). Each elected its own leaders, but the victory of government candidates was never in doubt.

Labor, peasant, and most professional associations remain under government control today, but that control has lessened as syndicate elections have become increasingly dominated by opposition parties, including the Fundamentalists. Indeed, by the mid-1990s, the Muslim Brotherhood dominated the largest of Egypt's 22 main professional organizations, including the medical, legal, and engineering associations. This clearly demonstrates that the appeal of Fundamentalism is not limited to the lower classes.

Labor, for its part, is in disarray. While there have been a few sporadic strikes, the Egyptian labor movement has found it difficult to confront the challenge of economic liberalization. Archaic government-owned factories, the heart of the labor movement, are being phased out and their workers are retired early. Indeed, some government firms have seen their numbers shrink by more than half. The decrease in public sector enterprises is being encouraged by private sector firms, most of whom are hostile to unionization. This is against the law, but it is also a fact of life. Workers that want jobs are reluctant to complain. How could it be otherwise in a country marked by high unemployment? As a labor organizer would complain, "It's not that the working class is apathetic. It is in a state of disorientation. It is still reeling under the effects of the structural changes [privatization] that have taken place" (*Al-Ahram Weekly,* May 1, 2003).

Business Associations. Egypt possesses the usual array of business associations, including the Egyptian-American Chamber of Commerce, the Egyptian Society of Association Executives, a Federation of Industries, a Businessmen's Council, and a Businessmen's Association. All are devoted to expanding the role of the private sector in an Egyptian economy that mixes private enterprise with state ownership (Zaki 1999). On one side of this conflict stand the business associations and the world's financial institutions, all of which place tremendous pressure on Egypt to disband the moribund state-owned enterprises that still dominate the Egyptian economy. On the other side stand the unions, which are fearful of mass layoffs. The unions are joined by a deeply entrenched bureaucracy clinging desperately to its power and by a government fearful that further privatization of the economy will lead to mass riots (*Al-Ahram Weekly*, Mar. 31, 2005, www). As things currently stand, the struggle appears to be a stalemate. The Government is moving slowly toward privatization but still maintains its network of unproductive factories. Gamal Mubarak, perhaps the heir apparent to the Egyptian presidency, is an investment banker and has become the leading voice for the rapid liberalization of the Egyptian economy.

This said, differences within Egypt's professional associations abound. The Egyptian-American Chamber of Commerce is indicative of the major role that American companies now play in Egypt and obviously advocates a greater openness in the Egyptian economy. The Egyptian Society of Association Executives is even more blatant in its advocacy of free enterprise and is funded by the United States for the express purpose of promoting economic globalization in Egypt (Potter 2004).

Many other business associations advocate greater freedom from government regulation, but are not anxious to face the onslaught of foreign competition that the globalization of the Egyptian economy will bring. Simply stated, they want the best of both worlds—freedom for themselves and restrictions for their external competition. As least for the moment, they appear to be better connected to the ruling elite than the pro-globalization organizations. That, in the world of Egyptian politics, is what counts.

The Pillars of Power: The Military and Others. While labor, professional, and business associations play an important role in Egyptian politics, the most powerful groups in Egypt continue to be those that are vital to the survival of the system. In this regard, four groups are of paramount importance: the military, the bureaucracy, the NDP, and the religious establishment. All benefit from the status quo and are unlikely to favor a dramatic shift therein. Of the four pillars of the regime, the military is by far the most important (Abdula 1990). Egypt continues to be a predominantly military regime, substantial progress toward democracy notwithstanding. Most of Mubarak's senior advisors are drawn from the military, as are key figures in the Presidential Office, the bureaucracy, the NDP, and the local government apparatus, including governors and district officials. Military officers enjoy subsidized housing and every other perk that a poor society can bestow upon them.

Although it holds a privileged position in Egyptian society, the Egyptian military is not necessarily of one mind. Many officers are loyal to Mubarak, but others incline toward the Nasserites, the New Wafd, and the Islamic Fundamentalists. Indeed, the military leadership has been very restrained in its criticism of the Fundamentalist movement. Government actions against the Fundamentalists, as a result, are generally carried out by special security forces under the control of the Minister of Interior rather than by the army. Information concerning this and most other military issues, unfortunately, remains limited. Suffice it to say that the Mubarak regime works hard to assure the officer corps that its privileged and influential role in Egyptian politics will be retained.

The bureaucracy and NDP were discussed at length earlier in the chapter and require little elaboration other than to say that key officials in both are appointed directly by the president or the Presidential Office. They are at the heart of the regime's system of control and patronage. Like the officer corps, they enjoy a privileged position in Egyptian society. To weaken either the bureaucracy or the NDP would be to weaken the regime.

Finally, Egypt's religious establishment has long enjoyed strong ties with the government. Religion, as discussed above, is an essential element in the Egyptian political equation. Mosques are built and maintained by the Ministry of Wafqs (religious endowments). Al-Azhar University, the Islamic university, has been expanded and glorified (Barraclough 1998). Branches are now being opened in Thailand and other countries with large Muslim populations. Islamic programs abound on Egyptian television, and Egypt maintains a separate Koranic radio station. The Egyptian media also break for prayers five times a day, in line with Islamic traditions, and senior Islamic leaders have free access to Mubarak. Mubarak has also attempted to increase the credibility of establishment clergy by allowing them to condemn the U.S. occupation of Iraq and support suicide bombings in Palestinian areas occupied by Israel. Both issues find strong support among the Egyptian population and has increased support for Fundamentalist groups.

Social Groups. In addition to the parties and pressure groups described above, Egyptian politics is also influenced by a variety of social groups that have become increasingly politicized in recent years. Some are highly organized while others lack a well-defined sense of group identity. All, however, are part of the mosaic of Egyptian politics. Particularly important are the Islamic benevolent associations that provide much-needed services to Egypt's poor. Fearing links between these groups and the Fundamentalists, the government has brought all Islamic groups, whatever their nature, under its control (*Associated Press,* May 28, 1999; *Al-Ahram,* Sept. 1, 1999, 12). How well it has succeeded remains to be seen.

Cairo as a Pressure Group. The citizens of Cairo are so vast in number and so fragmented in their interests, that it is difficult to think of them as a coherent group. From the perspective of the Government, however, Cairo represents a critical group whose interests must be addressed (Weede 1986). Cairo is the seat of the Egyptian government, industry, commerce, banking, communications, mass media, education, religion, culture, health, and tourism. Little of significance occurs in Egypt that is not controlled in one way or another by Cairo. Fifteen million-plus Cairo residents, for example, constitute more than a fourth of Egypt's population, and a strike in Cairo can cripple the entire country. When people speak of controlling "the streets," moreover, it is the streets of Cairo to which they are referring. To lose control of Cairo is to lose the capacity to rule.

Not surprisingly, the citizens of Cairo receive favored treatment in terms of food, services, education, and housing. Life in many areas of Cairo is difficult, but it is far less difficult than in the countryside. In a cruel irony, the favored position of Cairo has led to the city's inordinate growth. A city of 3 million in 1960 will soon be a city of 20 million. Cairo is the heart of Egypt.

University Students. University students also represent a special-interest group that has received the rapt attention of Egypt's leaders (Mubarak 1999). In contrast to the situation in the U.S., Egyptian students constitute a vibrant political force (Erlich 1989). They are the most idealistic, the most intellectually aware, and the most articulate segment of Egyptian society. Their awareness of injustice is unfailing. The politicization of Egyptian students also finds its origins in a profound sense of insecurity and frustration. Many Egyptian students (some place the figure at 25 percent or higher) face the prospect of unemployment. Many of those who do find jobs will find them in the lower rungs of the bureaucracy, a fate that will allow them a marginal existence at best.

Civic disturbances are generally initiated by university students, and if promising, are joined by disgruntled workers, high school students, and other dissidents. Some student disturbances are spontaneous; most have been inspired by external political groups such as the Nasserites or the Muslim Brotherhood. It was the students, for example, who kept the Nasserite movement alive during the purges of the Sadat era.

Mubarak is attempting to strengthen the student wing of the ruling National Democratic Party, but it is the Fundamentalists who are now the dominant force in student politics. It was they who orchestrated the massive demonstrations that shook Cairo during the U.S.-Iraqi War and it has been fear of similar riots that has underscored Mubarak's hostility to U.S. policy in the region, similar riots are expected to increase in the future (*Al-Ahram Weekly,* April 7, 2005, www).

Coptic Christians. Coptic Christians represent approximately 8 percent of the Egyptian population and constitute a far higher percentage of the population in the politically sensitive Cairo region. Historically, Copts have been well integrated into the fabric of Egyptian society and have not constituted a cohesive political group (Farah 1986).

This picture, however, is changing rapidly. The dramatic rise of the Muslim Fundamentalists and their demands for an Islamic state now threaten to destroy Egypt's long tradition of tolerance and religious harmony. Religious conflicts have become commonplace since the latter days of the Sadat regime, and if present trends toward the Islamization of Egypt continue, yet another key element of Egypt's political stability will come unraveled. The Egyptian Government, for its part, complains that the Western press has blown the problem far out of proportion. Even the Coptic Patriarch has criticized the alarmist nature of the media coverage, saying that inflated reports of communal tension may make the situation worse rather than better (*Al-Waton Al-Arabi,* Nov. 6, 1998, 26).

Women as a Political Force. The political role of women in Egypt is difficult to assess. Their stamp on the character and development of Egypt has been profound if little noted (Baron 2005, Pollard 2005). By Middle Eastern standards, Egyptian women have made dramatic progress toward economic and political equality. By Western standards, they remain an exploited underclass in a male-dominated society (Rugh 1986). Possessing the right to vote, Egyptian women are represented in the People's Assembly and, to a lesser extent, in the Cabinet. The legal status of women, while restricted, has also witnessed improvement in recent years. A 1979 law now requires a man to notify his wife in writing that he has divorced her. The law also states that a wife has the right to divorce her husband if he chooses to take a second wife, a practice limited largely to the rural areas. In such an instance, the ex-wife retains a legal right to the family's lodging until remarriage or until the children are no longer in her custody (twelve years for girls and ten years for boys). A law passed in 2000 allows women to divorce their husbands on the condition that they return their dowries (*Middle East Times,* 2002, Issue 51, www). Pressure for divorce continues to mount as Egyptian women become increasingly aware of their rights, yet face

the President's wife, lamented, "It is totally unacceptable to subjugate such small girls in this way, whether intentionally or unintentionally, and to force them to go through this cruel experience. What is even more painful is that this is happening because of inherited social traditions and not just any health or social reasons, or any proper religious rulings. It is happening under the pretext of love and protection on the part of parents for their daughters" (*Al Ahram Weekly,* June 26, 2003, www).

An Egyptian Organization for Human Rights was instituted by the Mubarak regime in 2004, but critics are not impressed. Egypt is not short of human rights legislation. The problem is a lack of enforcement.

Economic Growth and Quality of Life

The Nasser revolution attempted to provide all of Egypt's citizens with a minimally sustainable quality of life. Basic foodstuffs were subsidized by the state, as were fuel and housing. The Government also attempted to provide everyone with a job, and education and health care were free, at least for the poor. The quality of government services was dismal by first world standards, but most people got along. There was also optimism that Egypt was modernizing and that things would get better with time. By the mid-1970s, however, the regime was finding it difficult to maintain even a rudimentary level of basic services. The population was growing faster than the economy, and the huge bureaucracy that had been created to manage the welfare system absorbed much of the wealth it was designed to distribute. The situation would improve little during the 1980s and 1990s, and much of the growth that has occurred has been in real estate and banking, areas that create wealth for a narrow elite but produce few jobs.

Today, accordingly, the majority of Egyptians find themselves in a precarious financial position. Most continue to rely on government jobs that pay little more than a subsistence wage. A third of Egyptian workers earn a minimum wage that hovers around the poverty level, and some 20 percent of the population is unemployed, a situation that continues to worsen as some 500,000 new Egyptians enter the job market each year. As a senior Egyptian columnist notes, "The long and short of it is that the gap separating people—individuals, groups and classes—has grown wider than expected, and wider than was the case in earlier years." He also quotes a colleague saying "we no longer have gaps, only widening schisms" (Mattar 2003).

Egyptian education, moreover, does little to provide the technical skills needed for economic revival. Almost half of Egypt's engineering graduates are unable to pass standard examinations, and leading educators complain of inadequate equipment as well as poorly motivated teachers who, according to Professor D. Awatef Ali Shoir, "are always tired because of the long time they spend in tutoring to make up for an inadequate salary" (*The Egyptian Gazette,* Nov. 29, 1991). Exams at all levels are based heavily on lectures, the copies of which are for sale by the instructor. Not surprisingly, students from affluent backgrounds do far better than their poorer counterparts. It could not be otherwise, for Egypt spends the equivalent of only $129 per student as opposed to $4,763 in the United States and $6,959 in Japan (*Al-Ahram Weekly,* July 31, 2003, www).

The movement toward Islamic Fundamentalism is not merely a function of the dismal quality of life experienced by most Egyptians. It is also a function of the growing gap between rich and poor that now characterizes Egyptian society. The upper classes have the skills and connections required to benefit from the increasing liberalization of the Egyptian economy, but most Egyptians have little chance of improving their station in life. Mass education is poor and imparts few practical skills. It has also ceased to be free. Egyptian students struggle to gain an education, only to find there are few jobs for college graduates. Their hostility toward the Mubarak regime is understandable. Why should one support a regime that allows the rich to prosper while ignoring the plight of the poor?

The Egyptian government has attempted to bridge the gap between rich and poor by legislating one of the highest tax rates in the world. Taxes on the rich, however, are seldom collected, with the World Bank estimating that "75 percent of persons in high income brackets are not known to the Tax Authority in Egypt" (*Egyptian Gazette,* Nov. 27, 1991). Progress is being made, but tax problems continue (*Al-Ahram,* Sept. 6, 1999, 14; Sept. 13, 1999, 6).

The Environment

Egypt's environment is one of the unhealthiest in the world. The number of cars choking Cairo's streets increased from some 64,000 in 1970 to more than 400,000 in 1991. The turn of the century would see 1.6 million vehicles in Egypt, most located in the greater Cairo with no relief in sight (Chemonics 1998, *Al-Ahram Weekly,* April 6, 2005, www). The "black cloud" has become an annual event as Cairo moves into the winter season. Humorists blame demons breaking wind, while conspiracy theorists suggest that the cloud is produced by U.S. military maneuvers. More likely, the thick black smoke is produced by the increased burning of rice straw following the fall harvest (*Daily Star,* Dec. 10, 2002, www). Water quality is low and sewage problems endemic.

The Egyptians are painfully aware of their environmental problems. They live with them on a daily basis. The problem, however, is what to do about them. Egypt has too many people and too many cars squeezed into too little land. It also has too much poverty. Egypt possesses a full slate of environmental legislation but is reluctant to enforce environmental laws for fear of slowing the pace of economic growth or scaring away potential investors. Unfortunately, one of the comparative advantages enjoyed by Egypt in its search for new industries is precisely its lack of environmental regulation. From the perspective of Egypt's embattled government, food and jobs are more important than the environment.

Egypt's environmental crisis poses little direct threat to the stability of the country. Its political impact, however, is profound. Environmental pollution lowers productivity and increases health costs, most of which are subsidized by the government. Tourism, a mainstay of the Egyptian economy, is eroded by the toxicity of the air, and few tourists return for a second visit. Egypt's poor environmental conditions also stand as a daily reminder of the government's inability to cope with a problem that has become a pervasive topic in the Egyptian media.

Prospects for the Future

Egypt currently stands at three different crossroads: between democracy and continued military rule; between Western-style capitalism and the continuation of a predominantly socialist economy that provides at least a basic level of food, shelter, education, and welfare; and between a secular political system and a theocracy based upon the laws of Islam. The three crossroads possess a common denominator: the grinding poverty of the Egyptian people and their desperate search for a better way of life. In years past, the existence of an Islamic regime in Egypt would have been unthinkable. It seems much less so today.

REFERENCES

Abdel-Fadil, M. 1980. *The Political Economy of Nasserism.* Cambridge, England: Cambridge University Press.

Abdula, Ahmed. 1990. *The Military and Democracy in Egypt.* Cairo: Siani Publishing. (In Arabic.)

Abdul-Hamid, Barlinti. 1992. *The Marshal and I.* Cairo, Egypt: Madbouli. (In Arabic.)

Agha, Olfat Hassan. 1991. "Mass Communicators and Issues of Development: An Empirical Study of a Sample of Mass Communicators in the Egyptian Society." Unpublished Dissertation, Cairo University.

Akhavi, S. 1975. "Egypt: Neo-Patrimonial Elite." In *Political Elites and Political Development in the Middle East,* ed. F. Tachau. Cambridge, England: Schenkman Publishing.

Allam, Abeer. 2000. "Less Work, More Play for State Bureaucrats." *ME Times* http://www.metimes.com/2K/issue2000-2/eg/less_work_htm.

Al-Sayid, Mustafa Kamel. 1990 (Winter). *Privatization: The Egyptian Debate.* Cairo papers in Social Science, vol. 13, monograph 4. Cairo, Egypt: The American University in Cairo Press.

Al-Zayat, Mansour. 2002 (Aug. 11). "Sharia and Life Series: Islamic groups and Violence." Al Jazeera. Interviewed by Mahir Abdullah, at http://www.al-jazeera.net/programs/shareea/articles/2002/8/8-11-1.htm. (In Arabic.)

Aly, Abdel Monem Said. 1989 (Oct.). "The Myth and Reality: The Four Faces of the Islamic Investment Companies." Unpublished Paper, Al-Ahram Center for Political and Strategic Studies, Al-Ahram Foundation, Cairo, Egypt.

Amin, Gamal. 1974. *The Modernization of Poverty: A Study in The Political Economy of Growth in Nine Arab Countries, 1945–1970.* Leiden: Brill.

Ansari, Hamied. 1985 (Jan.). "Mubarak's Egypt." *A World Affairs Journal: The Middle East, 1985.* 84(498).

Ansari, Hamied. 1987. *Egypt: The Stalled Society.* Cairo, Egypt: The American University of Cairo Press.

Arab (Ezzel), Abdel Aziz. 2002. *European Control and Egypt's Traditional Elites: A Case Study in Elite Economic Nationalism.* Lewiston, NY: Edwin Mellen Press.

Ayrout, Henry. 1962. *The Egyptian Peasant.* Boston, MA: Beacon Press. Translated by John Williams.

Ayubi, Nazih. 1980. *Bureaucracy and Politics in Contemporary Egypt.* London: Ithaca Press.

Ayubi, Nazih. 1982. "Bureaucratic Inflation and Administrative Inefficiency," *Middle East Studies* 18(3): 286–99.

Ayubi, Nazih. 1983 (Nov.). "The Egyptian 'Brain Drain': A Multidimensional Problem." *International Journal of Middle East Studies* 15(4): 431–50.

Ayubi, Nazih. 1989. "Government and the State of Egypt Today." In *Egypt Under Mubarak,* ed. C. Tripp and R. Owen. London: Routledge.

Bahgat, Gawdat. 1991. "The Impact of External and Internal Forces on Economic Orientation: The Case of Egypt." Ph.D. Dissertation, Florida State University.

Baker, Raymond W. 1978. *Egypt's Uncertain Revolution Under Nasser and Sadat.* Cambridge, MA: Harvard University Press.

Baker, Raymond W. 1990. *Sadat and After.* Cambridge, MA: Harvard University Press.

Barakat, Mohammed and Mahmood Sadiq. 1998 (Nov. 17). "Has the Thought of Religious Violence in Egypt Receded?" *Al-Wanton Al-Arabi* 4–8.

Bar-Joseph, Uri. 2005. *The Watchman Fell Asleep: The Surprise of Yom Kippur and Its Sources.* Albany: State University of New York Press.

Baron, Beth. 2005. *Egypt as a Woman: Nationalism, Gender, and Politics.* Berkeley: University of California Press.

Barraclough, Steven. 1998 (Spring). "Al-Azhar: Between the Government and the Islamists." *The Middle East Journal* 52(2): 236–249.

Beattie, Kirk J. 1994. *Egypt During the Nasser Years: Ideology, Politics, and Civil Society.* Boulder, CO: Westview.

Behrens-Abouseif, Doris. 1990. *Islamic Architecture in Cairo: An Introduction.* Cairo, Egypt: The American University in Cairo Press.

Beinin, J., and Z. Lockman. 1987. *Workers on the Nile: Nationalism, Communism, Islam, and the Egyptian Working Class.* Princeton, NJ: Princeton University Press.

Beitler, Ruth Margoies and Jebb, Cindy R. 2003. *Egypt as a Failing State (Electronic Resource): Implications for US National Security.* Colorado Springs, CO: USAF Institute for National Security Studies, USAF Academy.

Berque, Jacques. 1967. *Egypt: Imperialism and Revolution.* New York: Praeger.

Bianchi, Robert. 1989. *Unruly Corporatism: Associational Life in Twentieth-Century Egypt.* New York: Oxford University Press.

Binder, Leonard. 1978. *In a Moment of Enthusiasm: Political Power and the Second Stratum in Egypt.* Chicago: University of Chicago Press.

Brands, H. W. 1993. *Into the Labyrinth: The United States and the Middle East: 1945–1993.* New York: McGraw-Hill.

Brown, Nathan J. 1990. Peasant Politics in Modern Egypt: The Struggle Against the State. New Haven, CT: Yale University Press.

Carter, B. L. 1986. *The Copts in Egyptian Politics.* London: Croom Helm.

Cassen, R. 1986. *Does Aid Work? Report to an Intergovernmental Task Force.* Oxford: Clarendon Press.

Chemonics International Inc. "Cleaner Air for Better Lives." Adapted from the 1998 *Foreign Exchange,* Chemonics' Annual Newsletter.

Dawisha, K. 1979. *Soviet Foreign Policy Towards Egypt.* New York: Macmillan.

Dekmejian, H. R. 1975. *Egypt Under Nasser: A Study in Political Dynamics.* Albany, NY: State University of New York Press.

Doran, Michael S. 1999. *Pan-Arabism Before Nasser.* New York: Oxford University Press.

Dunne, Michele Durocher. 2003. *Democracy in Contemporary Egyptian Political Discourse.* Philadelphia, PA: Benjamins Pub.

Edward, L. "Egypt: Growing a Global Profession." *Association Management* 55(10): 97–98.

El Din, Khaled Mohi. 1995. *Memories of the Revolution.* Cairo: American University of Cairo.

El Gamassy, Marshal Mohaned. 1989. "Memoirs," serialized in *Sharq Al-Ausat,* London, August 18, 1989.

Erlikh, Hagai. 1989. *Students and University in 20th Century Egyptian Politics.* London: F. Cass.

Fahmy, Khaled Mahmoud. 1988 (Fall). *Legislating Infitah: Investment, Currency, and Foreign Trade Laws.* Cairo Papers in Social Science, vol. 11, monograph 3. Cairo, Egypt: American University in Cairo Press.

Fahmy, S. Ninette. 1998 (Autumn). "The Performance of the Muslim Brotherhood in the Egyptian Syndicates: An

Alternative Formula for Reform?" *Middle East Journal* 52(4): 551–62.

Fandy, Mamoun. 1998 (Spring). "Political Science Without Clothes: The Politics of Dress, or Contesting the Spatiality of the State of Egypt." *Arab Studies Quarterly* 20(2): 87–104.

Farag, Fatemah. 2004. "Labour Backlog: Is the Working Class Moving Forward?" *Al-Ahram Weekly* http://www.weekly.ahram.org.eg/print/2004/689/eg2.htm.

Farah, Nadia Ramses. 1986. *Religious Strife in Egypt: Crisis and Ideological Conflicts in the Seventies.* New York: Gordon and Breach.

Farah, T. 1987. *Pan Arabism and Arab Nationalism: The Continuing Debate.* Boulder, CO: Westview Press.

Gershoni, Israel. 1981. *The Emergence of Pan-Arabism.* Tel-Aviv: Shiloah Center for Middle Eastern and African Studies, Tel-Aviv University.

Gillespie, Kate. 1984. *The Tripartite Relationship: Government, Foreign Investors and Local Investors During Egypt's Economic Opening.* New York: Praeger.

Goldschmidt, Arthur, Jr. 1988. *Modern Egypt: The Formation of a Nation State.* Boulder, CO: Westview Press.

Gomaa, Salwa. 1991. "Leadership and Elections in Local Government." *Perspectives in the Center-Local Relations: Political Dynamics in the Middle East,* M.E.S. Series No. 28, 1991, 34–63.

Gomaa, Salwa. 1993. Interview with author.

Gorst, Anthony, and Lewis Johnman. 1997. *The Suez Crisis.* London: Routledge.

Hafez, M. H. 1997 (Fall). "Explaining the Origins of Islamic Resurgence: Islamic Revivalism in Egypt and Indonesia." *The Journal of Social, Political and Economic Studies* 22(3): 295–324.

Hamouda, Adel. 1990. *How the Egyptians Mock Their Leaders.* Cairo, Egypt: House of Sphinx Publishers. (In Arabic.)

Handoussa, H. A. 1987 (Sept.). *The Impact of Foreign Aid on Egypt's Economic Development: 1952–1986.* Paper presented to the conference on Aid, Capital Flows and Development, Talloirs, France. Jointly sponsored by the World Bank

and International Center for Economic Growth, 13–17.

Hank, Iliya. 1997. *Economic Policy Reform in Egypt.* Gainesville, FL: University Press of Florida.

Heikal, Mohamed. 1975. *The Road to Ramadan.* New York: Ballantine.

Heikal, Mohamed. 1983. *Autumn of Fury: The Assassination of Sadat.* London: Andre Deutsch.

Hosseinzedeh, Esmail. 1989. *Soviet Non-Capitalist Development: The Case of Nasser's Egypt.* New York: Praeger,

Husaini, Ishak Musa. 1956. *The Moslem Brethren.* Beirut: Khayat.

Ibrahim, Saad Eddin. 1980 (Dec.). "Anatomy of Egypt's Militant Islamic Groups: Methodological Note and Preliminary Findings." *International Journal of Middle East Studies* 12(4): 423–53.

Ismail, Salwa. 1998 (May). "Confronting the Other: Identity Culture, Politics and Conservative Islamism in Egypt." *International Journal of Middle East Studies* 30(2): 199–225.

Jamasi, Muhammad Abd Al Ghani. 1993. *The October War: Memoirs of Field Marshal El-Gamasy of Egypt.* Translation by Gillian Potter, Nadra Morcos, and Rosette Frances. Cairo, Egypt: The American University of Cairo Press.

Johnson, Amy J. 2004. *Reconstructing Rural Egypt: Ahmed Hussein and the History of Egyptian Development.* Syracuse, NY: Syracuse University Press.

Kassem, Maye. 2004. *Egyptian Politics: The Dynamics of Authoritarian Rule.* Boulder, CO: Lynne Rienner Pub.

Kays, D. 1984. *Frogs and Scorpions: Egypt, Sadat, and the Media.* London: Frederick Muller.

Kechichian, Joseph, and Jeanne Nazimek. 1997 (Sept.) "Challenges to the Military in Egypt." *Middle East Policy* 5(3): 125–39.

Khadduri, Majid. 1955. *War and Peace in the Law of Islam.* Baltimore: Johns Hopkins Press.

Kienle, Eberhard. 1998 (Spring). "More than a Response to Islamism: The Political Deliberalization of Egypt in the 1990s." *The Middle East Journal* 52(2): 219–35.

Lane, E. W. 1954. *Manners and Customs of the Modern Egyptians.* London: J. M. Dent & Sons, Ltd.

Lawson, Fred H. 1992. *The Social Origins of Egyptian Expansionism During the Muhammad Ali Period.* New York: Columbia University Press.

Longgood, William F. 1957. *Suez Story: Key to the Middle East.* New York: Greenberg.

Marsot, Afaf Lutfi Al-Sayyid. 1984. *Egypt in the Reign of Muhammad Ali.* Cambridge, England: Cambridge University Press.

McDermott, Anthony. 1975 (Nov.). "Sadat, the Art of Survival." *Middle East International* 53: 13.

Mattar, Gamil. 2003 (Nov.). "Post-Democratic Disorders." *Al-Ahram Weekly* 20(665). http://weekly.ahram.org.eg/2003/665/op21.htm.

McDermott, Anthony. 1988. *Egypt from Nasser to Mubarak: A Flawed Revolution.* London: Croom Helm.

McNamara, Robert. 2003. *Britain, Nasser and the Balance of Power in the Middle East, 1952–1967: From the Egyptian Revolution to the Six-Day War.* London: Frank Cass.

Middle East Watch. 1991 (Sept.). "Egyptian Government to Dissolve Prominent Arab Women's Organization."

Moore, Clement Henry. 1986 (Autumn). "Money and Power: The Dilemma of the Egyptian Infitah." *The Middle East Journal* 40(4): 634–56.

Mubarak, Hosni. 1999 (Jan. 29). "Interview." *Al-Hawadth,* 19–24.

Murphy, Caryle. 2002. *Passion for Islam: Shaping the Modern Middle East, The Egyptian Experience.* NY: Scribner.

Mustafa, Hala. 1995. *The State and the Opposition Islamic Movements: Between Truce and Confrontation in the Eras of Sadat and Mubarak.* Cairo: Markaz Al-Mahrusa.

Nada, Joseph, "Dimensions of the American Attack of Islamic Financing," *Al Jazeera.* 19 Nov. 2001. Interviewed by Ahmed Mansour. http://www.aljazeera.net/programs/no_limits/articles/2001/11/11-19-1.htm (23 Nov. 2001). (In Arabic.)

Nada, Joseph. "Interview with Joseph Nada, Commissioner of International Political Affairs for the Muslim Brotherhood." Part 1 of six interviews by Ahmed Mansour. *Al Jazeera.* 4 Aug. 2002. http://www.aljazeera.net/programs/century_witness/articles/2002/8/8-4-1.htm (9 Sept. 2002). (In Arabic.)

Nada, Joseph. "Interview with Joseph Nada, Commissioner of International Political Affairs for the Muslim Brotherhood." Part 2 of six interviews by Ahmed Mansour. *Al Jazeera.* 13 Aug. 2002. http://www.aljazeera.net/programs/century_witness/articles/2002/8/8/ 13-1.htm (9 Sept. 2002). In Arabic.

Nada, Joseph. "Interview with Joseph Nada, Commissioner of International Political Affairs for the Muslim Brotherhood." Part 3 of six interviews by Ahmed Mansour. *Al Jazeera.* 18 Aug. 2002. http://www.aljazeera.net/programs/century_witness/articles/2002/8/8/ 18-1.htm (9 Sept. 2002). (In Arabic.)

Nada, Joseph. "Interview with Joseph Nada, Commissioner of International Political Affairs for the Muslim Brotherhood." Part 4 of six interviews by Ahmed Mansour. *Al Jazeera.* 28 Aug. 2002. http://www.aljazeera.net/programs/century_witness/articles/ 2002/8/8-28-1.htm (9 Sept. 2002). (In Arabic.)

Nada, Joseph. "Interview with Joseph Nada, Commissioner of International Political Affairs for the Muslim Brotherhood." Part 5 of six interviews by Ahmed Mansour. *Al Jazeera.* 9 Sept. 2002. http://www.aljazeera.net.programs/century_ witness/ articles/2002/9/9-5-1.htm (9 Sept. 2002). (In Arabic.)

Nada, Joseph. "Responses to Testimony of Youssef Nada." Part 6 of six interviews by Ahmed Mansour. *Al Jazeera.* 5 Oct. 2002. http://www.aljazeera. net/programs/no_limites/articles/2002/10/10_ 5_1. htm (13 Oct. 2002). (In Arabic.)

Nasser, Gamal Abdel. Nasser Speeches 1955–1965. Cairo: Government of Egypt. Ministry of Information.

Nasser, Gamal Abdel. 1959. *The Philosophy of the Revolution.* Buffalo, NY: Smith, Keynes and Marshall.

Orr, Tamra. 2003. *Egyptian Islamic Jihad.* NY: Rosen Pub. Group.

Palmer, Monte, Ali Leila, and El Sayed Yassin. 1988. *The Egyptian Bureaucracy.* Syracuse, NY: Syracuse University Press.

Palmer, Monte and Princess Palmer. 2004. *At the Heart of Terror: Islam, Jihadists, and America's War on Terror.* Lanham, MD: Rowman and Littlefield Pub. Inc.

Pollard, Lisa. 2005. *Nuturing the National: The Family Politics Modernizing, Colonizing and Liberating Egypt (1805/1923).* Berkeley: University of California Press.

Potter, Edward L. 2003 (Oct.). "Egypt: Growing a Global Profession." *Association Management* (55): 97.

Rugh, Andrea B. 1986. *Reveal and Conceal: Dress in Contemporary Egypt.* Cairo, Egypt: American University in Cairo Press.

Shuman, Hend. 2004. "Tolerant Education: New Ethics Classes are the Latest Development in the Long Saga Reforming Egypt's Education System." *Cairo Times* http://www.cairotimes.com/news/education0809.html.

Soreh, Berween. 1998. "Another AUC Book Slashed by the Censor." *Special to the Middle East Times,* www.

Springborg, Robert. 1989. *Mubarak's Egypt: Fragmentation of the Political Order.* Boulder, CO: Westview Press.

Springborg, Robert. 1998 (Jan.). "Egypt: Repression's Toll." *Current History* 97(615): 32–37.

Sullivan, Denis J. 1990. "The Political Economy of Reform in Egypt." *International Journal of Middle East Studies* 22(3): 317–34.

Sullivan, Earl L., All Leila, and Monte Palmer. 1990 (Fall). *Social Background and Bureaucratic Behavior in Egypt.* Cairo Papers in Social Science, vol. 13, monograph 3. Cairo, Egypt: The American University in Cairo Press.

Trimberger, Ellen Kay. 1978. *Revolution from Above: Military Bureaucrats and Development in Japan, Turkey, Egypt,* ssand Peru. New Brunswick, NJ: Transaction Books.

Tschirgi, Dan, ed. 1994. *The Arab World Today.* Boulder, CO: Lynne Rienner.

Tuma, Eliash. 1988. "Institutionalized Obstacles to Development: The Case of Egypt." *World Development* 16(10): 1185–98.

Walker, Edward S. Jr. 1997 (Winter–Spring). "United States–Egyptian Relations: Strengthening our Partnership." SAIS *Review* 17(1): 147–62. Waterbury, John. 1978. *Egypt: Burdens of the Past / Options for the Future.* Bloomington, IN: Indiana University Press.

Weaver, Mary Anne. 2003 (Oct.). "Pharoahs-in-Waiting: Who will Succeed Egypt's Hosni Mubarak as the Ruler of the World's most Populous and Important Arab Country?" *The Atlantic Monthly* (292): 79-87.

Weber, Max. 1947. *The Theory of Social and Economic Organization.* Glencoe, IL: Free Press. (Translated by A. M. Henderson and Talcott Parsons, 1947, renewed 1975 by Talcott Parsons.)

Weede, Erich. 1986 (Dec.). "Rent-Seeking or Dependency as Explanations of Why Poor People Stay Poor." *International Sociology* I(4): 421–41.

Weinbaum, M. G. 1986. *Egypt and the Politics of U.S. Economic Aid.* Boulder, CO: Westview Press.

Woodward, Peter. 1992. *Nasser.* London: Longman.

Youssef, Hassan Pasha, Head of the Royal Diwan. 1983. Interviews with author in Cairo, Egypt.

Youssef, Samir M. 1983. *System of Management in Egyptian Public Enterprises.* Cairo, Egypt: Center for Middle East Management Studies, The American University in Cairo.

Zaki, Moheb. 1999. *Egyptian Business Elites: Their Visions and Investment Behavior.* Cairo: Konrad-Adnauer-Stiftung: Arab Center for Development and Future Research.

Zaqzug, Hamdi D. 1999 (Jan. 4). "Interview with the Minister of Wafqs." *Al-Wasat* 23–25.

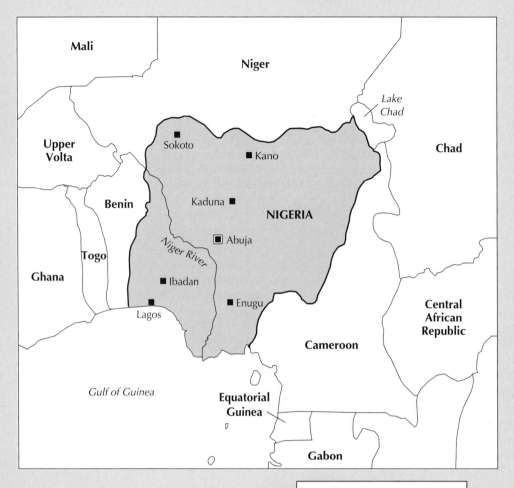

Population:
137,253,133 (2004 estimate)

Life expectancy at birth:
50 years (total population)
50 years (men)
51 years (women)

Literacy:
68 percent of people age 15
and over can read and write
(76 percent of men and 60
percent of wemen) (2003
estimate)

Capital:
Abuja

Per capita income:
$900

12

Nigeria

The Politics of Hope and Despair

The proclamation of Nigerian independence in 1960 was greeted by the world community with a tremendous sense of optimism. It was hoped that Nigeria, being a large and wealthy state, could take the lead in forging a stable, democratic, and economically developed Africa.

There were, of course, problems to be overcome. Nigeria's population was fragmented among diverse ethnic and religious groups. The nation's oil wealth, although substantial, masked a broader economy that was severely underdeveloped. Most of Nigeria's citizens were illiterate and lived in conditions of extreme poverty. Finally, Nigerians lacked political experience. Nigeria had been proclaimed a parliamentary democracy, but neither Nigeria's leaders nor its population had broad experience in democratic procedures.

The optimism that accompanied Nigeria's independence was based on the hope that democratically elected leaders would be able to set aside their religious and ethnic differences and use the country's abundant oil revenues to build a free and prosperous nation. In retrospect, the optimism of the independence era was misplaced. Democracy gave way to dictatorship, and Nigeria's oil revenues were squandered by corruption and mismanagement. Rather than joining the first world, Nigeria finds itself in danger of slipping into the fourth world.

In this chapter, we will trace the history of Nigerian politics from its colonial origins to its current struggle to re-establish some form of democratic government. We will see how political, cultural, economic, and international forces have combined to lock the Nigerian population into a seemingly endless cycle of hope

Werner Forman/Art Resource, NY

Art from the pre-colonial era displays the richness of traditional African culture. This plaque shows an entrance to the palace of the Oba of Benin. The turret features a python, messenger of the god Olukun, ruler of the seas. The pillars supporting the turret have representations of the Portuguese, and the door is flanked by four attendants, two on each side.

and despair. It should also be noted that the problems besetting Nigeria are symptomatic of those facing most of the countries of sub-Saharan Africa.

NIGERIA IN HISTORICAL PERSPECTIVE

Historically, Nigeria was a conglomerate of some 200 diverse ethnic (tribal) groups speaking more than 100 indigenous languages, welded together in 1914 by the force of British arms (Graf 1988). There had been no historic Nigeria, nor was there any sense of Nigerian nationalism. The northern regions were largely

Muslim, while the eastern and western regions were either Christian or animistic (Coleman 1965). More than anything else, Nigeria's borders reflected Britain's race with France to colonize the African continent.

The Colonial Era

Deep-seated ethnic, religious, and linguistic conflicts had made it difficult for Nigeria's diverse tribes to resist the British occupation. Such conflict is understandable, for Nigeria's citizens were isolated intellectually by their illiteracy, socially by the prevalence of tribal warfare, and culturally by a profound sense of mutual suspicion. As a result of their intellectual and social isolation, they were unable to envision a world broader than the confines of their tribal boundaries. Tribal life was all they knew (Doob 1964; Lerner 1958).

It was in the interest of the colonial authorities, moreover, to keep Nigeria's citizens as divided and as backward as possible. The pacification of Nigeria had been difficult, and cooperation among the tribes would only impede the economic exploitation of the colony.

British colonial policy in Nigeria was euphemistically referred to as **indirect rule** and centered on three interrelated strategies designed to alter the traditional nature of Nigerian society as little as possible.

First, tribal chiefs were allowed to play their traditional leadership roles, albeit with the assistance of a British advisor. This strategy reinforced traditional cultural arrangements and avoided direct confrontation between the British and the tribal chiefs (Turnbull 1963). Indirect rule was also far cheaper than attempting to maintain a massive colonial bureaucracy in a climatically difficult region.

Second, education and other intrusions of Western culture were kept to a minimum. For the most part, Western education was reserved for the sons of tribal leaders and other influential Nigerians.

Third, the occupation authorities reinforced the fragmentation of Nigerian society by playing upon tribal jealousies, favoring first one group and then another. In one way or another, British policy retarded Nigeria's evolution into an integrated country capable of speaking with a single voice (Davidson 1994).

Although British colonial policy stressed indirect rule and ethnic segmentation, it was inevitable that a Westernized elite with nationalistic aspirations would emerge to challenge British authorities for the right to rule. Nigeria's Westernized elite found its origins in the small cadre of Nigerians recruited by the British to assist in the administration of the large and climatically adverse colony. Other members of the Westernized elite included merchants and the sons of tribal leaders educated in British missionary schools (Coleman 1965).

As had happened in India and most other colonies, Westernized Nigerians became restive with a system that precluded them from competing with British nationals for advancement in the bureaucracy, military, and business communities. The few Nigerians to receive advanced positions, moreover, received far lower wages than their British counterparts and supervised only native personnel. As long as Nigeria remained a British colony, Nigerians would remain second-class citizens in their own country.

The tribal chiefs, too, had grown weary of British rule. Much like their Westernized counterparts, they viewed independence as the avenue to enhanced power and prosperity (Coleman 1965). The interwar period would thus find both sets of elites, the traditional and the modern, pressing Britain for a growing voice in the governing of the colony. Cooperation between the modern and traditional elites was facilitated by the overlapping membership of the two elite groups. Indeed, many members of the Westernized elite were the sons and grandsons of tribal leaders.

Faced with growing opposition to its rule, Britain reluctantly began to prepare Nigeria for independence as a democratic country. Shortly before World War II, Nigeria was divided into three administrative districts: a Northern district dominated by the predominately Muslim Hausa and Fulani tribes, a Western district dominated by the Yoruba, and an Eastern district dominated by the Ibo. At the end of World War II, each district was provided with its own regional legislature and allowed to be more or less self-governing. The provincial governments were capped by a federal parliament, the members of which were elected by the regional assemblies. With full independence to be granted in 1960, Nigeria's citizens would have 15 years in which to resolve their ethnic differences and adapt to a British-style democracy. The task would be a monumental one for a country whose population remained largely rural and illiterate, and in which all areas of life were governed by ethnic considerations. Nigeria, moreover, was to be a federal system in which the state boundaries were drawn along ethnic and religious lines. Each ethnic region, accordingly, would be competing with the others for jobs, development projects, government contracts, and educational opportunities (Miles 1988). Ethnic conflict, already strong, now was interwoven with economic conflict (Diamond 1988).

Other problems also loomed on the horizon. It was not clear, for example, that Nigeria possessed the bureaucratic capacity to administer its own affairs. Nigerians had been excluded from the senior civil service prior to 1946, and by 1954, six years before independence, they constituted less than 20 percent of Nigeria's senior officials (Koehn 1990). Junior officials were promoted to senior ranks shortly after independence but generally lacked the qualifications and experience required to execute their responsibilities in an efficient and impartial manner. Many succumbed to the temptations of tribalism and corruption.

The situation was similar in the Nigerian military, with 90 percent of the officer corps in the Nigerian Army, the former Royal West Africa Frontier Force, remaining in British hands on the eve of independence. Five years later, 90 percent of the officer corps was Nigerian. As a result of the rush to *nativize* the military, tribal conflicts became deeply embedded within the military structure. In many instances, loyalties to the ethnic group outweighed loyalties to the state.

Independent Nigeria: The First Republic

Nigeria embarked upon independence as a British-style parliamentary democracy. The House of Representatives, the Nigerian counterpart of the British House of Commons, was popularly elected in districts more or less corresponding to Nigeria's main ethnic regions. In classic parliamentary procedure, the members of the House of Representatives elected the prime minister and Cabinet from among their members, the Government serving at the pleasure of the House. The Senate was patterned after the British House of Lords, its role being to provide tribal chiefs and other traditional leaders with a symbolic voice in the political process (Diamond 1988).

Although patterned on the British system, Nigeria's governing structure also borrowed three key elements from the American experience. First, the federal structure established by the colonial administration was retained as a means of coping with Nigeria's regional, ethnic, and religious diversity. Second, Nigeria was provided with a written constitution that defined the role of its political institutions and delineated the rights of its citizens. Third, Nigeria was provided with a supreme court empowered to declare acts of the Government unconstitutional.

Whatever the merits of its political structure, Nigeria's first experiment in democracy was a dismal failure. Six years after the celebration of Nigerian independence, democracy gave way to military dictatorship.

What went wrong? Why did Nigeria's first experiment in democracy end in failure? The best answer to this question is that everything went wrong (Graf 1988). Nigeria's citizens remained overwhelmingly traditional in their political outlook, placing loyalty to their ethnic groups above loyalty to the state. Few people beyond the elite actually understood the political system. This was particularly the case among Nigeria's illiterate rural population which constituted the vast majority of the electorate. The only political system rural Nigerians really knew was the tribal-ethnic system.

The primacy of ethnic attachments was particularly evident in Nigeria's embryonic system of political parties. The Northern region was totally dominated by the Northern People's Congress (NPC), the party of the predominately Muslim Hausa and Fulani tribes. The National Convention of Nigerian Citizens (NCNC) represented the Ibos of the Eastern region, and the Action Group (AG) represented the Yorubas of the West.

The ethnic character of Nigeria's political parties was further intensified by the absence of **cross-cutting cleavages.** Each of Nigeria's three main ethnic groups was concentrated in a specific region of the country and possessed a unique religious character. The contrast between the Muslim North and the predominately Christian regions of the East and West was particularly stark. The three regions were also divided along socioeconomic lines. The North, while having the largest population, was far less developed than either the East or the West, both of which had been influenced more directly by colonialism. The North feared that the greater Westernization of the Ibo and Yoruba would enable them to gain control of the national government. The Ibo and Yoruba, by contrast, feared that the larger population base of the North would give it a commanding position in the Parliament. Ethnic conflict between the three dominant groups, then, was reinforced by religious and economic conflict.

The Government that would lead Nigeria to independence and democracy had been elected in 1959 under the supervision of the British. As expected, the election proved to be a largely tribal affair dominated by the NPC, the party of the Muslim North. The NPC Government allocated most of Nigeria's resources to the North, evoking charges of fraud and corruption from its adversaries.

Nigeria's first election as an independent country was held in 1963 and was supervised by a Government dominated by the Northern People's Congress. The magnitude of the NPC victory surprised even its own leaders. Opposition leaders charged the NPC with fraud, but to no avail. Democracy had merely become a new venue for tribal conflict (Diamond 1988).

The failure of Nigerian democracy must also be attributed to the unwillingness of Nigeria's political elites to put aside personal ambition for the sake of national unity. Rather than urging compromise and tolerance, most sought electoral victory by inflaming hostility toward competing tribes. Instead of building national unity, Nigeria's first experiment in democracy led to a strengthening of ethnic conflict.

Lacking strong leadership from its political elites, Nigeria failed to develop parliamentary and legal institutions worthy of public trust. Legislators raised their own salaries but avoided the difficult issues of nation building (Graf 1988). The courts enforced neither human rights nor fair elections, and corruption became rampant. Not all officials were corrupt, but the prevalence of corruption was staggering (Diamond 1988).

In retrospect, it could also be argued that the failure of Nigeria's first experiment in democracy was the result of an ill-advised attempt to impose British institutions upon a population that had nothing in common with the British. The British "Westminster" model allows a Government unlimited power to do as it pleases as long as it possesses a majority in the popularly elected house of Parliament. There are no minority rights, and all restraints on the abuse of power are cultural in nature. In the Nigerian context, this meant that the citizens in the Eastern and Western regions were excluded from the decision-making process. Their leaders could deliver fiery speeches denouncing the predominantly Northern Government, but as long as a majority in the House of Representatives, however fraudulently elected, supported that government there was little they could do to alter its policies. Nigeria's first experiment in democracy, then, exemplified the difficulties inherent in attempting to transplant the political institutions of the West into a region with widely differing sociocultural traditions.

Perhaps Nigeria during the early 1960s was simply the wrong place and the wrong time for an experiment in democracy. Democracy is a "reconciliation" system (Apter 1987). It seeks compromise between the demands of competing groups, assuring that all of the major contenders for power get a fair share of the country's economic resources. As noted above, the demands of Nigeria's major ethnic groups were difficult to reconcile. Each wanted to dominate the system, and each manifested profound distrust of the others. Nigeria needed to build a political community before it could build a democracy. Whatever the case, the First Republic collapsed with scarcely a whimper.

The Military As Savior

Nigeria's new military leaders portrayed themselves as the saviors of Nigeria. Continued civilian rule, they said, would have resulted in civil war and the dissolution of the Nigerian state. The military would build the nation and develop its resources. Once the task of nation building had been completed, Nigeria would be returned to civilian rule.

© Topham/The Image Works

Nigeria's military government spent the country's oil revenues constructing modern office buildings, airports, and military facilities. Meanwhile, the agrarian-based economy was all but ignored.

How successful was the military in solving Nigeria's political and economic woes? This is a difficult question to answer, for the early years of military rule saw Nigeria engulfed in an ethnic civil war of unprecedented ferocity. The military coup of 1966 had been executed by predominantly Ibo officers, many of whom were true nationalists distraught by the corruption and general disarray of the First Republic. Nevertheless, some also sought vengeance against the political leaders of the Northern and Western regions. The federal regions were abolished, becoming little more than the administrative provinces of a centralized state. The North erupted in riots, killing scores of Ibos living in the region and looting their property. Northern officers launched their own coup in July of the same year, unleashing a cycle of retribution and counter-retribution that threatened the survival of the Nigerian state. Ibo leaders in Nigeria's Eastern province, the heart of Nigeria's oil industry, seized upon the chaos to secede from the union. The Nigerian army, shorn of its Ibo units, invaded the newly proclaimed Biafran state, igniting a civil war that would endure for two and one-half years. Devastation in the Eastern region bordered on genocide, estimates of the war's casualties reaching the one million mark. The Union was sustained, but bitterness ran deep.

When the war ended, the military, now under Northern leadership, re-embarked upon its program of national salvation. The years of military rule were to be boom years as escalating oil revenues made Nigeria one of the richest countries in Africa. Nigeria's new military regime used its unexpected oil revenues to launch a massive program of public works. Seemingly overnight, airports, office buildings, and stadiums transformed the landscape of Nigeria's cities. Such spending generated popular support for the regime by creating the image of development, but it did little to address the inherent weakness of the nonpetroleum sector of the Nigerian economy, most of which was based on agriculture.

The boom economy also saw a coming together of Nigeria's Westernized elite, the members of which had grown wealthy by exploiting the lavish outlay of government revenues. All had a vested interest in assuring that ethnic conflict did not diminish what Nigerians refer to as the "cake." Rather than reducing corruption, military rule merely increased its scope.

If the military spent lavishly on public works projects, it was to spend more lavishly on itself, buying the latest military hardware and building elegant new facilities. Saving for the future was not part of the military's scheme of things. The gap between rich and poor continued to increase as little effort was made to build an egalitarian society in which all Nigerians had a stake.

Satisfied that the country was well on the path to prosperity and development, Nigeria's military leaders proclaimed that democracy would be restored in 1976, 10 years after the original coup. Whether the return to civilian authority would have actually occurred is moot, for 1975 saw Nigeria suffer its third coup d'état in a decade. The new generals, also from the North, said that Nigeria was not ready for democracy. Vowing to end corruption, they pledged that the country's oil revenues would be used to build a sound future for all Nigerians.

The new Nigerian leader, Murtala Mohammed, moved rapidly to put Nigeria's house in order, dismissing more than 10,000 administrative officials, many of senior rank, and establishing special corruption courts throughout the country. All military officers above the rank of Brigadier were retired (with compensation), and plans were made for restructuring the army. A counter-coup in 1976 failed but resulted in the death of Murtala Mohammed. He was replaced by his second in command, who promised an early return to civilian rule. In the view of some observers, the short reign of Murtala Mohammed "had achieved more and greater accomplishments than the three preceding governments" (Graf 1988).

The Second Republic: Structural Solutions to Behavioral Problems

The transition to civilian rule began in 1975 with the creation of a Constitutional Commission charged with drafting a constitution compatible with Nigeria's political and cultural realities. The new constitution was proclaimed in 1979, with national elections occurring shortly thereafter. Nigeria's second experiment in democracy, the Second Republic, would last for approximately four years before giving way to a new round of military coups.

The most interesting feature of the Second Republic was Nigeria's attempt to solve what were essentially behavioral and cultural problems by making mechanical adjustments in the structure of its political institutions (Joseph 1987).

Table 12.1 Nigeria: Patterns of Ethnic Distribution

Ethnic Group	Estimated Percentage of Population in 1998
A. Hausa/Fulani	32
B. Yoruba	21
C. Ibo	18
D. Other	29

SOURCE: Data from Internet source detnews.com/1998.

The structural organization introduced by the 1979 Constitution was three-fold. First, the British "Westminster" system of parliamentary democracy was replaced by a presidential system based on the American model (Ayeni, Nassar, and Popoola 1988). The parliamentary system, as noted above, had allowed a single ethnic group to dominate Nigerian politics. Adoption of the American system fragmented power and added the concept of checks and balances to Nigerian politics. Stronger provisions were also made for the protection of minority rights.

Second, the new constitution increased the number of states in Nigeria's federal system from 3 to 19. The purpose of restructuring the federal system was to broaden the base of Nigerian politics by empowering the smaller ethnic groups. Under the old system, a multitude of smaller ethnic groups constituting some 29 percent of the Nigerian population (see Table 12.1), were denied an effective political voice. The creation of 19 states freed many of those groups from domination by their larger neighbors.

Third, the new constitution attempted to assure that the presidents of the Second Republic would be truly national presidents by forcing them to garner both a majority of the popular vote and 25 percent of the vote in at least 12 different states. Under the new rules, the North would no longer be able to dominate national elections simply on the basis of its larger population.

The new constitution was an experiment in social engineering. Its creators attempted to eliminate ethnic politics by forcing Nigeria's politicians to jump through new hoops. The important question was whether organizational changes alone could force either the politicians or the electorate to alter deeply entrenched patterns of political behavior.

To what extent, then, did changes in Nigeria's constitutional structure lead to changes in Nigerian political behavior? Very little (Kalu 1987). Merely changing political structures does not solve problems that stem from cultural and economic conditions. The Second Republic collapsed for the same reasons that the First Republic did: ethnic conflict, institutional weakness, elite indifference, administrative ineptness, a lack of democratic experience, mass cynicism, rising expectations, blatant corruption, growing disparities in wealth, and a general inability of the government to meet the needs of its citizens.

The Military Returns

The collapse of Nigeria's second experiment in democracy was not widely mourned (Forrest 1993). The government simply had not worked. The rationale for the military takeover in 1983 was much the same as it had been some two decades earlier. General Buhari, the new Military Head of State, proclaimed that the military's seizure of power was merely corrective and promised a return to civilian rule at the earliest possible moment.

The challenges facing Nigeria's new military regime were the same as those that had faced previous military regimes. Nigeria's political and administrative institutions had to be strengthened, and popular faith in those institutions had to be restored. More fundamentally, Nigeria's diverse ethnic communities had to be welded into a national political community, a goal that could only be achieved by putting Nigeria's economy in order and closing the ever-widening gap between rich and poor.

General Buhari and his successors would not find this an easy task, for a collapse in world oil prices would see Nigeria's per capita income plummet from $1,000 in the early 1980s to less than $300 by the early 1990s. Nigerians had grown accustomed to the wealth of an oil economy, and the military government would be blamed for its decline.

General Buhari attacked Nigeria's social and political ills with unusual severity. Shop owners were forced to lower prices, and anti-sabotage decrees promised swift penalties for economic and social crimes. The penalties for cheating on school examinations ran as high as 21 years in prison, with death sentences being meted out to women suspected of smuggling cocaine (Graf 1988). The press protested and suffered accordingly. All political parties were abolished, and special "National Consciousness and Enlightenment Committees" were created to lecture the masses in good citizenship. A "War Against Undiscipline" was also launched against a bureaucracy swollen by years of political patronage (Ekwe-Ekwe 1991). Fearing that the severity of his reforms would trigger a counter-coup, Buhari also placed senior military commanders under surveillance (Graf 1988).

While Buhari attacked Nigeria's social and political ills with extraordinary vigor, he did little to restore a sense of ethnic balance to Nigerian politics. If anything, politics became more Northern and more Islamic (Ekwe-Ekwe 1991).

Buhari's reign was to be short-lived. It was not the severity of his reform program that triggered his demise, but the severity of his attacks on his military colleagues. In August 1985, General Babangida, one of those officers placed under surveillance by Buhari, overthrew the Buhari regime and reconstituted the ruling military council. The coup had little to do with either ethnic politics or religion. One Northern general had merely replaced another.

General Babangida promised a quick return to civilian rule and relaxed the more severe measures imposed by his predecessor. In their place, he attempted to stimulate economic growth by stimulating capitalism (Forrest 1993). He also increased the number of states from 19 to 30, hoping that the proliferation of state governments would make it difficult for Nigeria's ethnic leaders to consolidate their power (Forrest 1993). Political parties continued to be banned, and all former politicians, a group that included both party leaders and senior government officials, were prohibited from engaging in any form of political activity. Finally, efforts were accelerated to complete the transfer of Nigeria's capital from Lagos to Abuja (Umeh 1993). The new capital in Abuja, an ethnically neutral site in the center of Nigeria, was to symbolize Nigeria's new beginning (Taylor 1993).

In addition to the above reforms, Babangida also restored ethnic balance to the Supreme Military Council, now rechristened the Armed Forces Ruling Council. Many senior positions were allocated to members of minority tribes, and younger officers were brought into the ruling structure (Forrest 1993). It could be argued, of course, that the restoration of ethnic balance was merely illusory. General Babangida made all of the decisions, and the interests of the Muslim North were never in doubt (Ekwe-Ekwe 1991).

In the final analysis, the second round of military rule was not much more effective than the first. The hope that the military's greater efficiency would lead to clean government and economic development was not to be fulfilled.

The Long March Toward New Democracy

In 1986, General Babangida announced that the Government of Nigeria would be returned to civilian rule by the end of 1990. Toward this end, a 17-member Political Bureau was appointed by Babangida to stimulate national debate on the future of Nigerian democracy (Graf 1988). The 1990 deadline was not met, but elections for state governors and state assemblies took place toward the end of 1991. Elections for the House of Representatives and Senate took place in July 1992, with the oft-delayed election of a civilian president finally occurring in June 1993.

While the Political Bureau debated the nation's future, it was General Babangida who planned the course of Nigeria's transition to democracy. His concerns were many. Some focused on eliminating the problems that had destroyed the Second Republic. It was essential, for example, that the new government represent the entire nation and that tribalism and ethnic conflict no longer be allowed to destroy the fabric of Nigerian society. Corruption would also have to be eliminated, or at least brought under control. Other concerns were of a more personal nature. The interests of the North required attention as did the interests of the military and those of the general himself. As subsequent events would reveal, Babangida was clearly nervous about relinquishing the authority that he had wielded for more than a decade.

Babangida's plan for achieving the above objectives was as complex and potentially contradictory as the objectives themselves. The centerpiece of Babangida's attack on ethnic politics was a forced two-party system. Henceforth, Nigeria would have only two political parties: the National Republic Convention and the Social Democratic Party. The first, according to the General, would be a "little to the right" and the second, "a little to the left" (*Christian Science Monitor*, July 7, 1992).

A two-party system, it was hoped, would force Nigeria's ethnic groups to put aside their differences and forge broad national coalitions for the sake of winning the presidency. It was also hoped that the existence of a party of the left and a party of the right would focus the attention of Nigeria's voters on social and economic issues rather than on issues of ethnicity and religiosity.

The speed with which the new parties were created precluded the establishment of local party organizations other than those financed by the "big men," Nigeria's term for political bosses. General Babangida attempted to compensate for the organizational weaknesses of his new parties by providing them with offices and staff in each of Nigeria's 589 electoral districts. The parties took the support but complained of government interference in their internal affairs (Babatope 1991).

Corruption was attacked by banning all elected officials who had served in the Second Republic from participation in the new elections. Discredited politicians, according to Babangida's plan, would not be able to pick up where they had left off a decade earlier. Eliminating corruption, however, proved to be more difficult than Babangida had hoped. Excluded from the electoral process by military decree, Nigeria's political big men merely used surrogate candidates to do their bidding. As a result, the candidates of the big men dominated the local elections in 1987 as well as primary elections for the national legislature in 1991.

Babangida countered by annulling the results of the local government elections (1987) and by having the Election Commission cancel the results of the 1991 primary elections in several states (*African Concord,* Oct. 1991, 46). New surrogates were found, only to be disqualified by new exclusionary orders (*Economist,* Dec. 21, 1991, 41). As late as two weeks prior to the 1993 presidential elections, the National Election Commission suggested that one or both of the presidential candidates might have to be disqualified on the basis of alleged fraud.

Particularly interesting were the election procedures devised by the military government to stymie electoral fraud. Rather than secret ballots, Nigerians voted by lining up behind posters of the candidates they wished to support. Election officials then counted the number of individuals in each line and moved on to a new polling place. Having voters stand in line may have prevented the fraudulent stuffing of ballot boxes, but it also added an element of intimidation to the voting process.

For a while, all seemed to go well. Each of the two parties created by General Babangida nominated a candidate for the presidency reputed to be on good terms with the general. Both candidates, accordingly, could be counted on to serve both his interests and those of the military. The candidate of the Social Democratic Party, moreover, was a Yoruba, thereby precluding accusations that the new system was a Northern whitewash. Both candidates were Muslim and, as such, would understand the concerns of the Muslim North.

Democracy, however, would not be achieved. Elections scheduled for early in 1993 were delayed until June. The June elections were held as promised, but the government refused to announce the results, accusing both candidates of electoral violations. The elections were later nullified, with new elections promised in the near future.

Unofficial results published by a Nigerian civil rights group proclaimed Moshood Abiola, the candidate of the Social Democratic Party, to be the clear victor. Mr. Abiola, a Yoruba, reportedly captured 8,341,309 votes, as opposed to the 5,952,047 votes garnered by his Northern opponent. Mr. Abiola's victory, however, was clouded by an incredibly low rate of voter turnout, with only 14 million of the more than 39 million registered voters standing in line behind the

portrait of their preferred candidate. This was the lowest rate of voting in Nigerian history (*New York Times,* June 19, 1993, 2).

Babangida's reasons for nullifying the elections can only be conjectured. The
candidate of the North had lost, thereby threatening both the ethnic dominance
of the North and the self-interest of a military establishment controlled by the
North. Babangida, moreover, seemed reluctant to relinquish the powers that
he had wielded since 1985, despite building a 50-room retirement mansion in his
home village and purchasing a summer home on the French Riviera. In his
defense, Babangida could argue that the performance of the state and federal legislatures elected in 1991 and 1992 had demonstrated that Nigeria was not yet
ready for a return to democracy. As recounted by Paul Adams in *Africa Report:*

> The National Assembly, which kept two international hotels in Abuja in
> business but never passed a single law in nearly 18 months, was an expensive
> irrelevance, while the state assemblies were seen by their electorate as a rab-
> ble, shouting, fighting, and sacking their speakers instead of looking after the
> running of the states (Adams 1994, 49).

Whatever the case, the annulment of elections precipitated mass protests in
Nigeria's major cities, many of which turned violent. The military crushed the
initial wave of protests, only to confront a new round of protests by business
leaders in the Southwest, Abiola's Yoruba power base (Illoegbunam 1994). The
Nigerian economy, already a shambles, edged toward total collapse.

With support in the military eroding, Babangida ceded power to an interim
civilian regime headed by Chief Shonekan, a Harvard-educated Yoruba business-
man. Widely viewed as a Babangida surrogate, Shonekan had a four-month tenure
in office that was rocked by both communal violence and a general strike before
succumbing to a 1993 military coup led by General Sani Abacha.

In what had now become a tragic ritual, General Abacha proclaimed his seizure
of power to be corrective. As if to underscore Abacha's point, General Babangida
and his cronies were subsequently charged with having embezzled some $12 billion
from various government institutions (Nuanna 1995). A Constitutional Commission, Abacha said, would be established to devise a workable political system for
Nigeria. Its proposals, once complete, would then be considered by a full Constitutional Conference (*West Africa,* July 21, 1994, 588). In the meantime, Abiola was
charged with 23 counts of treason for attempting to establish a democratic government based on the assumed results of the aborted 1993 elections.

Abacha's Constitutional Conference was eventually convened in June of 1994,
but it was stillborn as many major groups refused to participate as a means of
protesting Abiola's arrest (*Christian Science Monitor,* June 27, 1994, 2). Indeed, *The
African Concord* warned that the Constitutional Conference was "beating the
drums of secession" (Ishaka 1994, 14-15). The newsweekly, part of Abiola's media
empire, was subsequently banned by the military regime.

Popular apathy toward Abacha's Constitutional Conference gave way to a
summer of violence that would see a strike by workers in the petroleum industry,
the source of more than 80 percent of Nigeria's revenues, bringing the
nation's economy to a halt. Demands for Abiola's release were also underscored

by a two-day "general strike" called by Nigeria's major labor federation. The strike was generally effective in the West and East but found little support in the Muslim North (*Economist,* Aug. 13, 1994). For a brief period, it appeared that Abacha would be forced to relinquish power.

Such optimism, however, was misplaced. The strike was broken and its leaders arrested. The opposition press was also shut down, and opponents of the Abacha regime were systematically imprisoned. The democracy movement had made a strong showing, but it lacked the internal cohesion to challenge a determined general supported by the North.

The Constitutional Conference labored on through the summer and fall of 1994, only to fizzle out in the early months of 1995. The delegates could agree on little and lacked sufficient power to do anything other than make recommendations to Abacha's Provincial Ruling Council. A new constitution was officially proclaimed in 1995, but not released to the public. No mention was made of setting a date for Abacha's departure, but some hinted that he planned to remain in office until 1997.

In the meantime, Abacha abolished the political parties created by Babangida and created five new ones in their stead. This, he proclaimed, was a vital step in Nigeria's return to democracy. With typical Nigerian wit, the five parties were soon labeled "Abacha's Quintuplets" and the "five fingers of a leprous hand" (Onadipe 1997). All five of the parties named Abacha as their presidential candidate, and he was still deciding which of the five to favor when he died of a heart attack in June 1998 (*Vanguard,* Feb. 12, 1999, www). The Swiss subsequently reported that Abacha and his family had deposited $654 million in Swiss banks (*New York Times,* Apr. 5, 2000, www).

Abacha was succeeded by General Abubakr, who lost little time in proclaiming that his sole purpose in office was to lead Nigeria's transition to democracy. Scores of political prisoners were released and elections were scheduled for all levels of government. Abacha's 1995 constitution was also released to the public. It was a ponderous 204-page document, largely discredited by the brutality of Abacha's rule.

This, however, created a constitutional crisis. How was Nigeria to prepare for the spate of elections scheduled for the end of 1998 and the beginning of 1999 without a constitution?

A Constitutional Review Committee appointed by General Abubakr recommended a return to Nigeria's 1979 Constitution, but the Nigerian media later announced that selected clauses would be drawn from the 1979, 1989, and 1995 Constitutions. The exact clauses to be used were not revealed (*Vanguard,* Feb. 18, 1999, www). As a result, Nigeria's local state, parliamentary, and presidential elections were held without benefit of a constitution. A noted Nigerian jurist warned the population "not to insist on having a real constitution now as this could provide an excuse for the prolongation of military rule" (*Guardian,* Feb. 22, 1999, www).

Among other things, the lack of a formal constitution made it difficult to delineate the respective powers of the Parliament and the president. Nevertheless, 109 senators and 360 members of the House of Representatives were duly elected by Nigeria's citizens, albeit with a low voter turnout.

A multitude of political parties contested the local government elections, with the three dominant vote-getters being allowed to contest the parliamentary and presidential races. The three political parties that established their dominance during the local government elections were the People's Democratic Party, The Alliance for Democracy, and the All People's Party. Each, as might be expected, drew its strength from one of Nigeria's three main ethnic regions (*Vanguard,* Dec. 7, 1998, www). In contrast to the past, however, both presidential candidates emerged from the Yoruba Southeast, guaranteeing the very rare occurrence of rule by a non-northerner.

The Nigerian press offered several interpretations of this remarkable turn of events. In the view of some, the northern population was fed up with the lack of development in the region. Northern politicians and generals had grown rich, but the Northern population had benefited little from its political dominance. In the words of Naajatu Muhammed, "If you go round the north, you see that there is nothing to show for the endless control of a government by northerners except stark poverty" (Muhammed 1998, 16).

Others pointed to fear of a violent political upheaval if a shift were not made to the South, and especially the Yoruba Southeast. Abiola, a Yoruba, was widely believed to have won the 1993 presidential elections annulled by Babangida, a debacle now referred to as the "Third Republic" (Benson 1999). Cynics also added that the victorious candidate, General Obasanjo, was on very good terms with the Northern elites and that he was widely supported by retired generals anxious to avoid prosecution by a civilian government (*International Herald Tribune,* Feb. 22, 1999, www; *New York Times,* Feb. 22, 1999, www). Whether or not this was the case, two of the first people to congratulate Obasanjo on his victory were former dictators General Gowon (1966–1975) and General Babangida (1985–1993) (*New York Times,* Mar. 3, 1999).

On Obasanjo's behalf, it should be noted that he was the only one of Nigeria's military rulers to relinquish power voluntarily to a civilian government. This he did in 1979, having ruled Nigeria from 1976 to 1979, most of the four-plus years in which Nigeria was ruled by non-northerners. Sixty-one years old at the time of his election and retired from the military, Obasanjo had established himself as an elder statesman of Nigerian politics, a position enhanced by a jail term served for plotting a coup against General Abacha.

Whatever the reasons for his election, Obasanjo and the People's Democratic Party swept to victory in the 1999 elections, claiming both the presidency and clear majorities in the Senate and the House of Representatives. The transition to the Fourth Republic had begun. It was completed in May 1999 when the military formally withdrew to its barracks. A new 1999 Constitution was also promulgated, its main features being similar to the 1979 Constitution.

A brief summary of Nigeria's tumultuous political history is provided in Table 12.2.

President Obasango swept to a second term in office in April of 2003 with some 62 percent of the valid popular vote. His ruling Popular Democratic Party also captured majorities in the House of Representatives and the Senate, and maintained its control over a majority of the governorships. It is not always easy to determine what constitutes a valid popular vote, but in Nigeria's 2003 elections, the task was particularly difficult. Irregularities were so glaring that

Table 12.2 Summary of Nigeria's Political History

Head of State	Period in Power	Mode of Relinquishing Authority
Alhaji A. T. Balewa	Oct. 1, 1960–Jan. 15, 1966	Killed in coup d'état.
Major Gen. J. T. U. Aguiyi Ironsi	Jan. 16, 1966–July 29, 1966	Killed in coup d'état.
Gen. Yakubu Gowon	Aug. 1, 1966–July 29, 1975	Ousted in a coup d'état.
Major Gen. Murtala Mohammed	July 30, 1975–Feb. 13, 1976	Killed in coup d'état.
Gen. O. Obasanjo	Feb. 13, 1976–Oct. 1, 1979	Handed over the mantle of leadership to Alhaji Shehu Shagari after the 1979 general elections, having survived threats against his government.
Alhaji Shehu Shagari	Oct. 1, 1979–Dec. 31, 1983	Ousted in coup d'état.
Major Gen. M. Buhari	Jan. 1, 1984–Aug. 27, 1985	Ousted in coup d'état.
Gen. I. B. Babangida	Aug. 27, 1985–Aug. 27, 1993	Ousted by a combination of military, civilian, and international pressure following nullification of elections.
Chief Shonekan	Aug. 27, 1993–Nov. 17, 1993	Military coup d'état.
General Sani Abacha	Nov. 17, 1993–1998	Natural death.
General Abubakr	June 1998–April 1999	Resigned.
General Obasanjo	May 29, 1999–Present	

SOURCE: Kelue and other sources.

observers from the European Union declared the elections to be a fraud, and the United States contemplated the imposition of political and economic sanctions until the situation was rectified (*Daily Independent Online,* March 03, 2004, www). One state cast 100 percent of its votes for Obasango, while the figure topped the 97 percent mark in at least two others. A few states declared results without bothering to hold elections. Optimists, such as the British foreign minister, suggested that the results were "disturbing," but represented an advance in Nigerian democracy (Ford, 2003(a)). Nigeria's Citizens Form, a blue ribbon civil rights group. warned that "it does not take a military dictatorship to degrade civil society, render it powerless and submissive (*Guardian* (Lagos), March 4, 2004, www).

Was Obasanjo's sweeping victory warranted by his performance during his first term in office? The answer of Nigeria's Citizens Form was a resounding no! Their litany of changes included: "Increased intolerance of dissent, a contempt for constitutional procedures, abuse of police powers, a flagrant debasement of the electoral process, cynical manipulation of the judiciary..." (*Guardian* (Lagos), March 4, 2004, www). The economic picture was not much better with one of the kinder assessments suggesting that "the scale of problems facing the President

General Olusegun Obasanjo ruled over Nigeria as a military dictator from 1976 to 1979, and then was elected president by the Nigerian people twenty years later.

were so great that nobody could have expected him to turn things around in four short years (Ford 2003(b))."

Obasanjo is now proposing yet another constitution amid speculation that it will offer the opportunity for a third term in office (*Vanguard*, May 1, 2005, www). Former dictator Babagida is also waiting in the wings.

THE POLITICAL INSTITUTIONS OF NIGERIA

Political institutions are the arena of politics. It is the executives, legislatures, courts, bureaucracies, and other agencies of government that authoritatively allocate the resources of the state. In this section, we shall examine the political institutions of Nigeria as they are evolving during the Fourth Republic.

Executive Power in Nigeria

Why has President Obansanjo found it so difficult to tackle Nigeria's problems? To some extent, the answer is to be found in the nature of its political institutions. All, including its constitution, executive, legislature, legal system, bureaucracy, and federal structure would seem to have serious flaws.

The Military and Executive Power in Nigeria. Nigeria's 1999 Constitution was cobbled together from earlier constitutions and continues to be a vague document that is honored in the breach. Indeed, the debate over which of

Nigeria's constitution was in force at the time of Obasanjo's first election made it difficult to say with certainty what the powers of the president would be. The issue had yet to be resolved by Obasango's re-election in 2003. The discussions of a new constitution are underway, but such things take time.

Constitutional ambiguities have been a matter of minimal concern for Obasanjo. Armed with a popular mandate and the apparent support of the military, he has left little doubt that he is the biggest of Nigeria's "big men." His adversaries, including many of Nigeria's legislators, are ridiculed as "small men." The big man/small man dichotomy also speaks volumes about the informal powers of the Nigerian president. It is he that giveth and it is he who taketh away. People rush to curry his favor and even his opponents feign admiration while plotting his downfall.

With all of his power, why has Obasanjo failed to solve Nigeria's two most pressing problems: corruption and poverty?

In large part, the answer to this riddle lies in the fact that Nigerian runs on corruption. Obasanjo can only rule by assuring that the big men who control Nigeria's tribes, ethnic groups, unions, bureaucracy, army, National Assembly, and state governments get their share of the cake. They, in turn, pay off lesser big men until one reaches the bottom of the pyramid of graft. By the time one reaches the bottom of the pyramid, there is nothing left for the average Nigerian who continues to live in poverty and despair. The problem of poverty cannot be solved until the problem of corruption has been solved. Increases in oil revenues simply bring greater corruption.

This said, one must credit Obasanjo with attempting to control the corruption in one of the most corrupt countries in the world. Laws prohibit corruption, but are easily circumvented by corrupt officials and their clients. Efforts to prosecute corrupt officials are doomed before they start by the sheer number of officials involved. In all probability, Obasanjo would be removed from office long before the task was complete. Faced with these realities, "Obasanjo has steered a middle course, forcing through those changes that he could, whilst keeping himself in power…" (Ford 2003(b)). Be this as it may, the lead story in the *Abuja Mirror* wrote:

> Very reliable sources have informed Abuja Mirror that many aids and close lieutenants of the President are neck–deep in corruption and regularly extort hefty pay-offs from members of the public who seek one type of favor or the other… it has become a common sight these days to see… bags being offloaded from car trunks, for onward transmission to top aides at the (Aso Rock) villa who are said to now openly demand bribes to influence executive appointments and contracts"(*Abuja Mirror,* July 26–Aug. 1, 2002, www).

The National Assembly

The National Assembly, Nigeria's Parliament, consists of two houses, a House of Representatives and a Senate. This framework was adopted from the 1979 Constitution, Nigeria's last democratic constitution, but the operational details are still being worked out. Indeed, press coverage prior to the legislative elections in

February 1999 seemed confused over the precise number of seats in the House of Representatives. Some placed the number at 309, while others suggested 409. It was later clarified that the HR would have 360 seats; the Senate 109 (*Guardian,* Feb. 24, 1999).

According to both the 1979 and the 1995 Constitutions, the powers of the National Assembly are similar to those of most democratic legislatures. The National Assembly passes laws, appropriates monies, confirms important officials, and checks the power of the president.

Given the power of the president and the record of past Nigerian Parliaments, many Nigerians view their new legislature with some apprehension. This is particularly the case in regard to the legislature's ability to check the power of the president, not to mention its ability to curb its own greed.

The answer to both questions is no. Nigeria's legislatures have not been able to constrain President Obasanjo nor have they been able to curb their love for money (Nwokocha 1999, Aziken 2002).

The main effort of the National Assembly to control the power of President Obasanjo came in 2002 when the House of Representatives balked at passing the president's austerity budget. He was trying to cut Nigeria's massive foreign debt; they wanted more money for their pet projects. Obasanjo attempted to intimidate the members of House into compliance by delaying their salaries. They responded by delaying work on the budget. The salaries were eventually paid and the budget came on line six months late. The battle, however, continued. Obasanjo refused to spend the additional monies while an irate National Assembly initiated impeachment procedures. The issue was resolved behind the scenes. The saga continues (*Vanguard,* Mar. 31, 2004, www, *Guardian* (Laos), May 1, 2005, www).

Bureaucracy and Politics in Nigeria

Nigeria's crisis of leadership has been paralleled by an equally profound crisis in administration. Decisions are made, but few are implemented in an efficient and impartial manner. This is as true of Nigeria's military regimes as it is of its civilian regimes. President Obasanjo has done little to alter the situation. As the *Economist* would write in the fall of 2003: "The government spends over 80% of the budget running its own incompetent and corrupt bureaucracy. When not asleep at their desks, civil servants openly and cheerfully ask visitors to their offices for cash" (*Economist,* Oct. 18, 2003, Vol. 369, Issue 8346, 46).

The causes of Nigeria's bureaucratic malaise are many. Unlike the Indian experience, Nigeria did not begin independence with a professionalized bureaucracy. Rather, most senior and technical positions remained in the hands of the British until the dawn of independence. The transfer of the bureaucracy into Nigerian hands occurred rapidly following the proclamation of independence, but the new appointees lacked experience. Most were poorly trained (Koehn 1990). Corruption was pervasive, and ethnic loyalties rivaled loyalty to the state. Bureaucratic recruitment hinges as much on ethnic and political considerations as on technical qualifications.

During Nigeria's presidential election in 2003, much of the voting and tallying was done by hand.

Stark testimony to the continued problems facing the Nigerian bureaucracy can be found in the fact that about 30 percent of all bureaucratic positions remained in the hands of foreigners decades after Nigeria gained its independence (Koehn 1990). The continued presence of foreigners reflects the inability of Nigeria's educational system to provide the bureaucracy with an adequate supply of technically trained officials. It is also an overt manifestation of ethnic distrust (Ayo 2002). Northern states, in particular, continue to prefer foreign bureaucrats to bureaucrats recruited from Nigeria's other ethnic communities (Koehn 1990). Even more damning is the fact that Nigeria is now preparing to turn over management of its major public corporations to European management firms (Obadina 1998).

Be this as it may, senior administrators are part and parcel of the ruling elite. Authority lines in Nigeria are fluid and overlapping, with administrative and military leaders often being linked by ethnic, family, social, and even business connections (Koehn 1990, Dibie 2003). Nigeria's elites also possess a strong common interest in strengthening the role of the central government at the expense of the states (Forrest 1993; Imoagene 1989).

The existence of strong links between Nigeria's administrative, political, and military elites, however, does not necessarily imply a great deal of mutual trust. The military is particularly suspicious of the administrative elite and sacks its members at will. Indeed, the generals have attempted to reduce the influence of the senior administrators by creating a perpetual game of musical chairs.

It should also be noted that Nigeria's bureaucrats represent a powerful corporate pressure group that has been very effective in preserving its privileged status in Nigerian society. A sustained strike by civil servants during the early 1990s, for example, resulted in a 45 percent pay increase. A major battle is now looming between Obasanjo and the bureaucrats as the president is proposing to cut the bureaucracy by 40 percent. The bureaucrats are threatening to strike.

Law and Politics in Nigeria

The structure of the Nigerian legal system is similar to that of most of the countries reviewed in the preceding chapters, with lower courts giving way to a system of appeal courts topped by a Nigerian Supreme Court. The Supreme Court possesses the power to declare acts of the Government unconstitutional, a power that it used on a limited basis during the Second Republic. With the return to military rule, the court's power of judicial review returned to the realm of theory.

The court system was made the focal point of political conflict during Nigeria's abortive transition to democracy in 1993, as Chief Abiola, the presumed winner in the June elections, sued in the Lagos High Court to have the interim government installed by General Babangida declared illegal. The Lagos High Court did so, but the ruling was moot, as General Abacha had seized power before the power of the courts to dissolve the Government had been tested.

Parallel court systems operate at both the national and state levels, a novel feature of the court system being the practice of Shari'a or religious law in predominantly Muslim areas. The Shari'a courts have jurisdiction over divorce, inheritance, and related family matters addressed by the Islamic faith. Nigeria thus finds itself in the difficult position of having two sets of family law: one for Muslims and one for non-Muslims. Rather than building a unified political community, accordingly, the legal system consolidates social cleavages. Indeed, Christians now fear that they may be made subject to Islamic law (*Associated Press,* Feb. 1, 2000, www).

The Nigerian legal system, in sum, continues to fight an uphill battle to retain its political independence. The intimidation of judges has been commonplace under both civilian and military regimes and is likely to remain so in the foreseeable future (Ikegwuoha 1987). The courts have been allowed to operate normally in the nonpolitical realm, but even here, they are subject to intense ethnic and religious pressures. Whatever the case, the judiciary promised to play a vigorous role in the Fourth Republic.

It is not clear that they have succeeded. Nigerian judges complain that the lack of independent funding makes them subject to pressure from the legislature and the executive. Like so much else, the separation of powers called for in Nigeria's diverse constitutions has yet to be implemented fully. Charges of corruption are frequent and several judges have been removed from office for corruption. A senior Nigerian jurist warned that many of the accusations leveled against judges are unfounded and that "vicious verbal attacks are the unattractive and unprofitable 'perquisites' of public office holders (*Vanguard Online,* Feb.20, 2004, www).

Federalism in Nigeria

Nigeria's political system is a federal system, with power being divided between a national government and 36 state (provincial) governments. During periods of civilian rule, the citizens of each state elect both a governor and a state legislature. During periods of military rule, the state legislatures are disbanded and the governors are appointed by the president. Each state also possesses its own bureaucracy and its own legal system (*African Concord,* Oct. 7, 1991, 37).

Relations between the Federal and provincial governments are based on two fundamentally opposing views of Nigeria's future (West 2003, Rothberg 2004). The vision of the federal government, as exemplified by Nigeria's ruling elite, is one of a centralized state in which ethnic and religious differences must ultimately give way to national goals and national interests. The states, by contrast, would prefer a Nigeria in which each region is free to manage its affairs in accordance with its ethnic and religious traditions (*Guardian,* Feb. 19, 1999, www). The oil producing states also demand a greater share of the country's oil wealth, most of which is absorbed by the rapacious appetites of the elites and the bureaucracy (Obi 2001).

The differing visions of Nigeria held by the state and federal governments are inherently irreconcilable. Military leaders attempted to ease ethnic tensions by fragmenting Nigeria into a multitude of states (provinces), but these efforts have met with minimal success. Declines in ethnic power, moreover, have merely given way to increased religious tensions. Some religious leaders now believe that the only solution to Nigeria's growing religious tension is the creation of two independent states—a Muslim state and a Christian state (*Christian Science Monitor,* July 30, 1992). While such views may be unduly pessimistic, they illustrate the fragility of the Nigerian political system. Perhaps President Obasanjo's greatest accomplishment has been holding Nigeria together.

THE ACTORS IN NIGERIAN POLITICS:
ELITES, PARTIES, GROUPS, AND CITIZENS

If political institutions are the arena of politics, it is the actors in the political process who give life to those institutions. In this section, we shall examine the four main types of political actors in Nigeria: elites, political parties, groups, and citizens. Of these, the elites get most of what there is to get in Nigeria.

Elites and Politics in Nigeria

The structure of Nigeria's elite mirrors the broader complexities of Nigerian society (Bienen and van de Walle 1989). As such, it has variously been described as pluralistic, centralized, interconnected, fluid, and self-serving. Each of these adjectives is accurate, and each has had a profound influence on the evolution of Nigerian politics.

Nigeria's elite structure is pluralistic in the sense that it encompasses a broad array of military, political, administrative, commercial, ethnic, and religious leaders, each of whom has the power to influence the course of Nigerian politics. No single branch of the elite, moreover, has been able to rule effectively without the support of others. Military leaders, for example, have found it difficult either to build support for their programs or to ease Nigeria's communal tensions without the active support of the country's ethnic and religious elites. Indeed, one of General Abacha's first acts upon seizing power in 1993 was to announce that his administration was "favorably disposed toward traditional rulers because of their nearness to the people" (*West Africa,* Apr. 4, 1994, 595). Ethnic and religious leaders, by contrast, enjoy tremendous influence within their communal enclaves but are dependent on the support of national leaders to assure that their regions receive a fair share of the nation's wealth. Administrative and commercial elites, in turn, lack the power to rule directly but control the economic resources upon which the success of the political and military elites depends. Unfortunately, Nigeria's elite structure is too pluralistic and too fragmented to chart a coherent course for the country.

As contradictory as it may seem given the above comments, Nigeria's political elite is also intensely centralized. Until very recently, virtually all political power at the national level was concentrated in the hands of one general or another. The generals, in turn, were supported by business and administrative elites who shared their belief in a centralized state. Only a centralized state, they argued, could bring order to the confused social mosaic that was Nigeria. As indicated in the introductory chapter, both centralized and pluralistic elites have advantages and disadvantages. Nigeria has managed to get the disadvantages of both.

Total political gridlock in Nigeria has been avoided by the fact that its elite is interconnected and overlapping. Some of its diverse members come from the same "big" families, while others are linked by business and political alliances. All benefit from ready access to the state's resources (Sklar 1967). A self-serving interest in maintaining a corrupt political system, unfortunately, is a poor foundation for nation building (Pandjo Boumba 2002).

Finally, it should be noted that *Nigeria's elite system is also very fluid.* Babangida banished all members of the previous political elite from power, yet no sooner had he resigned from office than Chief Shonekan, his hand-picked successor, demoted 36 of his chief military aides. The seizure of power by General Abacha was followed by the sacking of an additional 17 senior pro-Babangida officers, not to mention the supporters of Chief Shonekan. It is now Abacha supporters who are on the losing side. The fluidity of the Nigerian elite system has robbed the country of much-needed political continuity. It has also imbued Nigeria's political leaders with a profound sense of political insecurity, leading many officials to take whatever they can acquire during their short tenure in office. Not all Nigerian leaders are corrupt, but the Nigerian press leaves little doubt that it is a national problem (Williams 1998). It is the elites, moreover, that set the tone for the masses. If the Nigerian public is fragmented and disillusioned, it is not without cause.

Parties and Politics in Nigeria

Nigeria's initial political parties began as little more than ethnic associations created to assure that each of the main ethnic groups received its fair share of the "cake." Party leaders were ethnic leaders, party organizations were ethnic organizations, and party campaigns played upon ethnic jealousies. Each party totally dominated the politics of its own region but had little support beyond that region.

Reflecting the logic of their ethnic underpinnings, Nigeria's early political parties used their influence to strengthen the group rather than to strengthen the nation. Parties encouraged their followers to support the ethnic group, mobilized their supporters to harass the candidates of competing ethnic groups, and defined the issues confronting the new nation in ethnic rather than ideological terms. Fiery slogans proclaimed each party's stance on economic policy, welfare, and human rights, but the underlying message of these slogans was clear to all: the prosperity, welfare benefits, and human rights of our group are totally dependent on the victory of our ethnic group.

Under these circumstances, it was not surprising that Nigeria's first experiment in multiparty democracy would fragment the nation rather than unite it. Indeed, the intensity of ethnic conflict made political compromise all but impossible. The Northern party was dominant, and its opponents had little hope of achieving their fair share of Nigeria's resources by democratic means.

The picture was much the same during the Second Republic. The names of the political parties had been changed to provide broader appeal, but their support still came primarily from a single ethnic region. The Northern party did better at establishing a national constituency than did its counterparts, but it achieved this only by promising the leaders of minority tribes in the East and West enhanced patronage if they supported the North (Joseph 1987).

Being the largest of Nigeria's ethnic regions, the Northern party again dominated Nigerian politics, leaving voters in the East and West with little reason to support a political system that worked to their disadvantage. The East and West could have joined forces against the North, but a long history of ethnic distrust between the two regions precluded this from happening. Once again, then, the Nigerian multiparty system divided the nation rather than uniting it.

The two-party system imposed upon Nigeria by General Babangida forced the creation of two broad multiethnic coalitions, the right-of-center National Republic Convention and the left-of-center Social Democratic Party (SDP). The new party system was tested in the aborted presidential elections of 1993, with Chief Abiola and the SDP being the presumed winners. The SDP's presidential victory was apparently built upon a coalition of Northern Muslims and Western Christians. Being a Western (Yoruba) Muslim, Chief Abiola, the presumed winner, could appeal to both groups (Adams 1993). As the results of the election were impounded, we can only conjecture.

With the advent of the Abacha regime, the two broad coalitions began to disintegrate into their ethnic components (Adams 1993) and eventually disappeared altogether. Be this as it may, Babangida's experiment in two-party democracy did demonstrate that Nigeria's diverse ethnic groups could merge into broad electoral coalitions if they were forced to do so.

upon graduation. Student protests are also provoked, if not orchestrated, by Nigeria's politicians, all of whom attempt to recruit students allies.

Students have a considerable influence on Nigerian politics, yet they seldom speak with a single voice. As with most other broad-based groups in Nigerian society, sustained political action is undermined by a mélange of ethnic, religious, political, regional, and personality considerations.

Particularly disconcerting to the military authorities has been the emergence of secret cults on Nigeria's campuses (*Guardian,* Feb. 16, 1999). In addressing the problem of the cults, Dr. Ayu, the Minister of Education, said that 'Of late, our collective psyche has been assaulted by the tragic wave of secret cults in our school campuses. Bizarre killings, intimidations, violence, undiscipline precipitated by the activities of secret cults are daily on the rise" (*West Africa,* Mar. 28–Apr. 3, 1994, 349). He went on to say that the blood-sucking members of these cults have no respect for life or property. He enumerated some of the wilder excesses of the cultists: They are rude to teachers and intimidate the school authorities to do their bidding. They decide when lectures should start and when examinations should start or end and, in some cases, they infiltrate other campuses to kidnap heads of institutions and force them to sign agreements that violate the rules and regulations of a decent society (*West Africa,* Mar. 28–Apr. 3, 1994, 349).

The situation has yet to improve. University officials charged with ending the cult scourge fear for their lives, adding to the general malaise of a Nigerian university system beset by cultism, sexual harassment, improper examination procedures, and the sale of professors' notes to those who can afford them (*Vanguard,* March 30, 2004,www).

Women.   Women's groups have had minimal impact upon Nigerian politics, a fact that reflects the subservient role of women in Nigerian society (Hussaina 1995). Efforts of the United Nations to empower Nigerian women have produced limited results, the most visible of which has been the establishment of an officially sanctioned National Commission for Women. The NCW convened a major conference to discuss women's rights in 1993, its opening session being addressed by the wife of General Babangida. Among other things, the conference called upon the government to reserve 25 percent of the positions in the bureaucracy for women and debated whether the role of the first lady should be formalized. Subsequent meetings have been less subtle. The 2004 celebration of International Women's Day would see the president of the organization denounce the Obasango government for its insensitivity to the women's rights and call it a "bane" to the development of Nigerian women. She also "bemoaned unyielding cultural practices. . . . and pleaded with traditional (tribal) rulers to evolve ways to include women in decision-making process" (*Daily Times,* March 2, 2004, www). In the meantime, local women's groups have begun to take matters into their own hands. The beginning of President Obasanjo's second term, for example, would see a militant women's group seize the ChevronTexaco Corporation's export terminal to press their demands for jobs for their children and amenities for their communities.

Citizens and Politics in Nigeria

Public opinion in Nigeria finds expression in the country's infrequent and irregular elections, in commentary in the Nigerian press, and in strikes, protests, and other forms of direct action. Public opinion polls have been discouraged during the military era. Collectively, the above avenues of public expression portray a population that is both divided among itself and alienated from its political system.

Elections. The elections conducted during the First and Second Republics reflected the pervasiveness of ethnic and religious tensions in Nigeria's political life. This was to be expected, given the recentness of independence and the divisiveness of Nigeria's colonial past. The 1998 and 1999 elections continued to reflect ethnic considerations but also sent a clear message that voters throughout Nigeria were fed up with more than three decades of Northern military domination (Ciroma 1998). The 2003 elections painted a similar picture, but had little to do with democracy. Ethnic and religious loyalties still outweigh loyalty to the country, and communal ties will remain the scourge of Nigerian politics until the government can meet the material and security needs of the population.

The press for its part, has been a vocal, if sometimes intimidated, force in Nigerian politics. Most major groups sponsor their own papers, but the radio and television media are controlled by the Government.

Abacha closed all opposition papers during the "long, hot" summer of 1994 and threatened reporters with imprisonment. The press has regained much of its vigor during the early years of the Obasanjo era with one commentator candidly stating: "Having embraced democracy haphazardly due to the hurried transition, many of the elected officials do not understand the democratic process. And the President, coming from a military background does not understand it either" (*Abuda Mirro,* July 19–25, 2000, www).

Mass Protest. Mass protest in Nigeria takes the form of political demonstrations, economic strikes, communal violence, and a lawlessness that has made Nigeria one of the most crime-ridden countries in the world. All are born of frustration with a political system that has been unable to provide its citizens with a sustainable quality of life. Political and economic protest, while harshly suppressed by the Babangida regime, exploded in response to his annulment of the 1993 presidential elections, forcing both his resignation and that of his hand-picked successor. Mass protests similarly forced General Abacha to promise a new constitution (Edozie 2002). Violence has also been directed against Western oil companies, with the Royal Dutch/Shell Group threatening to abandon its Nigerian oil operations if the violence continued (*Guardian* (London), 2004, www).

While political and economic protests give vent to the frustrations of Nigeria's more modern and urban population, communal tensions continue to flare throughout most areas of Nigeria. Crime, in turn, is the most basic symptom of anomie or institutional collapse. The failure of Nigeria's political institutions has so impoverished the majority of the country's citizens that they have no option but to provide for their families by any means at their disposal, legal or otherwise.

Perhaps this is the reason that the public has ignored a 2004 police directive to turn in their illegal weapons (*Daily Independent,* March 3, 2004, www). Indeed, mass frustrations are now so intense that they may defy control by any political regime, whether military or civilian. This situation is unlikely to change rapidly in the near future.

THE CONTEXT OF NIGERIAN POLITICS: CULTURE, ECONOMICS, AND INTERNATIONAL INTERDEPENDENCE

The actors in Nigerian politics play a vital role in determining who gets what, when, and how, but the behavior of those actors is often influenced by the broader environmental context in which Nigerian politics occurs. In this section, we shall examine three dimensions of Nigeria's environmental context: political culture, political economy, and the influence of the international arena.

The Culture of Nigerian Politics

The leaders of the First Republic inherited a population that placed loyalty to the ethnic group above loyalty to its new and untested political institutions. Each ethnic community was a world unto itself that viewed members of other communal groups with profound distrust. From a cultural perspective, Nigeria was not a nation, but a confederation of several nations, each with its own traditions and aspirations.

The colonial experience had further fragmented Nigeria's citizens into modern, traditional, and transitional clusters, depending on their experiences and their aspirations for the future. The vast majority of Nigerians clung to the ways of their traditional past, while a narrow Westernized elite sought the creation of a Westernized and presumably democratic Nigeria. Falling between the two extremes was a large transitional population that aspired to the material benefits of Westernization but lacked either the skills or the opportunities to attain them. For the most part, the transitionals were recent migrants to Nigerian cities and residents of their gruesome slums.

The challenge confronting Nigeria's leaders was to transform Nigeria's essentially tribal political culture into a civic culture in which the majority of its citizens would place loyalty to the nation above loyalties to their ethnic and religious communities.

Toward this end, Nigerian nationalism was taught in the schools and stressed in the mass media. More and more, Nigerians were also welded into a national community via military service or employment in the civil service. Urbanization and education also expanded rapidly.

As a result of these efforts, ethnic loyalties have given way to nationalistic loyalties among many of Nigeria's more educated and urbanized citizens. Some

blending of cultures is also occurring in the rural areas as the lines between ethnic and linguistic regions become increasingly blurred (Otite 1976). There also
appears to be genuine support for the concept of democracy.

Be this as it may, ethnic and religious loyalties continue to be the dominant
features of Nigerian political culture (Aborisade and Mundt 2002). Three
decades of corruption and mismanagement have also created a profound aura
of cynicism (Nigerian Economic Society 1986). It is difficult for individuals to
develop a deep emotional attachment to political institutions that are corrupt,
biased, and ineffective. The ability of General Obasanjo to alter this picture remains a daunting task.

The Economy of Nigerian Politics

Political economists would suggest great care in attributing Nigeria's political
woes to ethnicity and other cultural factors. In their view, tribes, ethnic communities, and other "culturally" based social organizations are merely the units of
political conflict in Nigeria. The source of that conflict, political economists argue,
is economic.

Recent patterns of ethnic and religious violence lend strong support to this
argument. Increases in communal tensions have paralleled the decline of Nigeria's oil-based economy, a decline that has forced Nigeria's citizens to look to
their ethnic groups for economic survival. Indeed, much of Nigeria's recent
communal violence has been triggered by economic incidents pitting one
group against another.

Ethnic tensions have also been reinforced by the uneven distribution of Nigeria's oil wealth. The Biafran Civil War had its origins in Ibo demands to retain a
larger share of their oil wealth than a central government dominated by the North
would allow. Parallel tensions are now building between the central government
and the minority tribes that currently produce some 70 percent of Nigeria's oil
revenues.

Economic scarcity also underlies a crime wave of epidemic proportions. Unemployment has reached record levels, and state welfare agencies lack the funds
to ease the plight of the poor and the homeless. For many, and particularly the
dwellers of urban shanty towns cut off from their rural support systems, crime is
the only means of survival.

Ironically, economic factors have also created much of the precarious unity
that Nigeria does enjoy (Ahmad Khan 1994). The Westernized elite has prospered from a unified Nigeria and it is they, buoyed by a lion's share of the nation's
wealth, who have kept Nigeria from dissolving into a patchwork of ethnic enclaves. Exact data on this topic are difficult to come by, as are most other politically sensitive data.

How, then, does one sort out the competing economic and cultural explanations of Nigerian politics? The answer is that both economics and culture are essential to understanding Nigerian politics. Ethnic and religious violence in
Nigeria is usually precipitated by economic conflict, but the intensity of that violence draws upon culturally transmitted fears and distrust that have accumulated

over centuries. The strength of ethnic and cultural ties has also slowed the development of class consciousness in Nigeria. As things currently stand, most Nigerians seek economic security in the solidarity of their ethnic group rather than in the solidarity of their economic class (Sit 1993).

The importance of ethnic loyalties, moreover, will not decline until the Nigerian state can meet the economic and security needs of its citizens. People must have jobs, and they must be protected from the violence that engulfs them. Ironically, the communal base of Nigerian politics has undermined the capacity of the government to perform either of these tasks. Reflective of this fact has been the flight of an estimated $54.6 billion from Nigeria between 1972 and 1995, much of it to personal bank accounts in the West (*Vanguard,* Feb. 25, 1999). The flights of capital, legal and illegal, shows little sign of stopping as Nigerians continue to worry about the future of their country.

International Interdependence and the Politics of Nigeria: From the IMF to Jihadist Terror

It would be easy to blame Nigeria's political woes on its lethal mix of ethnic conflict and economic mismanagement. This indictment would not be entirely fair, as many of the problems besetting Nigeria today are of external origin. As noted in the introduction to this chapter, Nigeria did not originate as a coherent geographic or ethnic region. Rather, the concept of a Nigerian state was the outgrowth of a colonial policy that lumped diverse ethnic groups into the confines of a single administrative region for the sake of efficiency. Nigeria entered independence with much of its bureaucracy and most of its military establishment still in the hands of the British. Its economy was also dependent on that of Britain, and its citizens received little training in self-government. On what basis, then, did Britain and the international community expect Nigeria to blossom suddenly into a prosperous Western-style democracy?

The dramatic rise in world oil prices during the 1970s provided Nigeria with phenomenal wealth, but for reasons discussed throughout this chapter, the young country lacked the political and administrative capacity to manage its oil wealth effectively. Rather, a tremendous opportunity for economic development was squandered through corruption and grandiose spending on flashy public buildings and ill-conceived development projects such as a Soviet-designed steel plant. Much was accomplished, but the return on the investment was low. Agricultural development, the core of Nigeria's non-petroleum economy, was largely neglected.

The more oil revenues declined, the more Nigeria was forced to borrow from international banks to keep its financial head above water. By the mid-1980s, its foreign debt was approaching $35 billion, a staggering figure for a country with a per capita income of $300 per year. Faced with the prospect of bankruptcy, Nigeria stopped paying its debts.

President Obasango is attempting to impose austerity programs that will bring Nigeria in line with International Monetary Fund guidelines for economic recovery. The economic reforms demanded by the IMF are essentially the same reforms that the donor community has demanded of Russia, India, Egypt and most other countries of the third world:

- Government-owned firms are to be privatized.

- Tariffs and other obstacles to free trade are to be gradually eliminated.

- Government subsidies on food, fuel, and other basic goods are to be reduced, as are price controls and other regulations obstructing the efficient operation of the free market.

- The bureaucracy is to be downsized and rationalized.

- Nigeria was to reduce its dependence on oil by stimulating economic diversification.

- The Nigerian government is to reduce spending and use the fiscal measures at its disposal to reduce inflation and promote economic growth.

If Nigeria complies with these demands, the IMF has promised that the loans and grants required to stimulate Nigeria's economic revival will be forthcoming from the donor community. If Nigeria does not "bite the bullet" and accept the IMF recommendations, it will be cut off from the money required for its continued economic survival. IMF support was temporarily curtailed in 2001, but was reinstated with Nigerian promises to comply with IMF guidelines. It didn't, and by 2005, Nigeria was on the brink of bankruptcy (*Guardian*, April 26, 2005, www).

Although the IMF guidelines may be logical from an economic perspective, compliance promises a sustained period of hardship for most of the Nigerian population. The poor will be deprived of the subsidies upon which their survival depends. Privatization and cutbacks in the size of the bureaucracy, 40 percent by current estimates, will increase an already staggering rate of unemployment. The opening of Nigeria's markets to foreign goods threatens to destroy much of Nigeria's inefficient industrial base. The Nigerian elite, moreover, offered little support for an economic recovery plan that would reduce its opportunities for corruption and influence peddling.

The more Obasanjo pushes his austerity plan, the more tensions and violence in Nigeria are likely to increase. Strikes have already been in the offing. Obasanjo appears to be walking a middle ground, calling for reforms but backing down when tensions mount. This policy will extend his reign, but it will not solve its economic problems.

While pushing for a radical restructuring of the Nigerian economy, the international financial community refuses to acknowledge that it is part of the problem. Nigeria depends on the Royal Dutch/Shell Group, ChevronTexaco Corporation, and other oil companies to produce the foreign currency that constitutes 80 percent of its budget. The oil companies oppose any policies that might hurt their profit margins and have been primarily responsible for turning the oil delta into an environmental nightmare. The Government claims that it is being ripped off by the oil companies, but Nigerian officials gladly accept the bribes offered, not the least of which was a $2.4 million bribe by the U.S. Halliburton Company (*Guardian* (UK), May 9, 2003, www).

Adding to Nigeria's woes has been the growing threat of Jihadist terrorism (Lyman and Morrison 2004). The Jihadists prosper in regions of chaos and many believe that Africa is theirs for the taking. Toward this end, Jihadist strategy in Africa has concentrated on fermenting internal turmoil (Palmer and Palmer 2004). Nigeria, because of its oil wealth and key role in African politics, has become one of their prime targets. A history of deep seated tensions between Nigeria's Christians and Muslims also make it a relatively easy target. The government has responded by declaring the imposition of Islamic law in Nigeria's 12 northern states to be illegal and prohibited by Nigeria's Constitution. But, as the press notes, "the states have taken no notice whatsoever . . . Obasanjo's own statements on the subject have been treated with equal disdain, as coming from a 'toothless bulldog'"(*Observer*, Nov. 24, 2002, www).

The State Security Services (SSS) have also become increasingly active in closing down suspected Jihadist groups including the Taliban, a Nigerian group responsible for a wave of violence in the Kano region (*Guardian* (Lagos), March 08, 2004, www).

CHALLENGES OF THE PRESENT AND PROSPECTS FOR THE FUTURE

The world community has increasingly defined good government in terms of six goals: democracy, stability, human rights, quality of life, economic growth, and concern for the environment. Most states of the third world have made substantial progress in achieving one or more of these goals. Some are approaching economic parity with the first world but find democracy and human rights to be elusive. Others have established strong democratic traditions but remain mired in poverty. Nigeria has found all of the goals of good government to be elusive.

Democracy and Stability

Nigeria has witnessed three periods of democratic rule. Each was initiated by reasonably fair elections in which voters were offered a meaningful choice of candidates. The victors took office, and they did rule. In the first two cases, however, the ruling party was not willing to relinquish office once its term had expired. New elections were held, but they were neither free nor fair. Whether subsequent elections have been free and fair is largely a matter of opinion, the 2003 elections being severely flawed (*Economist*, Jan. 29, 2005).

The reasons offered for the failure of Nigerian democracy are many.

1. Nigeria's ruling elites were more concerned with serving themselves and their ethnic communities than with serving Nigeria as a nation.

2. Nigeria's democratic institutions were borrowed from the West and had little grounding in Nigerian culture or experience. As a result, they performed poorly and failed to gain the confidence of the Nigerian population.

3. The Nigerian electorate was fragmented by "we/they" ethnic identities that were too ingrained to be reconciled by democratic means. Being Ibo, Yoruba, or Hausa-Fulani was more important than being Nigerian.

4. *Nigeria's political parties and pressure groups were based on ethnicity.* Rather than building a unified political community, they intensified the fragmentation of the Nigerian state. Pluralism facilitates democracy, but not when loyalties to the group outweigh loyalties to the state.

5. Abundant economic resources that should have been used to build a political community were not put to that use. As a result, growing economic scarcity fueled ethnic conflict.

6. *The failure of Nigerian democracy was the product of an adverse international environment.* Colonialism had done little to build an integrated political community, and preparation for democracy had been minimal. The world community could have forced a return of Nigerian democracy, but was reluctant to impose the same pressures on Nigeria's military leaders that it imposed on the apartheid regime in South Africa.

President Obasanjo's own assessment of the future of democracy in Nigeria is grim. Nigeria, he said, seems to "be steadily losing ground to the suffocating influences of violence and lawlessness in the conduct of our political affairs" (*New York Times,* Feb 8, 2002, www). Communal fighting, alone, caused some 10,000 deaths during Obasanjo's first term in office. His second term promises to be little better. A rebellion rages in the oil rich delta region and an attempted coup was crushed in 2004.

Some scholars now suggest that it is a mistake to impose a purely Western-style democracy on Nigeria and Africa without making adjustments for its ethnic and religious makeup (Bogaards 2003; Boadi 2004).

Human Rights

Human rights abuses in Nigeria stem from three distinct sources: legal abuses by dictatorial regimes, traditional cultural practices, and ethnic/religious intolerance. Nigeria's military leaders have paid little heed to the constitutional rights of Nigeria's citizens, with most of their critics ending up either in jail or in exile. Political prisoners now are being released, and Obasanjo has declared that Nigeria is embarking on a new era of political freedom. The opposition parties are not convinced, and accuse Obasanjo's ruling party of being a "nest of killers" who are systematically eliminating opposition politicians and officials (*Vanguard*, March 15, 2004, www). Obasanjo has blamed the killings on robbers.

While the abrogation of political rights has received most of the attention in the world press, the violation of property rights has also been widespread. The Royal Dutch/Shell Group, for example, is often "assisted" by the Nigerian army in the development of its oil fields. Shell has responded to local complaints of environment pollution by stating that it paid the government a three percent production levy to cover the costs of any personal or property damage and that it was the government's responsibility to see that the money reached the aggrieved parties (*Times of London,* July 9, 1993, 11). Apparently these payments were delayed.

While many civil rights abuses are politically motivated, others result from a lack of professionalism among the Nigerian police. Calls for President Obasanjo to step up measures for revitalizing the nation's police force continue to mount (*Guardian,* Feb. 2, 2000, www). The military has also been accused of widespread human rights abuses, much of it ethnic based. The military has responded to the accusations by blaming civilians for attacking soldiers attempting to restore law and order (*Guardian* (Lagos), April 5, 2004, www).

Culturally based human rights abuses, in turn, focus on the exploitation of women and children (Rwomire 2001). Children have historically provided an important segment of the labor force in Nigeria and, while this is less the case today, child labor remains important to the economic survival of the poor (Dennis 1991).

The exploitation of women in Nigeria borders on servitude. By and large they are viewed as the property of their father before marriage and their husband after marriage (Nwabara 1989). Nigeria also remains a quasi-polygamous society in which the wives of Nigeria's poor bear most of the responsibility for raising their children. Nigeria's declining economic situation has made this a particularly difficult task.

Finally, human rights abuses stem from ethnic intolerance as Nigeria's larger ethnic groups continue to impose their will upon their smaller neighbors. They also practice "ethnic cleansing" by subjecting residents from competing groups to systematic abuse. Religious tensions have similarly led to human rights abuses as the North continues to use its dominant position to impose Muslim religious values upon non-Muslim populations (Finkel 2002; *Guardian* (Lagos), 2004, www). Both Muslim and Christian groups have their own armed militias (*Guardian* (Lagos), May 5, 2004, www). As noted in earlier sections of the chapter, the causes of ethnic intolerance are both cultural and economic in nature, one feeding upon the other.

The new Nigerian constitution, like the previous one, contains a lengthy enumeration of the rights of Nigerian citizens. The problem, however, is not one of legislation but of enforcement.

Quality of Life and Economic Growth

The quality of life of the average Nigerian is dismal. Life expectancy is 50 years, as compared to 76 years in the United States and 79 years in Japan. The World Health Organization ranks Nigeria forth from the bottom in health care. Only Sierre Leone, Liberia, and the Democratic Republic of the Congo score lower in the WHO's world rankings. (*Guardian* (Lagos), May 5, 2004, www). The per capita income is below $900, but little of that figure reaches the average Nigerian. Water and electricity services in Nigeria's major cities are erratic, and schools and hospitals are falling apart. More disquieting is a recent United Nations report indicating that one-half of all newborn babies in Africa carry the HIV virus (*International Herald Tribune,* Sept. 13, 1999, www). The latest data suggest that 3.5 million Nigerians are living with AIDs and that 170,000 have perished from the disease.

The quality of Nigerian life cannot improve without sustained improvement of the Nigerian economy. Oil revenues have increased with instability in the Middle East, but will be of little avail if they are not used more efficiently. New industries must be developed. Unfortunately, neither goal will be easily achieved and the outlook for the future remains grim. The problem is not a lack of money, but corruption, venality, and bureaucratic strangulation.

The Environment

Nigeria is not an environmentally concerned country. Lagos and other major Nigerian cities are so heavily polluted that one of the main justifications for building a new capital city in Abuja was that it would be "healthful." Oil-related pollution in the petroleum regions threatens both the people and the wildlife, while water supplies in some rural states are infested with disease-carrying worms (*West Africa,* Mar. 28, 1994). The *CIA World Fact Book: 2003* summarizes Nigeria's environmental problems as "soil degradation; rapid deforestation; urban air and water pollution; desertification: oil pollution—water, air and soil; has suffered serious damage from oil spoils; loss of arable land; rapid urbanization (*CIA World Fact Book 2003,* www).

Nigeria is now attempting to gain some leverage against international pressure by acquiring nuclear power as part of an agreement with Pakistan, the lead country in the black market in nuclear weapons materials. Both countries have denied hostile intent.

The situation, unfortunately, is not likely to improve in the near future. Nigeria is too poor to pay for sweeping environmental programs, and its public service is too inefficient to implement programs that are already on the books. Strict environmental regulations, moreover, would depress the Nigerian economy, something that no government, civilian or military, is anxious to do.

Prospects for the Future

Nigerian politics was earlier characterized as a struggle between hope and despair. Hope springs from Nigeria's oil wealth as well as from an irrepressible desire for democracy among a large segment of the Nigerian population. Despair is the product of the corruption and mismanagement that have squandered the nation's wealth, leaving much of its population poverty-stricken. Despair also flows from a persistence of ethnic and religious conflict as well as from the fragile nature of Nigeria's fledgling democracy. Finally, despair arises from a sense that the international community seems to be losing interest in Africa and its affairs. This is unfortunate, for Nigeria requires strong international encouragement if it is to achieve the UN's much-vaunted goals of stability, democracy, human rights, economic growth, quality of life, and environmental concern.

REFERENCES

Aborisade, Oladimeji and Robert J. Mundt. 2002. *Politics in Nigeria.* 2nd ed. NY: Longman.

Adams, Paul. 1993 (July-Aug.). "Babangida's Boondoggle." *Africa Report* 26–28.

Adams, Paul. 1994 (Jan. -Feb.). "The Army Calls the Tune." *Africa Report* 47–49.

Ahmad Khan, Sarah. 1994. *Nigeria: The Political Economy of Oil.* Oxford, England: Oxford University Press. (For the Oxford Institute for Energy Studies.)

Apter, David E. 1987. *Rethinking Development: Modernization, Dependency, and Postmodern Politics.* Beverly Hills, CA: Sage.

Ayeni, Victor, Lanre Nassar, and Dotun Popoola. 1988. "Interest and Pressure Group Activities." In *Nigeria's' Second Republic: Presidentialism, Politics and Administration in a Developing State,* (pp. 107–20), ed. Victor Ayeni and Kayode Soremekun. Apapa: Daily Times Publications.

Ayo, S. Bamidele. 2002. *Public Administration and the Conduct of Community Affairs among the Yoruba in Nigeria.* Oakland, CA: ICS Press.

Aziken, Emmanuel. 2004 (March). "Bribery Allogations: Chukwumerije, Nzeribe and the Senate's Code of Silence." *Vanguard,* 2–6, www.

Babatope, Ebenezer. 1991 (Oct. 7). "Notes on the Transition." *African Concord* (Lagos, Nigeria).

Benson, Dayo. 1999 (Feb.). "For Once, the North Bows." *Vanguard* 1–4, www.

Bienen, Henry, and Nicolas van de Walle. 1989 (Mar.). "Time and Power in Africa." *American Political Science Review* 83(1): 19–34.

Bogaards, Matthijs. 2003 (Nov.). "Electoral Choices for Divided Societies: Multi-Ethnic and Constituency Pooling in Africa." *Commonwealth and Comparative Politics* 41(3): 59–81.

Ciroma, Adamu. 1998 (Oct.). "Rich but Poor." *Africa Today* 4(10): 10–14.

Cohen, Robin. 1981. *Labour and Politics in Nigeria.* London: Heinemann.

Coleman, James S. 1965. *Nigeria: Background to Nationalism.* Berkeley, CA: University of California Press.

Davidson, Basil. 1994. *Modern Africa: A Social and Political History.* 3rd ed. New York: Longman.

Dennis, Carolyne. 1991. "Constructing a 'Career' Under Conditions of Economic Crisis, and Structural Adjustment: The Survival Strategies of Nigerian Women." In *Women, Development and Survival in the Third World* (pp. 88–106), ed. Haleh Afshar. London: Longman.

Diamond, Larry. 1988. *Class, Ethnicity and Democracy in Nigeria: The Failure of the First Republic.* London: Macmillan.

Dibie, Robert A. 2003. *Public Management and Sustainable Development in Nigeria: Military-Bureaucracy Relationship.* Burlington, VT: Ashgate.

Doob, Leonard, W. 1964. *Patriotism and Nationalism: Their Psychological Foundations.* New Haven, CT: Yale University Press.

Edozie, Rita Kiki. 2002. *People Power and Democracy: The Popular Movement against Military Despotism in Nigeria, 1989–1999.* Trenton, NJ: Africa World Press, Inc.

Egwu, Sam. 1990. "Nigeria's Political Culture: Past, Present and Future." In *Nigerian Cultural Heritage* (pp. 189–206), ed. E. Ikenga-Metuh and O. Ojoade. South Onitsha: IMICO.

Ekwe-Ekwe, Herbert. 1991. *Issues in Nigerian Politics Since the Fall of the Second Republic.* Lewiston, NY: Edwin Mellen.

Finkel, David. 2002 (Nov. 23). "Crime and Holy Punishment: In Divided Nigeria, Search for Justice Leads Many to Embrace Islamic Code." *Washington Post* (www.washingtonpost.com/wp-dyn/articles/A31793-2002n=Nov23.html).

Ford, Neil. 2003(a) (June). "Now Obasanjo Must Turn Economy Around." *African Business,* 12–18. (http://infotrac-college.thomsponlearning.com/itw/informar).

Ford, Neil. 2003(b) (April). "The Obasanjo Balance-Sheet." *African Business,* 54.

(http://infotrac-college.thomsponlearn-ing.com/itw/informar.)

Forrest, Tom. 1993. *Politics and Economic Development in Nigeria.* Boulder, CO: Westview Press.

Graf, William D. 1988. *The Nigerian State: Political Economy, State, Class, and Political System in the Post—Colonial Era.* London: James Currey.

Gyimah-Boadi, E., ed. 2004. *Democratic Reform in Africa: The Quality of Progress.* Boulder, CO: Lynne Rienner Pub.

Hussaina, Abdullah. 1995. "Wifeism and Activism: The Nigerian Women's Move-ment." In *The Challenge of Local Femi-nisms,* ed. Amrita Basu. Boulder, CO: Westview.

Ihonvbere, Julius O. 1997 (Dec.). "Organized Labor and the Struggle for Democracy in Nigeria." *African Studies Review* 40(3): 77–110.

Ikegwuoha, Bernard-Thompson. 1987. *Politics and Government of the Nigerian "Second Republic": October 1, 1979– December 31, 1983.* Rome: N. Domenici—Pecheux.

Illoegbunam, Chuks. 1994. *West Africa,* December 27–January 9, 1994, 2339.

Imoagene, Oshomha. 1989. *The Nigerian Class Struggle.* Ibadan, Nigeria: Evans Brothers.

Ishaka, Peter. 1994 (Feb. 14). "Beating the Drums of Secession." *African Concord,* 14–15.

Jason, Pini. 2003 (April). "Don't Mention the Economy." *New African,* 31–32.

Johnson, Segun. 1990. "Introduction: Nige-ria: A Country Conceived in Problems." In *Readings in Selected Nigerian Problems* (pp. 1–8), ed. Segun Johnson. Lagos: Koservices, Ltd.

Joseph, Richard. 1987. *Democracy and Preben-dal Politics in Nigeria: The Rise and Fall of the Second Republic.* New York: Cam-bridge University Press.

Kalu, Vicktor Eke. 1987. *The Nigerian Condi-tion.* Enugu, Nigeria: Fourth Dimension.

Kastfelt, Niels. 1993. *Religion and Politics in Nigeria.* New York: St. Martin's.

Koehn, Peter H. 1990. *Public Policy and Administration in Africa: Lessons from Nigeria.* Boulder, CO: Westview Press.

Lemer, D. 1958. *The Passing of Traditional Society.* Glencoe, IL: Free Press.

Lyman, Princeton N. and J. Stephen Morri-son. 2004 (Jan.-Feb.). "The Terrorist Threat in Africa." *Foreign Affairs* 83(1): 75. Infotrac Article, No. l, A112033250.

Marshall-Fratani, Ruth. 1998. "Mediating the Global and Local in Nigerian Pen-tecostalism." *Journal of Religion in Africa* 28(3): 278–315.

Miles, William. 1988. *Elections in Nigeria: A Grassroots Perspective.* Boulder, CO: Lynne Rienner.

Muhammed, Naajatu. 1998 (Oct.). "North-erners Have Nothing Concrete to Show for More Than 30 Years in Power. Ask Them." *Africa Today* 4(10): 15–16.

Nigerian Economic Society. 1986. *The Niger-ian Economy: A Political Economy Approach.* Essex, England: Longman/Bienen.

Nuanna, Ochereome. 1995 (Jan.). "Corrup-tion Unlimited." *African Business* 195.

Nwabara, Zahra Imam. 1989. "Women in Nigeria-The Way I See It." In *Women and the Family in Nigeria* (pp. 7–16), ed. A. Imam, R. Pittin, and H. Omole. Dakar: Codesria.

Nwokocha, John. 1999 (Feb. 21). "National Assembly: How Far Can it Check?" *Vanguard* 1–3, www.

Nwosu, Ikechukwu E. 1988. "Comparative Analysis of Media–Government Rela-tionship in Nigeria, Britain and the United States of America." In *Contempo-rary Issues in Mass Media for Development and National Security* (pp. 174–88), ed. Ralph A. Akinfeleye. Lagos: Unimedia.

Obadina, Tunde. 1998 (Sept. 24). "A Dan-gerous Way to Privatise." *Africa Economic Analysis* 1–2, www.

Obi, Cyril I. 2001. *The Changing Forms of Identity Politics in Nigeria Under Economic Adjustment: The Case of the Oil Minorities Movement of Niger Delta.* Bloomington, IN: Indiana University Press.

Okoye, Israel Kelue. 1991. *Soldiers and Politics in Nigeria.* Lagos, Nigeria: New Age.

Olawunmi, Tunji. 1999 (March 2). "Presidency: Why Falae Lost." *Vanguard* 1–4, www.

Olugbade, Kola. 1992. "The Nigerian State and the Quest for a Stable Polity." *Comparative Politics* 4: 293–315.

Onadipe, Abiodun. 1997 (Oct.). "Nigeria's Crucial Month." *Contemporary Review* 271(1581): 169–77.

Osuntokum, Jide. 1979. "The Historical Background of Nigerian Federalism." In *Readings on Federalism* (pp. 91–102), ed. A. B. Akinyemi, P. D. Cole, and Walter Ofonagoro. Ibadan, Nigeria: Nigerian Institute of International Affairs.

Otegbeye, Tunji. 1999 (Feb. 21). "Why Alliances have Failed in Nigeria." *Vanguard* 1–5, www.

Otite, O. 1976. "On the Concept of a Nigerian Society." In *Ethnic Relations in Nigeria* (pp. 3–16), ed. A. O. Sanda. Ibadan, Nigeria: University of Ibadan.

Otobo, D. 1987. "The Nigerian General Strike of 1981." In *Readings in Industrial Relations in Nigeria* (pp. 233–53), ed. Dafe Otobo and Morakinyo Omole. Lagos: Malthouse Press Ltd.

Palmer, Monte and Princess Palmer. 2004. *At the Heart of Terror: Islam, Jihadists, and America's War on Terror.* Lanham, MD: Rowman and Littlefield.

Pandjo Boumba, Luc. 2002. *La violence du developpement: pouvoir politique et rationalite economique des elites africaines.* Paris: L'Harmattan.

Rothberg, Robert. 2004. *Crafting the New Nigeria: Confronting the Challenges.* Boulder, CO: Lynne Rienner Pub.

Rwomire, Apollo, ed. 2001. *African Women and Children: Crisis and Response.* Westport, CO: Praeger.

Sit, Narasingha. 1993. "Nigerian Intellectuals and Socialism: Retrospect and Prospect." *The Journal of Modern African Studies* 31(3): 361–85.

Sklar, Richard L. 1967. "Ethnic Relations and Social Class." *Journal of Modern African Studies* 5(1): 4–11.

Taylor, Robert. 1993. "Chapter One." In *Urban Development in Nigeria,* ed. Robert Taylor. Aldershot, England: Avebury.

Tokunboh, M. A. 1985. *Labour Movement in Nigeria: Past and Present.* Lagos: Literamed.

Turnbull, Colin M. 1963. *The Lonely African.* Garden City, NY: Doubleday/Anchor.

Uche, Luke Uka. 1989. *Mass Media, People and Politics in Nigeria.* New Delhi: Concept.

Umeh, Louis C. 1993. "The Building of a New Capital City: The Abuja Experience." In *Urban Development in Nigeria* (pp. 215–28), ed. Robert W. Taylor. Aldershot, England: Avebury.

Usen, Anietie. 1998 (Oct.). "Rich but Poor." *Africa Today* 4(10): 10–11.

West, Deborah. 2003. *Governing Nigeria: Continuing Issues after the Elections.* Cambridge, MA: World Peace Foundation.

Williams, Adebayo. 1998 (Oct.). "A Nation in Search of Itself." *Africa Today* 4(10): 20–21.

Glossary

actors Those who give life to political institutions and carry out the work of governments.

amparo A type of legal injunction unique to Mexico that blocks government action because of issues of constitutionality.

anomie A sociological term referring to an absence of social norms caused by the breakdown of social and political institutions.

Arab League Regional organization designed to promote political, military, and economic cooperation among the Arab states.

artistic culture The dimension of culture that gives expression to those symbols that politics lives on.

authoritarian regime Non-democratic political system in which all power is concentrated in the hands of a single individual or small oligarchy (e.g., Saudi Arabia).

back benchers British members of Parliament (MPs) who are not in the Government or shadow cabinet. They sit on the back benches of the House of Commons.

baronage Collective term referring to former officers of William the Conqueror's army, who received large grants of land and aristocratic titles such as Duke, Earl, and Viscount after the Norman Conquest of England in 1066. Their heirs inherited their titles.

Basic Law German equivalent of a constitution, which was established shortly after Germany was divided into two countries following World War II.

Berlin Wall A fortified prison wall erected by communist authorities between East and West Berlin in 1961 to prevent East Germans from defecting to the West. In 1989, the citizens of East Berlin tore the wall down.

bi-polar system The coexistence of two global superpowers, such that neither is able to force its will on the world community, causing each to balance the other.

Bolsheviks Lenin-led faction of the communist movement in tsarist Russia.

boryokudan Violence groups in Japan.

bourgeoisie Marx's term for the middle class, particularly industrialists and merchants.

Brahma Hindu god of creation.

Brahman The highest level of the Indian caste system, often referred to as the priestly caste.

British East India Company Private British corporation that established trading posts in India during the 1600s and eventually ruled most of the Indian subcontinent.

Bundesrat The upper house of the German legislature, consisting of delegates selected by the Land (state) governments.

Bundestag The lower house of the German legislature, consisting of delegates elected by the German population.

bureaucrat An administrator who works for a government or large institution. Bureaucrats possess specialized information and are responsible for implementing the political decisions made by the elites. The behavior of bureaucrats directly influences public attitudes toward the government.

by-election An election held to replace a Member of Parliament who has resigned or died.

cadres Dedicated members of a political party or organization who do most of the work that gets done. The original cadres in the Chinese Communist Party were lauded for their idealism and revolutionary zeal, but cadres in later years were criticized for corruption and powermongering. Cadres hold most bureaucratic positions in China and are divided into various ranks and levels.

camarilla In Mexico, a group or network of politicians who rely on one another for advancement.

catch-all party A large, broad-based political party that is more concerned with winning elections than with conforming to a specific ideology (e.g., the Republican and Democratic Parties in the US).

CDU. *See* Christian Democratic Union.

center An ideological classification based on seating arrangements in the parliament of revolutionary France. Traditionally, parties at the "center" of the political spectrum advocate a balance between capitalism and social welfare.

Central European Bank An agency of the EU designed to regulate monetary policy in the European Monetary Union (countries that use the euro as a common currency). Located in Frankfurt, the Bank began operation in 1999.

Chamber of Deputies One house of the Mexican Congress (the other house is the Senate).

chancellor Germany's chief executive, whose role is similar to that of the British prime minister. (Germany's president is the symbolic head of the country.)

charisma In the words of German sociologist Max Weber, *charisma* is "a certain quality of an individual personality by virtue of which he is set apart from ordinary men and treated as endowed with supernatural, superhuman, or at least specifically exceptional powers or qualities." Charismatic individuals have a broad appeal to the masses.

Chifuren An association of Japanese housewives.

Christian Democratic Union (CDU) Germany's large catch-all party of the center right, which has become identified with business interests and European unification.

civic culture Democratic society whose citizens are committed to democratic values, understand how their political institutions work, and believe in their ability to influence those institutions. In a civic culture, loyalty to the state takes precedence over loyalties to ethnic, religious, and other parochial groups.

civil society A country with an active array of political parties, citizen action groups, the mass media and all other nongovernmental groups.

coalition government A government in which the seats in the Cabinet are fragmented among several political parties, none of which can claim a majority. The prime minister can rule only as long as he or she retains the support of all members of the coalition.

co-determination Policy of involving workers in management decisions.

cohabitation A period during which the French president lacks the support of a majority of the deputies in the Assembly, and therefore the powers of the prime minister equal those of the president.

common law A judicial system based on tradition and custom.

commons In feudal England, the social class comprising knights and merchants. (*See also* House of Commons.)

communism Economic system postulated by Karl Marx (1818–1883) and others, in which everything is owned in common and in which people willingly give according to their abilities and take according to their needs.

communist An advocate or supporter of communism. (*See* communism.)

Communist Party Political party advocating the economic and political system devised by Karl Marx. (*See* communism.)

comparative advantage Doctrine stating that a truly free world market will allow each country to specialize in what it does best. For example, countries with cheap labor will specialize in labor-intensive industries, while those with a highly skilled work force will specialize in high-tech industries.

comparative politics, or **comparative political analysis** A branch of political science that uses comparisons between countries and other political units to make generalized statements about the political process.

conciliation commissions Units of the Japanese legal system that are designed to facilitate out-of-court settlement of disputes.

conflict management Systems and procedures designed to keep political conflict within tolerable limits.

Confucian culture Asian value system that is based on Confucianism and emphasizes hard work, respect for hierarchical authority, rule by merit, and devotion to the group.

Confucianism A traditional Chinese belief system based on the teachings of Confucius (511–479 BC), who stressed the importance of wise governance, compliance with the laws of the land, family loyalty, responsibility toward others, and self-improvement.

Congress Party Political party that became a symbol of India's independence movement. The Congress Party ruled India for most of its history as an independent country.

Constitutional Council Russia's equivalent of the US Supreme Court.

co-optation Promotional system used within authoritarian political parties, wherein members of higher committees decide which members of lower committees will be elevated to a higher rank.

corporatism A formalized relationship between the state and social organizations, in which organizations exercise control over their particular domains but lose a degree of autonomy. In Mexico, examples include the incorporation of labor unions and peasant organizations into the PRI.

Council of Ministers of the EU Consists of a cabinet-level minister from each EU country assisted by a number of "permanent representatives" depending on the size of the country. Representatives on the Council of Ministers are selected by the national governments of EU countries.

coup d'état Sudden, forceful overthrow of the government.

cross-cutting cleavages Conflicting or competing loyalties felt by group members as a result of their religious, ethnic, economic, political, or other affiliations.

cultural map The framework of values, attitudes, and preconceptions that individuals absorb from their culture and rely on when making choices about politics, economics, and other important issues in their lives.

culture The ideas, values, and expectations shared by a group of people. Culture tells people what they should consider important, defines what is considered right and wrong, and delineates the roles that people are expected to play in life.

daimyo Japanese term for feudal fiefdoms and the leaders of those fiefdoms.

dedazo Literally, the "finger-pointing" process whereby the Mexican president picks his successor.

demands The expectations that citizens, pressure groups, and political parties place upon the government concerning reallocation of scarce resources.

dependency theory A political theory which asserts that First World countries use their dominant economic power to keep Third World countries in a permanent state of dependence and poverty.

development *See* political development.

devotee party A political party whose members are expected to devote their lives to the achievement of the party's well-defined ideological goals (e.g., Communists, Fascists, Hitler's Nazis).

Diet Japan's Parliament, consisting of a House of Representatives (lower house) and a House of Peers (upper house).

dirigisme A mild version of state capitalism in which economic planners establish goals for the French economy and then use the financial resources of the government to encourage private-sector compliance with those goals.

dual society A country in which a sharp division exists between prosperous and educated upper- and middle-class citizens and a minimally skilled and unemployed working class whose members live in poverty.

Duma Lower house of the Russian Parliament (Federal Assembly).

economic culture The value that a society places on hard work and innovation.

ejido In Mexico, a collective farm that is usually divided into individual plots for peasants.

elite *See* political elite.

elite analysis A method of political analysis that focuses on the study of elite attitudes and behavior. Elites are assumed to be the most important element in the political process.

enarques Graduates of the Ecole Nationale d'Administration (ENA), who control the bureaucratic apparatus in France.

EU *See* European Union.

euro The monetary unit of the European Union.

Euro-communism A philosophy based on the idea that one can subscribe to the basic principles of Marxism and still play by democratic rules. If citizens become dissatisfied, they can vote the communists out of office.

European Commission of the EU A branch of European government consisting of twenty members nominated by the member countries of the European Union with the implied accord of the other member countries and the president of the Com-mission. The commission supervises the European bureaucracy that implements EU policy and may also suggest new legislation to the Council of Ministers. Members of the Commission are expected to act in the best interests of the EU and not to receive instructions from their home countries.

European Council A periodic "summit meeting" of the prime ministers of the fif- teen member states in the European Union. All decisions of the European Council must be unanimous if they are to become EU policy.

European Court of Justice of the EU The judicial branch of the EU, which adjudicates disputes related to EU treaties and laws. The court, which is located in Luxembourg, consists of fifteen member judges appointed for six-year terms.

European Parliament A branch of European supranational government consisting of 500 deputies chosen in direct election by the population of the member countries. Seats in the parliament are allocated in proportion to the populations of member states. The European parliament meets in Strasbourg and Brussels.

European Union (EU) A supranational body composed of twenty five member countries. All have transferred broad areas of economic sovereignty to a supranational government located in Brussels.

euroskeptics Individuals who are opposed to the greater unification of Europe. Some would like to undo what has already been done.

external face of culture The national myths, ideologies, religions, and other belief systems that a society uses to socialize or "program" its citizens.

external political culture The political content of a society's ideologies, myths, and religions; the content of political socialization.

EZLN Zapatista Army of National Liberation, a largely indigenous-based Mexican guerilla force that emerged in 1994 in Chiapas.

Fabians A group of British intellectuals who advocated democratic socialism as the means of achieving an equitable society.

fair share Concept based on the myth that Japan is one large family whose members are each entitled to receive a portion of the nation's wealth.

far left An ideological classification based on seating arrangements in the parliament of revolutionary France. Traditionally, the "far left" end of the political spectrum included communists, anarchists, and other parties advocating a mass revolution by violent means.

far right An ideological classification based on seating arrangements in the parliament of revolutionary France. Traditionally, the "far right" end of the political spectrum includes monarchists, supporters of the church, and extreme nationalists.

fascism A right-wing, extremely nationalistic political ideology incorporating a totalitarian and hierarchical power structure.

FDP *See* Free Democratic Party.

Federal Assembly Russian parliament.

Federation Council Upper house of the Federal Assembly (Russian parliament).

feudalism A social, economic, and political system in which members of the landed aristocracy (baronage) maintained order in their domains, provided the king with knights and foot soldiers in times of war, and contributed financially to the royal household. Peasants were relegated to the bottom of the social hierarchy and lived in near-servitude.

first world The advanced industrial societies of the world, which produce most of the world's technology, consume most of the world's resources, and possess most of the world's wealth. The classic countries of the First World are the United States, Japan, Canada, Australia, New Zealand, the United Kingdom, France, Germany, Italy, the Scandinavian states, the Benelux states (Belgium, the Netherlands, Luxembourg), Finland, and Switzerland.

fourth world Countries that are unable to provide citizens with a minimally acceptable quality of life. Most are dictatorships racked with tribal conflict or open civil war. Human rights are ignored, and inequality reigns in all areas of political, economic, and social life. Environmental protection is minimal or nonexistent.

fraktionen German parliamentary parties comprising all of a party's deputies in the Bundestag. The leader of the majority Fraktionen is the chancellor.

Free Democratic Party (FDP) German political party that plays a pivotal role as a balancer between Germany's two large catch-all parties, the CDU and the SPD.

free-market economy An economic system in which economic decisions are made on the basis of supply and demand, with minimal intervention by the government.

G-7 and G-8 A group consisting of the world's eight major capitalist powers: the United States, Canada, Japan, the United Kingdom, France, Germany, and Italy. The heads of these countries meet regularly to determine world economic policy. Sometimes Russia participates in these meetings, making the G-8. Russian economic influence, however, is minimal.

glasnost A Russian term for greater openness and democracy, a process within the Soviet system that began with the Gorbachev reforms.

globalization The process by which economics, politics and culture are becoming global in nature. The economic and military power of the United States are the major forces in the globalization of the world, as is the pervasiveness of the US mass media.

governments, Government Political institutions responsible for allocating scarce resources in an authoritative manner. In this text, the word *Government* (capitalized) refers to a country's prime minister, Cabinet, and other relevant positions selected by the prime minister.

grands fonctionnaires A small group of enarques (graduates of the ENA) who are highly influential in French polities.

Greens Political party that began in Germany during the 1970s and spread gradually to other countries. As the name suggests, Green Parties focus mainly on environmental issues.

growth with equity An ideal version of state capitalism in which the government stimulates the development of the economy while ensuring that all members of society share in the benefits of that development.

guerilla warfare Guerilla warfare involves large armed groups and militias who actively seek to control territory. Guerilla groups often confront government forces in battle. Guerilla warfare is most often associated with civil war and independence movements. (*See* terrorism.)

House of Commons The lower house in the British Parliament, the members of which are elected by universal suffrage for a maximum of five years.

House of Councilors (formerly, **House of Peers**) Upper house of the Japanese Parliament.

House of Lords The upper house in the British Parliament. Members of the House of Lords are referred to as "Peers."

House of Peers *See* House of Councilors.

House of Representatives Lower house of the Japanese Parliament.

IFE (Federal Electoral Institute) Agency in charge of organizing and conducting elections in Mexico. It is largely autonomous of other political powers.

IMF *See* International Monetary Fund.

immobilisme (immobilism) French term for a weak Government that is unable to agree on a course of action and move forward with it.

import substitution (*also* **import substitution industrialization**) Strategy of economic development based on promoting and protecting domestic industry. Tariffs are placed on imported goods to encourage consumers to purchase items that are produced domestically.

indirect rule Euphemistic term for British colonial policy in Nigeria and other colonies, which kept tribal chiefs in place, discouraged the creation of a Westernized elite, and reinforced the fragmentation of Nigerian society by playing upon tribal jealousies.

infitah Literally, "economic opening." A partial shift to capitalism initiated by Egyptian president Anwar Sadat in 1974.

institutionalization The process in which organizations and procedures evolve slowly over time, earning a respected place in society.

internal face of culture The cultural beliefs that have been absorbed by the citizens of a society; the predispositions, values, and attitudes that shape their view of their world.

internal political culture People's orientations toward politics: their attitudes and opinions regarding political leaders, political movements, political events, and political institutions.

International Monetary Fund (IMF) Established at the end of World War II to facilitate the reconstruction of a war-torn Europe and to reestablish order in the world economy, the IMF now operates as an international credit union that makes short-term loans to countries. Member states must pay in to the IMF and have the right to borrow up to 20 percent of the contribution without restriction. Larger loans must be approved by the governing board of the IMF.

Japan Inc. Ruling alliance of political, administrative, and business leaders in Japan.

jati Sub-castes within the Indian caste system (there are more than 2,000 jati).

Jihad A holy war intended to protect and extend the Muslim faith. It is also a personal struggle against personal sins.

Jihadists Islamic extremists who believe that violence is the only way to impose Islamic rule on the countries of the Islamic world if not the world beyond. They attack anyone who stands in their way of a very narrow and restrictive view of Islamic rule.

karma An Indian term referring to the soul's predisposition toward good or evil. Karma has been described as everything from a cosmic force to luck or destiny.

KMT *See* Kuomintang.

Kshatriya The second level of the Indian caste system, often referred to as the warrior caste.

Kuomintang (KMT) Chinese nationalist movement initiated by followers of Sun Yat-sen and later led by Chiang Kai-shek. The KMT fought the Communist Party for control of China but eventually had to retreat to the island of Taiwan.

Labour Party In the United Kingdom, a party formed in the early 1900s as an alliance between labor unions and various socialist groups of the era, in order to force a fundamental change in the allocation of Britain's wealth.

Land The German term for a German state.

Lander Plural form of *Land* (see above).

LDP *See* Liberal Democratic Party.

left *See* political left.

leftist economist An economist who believes that socialism is preferable to capitalism because it is a more equitable system.

legitimacy A government is viewed as *legitimate* if a country's citizens agree that the government's rules are in the best interests of all citizens and should be followed voluntarily.

Liberal Democratic party (LDP)
Political party that dominated Japanese politics from 1955 to 1993. It continues to be Japan's dominant party today.

limited-issue party *See* single-issue party.

linkage function Mechanism for communicating between the elites and the masses. In modern societies, the linkage function is performed by parties, pressure groups, and the mass media.

Lok Sabha Popularly elected lower house of the Indian parliament, also known as the House of the People. The members of the Lok Sabha elect the prime minister.

Maastricht Treaty An agreement that went into effect on January 1, 1993, transforming the European Community into the European Union and providing the framework for the eventual political unification of its member countries. The treaty outlined a method to create (within a ten-year transition period) a single European currency—the euro—and to strengthen the authority of the EU with regard to foreign affairs, trade, and environmental and social policy.

Majlis As-Shab (People's Assembly)
Popularly elected body of the Egyptian legislature whose powers are largely theoretical. Ultimately, power rests in the hands of the Egyptian president.

Majlis As-Shoura (Consultive Assembly) Entity within the Egyptian parliament that serves as a debating society designed to air issues of public importance.

maquiladoras Mexican factories located mainly along the US border that assemble imported parts and export finished products.

marginalized group Group whose members exist on the fringes of society and have little influence on politics.

Marxism Economic philosophy developed by Karl Marx (1818–1883), which argues that prosperity and equality are best assured by a socialist economic system in which the government owns factories, farms, and other means of production (e.g., the Soviet Union and China prior to 1990).

masses Citizens, the people, the public, or the population of a state. It is the masses who do most of the work within a society.

mass-membership parties *See* devotee parties.

master race Hitler's theory that Germans were a superior race and therefore historically destined to rule the world.

Member of Parliament (MP) Legislator in the British Parliament.

mestizo Racial designation for the majority of the Mexican population who are of mixed Spanish and indigenous descent.

moderate left An ideological classification based on seating arrangements in the parliament of revolutionary France. Traditionally, the "moderate left" end of the political spectrum includes social liberals and supporters of organized labor.

moderate (or democratic) right An ideological classification based on seating arrangements in the parliament of revolutionary France. Traditionally, the "moderate right" end of the political spectrum includes individuals favoring private property, free enterprise, low taxation, and law and order.

MP *See* Member of Parliament.

multiparty system A political system in which several parties compete for voter support and no party is able to gain a majority of the vote in any election (e.g., Russia, Poland).

Muslim Brotherhood Islamic religious organization dedicated to the creation of an Islamic state in Eqypt.

Muslim League Political party that represented the interests of the Muslim segment of the population in pre-independence India.

National Front Political party at the extreme right end of the political spectrum in France. According to the platform of the National Front, immigrants are responsible for France's economic and social problems and thus should be deported from France.

NATO *See* North Atlantic Treaty Organization.

Nazi Party Political party formed by Adolf Hitler in 1919 that rose to prominence as a result of Germany's social disintegration during the 1930s.

neoclassical economists Economic theorists who argue for a world in which monopolistic practices are prohibited and governmental intervention in the economy is limited to facilitating free-market competition.

neocorporatism A technique for managing the influence of pressure groups by allowing them to assist in the drafting of legislation. In return, pressure groups are expected to be moderate in the demands they place upon the government.

new left Political parties with a moderate, slightly left-of-center philosophy, such as the Labour Party in England and the Social Democratic Party in Germany.

New Wafd Pro-business political party in Egypt.

NGO Non-governmental organization—a politically significant group that operates independently from the government. Examples range from small self-help groups in poor countries to large international organizations such as the Red Cross.

nirvana A cosmic soul that embodies the true harmony of the universe. For Hindus, salvation is achieved by attaining nirvana, or merging with the cosmic soul.

no-party system An authoritarian regime in which political parties are not allowed (e.g., Libya, Saudi Arabia).

North Atlantic Treaty Organization (NATO) Military alliance between the United States, Canada, and most countries of Western Europe.

oligarchy A government ruled by a small group of powerful individuals.

PAN (National Action Party) Center-right opposition party to the PRI in Mexico.

pantoflage A process in which senior civil servants in France begin their careers in government service and then jump to the private sector.

parliamentary democracy A democracy in which the population elects the Members of Parliament, who in turn elect the prime minister.

parliamentary party The organization of a political party in the British House of Commons and elsewhere.

party *See* political party.

party families Groups of political parties that share a common orientation and cooperate with each other most of the time. In France, the two major party families are on the political left and the political right.

patron–client network System in which junior members of an organization attach themselves to a powerful leader, hoping to receive promotions and other favors. Similar networks exist between politicians and citizens.

peak association Large pressure group encompassing a variety of smaller organizations that share a common interest, such as the British Trades Unions Congress or the US Chamber of Commerce.

People's Republic of China The name given to mainland China after the Communist Party took over in 1949.

perestroika Structural reform movement initiated by Mikhail Gorbachev in an attempt to break the grip of government and Party bureaucracies on the Soviet economy. Factory managers were given greater flexibility in the management of their plants; elections to government councils featured open discussion, multiple candidates, and secret ballots; and experimentation with small-scale capitalism was encouraged.

petite bourgeoisie A French term referring collectively to small merchants, artisans, farmers, and retirees.

plebiscite An election in which voters indicate their approval or disapproval of a proposal or candidate put forward by the government. There are no other choices.

pluralism Distribution of political power among a broad range of groups and interests.

pluralistic elite Elite structure in which a broad range of individuals and groups share decision-making power (e.g., United States). Systems with pluralistic elites are responsive to diverse interests, but decisive action is impaired by the need to achieve consensus.

plurality The greatest number; for example, the political candidate receiving a *plurality* of votes is the candidate who receives the most votes. A candidate can have a plurality without receiving an actual majority (50 percent or more) of the total number of votes cast in an election.

Politburo In the former Soviet Union, an executive committee comprised of powerful political and military leaders.

political actors Individuals and groups that give direction to the political process, such as elites, bureaucrats, citizens, political parties, and pressure groups.

political culture The dimensions of culture that seem to have the greatest influence on people's political behavior.

political development Defined by the United Nations as the achievement of a stable democracy that promotes the economic well-being of citizens in an equitable, humane, and environmentally concerned manner.

political economy approach An approach to comparative political analysis asserting that most areas of political life are shaped by economic factors.

political elites Individuals and groups who dominate the political process, controlling the allocation of scarce resources. Elites often include senior members of the government, wealthy individuals, military leaders, representatives of large groups such as labor unions, and religious leaders.

political institutions Organizational mechanisms for determining how the scarce resources of society will be allocated.

political left An ideological classification based on seating arrangements in the parliament of revolutionary France. Traditionally, leftists included communists, socialists, anarchists, and other diverse groups claiming to be heirs of the Revolution. Today, the left generally inclines toward advocating greater government involvement in the economy and more welfare programs for the public.

political party A group of individuals working together to achieve common goals by controlling all or part of the government.

political right An ideological classification based on seating arrangements in the parliament of revolutionary France. Traditionally, rightists included monarchists, clerics, and supporters of the church. Today, the right generally champions decreased government involvement in the economy and cutbacks in welfare programs.

politics Two widely accepted definitions of *politics* are "the process of deciding who gets what, when, and how" and "the authoritative allocation of scarce values." Politics involves both conflict and cooperation.

Porfiriato Period from 1876 to 1911, when Mexico was under the authoritarian rule of General Porfirio Diaz.

pork barrel Allocation of government funds to public works projects in a certain constituency, which enhances the political fortunes of politicians and their supporters.

PRD (Party of the Democratic Revolution) Center-left opposition party to the PRI in Mexico.

presidential model of democracy The pattern of democracy, as in the United States, with legislative and judicial branches balancing a president-led executive branch.

president In Germany, the symbolic head of state who plays a similar role to that of the British monarch.

presidentialism Concentration of political power in the hands of the Mexican president.

pressure groups Groups that form for the express purpose of influencing governmental policies (e.g., labor unions or business associations).

PRI (Institutional Revolutionary Party) (*Also* **PNR, PRM**) Political party that has dominated Mexican politics since its formation in 1929.

proletariat Marx's term for the industrial working class.

quasi-democratic political system A political system that blends democratic and authoritarian tendencies (e.g., Mexico, Egypt).

Question Period (Question Hour) In Britain, the Question Period consists of an hour-long session in which members of the House of Commons are allowed to question members of the Government about issues of concern. In Germany, the Question Hour gives members of the Bundestag a chance to question the Government on issues ranging from matters of national policy to personal grievances of constituents.

Rajya Sabha Upper house of the Indian Parliament, also known as the Council of States.

Rally of the French People (RPF) A movement founded by supporters of Charles de Gaulle, whose platform became the cornerstone of the French right.

Rally for the Republic (RPR) French Gaullist party that advocates law and order, morality, low taxes, and high tariffs and is reluctant to move quickly toward European unity.

reich A German term meaning *empire*.

Rengo The umbrella or "peak" organization coordinating the Japanese labor movement.

Republic of China The Chinese island of Taiwan, which became the headquarters of Chiang Kai-shek's Kuomintang after the KMT's Communist rivals took control of mainland China in 1949.

right *See* political right.

RPF *See* Rally of the French People.

RPR *See* Rally for the Republic.

samurai Warriors in feudal Japan who served their daimyo in exchange for land and money, much as the knights of medieval Europe served their lords.

sati Hindu custom in which a widow committed suicide by throwing herself upon her husband's funeral pyre.

second world A term that originally referred to countries of the Communist Bloc, such as the Soviet Union and the People's Republic of China. Today, the second world no longer exists as Russia and most other members of the Communist Bloc are now considered part of the third world.

shadow cabinet In England, refers to leaders of the opposing party in Parliament.

Shiva The Hindu god of destruction.

shogun Military warlord who ruled the central region of Japan during the country's feudal period.

single-issue (limited-issue) party Political party that focuses on a narrow range of issues (e.g., the Green parties of Europe).

single-member, simple-majority voting system An electoral system in which the winning candidate must receive a majority of the popular vote. If no candidate receives a majority of the vote during the first round of elections, a run-off election is held between the two leading candidates.

single-member, simple-plurality voting system An electoral system in which the candidate who receives the greatest number of votes in a given district wins the election, even though the candidate may not receive an actual majority (50 percent or more) of the votes cast in the district.

single-party-authoritarian system A non-democratic political system in which the ruling party totally controls all political activity (e.g., Nazi Germany, the Soviet Union, Cuba, China).

single-party-dominant system A democracy (or quasi-democracy) that is overwhelmingly dominated by a single party (e.g., Mexico, Egypt).

Siva Hindu god of destruction.

social Darwinism The belief that "survival of the fittest" applies to groups within society, not just species within the natural world. According to Hitler's version of social Darwinism, the purity of the "master race" could be preserved by exterminating Jews, disabled people, and others whom Hitler viewed as undesirable.

Social Democratic Party (SPD) A large catch-all party in Germany that is now slightly left of the center politically but originated as a Marxist-oriented socialist party. The SPD calls for a balance between economic growth and social welfare.

socialism Economic system based on the collective ownership of the means of production, distribution, and exchange.

Socialist Party Leftist political party advocating the nationalization of industry and social equality for all citizens within a democratic culture.

socialist work culture Work culture that developed under the communist regimes in the Soviet Union and mainland China, in which employment was guaranteed and all workers in the same class received the same wage regardless of how hard they worked. As a result, industries suffered from low productivity and poor quality control.

socialization The process of indoctrinating people into their culture. Parents, peers, schools, religious institutions, and the mass media participate in the socialization process.

social market economy A version of state capitalism practiced in Germany, in which government, business, and labor cooperate to achieve both economic growth and equity.

Soviet Union The former Union of Soviet Socialist Republics, or USSR.

soviets Popular councils that seized control of Russia's local governments during the 1917 revolution.

SPD *See* Social Democratic Party.

standing committee A step in the legislative process. Bills are sent to standing committees for review, modifications are suggested, and then the bills are returned to the legislature.

state A well-defined geographic area in which the population and resources are controlled by a government; the governmental apparatus of a country.

state capitalism An economic system that combines capitalism with government planning (e.g., Japan and the industrial countries of Asia). Under state capitalism, most economic activity is in the hands of individual capitalists, but the government provides extra resources and support to private-sector firms that are involved in high-priority industries.

state terrorism State terrorism is government sponsored violence directed against citizens and opposition groups. It often involves the assassination of opposition leaders. State violence may be carried out by government agents or outsources to violent groups.

Sudra Fourth level of the Indian caste system, often referred to as the artisan caste.

supports The actions that people and groups take to strengthen the government (e.g., obeying laws, paying taxes, voting).

supranational government An entity that controls the policies of more than one country (e.g., the European Union).

supranational organization Quasi-governmental organization that attempts to coordinate the activities of its member countries (e.g., United Nations).

system analysis Analytical scheme designed to provide an integrated picture of the political process in which the various parts are seen as interconnected and interdependent.

technocracy, technocrats Administrative elite whose power is based on the possession of specialized technical knowledge.

terrorism Usually defined as politically motivated acts of violence committed by an individual or a small group of individuals. Terrorists attempt to terrorize governments into submission, but are generally unable to occupy territory. By and large, terrorists resist direct confrontation with government troops. The US Army refers to terrorism as low intensity conflict. Terrorism may evolve into guerilla warfare. (*See* guerilla warfare.)

theocracy A country ruled by religious leaders (e.g., Iran), in which the full power of the state is used to assure mass compliance with a particular set of religious doctrines.

third world Countries that have yet to establish a strong position in terms of one or more of the US indicators of development, such as economic growth, equity, democracy, human rights, and concern for the environment (e.g., Egypt, Mexico). There is wide variation among third world countries regarding these developmental indicators; some are strong in one area but weak in others. For example, India has the most enduring democracy in the third world, but most of its citizens live in poverty.

tigers of Asia A term used to describe Taiwan, South Korea, Hong Kong (now part of China), Singapore, and, to a lesser extent, Malaysia. State capitalism is the economic system chosen by each of these countries.

Tories An early British political party, the members of which supported the Crown, the rights of the landed aristocracy, and the dominant position of the Church of England. Today, this term is commonly applied to members of the Conservative Party.

totalitarian society A society in which all political, economic, and cultural activity is under the direct control of the state (e.g., Nazi Germany, the Soviet Union).

totalitarianism A system of government in which no area of human endeavor escapes the scrutiny of the all-pervasive state.

transitional society A society in which large numbers of people are trying to adjust to the conflicting demands of tradition and modernity.

tsars Russian rulers who used religion to legitimize an authoritarian system

two-party system A political system in which the government is always dominated by one of the country's two major parties (e.g., the US, Great Britain, and Germany).

UDF *See* Union for French Democracy.

umbrella association *See* peak association

uni-polar system The existence of a single global superpower with no countervailing national rivals.

Union for French Democracy (UDF) A French Gaullist party of the center right that aspires to unite the interests of big business with those of France's large white-collar class. The UDF advocates free-market capitalism and European unity.

unitary elite A small group of individuals who control decision-making in a broad range of areas e.g., the British prime minister and Cabinet).

universal manhood suffrage System in which all competent adult males are allowed to vote in elections.

universal suffrage System in which all competent adults (male or female) are allowed to vote in elections.

untouchables The lowest level of the Indian caste system, whose members are expected to perform "impure" tasks such as cleaning sewers.

Vaishya Third level of the Indian caste system, often referred to as the trader caste.

Vishnu Hindu god of preservation.

vote of no confidence Legislative action that can force the resignation of a prime minister and Cabinet, usually by voting down a major piece of legislation.

Wafd Party Political party dedicated to liberating Egypt from British rule. (*See* New Wafd.)

Westminster model The British pattern of parliamentary democracy characterized by single-member, simple-plurality voting ("winner take all") systems and a lower house of Parliament dominated by one of two major political parties. The Westminster model is far more efficient at making decisions than are most presidential democracies,

but it is inclined to ignore the views of minorities.

Whigs An early British political party consisting of prosperous members of the middle class who advocated less restrictive economic laws and a reduced role for the Crown and the Church of England in the affairs of the country. The Whigs later evolved into the Liberal Party. (The term *whig* is an abbreviation of *Wiggamores*, a band of Scottish rebels.)

whips In England, the term *whip* has two meanings: (1) party "policemen" who ensure that the members of a party in the legislature understand the party's position and vote accordingly; (2) written instructions sent to party MPs by the party whips prior to votes in Parliament.

World Bank Established at the end of World War II to facilitate the reconstruction of a war-torn Europe and to reestablish order in the world economy, the World Bank now makes long-term loans to Third World countries and attempts to stimulate democracy in the countries that it assists. The World Bank is controlled by First World member countries, with each member's voting power reflecting the size its financial contribution.

world (capitalist) economic system An informal network of the world's capitalist superpowers, multinational corporations, and international financial institutions such as the World Bank, the International Monetary Fund, and the World Trade Organization.

world (international) political system A concept based on the observation that international relations seem to follow certain regularized patterns. For example, prior to World War II the international system was characterized by a balance of power between nations.

World Trade Organization (WTO) An institution designed to regulate the level of tariffs that countries can place on imported goods.

WTO *See* World Trade Organization.

yakuza Japan's large and quasi-legal crime syndicates.

zaibatsu Large business conglomerates in Japan that are controlled by a single interlocking directorate.

Index